Innovation Management and New Product Development

Innovation Management and New Product Development

Sixth Edition

Paul Trott

Portsmouth Business School

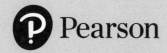 Pearson

Harlow, England • London • New York • Boston • San Francisco • Toronto • Sydney • Dubai • Singapore • Hong Kong
Tokyo • Seoul • Taipei • New Delhi • Cape Town • Sao Paulo • Mexico City • Madrid • Amsterdam • Munich • Paris • Milan

Pearson Education Limited
Edinburgh Gate
Harlow CM20 2JE
United Kingdom
Tel: +44 (0)1279 623623
Web: www.pearson.com/uk

First published 1998 (print)
Second edition published 2002 (print)
Third edition published 2005 (print)
Fourth edition published 2008 (print)
Fifth edition published 2012 (print)
Sixth edition published 2017 (print and electronic)

The screenshots in this book are reprinted by permission of Microsoft Corporation.

Pearson Education is not responsible for the content of third-party internet sites.

The *Financial Times*. With a worldwide network of highly respected journalists, The
Financial Times provides global business news, insightful opinion and expert analysis of
business, finance and politics. With over 500 journalists reporting from 50 countries
worldwide, our in-depth coverage of international news is objectively reported and
analysed from an independent, global perspective. To find out more, visit www.ft.com/
pearsonoffer.

ISBN: 978-1-292-13342-3 (print)
      978-1-292-16540-0 (PDF)
      978-1-292-17069-5 (ePub)

British Library Cataloguing-in-Publication Data
A catalogue record for the print edition is available from the British Library

Library of Congress Cataloging-in-Publication Data
A catalog record for the print edition is available from the Library of Congress

10 9 8 7 6 5 4 3 2 1
20 19 18 17 16

Cover image: Max Margarit/Shutterstock

Print edition typeset in 10/12pt Sabon LT Pro by iEnergizer Aptara® Ltd
Print edition printed and bound in Slovakia by Neografia

NOTE THAT ANY PAGE CROSS REFERENCES REFER TO THE PRINT EDITION

Contents

4 Managing innovation within firms   116

5 Operations and process innovation 154

6 Managing intellectual property 188

Part Two Turning technology into business   225

7 **Managing organisational knowledge**   226

8 Strategic alliances and networks

9 Management of research and development 304

Part Three New product development

12 Business models

15 New service innovation   522

17 Managing the new product development process   586

Preface

The demise of Kodak is a sharp reminder to all firms, even great big ones, that success today does not ensure success tomorrow. The ability of firms to develop new products and services that people want will surely help them survive into the future. But precisely how should firms go about this? The Kodak case is even more remarkable because Kodak was the pioneer in digital cameras – the technology that, ultimately, led to its decline in income. So, in this case, it is not a lack of innovation *per se* but how it is used to deliver value to the firm and its customers.

We are all well aware that good technology can help companies achieve competitive advantage and long-term financial success; just look at Google. But there is an abundance of exciting new technology in the world and it is the transformation of this technology into products that is of particular concern to organisations. There are numerous factors to be considered by the organisation, but what are these factors and how do they affect the process of innovation? This book will explain how and why the majority of the most significant inventions of the past two centuries have not come from flashes of inspiration, but from communal, multilayered endeavour – one idea being built on another until a breakthrough is reached (Johnson, 2010).

In this book we see that many of the old traditional approaches to management need to change and new approaches need to be adopted. Increasingly, managers and those who work for them are no longer in the same location. Often, complex management relationships need to be developed because organisations are trying to produce complex products and services and do so across geographic boundaries. Cross-functional and cross-border task forces often need to be created.

Objective of the book

It is designed to be accessible and readable. The book emphasises the need to view innovation as a management process. We need to recognise that change is at the heart of it. And that change is caused by decisions that people make. The framework in Chapter 1 (Figure 1.9) attempts to capture the iterative nature of the network processes in innovation and represents this in the form of an endless innovation circle with interconnected cycles. This circular concept helps to show how the firm gathers information over time, how it uses technical and societal knowledge, and how it develops an attractive proposition. This is achieved through developing linkages and partnerships with those having the necessary capabilities.

Target audience

This book is written for people who want to understand how firms can improve the way they manage their innovation processes to develop new products and services.

It can be used as a textbook for undergraduate or graduate courses in innovation management and new product development. A second audience is the manager who wishes to keep abreast of the most recent developments in the innovation field.

Special features

The book is designed with one overriding aim: to make this exciting and highly relevant subject as clear to understand as possible. To this end, the book has a number of important features:

- A clear and straightforward writing style enhances learning comprehension.
- Extensive up-to-date references and relevant literature help you find out more and explore concepts in detail.
- 'Innovation in action' boxes illustrate how real companies are managing innovation today.
- Clear chapter openers set the scene for each chapter and provide a chapter contents list, which offers page references to all the sections within the chapter.
- Learning objectives at the beginning of each chapter explicitly highlight the key areas that will be explored in the chapter.
- More photographs and images are included to help illustrate and enliven the text.
- Topical articles from the *Financial Times* illustrate how the subject is being discussed in the context of the wider business world.
- Summaries at the end of each chapter provide a useful means of revising and checking understanding.
- 'Pause for thought' questions are integrated within the text. These are designed to help you reflect on what you have just read and to check your understanding. Answers to all 'Pause for thought' questions are given on the book's website (www.pearsoned.co.uk/trott).
- Comprehensive diagrams throughout the book illustrate some of the more complex concepts.
- Plentiful up-to-date examples within the text drive home arguments. This helps to enliven the subject and places it in context.
- A comprehensive index, including references to all defined terms, enables you to look up a definition within its context. See also the 'Key words and phrases' boxes at chapter ends. Key words are presented emboldened in colour within the main text.
- A substantial case study at the end of each chapter shows the subject in action within actual firms. These have been trialled on classes at several universities and have formed the basis of lively one-hour class seminar discussions.

What is new in the 6th edition?

- Three new chapters: 'National systems of innovation and entrepreneurship', 'Market adoption and technology diffusion' and 'Business models'.
- 'Innovation in action' boxes in every chapter. These bring the subject to life by providing a real life illustration of how firms are managing innovation today.
- All chapters have been reviewed and updated with relevant references to the literature. Illustrations within chapters have been renewed. All case studies have been updated and modified where appropriate.
- Chapter 1 – there is a new case study on Apple. This new case study examines the increasing competition faced by Apple in the smartphone market and the rise of Samsung.
- Chapter 2 – this is a new chapter focusing on national systems of innovation and entrepreneurship. It emphasises the role played by the state in helping private firms grow. The subject of entrepreneurship receives substantial coverage by illustrating the linkages between these areas.
- Chapter 3 – this is a new chapter on market adoption and technology diffusion. The role played by lead users in the innovation process is explored. The chapter also covers the growing use by firms of crowdsourcing for new product ideas. The topic of frugal innovation is also included.
- Chapter 5 – a major new case study at the end of the chapter tells the story of how an innovation in the paper and board packaging industry may help it compete with polymers.
- Chapter 7 – a new section examines the issue of disruptive innovation and the innovation dilemma. This looks in detail at how it is possible for firms to offer what appears to be an inferior technology to a particular market segment and how, over time, that product can develop and overtake the original technology in terms of performance.
- Chapter 11 – a major new case study at the end of the chapter tells the story of how a nappy producer is considering using sensors in its products to indicate wetness. How will consumers react?
- Chapter 12 – this is a new chapter on business models. The chapter explains the link between business models and strategy and business plans. It discusses the many different forms of business models that exist, including the famous bait and hook business model that has been so effectively used by ink jet cartridge manufacturers and razor producers.
- Chapter 15 – the case study on eBay has been rewritten to include the eBay-PayPal separation. The growth in online payment systems forms a key part of this new case.
- Chapter 17 – a new section explores the area of innovation audits. This offers some practical guidance to firms wishing to assess their level of innovation capacity or those of others.

Web products

Log on to www.pearsoned.co.uk/trott to access learning resources, which include:

For students:
- Study materials designed to help you improve your results.
- Self-test multiple choice questions, organised by chapter.
- Answers to all 'Pause for thought' questions, to allow you to check understanding as you progress.
- Annotated links for each chapter to relevant companies and internet sites.

For tutors (password protected):
- Lecture notes and PowerPoint slides.
- Figures and tables from the book in PowerPoint colour slides.
- Key models as full-colour animated PowerPoint slide shows.
- Teaching/learning case studies.
- Answers to all end-of-chapter discussion questions.
- Multiple choice questions, organised by chapter for use in assessments.

Reference

Johnson, S. (2010) *Where Good Ideas Come From: The Natural History of Innovation*, Riverhead Books, New Jersey, USA.

Acknowledgements

Author's acknowledgements

I am indebted to many for their ideas and assistance. My primary thanks go to the many academics who have advanced our knowledge of innovation and new product development and on whose shoulders I have been able to stand. The following reviewers provided feedback for this new edition: Jon Sundbo, Roskilde University, Denmark; Guus Berkhout, TUDelft; Helen Perks, UMIST; Niki Hynes, Napier University Business School; Mark Godson, Sheffield Hallam University; Paul Oakley, University of Birmingham; David Smith, Nottingham Business School, Nottingham Trent University; Fritz Sheimer, FH Furtwagen; Claus J. Varnes, Copenhagen Business School; Roy Woodhead, Oxford Brookes University; Patrick van der Duin, TU Delft, the Netherlands; Dap Hartman, TU Delft, the Netherlands; E J Hultink, TU Delft, The Netherlands; Phil Longhurst, Cranfield University; Zahed Subhan, Drexel University, USA; Christian M. Thurnes, Hochschule Kaiserslautern — University of Applied Sciences, Germany.

It has been a pleasure to work with my editor Rachel Gear, who provided encouragement, help and valuable suggestions. The task of writing has been made much easier by the support I have had from many people. First, all my students who have both wittingly and unwittingly provided constant feedback to me on ideas. Also, a big thank you to the team at Pearson Education. Any errors or omissions in the book are entirely mine.

Publisher's acknowledgements

Figures

University, Sage Publications; Figure 4.5 from Relationships between innovation stimulus, innovation capacity and innovation performance, *R&D Management*, 36(5), pp. 499–515 (Prajogo, D.I. and Ahmed, P.K. 2006), © John Wiley & Sons Ltd and RADMA; Figure 4.6 from Success and failure of innovation: a review of the literature, *International Journal of Innovation Management*, 7(3), pp. 309–38 (van der Panne, G., van Beers, C. and Kleinknecht, A. 2003), World Scientific Publishing Co.; Figure 4.7 from Sectoral patterns of technological change: towards a taxonomy and theory, *Research Policy*, 13, pp. 343–73 (Pavitt, K. 1994), Elsevier Science Ltd; Figures 5.1, 5.5 and 5.6 from *Operations Management*, 4th edn, Pearson Education Ltd (Slack, N. et al. 2004), © Pearson Education Ltd; Figure 5.4 from Why the process industries are different, *Production and Inventory Management Journal*, 22(4), pp. 9–24 (Taylor, S.G., Stewart, S.M. and Bolander, S.F. 1981), used with permission from APICS, copyright 1981; Figure 5.8 from *Lean Product Management*, The 280 Group (Cohen, G. 2011), © 2011 The 280 Group, reproduced with permission; Figure 7.4 from *Innovation Management: Strategies, Implementation and Profit*, Oxford University Press (Afuah, A. 2003) p. 53, Figure 3.5, by permission of Oxford University Press, USA; Figure 7.9 from Patterns of industrial innovation, *Technology Review*, 80(7), pp. 40–7 (Abernathy, W.J. and Utterback, J. 1978), © 1978 from MIT Sloan Management Review/Massachusetts Institute of Technology, all rights reserved, distributed by Tribune Content Agency; Figure 7.10 from Organizational determinants of technological change: towards a sociology of technological evaluation, *Research in Organizational Behavior*, 14, pp. 311–47 (Tushman, M.L. and Rosenkopf, L. 1992), © Elsevier, 1992; Figure 8.2 from Carmaker alliances: a tangled web, *Financial Times*, 04/05/2010 (Reed, J.), © The Financial Times Limited. All Rights Reserved; Figure 10.7 adapted from *Managing Engineering and Technology: An Introduction to Management for Engineers*, 2nd edn, Prentice Hall, Inc. (Morse, D. and Babcock, D.L. 1996), © 1996, adapted by permission of Pearson Education, Inc., Upper Saddle River, NJ; Figure 11.3 adapted from *Architect or Bee? The Human Price of Technology*, Chatto & Windus (Cooley, M. 1987), reprinted by permission of The Random House Group Ltd; Figure 12.4 adapted from Business model innovation: opportunities and barriers, *Long Range Planning*, 43, pp. 354–63 (Chesbrough, H. 2010), figure 2, p. 360, copyright 2010, with permission from Elsevier; Figure 13.4 from Brand first management, *Journal of Marketing Management*, 12, pp. 269–80 (Rubenstein, H. 1996), Westburn Publishers; Figure 14.4 from How to organise for new products, *Harvard Business Review*, 35, pp. 49–62 (Johnson, S.C. and Jones, C. 1957), Harvard Business School Publishing; Figure 14.6 adapted from PDMA research on new product development practices: updating trends and benchmarking best practices, *Journal of Product Innovation Management*, 14(5), pp. 429–58 (Griffin, A. 1997), © John Wiley & Sons Ltd; Figure 14.7 from Brand franchise extension: new product benefits from existing brand names, *Business Horizons*, vol. 24, no. 2, pp. 36–41 (Tauber, E.M. 1981), with permission from Elsevier; Figure 14.8 from Product replacement: strategies for simultaneous product deletion and launch, *Journal of Product Innovation Management*, vol. 11, no. 5, pp. 433–50 (Saunders, J. and Jobber, D. 1994), © John Wiley & Sons Ltd; Figure 14.12 from *The Design Dimension*, Blackwell Publishing Ltd (Lorenz, C. 1990), with permission from John Wiley & Sons Ltd, permission conveyed through Copyright Clearance Center, Inc.; Figure 15.1 from *Service Operations Management*, 4th edn, Prentice Hall (Johnston, R. and Clark, G. 2012) figure 2.2, p. 36, © Pearson Education Ltd; Figure 16.2 adapted from *Proceedings of the Annual Conference of the European Marketing Academy, Maastricht* (Saren, M.A.J. and Tzokas, N. 1994); Figure 16.3 from Competing for the future, *Harvard Business Review*, vol. 72, no. 4, pp. 122–8 (Hamel, S. and Prahalad, C.K. 1994), Harvard Business School Publishing.

Tables

Table 1.2 from The most innovative companies, https://www.bcgperspectives.com/content/interactive/innovation_growth_most_innovative_companies_interactive_guide/, The Boston Consulting Group; Table 2.1 adapted from *Global Shift: Transforming the World Economy*, Paul Chapman (Dicken, P. 1998), reproduced by permission of Peter Dicken and SAGE Publications, London, Los Angeles, New Delhi and Singapore, copyright © Sage Publications, 1998; Table 2.2 from Why entrepreneurship has won, *Coleman White Paper*, pp. 1–8 (Stevenson, H.H. 2000), http://www.unm.edu/~asalazar/Kauffman/Entrep_research/e_won.pdf, Professor Howard H. Stevenson; Table 4.1 from Innovation management measurement: a review, *International Journal of Management Reviews*, 8(1), pp. 21–47 (Adams, R., Bessant, J. and Phelps, R. 2006), reproduced with permission of John Wiley & Sons; Table 4.3 from Juggling entrepreneurial style and organizational structure: how to get your act together, *Sloan Management Review*, Winter, pp. 43–53 (Slevin, D.P. and Covin, J.G. 1990), © 1990 from MIT Sloan Management Review/Massachusetts Institute of Technology, all rights reserved, distributed by Tribune Content Agency; Table 6.2 from *Patents: Their Effectiveness and Role*, Carnegie Mellon University & National Bureau of Economic Research (Cohen, W.M. 2002), with permission from Wesley Cohen; Table 7.1 from Patterns of industrial innovation, *Technology Review*, 80(7), pp. 40–7 (Abernathy, W.J. and Utterback, J. 1978), © 1978 from MIT Sloan Management Review/Massachusetts Institute of Technology, all rights reserved, distributed by Tribune Content Agency; Table 9.1 from Economics of Industrial Research & Innovation, European Commission, http://iri.jrc.ec.europa.eu/research/scoreboard_2015.htm, © European Union, 1995–2016; Table 9.2 from www.innovation.gov.uk/rd_scoreboard, contains public sector information licensed under the Open Government Licence (OGL) v3.0, http://www.nationalarchives.gov.uk/doc/open-government-licence; Table 9.3 from Towards the sixth generation of R&D management, *International Journal of Project Management*, 22(5), pp. 369–75 (Nobelius, D. 2004), exhibit 1, copyright 2004, with permission from Elsevier; Table 9.4 from *EU R&D Scoreboard: The 2014 EU Industrial R&D Investment Scoreboard*, European Commission (Hernández, H., Tübke, A., Hervás, F., Vezzani, A., Dosso, M., Amoroso, S. and Grassano, N. 2015), © European Union, 1995–2016; Table 12.3 from *Do Some Business Models Perform Better than Others? A Study of the 1000 Largest US Firms*, Sloan School of Management, Massachusetts Institute of Technology, Working Paper No. 226 (Weill, P., Malone, T.W., D'Urso, V.T., Herman, G. and Woerner, S. 2005), © 2005 from MIT Sloan Management Review/Massachusetts Institute of Technology, all rights reserved, distributed by Tribune Content Agency; Table 12.5 from *Royalty Rates for Licensing Intellectual Property*, John Wiley and Sons, Inc. (Parr, R.L. 2007), republished with permission of Wiley, permission conveyed through Copyright Clearance Center, Inc.; Table 13.3 from *Product Strategy and Management*, Prentice Hall (Baker, M.

and Hart, S. 1989), © Pearson Education Ltd; Table 13.5 with permission from The Nielsen Company; Table 14.1 from The role of marketing specialists in product development, *Proceedings of the 21st Annual Conference of the Marketing Education Group, Huddersfield*, Vol. 3, pp. 176–91 (Johne, F.A. and Snelson, P.A. 1988); Table 14.3 from Product development: past research, present findings and future directions, *Academy of Management Review*, Vol. 20, No. 2, pp. 343–78 (Brown, S.L. and Eisenhardt, K.M. 1995), Academy of Management; Table 14.6 adapted from Britvic Soft Drinks Review 2015, page 46, http://www.britvic.com/~/media/Files/B/Britvic-V3/documents/pdf/presentation/2015/brv-300044-eve-soft-drinks-review-2015m.pdf, source: Nielsen Scantrack 52we 27 December 2014, with permission from The Nielsen Company; Table 15.2 adapted from *Service Operations Management*, 4th ed., Prentice Hall (Johnston, R. and Clark, G. 2012), © Pearson Education Ltd; Table 15.4 from *An Analysis of Internet Banking Adoption in Turkey: Consumer, Innovation and Service Developer Dimensions*, PhD thesis, University of Portsmouth (Ozdemir, S. 2007).

Text

Illustration 1.1 adapted from Apple Watch app designers scramble ahead of launch, *Financial Times*, 06/04/2015 (Bradshaw, T.), © The Financial Times Limited. All Rights Reserved; Illustration 2.1 from Brussels v Google – Antitrust rules – EU poised to launch broader competition crackdown, *Financial Times*, 16/04/2015 (Oliver, C. and Waters, R.), © The Financial Times Limited. All Rights Reserved; Illustration 4.1 from Business pioneers in technology, *Financial Times*, 31/03/2015 (Waters, R.), © The Financial Times Limited. All Rights Reserved; Illustration 6.1 from Theft of intellectual property 'should be a crime', *Financial Times*, 24/09/2010 (Greenhalgh, H.), © The Financial Times Limited. All Rights Reserved; Illustration 6.5 from Interview with Adam Hargreaves – Mr Men illustrator and writer, http://www.sussexlife.co.uk/people/celebrity-interviews/interview_with_adam_hargreaves_mr_men_illustrator_and_writer_1_1636359, Archant Community Media Ltd; Illustration 8.2 adapted from www.corning.com/innovationventures, Corning Incorporated; Illustration 8.3 from *Racing for radical innovation: how motorsport companies harness network diversity for discontinuous innovation* (Delbridge, R. and Mariotti, F. 2009), Advanced Institute of Management Research, London; Illustration 8.6 from How to keep your best people happy in the saddle, *Financial Times*, 25/10/2010 (Moules, J.), © The Financial Times Limited. All Rights Reserved; Illustration 9.3 from *EU R&D Scoreboard: The 2014 EU Industrial R&D Investment Scoreboard*, European Commission (Hernández, H., Tübke, A., Hervás, F., Vezzani, A., Dosso, M., Amoroso, S. and Grassano, N. 2015), © European Union, 1995–2016; Illustration 10.1 from Quick-hit chemistry becomes elusive, *Financial Times*, 12/09/2001 (Michaels, A.), © The Financial Times Limited. All Rights Reserved; Case study on p. 368 from The rise of DNA analysis in crime solving, *The Guardian*, 10/04/2010, p. 24 (Jones, T.), copyright Guardian News & Media Ltd 2016; Illustration 11.2 from Cult carmaker Morgan defies the gloom, *Financial Times*, 22/08/2010 (Moules, J.), © The Financial Times Limited. All Rights Reserved; Illustration 14.1 from New products crucial to success, *Financial Times*, 21/05/2002 (Marsh, P.), © The Financial Times Limited. All Rights Reserved; Quotes on pp. 509 and 513 from Innocent Drinks, www.innocentdrinks.co.uk; Illustration 16.3 from Marketing industry turns to mind reading, *Financial Times*, 11/04/2010 (Kuchler, H.), © The Financial Times Limited. All Rights Reserved.

Photographs

(Key: b – bottom; c – centre; l – left; r – right; t – top)

123rf.com: csakisti. 123rf.com 90; **Alamy Images:** Andrew Holt 427, Andrew Paterson 94, Art Directors & TRIP 134, Cras Media Group 277, Directphoto Collection 209, Len Holsborg 490, imageBROKER 176, Images by Morgana 40, James Appleton 538, Joe Belanger 421, John Bowling 598, Chloe Johnson 123, Kevpix 321, Mark Fagelson 425, Neil Fraser 4, Newscast Online 166, Oliver Leedham 293, Oramstock 574, Paul Weston 389, Pixellover RM 9 452, Steve Stock 482, Rufus Stone 162, The Picture Pantry 252, Trinity Mirror/Mirrorpix 316, WENN Ltd 345, Xavier Vila 602; **Brand X Pictures:** Burke Triolo Productions 554; **Digital Stock:** 274; **Digital Vision:** 525; **Getty Images:** Anthony Redpath 146, Bloomberg 611, Chris Stowers 527, Condé Nast Archive 215, Mark Elias/Bloomberg 450, Johnny Haglund 19, Stock Illustration Source 247; **innocent ltd:** 509; **Mary Evans Picture Library:** 228; **Mini UK:** 491; **Pearson Education Ltd:** 368, Coleman Yuen. Pearson Education Asia Ltd 612; **PhotoDisc:** Kent Knudson 177, Michael Matisse 562, Nick Rowe 313, Photodisc 104, 109, 191, 334, 359, Photolink 357; **Shutterstock.com:** Andrei Mayatnik 181, Bart_J 398, bioraven 197, Bloomua 545, Chesky 76, kurhan 436, Lou Oates 290, maxuser 592, nitinut380 471, think4photop 98, Zdenek Fiamoli 241, Zeynep Demir 35, Zurijeta 133; **Westend 61. Creativ Studio Heinemann:** Westend 61. Creativ Studio Heinemann 71; **www.imagesource.com:** Image Source Ltd. www.imagesource.com 386.

All other images © Pearson Education

Plan of the book

Part One Innovation management

Chapter 1 Innovation management: an introduction	**Chapter 2** National systems of innovation and entrepreneurship	**Chapter 3** Market adoption and technology diffusion
Chapter 4 Managing innovation within firms	**Chapter 5** Operations and process innovation	**Chapter 6** Managing intellectual property

Part Two Turning technology into business

Chapter 7 Managing organisational knowledge	**Chapter 8** Strategic alliances and networks	**Chapter 9** Management of research and development
Chapter 10 Managing R&D projects		**Chapter 11** Open innovation and technology transfer

Part Three New product development

Chapter 12 Business models	**Chapter 13** Product and brand strategy	**Chapter 14** New product development
Chapter 15 New service innovation	**Chapter 16** Market research and its influence on new product development	**Chapter 17** Managing the new product development process

Part One
Innovation management

The purpose of this part of the book is to introduce and explore the concept of innovation management. Particular emphasis is placed on the need to view innovation as a management process. A cyclic model of innovation is introduced, which emphasises the importance of internal processes and external linkages. This raises the issue of the context of innovation and Chapter 2 demonstrates that innovation cannot be separated from the wider national system. The United States is often cited as a good example of a system that enables innovation to flourish: hence it is necessary to explore the economic factors that influence innovation and the role of entrepreneurship. The rate at which these technologies are adopted and used by consumers and society is the subject of Chapter 3.

Chapter 4 explores the issue of the organisational context and it is from this vantage point that the subject of managing innovation within firms is addressed. Virtually all major technological innovations occur within organisations; hence it is necessary to look at organisations and explore how they manage innovation.

Given that many new product ideas are based on existing products and may be developed from within the production or service operations function, Chapter 5 considers the role of operations within innovation. Many new product ideas may be modest and incremental rather than radical but the combined effect of many, small, innovative ideas may be substantial.

A major part of the process of innovation is the management of a firm's intellectual effort and this is the focus of Chapter 6. Patents, trademarks, copyright and registered designs are all discussed.

The principal message of this part is this: innovation is a management process that is heavily influenced by the organisational context and the wider macro system in which the organisation exists.

Chapter 1
Innovation management: an introduction

Introduction

Innovation is one of those words that suddenly seems to be all around us. Firms care about their ability to innovate, on which their future allegedly depends (Christensen and Raynor, 2003), and many management consultants are busy persuading companies about how they can help them improve their innovation performance. Politicians care about innovation, too: how to design policies that stimulate innovation has become a hot topic at various levels of government. The European Commission, for instance, has made innovation policy a central element in its attempt to invigorate the European economy (see Chapter 2). A large amount of literature has emerged, particularly in recent years, on various aspects of innovation and many new research units focusing on innovation have been formed (Martin, 2012).

There is extensive scope for examining the way innovation is managed within organisations. Most of us are well aware that good technology can help companies achieve competitive advantage and long-term financial success. But there is an abundance of exciting new technology in the world and it is the transformation of this technology into products that is of particular concern to organisations. There are numerous factors to be considered by the organisation, but what are these factors and how do they affect the process of innovation? This book will explain how and why most of the most significant inventions of the past two centuries have not come from flashes of for-profit inspiration, but from communal, multilayered endeavour – one idea being built on another until a breakthrough is reached (Johnson, 2010). The Apple case study at the end of this chapter helps illustrate Apple's rise and fall over the past 20 years.

Chapter contents

Learning objectives

When you have completed this chapter you will be able to:

- recognise the importance of innovation;
- explain the meaning and nature of innovation management;
- provide an introduction to a management approach to innovation;
- appreciate the complex nature of the management of innovation within organisations;
- describe the changing views of innovation over time;
- recognise the role of key individuals within the process; and
- recognise the need to view innovation as a management process.

The importance of innovation

Corporations must be able to adapt and evolve if they wish to survive. Businesses operate with the knowledge that their competitors will, inevitably, come to the market with a product that changes the basis of competition. The ability to change and adapt is essential to survival. But can firms manage innovation? The answer is certainly yes, as Bill Gates confirmed in 2008:

> The share price is not something we control. We control innovation, sales and profits.
>
> (Rushe and Waples, 2008)

Today, the idea of innovation is widely accepted. It has become part of our culture – so much so that it verges on becoming a cliché. But, even though the term is now embedded in our language, to what extent do we fully understand the concept? Moreover, to what extent is this understanding shared? A scientist's view of innovation may be very different from that of an accountant in the same organisation.

The Apple Inc. story in Illustration 1.1 puts into context the subject of innovation and new product development. In this case, Apple's launch of a new product in the mobile phone market will help Apple generate increases in revenue and grow the firm. Innovation is at the heart of many companies' activities. But to what extent is this true of all businesses? And why are some businesses more innovative than others?

Illustration 1.1

Apple Watch app designers scramble ahead of launch

Apple has invited small groups of developers to its Silicon Valley offices to help them prepare their apps for its Watch, as it gears up for the launch at the end of this month.

Their creations range from exercise trackers and car-hailing services such as Uber, to a digital version of a painter's palette board and an app for sending a tweet to astronauts passing overhead on the International Space Station, all from a user's wrist.

In addition to its own messaging and fitness services, Apple is hoping a vibrant App Store will help persuade customers to spend between $350 and $17,000 on the Watch, its first new device since the iPad.

Developers say the technical and creative challenge is greater than when they had to rejig their iPhone apps for the iPad five years ago, due to the Watch's tiny screen and control scheme.

Some developers are able to draw on their experience with other smartwatches, such as the

Source: Neil Fraser/Alamy Images

pioneering Pebble or Google's Android Wear. Many are using much more rudimentary techniques, such as taping paper mock-ups to their arms, to figure out what might work best on the Watch's 38–42mm screen.

Before March's press event, only top-ranking iPhone developers such as Uber and Facebook were invited to Apple's offices to test their Watch apps. In the weeks since then, however, it has opened to more, with about 20 developers a day visiting its labs, according to those who have been there.

App makers are betting that Apple will succeed where other smartwatch makers have failed to sell in the many millions.

What is meant by innovation? And can it be managed? These are questions that will be addressed in this book.

'. . . not to innovate is to die', wrote Christopher Freeman (1982) in his famous study of the economics of innovation. Certainly, companies that have established themselves as technical and market leaders have shown an ability to develop successful new products. In virtually every industry, from aerospace to pharmaceuticals and from motor cars to computers, the dominant companies have demonstrated an ability to innovate (see Table 1.1). Furthermore, in The Boston Consulting Group's annual report on the world's most innovative companies, these same firms are delivering impressive growth and/or return to their shareholders (see Table 1.2).

Table 1.1 Market leaders in 2015

Industry	Market leaders	Innovative new products and services
Cell phones	Samsung; Apple	Design and new features
Internet-related industries	Google; Facebook	New services
Pharmaceuticals	Pfizer; GlaxoSmithKline	Impotence; ulcer treatment drug
Motorcars	Toyota; BMW	Car design and associated product developments
Computers and software development	Intel; IBM and Microsoft; SAP	Computer chip technology, computer hardware improvements and software development

Table 1.2 World's most innovative companies

2014 Rank	Company	Revenue growth 2012–13 % change	R&D spending 2012–13 % change
1	Apple	9.2	32.4
2	Google	19.2	17.1
3	Samsung	17.0	27.8
4	Microsoft	5.6	6.1
5	IBM	−4.6	−1.2
6	Amazon	21.9	43.8
7	Tesla Motors	387.2	−15.3
8	Toyota	−3.9	−6.9
9	Facebook	54.7	1.1
10	Sony	−5.7	−18.8

Source: www.bcgperspectives.com/content/interactive/innovation_growth_most_innovative_companies_interactive_guide/, The Boston Consulting Group

Table 1.3 Nineteenth-century economic development fuelled by technological innovations

Innovation	Innovator	Date
Steam engine	James Watt	1770–80
Iron boat	Isambard Kingdom Brunel	1820–45
Locomotive	George Stephenson	1829
Electromagnetic induction dynamo	Michael Faraday	1830–40
Electric light bulb	Thomas Edison and Joseph Swan	1879–90

A brief analysis of economic history, especially in the United Kingdom, will show that industrial technological innovation has led to substantial economic benefits for the innovating *company* and the innovating *country* (see Illustration 1.2). Indeed, the industrial revolution of the nineteenth century was fuelled by technological innovations (see Table 1.3). Technological innovations have also been an important component in the progress of human societies. Anyone who has visited the towns of Bath, Leamington and Colchester will be very aware of how the Romans contributed to the advancement of human societies. The introduction over 2,000 years ago of sewers, roads and elementary heating systems is credited to these early invaders of Britain.

Illustration 1.2

A review of the history of economic growth

Economic historians argue that the world's economy has experienced unprecedented growth rates only after 1800, following millennial relative stagnation, because of the role of technology in affecting economic change.

The classical economists of the eighteenth and nineteenth centuries believed that technological change and capital accumulation were the engines of growth. This belief was based on the conclusion that productivity growth causes population growth, which in turn causes productivity to fall. Today's theory of population growth is very different from these early attempts at understanding economic growth. It argues that rising incomes slow the population growth because they increase the rate of opportunity cost of having children. Hence, as technology advances, productivity and incomes grow.

The Austrian economist, Joseph Schumpeter, was the founder of modern growth theory and is regarded as one of the world's greatest economists. In the 1930s he was the first to realise that the development and diffusion of new technologies by profit-seeking entrepreneurs formed the source of economic progress. One important insight arising from Schumpeter's ideas is that innovation can be seen as *'creative destruction'* waves that restructure the whole market in favour of those who grasp discontinuities faster. In his own words 'the problem that is usually visualised is how capitalism administers existing structures, whereas the relevant problem is how it creates and destroys them.'

Robert Solow, who was a student of Schumpeter, advanced his professor's theories in the 1950s and won the Nobel Prize for economic science. Paul Romer has developed these theories further and is responsible for the modern theory of economic growth, sometimes called neo-Schumpeterian economic growth theory, which argues that sustained economic growth arises from competition amongst firms. Firms try to increase their profits by devoting resources to creating new products and developing new ways of making existing products. It is this economic theory that underpins most innovation management and new product development theories.

Source: Adapted from Parkin, M. et al. (2008) and McCloskey, D.N. (2013).

Pause for thought

Not all firms develop innovative new products, but they still seem to survive. Do they thrive?

The study of innovation

Innovation has long been argued to be the engine of growth. It is important to note that it can also provide growth, almost regardless of the condition of the larger economy. Innovation has been a topic for discussion and debate for hundreds of years. Nineteenth-century economic historians observed that the acceleration in **economic growth** was the result of technological progress. However, little effort was directed towards understanding *how* changes in technology contributed to this growth.

Schumpeter (1934, 1939, 1942) was amongst the first economists to emphasise the importance of *new products* as stimuli to economic growth. He argued that the competition posed by new products was far more important than marginal changes in the *prices* of existing products. For example, economies are more likely to experience growth due to the development of products, such as new computer software or new pharmaceutical drugs than to reductions in prices of existing products, such as telephones or motorcars. Indeed, early observations suggested that economic development does not occur in any regular manner, but seemed to occur in bursts or waves of activity, thereby indicating the important influence of external factors on economic development.

This macro view of innovation as cyclical can be traced back to the mid-nineteenth century. It was Marx who first suggested that innovations could be associated with waves of economic growth. Since then, others such as Schumpeter (1934, 1939), Kondratieff (1935/51) and Abernathy and Utterback (1978) have argued the long-wave theory of innovation. Kondratieff was, unfortunately, imprisoned by Stalin for his views on economic growth theories, because they conflicted with those of Marx. Marx suggested that capitalist economies eventually would decline, whereas Kondratieff argued that they would experience waves of growth and decline. Abernathy and Utterback (1978) contended that at the birth of any industrial sector there is radical product innovation, which is then followed by radical innovation in production processes, followed, in turn, by widespread incremental innovation. This view was once popular and seemed to reflect the life cycles of many industries. It has, however, failed to offer any understanding of *how* to achieve innovative success.

After the Second World War, economists began to take an even greater interest in the causes of economic growth (Domar, 1946; Harrod, 1949). One of the most important influences on innovation seemed to be industrial research and development. After all, during the war, military research and development (R&D) had produced significant technological advances and innovations, including radar, aerospace and new weapons. A period of rapid growth in expenditure by countries on R&D was to follow, exemplified by US President Kennedy's 1960 speech outlining his vision of getting a man on the moon before the end of the decade. But economists soon found that there was no *direct* correlation between R&D spending and national rates of economic growth. It was clear that the linkages were more complex than first thought (this issue is explored more fully in Chapter 9).

There was a need to understand *how* science and technology affected the economic system. The neo-classical economics approach had not offered any explanations. A series of studies of innovation were undertaken in the 1950s, which concentrated on the internal characteristics of the innovation process within the economy. A feature of these studies was that they adopted a cross-discipline approach, incorporating economics, organisational behaviour and business and management. The studies looked at:

- the generation of new knowledge;
- the application of this knowledge in the development of products and processes;
- the commercial exploitation of these products and services in terms of financial income generation.

In particular, these studies revealed that firms behaved differently (see Carter and Williams, 1957; Simon, 1957; Woodward, 1965). This led to the development of a new theoretical framework that attempted to understand how firms managed the above, and why some firms appeared to be more successful than others. Later studies in the 1960s were to confirm these initial findings and uncover significant differences in organisational characteristics (Burns and Stalker, 1961; Cyert and March, 1963; Myers and Marquis, 1969). Hence, the new framework placed more emphasis on the firm and its internal activities than had previously been the case. The firm and how it used its resources was now seen as the key influence on innovation.

Neo-classical economics is a theory of economic growth that explains how savings, investments and growth respond to population growth and technological change. The rate of technological change influences the rate of economic growth, but economic growth does not influence technological change. Rather, technological change is determined by chance. Thus, population growth and technological change are exogenous. Also, neo-classical economic theory tends to concentrate on industry or economy-wide performance. It tends to ignore differences amongst firms in the same line of business. Any differences are assumed to reflect differences in the market environments that the organisations face. That is, differences are not achieved through choice but reflect differences in the situations in which firms operate. In contrast, research within business management and strategy focuses on these differences and the decisions that have led to them. Furthermore, the activities that take place within the firm that enable one firm seemingly to perform better than another, given the same economic and market conditions, has been the focus of much research effort since the 1960s.

The Schumpeterian view sees firms as different – it is the way a firm manages its resources over time and develops capabilities that influences its innovation performance. The varying emphasis placed by different disciplines on explaining how innovation occurs is brought together in the framework in Figure 1.1. This overview of the innovation process includes an economic perspective, a business

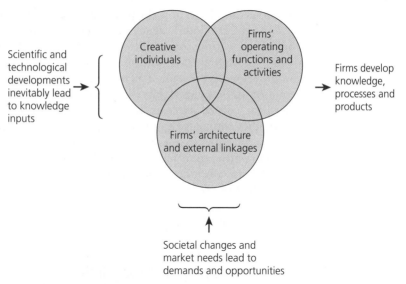

Figure 1.1 Overview of the innovation process

management strategy perspective and organisational behaviour, which attempts to look at the internal activities. It also recognises that firms form relationships with other firms and trade, compete and cooperate with each other. It further recognises that the activities of individuals within the firm also affect the process of innovation.

Each firm's unique **organisational architecture** represents the way it has constructed itself over time. This comprises its internal design, including its functions and the relationships it has built up with suppliers, competitors, customers, etc. This framework recognises that these will have a considerable impact on a firm's innovative performance. So, too, will the way it manages its individual functions and its employees or individuals. These are separately identified within the framework as being influential in the innovation process.

Two traditions of innovation studies: Europe and the USA

Benoit Godin has written extensively on the intellectual history of innovation. His work provides a detailed account of the development of the category of innovation. In his two papers 'Innovation Studies: The development of a speciality I and II' (Godin, 2010a; 2010b) he explains how two traditions emerged. The first in the USA was concerned with technological change as the use of inventions in industrial production and the second in Europe, which was concerned more specifically with commercialised invention. The European tradition, which was developed as late as the 1970s, restricted the previously broader definition of innovation as the introduction of change to a narrower focus on technology and commercialisation. Christopher Freeman is largely credited as responsible for this so-called European tradition, which shifted the focus of studies of innovation to the process from invention to diffusion and the consideration of policy issues, specifically economic growth. The idea of a professionalised R&D system was proposed as having a key role.

According to Godin, this is now the position adopted by many public organisations, including the OECD. Godin argues that Freeman transformed an old meaning of technological innovation; that of introducing technical change within firms to commercialising technological invention and so helped build a new tradition. The European tradition saw invention as part of the innovation process and introduced the function of market uncertainty. This begins to shift the focus to product development and the role of users in the testing of such products. In addition, Godin identified another rationale that Freeman put forward for wanting to include users of the technology. This was: 'Freeman believed that there is a failure in the market mechanism in relation to technical change in consumer goods and services' (Godin, 2010b: 26). Godin concludes by suggesting, somewhat mischievously, that the two different traditions have emerged on different continents and continue to exist in almost total ignorance of each other. This helps to explain the emergence of different views on how to delineate innovation.

Recent and contemporary studies

As the twentieth century drew to a close, there was probably as much debate and argument concerning innovation and what contributes to innovative performance as a hundred years ago. This debate has, nonetheless, progressed our understanding of the area of innovation management. It was Schumpeter who argued that modern firms equipped with R&D laboratories have become the central innovative actors. Since his work, others have contributed to the debate (Chandler, 1962; Cohen and Levinthal, 1990; Nelson and Winter, 1982; Patel and Pavitt, 2000; Pavitt, 1990; Prahalad and Hamel, 1990). This emerging Schumpeterian or evolutionary theory of dynamic firm capabilities is having a significant impact on the study of business and management today. Success in the future, as in the past, surely will lie in the ability to acquire and utilise knowledge and apply this to the development of new products. Uncovering how to do this remains one of today's most pressing management problems.

The importance of uncovering and satisfying the needs of customers is the important role played by marketing and these activities feed into the new product development process. Studies by Christensen (2003) and Hamel and Prahalad (1994) suggest that listening to your customer may actually stifle technological innovation and be detrimental to long-term business success. Ironically, to be successful in industries characterised by technological change, firms may be required to pursue innovations that are not demanded by their current customers. Christensen (2003) distinguishes between 'disruptive innovations' and 'sustaining innovations' (radical or incremental innovations). Sustaining innovations appealed to existing customers, since they provided improvements to established products. For example, the introduction of new computer software usually provides improvements for existing customers in terms of added features. Disruptive innovations tend to provide improvements greater than those demanded. For example, whilst the introduction of 3.5-inch disk drives to replace 5.25-inch drives provided an enormous improvement in performance, it also created problems for users who were familiar with the previous format. These disruptive innovations also tended to create new markets, which eventually captured the existing market (*see* Discontinuous innovations, later in this chapter for more on this).

The need to view innovation in an organisational context

During the early part of the nineteenth century, manufacturing firms were largely family oriented and concentrated their resources on one activity. For example, one firm would produce steel from iron ore, another would roll this into sheet steel for use by, say, a manufacturer of cooking utensils. These would then be delivered to shops for sale. Towards the latter part of the century, these small enterprises were gradually replaced by large firms that would perform a much wider variety of activities. The expansion in manufacturing activities was simultaneously matched by an expansion in administrative activities. This represented the beginnings of the development of the diversified functional enterprise. The world expansion in trade during the early part of the twentieth century saw the quest for new markets by developing a wide range of new products (Chandler, 1962).

Unfortunately, many of the studies of innovation have treated it as an artefact that is somehow detached from knowledge and skills and not embedded in know-how. This, inevitably, leads to a simplified understanding, if not a misunderstanding, of what constitutes innovation. This section shows why innovation needs to be viewed in the context of organisations and as a process within organisations.

The diagram in Figure 1.1 shows how a number of different disciplines contribute to our understanding of the innovation process. It is important to note that firms do not operate in a vacuum. They trade with each other, they work together in some areas and compete in others. Hence, the role of other firms is a major factor in understanding innovation. As discussed earlier, economics clearly has an important role to play. So, too, does organisational behaviour as we try to understand what activities are necessary to ensure success. Studies of management will also make a significant contribution to specific areas, such as marketing, R&D, manufacturing operations and competition.

As has been suggested, in previous centuries it was easier in many ways to mobilise the resources necessary to develop and commercialise a product, largely because the resources required were, in comparison, minimal. Today, however, the resources required, in terms of knowledge, skills, money and market experience, mean that significant innovations are synonymous with organisations. Indeed, it is worthy of note that more recent innovations and scientific developments, such as significant discoveries like mobile phones or computer software and hardware developments, are associated with organisations rather than individuals (see Table 1.4). Moreover, the increasing depth of our understanding of science inhibits the breadth of scientific study. In the early part of the twentieth century, for example, the German chemical company Bayer was regarded as a world leader in chemistry. Now it is almost impossible for single chemical companies to be scientific leaders in all areas of chemistry. The large companies have specialised in particular areas. This is true of many other industries. Even university departments are having to concentrate their resources on particular areas of science. They are no longer able to offer teaching and research in all fields. In addition, the creation, development and commercial success of new ideas require a great deal of input from a variety of specialist sources and often vast amounts of money. Hence, today's innovations are associated with groups of people or companies. Innovation is, invariably, a team game. This will be explored more fully in Chapters 4, 7 and 16.

Table 1.4 Twentieth-century technological innovations

Date	New product	Responsible organisation
1930s	Polythene	ICI
1945	Ballpoint pen	Reynolds International Pen Company
1950s	Manufacturing process: float glass	Pilkington
1970/80s	Ulcer treatment drug: Zantac	GlaxoSmithKline
1970/80s	Photocopying	Xerox
1980s	Personal computer	Apple Computer
1980/90s	Computer operating system: Windows 95	Microsoft
1995	Impotence drug: Viagra	Pfizer
2000s	Cell phones	Motorola/Nokia
2005	MP3 players	Creative; Apple

Pause for thought

If two different firms, similar in size, operating in the same industry, spend the same on R&D, will their level of innovation be the same?

Individuals in the innovation process

Figure 1.1 identifies individuals as a key component of the innovation process. Within organisations, it is individuals who define problems, have ideas and perform creative linkages and associations that lead to inventions. Moreover, within organisations, it is individuals in the role of managers who decide what activities should be undertaken, the amount of resources to be deployed and how they should be carried out. This has led to the development of so-called key individuals in the innovation process, such as inventor, entrepreneur, business sponsor, etc. These are discussed in detail in Chapter 4.

Problems of definition and vocabulary

Whilst there are many arguments and debates in virtually all fields of management, it seems that this is particularly the case in innovation management. Very often, these centre on semantics. This is especially so when innovation is viewed as a single event. When viewed as a *process*, however, the differences are less substantive. At the heart of this book is the thesis that innovation needs to be viewed as a process. If one accepts that inventions are new discoveries, new ways of doing things, and that products are the eventual outputs from the inventions, that process from new discovery to eventual product is the innovation process. A useful analogy would be education, where qualifications are the formal outputs of the education process. Education, like innovation, is not and cannot be viewed as an event (Linton, 2009).

Arguments become stale when we attempt to define terms such as new, creativity or discovery. Often, it results in a game of semantics. First, what is new to one company may be old hat to another. Second, how does one judge success in terms of commercial gain or scientific achievement? Are they both not valid and justified goals in themselves? Third, it is context dependent – what is viewed as a success today may be viewed as a failure in the future. We need to try to understand how to encourage innovation in order that we may help to develop more successful new products (this point is explored in Chapters 13 and 14).

Entrepreneurship

Entrepreneurship is discussed at length in Chapter 2. The popular and traditional view of **entrepreneurship** is that of an individual who spots an opportunity and develops a business; it is understood that entrepreneurs often seem to have innate talents. In the United States, the subject of innovation management is often covered within 'entrepreneurship'. Indeed, it has been taught for many years and there are many courses available for students in US business schools on this topic. In a study of past and future research on the subject of entrepreneurship, Howard Stevenson, who did so much to establish entrepreneurship as a discipline at Harvard Business School and was Director of the Arthur Rock Centre for entrepreneurship there, defines entrepreneurship as:

the pursuit of opportunity beyond the resources you currently control.
(Stevenson and Amabile, 1999)

It is the analysis of the role of the individual entrepreneur that distinguishes the study of entrepreneurship from that of innovation management. Furthermore, it is starting small businesses and growing them into large and successful businesses that was the traditional focus of attention of those studying entrepreneurship. This has been changing over the past 10 years, especially across Europe, where there is now considerable emphasis, especially within the technical universities, on trying to understand how entrepreneurship and innovation can help create the new technology intensive businesses of tomorrow. Moreover, it is the recognition of the entrepreneur's desire to change things that is so important within innovation. We will see later that the role of an entrepreneur is central to innovation management. Illustration 1.3 shows how a serial entrepreneur has driven innovation and new product development in several industries.

Design

The definition of design with regard to business seems to be widening ever further and encompassing almost all aspects of business (see the Design Council, **www.designcouncil.org.uk**). For many people design is about developing or creating something; hence we are into semantics regarding how this differs from innovation. Hargadon and Douglas (2001: 476) suggest design is concerned with the emergent arrangement of concrete details that embody a new idea. A key question, however, is how design relates to research and development. Indeed, it seems that, in most cases, the word *design* and the word *development* mean the same thing. Traditionally, design referred to the development of drawings, plans and sketches. Indeed, most dictionary definitions continue with this view today and refer to a designer as a 'draughtsman who makes plans for manufacturers or prepares drawings for clothing or stage productions' (*Oxford English Dictionary*, 2005). In the aerospace industry,

Illustration 1.3

PayPal entrepreneur nets $1.3 billion in sale to eBay

Elon Musk (born 28 June 1971) is a South African-American engineer, entrepreneur and philanthropist. He is best known for co-founding PayPal. He is currently the CEO and Product Architect of Tesla Motors, and has degrees in business and physics from the University of Pennsylvania. In March 1999, Musk co-founded X.com, an online financial services and email payment company. One year later, X.com merged with Confinity, originally a company formed to transfer money between Palm Pilots. The new combined entity focused on email payments through the PayPal domain, acquired as part of Confinity.

In February 2001, X.com changed its legal name to PayPal. In October 2002, PayPal was acquired by eBay for US$1.5 billion in stock. In 2015 eBay separated from PayPal.

Musk decided to invest some of his fortune in Tesla Motors, of which he is a co-founder, chairman of the board and the sole product architect. First investing in April 2004, he led several rounds of financing, and became CEO in October 2008. Tesla Motors built an electric sports car, the Tesla Roadster, and plans to produce a more economical four-door electric vehicle. Musk is responsible for a business strategy that aims to deliver affordable electric vehicles to mass-market consumers.

engineers and designers previously would have worked closely together for many years, developing drawings for an aircraft. Today, the process is dominated by computer software programs that facilitate all aspects of the activity; hence the product development activities and the environments in which design occurs have changed considerably. Figure 1.2 shows, along the horizontal axis, the wide spectrum of activities

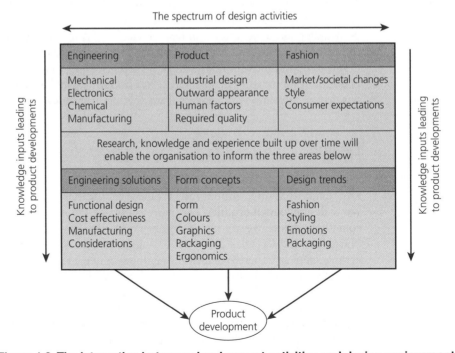

Figure 1.2 The interaction between development activities and design environment

that design encompasses from clothing design to design within electronics. The vertical axis shows how the areas of design feed into outputs from choice of colour to cost effectiveness; all of which are considered in the development of a product. The position taken by this book is to view design as an applied activity within research and development, and to recognise that, in certain industries, like clothing for example, design is the main component in product development. In other industries, however, such as pharmaceuticals, design forms only a small part of the product development activity (Moultrie and Livesey, 2014).

Innovation and invention

Many people confuse these terms. Indeed, if you were to ask people for an explanation, you would collect a diverse range of definitions. It is true that innovation is the first cousin of invention, but they are not identical twins that can be interchanged. Hence, it is important to establish clear meanings for them.

Innovation itself is a very broad concept that can be understood in a variety of ways. One of the more comprehensive definitions is offered by Myers and Marquis (1969):

> *Innovation is not a single action but a total process of interrelated sub processes. It is not just the conception of a new idea, nor the invention of a new device, nor the development of a new market. The process is all these things acting in an integrated fashion.*

It is important to clarify the use of the term 'new' in the context of innovation. Rogers and Shoemaker (1972) do this eloquently:

> *It matters little, as far as human behaviour is concerned, whether or not an idea is 'objectively' new as measured by the lapse of time since its first use or discovery . . . If the idea seems new and different to the individual, it is an innovation.*

> [emphasis added]

Most writers, including those above, distinguish innovation from invention by suggesting that innovation is concerned with the *commercial and practical application* of ideas or inventions. Invention, then, is the conception of the idea, whereas innovation is the subsequent translation of the invention into the economy. The following simple equation helps to show the relationship between the two terms:

Innovation = theoretical conception + technical invention + commercial exploitation

However, all the terms in this equation will need explanation in order to avoid confusion. The *conception* of new ideas is the starting point for innovation. A new idea by itself, whilst interesting, is neither an invention nor an innovation; it is merely a concept, a thought or collection of thoughts. The process of converting intellectual thoughts into a tangible new artefact (usually a product or process) is an **invention**. This is where science and technology usually play a significant role. At this stage, inventions need to be combined with hard work by many different people to convert them into products that will improve company performance. These later activities represent *exploitation*. However, it is the *complete* process that represents *innovation*. This introduces the notion that innovation is a process with a number of distinctive features that have to be managed. This is the view taken by this book. To summarise, then, innovation depends on inventions, but inventions need to be

Illustration 1.4

An example of an invention

Scientists and development engineers at a household cleaning products company had been working for many months on developing a new lavatory cleaning product. They had developed a liquid that, when sprayed into the toilet pan, on contact with water, would fizz and sparkle. The effect was to give the impression of a tough, active cleaning product. The company applied for a patent and further developments and market research were planned.

However, initial results, both from technical and market specialists, led to the abandonment of the project. The preliminary market feedback suggested a fear of such a product on the part of consumers. This was because the fizz and sparkle looked too dramatic and frightening. Furthermore, additional technical research revealed a short shelf-life for the mixture. This is a clear example of an invention that did not progress beyond the organisation to a commercial product.

harnessed to commercial activities before they can contribute to the growth of an organisation. Thus:

> Innovation is the management of all the activities involved in the process of idea generation, technology development, manufacturing and marketing of a new (or improved) product or manufacturing process or equipment.

This definition of **innovation as a management process** also offers a distinction between an innovation and a product, the latter being the output of innovation. Illustration 1.4 should help to clarify the differences.

It is necessary at this point to cross-reference these discussions with the practical realities of managing a business today. The senior vice-president for research and development at 3M, one of the most highly respected and innovative organisations, recently defined innovation as:

> Creativity: the thinking of novel and appropriate ideas. Innovation: the successful implementation of those ideas within an organisation.

Successful and unsuccessful innovations

There is often a great deal of confusion surrounding innovations that are not commercially successful. Some famous examples would be the Kodak Disc Camera or the Sinclair C5. The C5 was a small, electrically driven tricycle or car. Unfortunately for Clive Sinclair, the individual behind the development of the product, it was not commercially successful. Commercial failure, however, does not relegate an innovation to an invention. Using the definition established above, the fact that the product progressed from the drawing board into the marketplace makes it an innovation – albeit an unsuccessful one.

Pause for thought

Android and Apple are the clear dominant market leaders in App platforms. Microsoft has experience of how to be dominant in an industry. Could it possibly be a third App platform?

Different types of innovation

Industrial innovation includes not only major (radical) innovations but also minor (incremental) technological advances. Indeed, the definition offered above suggests that successful commercialisation of the innovation may involve considerably wider organisational changes. For example, the introduction of a radical, technological innovation, such as digital cameras by Kodak and Fuji, invariably results in substantial internal organisational changes. In this case, substantial changes occurred with the manufacturing, marketing and sales functions. Both of these firms decided to concentrate on the rapidly developing digital photography market. Yet both Fuji and Kodak were the market leaders in supplying traditional 35mm film cartridges. Their market share of the actual camera market was less significant. Such strategic decisions forced changes on all areas of the business. For example, in Kodak's case, the manufacturing function underwent substantial changes as it began to substantially cut production of 35mm film cartridges. Opportunities existed for manufacturing in producing digital cameras and their associated equipment. Similarly, the marketing function had to employ extra sales staff to educate and reassure retail outlets that the new technology would not cannibalise their film-processing business. Whilst many people would begin to print photographs from their PCs at home, many others would continue to want their digital camera film processed into physical photographs. For both Fuji and Kodak, the new technology has completely changed the photographic industry. Both firms have seen their revenues fall from film cartridge sales, but Kodak and Fuji are now market leaders in digital cameras, whereas before they were not.

Hence, technological innovation can be accompanied by additional managerial and organisational changes, often referred to as innovations. This presents a far more blurred picture and begins to widen the definition of innovation to include virtually any organisational or managerial change. Table 1.5 shows a typology of innovations.

Innovation was defined earlier in this section as the application of knowledge. It is this notion that lies at the heart of all types of innovation, be they product, process or

Table 1.5 A typology of innovations

Type of innovation	Example
Product innovation	The development of a new or improved product
Process innovation	The development of a new manufacturing process such as Pilkington's float glass process
Organisational innovation	A new venture division; a new internal communication system; introduction of a new accounting procedure
Management innovation	TQM (total quality management) systems; BPR (business process re-engineering); introduction of SAPR3*
Production innovation	Quality circles; just-in-time (JIT) manufacturing system; new production planning software, e.g. MRP II; new inspection system
Commercial/marketing innovation	New financing arrangements; new sales approach, e.g. direct marketing
Service innovation	Internet-based financial services

Note: SAP is a German software firm and R3 is an enterprise resource planning (ERP) product.

service. It is also worthy of note that many studies have suggested that product innovations are soon followed by process innovations in what they describe as an industry innovation cycle (see Chapter 6). Furthermore, it is common to associate innovation with physical change, but many changes introduced within organisations involve very little physical change. Rather, it is the activities performed by individuals that change. A good example of this is the adoption of so-called Japanese management techniques by automobile manufacturers in Europe and the United States.

It is necessary to stress at the outset that this book concentrates on the management of product innovation. This does not imply that the list of innovations above are less significant; this focus has been chosen to ensure clarity and to facilitate the study of innovation.

Technology and science

We also need to consider the role played by *science and technology* in innovation. The continual fascination with science and technology at the end of the nineteenth century and subsequent growth in university teaching and research have led to the development of many new strands of science. The proliferation of scientific journals over the past 30 years demonstrates the rapidly evolving nature of science and technology. The scientific literature seems to double in quantity every five years (Rothwell and Zegveld, 1985).

Science can be defined as systematic and formulated knowledge. There are clearly significant differences between science and technology. Technology is often seen as being the application of science and has been defined in many ways (Lefever, 1992).

It is important to remember that technology is not an accident of nature. It is the product of deliberate action by human beings. The following definition is suggested:

Technology is knowledge applied to products or production processes.

No definition is perfect and the above is no exception. It does, however, provide a good starting point from which to view technology with respect to innovation. It is important to note that technology, like education, cannot be purchased off the shelf like a can of tomatoes. It is embedded in knowledge and skills.

In a lecture given to the Royal Society in 1992, the former chairman of Sony, Akio Morita, suggested that, unlike engineers, scientists are held in high esteem. This, he suggested, is because science provides us with information that was previously unknown. Yet, technology comes from employing and *manipulating science* into concepts, processes and devices. These, in turn, can be used to make our life or work more efficient, convenient and powerful. Hence, it is technology, as an *outgrowth of science*, that fuels the industrial engine. And it is *engineers* and not scientists who make technology happen. In Japan, he argued, you will notice that almost every major manufacturer is run by an engineer or technologist. However, in the United Kingdom, some manufacturing companies are led by chief executive officers (CEOs) who do not understand the technology that goes into their own products. Indeed, many UK corporations are headed by chartered accountants. With the greatest respect to accountants, their central concerns are statistics and figures of *past* performance. How can an accountant reach out and grab the future if he or she is always looking at *last* quarter's results (Morita, 1992)?

The above represents the personal views of an influential senior figure within industry. There are many leading industrialists, economists and politicians who would concur (Hutton, 1995). But there are equally many who would profoundly disagree. The debate on improving economic innovative performance is one of the most important in the field of political economics. This debate should also include 'The young world rising' (see Illustration 1.5).

Innovation in action

A $900 shop

Looking to build a new office or shop? How about adopting the ultimate in recycling – a building made out of stacked shipping containers?

It is generally too expensive to ship an empty container back to its point of origin so there are thousands of them sitting in docks around the world. They are strong, stackable and cost as little as $900.

Source: Johnny Haglund/Getty Images

The Dordoy Bazaar in Bishkek, Kyrgyzstan is one of Asia's largest markets. It stretches for more than a kilometre and is almost entirely constructed from empty shipping containers stacked two high. Its success has been copied around the world: in 2011 Boxpark Shoreditch – London's first pop-up shopping mall made completely from shipping containers – opened.

(See the case study at the end of Chapter 3 for further details on shipping containers.)

Illustration 1.5

The young world rising

In his book titled *The Young World Rising*, Rob Salkowitz argues that three forces are coming together to shape the twenty-first century. These are youth, entrepreneurship and ICT. First, Salkowitz argues that within the fastest growing economies such as the BRICI countries (Brazil, Russia, India, China and Indonesia), the young represent a much higher proportion of the population than is typical in old world western counties in Europe and the USA. It is this new generation, he suggests, that will deliver the new fast-growing entrepreneurial firms of the future. Second, independent evidence from firms such as the Boston Consulting Group confirm that the information and communication technology (ICT) revolution is continuing to cause huge changes in the way people live and consume services. And, significantly because this new generation has not been

→

brought up on mainframe computers and PCs, Salkowitz argues they are not hampered in their mindsets and the way they think and develop new ideas. They have grown up with mobile devices and it is these that will provide the foundation for entrepreneurship in the twenty-first century. It is this fresh young cast of entrepreneurs whose ideas are changing the world. The next generation of Googles and Ubers may begin to emerge from this rising new young world.

Schumpeter: The other demographic dividend, *The Economist*, 7 October 2010.

Popular views of innovation

Science, technology and innovation have received a great deal of popular media coverage over the years, from Hollywood and Disney movies to best-selling novels (see Figure 1.3). This is probably because science and technology can help turn vivid imaginings into a possibility. The end result, however, is a simplified image of scientific discoveries and innovations. It usually consists of a lone professor, with a mass of white hair, working away in his garage and stumbling, by accident, on a major new discovery. Through extensive trial and error, usually accompanied by dramatic experiments, this is eventually developed into an amazing invention. This is best demonstrated in the blockbuster movie *Back to the Future*. Christopher Lloyd plays the eccentric scientist and Michael J. Fox his young, willing accomplice. Together, they are involved in an exciting journey that enables Fox to travel back in time and influence the future.

Cartoons have also contributed to a misleading image of the innovation process. Here, the inventor, usually an eccentric scientist, is portrayed with a glowing light-

Figure 1.3 The popular view of science

bulb above his head, as a flash of inspiration results in a new scientific discovery. We have all seen and laughed at these funny cartoons.

This humorous and popular view of inventions and innovations has been reinforced over the years and continues to occur in the popular press. Many industrialists and academics have argued that this simple view of a complex phenomenon has caused immense harm to the understanding of science and technology.

Models of innovation

Traditional arguments about innovation have centred on two schools of thought. On the one hand, the social deterministic school argued that innovations were the result of a combination of external social factors and influences, such as demographic changes, economic influences and cultural changes. The argument was that *when* the conditions were right, innovations would occur. On the other hand, the individualistic school argued that innovations were the result of unique individual talents and such innovators are born. Closely linked to the individualistic theory is the important role played by serendipity; more on this later.

Over the past 10 years, the literature on what drives innovation has tended to divide into two schools of thought: the market-based view and the resource-based view. The market-based view argues that market conditions provide the context that facilitates or constrains the extent of firm innovation activity (Porter, 1980, 1985; Slater and Narver, 1994). The key issue here, of course, is the ability of firms to recognise opportunities in the marketplace. Cohen and Levinthal (1990) and Trott (1998) would argue that few firms have the ability to scan and search their environments effectively.

The resource-based view of innovation considers that a market-driven orientation does not provide a secure foundation for formulating innovation strategies for markets that are dynamic and volatile; rather a firm's own resources provide a much more stable context in which to develop its innovation activity and shape its markets in accordance with its own view (Conner and Prahalad, 1996; Eisenhardt and Martin, 2000; Grant, 1996; Penrose, 1959; Prahalad and Hamel, 1990; Wernerfelt, 1984, 1995). The resource-based view of innovation focuses on the firm and its resources, capabilities and skills. It argues that when firms have resources that are valuable, rare and not easily copied they can achieve a sustainable competitive advantage – frequently in the form of innovative new products. Chapter 6 offers a more detailed overview of the **resource-based theory of the firm**.

Serendipity

Many studies of historical cases of innovation have highlighted the importance of the unexpected discovery. The role of serendipity or luck is offered as an explanation. As we have seen, this view is also reinforced in the popular media. It is, after all, everyone's dream that they will accidentally uncover a major new invention leading to fame and fortune.

On closer inspection of these historical cases, serendipity is rare indeed. After all, in order to recognise the significance of an advance, one would need to have some prior knowledge in that area. Most discoveries are the result of people who have had a fascination with a particular area of science or technology and it is following extended efforts on their part that advances are made. Discoveries may not be expected, but in the words of Louis Pasteur, 'chance favours the prepared mind'.

Linear models

It was US economists after the Second World War who championed the linear model of science and innovation. Since then, largely because of its simplicity, this model has taken a firm grip on people's views on how innovation occurs. Indeed, it dominated science and industrial policy for 40 years. It was only in the 1980s that management schools around the world began seriously to challenge the sequential linear process. The recognition that innovation occurs through the interaction of the science base (dominated by universities and industry), technological development (dominated by industry) and the needs of the market was a significant step forward (see Figure 1.4). The explanation of the interaction of these activities forms the basis of models of innovation today. Students may also wish to note that there is even a British Standard (BS7000), which sets out a design-centred model of the process (BSI, 2008).

There is, of course, a great deal of debate and disagreement about precisely what activities influence innovation and, more importantly, the internal processes that affect a company's ability to innovate. Nonetheless, there is broad agreement that it is the linkages between these key components that will produce successful innovation. Importantly, the devil is in the detail. From a European perspective, an area that requires particular attention is the linkage between the science base and technological development. The European Union (EU) believes that European universities have not established effective links with industry, whereas in the United States universities have been working closely with industry for many years.

As explained above, the innovation process has traditionally been viewed as a sequence of separable stages or activities. There are two basic variations of this model for product innovation. First, and most crudely, there is the technology-driven model (often referred to as technology push) where it is assumed that scientists make unexpected discoveries, technologists apply them to develop product ideas and engineers and designers turn them into prototypes for testing. It is left to manufacturing to devise ways of producing the products efficiently. Finally, marketing and sales will promote the product to the potential consumer. In this model, the marketplace was a passive recipient for the fruits of R&D. This technology-push

Figure 1.4 Conceptual framework of innovation

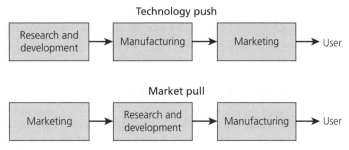

Figure 1.5 Linear models of innovation

model dominated industrial policy after the Second World War (see Figure 1.5). Whilst this model of innovation can be applied to a few cases, most notably the pharmaceutical industry, it is not applicable in many other instances; in particular where the innovation process follows a different route.

It was not until the 1970s that new studies of actual innovations suggested that the role of the marketplace was influential in the innovation process (von Hippel, 1978). This led to the second linear model, the market-pull model of innovation. The customer need-driven model emphasises the role of marketing as an initiator of new ideas resulting from close interactions with customers. These, in turn, are conveyed to R&D for design and engineering and then to manufacturing for production. In fast-moving consumer goods industries the role of the market and the customer remains powerful and very influential. The managing director of McCain Foods argues that knowing your customer is crucial to turning innovation into profits:

> It's only by understanding what the customer wants that we can identify the innovative opportunities. Then we see if there's technology that we can bring to bear on the opportunities that exist. Being innovative is relatively easy – the hard part is ensuring your ideas become commercially viable.

(Murray, 2003)

Simultaneous coupling model

Whether innovations are stimulated by technology, customer need, manufacturing or a host of other factors, including competition, misses the point. The models above concentrate on what is driving the downstream efforts rather than on *how* innovations occur (Galbraith, 1982). The linear model is able to offer only an explanation of *where* the initial stimulus for innovation was born, that is, where the trigger for the idea or need was initiated. The simultaneous coupling model shown in Figure 1.6

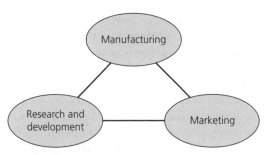

Figure 1.6 The simultaneous coupling model

suggests that it is the result of the simultaneous coupling of the knowledge within all three functions that will foster innovation. Furthermore, the point of commencement for innovation is not known in advance.

Architectural innovation

Henderson and Clark (1990) divide technological knowledge along two new dimensions: *knowledge of the components* and knowledge of the linkage between them, which they called *architectural knowledge*. The result is four possible types of innovation: incremental, modular, radical and architectural innovation. Essentially, they distinguish between the components of a product and the ways they are integrated into the system, that is, the product architecture, which they define as innovations that change the architecture of a product without changing its components. Prior to the Henderson and Clark model, the radical/incremental dimension suggests that incumbents will be in a better position if the innovation is incremental, since they can use existing knowledge and resources to leverage the whole process. New entrants, on the other hand, will have a large advantage if the innovation is radical because they will not need to change their knowledge background. Furthermore, incumbents struggle to deal with radical innovation both because they operate under a managerial mindset constraint and because, strategically, they have less of an incentive to invest in the innovation if it will cannibalise their existing products.

Kodak illustrates this well. The company dominated the photography market over many years and, throughout this extended period, all the incremental innovations solidified its leadership. As soon as the market experienced a radical innovation – the entrance of digital technology – Kodak struggled to defend its position against the new entrants. The new technology required different knowledge, resources and mindsets. This pattern of innovation is typical in mature industries. This concept is explored further in Chapter 7.

Interactive model

The interactive model develops this idea further (see Figure 1.7) and links together the technology-push and market-pull models. It emphasises that innovations occur as the result of the interaction of the marketplace, the science base and the organisation's capabilities. Like the coupling model, there is no explicit starting point. The use of information flows is used to explain how innovations transpire and that they can arise from a wide variety of points.

Whilst still oversimplified, this is a more comprehensive representation of the innovation process. It can be regarded as a logically sequential, though not necessarily continuous, process that can be divided into a series of functionally distinct but interacting and interdependent stages (Rothwell and Zegveld, 1985). The overall innovation process can be thought of as a complex set of communication paths over which knowledge is transferred. These paths include internal and external linkages. The innovation process outlined in Figure 1.7 represents the organisation's capabilities and its linkages with both the marketplace and the science base. Organisations that are able to manage this process effectively will be successful at innovation.

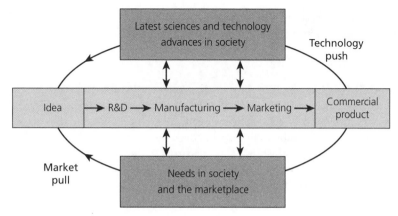

Figure 1.7 Interactive model of innovation

At the centre of the model are the organisational functions of R&D, engineering and design, manufacturing and marketing and sales. Whilst, at first, this may appear to be a linear model, the flow of communication is not necessarily linear. There is provision for feedback. Also, linkages with the science base and the marketplace occur between all functions, not just with R&D or marketing. For example, as often happens, it may be the manufacturing function that initiates a design improvement that leads to the introduction of either a different material or the eventual development by R&D of a new material. Finally, the generation of ideas is shown to be dependent on inputs from three basic components (as outlined in Figure 1.4): technological developments; the needs of the marketplace; the science and technology base. Recent research confirms the validity of this concept today. Research by Stefano et al., (2012) updates the debate on the sources of innovation. They show and confirm that:

● the market is a major source of innovation;
● firm competences enable firms to match technology with demand; and
● external and internal sources of innovations are important.

All of which are necessary for value creation and capture.

Innovation life cycle and dominant designs

The launch of an innovative new product into the market is usually only the beginning of technology progress. At the industry level, the introduction of a new technology will cause a reaction: competitors will respond to this new product, hence technological progress depends on factors other than those internal to the firm. We need to consider the role of the competition. Product innovation, process innovation, competitive environment and organisational structure all interact and are closely linked together. Abernathy and Utterback (1978) argued there were three different phases in an innovation's life cycle: fluid, transitional and specific. This concept will be discussed in detail in Chapter 7, but at this stage we need only to recognise that one can consider innovation in the form of a life cycle that begins with a major technological change and product innovation. This is followed by the

Illustration 1.6

The 'sailing ship effect'

The so-called 'sailing ship effect' often has been stated as though there is no doubt that it really took place at the end of the nineteenth century. The notion is that the substitution threat of new radical technologies (steamships) may lead to a renewed spurt of innovation in an old and established technology (sailing ships). Recently, Mendonça (2013) reviewed the field of maritime history and shows that the effect is nowhere to be found, even in the very case from which it derives its name. Mendonça says the modernisation of the sailing trader occurs before, not after, the steamship had become an effective competitor.

emergence of competition and process innovations (manufacturing improvements). As the life cycle proceeds, a dominant design usually emerges prior to standardisation and an emphasis on lowering cost. This model can be applied to many consumer product innovations over the past 20–30 years, such as VCRs, CD players and mobile phones. The so-called sailing ship effect can sometimes enable old technologies to have new life (see Illustration 1.6).

Open innovation and the need to share and exchange knowledge (network models)

Innovation has been described as an information–creation process that arises out of social interaction. Chesbrough (2003), adopting a business strategy perspective, presents a persuasive argument that the process of innovation has shifted from one of closed systems, internal to the firm, to a new mode of open systems involving a range of players distributed up and down the supply chain. Significantly, it is Chesbrough's emphasis on the new knowledge-based economy that informs the concept **open innovation**. In particular, it is the use of cheap and instant information flows that places even more emphasis on the linkages and relationships of firms. It is from these linkages and the supply chain in particular that firms have to ensure that they have the capability to fully capture and utilise ideas.

Furthermore, the product innovation literature, in applying the open innovation paradigm, has been debating the strengths and limitations of so-called user toolkits, which seem to ratchet up further this drive to externalise the firm's capabilities to capture innovation opportunities (von Hippel, 2005).

Authors such as Thomke (2003), Schrange (2000) and Dodgson et al. (2005) have emphasised the importance of learning through experimentation. This is similar to Nonaka's work in the early 1990s, which emphasised the importance of learning by doing in the 'knowledge creating company' (Nonaka, 1991). However, Dodgson et al. argue that there are significant changes occurring at all levels of the innovation process, forcing us to reconceptualise the process with emphasis placed on the three areas that have experienced most significant change through the introduction and use of new technologies. These are: technologies that facilitate creativity, technologies that facilitate communication and technologies that facilitate

Table 1.6 The chronological development of models of innovation

Date	Model	Characteristics
1950/60s	Technology-push	Simple linear sequential process; emphasis on R&D; the market is a recipient of the fruits of R&D
1970s	Market-pull	Simple linear sequential process; emphasis on marketing; the market is the source for directing R&D; R&D has a reactive role
1970s	Dominant design	Abernathy and Utterback (1978) illustrate that an innovation system goes through three stages before a dominant design emerges
1980s	Coupling model	Emphasis on integrating R&D and marketing
1980/90s	Interactive model	Combinations of push and pull
1990	Architectural innovation	Recognition of the role of firm-embedded knowledge in influencing innovation
1990s	Network model	Emphasis on knowledge accumulation and external linkages
2000s	Open innovation	Chesbrough's (2003) emphasis on further externalisation of the innovation process in terms of linkages with knowledge inputs and collaboration to exploit knowledge outputs

manufacturing. For example, they argue that information and communication technologies have changed the way individuals, groups and communities interact. Mobile phones, email and websites are obvious examples of how people interact and information flows in a huge osmosis process through the boundaries of the firm. When this is coupled with changes in manufacturing and operations technologies, enabling rapid prototyping and flexible manufacturing at low costs, the process of innovation seems to be undergoing considerable change (Chesbrough, 2003; Dodgson et al., 2005; Schrange, 2000). Models of innovation need to take account of these new technologies, which allow immediate and extensive interaction with many collaborators throughout the process from conception to commercialisation.

Table 1.6 summarises the historical development of the dominant models of the industrial innovation process.

Doing, using and interacting (DUI) mode of innovation

Researchers have recognised for many years that in low and medium technology (LMT) intensive industries the traditional science and technology model of innovation is not applicable and cannot explain continued product and process innovations (see Arrow, 1968; Bush, 1945; Fitjar and Rodriguez-Pose, 2013; Maclaurin, 1953; Pavitt, 2001). Further, in the classic article by Pavitt (1984: 343–73) he spelt out, in his typology of firms, that 'LMT industries are characterised by process, organisational and marketing innovations, by weak internal innovation capabilities and by strong dependencies on the external provision of machines, equipment and software'. LMT sectors are central to economic growth. Whether measured in terms of output, capital invested or employment, they dominate the economies of highly developed as well as developing nations, providing more than 90 per cent of output in the European Union, the USA and Japan.[1] Given this dominant position within modern industrialised economies, attempting to better understand the nature of innovation within this sector is of concern to policy makers and industrialists.

The role of low technology intensive firms and industries in modern economies is complex and frequently misunderstood. This is due partly to Hatzichronoglou's (1997) widely used revision of the OECD classification of sectors and products that refers only to high technology (defined as spending more than 5 per cent of revenues on research and development). This has contributed to an unfortunate tendency to understate the importance of technological change outside such R&D-intensive fields (Hirsch-Kreinsen et al., 2006; Robertson et al., 2009). Products and production processes in these industries may be highly complex and capital intensive. Research in the area of low technology intensive industries shows a dominance of incremental, mostly process-driven innovations where disruptive innovation activities are scarce.

The food industry traditionally has experienced very low levels of investment in R&D, yet has delivered both product and process innovation over a sustained period. In such environments, innovation can be explained through learning by doing and the use of networks of interactions and extensive tacit knowledge (Lundvall, 1992; Nonaka and Hirotaka, 1995). Similarly, Jensen et al. (2007) characterised a learning by 'Doing, Using and Interacting' (DUI) mode of innovation where extensive on-the-job problem solving occurs and where firms interact and share experiences. More recently, Fitjar and Rodriguez-Pose (2013) developed a classification of DUI firm interactions in a study of firm-level innovation in the food industry in Norway. They found that 'firms which engage in collaboration with external agents tend to be more innovative than firms that rely on their own resources for innovation' (Fitjar and Rodriguez-Pose, 2013: 137).

Discontinuous innovation – step changes

Occasionally, something happens in an industry that causes a disruption – the rules of the game change. This has happened in many different industries: for example, telephone banking and internet banking have caused huge changes for the banking industry. Likewise, the switch from photographic film to digital film changed the landscape in that industry. And the music industry is still grappling with the impact of downloading as the dominant way to consume music. These changes are seen as not continuous, that is **discontinuous**: the change is very significant (see Figure 1.8). Sometimes this is referred to as disruptive innovation. Schumpeter referred to this concept as creative destruction.

The term disruptive innovation as we know it today first appeared in *The Innovator's Dilemma*. In this book, Clayton Christensen investigated why some

---

[1] General treatments of the role of LMT firms and industries are given in Von Tunzelmann and Acha (2005), Sandven et al. (2005) and Robertson and Patel (2007). Hirsch-Kreinsen et al. (2006) report on a European Commission study of LMT sectors.

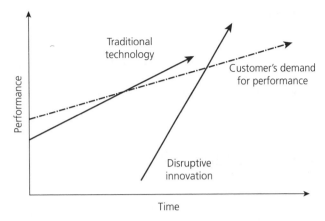

Figure 1.8 Disruptive innovations

innovations that were radical in nature reinforced the incumbent's position in a certain industry, contrary to what previous models (for instance the Henderson–Clark model) would predict. More specifically, he analysed extensively the disk drive industry because it represented the most dynamic, technologically discontinuous and complex industry one could find in the economy. Figure 1.8 shows how a disruptive innovation creates a step change in performance.

This very same pattern of disruption can be observed with video rental services, department stores and newspapers. The appearance of online news services, web portals and other media platforms, such as blogs and wikis, clearly represent a disruptive innovation for the traditional newspaper industry. Will the likes of *The Times*, *The Guardian* and the *New York Times* be able to survive such disruption? For many years, newspapers embraced the web and provided content online, but sales of newspapers continued to decline. A key question for the industry is: What indispensable roles can we play in the lives of the consumers we want to serve?

Other examples of disruptive innovations are:

- steamships (which disrupted sailing ships);
- music downloads (which disrupted CDs); and
- internet shopping (which disrupted high street retailing).

Discontinuity can also come about by reframing the way we think about an industry. Later in this book, Table 15.3 shows a wide range of new services that also created new business models. This includes online gambling and low cost airlines. What these examples – and many others – have in common is that they represent the challenge of discontinuous innovation. How do incumbent firms cope with these dramatic shifts in technology, service and/or the business model?

What many firms would also like to know is how they can become the disruptor or radical innovator. In a study of radical innovation in the highly innovative motorsport industry, Delbridge and Mariotti (2009) found that successful innovators:

- engage in wide exploratory innovation search activities, looking beyond their own knowledge base and domain of expertise;

- identify the advantages offered by new combinations of existing knowledge, through the application of technologies and materials initially developed elsewhere;
- often partner with unusual firms, beyond the usual sphere of collaboration;
- engage with partner companies to establish a close working relationship;
- promote lateral thinking within an existing web of partners.

Innovation as a management process

> *The fact is coming up with an idea is the least important part of creating something great. The execution and delivery are what's key.*
>
> (Sergey Brin, Co-founder of Google, quoted in *The Guardian* (2009))

The statement by Sergey Brin, co-founder of Google, confirms that we need to view innovation as a management process. The preceding sections have revealed that innovation is not a singular event, but a series of activities that are linked in some way to the others. This may be described as a process and involves:

1 a response to either a need or an opportunity that is context dependent;
2 a creative effort that, if successful, results in the introduction of novelty;
3 the need for further changes.

Usually, in trying to capture this complex process, the simplification has led to misunderstandings. The simple linear model of innovation can be applied to only a few innovations and is more applicable to certain industries than others. The pharmaceutical industry characterises much of the technology-push model. Other industries, like the food industry, are better represented by the market-pull model. For most industries and organisations, innovations are the result of a mixture of the two. Managers working within these organisations have the difficult task of trying to manage this complex process.

A framework for the management of innovation

Industrial innovation and new product development have evolved considerably from their early beginnings outlined above. We have seen that innovation is extremely complex and involves the effective management of a variety of different activities. It is precisely how the process is managed that needs to be examined. Over the past 50 years, there have been numerous studies of innovation attempting to understand not only the ingredients necessary for it to occur but also what levels of ingredients are required and in what order. Furthermore, a study by the Boston Consulting Group reported in *Business Week* (2006) of over 1,000 senior managers revealed further explanations as to what makes some firms more innovative than others. The key findings from this survey are captured in Table 1.7. While these headline-grabbing bullet points are interesting, they do not show us what firms have to do to become excellent in design (BMW) or to improve cooperation with suppliers (Toyota). Table 1.8 captures some of the key studies that have influenced our understanding.

Table 1.7 Explanations for innovative capability

Innovative firm	Explanation for innovative capability
Apple	Innovative chief executive
Google	Scientific freedom for employees
Samsung	Speed of product development
Procter & Gamble	Utilisation of external sources of technology
IBM	Share patents with collaborators
BMW	Design
Starbucks	In-depth understanding of customers and their cultures
Toyota	Close cooperation with suppliers

Table 1.8 Studies of innovation management

	Study	Date	Focus
1	Carter and Williams	1957	Industry and technical progress
2	Project Hindsight – TRACES (Isenson)	1968	Historical reviews of US government-funded defence industry
3	Wealth from knowledge (Langrish et al.)	1972	Queen's Awards for technical innovation
4	Project SAPPHO (Rothwell et al.)	1974	Success and failure factors in chemical industry
5	Minnesota Studies (Van de Ven)	1989	14 case studies of innovations
6	Rothwell	1992	25-year review of studies
7	Sources of innovation (Wheelwright and Clark)	1992	Different levels of user involvement
8	MIT studies (Utterback)	1994	5 major industry-level cases
9	Project NEWPROD (Cooper)	1994	Longitudinal survey of success and failure in new products
10	Radical innovation (Leifer et al.)	2000	Review of mature businesses
11	TU Delft study (van der Panne et al.)	2003	Literature review of success and failure factors

This chapter so far has helped to illustrate the complex nature of innovation management and also identified some of the limitations of the various models and schools of thought. Specifically, these are:

- Variations on linear thinking continue to dominate models of innovation. Actually, most innovation models show innovation paths, representing a stage-gate type of activity, controlling the progress from idea to market introduction, rather than giving insight into the dynamics of actual innovation processes.
- Science is viewed primarily as technology orientated (physical sciences) and R&D is closely linked to manufacturing, causing insufficient attention to be paid to the behavioural sciences. As a consequence, service innovation is hardly addressed.
- The complex interactions between new technological capabilities and emerging societal needs are a vital part of the innovation process, but they are underexposed in current models.

- The role of the entrepreneur (individual or team) is not captured.
- Current innovation models are not embedded within the strategic thinking of the firm; they remain isolated entities.

Innovation needs to be viewed as a management process. We need to recognise that change is at the heart of it. And that change is caused by decisions that people make. The framework in Figure 1.9 attempts to capture the iterative nature of the network processes in innovation and represents this in the form of an endless innovation circle with interconnected cycles. This circular concept helps to show how the firm gathers information over time, how it uses technical *and* societal knowledge, and how it develops an attractive proposition. This is achieved through developing linkages and partnerships with those having the necessary capabilities ('open innovation'). In addition, the entrepreneur is positioned at the centre.

The framework in Figure 1.9 is referred to as the 'cyclic innovation model' (CIM) (Berkhout et al., 2010); a cross-disciplinary view of change processes (and their interactions) as they take place in an open innovation arena. Behavioural sciences and engineering as well as natural sciences and markets are brought together in a coherent system of processes with four principal nodes that function as roundabouts. The combination of the involved changes leads to a wealth of business opportunities. Here, entrepreneurship plays a central role by making use of those opportunities. The message is that without the drive of entrepreneurs there is no innovation, and without innovation there is no new business. Figure 1.9 shows that the combination of change and entrepreneurship is the basis of new business.

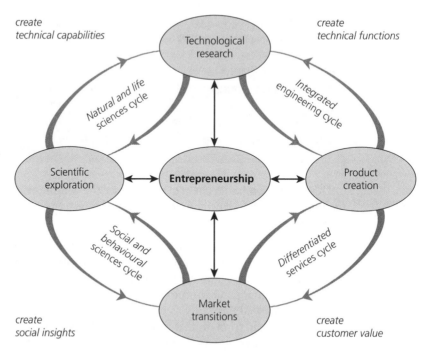

Figure 1.9 The cyclic model of innovation with interconnected cycles
Source: Berkhout et al. (2010).

Adopting this approach to the management of innovation should help firms as processes should not be forced into simple one-way pipelines, but rather be organised by interconnected cycles with feedforward and feedback connections: from linear to non-linear thinking. In that way, a dynamic network environment is created in which the social and behavioural sciences are linked to engineering, and where the natural and life sciences connect with market goals (Berkhout, 2000). This is what is captured in the proposed innovation framework. Supported by today's powerful communication technology, serial process management along a linear path is replaced by parallel networking along a largely self-organising circle. Vital decisions in innovation do not occur in the gates of a staged project management pipeline, but do occur on the innovation shop floor itself; or in the nodes of the cyclic networks. In my experience, young people like to work in such an environment. Moreover, according to Salkowitz (2010), young entrepreneurs around the world are blending new technologies and next-generation thinking, building radically new kinds of organisations adapted to a flat and crowded world (see Illustration 1.6).

The cyclic innovation model is the result of a combination of analysis of theory and practical evidence, based on many years of experience within industries that work with scientists to develop valuable new products and services. Furthermore, evidence has been gathered from Delphi, a science-industry consortium that consists of a large number of international companies within the field of geo-energy (Berkhout et al., 2010).

The most important feature of Figure 1.9 is that the model architecture is not a chain but a *circle*: innovations build on innovations. Ideas create new concepts, successes create new challenges and failures create new insights. Note that new ideas may start anywhere in the circle, causing a wave that propagates clockwise and anti-clockwise through the circle. In an innovative society, businesses are transparent and the speed of propagation along the circle is high, resulting in minimum travel time along the innovation path. Today, time is a crucial factor in innovation. Indeed, when it comes to managing the process within the firm, the stage-gate approach dominates practice. This is because the project management advantages tend to outweigh the limitations it poses to the innovation process. This can be illustrated within Figure 1.9; here the central position in the innovation circle is frequently occupied by a manager, who adopts a stage-gate approach and culture, rather than an entrepreneur; having an entrepreneur in the centre enhances the innovation process.

New skills

The framework in Figure 1.9 underpins the way managers need to view the management of innovation. Many of the old traditional approaches to management need to change and new approaches need to be adopted. Increasingly, managers and those who work for them are no longer in the same location. Gone are the days when managers could supervise the hour-to-hour work of individuals. Often complex management relationships need to be developed because organisations are trying to produce complex products and services and do so across geographic boundaries. Cross-functional and cross-border task forces often need to be created.

And managers have to manage without authority. In these circumstances, individual managers need to work with and influence people who are not their subordinates and over whom they have no formal authority. Frequently, this means leadership must be shared across the team members. An important part of getting work done without authority is having an extensive network of relationships. In today's complex and virtual organisations, managers need information and support from a wide range of individuals. To summarise, then, new skills are required in the following areas:

● virtual management;
● managing without authority;
● shared leadership;
● building extensive networks.

Pause for thought

Surely all innovations start with an idea and end with a product; so does that not make it a linear process?

Innovation and new product development

Such thinking is similarly captured in the framework outlined in Figure 1.9. It stresses the importance of interaction and communication within and between functions and with the external environment. This networking structure allows lateral communication, helping managers and their staff unleash creativity. This framework emphasises the importance of informal and formal networking across all functions (Pittaway et al., 2004).

This introduces a tension between the need for diversity, on the one hand, in order to generate novel linkages and associations, and the need for commonality, on the other, to facilitate effective internal communication.

The purpose of this book is to illustrate the interconnections of the subjects of innovation management and new product development. Indeed, some may argue they are two sides of the same coin. By directly linking together these two significant areas of management, the clear connections and overlaps between the subjects can be more fully explored and understood.

It is hoped that this framework will help to provide readers with a visual reminder of how one can view the innovation process that needs to be managed by firms. The industry and products and services will determine the precise requirements necessary. It is a dynamic process and the framework tries to emphasise this. It is also a complex process and this helps to simplify it to enable further study. Very often, product innovation is viewed from a purely marketing perspective with little, if any, consideration of the R&D function and the difficulties of managing science and technology. Likewise, many manufacturing and technology approaches to product innovation have previously not taken sufficient notice of the needs of the customer. Into this mix we must not forget the role played by the entrepreneur in visioning the future.

Case study

Has the Apple innovation machine stalled?

This case study examines the success and failure of new products from Apple. Many analysts have argued that the death of Steve Jobs has had a significant impact on Apple's innovation ability. What is more likely is that competition has increased and profits have been reduced; but did Apple make mistakes? Difficult times may lie ahead, but the case shows that Apple faced even worse times in the 1990s. Jonathan Ives, Head of Design at Apple, argues Apple is more than one man. High levels of investment seem to suggest a good future.

Apple, innovation and market vision
Stiffer competition in smartphones and tablets from the likes of Samsung has raised concerns over whether the party is over for Apple. One should not be surprised. Apple's fantastic profit margins – 38.6 per cent on sales have attracted many competitors. The iPhones and iPads still generate huge profits. But margins are being eroded by clever competitors like Samsung (see Figure 1.10). Apple needs another disruptive innovation.

Apple made $42 billion in 2012. This was a record for Apple and amongst the all-time records for corporations everywhere. Under Tim Cook, Apple has

Source: Zeynep Demir/Shutterstock.com

introduced the iPad Mini – a 7-inch tablet (a category Jobs dismissed as pointless) – which has preserved the iPad's leadership in tablets. This is in addition to Tim Cook's exceptional management of Apple's supply chain. When Cook initially took over Apple's

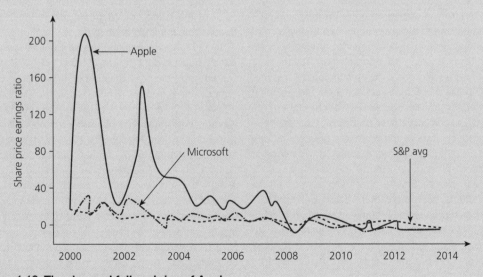

Figure 1.10 The rise and fall and rise of Apple

supply chain, he cut down the number of component suppliers from 100 to 24, forcing companies to compete for Apple's business. More recently, Apple has adopted even stricter management over its supply chain than before. The changes include more frequent inspections, greater time spent on inspections, and a renewed focus on managing costs and product quality.

The iPod, iPhone and iPad have all shown Apple's great skill in bringing disruptive innovations to the market. Disruptive innovation explains the dichotomy of *sustaining* and *disruptive* innovation. A sustaining innovation improves the performance of existing products along the dimensions that mainstream customers value. It results in limited change for established companies. Disruptive innovations, on the other hand, often will have characteristics that traditional customer segments may not want, at least initially. Such innovations will appear as cheaper, simpler and even with inferior quality if compared to existing products, but some new segment will value it.

The iPod, iPhone and iPad also demonstrates Apple's great skill in market vision. Disruptive innovations require a greater change in existing patterns of behaviour and thinking; thus consumers would perceive a higher level of risk and uncertainty in their adoption decisions relative to continuous innovations that depend on established behavioural patterns and perceptions.

This ability has been at the heart of Apple's success. Its ability in market vision or the ability to look into the future and picture products and services that will be successful is a fundamental requirement for those firms wishing to engage in innovation. It involves assessing one's own technological capability and present or future market needs and visioning a market offering that people will want to buy.

Apple needs more new products. One of these new products is likely to be a much cheaper iPhone aimed at emerging markets. Apple sold two million of its top-of-the-range iPhone devices in 2013. However, most Chinese shoppers cannot afford them. Barclays, an investment bank, believes that Apple could produce an iPhone for less than $150 to broaden its appeal. This would certainly generate revenues by appealing to mass markets. But Apple has rarely targeted the mainstream. A review of its past may point the way for the future.

The rise and fall and rise of Apple Corp Inc.

Apple computers began in 1977 when Steven Wozniak and Steven Jobs designed and offered the Apple I to the personal computer field. It was designed over a period of years, and was built only in printed circuit-board form. It debuted in April 1976 at the Homebrew Computer Club in Palo Alto, but few took it seriously. Continual product improvements and wider technological developments, including microprocessor improvements, led to the launch of the Apple Macintosh in 1984.

The Macintosh computer was different because it used a mouse-driven operating system, all other PCs used the keyboard-driven system known as MS DOS (Microsoft Disc operating system). Early in the 1980s, Microsoft licensed its operating system to all PC manufacturers, but Apple decided against this approach, opting instead to stay in control of its system. The 1980s was a period of dramatic growth for personal computers as virtually every office and home began to buy into the PC world. Slowly, Microsoft became the dominant standard, not because its technology was better, but largely because its system became the dominant standard. As people bought PCs, so with it they would buy the operating system: MS Windows, hence it became the de facto dominant standard. The Apple operating system was available only if you bought an Apple PC. Consequently, Apple's market share plummeted. By the mid-1990s, Apple had grown to a $12 billion company, twice the size of Microsoft; but Microsoft was powering ahead on the back of the launch of Windows and it would soon become the dominant tech firm.

In 1993, Apple launched the Newton; its first completely new product in many years. Indeed, it represented Apple's entry into (and perhaps creation of) an entirely new market: Personal Digital Assistants (PDAs). The PDA market was barely present when the Newton was released, but other companies were working on similar devices. The Newton Message Pad featured a variety of personal-organisation applications, such as an address book, a calendar, notes, along with communications capabilities such as faxing and email. It featured a pen-based interface, which used a word-based, trainable handwriting recognition engine. Unfortunately, this engine had been developed by a third party, and was notoriously difficult to use and was partly responsible for the product's failure. This was to represent a low point in Apple's fortunes.

Table 1.9 Apple's new product failures

Apple product	Why it failed
Macintosh Portable (1989–91)	The 16-pound monster had many cutting-edge technologies for the time, such as its active matrix LCD screen, but its weight and the fact that it often would not turn on, even when plugged in, due to its battery design, kept it off users' desks. In 1989 Toshiba and others were shipping the 6-pound notebook form we still use today, making the Macintosh Portable a whale in a market of dolphins.
Apple Newton MessagePad (1993–8)	The Newton MessagePad, a tablet-PDA hybrid with handwriting recognition. There was nothing else like it, but its ungainly size, woeful battery life, and hard-to-read screen relegated it to technology-cult status.
Macintosh Performa series (1992–7)	In the 1990s, Apple was facing increased competition from DOS- and Windows-based PC makers. Apple's then-CEO Michael Spindler decided to sell a line of cheap Macs, called the Performa. They were cheap: flimsy, prone to failure and underpowered – yet still costlier than a cheap PC. Worse, they cannibalised the sales of pricier Macs for a while, rather than expanding the market.
Pippin (1995–6)	The Pippin was a multimedia PC aimed more at gaming and CD playback than traditional computing – more like what a PlayStation or Xbox is today. PlayStation, Nintendo and Sega consoles were already out and more popular, so game developers and users ignored the Pippin.
Macintosh clones (1995–7)	In the mid-1990s, Apple was struggling. Apple decided to let other companies make and sell Macs. The main clone maker was Power Computing. Power Computing's clones cost less and soon surpassed Apple's own Macs in ratings. Steve Jobs returned to Apple in 2007 and quickly killed the clone experiment by releasing Mac OS 9. Apple bought Power Computing and shut it down that year.
Apple USB Mouse (1998–2000)	After taking back control of Apple in 1997, Steve Jobs went about redefining the look and feel of the Mac itself, and his design team created the candy-coloured iMac line that contrasted dramatically with the traditional beige box. It also decided to reinvent the look and feel of the mouse. The new disc design certainly got attention, but for the wrong reasons: it was hard to hold, as it did not fit most people's hands. In 2000, the company released the soapbar-shaped Apple Pro mouse – the elongated, yet still simple, curves could be held comfortably and securely.
Apple TV (2007–present)	Apple's networked media player box was supposed to be the new TiVo, but it is not even as well liked as Windows-based media-centre PCs. Apple TV is fairly limited: Apple TV is not connected to the vast video libraries of Netflix or Blockbuster (BBI), so you are stuck with the iTunes Store's offerings, which many television and movie studios have avoided supporting for fear of suffering the same loss of control as the music industry experienced with iTunes. In other words, Apple TV is not that innovative or that capable.

In February 1996, *Business Week* put Apple on its front cover suggesting the demise of the company.

With so much success currently washing around the firm, it is sometimes difficult to recall all of Apple's failures. So I have listed them in Table 1.9. Some of them were very bad. But learning from your mistakes is an important lesson in every aspect of life and it seems that Apple has learnt well.

In the mid-1990s, Apple's future in the computer technology industry looked bleak, with a diversified product portfolio and a low market share within the PC market of only 3 per cent. Many were, therefore, surprised when Steven Jobs returned to the company as Chief Executive in 1997. He quickly set about culling many product lines and much of its operations and decided to focus on only a few products, including the new-looking iMac. This coincided with the economic boom in the late 1990s and allowed Apple to generate cash very quickly. This provided revenue for the development of the iPod, which was to transform the fortunes of Apple. Table 1.10 shows the Apple and Steve Jobs relationship.

→

Table 1.10 Steve Jobs and Apple

Year	Event	Year	Event
1976	Co-founds Apple with Steve Wozniak	2001	Launches iPod
1976	Apple launches first computer	2003	iTunes launched
1984	Launch of Apple Mac	2007	iPhone lauched
1985	Jobs ousted in Boardroom battle	2010	iPad launched
1986	Co-founds Pixar	2010	Apple overtakes Microsoft
1997	Returns to Apple	2011	iCloud launched
1998	Launch of iMac	2011	Steve Jobs dies
2001	First Apple store opens		

Jonathan Ive and life without Steve Jobs

Jonathan Ive is the British designer behind Apple's iconic iPods, iPads and iPhones. It is hard to overestimate the influence of Jonathan Ive. He is due to receive $25 million (£15.5 million) in shares, which he was able to buy for £7 million. The money will contribute to his fortune of more than £80 million. In September 2012, Ive seems to have committed himself to Apple when he bought a $17 million house in San Francisco. In 2012, Ive was promoted to a bigger role at Apple where he now oversees all product design, hardware and software. This follows news that Apple is parting with mobile software chief Scott Forstall. Ive will fill some of the vacuum left by Forstall. Apple announced the following:

Jonathan Ive will provide leadership and direction for Human Interface (HI) across the company in addition to his role as the leader of Industrial Design. His incredible design aesthetic has been the driving force behind the look and feel of Apple's products for more than a decade.

Ive is softly spoken and has worked at Apple in California since 1992 and, since 1997, has been in charge of its designs. This may well make him the most influential designer in the world. In creating the iMac, he helped save Apple. With the iPod, he unleashed a product that profoundly altered the music industry, whilst the iPhone is doing the same to the mobile phone industry. The most recent product from his team, the Apple Watch, is setting the standard for an entirely new category of device.

He studied design at Newcastle Polytechnic, now Northumbria University, where he still returns frequently to give guest lectures. Ive emphasises the teamwork involved in producing products such as the iMac, the candy-coloured computer that relaunched Apple on the path to success, or the iPad. Ive and his team do not just design the products that Apple makes. The ideas are often so different that, frequently, they have to design the entire production process that the factories will use to make them.

In interviews, Ive has said that, 'We don't really talk about design, we talk about developing ideas and making products.' The simplicity that is found in the hardware has not always been matched in the software, which since the rise of iOS – the operating system for iPad, iPhone and iPod touch – has been marked by something known as skeuomorphism, a tendency for new designs to retain ornamental features of the old design.

There have also been unsuccessful products (see Table 1.9). But Ive says that most of the company's failures are kept far behind the scenes. He goes on: 'And there have been times when we've been working on a program and when we are at a very mature stage and we do have solutions and you have that sinking feeling because you're trying to articulate the values to yourself and to others just a little bit too loudly. This is probably indicative of the fact that actually it's not good enough. On a number of occasions we've actually all been honest with ourselves and said "you know, this isn't good enough, we need to stop". And that's very difficult.' Knowing when to call a halt to a project is an important part of his role.

There is, within Apple, a strong belief in people focusing on their area of expertise, says Ive, but when a product is being developed, the process can be quite fluid. He says: 'As we're sitting together to develop a product, you would struggle to identify who the electrical engineer is, who's the mechanical engineer, who's the industrial designer.' Teamwork is an important part of the process.

'One of the things that is particularly precious about working at Apple is that many of us on the design team have worked together for 15-plus years and there's a wonderful thing about learning as a group. A fundamental part of that is making mistakes together. There's no learning without trying lots of ideas and failing lots of times.'

In interviews, Ive has said that the absence of Jobs has not affected the way Apple develops products. He says they will do it in exactly the same way because there is a large group of people that work in the same way. That team is the reason that Ive believes Apple will continue to succeed. 'We have become rather addicted to learning as a group of people and trying to solve very difficult problems as a team. And we get enormous satisfaction from doing that. In 2012, and very unusually, Apple flew in its entire design team from San Francisco in recognition of the importance of the Design & Art Direction Awards – all 16 of them accompanied Sir Jonathan Ive on stage to collect the award for best design studio.

Troubles ahead?

An area of criticism levelled against Apple Inc. that has also received considerable media coverage is the issue of excessive secrecy and obsessive control exerted by Apple on its suppliers. One of these suppliers is Foxconn, the world's biggest contract maker of IT goods, including the iPhone. It is far less well known than the brands it assembles, but it is one of Taiwan's largest companies. Reuters news agency reported in 2010 that Apple goes to 'extreme lengths' to protect even the smallest details of its new products under development (Pomfret and Soh, 2010). At Foxconn's assembly plant in Longhua, South China, workers swipe security cards at the gate and guards check the occupants of each vehicle with fingerprint recognition scanners. It resembles a fortress – so much for open innovation! Many of Apple's finished gadgets, from iPods to iPads, are assembled at industrial compounds like the one in Longhua. Many of Apple's tactics seem like they have emerged from a James Bond film: information is assiduously guarded and handed out only on a need-to-know basis; employees suspected of leaks may be investigated by the contractor; and the company makes it clear that it will not hesitate

to sue if secrets are spilled. To try to control information, Apple will give contract manufacturers different products, just to try them out. That way, the source of any leaks becomes immediately obvious. Apple's obsession with secrecy is the stuff of legend in Silicon Valley. Over the years, it has fired executives over leaks and sued bloggers to stop trade secrets from being exposed. Apple also helps keep its components out of the mainstream by insisting on custom designs rather than off-the-shelf parts – a practice that leaves many suppliers frustrated. Not surprisingly, landing a contract with Apple will always include a confidentiality clause. And they usually come with stiff penalties in the event that a breach is discovered. Such agreements often come on top of unannounced checks by Apple officials to maintain standards. However, the difficulty lies in proving the source of a leak. In the absence of solid evidence, the most Apple can do is to switch suppliers once the contract runs out. At times, all of this secrecy seems to run out of control. In a case that made global headlines, an employee in China for Foxconn was believed to have jumped to his death after being interrogated by his employer. According to local press reports, he was under suspicion of taking an iPhone prototype – to which he had access – out of the factory (Watts, 2010).

Outsourcing and the danger of creating a competitor

The benefits of outsourcing seem to have been demonstrated clearly by Apple, as it has masterfully used its supply chain to deliver low cost components and thereby enabling it to create large margins for itself. Table 1.11 shows the key components that go into the iPhone. One of the ongoing challenges when a firm outsources is the ever present threat that one of your partners decides that it can make for itself what it makes for you. This has been demonstrated time and again across a variety of industries. Acer is a good example. For Apple, Samsung has turned from partner to competitor as it learnt from Apple and then developed further the technologies it was supplying.

The way forward?

The best way for the company to prove it is not past its prime would be for it to disrupt another big market. Since Jobs' death in 2011, Apple has concentrated on sprucing up its existing products. Now investors want

→

Table 1.11 Key components that go into the iPhone

Component part	Supplier*
Touch screen	Japan Display Inc. or LG
Flash memory disk	SanDisk or SK Hynix, Samsung, Toshiba
Processor	Samsung Semiconductors
Processor	Qualcomm
Camera module	Qualcomm
Phone casing	Qualcomm
Battery	Sony
Touchscreen controller	Texas Instruments
Duplexer	Avago

*Has been a supplier in the past and is a likely supplier, but suppliers are reluctant to reveal contracts.

to see it conjure up entirely new ones. All eyes are on television. Tim Cook, CEO of Apple, has said that he feels like he has 'gone backwards in time by 20 or 30 years' when he switches on his TV at home. This could suggest that Apple will launch an iTV. The iTV, which may be controlled via iPads and iPhones, could be a digital hub for the home. It would let people check whether their washing machine has finished its cycle whilst they gossip on Facebook and watch their favourite soap. It should also boost purchases of iPads and other Apple gear, as more people get sucked into the firm's 'ecosystem' of linked devices and software.

Source: Images by Morgana/Alamy Images

Apple will also, as usual, face stiff competition from Samsung. The South Korean firm is one of several that already sell smart TVs. Indeed, Samsung seems to be churning out more and more groundbreaking devices whilst Apple has produced only incremental innovations of late. Apple's court battles

with Samsung over smartphone patents have reinforced the impression that it is on the defensive.

It is worthy of note that Apple's capital expenditure has soared in recent quarters, reaching levels typically seen at firms with huge manufacturing operations, such as Intel. Some of this money is going into data centres to support cloud services like iTunes. But where is the rest of the investment going?

One area clearly in need of substantial investment is the retail operation. The Apple stores have been experiencing very long queues as people bring in faulty iPhones, iPads and laptops. The so-called Apple genius experts offer technical help to customers. But there are too few of them. This is because Apple has relatively few shops but increasing numbers of people have Apple products. The London Regent Street store employs 120 geniuses, each sees about 30 customers a day, but demand is so great that it is not possible to book an appointment. One solution would be to reduce numbers of customers. Take the product more upmarket and make it more expensive so it is able to serve fewer customers. Alternatively, investments could be made into effective operations (see Chapter 5) or improved service delivery (see Chapter 15). The Apple Watch and a move into wearable technology could see the Apple stores become more like clothing stores, such as Gap or Abercromby & Fitch. This could present a whole host of new problems.

Conclusions

The iPod was not the first digital music player, nor was the iPhone the first smartphone or the iPad the first tablet. Apple imitated other products, but they appeal to us on a human level because they are so aesthetically pleasing and intuitive to use. One of the reasons that Apple is so revered by designers is because it is not obsessed by technology for technology's sake.

Apple, once best known for its Macintosh computers, and now known for its iPod, iPhone and its iTune online music store, is at last making up for its lack of market gains in the highly competitive PC market. It is necessary to remind business students that, ultimately, this is about money and Apple was twice the size of Microsoft in 1992 and, for 10 years, it failed to deliver growth for its shareholders. It is only in the last 10 years that Apple has started to repay investors, reaching an equivalent market value of Microsoft in 2010. Fortunes change quickly in technology intensive industries, but they change even more quickly in the world of fashion.

One of Jobs' greatest skills was being able to decide which projects the firm should not undertake. For example, it is said that engineers at Apple were urging its boss to create a tablet computer in early 2000/2. But Jobs turned a deaf ear to their entreaties and, instead, insisted that the company focus on producing a smartphone. The result was the iPhone, which transformed yet another market and is still minting money. In a creative cauldron like Apple, ideas are rarely in short supply. But the skill of choosing the right ones to focus on at the right time is rare.

Yet, even if it produces a cheaper iPhone, pushes deep into China and wows the world with a smart TV and Apple Watch, competition is now tougher in its core markets. Rivals will not let it disrupt new ones so easily. Has the firm's great innovation engine stalled?

Questions

1 The return on investment delivered by Apple has fallen considerably. Explain why.

2 Steve Jobs' impact on Apple is without question. Surely a company of over 100,000 employees is not reliant on one person? How did his death affect Apple?

3 Apple's fortunes have ebbed and flowed over the past 40 years. The past few have seen growth; in your assessment will the next few years see decline?

4 Explain how Jonathan Ive may be responsible for much of Apple's past success and future fortune.

5 Discuss whether Apple has shunned open innovation and adopted a very closed innovation model.

6 Samsung seems to be nibbling away at Apple's market share. Has Apple mismanaged its outsourcing?

7 How might Apple be able to capture value from the rise of Apple as a lifestyle brand?

8 Discuss how, on the one hand, Apple seems to very good at disruptive innovation, yet it is also accused of copying others.

9 How do you solve the Apple stores problem?

Chapter summary

This initial chapter has sought to introduce the subject of innovation management and place it in context with the theory of economic growth. One can quickly become ensnarled in stale academic debates of semantics if innovation is viewed as a single event, hence the importance of viewing it as a process. The chapter has also stressed the importance of understanding how firms manage innovation and how this can be better achieved by adopting a management perspective.

The level of understanding of the subject of innovation has improved significantly over the past half century and, during that time, a variety of models of innovation have emerged. The strengths and weaknesses of these were examined and a conceptual framework was presented that stressed the linkages and overlaps between internal departments and external organisations.

Discussion questions

1 Explain why it is necessary to view innovation as a management process.

2 What is wrong with the popular view of innovation in which eccentric scientists develop new products?

3 How does an 'open innovation' approach help firms?

4 What is the difference between an unsuccessful innovation and an invention?

5 To what extent do you agree with the controversial view presented by the chairman of Sony?

6 Show how the three forces shaping the twenty-first century, according to Salkowitz (2010) – youth, entrepreneurship and ICT – are captured in the cyclical model of innovation.

7 Explain Sergey Brin's (co-founder of Google) comment that coming up with an idea is easy, but innovation is difficult.

Key words and phrases

Economic growth *7*

Organisational architecture *9*

Entrepreneurship *13*

Invention *15*

Innovation as a management process *16*

Models of innovation *21*

Resource-based theory of the firm *21*

Open innovation *26*

Discontinuous *28*

References

Abernathy, W.J. and Utterback, J. (1978) 'Patterns of industrial innovation', in Tushman, M.L. and Moore, W.L. *Readings in the Management of Innovation*, HarperCollins, New York, 97–108.

Arrow, K. (1962) 'Economic welfare and the allocation of resources for invention', in R. Nelson (ed.), *The Rate and Direction of Inventive Activity*, Princeton University Press, Princeton.

Berkhout, A.J. (2000) *The Dynamic Role of Knowledge in Innovation. An Integrated Framework of Cyclic Networks for the Assessment of Technological Change and Sustainable Growth*, Delft University Press, Delft, The Netherlands, 2000.

Berkhout, A.J., Hartmann, D. and Trott, P. (2010) Connecting technological capabilities with market needs using a cyclic innovation model, *R&D Management*, vol. 40, no. 5, 474–90.

BSI (2008) *Design Management Systems*, Guides to Managing Innovation, British Standards Institute, London.

Burns, T. and Stalker, G.M. (1961) *The Management of Innovation*, Tavistock, London.

Bush, V. (1945) *Science: The Endless Frontier*, A Report to the President.

Business Week (2006) The world's most innovative firms, 24 April.

Carter, C.F. and Williams, B.R. (1957) The characteristics of technically progressive firms, *Journal of Industrial Economics*, March, 87–104.

Chandler, A.D. (1962) *Strategy and Structure: Chapters in the History of American Industrial Enterprise*, MIT Press, Cambridge, MA.

Chesbrough, H. (2003) *Open Innovation: The New Imperative for Creating and Profiting from Technology*, Harvard Business School Press, Boston, MA.

Christensen, C.M. (2003) *The Innovator's Dilemma: When New Technologies Cause Great Firms to Fail*, 3rd edn, Harvard Business School Press, Cambridge, MA.

Christensen, C. M. and Raynor, M.E. (2003) *Six Keys to Creating New-Growth Businesses*, Harvard Business School Press, Boston, MA.

Cohen, W.M. and Levinthal, D.A. (1990) A new perspective on learning and innovation, *Administrative Science Quarterly*, vol. 35, no. 1, 128–52.

Conner, K.R. and Prahalad, C.K. (1996) A resource-based theory of the firm: knowledge versus opportunism, *Organisation Science*, vol. 7, no. 5, 477–501.

Cooper, R. (1994) Third generation new product processes, *Journal of Product Innovation Management*, vol. 11, no. 1, 3–14.

Cyert, R.M. and March, J.G. (1963) *A Behavioural Theory of the Firm*, Prentice-Hall, Englewood Cliffs, NJ.

Delbridge, R. and Mariotti, F. (2009) Reaching for radical innovation: How motorsport companies harness network diversity for discontinuous innovation, Advanced Institute of Management Research (AIM), London.

Dodgson, M., Gann, D. and Salter, A. (2005) *Think, Play, Do*, Oxford University Press, Oxford.

Domar, D. (1946) Capital expansion, rate of growth and employment, *Econometra*, vol. 14, 137–47.

Eisenhardt, K.M. and Martin, J.A. (2000) 'The knowledge-based economy: from the economics of knowledge to the learning economy', in Foray, D. and Lundvall, B.A. (eds) *Employment and Growth in the Knowledge-Based Economy*, OECD, Paris.

Fitjar, R.D. and Rodríguez-Pose, A. (2013) Firm collaboration and modes of innovation in Norway, *Research Policy*, vol. 42, no. 1, 128–38.

Freeman, C. (1982) *The Economics of Industrial Innovation*, 2nd edn, Frances Pinter, London.

Galbraith, J.R. (1982) Designing the innovative organisation, *Organisational Dynamics*, Winter, 3–24.

Godin, B. (2010a) Innovation studies: the invention of a specialty (Part I) *Project on the Intellectual History of Innovation*, Working Paper, 7.

Godin, B. (2010b) Innovation without the word: William F. Ogburn's contribution to technological innovation studies, *Project on the Intellectual History of Innovation*, Montreal.

Grant, R.M. (1996) Towards a knowledge-based theory of the firm, *Strategic Management Journal*, Summer Special Issue, vol. 17, 109–22.

Guardian, The (2009) Interview with Technology Guardian, 18 June, p. 1.

Hamel, G. and Prahalad, C.K. (1994) Competing for the future, *Harvard Business Review*, vol. 72, no. 4, 122–8.

Hargadon, A. and Douglas, Y. (2001) When innovations meet institutions: Edison and the design of the electric light, *Administrative Science Quarterly*, vol. 46, 476–501.

Harrod, R.F. (1949) An essay in dynamic theory, *Economic Journal*, vol. 49, no. 1, 277–93.

Hatzichronoglou, T. (1997) Revision of the high-technology sector and product classification, *STI Working Paper 1997/2*, OECD, Paris.

Henderson, R. and Clark, K. (1990) Architectural innovation: the reconfiguration of existing product and the failure of established firms, *Administrative Science Quarterly*, vol. 35, 9–30.

Hirsch-Kreinsen, H., Jacobson, D. and Robertson, P.L. (2006) 'Low-tech' industries: innovativeness and development perspectives – a summary of a European research project, *Prometheus*, vol. 24, no. 1, 3–21.

Hutton, W. (1995) *The State We're In*, Jonathan Cape, London.

Isenson, R. (1968) Technology in retrospect and critical events in science (Project Traces), Illinois Institute of Technology/National Science Foundation, Chicago, IL.

Jensen, M.B., Johnson, B., Lorenz, E. and Lundvall, B.-A. (2007) Forms of knowledge and modes of innovation, *Research Policy*, vol. 36, no. 5, 680–93.

Johnson, S. (2010) *Where Good Ideas Come From: The Natural History of Innovation*, Riverhead Books, New Jersey, USA.

Kondratieff, N.D. (1935/51) The long waves in economic life, *Review of Economic Statistics*, Vol. 17, 6–105 (1935), reprinted in Haberler, G. (ed.) *Readings in Business Cycle Theory*, Richard D. Irwin, Homewood, IL (1951).

Langrish, J., Gibbons, M., Evans, W.G. and Jevons, F.R. (1972) *Wealth from Knowledge*, Macmillan, London.

Lefever, D.B. (1992) Technology transfer and the role of intermediaries, PhD thesis, INTA, Cranfield Institute of Technology.

Leifer, R., Colarelli O'Connor, G. and Peters, L.S. (2000) *Radical Innovation*, Harvard Business School Press, Boston, MA.

Linton, J. (2009) De-babelizing the language of innovation, *Technovation*, vol. 29, no. 11, 729–37.

Lundvall, B.-A. (ed.) (1992) *National Systems of Innovation: Towards a Theory of Innovation and Interactive Learning*, Pinter Publishing Ltd.

Maclaurin, W.R. (1953), The sequence from invention to innovation and its relation to economic growth, *Quarterly Journal of Economics*, vol. 67, no. 1, 97–111.

McCloskey, D.N. (2013) Tunzelmann, Schumpeter, and the hockey stick, *Research Policy*, vol. 42, no. 10, 1706–15.

Martin, B.R. (2012). The evolution of science policy and innovation studies. *Research Policy*, 41(7), 1219–1239.

Mendonça, S. (2013). The 'sailing ship effect': reassessing history as a source of insight on technical change, *Research Policy*, vol. 42, no. 10, 1724–38.

Morita, A. (1992) 'S' does not equal 'T' and 'T' does not equal 'I', paper presented at the Royal Society, February 1992.

Moultrie, J. and Livesey, F. (2014) Measuring design investment in firms: conceptual foundations and exploratory UK survey, *Research Policy*, vol. 43, no. 3, 570–7.

Murray, S. (2003) Innovation: a British talent for ingenuity and application, www.ft.com, 22 April.

Myers, S. and Marquis, D.G. (1969) Successful industrial innovation: a study of factors underlying innovation in selected firms, National Science Foundation, NSF 69–17, Washington, DC.

Nelson, R.R. and Winter, S. (1982) *An Evolutionary Theory of Economic Change*, Harvard University Press, Boston, MA.

Nonaka, I. (1991) The knowledge creating company, *Harvard Business Review*, November–December, 96–104.

Nonaka, I. and Hirotaka, T. (1995) *The Knowledge-Creating Company: How Japanese Companies Create the Dynamics of Innovation*, Oxford University Press, Oxford.

Oxford English Dictionary (2005) Oxford University Press, London.

Parkin, M., Powell, Dr. M. and Matthews, Dr K. (2008) *Economics*, 7th edn, Addison-Wesley, Harlow.

Patel, P. and Pavitt, K. (2000) 'How technological competencies help define the core (not the boundaries) of the firm', in Dosi, G., Nelson, R. and Winter, S.G. (eds) *The Nature and Dynamics of Organisational Capabilities*, Oxford University Press, Oxford, 313–33.

Pavitt, K. (1984) Sectoral patterns of technical change: towards a taxonomy and a theory, *Research Policy*, vol. 13, 343–73.

Pavitt, K. (1990) What we know about the strategic management of technology, *California Management Review*, vol. 32, no. 3, 17–26.

Pavitt, K. (2001) Public policies to support basic research: what can the rest of the world learn from US theory and practice? (And what they should not learn), *Industrial and Corporate Change*, vol. 10, no. 3, 761–79.

Penrose, E.T. (1959) *The Theory of the Growth of the Firm*, Wiley, New York.

Pittaway, L., Robertson, M., Munir, K., Denyer, D. and Neely, A. (2004) Networking and innovation: a systematic review of the evidence, *International Journal of Management Reviews*, vol. 5/6, nos 3 and 4, 137–68.

Pomfret, J. and Soh, K. (2010) For Apple suppliers loose lips can sink contracts, Reuters, 17 February.

Porter, M.E. (1980) *Competitive Strategy*, The Free Press, New York.

Porter, M.E. (1985) *Competitive Strategy*, Harvard University Press, Boston, MA.

Prahalad, C.K. and Hamel, G. (1990) The core competence of the corporation, *Harvard Business Review*, vol. 68, no. 3, 79–91.

Robertson, P.L. and Patel, P.R. (2007). New wine in old bottles: technological diffusion in developed economies, *Research Policy*, vol. 36, no. 5, 708–21.

Robertson, P., Smith, K. and von Tunzelmann, N. (2009). Innovation in low- and medium-technology industries, *Research Policy*, vol. 38, no. 3, 441–46.

Rogers, E. and Shoemaker, R. (1972) *Communications of Innovations*, Free Press, New York.

Rothwell, R. (1992) Successful industrial innovation: critical factors for the 1990s, *R&D Management*, vol. 22, no. 3, 221–39.

Rothwell, R. and Zegveld, W. (1985) *Reindustrialisation and Technology*, Longman, London.

Rothwell, R., Freeman, C., Horlsey, A., Jervis, V.T.P., Robertson, A.B. and Townsend, J. (1974) SAPPHO updated: Project SAPPHO phase II, *Research Policy*, vol. 3, 258–91.

Rushe, D. and Waples, J. (2008) Interview with Bill Gates, *Sunday Times*, 3 September.

Salkowitz, R. (2010) *Young World Rising: How Youth Technology and Entrepreneurship are Changing the World from the Bottom up*, John Wiley & Sons, NJ.

Sandven, T., Smith, K. H. and Kaloudis, A. (2005) *Structural Change, Growth and Innovation: The Roles of Medium and Low-Tech Industries, 1980-2000*, Doctoral dissertation, Peter Lang.

Schrange, M. (2000) *Serious Play – How the World's Best Companies Stimulate to Innovate*, Harvard Business School Press, Boston, MA.

Schumpeter, J.A. (1934) *The Theory of Economic Development*, Harvard University Press, Boston, MA.

Schumpeter, J.A. (1939) *Business Cycles*, McGraw-Hill, New York.

Schumpeter, J.A. (1942) *Capitalism, Socialism and Democracy*, Allen & Unwin, London.

Simon, H. (1957) *Administrative Behaviour*, Free Press, New York.

Slater, S.F. and Narver, J. (1994) Does competitive environment moderate the market orientation performance relationship? *Journal of Marketing*, vol. 58 (January), 46–55.

Stefano, G.D., Gambardella, A. and Verona, G. (2012). Technology push and demand pull perspectives in innovation studies: current findings and future research directions, *Research Policy*, vol. 41, no. 8, 1283–1295.

Stevenson, H.H. and Amabile, T.M. (1999) 'Entrepreneurial management: in pursuit of opportunity', in McCraw, T.K. and Cruikshank, J.L. (eds) *The Intellectual Venture Capitalist: John H. McArthur and the Work of the Harvard Business School, 1980–1995*, Harvard Business School Press, Boston, MA.

Thomke, S.H. (2003) *Experimentation Matters: Unlocking the Potential of New Technologies for Innovation*, Harvard Business School Press, Boston, MA.

Trott, P. (1998) Growing businesses by generating genuine business opportunities, *Journal of Applied Management Studies*, vol. 7, no. 4, 211–22.

Utterback, J. (1994) *Mastering the Dynamics of Innovation*, Harvard Business School Press, Boston, MA.

Van de Ven, A.H. (1989) *The Innovation Journey*, Oxford University Press, New York.

van der Panne, G., van Beers, C. and Kleinknecht, A. (2003) Success and failure of innovation: a review of the literature, *International Journal of Innovation Management*, vol. 7, no. 3, 309–38.

von Hippel, E. (1978) Users as innovators, *Technology Review*, vol. 80, no. 3, 30–4.

von Hippel, E. (2005) *Democratizing Innovation*, MIT Press, Cambridge, MA.

von Tunzelmann, N. and Acha, V. (2005) 'Innovation in "low-tech" industries', in Fagerberg, J., Mowery, D. and Nelson, R. (eds), *The Oxford Handbook of Innovation*, Oxford University Press, Oxford, 407–32.

Watts, J. (2010) iPhone factory offers pay rises and suicide nets as fears grow over spate of deaths, *Guardian*, 29 May, p. 30.

Wernerfelt, B. (1984) A resource based view of the firm, *Strategic Management Journal*, vol. 5, no. 2, 171–80.

Wernerfelt, B. (1995) The resource-based view of the firm: ten years after, *Strategic Management Journal*, vol. 16, no. 3, 171–4.

Wheelwright, S. and Clark, K. (1992) *Revolutionising Product Development*, The Free Press, New York.

Woodward, J. (1965) *Industrial Organisation: Theory and Practice*, 2nd edn, Oxford University Press, Oxford.

Further reading

For a more detailed review of the innovation management literature, the following develop many of the issues raised in this chapter:

Berkhout, A.J., Hartmann, D. and Trott, P. (2010) Connecting technological capabilities with market needs using a cyclic innovation model, *R&D Management*, vol. 40, no. 5, 474–90.

Boh, W.F., Evaristo, R. and Ouderkirk, A. (2014) Balancing breadth and depth of expertise for innovation: a 3M story, *Research Policy*, vol. 43, no. 2, 349–66.

Evans, H. (2005) The Eureka Myth, *Harvard Business Review*, 83, June, 18–20.

Linton, J. (2009) De-babelizing the language of innovation, *Technovation*, vol. 29, no. 11, 729–37.

Martin, B.R. (2012) The evolution of science policy and innovation studies, *Research Policy*, vol. 41, no. 7, 1219–39.

McCloskey, D. N. (2013) Tunzelmann, Schumpeter, and the hockey stick, *Research Policy*, vol. 42, no. 10, 1706–15.

Salkowitz, R., (2010) *Young World Rising: How Youth Technology and Entrepreneurship are Changing the World from the Bottom Up*, John Wiley & Sons, NJ.

Schrange, M. (2013) *Serious Play: How the World's Best Companies Simulate to Innovate*, Harvard Business Press, Boston, MA.

Tidd, J., Bessant, J. and Pavitt, K. (2009) *Managing Innovation*, 4th edn, John Wiley & Sons, Chichester.

Chapter 2
National systems of innovation and entrepreneurship

Introduction

Schumpeter argued that innovation is at the heart of economic progress. It gives new businesses a chance to replace old ones. He likened capitalism to a 'perennial gale of creative destruction' and it was entrepreneurs who kept this gale blowing.

This chapter explores the wider context in which innovation occurs and also explores how national governments can help firms. The United States, in particular, is frequently cited as a good example of a nation where the necessary conditions for innovation to flourish are in place. This includes both tangible and intangible features, including, on the one hand, economic, social and political institutions and, on the other, the way in which knowledge evolves over time through developing interactions and networks. This chapter examines how these influence innovation.

The case study at the end of this chapter explores the potential widespread use of new drone technology. It has potential uses in many industries from farming to policing. In some countries, however, questions have been raised about safety and privacy. This case study explores the challenges that lie ahead for this innovation.

Chapter contents

Learning objectives

When you have completed this chapter you will be able to:

- understand the wider context of innovation and the key influences;
- recognise that innovation cannot be separated from its local and national context and from political and social processes;
- understand that the role of national states considerably influences innovation;
- identify the structures and activities that the state uses to facilitate innovation;
- recognise the role played by entrepreneurship in innovation;
- recognise the role played by universities in delivering entrepreneurship.

Innovation in its wider context

According to many, the process of innovation is the main engine of (continued) economic growth. As far back as 1943 Joseph Schumpeter (**Schumpeterian theory**) emphasised that:

> *the fundamental impulse that sets and keeps the capitalist engine in motion comes from the new consumers' goods, the new methods of production or transportation, the new markets, the new forces of industrial organisation that capitalist enterprise creates.*
>
> (1943: 10)

However, such potential to create new products, processes, markets or organisations are path-dependent in the sense that there are certain nations and locations that seem to have acquired that capability over time, for innovation relies upon the accumulation and development of a wide variety of relevant knowledge (Dicken, 1998).

The view that much needs to be in place for innovation to occur and that there is a significant role for the state is confirmed by Alfred Marshall, whose ideas were responsible for the rebuilding of Europe after the Second World War. He commented on both the tangible and intangible aspects of the Industrial Revolution and suggested that 'the secrets of Industry are in the air'. Marshall (cited in Dickens, 1998: 20) recognised a number of characteristics that influenced innovation:

- the institutional set-up;
- the relationship between the entrepreneurs and financiers;
- society's perception of new developments;
- the openness to science and technology;
- networks between scientific and academic communities and business circles;
- the productive forces and financial institutions;
- the growing liberal–individualist economic paradigm;
- the role played by the state in accommodating and promoting capitalistic changes and preparing the framework for the development of capitalism.

The process of innovation has so far been treated as an organisational issue. We have seen, and will continue to see over the course of the book, that within the organisation, management of the innovation process is an extremely demanding discipline, for converting a basic discovery into a commercial product, process or service is a long-term, high-risk, complex, interactive and non-linear sequence. However, the capability of organisations in initiating and sustaining innovation is, to a great extent, determined by the wider local and national context within which they operate. This is, essentially, why 'innovation within' requires a favourable 'context outside'. That is, economic and social conditions will play a major role in whether the organisations or corporate actors will take the risk and establish the longer-term vision that innovation is key to competitiveness, survival and sustained growth. To get a better understanding of this, it is necessary to 'look out of the window' at the business environment in which economic actors strive to get an upper hand in the marketplace in a mix of competition and cooperation through network, market and hierarchical relations. This notion is reinforced by the interactions between the organisation and the external environment, which is emphasised in Figure 1.7.

Much can be learned from glancing at recent history. The development of science and technology in the West opened a wide gap between the so-called industrialised nations and their followers, 'late-industrialisers'. Late-industrialisers refer to countries with no or limited indigenous technology development capacity. Some states, including Japan and some east Asian countries, have managed to close that gap with strategies that focus mainly on industrialisation. In these countries, economic growth was achieved through imitation by diffusion of technology, development of new technology and efforts to develop their own capacities. So the cycle that began with imitation was later turned into a creative and broader basis upon which economic transformation could be achieved. This transformation required continual efforts by entrepreneurs and businesses and a collaborative framework promoted by the state. However, to reach maturity in today's economy, i.e. to be able to create high-value-added and knowledge-based products and services, would appear to be a gigantic task for the states and societies of the latecomers. Apart from its regulatory and redistribution functions, the state must play a significant role through strategic intervention into infrastructure development and technological capacity formation as well as into human capital formation.

This wider view of the economic environment is referred to as *integral economics*, where the economic processes are viewed in their social and political entirety. As pointed out by Dicken (1998: 50), 'technology is a social process which is socially and institutionally embedded'. In this context, it would be useful to remind ourselves that innovation cannot be separated from its local and national (as well as global) contexts and from political and social processes, let alone main economic trends.

Given the nature of 'the game', however, there is always the risk that entrepreneurs and businesses may focus only on high-return opportunities in the short term, marginalise strategic and innovative perspective and ignore the long-term implications of such behaviour (as will be seen in Chapter 15). Economies dominated by this type of philosophy will have serious difficulties in moving beyond commercial activities (that is, in current popular business discourse, 'moving boxes'). This so-called **short-termism** has characterised the economy of Turkey which, despite its strategic geographic position, has failed to develop significantly. In this context, we find that the businesses themselves and the business philosophy were progressively created by the Republican state within a modernist approach only to observe that the so-called entrepreneurs opted to become rich rather than entrepreneurs. So, the act of business-making was undertaken only on the surface; and policy changes, such as liberalisation, only led the entrepreneurs and businesses to seek their ends in the short run with no calculated risk-taking in business. Thus, business in Turkey developed its own weakness by becoming dependent on the weaknesses of the Turkish state, e.g. using high and growing budget deficits as a money-making opportunity. In this chapter, we will try to highlight why the situation for economies such as the Turkish economy remain unchanged, whilst some societies and economies enjoyed sustained growth over several decades and have become powerful players in the global economy.

Pause for thought ❓

For Schumpeter, the idea of being entrepreneurial was not simply buying something cheap and selling it for a quick profit. It was bound up with new products and new methods of production; by implication it was long-term rather than short-term in nature. Is our understanding of **entrepreneurship** different now?

The role of the state and national 'systems' of innovation

To support our understanding of the process of innovation within the capitalist enterprise, we must also grasp a basic understanding of the way the economy interrelates with global and regional economies on local and national levels. Not only do national economies tend to be dominated by a form of economic organisation (e.g. the *Chaebol* in South Korea or *Keiretsu* in Japan), it is also the case that the relationship between state and business differs radically from one national space to the other. Such interrelationships in society generate a business environment with a unique business value system, attitude and ethic. Historically, this difference created advantages and disadvantages for business organisation across a range of activities, the most important of which may be perceived as the process of innovation. This would seem to be the case, given the crucial role played by innovation in the history of capitalism.

Why firms depend on the state for so much

Mariana Mazzucato (2011) argues that the state has played a central role in producing game-changing breakthroughs, and that its contribution to the success of technology-based businesses should not be underestimated. According to Mazzucato, Apple's success would have been impossible without the active role of the state, the unacknowledged enabler of today's consumer-electronics revolution. Consider the technologies that put the smart into Apple's smartphones. The armed forces pioneered the internet, GPS positioning and voice-activated virtual assistants. They also provided much of the early funding for Silicon Valley. Academic scientists in publicly funded universities and labs developed the touchscreen and the HTML language. An obscure government body even lent Apple $500,000 before it went public. Mazzucato considers it a travesty of justice that a company that owes so much to public investment devotes so much energy to reducing its tax burden by shifting its money offshore and assigning its intellectual property to low-tax jurisdictions such as Ireland.

Similarly, the research that produced Google's search algorithm, the fount of its wealth, was financed by a grant from the National Science Foundation. Pharmaceutical companies are even bigger beneficiaries of state research than internet and electronics firms. America's National Institutes of Health, with an annual budget of more than $30 billion, finances studies that lead to many of the most revolutionary new drugs.

The issue of whether there is a role for the state in the process of innovation has been addressed in different contexts (e.g. Afuah, 2003; Porter, 1990). The literature on the subject has attracted attention to the following points, where state action may be necessary:

1 *The 'public' nature of knowledge that underpins innovation.* This refers to the role that can be played by the government in the process of idea generation and its subsidisation and distribution. This way, economic actors may be stimulated to work on new ideas, alongside state organisations, and may endeavour to convert such ideas into marketable goods or services. For instance, by granting intellectual property rights to producers of knowledge and by establishing the

necessary legal infrastructure to support those rights, the state may promote knowledge generation.

2 *The uncertainty that often hinders the process of innovation.* Macroeconomic, technological or market uncertainties may hinder innovation. When the companies are risk-averse in investing funds in innovation projects, then the state may promote such activities through subsidising, providing tax advantages and supporting firms to join R&D projects. Forming a stable economic environment, where funds could be extended by the banking system to productive firms, also creates a favourable long-term perspective, for one of the first preconditions of strategy making is economic stability. Thus, expectations of low inflation, low interest rates and stable growth will encourage firms to invest in entrepreneurial activity (particularly given that other areas, e.g. portfolio investments, are less profitable to invest in).

3 *The need for certain kinds of complementary assets.* Provision of electricity, roads and water has historically assisted industrial development; recently, the establishment of communication systems (e.g. communication superhighways), legal infrastructure and the formation of industrial districts have been issues where state action has led to favourable outcomes with tangible and intangible conditions created for enterprises.

4 *The need for cooperation and governance, resulting from the nature of certain technologies.* For the development of possible networks, which will enhance and promote the diffusion of new technologies and innovations, the state may set the vision and enhance the possibilities for better communication and joint decision making. In the UK, the Government provided funds (through education and promotion) to encourage households to switch from analogue television signal to a digital television signal. Such action helps countries/society to upgrade from one old established technology to a newer improved technology.

5 *Politics.* Lastly, in terms of politics, national states still have a key role in foreseeing and contributing to international and regional standards of business making within the system of 'national states' and in creating consent and cohesion in the national arena amongst domestic forces. Such standards increasingly are becoming environmental, safety and human rights standards in industrial or business activities. The German Government has an impressive record of being at the forefront of introducing legislation in automobile safety and environmental recycling, which has contributed to Germany becoming a world leader in these two industries.

How national states can facilitate innovation

Figure 2.1 highlights the possible roles that can be played by national states. It takes Porter's industry attractiveness framework and develops the role the state can play in relation to innovation. It underlines a firm's relationship with the buyers, factor conditions (e.g. labour, capital, raw materials), related and supporting industries (e.g. technology providers, input providers, etc.) and other institutions that help facilitate strategic orientation and innovative capabilities. These will determine, to a great extent, the firm's opportunities – notwithstanding the fact that its inner strengths, i.e. its strategy-making capabilities and structural features, will clearly affect this potential.

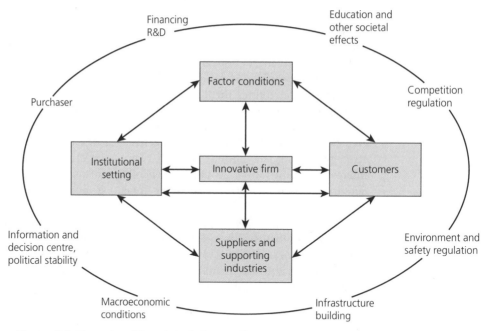

Figure 2.1 The role of the state in innovation

As a financier of R&D and a major purchaser, the state has a significant impact on strategic direction towards critical industries and encouraging entrepreneurial spirit. For instance, the United States annually has a budget for R&D spending of in excess of $100 billion, which is spent on defence, health, space, general science, energy, transportation, environment and agriculture. Much of the funds goes to industrial research laboratories, universities, non-profit laboratories and federally funded research R&D centres. There are also indirect ways of financing R&D, such as tax exemptions, subsidies, loan guarantees, export credits and forms of protection. As a major purchaser, the state will also reduce uncertainty and create favourable cash flows for firms by its willingness to pay higher (monopolistic) prices for early models. Public procurement is seen increasingly as an important potential instrument of innovation policy. Research by Georghiou et al. (2014) identifies a broad taxonomy of procurement policies and instruments that have emerged in OECD countries in response to perceived deficiencies. These include: the creation of framework conditions, establishing organisational frameworks and developing capabilities, identifying, specifying and signalling needs and incentivising innovative solutions. A good example here is the UK Government's expenditure on the London congestion charge technology. Many of the firms involved in supplying and implementing that technology are now suppliers to other cities across the globe. This willingness to be a major purchaser has helped drive the technology.

Through education, information dissemination, governance and other societal actions, the state can impact upon the way the society perceives discoveries and adapts new technologies at the same time as creating cohesion in the society and making strategic interventions to promote, for instance, the formation of a highly qualified workforce. Interdependency between state and society may create a favourable national culture, which welcomes scientific development and removes the potential for conflict between leading sectors and traditional sectors, economic interests and social forces and cultural traditions and new trends. By incubating a form of unity between state and society, the state may set in motion an overall vision and dynamic in the society and for the industry.

Regulation of competition is another critical area for the reproduction/expansion of the capitalist system, as the state can promote the system by preventing monopolies that can result in under-innovation and by protecting the society against possible abuse by companies. Google's very high profile antitrust case with the European Union (EU) is a good illustration (see Illustration 2.1). A summary of the complex way in which the state can impact upon the behaviour of capitalist firms and how they manage their economic and social relationships is shown in Figure 2.1.

Illustration 2.1

Brussels v Google – antitrust rules – EU poised to launch broader competition crackdown

Margrethe Vestager, the EU's competition commissioner, issued charges against Google yesterday over concerns that its search engine was biased in favour of the company's own shopping services. Google denies that it is breaching antitrust rules.

Whilst the focus on shopping was narrower than some complainants against Google had hoped, Ms Vestager said the case could lay the groundwork for tackling other areas where Google derives money from advertising, such as travel agencies and mapping. "If an infringement is proven, a case focusing on comparison shopping could potentially establish a broader precedent for enforcing EU competition rules in other instances of Google favouring its own services," she said.

Ms Vestager said Google could remedy the EU's concerns with "future-proof" principles that set out fairness in the way searches worked.

"To be clear, we would not want to interfere with Google's design choices or how its algorithms work."

In this respect, Ms Vestager appears to be aiming at a broader solution to the complaints against Google than her predecessor, Joaquín Almunia. In his third attempted settlement with the company Mr Almunia focused on page layout and the display of products and services from Google's rivals.

Given the stakes for Google's business model, Gary Reback, a Silicon Valley lawyer who has represented several of its rivals said: "You should expect Google to fight this tooth and nail. It's going to affect nearly everything they do on the monetisable side of search."

Shopping was the first area in which the commission received a complaint over Google's conduct, from the British price comparison site, Foundem. The complaints have since snowballed to include online travel services such as Expedia, as well as large groups including Microsoft, and French and German publishers.

Google now has 10 weeks to respond and allay the commission's concerns. It also has a right to a hearing in the coming months, normally attended by national representatives, in which all the main arguments can be aired.

If Google's defence is unsuccessful, it faces a fine. Theoretically this could be as much as 10 per cent of the previous year's turnover, some $66bn in 2014, but lawyers do not expect any potential penalty from the commission to be anywhere near as high as the possible maximum.

Google said, in an internal email sent before Ms Vestager's announcement: "We have a very strong case, with especially good arguments when it comes to better services for consumers and increased competition."

FT *Source*: Oliver, C. and Waters, R. (2015), www.ft.com 16 April.

National scientific capacity and R&D offshoring

Clearly all governments would wish for their countries to be world leaders in fields of science to help attract industry and R&D to its shores. The past decade has seen an increase in R&D offshoring partly for low labour costs and partly to access new knowledge. Recent research by Thomson (2013) suggests firms offshore and source technology from less technologically advanced nations to access niche skills.

The impact of the economic crisis on innovation

Economic crises cause companies to reduce their investment, including investment in innovation where returns are uncertain and long-term. This has been confirmed by the 2008–13 financial crisis, which has substantially reduced the willingness of firms to invest in innovation. However, the reduction in investment has not been uniform across companies and a few even increased their innovation expenditures, such as Toyota and Volkswagen. Research by Archibugi et al. (2013) on European firms shows that before the crisis, incumbent firms were more likely to expand their innovation investment, whilst, after the crisis, a few small enterprises and new entrants are ready to 'swim against the stream' by expanding their innovative-related expenditures.

Fostering innovation in the United States and Japan

Although local characteristics also play a very significant role in the innovation process, the overall tendencies of nations and nation states are linked to success on a very local level. Whilst some states, such as Japan, provided extensive support and subsidies to promote industrial innovation, others, such as the United States, have aimed to create positive effects in the economy by letting the market achieve the most efficient allocation of resources with minimal possible intervention. The so-called Chicago School paradigm for promoting competitiveness and innovation, which created a belief in the free market to maximise innovation and productivity (Rosenthal, 1993), has, for more than two decades, been the dominant perspective in the United States. At this instance, we can cite the impact on the industry of public R&D with such expected transformative effects as provided by the internet's later commercial application, initially a military project initiated by the state. In fact, the United States is leading the way in performing half of the world's basic research, making most of the seminal discoveries, thanks to the trillion-dollar investment in US universities and government laboratories.

In the case of more interventionist states, incentives were provided either as direct support (e.g. subsidies, location provision, etc.) or in the form of governance, assuming a coordinating and leading role in the management of innovation projects. In this instance, governance refers to the efforts at creating cohesion and complementarity, which are directed to the realisation of a joint objective that is deemed to be mutually beneficial to the various parties involved. A good example of the latter was the role played by the Japanese state in bringing universities, state organisations (primarily the Ministry of International Trade and Industry (MITI)), sector organisations and business enterprises together for research on the development of the Trinitron television (a technology that dominated home electronics for more than two decades) with financial support attached. Although the Japanese model has come under severe criticism, particularly by Porter et al. (2000), as a result of the recent economic slowdown, the weaknesses mainly attributed to the lack of concern for strategy in Japanese companies and being stuck in between two competitive strategies of cost and quality, as well as low profitability, the success of the model has been long acknowledged (see, for instance, Johnson, 1982). In the case of innovation, governance requires the establishment of a proper framework for the smooth flow of knowledge between universities, state institutions, private sector organisations and corporations until the end result takes some form of a marketable commodity. In this framework, whilst some economies are better placed with innovation capabilities, some are at a disadvantage because of their characteristics.

The concept of 'developmental states' is used to show the way in which some states achieved a major transformation of the economy and society. At the other end of the spectrum there are the 'predatory states', which capture most of the funds in the economy and reallocate them in the form of rents to a small group of the population, thus impeding the growth potential in the state (Evans, 1989). This development was found in particular to be a major characteristic of some east Asian states, especially the so-called Tigers of Korea, Taiwan, Singapore and Hong Kong (Castells, 1992). Although such states were not immune to **corruption**, fraud and other forms of inefficiency, they brought about major changes in the economy, particularly in upgrading the potential of the industry from imitation towards innovation and technology development, which is by no means an easy task.

Pause for thought

Is it true that in a developed market economy the role of the state is a minor one? Why is it *not* surprising that many consumer products such as in-car satellite navigational guidance, mobile telephones and computers have their origins in defence research?

Triple Helix of university–industry–government relationships that drives innovation

University research and research-related activities contribute in many important ways to modern economies: notably through increased productivity of applied R&D in industry due to university-developed new knowledge and technical know-how; provision of highly valued human capital embodied in staff and students; development of equipment and instrumentation used by industry in production and research; and creation of concepts and prototypes for new products and processes, which may have some unexpected and large social and economic impacts. Major discoveries emanating from academic and/or publicly funded research have had enormous global economic and social impacts that are obvious but difficult to predict and quantify (e.g., Google, the World Wide Web, nanotechnologies, etc.). Roessner et al. (2013) offers quantitative evidence that the economic impact of university research and technology transfer activities is significant.

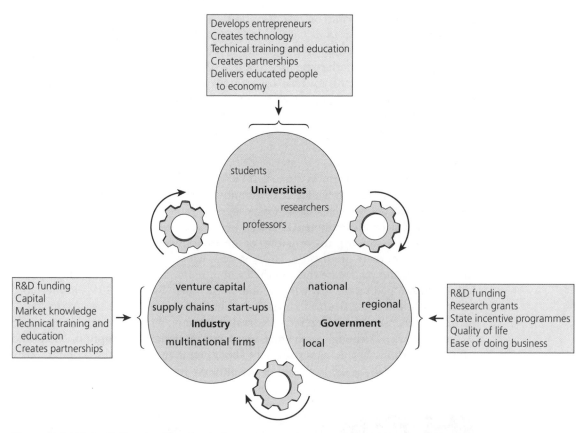

Figure 2.2 Triple Helix of university–industry–government relationships that drives innovation

Lundvall (1988) first introduced the concept of 'national systems of innovation' by elaborating on Christopher Freeman's (1987) study entitled *Technology, Policy, and Economic Performance: Lessons from Japan.* In Freeman's study he argued that Western nations could learn from Japan's experience in the coordination, at the national level, of S&T policies orchestrated by the Japanese Ministry of Trade and Industry (MITI). More recently, the Japanese economy has not been viewed with much admiration. Nonetheless, the Japanese model or system knew what was expected technologically in order to meet (economic) demands and (political) objectives. In this integrative model, university–industry–government relations were synchronised at the national level. Similarly, the Triple Helix of university–industry–government relationships initiated in the 1990s by Etzkowitz and Leydesdorff (1995), interprets the shift from a dominating industry–government dyad in the Industrial Society to a growing triadic relationship between university–industry–government in the Knowledge Society. The Triple Helix thesis is that the potential for innovation and economic development in a Knowledge Society lies in a more prominent role for the university. Specifically regarding the production, transfer and application of knowledge.

Emerging technologies can be expected to be more diversified and their life cycles are likely to become shorter than before. According to Ivanova and Leydesdorff (2014), government policy makers need to take account of a shift from the production of material objects to the production of innovative technologies.

The right business environment is key to innovation

Schumpeter preached technology as the engine of growth but also noted that to invest in technology there had to be spare resources and long time-horizons. So the business environment must give the right signals to the business units for them to invest in such operations. In this regard, not only does macroeconomic stability play a significant role, but also the availability of quick (short-term) returns and opportunistic trends needs to be suppressed so that the money can flow into basic research and R&D. Likewise, the approach of business would differ if it faced strong (external or internal) competition. A protected domestic market more often than not amounts to signalling to business units that they should seek monopolistic or oligopolistic returns by not making enough investment into new product development or even product improvement.

The next chapter explores the organisational characteristics that need to be in place for innovation to occur. From the preceding discussion one can already begin to see what these characteristics might be.

Waves of innovation and growth: historical overview

When we investigate the history of capitalist development, there is a pattern of economic growth. The work of Kondratieff and Schumpeter has been influential in identifying the major stages of this development. The five waves, or growth cycles, are identified in Figure 2.3. This highlights that technological developments and innovations have a strong spatial dimension; however, leadership in one wave is not necessarily maintained in the succeeding waves. So one can observe shifts in the geography of innovation through time. The leaders of the first wave were Britain, France and Belgium. The second wave brought new players into the game, namely the United States and Germany. Wave three saw the strengthening of the positions of the United States and Germany. In wave four, Japan and Sweden joined the

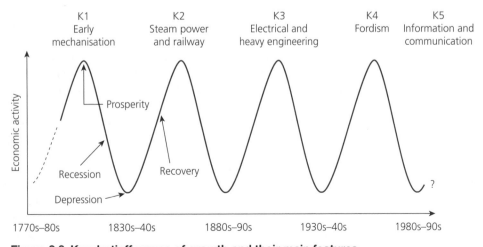

Figure 2.3 Kondratieff waves of growth and their main features

technology and innovation race. More recently, in wave five, Taiwan and South Korea are becoming key players in the global economy.

In these **Kondratieff waves of growth,** the capitalist economy grew on the basis of major innovations in product, process and organisation with accompanying shifts in the social arena. Kuhn's theory on the nature of scientific revolutions has been justified: each wave comes to an end due to its major shortcomings and the successive wave fundamentally restructures and improves those weaknesses. Each major phase of innovation produced a 'star' industry or industry branch, which seemed to affect the way the economy was organised. The leap forward provided by such industry(ies) resulted in a major transformation of the economy and economic relations – given that other factors, such as demand, finance, industrial and social conditions, were favourable. Products, processes and organisations created by technological development became universal and cheaply available to a vast population, which, in turn, created the economic shift. These Kondratieff waves took place in the order of early mechanisation, steam power and railways, electrical and heavy engineering, 'Fordism' (i.e. use of mass-production methods) and information and communication. The last of these waves is currently under way with what is now termed the information revolution. Almost every day we are presented with a number of new ways in which we can do business, search for information, communicate and socialise with other people or carry out our bank operations. This means that the new developments deeply affect not only economic relations but also our private (home and relations) and work (public) spheres.

In the very first Kondratieff wave, the rise of the factory and mechanisation in textiles was only part of the story. The need to produce in greater quantities to start serving the growing overseas markets with the improved transport methods now available was complemented by the abundance of finance with the money flowing in from the colonies, particularly the United States. Universally and cheaply available input (i.e. cotton), improving nationwide transport infrastructure (with rising investment in canals and roads by landlords), the advent of the so-called adventurers (now widely recognised as entrepreneurs), pools of labour available for employment in some local markets, the growing education infrastructure, the role played by academic and scientific societies and the attitude of the state towards manufacturing interests were the other complementary factors affecting change (Freeman and Soete, 1997).

With the decline of the previous techno-economic paradigm, the next one starts to take shape with features that offer solutions to the weaknesses of the earlier phase. As Marx (1972) foresaw, capitalism has always found a way of reproducing itself with changes in the way factors of production were organised. For instance, the organisational characteristics have changed from the first through to the fifth wave, and the early emphasis on individual entrepreneurs has given way to small firms, then to the monopolists, oligopolists and cartels of the third wave, centralised TNCs (transnational corporations) of the fourth wave and, finally, to the so-called network type, flexible organisations of the information age (see Table 2.1 for an overview of the waves of growth).

According to Linstone and Devezas (2012), the pattern of basic innovation clustering associated with Kondratieff long wave theory raises questions when we consider the fourth downswing. There is increasing concern expressed that we may be facing innovation starvation or innovation stagnation. Amongst the questions: Is the internet a cluster of one? Or should the smartphone, iPad, Facebook, iCloud, etc. be

Table 2.1 Characteristics of the five waves of growth

	Wave 1	Wave 2	Wave 3	Wave 4	Wave 5
Main branches	Textiles Textile machinery Iron working Water power Pottery	Steam engines Steamships Machine tools Iron and steel Railway equipment	Electrical engineering Electrical machinery Cable and wire Heavy engineering Steel ships Heavy chemicals	Automobiles Trucks/tractors/ planes Consumer durables Process plant Synthetic materials Petrochemicals	Computers Electronic capital goods Telecommunications Robotics Information services
Universal and cheap key factors	Cotton	Coal, iron	Steel; electricity	Oil; plastics	Gas; oil; microelectronics
Infrastructure	Trunk canals Turnpike roads	Railways Shipping	Electricity supply and distribution Limitations of iron as an engineering material (strength, durability, precision, etc.) overcome by steel and alloys; limitations of steam engine overcome by unit and group electrical machinery, power tools, permitting layout improvement and capital saving; standardisation	Highways; airports/airlines Limitations of batch production overcome by flow processes and assembly line; full standardisation and replaceability of components and materials; universal availability and cheapening of mass consumption goods	Digital networks; satellites Inflexibility of dedicated assembly line and process plant overcome by flexible manufacturing systems, networking and economies of scope; electronic control systems and networking provide for necessitated flexibility
Limitations of previous technoeconomic paradigm; solutions	Limitations of scale, process control and mechanisation in 'putting out' system; solutions offered through mechanisation and factory organisation towards productivity and profitability	Limitations of water power: inflexibility of location, scale of production, reliability; solutions offered through steam engine and transport system	Emergence of giant firms, cartels, trusts, mergers; regulation of or state ownership of natural monopolies; concentration of finance and banking capital; emergence of middle management	Oligopolistic competition; TNCs; 'arm's-length' subcontracting or vertical integration; bureaucratic control and bureaucratisation	Networks of large and small firms based increasingly on computers; trust- based networks with close cooperation in technology, quality control, training and production planning (e.g. JIT)
Organisation of firms	Individual entrepreneurs and small firms (<100 employees); partnership between technical innovators and financial circles	Small firms dominate but large firms and large markets emerge; limited liability and joint stock companies emerge	Germany, United States, Britain, France, Belgium, The Netherlands, Switzerland	United States, Germany, other EU, Japan, Switzerland, other EFTA, Canada, Australia	Japan, United States, Canada, Germany, Sweden, other EU and EFTA, Taiwan, Korea

→

Table 2.1 Characteristics of the five waves of growth *(continued)*

	Wave 1	Wave 2	Wave 3	Wave 4	Wave 5
Geographical focus	Britain, France, Belgium	Britain, France, Belgium, Germany, United States			

Note: EFTA, European Free Trade Association; JIT, just-in-time; TNC, transnational corporation.

Source: Reproduced and adapted from Dicken, P. (1998) *Global Shift: Transforming the World Economy*, Paul Chapman, London (a Sage Publications company); Freeman, C. and Soete, L. (1997) *The Economics of Industrial Innovation*, 3rd edn, Pinter, London (Cengage Learning Services Ltd).

considered basic rather than improvement innovations as well because of their huge societal impact? The invention phase took place from 1960 to 1984, the basic innovation phase from 1984 to 1995, and the diffusion phase beginning in 1995. Is the internet a cluster of one? If not, what are other components of this cluster? Does the consumerisation of information technology (IT), exemplified by the Macintosh, iPod, iPhone, iPad, iCloud, and apps like iTunes that revolutionised the music industry qualify as a series of basic innovations together with the internet or do they constitute improvement innovations that will drive the 5th K-wave upswing? The argument for considering these and other innovations, such as network enablers Facebook, Linked-In, e-commerce, and the worldwide web as basic is reinforced, as social media, supported by wireless connectivity and cloud computing, are now opening up an entirely new approach to individual entrepreneurial activities.

> **Pause for thought**
>
> The Kondratieff theory suggests that networks constitute a key organisational attribute to the current wave of economic growth. Does this mean it is not possible for a firm to be innovative on its own?

Fostering innovation in 'late-industrialising' countries

We have already noted that there is no guarantee for continued technological leadership. The geography of innovation has shown regional, national or local variations in time. One proof in this regard has been the case of south-east Asia. Although the late developers followed more or less similar paths towards industrialisation, some managed significant achievements, particularly in the attitude of the private sector to innovation and technology development (for example, Taiwan, Malaysia and Korea). Almost all latecomers started with the exports of basic commodities and, through the application of a mix of policies in different periods, they aimed for industrialisation. When innovation is considered, the focus of entrepreneurs and businesses was initially on imitative production (so-called 'reverse engineering') in relatively unsophisticated industries. Hobday et al. (2004) have illustrated that Korean firms have adopted a policy of 'copy and develop', which has taken them to the technological frontier in industries from automotive to telecommunications.

When the business environment became conducive to business activity, after initial capital accumulation in key industries, then an upward move was observed along the ladder of industrialisation. In many countries, such a transformation required an envisioning state, actively interfering with the functioning of the private enterprise system. In some cases, it set 'the prices wrong' deliberately (Amsden, 1989) to protect and promote infant industries; in others, it created enterprises itself in order to compensate for the lack of private initiative in the economy (Toprak, 1995).

Although there are significant differences between the cases of Latin American countries and their south Asian counterparts, their paths of industrialisation also bear similarities. Initially, all were exporters of raw materials and importers of higher-technology products. In achieving the transformation, the move from simple technology sectors towards higher-value-added and heavy industries seems to be the key to their successes. This was achieved with the complementary use of (inward-looking) import-substituting industrialisation (ISI) and (outward-looking) export-oriented (EOI) economic policies. The main difference in south Asian economies, which, in retrospect, seems to be their main advantage, was that after the initial phase of ISI, they opened up to international competition through an EOI regime in contrast particularly to Latin American countries and Turkey. Turkey had a set of problems that were established over a long period of time, which led to a weak **business system**. This was due partly to the nation building and 'Turkification' of the economy during the twentieth century. This resulted in the Turkish business system becoming state dependent. Thus, trying to create a business class from scratch during the 1970s and 80s had its costs: entrepreneurs and businesses, which are expected to invest their accumulation into business activities along the value chain, were after easy and quick returns ('petty entrepreneurship') or invested their accumulation into luxury goods. In a favourable environment, such accumulation could have meant the deepening of the economy. However, the case of Turkey proved that, without a proper legal and institutional framework, and a social code, established business values and ethic, the outcome turned out to be a sluggish business system.

Pause for thought

In order to compete, much emphasis is placed on the need to cut costs and improve efficiency. Why would an emphasis on efficiency alone be bad for businesses and economic growth in general?

Innovation within the 28 European Union states

In a response to increased competition and globalisation, the European Council argued for increased and enhanced efforts to improve the Union's performance in innovation. In March 2000, in the picturesque city of Lisbon, the Union set itself the goal of becoming the most competitive and dynamic knowledge-based economy in the world within the next decade. Fine words, one may say, but precisely how does one set about achieving this laudable goal? A strategy was developed and presented in Stockholm in March 2001. The strategy was to build on the economic convergence that had been developed over the past 10 years within the EU single market and to coordinate an 'open method' of developing policies for creating new skills, knowledge and innovation. To support this approach, the European Commission stated that there was a need for an assessment of how member countries were performing in the area of innovation. The idea of a scoreboard was launched to indicate the performance of member states. This would be conducted every year as a way of assessing the performance of member countries. It is, essentially, a benchmarking exercise where the European Union can assess its performance against other countries, most notably Japan and the United States. The EU has used a variety of instruments to support collaborative R&D, including the European Framework Programmes, see Illustration 2.2.

The EU has to compete with a similar trading block: the North American Free-Trade Agreement (NAFTA), which in 1994 eliminated most tariffs between Mexico, the United States and Canada. (See the Case Study at the end of the chapter on the growth of Mexico.)

This is an extremely ambitious project to try to assess innovative ability. There have been many studies over the past two decades that have tried to identify the factors necessary for innovation to occur (see Table 1.6) and, whilst many factors have been identified, many of these are necessary but not sufficient in themselves. Moreover, some governments have attempted to develop innovation toolkits and scorecards to try to help firms in their own countries to become more innovative. Most of these have not been successful. This ambitious project by the European Union is full of limitations and is generally regarded as oversimplistic. This is largely because the economic conditions of the member countries are so very different and all have a wide variety of strengths and weaknesses. Nonetheless, in order to assess where the European Union should target help and the precise type of help required by each member, it is necessary to analyse the innovative performance of countries. Every two years, the Innovation Union Scoreboard is accompanied by a Regional Innovation Scoreboard. The Regional Innovation Scoreboard 2014 (RIS, 2014) provides a comparative assessment of how European regions perform with regard to

Illustration 2.2

Horizon 2020

The EU Framework Programme for Research and Innovation
Horizon 2020 is the financial instrument implementing the Innovation Union, a Europe 2020 flagship initiative aimed at securing Europe's global competitiveness. Theoretically, these policy instruments are designed to overcome a set of failures (market and systemic failures) impeding the innovation process. Seen as a means to drive economic growth and create jobs, Horizon 2020 has the political backing of Europe's leaders and the Members of the European Parliament. By coupling research and innovation, Horizon 2020 is helping to achieve this with its emphasis on excellent science, industrial leadership and tackling societal challenges. The goal is to ensure Europe produces world-class science, removes barriers to innovation and makes it easier for the public and private sectors to work together in delivering innovation. Evidence on its effectiveness is mixed, see Bach et al. (2014); and Dolfsma and Seo (2013).

Source: http://ec.europa.eu/programmes/horizon2020/en/what-horizon-2020

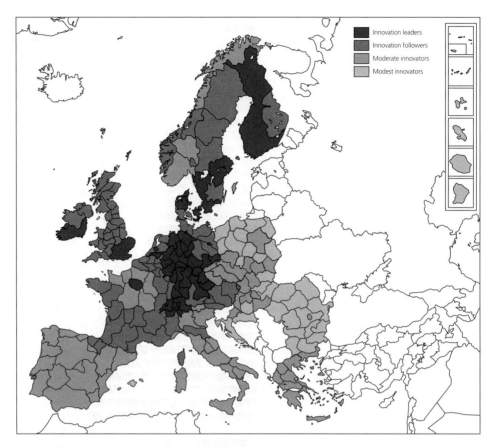

Figure 2.4 Map of the European Union indicating four performance groups, ranging from the highest to the lowest overall performers

Source: Regional Innovation Scoreboard (2014).

innovation. The report covers 190 regions across the European Union, Croatia, Norway and Switzerland. Figure 2.4 shows a map of the European Union, indicating four performance groups, ranging from the highest to the lowest overall performers. Figure 2.5 illustrates innovation performance by country (IUS, 2014) and classifies the performance into four key groups.

Improving the innovation performance of the EU

All the elements in the scoreboard are necessary but not sufficient in themselves to ensure that innovation occurs. For example, in this chapter we have seen the example of Turkey, a late-industrialising country on the edge of Europe, a country with a population of 60 million, already a member of the North Atlantic Treaty Organization (NATO) and a prospective member of the European Union. Turkey is a good example of a late-industrialising economy. Sitting on the edge of Europe and bestriding two continents, Turkey should be in a position to develop a successful economy. However, in Turkey there seems to be a missing link in terms of the innovative

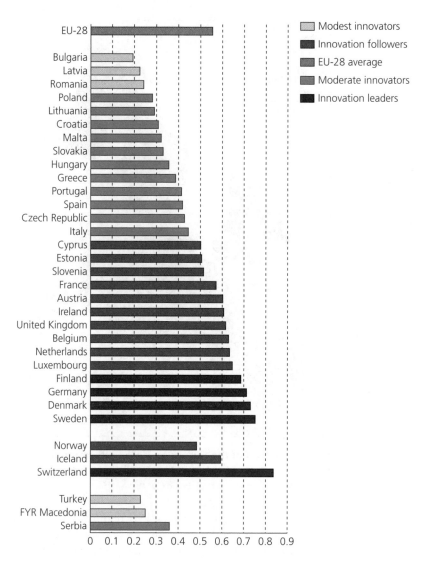

Figure 2.5 Innovation performance by country to 2014

Note: The innovation Union Scoreboard analyses the innovation system of EU Member States through a set of 25 indicators broken down into eight dimensions looking at human resources, research systems, finance and support, firm investments, linkages and entrepreneurship, intellectual assets, innovators and economic effects. In the resulting summary innovation index EU Member States are classified into four groups, based on their average innovation performances: 'Innovation leaders' have an innovation performance well above that of the EU average, 'Innovation followers' group comprises countries whose performance is above or close to that of the EU average, 'Moderate innovators' have a performance below that of the EU average, and the last group covers 'Modest innovators' whose performance is well below that of the EU average.

Source: Innovation Union Scoreboard (2014).

intention and capabilities of enterprises. Turkey needs to put in place many of the things detailed in the scoreboard. This would surely help to develop enterprise in the country, but it will not convert Turkey into a Germany or Finland overnight.

By identifying, comparing and disseminating best practices in financing and technology transfer, Europe can improve its innovation performance. One area that needs particular attention is the overall perception of the entrepreneur. The image of the entrepreneur needs to have greater value, as in the United States where the drive to try to market new products, with the inbuilt risk of failure, is seen much more positively than in Europe. When looking at performance of innovation systems in a global context, South Korea, the USA and Japan have an innovation performance lead over the EU (Figure 2.6). Whilst the gap between the USA and Japan is decreasing, it is widening with South Korea.

The scoreboard may be helpful to governmental policy makers in deciding where to invest substantial sums of money. However, the first two chapters of this book have emphasised that firms behave differently given similar circumstances and that some firms appeared to be more successful than others. Given this, the scoreboard's practical help is likely to be extremely limited.

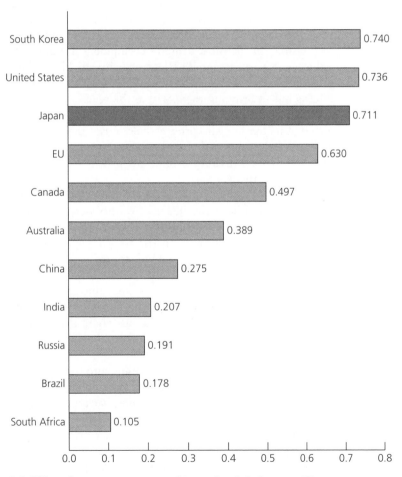

Figure 2.6 EU performance compared to main global competitors

Illustration 2.3

When state support does not help

Research by Hu and Hun (2014) illustrates that, sometimes, state support does not work. The Taiwan system of innovation in the pharmaceutical industry has failed to achieve international competitiveness, despite strong state support. Their study showed that the innovation performance of Taiwan's pharmaceutical industry has been poor when compared to India, especially when looking at patenting and publication activities. Previous research has demonstrated that patents and publications play a critical role in linking actors and institutions and is highly associated with the effectiveness of the innovation system.

Entrepreneurship

Joseph Schumpeter was one of the few intellectuals who saw business differently. He regarded business people as unsung heroes: men and women who create new enterprises through the sheer force of their wills and imaginations and, in so doing, are responsible for the most benign development in human history, the spread of mass affluence. 'Queen Elizabeth [I] owned silk stockings,' he once observed. 'The capitalist achievement does not typically consist in providing more silk stockings for queens but in bringing them within the reach of factory girls in return for steadily decreasing amounts of effort . . . The capitalist process, not by coincidence but by virtue of its mechanism, progressively raises the standard of life of the masses.' But Schumpeter recognised that business people are often ruthless robber barons, obsessed by their dreams of building 'private kingdoms' and willing to do anything to crush their rivals.

Schumpeter's ability rested on a broader philosophy of capitalism. He argued that innovation is at the heart of economic progress. It gives new businesses a chance to replace old ones, but it also dooms those new businesses to fail, unless they can keep on innovating (or find a powerful government patron). In his most famous phrase, he likened capitalism to a 'perennial gale of creative destruction'.

For Schumpeter, the people who kept this gale blowing were entrepreneurs. He was responsible for identifying the entrepreneur's central function: of moving resources, however painfully, to areas where they can be used more productively. Importantly, he also recognised that big businesses can be as innovative as small ones.

Entrepreneurship is all about stepping into the unknown and breaking away from the familiar. For some people, this is less of a challenge than for others. This can be for a wide variety of reasons, including background and parental influence. Across Europe, unlike in the USA, it remains true that more graduates would sooner work for Siemens, Shell or Nokia than start their own business. This picture, however, is changing and the numbers interested in starting their own business is rising rapidly. Furthermore, an injection of entrepreneurship, by which creative people are encouraged to strike out and develop new products or services, is important to the financial health of all organisations. Yet, fundamental questions appear as major obstacles:

Where is the opportunity? How do I capitalise on it? What resources do I need? How do I gain control over them?

For many, the entrepreneur and entrepreneurship is best captured by George Bernard Shaw's famous quote:

> *The reasonable man (woman) adapts himself (herself) to the world. The unreasonable one persists in trying to adapt the world to himself (herself). Therefore, all progress depends on unreasonable men (and women).*

(George Bernard Shaw)

This captures the essence of entrepreneurship. That it is about change; it is about doing something different. Often, this change will be met with resistance and it is the entrepreneur who will persist and get things done. Without such people, improvements are less likely.[1]

But what does *entrepreneurial* mean? Managers describe entrepreneurship with such terms as innovative, flexible, dynamic, risk taking, creative and growth oriented. The popular press, on the other hand, often defines the term as starting and operating new ventures. That view is reinforced by the alluring success of such upstarts as SAP, Dyson and TomTom.

Neither approach to a definition of entrepreneurship is precise or prescriptive enough for managers who wish to be more entrepreneurial. Everybody wants to be innovative, flexible and creative. But for every SAP, Dyson and TomTom there are thousands of new restaurants, clothing stores and consulting firms that, presumably, have tried to be innovative, to grow and to show other characteristics that are entrepreneurial — but have failed.

In this book, we want to reinforce the idea that entrepreneurship is not just about starting a new business. Our focus on innovation management underscores this point. We are all aware of many medium and small businesses that consistently develop new products and markets and also grow at rates far exceeding national averages. For example, Subocean Group grew an incredible 237 per cent in 2009, increasing its turnover from £1.7 million to £65 million in 2009. Subocean runs power cables along the sea floor from offshore wind farms to substations on land (Fast Track 100, 2010). Moreover, we are all aware of many of the largest corporations – BMW, AstraZeneca and Ericsson are just a few of the best known – that make a practice of innovating, taking risks and showing creativity. And they continue to expand.

Entrepreneurship and innovation

In the United States, the subject of entrepreneurship has been taught in business schools for over 50 years. The content of these courses clearly varies but many of them study growing a small business into a large one. When it comes to innovation management, generally, this has not been studied and, until recently, there were far fewer courses available. This is changing. Yet, in Europe, we have a long history of teaching innovation management but not entrepreneurship. This is changing and entrepreneurship is a rapidly growing subject in universities across Europe, as an academic field entrepreneurship has flourished. In 1983, Babson held the first

---

[1] George Bernard Shaw (1856 –1950) was an Irish playwright and a co-founder of the London School of Economics. He is also the only person to be awarded a Nobel prize for literature and an Oscar.

research conference on entrepreneurship with 37 papers presented. In 2010, there were over 1,000 papers presented. Entrepreneurship now has its own division within the Academy of Management.

In Europe, there is a recognition and a considerable emphasis, especially within the technical universities, on trying to understand how entrepreneurship and innovation can help create the new technology intensive businesses of tomorrow. Moreover, it is the recognition of the entrepreneur's desire to change things that is so important within innovation. We will see later that the role of an entrepreneur is central to innovation management.

Trying to uncover separate definitions for innovation and entrepreneurship is, increasingly, a purely academic exercise. The main traits associated with entrepreneurship, such as growth, flexibility and creativity, are also desirable traits for innovation. Theorists and practioners alike recognise that these constructs are close relatives or two sides of the same coin. Now we will outline briefly the roots of these terms and their linkage.

Traditionally, it is Jean-Baptiste Say who is credited for coining the word and advancing the concept of the entrepreneur, but, in fact, it was Richard Cantillon who first introduced the term in *Essai*; this was written in 1730. Cantillon divided society into two principal classes – fixed-income wage earners and non-fixed income earners. Entrepreneurs, according to Cantillon, are non-fixed income earners who pay known costs of production, but earn uncertain incomes, hence it was Cantillon who saw the entrepreneur as a risk-taker, whereas Say predominately considered the entrepreneur a planner.

A few years later, in his 1776 thought-provoking book *The Wealth of Nations*, Adam Smith explained clearly that it was not the benevolence of the baker but self-interest that motivated him to provide bread. From Smith's standpoint, entrepreneurs were the economic agents who transformed demand into supply for profits. In 1848, the famous economist John Stuart Mill described entrepreneurship as the founding of a private enterprise. This encompassed the risk takers, the decision makers and the individuals who desire wealth by managing limited resources to create new business ventures.

Whilst entrepreneurship may have a long history, the term entrepreneur continued to be used to define a businessman until the arrival of Joseph Schumpeter. It was his work in the 1930s that made the clear linkage between the terms innovation and entrepreneurship. He considered entrepreneurship as influencing growth in the economy. It is something that disrupts the market equilibrium, or 'circular flow'. Its essence is 'innovation'. He writes that: 'the carrying out of new combinations we call enterprise; the individuals whose function is to carry them out we call entrepreneurs' (1934: 74). After Schumpter's work, most economists (and many others) have accepted his identification of entrepreneurship with innovation (see Kilby, 1971, for a summary of the term entrepreneur).

According to Schumpeter, economic development is the result of three types of factors:

1 External factors such as demand by government (changes in legislation, defence orders).
2 Factors of growth or gradual changes in economic life that are accomplished through day-to-day activities and adjustments.
3 'The outstanding fact in the economic history of capitalist society', innovation.

And, for Schumpeter, entrepreneurs are galvanised into action under the following conditions (Schumpeter, 1961: 214):

1 The existence of new possibilities more advantageous from the private standpoint – a necessary condition;
2 Limited access to these possibilities because of personal qualifications and external circumstances;
3 An economic situation that allows tolerably reliable calculations.

For Schumpeter, and his direct disciples (Freeman, 1979; Kleinknecht, 1981; 1 and Mensch, 1979) innovation is the chief force in what he calls 'economic evolution'. It is worthy of note that for Schumpeter his concept of innovation is broader than some innovation theorists have since argued. For Schumpeter, innovation is not simply the patenting of new inventions, it includes new combinations in organisations, commerce and the market, as well as the creation of new business organisations (Schumpeter, 1961: 66). This, then, may be helpful as we try to consider together the concepts of entrepreneurship and innovation. We also need to recognise a wider definition of innovation that includes more than the hard physical outputs from a traditional science-led institution, such as a technical university (TU) and consider new service offerings as well.

Defining entrepreneurship

For many people the following Innovation in action captures what it is to be an entrepreneur.

Innovation in action

Penny apples – selling them thrice over

In his autobiography, the Irish entrepreneur Billy Cullen (2003) tells the story of how, as an eight-year-old boy, he demonstrated sharp entrepreneurial skills. In a poverty-stricken area of Dublin, young Billy would buy wooden crates of apples for a shilling and then sell the apples on a Saturday afternoon to the hundreds of local people who would flock to watch their local football team play. This provided Billy with a healthy profit

Source: Pearson Education Ltd/Westend 61

of a shilling, if he could sell all the apples. But, his entrepreneurial skills did not stop there. He would then take the wooden apple boxes to the football ground and sell them for a penny to people at the back of the crowds, so that they could stand on the box for a better view. And, finally, when the match had finished, Billy would collect up the wooden boxes, break them up and sell them in bundles for firewood.

Entrepreneurship can be described as a process of action that an entrepreneur undertakes to establish an enterprise. Entrepreneurship is a creative activity. It is the ability to create and build something from practically nothing. It is an ability to see an opportunity where others see chaos, contradiction and confusion. Entrepreneurship is an attitude of mind to seek opportunities, take calculated risks and derive benefits by setting up a venture. It comprises numerous activities involved in conception, creation and running an enterprise. Similarly, an entrepreneur is a person who starts such an enterprise. He searches for change and responds to it. There are a wide variety of definitions for an entrepreneur – economists view him as a fourth factor of production along with land labour and capital. Sociologists feel that certain communities and cultures promote entrepreneurship. The USA often is cited as having a culture that supports entrepreneurs. Still others feel that entrepreneurs are innovators who come up with new ideas for products and markets. To put it very simply, an entrepreneur is someone who perceives opportunity, organises resources needed for exploiting that opportunity and exploits it.

Peter Drucker's classic book *Innovation and Entrepreneurship* was first published in 1985 and it was the first book to present innovation and entrepreneurship as a purposeful and systematic activity. According to Drucker, 'Innovation is the specific function of entrepreneurship' and entrepreneurship, 'is the means by which the entrepreneur either creates new wealth-producing resources or endows existing resources with enhanced potential for creating wealth'.

In his book, Drucker focuses on large-scale entrepreneurship, rather than small business management. Drucker's recurring theme is that good entrepreneurship is usually market-focused and market-driven. Contrary to the belief of many, Drucker says that innovation is not inspired by a bright idea, rather it 'is organised, systematic, rational work'. Innovation can be mastered and integrated into a company or non-profit organisation.

In a study of past and future research on the subject of entrepreneurship, Low and MacMillan (1988) define it as 'the process of planning, organising, operating, and assuming the risk of a business venture'. Risk and the willingness to take a risk with one's time and money is surely a key feature of entrepreneurship. It is the analysis of the role of the individual entrepreneur that distinguishes the study of entrepreneurship from that of innovation management. Howard Stevenson, who developed entrepreneurship teaching at Harvard Business School, defines entrepreneurship as follows:

> *Entrepreneurship is the pursuit of opportunity beyond the resources you currently control.*
>
> (Stevenson 1983, 1985, 1990)

This definition takes into account both the individual and the society in which the individual is embedded. The individual identifies an opportunity to be pursued, then, as an entrepreneur, must seek the resources from the broader society. Stevenson argues that entrepreneurship activities can be identified as distinct from that of the administrator (see Table 2.2 below). This is significant, for it recognises that entrepreneurship can be viewed as a mode of management within a corporation.

According to Howard Aldrich (2012), the academic field of entrepreneurship research has grown from groups of isolated scholars doing research on small businesses to an international community of departments, institutes and foundations promoting research on new and high-growth firms. The field is increasingly formalised

Table 2.2 Definition of entrepreneurship

A process definition of entrepreneurship		
Key business dimension	**Entrepreneur**	**Administrator**
Strategic orientation	Driven by perception of opportunity	Driven by resources currently controlled
Commitment to opportunity	Quick commitment	Evolutionary with long duration
Commitment process	Multistage with minimal exposure at each stage	Single-stage with complete commitment upon decision
Control of resources	Episodic use of rent of required resources	Ownership or employment of required resources
Management structure	Flat with multiple informal networks	Formalised hierarchy
Reward system	Value-based and team-based	Resource-based individual and promotion oriented

Source: Stevenson (2000).

and anchored in a small set of intellectual bases. Significantly, however, major foundations and many other smaller funding sources have changed the scale and scope of entrepreneurship research today. Virtually all business schools now engage in entrepreneurship research.

Technological entrepreneurship: a question of context

Like so many things in life, our perception of something depends upon our vantage point. For those of us considering entrepreneurship, this is particularly relevant. Do we wish to consider the individual entrepreneur, the organisation, an industry, an economy or even the wider society? Hence, the level of analysis needs to be specified. Also, do we wish to investigate the past or the future? For example, there are many studies that have tried to explain why some firms or individuals were successful – the growth (and fall) of Microsoft or Nokia. There are also historical studies of periods of time, such as the growth of the Roman Empire or the demise of the Ottoman Empire. So the time frame needs to be specified. Finally, do we wish to investigate or study a particular phenomenon or issue? For example, entrepreneurship education has received a great deal of attention from policy makers and politicians as they have tried to enhance their country's economic growth. Nonetheless, this area of business management is problematic. In his book *High-Technology Entrepreneurship*, Professor Ray Oakey provides a comprehensive overview of all aspects of high-technology small firm formation and growth and illustrates that they have not been attractive assessment vehicles for those with money to invest (Oakey, 2012).

Research by Autio et al. (2014) illustrates the importance of context when they compare the attributes of national innovation systems, entrepreneurship and entrepreneurial innovation and its influences on entrepreneurial innovation. The evidence is mounting up all over the world that innovation is key to competitiveness and growth and that entrepreneurial dynamism is key to economic renewal and growth. The focus is, therefore, provided by a combination of several areas of policy. One of the major weaknesses of the effectiveness of policies to develop technological entrepreneurship is insufficient recognition of the overlaps and linkages between these four areas:

1 Science and technology.
2 Small and medium-sized enterprise.
3 Innovation.
4 Entrepreneurship.

Science and technology policy

Science and technology policy is an area of public policy concerned with the government decisions that affect the conduct of the science and research enterprise, including the funding of science, often in pursuance of other national policy goals, such as technological innovation to promote commercial product development, weapons development, health care and environmental monitoring. Indeed, innovation policy has evolved from S&T policy.

Small and medium-sized enterprise

There has been recognition for a long time that small firms require support and help if they are to grow into larger firms and help develop and grow the economy. Many economies embraced the concept of 'acorn to oak tree' as they put in place numerous measures to help SMEs grow. Entrepreneurship policy has evolved from SME policy. Yet, it has been recognised for many years now that most small businesses are not investment-ready. Their owners are unwilling to seek external equity finance and those who are willing do not understand what equity investors are looking for or how to 'sell' themselves and their businesses to potential investors. These weaknesses, in turn, compromise the effectiveness of supply-side interventions, such as initiatives to stimulate business angels or which create public sector venture capital funds (Oakey, 2007b).

Within this area, we find business incubators. Business incubators can offer start-ups various forms of assistance from economies related to shared business services, to expert advice, and access to venture funding opportunities. Incubator facilities vary widely in size, as measured by the square footage or total start-up costs and the number of tenants resident in the facilities. Technology-oriented incubators are increasingly locating near research parks, universities or research labs to offer technology entrepreneurs access to a wider range of facilities, individuals and opportunities within their field. Tenant firms can have access to the research facilities and personnel of established firms, universities and research institutes. Additionally, they are able to network more easily with experienced and successful entrepreneurs and may even engage in strategic alliances to exploit business opportunities either as a subcontractor or a supplier.

University spin-outs

University spin-outs have received considerable positive publicity. Yahoo and Google often are cited as examples. Yet research comparing non-university spin-outs with university spin-outs reveals a different picture (Ortín-Ángel and

Vendrell-Herrero, 2014). A close examination of the literature on university spin-outs reveals surprising evidence:

- The average number of spin-outs from American universities in 2012 was a measly three (AUTM, 2015).
- The income generated from technology transfer as a proportion of research income is insignificant (at MIT, for example, in 2012 it was 2.4 per cent of their research income).
- Most US universities lose money on technology transfer activities because of their high running costs (the exceptions are the handful of universities that own patents on blockbuster drugs).

Even the high profile business successes of Yahoo and Google are sometimes used to support the notion of university spin-outs, but even here the evidence cannot be found. Whilst both Yahoo and Google were founded by Stanford University students, Stanford did not claim intellectual property in the Yahoo technology because this was developed in the students' own time. In the Google case, Stanford was able to generate income from ownership of the intellectual property, but most of its income comes from its venture capital (VC) investment made through local VC firms rather than from the licence. The definition of a university spin-out is critical here. In the survey above, a new business venture by university students is not classified as a spin-out. A university spin-out involves staff from the university starting a new business.

The devil is in the detail here. For, whilst university spin-outs cannot claim significant economic impact, the role of universities in supplying educated and trained personnel who can then exploit opportunities certainly can. What is clear, then, is that when we examine the business/university interface we see university graduates as a driver of economic growth, rather than university technology as the driver.

Established firms versus start-ups

Despite the widely acknowledged role of start-ups in economic development, little is known about their innovative activities compared with those of established firms. In a study of UK firms, research by Criscuolo et al. (2012) shows that start-ups differ significantly from established firms in their innovation activities. They find that in services, being a start-up increases the likelihood of product innovations. However, in manufacturing, they find no significant differences in the likelihood of product innovation between start-ups and established firms (Criscuolo et al., 2012). The performance of new firms is important for economic development, but research has produced limited knowledge about the key relationships amongst growth, profitability and survival for new firms. Delmar et al. (2013) has found that profitability enhances both survival and growth, and growth helps profitability but has a negative effect on survival.

Innovation policy

Within the EU and in other countries too, such as South Korea, innovation policy has focused generally on four key objectives:

- The generation of new knowledge.
- Making government investment in innovation more effective.

- Enhancing diffusion of knowledge and technology (network interaction effects).
- Establishing the right incentives to stimulate private sector innovation to transform knowledge into commercial success.

Much of the policy assistance for high-technology small firms (HTSFs) over recent years has been directed at encouraging their research and development (R&D) collaboration through local networking and technology transfer, such as working with larger partners or universities. Research by Professor Ray Oakley has questioned the value of external collaborative R&D to internal R&D management, inside incubators, science parks or industry clusters. His research suggested that the extent of R&D collaboration with external partners is very limited and, moreover, much of the collaborative HTSF R&D is highly confidential, competitive and wholly internalised, thereby limiting the benefits to the wider economy (Oakey, 2007a).

Entrepreneurship policy

Entrepreneurship policies have attempted to concentrate on developing an environment and support system to foster the emergence of new entrepreneurs and the start-up and early stage growth of new firms. Yet there has been limited recognition of the full integration of entrepreneurship and innovation. Indeed, there has been a disconnect between entrepreneurship and innovation policies. There needs to be a convergence between the two to ensure optimisation of complementarities. Unfortunately, all too often, innovation policies do not incorporate entrepreneurship as a focus. Yet we know that entrepreneurship involves the act of innovation and that entrepreneurs are essential to convert knowledge into economic and social benefits.

Case study

Pizza delivery with unmanned drones

In the summer of 2013, a Domino's franchise in the United Kingdom posted a video showing an unmanned drone delivering pizzas in the company's Heatwave bags. Was this genuine product testing by Domino's of a novel way of getting takeaway food to customers or merely a stunt by Domino's to raise its profile? The use of drone technology has, up to now, been associated mostly with war-like situations in a more benign manner. For example, drones are being used already to great effect in Afghanistan, where two K-MAX unmanned helicopters have carried more than three million pounds of cargo since December 2011. The widespread use of such drones, though, raises questions. Some are of safety: every extra craft

Source: Chesky/Shutterstock.com

in the air adds to the risk of a crash or collision. Others are of privacy: are people's activities to be monitored continuously when they are outdoors, even when they are on their own private property? This case study explores the challenges that lie ahead for this innovation.

Introduction

There are a few other industries that are exploring the use of unmanned drone technology. For example, Shenzhen-based Chinese delivery company SF Express (a parcel delivery company) is in the early stages of putting drones in the skies that can deliver packages to remote areas, according to the *South China Morning Post*. SF has begun testing the drones in Guangdong Province's Dongguan City, and can reach a flight altitude of about 100 metres. The benefits of this technology are simple to recognise. For example, farmers would no longer have to go out in all weathers to check on livestock and farmland. They could remain indoors and use a drone with a camera to patrol their land.

In some countries, most notably the United States, a major hurdle for getting drones into the air is hampered by the fact that the Federal Aviation Administration (FAA) does not currently allow drones for commercial use in US airspace. Because of its early stage of technology development and current US flight restrictions, UPS and FedEx may be at a disadvantage. If courier companies like SF Express can make significant inroads in development and implementation of package-delivering drones, then parcels-via-drone suddenly becomes much closer to reality, at least for smaller package transportation. Whilst the SF Express drones are being developed with the intention of reaching difficult-to-get-to remote areas, it is hard not to imagine the potential benefits of having drone 'deliverymen'. They can reach remote locations where there are no roads. They can be pre-programmed with destination coordinates and can, effectively, fly in a straight line. This would cut down on fuel costs associated with delivery. Why send a truck that takes fuel when you could send a drone and then simply recharge the battery? Police forces around the world are also keen to lay their hands on small pilotless aircraft to help them catch fleeing criminals and monitor crime scenes from above. With price tags of a little more (and, in some cases, a good deal less) than the £30,000 of a police patrol car, a new generation of micro-unmanned aerial vehicles (UAVs) is being recruited to replace police helicopters costing £1.5 million and up. It is possible to imagine standing out on your front porch, morning coffee in hand, looking up and watching as a whole buzzing network of drones go about their business catching criminals, delivering goods . . . and pizzas. Welcome to the world of drone technology.

Where technologies collide: toys and unmanned aircraft

Quadcopters – small, four-rotored helicopters – are popular toys. A few hundred pounds will buy you one that can be controlled remotely using a standard tablet computer. Parrot, a French firm that makes one such model, says it has sold more than half a million of them. But they are also a favourite of researchers looking into the possibilities offered by small, pilotless aircraft to do everything from delivering packages to scouting and surveillance. Although they are pilotless, quadcoptors are not generally clever enough to be properly self-flying. Most have to be controlled from the ground. Parrot's toy drones will stabilise themselves and hover if left unattended, but require a human to tell them what to do, if they are actually to go anywhere. Satellite-navigation systems can give the craft the ability to get to roughly where they are needed, but do not work indoors and do not provide for fine manoeuvrability. More advanced laboratory-bound drones can perform impressive feats of agility, like zipping through small holes and perching, birdlike, on vantage points – but they require a ground-based computer to monitor them with high-speed cameras and tell them how to achieve all this.

Some more recent prototypes incorporate smartphone technology to help the drones. They use image-recognition programs to find their way around. They identify objects in the vicinity, remember their locations and thus build up a map of the area the drone is flying through. For now, the 'objects' are distinctive patterns analogous to the two-dimensional 'barcodes' beloved of advertisers, which are designed to be scanned by mobile-phone cameras. But image-recognition algorithms are a hot area of research for everyone from governments to social-networking firms keen to identify pictures of their users – and smartphones, like other kinds of computer, are always getting faster. Technology developments in other areas offer even more potential to drones. For example, a solar-powered drone could fly long missions, which conventional aircraft are not capable of doing.

Drones with even a limited ability to find their own way through the world would be a significant step closer to ones that could be employed for tasks such as search and rescue, industrial inspection and the surveillance of dangerous areas. And, since they will be cheap, their users will, doubtless, think up plenty of other uses for them, both helpful and unsavoury. Drones are best known for their role in the Afghan war, where they both monitor and strike at enemy forces. The attraction of drones for domestic users is their ability to carry sensors, such as cameras and spectrometers, rather than weapons. This suggests they could be useful in commerce and research, as well as policing. A number are in police departments, and it is this development that is stirring up concerns about privacy and protests from local residents.

Potential innovation hurdles from regulators

Technology development and innovation does not occur in isolation and some industries are very heavily regulated. Drones may be too. In Australia, it is legal to use drones for commercial purposes, but that is not the case in the USA, where the Federal Aviation Authority will not release rules for commercial drones until 2016. Laws on the use of drones vary from country to country. In Canada, for instance, companies looking to operate an unmanned aircraft for commercial reasons are required to obtain a special government-issued certificate for each flight taken. Small unmanned aircraft are allowed as long as they are operated by an individual for recreational purposes only. In the UK, where the Domino's pizza project was born, there are currently at least 130 groups or companies licensed to use drones in the country's airspace. According to a recent *Financial Times* report, the country has become something of a leader in the commercial use of unmanned aircraft with real estate agents deploying them to snap aerial shots of properties and farmers using them to monitor crops. Obviously, delivering food is different from snapping pictures.

Current drones depend on two-way satellite communications. If this data link is broken, the remote pilot will lose direct control of the aircraft, which then has to rely on pre-loaded software and GPS guidance. For routine missions that may be all right, but for missions requiring constant oversight, the vulnerability to electronic jamming or a direct attack on a communications satellite is an Achilles heel. Data links can also go down without help from an enemy.

Another problem is that drones have not been cleared to share civil airspace over the USA and Europe by air-traffic controllers. The Federal Aviation Authority began trials in 2010, but it will not be easy to dispel fears that, if a pilot were temporarily to lose control of a drone, it might smash into a passenger airliner in shared airspace.

One technical point is how a UAV should respond if it loses its communications link with the operator on the ground. Should it return automatically to some pre-assigned GPS location, or head for the nearest open space? Should it have a parachute arrangement – like an increasing number of private planes – to lower it gently to the ground in an emergency, or should it put itself immediately into a stall? Plenty of practical solutions exist for such problems. The issue is cost. A bigger stumbling block is how UAVs should detect, sense and avoid other aircraft operating in the same airspace. Drones piloted remotely by operators on the ground cannot see other aircraft in the sky in the way that human pilots can. Before giving the go-ahead, regulators will want UAVs to be able to operate as safely as manned aircraft. That may mean developing a lot of expensive gear to avoid mid-air collisions and near misses. So, whilst drones may appear to be cheap, making them safe raises the cost. This may limit their appeal.

Clearly, the police and other civilian groups are unlikely to be able to afford to have a couple of dedicated operators on the ground for each UAV in the air. Nor can they be expected to have multiple ground-based radars tracking their UAV's every move. But, if small pilotless planes are to fulfil a useful role in fighting crime and saving lives, then the regulations governing their use ought to reflect the environment in which they are likely to operate. Because of the roles they will play, most micro-UAVs used by civilian agencies will operate well below 400 ft and probably (like the rules governing model aircraft) no closer than three miles from an airport. That is not exactly Class A airspace used by commercial air traffic. Arguably, mid-air collisions are, therefore, even less likely than they are in the open skies. Nonetheless, cost is a key part of the innovation jigsaw. Surprisingly, the missing piece of the jigsaw may be available in Mexico.

Very low cost drones from Mexico's maquiladoras

Most new technologies enter the market with a price premium; drones are no exception. This is partly because firms have to recoup initial investments so that they can re-invest in faster and larger factories, which will, eventually, help to lower costs. Unusually, drone technology has been developing in two separate spheres: military aviation with unmanned aircraft and in the sphere of toys with wireless model aircraft. Whilst engineers and technologists will argue the technologies are very different, there is clearly scope for technology transfer and economies of scale. Aerospace products are associated with large price tags, whether it be military aircraft or executive jets. Yet, this may not necessarily be the case for drones.

Just over the US border in Mexico is 3D Robotics, a small Mexican entrepreneurial firm based in Tijuana. It makes small, insect-like drones (pilotless aircraft) for civilian use. 3D Robotics's drone-producing plant is a *maquiladora*, a factory that enjoys special tax breaks. When Mexico set up the first maquiladoras half a century ago, they were sweatshops that simply bolted or stitched together imported parts, then exported the assembled product north across the border to the United States. The USA secured cheap goods; Mexico got jobs and export revenues. Now, with competition growing from other low-cost locations, and with the government cutting some of their tax breaks, the maquiladoras are having to step up their efforts to become innovative.

The factory in Tijuana where they make their small drones is so close to the border that they could, if they were allowed, fly across to San Diego. That is where the firm's boffins design and engineer them. 3D Robotics' co-founder, Jordi Muñoz, grew up dreaming of building robotic flying machines, but managed to do so only after moving to California. He says he could not have succeeded without the United States' technological prowess and entrepreneurial culture. He began to make progress in 2006, when the imminent launch of Apple's iPhone triggered a plunge in the cost of the motion sensors he needed to build his dream. It is easy to buy supplies on eBay – and, again in contrast to Mexico, the postal system delivers them quickly and reliably. Mexican bureau-cracy makes it hard to get started: even a tiny garage start-up requires an industrial permit. Before the firm had its own premises, Muñoz got some friends to assemble the drones in their kitchen. From such humble beginnings, 3D Robotics hopes its pilotless craft will be used for anything from monitoring crops to lifeguard duties on beaches.

Over the years, the maquiladoras have already lost much basic work, such as stitching together fabrics, to cheaper places in Asia, like Bangladesh. But, more recently, rising pay in Chinese factories has made Mexico look an attractive location once more. Indeed, Figure 2.7 shows the narrowing of wage rates in China and Mexico. The minimum wage in Shanghai and Qingdao is now higher than in Mexico City and Monterrey.

Mexico may provide the US drone industry with a low cost advantage

Cuernavaca is a typical Mexican town. Yet, on the outskirts of the city, in an enormous industrial park, a visitor could forget he was in Latin America. Nissan, a Japanese car giant, has created a factory the size of a village where it is turning out thousands of yellow and chessboard-chequered New York City taxis. Once shuttered off by tariffs and trade controls, Mexico has opened up to become a place where the world does business. The North American Free-Trade Agreement (NAFTA), which in 1994 eliminated most tariffs between Mexico, the United States and Canada, was only the beginning: Mexico now boasts free-trade deals with 44 countries, more than any other nation. In northern and central Mexico, German companies turn out electrical components for Europe, Canadian firms assemble aircraft parts and factory after factory makes televisions, fridge-freezers and much else. Each year, Mexico exports manufactured goods to about the same value as the rest of Latin America put together.

Hauling goods from Asia to the United States is costlier, too. The price of oil has trebled since the start of the century, making it more attractive to manufacture close to markets. A container can take three months to travel from China to the United States, whereas products trucked in from Mexico can take just a couple of days. When one considers the joint effect of pay, logistics and currency fluctuations, Mexico is now one of the world's cheapest places to manufacture goods destined for the United States,

→

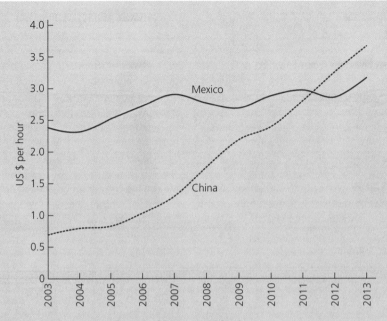

Figure 2.7 The narrowing of wage rates in China and Mexico

Source: Bank of America Merrill Lynch Global Research, Banxico, INEGI, International Labor Organizations, National Bureau of Statistics of China own estimates for China since 2009 and for Mexico in 2013.

undercutting China as well as countries such as India and Vietnam.

Conclusions

Technical challenges remain for drone technology. For example, drones are almost always battery powered and, at present, can run for only a short time. Until these are improved, it will remain too expensive to deliver food to customers. There are also safety issues associated with flying drones as delivery vehicles: drones still are not great at using 'sense and avoid' technology to keep them from hitting obstacles, including power lines, birds and other drones.

Whether this is merely a publicity stunt for the pizza company or a genuine prototype, it helps people who may associate drones with targeted killings overseas to see them in a more positive light. It could be possible to have an unmanned helicopter in the Navy to deliver emergency medical supplies and perform evacuations. They could carry food supplies, medical supplies and help humans who are in dire trouble. Potentially, this technology has endless positive uses. Solar-powered drones could be useful to survey pipelines and power cables, perform aerial filming for anyone from television news stations to estate agents,

monitor fires and assist in search-and-rescue operations and help carry out research. Aviation regulators are now forming rules that would allow far greater civilian use of such drones. For many of these missions, long flight times would be important and solar power can help with that. This would also mean not having to transport fuel or carry recharging equipment.

It is the possibility of very low cost drones that makes this technology even more likely to have a huge impact on businesses. Aerospace and defence companies are amongst those thought likely to 'nearshore' some of the manufacturing currently sent to China. The maquiladora zone near Tijuana already has more than 50 firms in these industries and it is here that the efforts to become more innovative are most visible. The Tijuana plant of Zodiac Aerospace, a French company, makes aircraft interiors. In the design office, young engineers are designing from scratch a netting system for planes' overhead lockers, to stop luggage shifting during flights. There is a note attached, saying 'Made in Mexico' on his screen.

To become a plausible aerospace 'cluster', and attract more investment from the world's top manufacturers, the maquiladoras around Tijuana need to bolster the local supply chain, as well as produce more engineers capable of product design. For decades, low costs have made the maquiladoras one of the two main pillars of Mexico's exports, second only to oil. From now on, creativity and innovation will be a better way of beating the competition than cost. If 3D Robotics, and others like it, can get involved in design and development they stand to gain some of the investment that US manufacturers are expected to make, as they shift work closer to home in reaction to rising costs in China. Otherwise, those firms may instead be tempted to put their new plants in US states, such as Nevada and New Mexico. These may not be able to match Mexican labour costs, but they have a better educated workforce and are offering attractive tax rates and utility costs.

Finally, resistance to the technology may yet come from a frightened public concerned about loss of privacy. Politicians may find themselves popular if they are able to portray drones as 'an enemy of privacy'. They may try to paint an Orwellian nightmare to gain votes. It is not too hard to image some unscrupulous drone uses, such as neighbours spying on one another.

Questions

1 In this case, the technology would seem to be stable and its costs falling rapidly. Where, then, are the difficulties of launching the product?

2 Two separate product technologies seem to be converging: military unmanned aircraft and remote-controlled toy drones. What opportunities does this generate?

3 Apply the cyclic innovation model to the case to illustrate the entrepreneurs and technology development.

4 Describe how the national innovation system in Mexico may hinder the chances of firms succeeding.

5 Specify precisely how the Mexican maquiladoras can provide US manufacturers with a way of competing with Chinese firms.

6 This case illustrates the influence of regulation on innovation. Show how tight and loose regulation may help and hinder innovation.

7 Discuss why the right to privacy may yet prevent this technology from getting off the ground.

Note: This case has been written as a basis for class discussion rather than to illustrate effective or ineffective managerial or administrative behaviour. It has been prepared from a variety of published sources, as indicated, and from observations.

Chapter summary

This chapter has explored the wider context of innovation, in particular the role of the state. It has shown that innovation cannot be separated from political and social processes. This includes both tangible and intangible features, including economic, social and political institutions, and processes and mechanisms that facilitate the flow of knowledge between industries and firms.

Discussion questions

1 Discuss the tangible features that it is necessary for the state to put in place to foster innovation.

2 How can the state encourage entrepreneurs and businesses to invest in longer time horizons?

3 Explain Schumpeter's view of entrepreneurial behaviour and economic growth.

4 Explain how the success of companies like Apple and Google is due partly to the state.

5 Discuss the evidence for the fifth Kondratieff wave of growth.

6 What is meant by a 'weak business system'?

7 Explain the role played by entrepreneurship in innovation.

8 How do universities help to deliver entrepreneurship?

Key words and phrases

Schumpeterian theory *50*

Short-termism *51*

Entrepreneurship *51*

National systems of innovation *52*

Corruption *57*

Kondratieff waves of growth *60*

Business system *63*

Websites worth visiting

Confederation of British Industry www.cbi.org.uk

Engineering Council (EC UK) www.engc.org.uk

European Industrial Research Management Association (EIRMA) www.eirma.org

Quoted Companies Alliance (QCA) www.theqca.com

TechUK www.techuk.org

The R&D Society www.rdsoc.org

The Royal Academy of Engineering www.raeng.org.uk

References

Afuah, A. (2003) *Innovation Management: Strategies, Implementation and Profits*, 2nd edn, Oxford University Press, Oxford.

Aldrich, H.E. (2012) The emergence of entrepreneurship as an academic field: a personal essay on institutional entrepreneurship, *Research Policy*, vol. 41, no. 7, 1240–8.

Archibugi, D., Filippetti, A. and Frenz, M. (2013) The impact of the economic crisis on innovation: evidence from Europe, *Technological Forecasting and Social Change*, vol. 80, no. 7, 1247–60.

Amsden, A. (1989) *Asia's Next Giant: South Korea and Late Industrialisation*, Oxford University Press, Oxford.

Autio, E., Kenney, M., Mustar, P., Siegel, D. and Wright, M. (2014) Entrepreneurial innovation: the importance of context, *Research Policy*, vol. 43, no. 7, 1097–108.

AUTM (2015) Association of University Technology Managers, US Licensing Activity Survey: FY2014. www.autm.net. 9 Sept. (Retrieved 13 Dec 2015.)

Bach, L., Matt, M. and Wolff, S. (2014) How do firms perceive policy rationales behind the variety of instruments supporting collaborative R&D? Lessons from the European Framework Programs, *Technovation*, vol. 34, no. 5, 327–37.

Castells, M. (1992) 'Four Asian Tigers with a dragon head: a comparative analysis of the state, economy, and society in the Asian Pacific Rim', in Appelbaum, R.P. and Henderson, J. (eds) *States and Development: The Asian Pacific Rim*, Oxford University Press, Oxford, 33–70.

Criscuolo, P., Nicolaou, N. and Salter, A. (2012) The elixir (or burden) of youth? Exploring differences in innovation between start-ups and established firms, *Research Policy*, vol. 41, no. 2, 319–33.

Cullen, B. (2003) *It's a Long Way from Penny Apples*, Coronet, London.

Delmar, F., McKelvie, A. and Wennberg, K. (2013) Untangling the relationships among growth, profitability and survival in new firms, *Technovation*, vol. 33, no. 8, 276–91.

Dicken, P. (1998) *Global Shift: Transforming the World Economy*, Paul Chapman, London.

Dolfsma, W. and Seo, D. (2013) Government policy and technological innovation: a suggested typology, *Technovation*, vol. 33, no. 6, 173–9.

Drucker, P. (1985) *Innovation and Entrepreneurship*, Harper & Row, New York.

Etzkowitz, H. and Leydesdorff, L. (1995). The Triple Helix of university–industry–government relations: a laboratory for knowledge-based economic development, *EASST Review*, vol. 14, no. 1, 14–19.

European Innovation Scoreboard (EIS) 2014 http://ec.europa.eu/eurostat/statistics-explained/index.php/Main_Page

Evans, P.B. (1989) Predatory, developmental, and other apparatuses: a comparative political economy perspective on the Third World state, *Sociological Forum*, vol. 4, no. 4, 561–87.

Fast Track 100 (2010) Britain's fastest growing private companies, *Sunday Times*, 5 December, 3.

Freeman, C. and Soete, L. (1997) *The Economics of Industrial Innovation*, 3rd edn, Pinter, London.

Freeman, C. (1979) The determinants of innovation: market demand, technology, and the response to social problems, *Futures*, vol. 11, no. 3, 206–15.

Freeman, C. (1987), *Technology, Policy, and Economic Performance: Lessons from Japan*, Pinter, London.

Georghiou, L, Edler, J., Uyarra, E. and Yeow, J. (2014) Policy instruments for public procurement of innovation: choice, design and assessment, *Technological Forecasting & Social Change*, 86, 1–12.

Hobday, M., Rush, H. and Bessant, J. (2004) Approaching the innovation frontier in Korea: the transition phase to leadership, *Research Policy*, vol. 33, no. 10, 1433–57.

Hu, M.-C. and Hung, S.-C. (2014) *Technological Forecasting and Social Change*, 88, 162–76.

IUS (2014) Innovation Union Scoreboards: ec.europa.eu/growth/industry/innovation/facts-figures/scoreboards/

Ivanova, I.A. and Leydesdorff, L. (2014) Rotational symmetry and the transformation of innovation systems in a Triple Helix of university–industry–government relations, *Technological Forecasting & Social Change*, vol. 86, no. 6, 143–56.

Johnson, C. (1982) *MITI and the Japanese Miracle: The Growth of Industrial Policy 1925–75*, Stanford University Press, Stanford, CA.

Kilby, P. (1971) Hunting the heffalump, *Entrepreneurship and Economic Development*, 1–40.

Kleinknecht, A. (1981) Observations on the Schumpeterian swarming of innovations, *Futures*, vol. 13, no. 4, 293–307.

Linstone, H.A. and Devezas, T. (2012) Technological innovation and the long wave theory revisited, *Technological Forecasting and Social Change*, vol. 79, no. 2, 414–16.

Low, M.B. and MacMillan, I.C. (1988) Entrepreneurship: past research and future challenges, *Journal of Management*, vol. 14, no. 2, 139–61

Lundvall, B.Å. (1988) 'Innovation as an interactive process', in Dosi, G. et al. *Technical Change and Economic Theory*, Pinter, London.

Marx, K. (1972) *The Karl Marx Library, Vol. 1: The Eighteenth Brumaire of Louis Bonaparte*, Padover, S.K. (ed.), McGraw Hill, New York, pp. 245–6.

Mazzucato, M. (2011) *The Entrepreneurial State*, Demos, London.

Mensch, G. (1979) *Stalemate in Technology: Innovations Overcome the Depression*, Ballinger, New York.

Oakey, R.P. (2007a) A commentary on gaps in funding for moderate 'non-stellar' growth small businesses in the United Kingdom, *Venture Capital*, vol. 9, no. 3, 223–35.

Oakey, R.P. (2007b) R&D collaboration between high technology small firms (HTSFs) in theory and practice, *R&D Management*, vol. 37, no. 3, 237–48.

Oakey, R.P. (2012) *High-Technology Entrepreneurship*, Routledge, Oxon, UK.

Ortín-Ángel, P. and Vendrell-Herrero, F. (2014) University spin-offs vs. other NTBFs: total factor productivity differences at outset and evolution, *Technovation*, vol. 34, no. 2, 101–112.

Porter, M. (1990) *The Competitive Advantage of Nations*, Macmillan, London.

Porter, M., Takeuchi H. and Sakakıbara, M. (2000) *Can Japan Compete?* Perseus Pub., Cambridge, MA.

RIS (2014) Regional Innovation Scoreboards: ec.europa.eu/growth/industry/innovation/facts-figures/scoreboards/

Roessner, D., Bond, J., Okubo, S. and Planting, M. (2013) The economic impact of licensed commercialized inventions originating in university research, *Research Policy*, vol. 42, no. 1, 23–34.

Rosenthal, D.E. (1993) Reevaluating the Chicago School paradigm for promoting innovation and competitiveness, *Canada–United States Law Journal*, vol. 19, 97–104.

Schumpeter, J. A. (1934) *The Theory of Economic Development: An inquiry into profits, capital, credit, interest, and the business cycle*, vol. 55, Transaction.

Schumpeter, J. (1943) *Capitalism, Socialism and Democracy*, Allen & Unwin, London.

Schumpeter, J. (1961) *The Theory of Economic Development*, Oxford University Press, New York.

Schumpeter, J. (1975) *Capitalism, Socialism and Democracy*, Harper, New York.

Stevenson, H. (1983) *A Perspective on Entrepreneurship*, vol. 13, Harvard Business School, Cambridge, Mass.

Stevenson, H. (2000). Why entrepreneurship has won? Coleman White Paper, 1-8.

Stevenson, H. and Gumpert, D.E. (1985) The heart of entrepreneurship, *Harvard Business Review*, 184.

Stevenson, H. and Harmeling, S. (1990) Entrepreneurial management's need for a more 'chaotic' theory, *Journal of Business Venturing*, vol. 5, no. 1, 1–14.

Stevenson, H. and Jarillo, C.J. (1990) Paradigm of entrepreneurship: entrepreneurial management (Special Issue: Corporate Entrepreneurship), *Strategic Management Journal*, vol. 11 (Summer), 17–27.

Thomson, R. (2013) National scientific capacity and R&D offshoring, *Research Policy*, vol. 42, no. 2, 517–28.

Toprak, Z. (1995) National Economics-National Bourgeoisie: Economy and Society in Turkey 1908–1950 (in Turkish: *Milli Iktisat-Milli Burjuvazi: Türkiye'de Ekonomi ve Toplum 1908–1950*), Türkiye Toplumsal ve Ekonomik Tarih Vakfı, Istanbul.

Further reading

For a more detailed review of the role of the state in innovation management, the following develop many of the issues raised in this chapter:

Afuah, A. (2003) *Innovation Management: Strategies, Implementation and Profits*, 2nd edn, Oxford University Press, Oxford.

Asheim, B.T., & Parrilli, M.D. (2012). Introduction: Learning and interaction-Drivers for innovation in current competitive markets. *Interactive Learning for Innovation: A Key Driver within Clusters and Innovation Systems. Basingstoke: Palgrave Macmillan*, 1–32.

Freeman, C. and Soete, L. (2009) Developing science, technology and innovation indicators: what we can learn from the past, *Research Policy*, vol. 38, no. 4, 583–9.

Hobday, M., Rush, H. and Bessant, J. (2004) Approaching the innovation frontier in Korea: the transition phase to leadership, *Research Policy*, vol. 33, no. 10, 1433–57.

HSBC (2010) *100 Thoughts*, HSBC, London.

Lundvall, B.Å. (ed.). (2010). *National systems of innovation: Toward a theory of innovation and interactive learning* (Vol. 2). Anthem Press.

Malerba, F. (ed.). (2010). *Knowledge Intensive Entrepreneurship and Innovation Systems: Evidence from Europe*. Routledge.

Moore, G.A. (2004) *Crossing the Chasm: Marketing and Selling Technology Products to Mainstream Customers*, 2nd edn, Capstone, Oxford.

Parrilli, M.D., & Heras, H.A. (2016). STI and DUI innovation modes: Scientific-technological and context-specific nuances. *Research Policy, 45*(4), 747–756.

Rogers, E.M. (2003) *Diffusion of Innovations*, 5th edn, Free Press, New York.

Trott, P., Hartmann, D., Scholten, V. and Van Der Duin, P. (2015) *Managing Technology Entrepreneurship and Innovation*, London, Routledge.

Veryzer, R. (2003) 'Marketing and the development of innovative products', in Shavinina, L. (ed.), *The International Handbook on Innovation*, Elsevier, Oxford.

Chapter 3
Market adoption and technology diffusion

Introduction

The role of the market within the wider context of innovation is ever-present; hence this chapter explores this key challenge within innovation. The relationship between new technology and the market is examined within the diffusion of innovations and market adoption. Diffusion of innovations is a theory that seeks to explain how, why and at what rate new technology spread through an industry and markets. Diffusion involves the initial adoption of a new technology by a firm or individual. Adoption examines all those decision-making factors and an understanding of these can help firms ensure their products are chosen over competitors.

The case study at the end of this chapter tells the story of how three university students had an idea for a folding shipping container and went about building a business. One of the key problems they faced was how to get the industry to adopt new container technology.

Chapter contents

Learning objectives

When you have completed this chapter you will be able to:

- illustrate how the diffusion of innovation theory influences consumer adoption of products and services;

- identify and discuss the technical, financial and organisational obstacles that have to be overcome to bring an invention to the market;

- explain innovation and diffusion as ongoing processes with a range of factors affecting success at each stage;

- recognise the role marketing plays in the early stages of product innovation;

- explain how market vision helps the innovation process; and

- understand how the pattern of consumption influences the likely success or failure of a new product.

Time lag between innovation and useable product

We are all taught at school that Alexander Fleming discovered penicillin in 1928. He was working in his lab trying to kill a deadly bacteria, when he noticed a blue mould growing on the petri dish. He noticed that the bacteria around the mould was dissolving. But, for almost 10 years, nobody could purify the mould. Finally, in 1938, a team of scientists led by Howard Florey (Australian born) and Ernst Chain (German born) helped to develop penicillin. It was first used in the Second World War where it was mass produced by the US Department of Agriculture. But it did not become widely available until after 1945. So, we have a period from 1928 from the invention, to 1943 when we have a useable product – 15 years. Interestingly, the Nobel Prize for medicine was won in 1945 by all three: Florey, Chain and Fleming. Clearly, the Nobel Foundation recognises their equal contribution. Chain and Florey are not so widely remembered. This partly helps to explain the misunderstanding we have with innovation: that we fail to acknowledge the 15 years of work turning the idea into a commercial product.

Adoption is defined as the relative speed at which participants adopt an innovation. Rate usually is measured by the length of time required for a certain percentage of the members of a social system to adopt an innovation (Rogers, 1962). In general, individuals who first adopt an innovation require a shorter adoption period (adoption process) when compared to late adopters. Within the adoption curve, at some point the innovation reaches critical mass. This is when the number of individual adopters ensures that the innovation is self-sustaining.

Innovation and the market

We have explored the reasons why some state that contexts are more conducive to deeper levels of entrepreneurial activity and innovation, whilst others promote 'petty entrepreneurialism' with short-term, accumulation-ridden intentions. This chapter also tries to explain how some nations achieved a strong transformation from basic industries and joined the vanguard of technology development. In that respect, it was suggested that, although knowledge accumulation is a socially and spatially focused process, geographical shifts have occurred throughout history when 'state-societal arrangements' were conducive and there may be possible openings for late-developing nations in the future. This, however, is by no means a simple process.

Chapter 1 emphasised the inclusion of commercialisation within the process of innovation. It is this part of the innovation process that proves so extremely difficult for many firms. There have been many exciting scientific advances, such as Alexander Fleming's discovery of penicillin (1928) and Crick and Watson's discovery of DNA (1953) but, in both cases, it was over 20 years later that commercial products emerged from the science and technology: antibiotics in the first case and numerous genetic advances including genetic fingerprinting in the second. Commercialising technology and new products, in particular, then, is one of the key challenges within innovation. We now turn our attention to this process and, in particular, the diffusion of innovations and market adoption.

Innovation and market vision

We all respond differently to different types of innovations. It is because of this that the role of marketing is so valuable to firms developing new products and services. For example, in the context of disruptive innovations, which require a greater change in existing patterns of behaviour and thinking, consumers would perceive a higher level of risk and uncertainty in their adoption decisions relative to continuous innovations that depend on established behavioural patterns and perceptions. Take internet banking as an example: this is a type of service that necessitates changes in perceptions and the established patterns of behaviour and requires the formation of new consumption practices. Indeed, the underlying internet technology itself is a disruptive innovation. Yet, herein lies the problem: highly innovative products have an inherent high degree of uncertainty about exactly how an emerging technology may be formulated into a usable product and what the final product application will be. **Market vision,** or the ability to look into the future and picture products and services that will be successful, is a fundamental requirement for those firms wishing to engage in innovation. It involves assessing one's own technological capability and present or future market needs and visioning a market offering that people will want to buy. Whilst this may sound simple, it lies at the heart of the innovation process and focuses our attention on the need to examine not only the market but the way the new product offering is used or consumed.

Analysing internet search data to help adoption and forecasting sales

Recently, researchers have used internet search traffic to analyse the immense body of information made available by hidden traces left behind by consumers. Jun et al. (2014) used search traffic to analyse the adoption process of a new technology, specifically hybrid cars. The research compared technology searches that specified the technology name with searches that specified the brand name. The results showed that the traffic of searches that specify a product's brand name was significant for explaining sales. Significantly, brand-focused search traffic showed a superior ability to forecast sales volume compared to macro-indicators, such as GDP growth or oil prices that had been used previously to forecast car demand.

Innovative new products and consumption patterns

Consumption pattern refers to the degree of change required in the thinking and behaviour of the consumer in using the product. Products involving consumption pattern changes, such as internet banking or MP3 players, can require customers to alter their thinking and habits and this may affect their willingness to embrace a new product. A product can be familiar or novel in the way it requires users to interact with it. The nature of the change involved with respect to this aspect of a new product can play a significant role in product evaluation and adoption (Veryzer, 2003). It is this dimension that Apple Inc. successfully

iPods have changed the way people now consume music. The impact has been considerable for music retailers.
Source: csakisti. 123rf.com/Pearson Education Ltd

addressed in its MP3 player, the iPod. Apple was not the first to develop an MP3 player. Indeed, five years after launch, its capabilities were still fewer than its rivals (for example, in 2006 it did not have an FM radio). Yet, in terms of ease of use, it was considerably ahead of its nearest rival. In considering highly innovative products, it is crucial to take the customer's view and experience of the product into account. A technology-focused approach to innovation that does not consider the customer's perspective would, surely, result in a product that is at odds with the market's perception of it. Even though technology is the means for enabling an innovation, new products are more than simply bundles of technology, as Apple has demonstrated with its iPod. Innovative new products must deliver benefits and be used by people who can enjoy them and the advantages that they can bring about.

This introduces another variable that needs to be considered by the firm developing innovative products. In addition to new technology within the product and product capabilities, the firm must also consider how these will affect consumption of the product. Figure 3.1 illustrates the relationship between these three key variables that the firm needs to consider as it develops new product ideas. Sometimes, whilst the technology has been proven and the capabilities of the product demonstrated to be superior to existing products, if the extent of change in the pattern of consumption by the consumer is too great, the product may yet fail or take a long time to succeed.

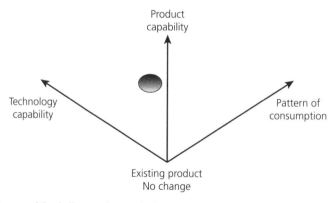

Figure 3.1 Three critical dimensions of change-of-technology intensive products

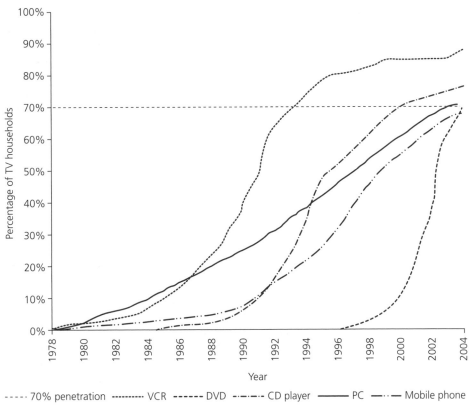

Figure 3.2 **Penetration of consumer electronics, 1978–2004**

A good example of this would be the failed Apple Newton (personal digital assistant) or even the personal computer which, as Figure 3.2 illustrates, took over 20 years to achieve a 70 per cent market penetration rate.

| **Pause for thought** | |

If consumers are unwilling to embrace new products that impose a high degree of change in the consumption pattern for consumers, does this mean that firms should introduce only products that are similar to existing products?

Marketing insights to facilitate innovation

Marketing can provide the necessary information and knowledge required by the firm to ensure the successful development of innovative new products and the successful acceptance and diffusion of new products. In both cases, it is usually the insights with respect to understanding potential customers that marketing supplies. Uncovering and understanding these insights is where effective marketing is extremely valuable. The Viagra case in Chapter 9 illustrates this very clearly. The deep insights necessary for truly innovative products requires great skill, as much of the information gained from customers for such products needs to be ignored (Veryzer, 2003). Research within marketing has shown for many years that gaining valuable insight from consumers about innovative new market offerings, especially discontinuous new products, is extremely difficult and can sometimes lead to misleading information (Veryzer, 2003; King, 1985; Tauber, 1974; Martin, 1995; Hamel and Prahalad, 1994). Indeed, frequent responses from consumers are along the lines of 'I want the same product, only cheaper and better'. Von Hippel (1994) has suggested that consumers have difficulty in understanding and articulating their needs and has described this phenomenon as 'sticky information'. That is, information that is difficult to transfer (similar to the notion of tacit knowledge). User toolkits have been shown to facilitate the transfer of so-called 'sticky information' and have enabled firms to understand better the precise needs and desires of customers (Franke and Piller, 2004). The greater uncertainties involved with discontinuous innovations demands both insight and foresight from firms. Advanced technology presents significant technical and market uncertainty, especially when the technology is emerging and industry standards have yet to be established. Appreciating and understanding the potential new technology and uncovering what the market will and will not embrace is a key challenge for marketing. Indeed, bridging the technology uncertainty and the market need is critical for a commercially viable new product. Figure 3.2 illustrates the penetration over time of a range of consumer electronic products from DVD players to mobile phones. The penetration rates differ considerably with some achieving a 70 per cent market penetration within a few years, such as DVD players, whereas PCs, as we have seen, took over 20 years.

Highly innovative or discontinuous new products are particularly demanding in terms of early timely information, if they are to avoid being judged harshly later by the market. Whether this information and knowledge is provided by marketing personnel or by R&D scientists and engineers does not matter, but its input into the new product development process is essential. The product development team need to determine (Leifer et al., 2000: 81):

- What are the potential applications of a technology as a product?
- Which application(s) should be pursued first?
- What benefits can the proposed product offer to potential customers?
- What is the potential market size and is this sufficient?

Beyond consumer concerns that are relevant to the development and marketing of innovative products are more macro influences that can affect adoption and thus need to be considered. The substitution of one technology for another is an obvious concern (the case study in Chapter 7 discusses this in more detail with regard to screw-caps replacing cork). Along with this, the issue of product complementarity, or when there is a positive interrelationship between products (e.g. a computer printer and a computer), can also be important with respect to product adoption. Thus, in addition to displacing products, new technological innovations often modify or complement existing products that may still be diffusing throughout a given market. This has significant implications for market planning decisions for both products, since their diffusion processes are interlinked (Dekimpe et al., 2000;

Norton and Bass, 1987, 1992). In such cases, e.g. new electric motor vehicles, the following need to be carefully considered:

- whether there is a positive interdependence between a new product and existing products;
- whether the old technology will be fully replaced by a newer product;
- how the size of the old technology's installed base will affect the speed of diffusion of the new product or product generation.

Lead users

Considering users as innovators has gained considerable support over the past 30 years. Eric von Hippel's work in this area (1977) forms a significant part of the theoretical underpinning and evidence behind the concept (**lead-user theory**). Many further studies have been undertaken to support it (e.g., Urban and von Hippel, 1988; Shah and Tripsas, 2007). It has contributed to our understanding of innovation management in general and new product development in particular. Clearly, whilst lead users can contribute to the innovation process, this contribution should not be overstated and it should be noted that arguably significant technology-based innovations remain driven by scientific advancement.

In their review of users as innovators in the *Journal of Management*, Bogers et al. (2010) explain that 'intermediate users are firms that use equipment and components from producers to produce goods and services' whereas 'consumer users – users of consumer goods – are typically individual end consumers' (Bogers et al., 2010: 859). They further illustrate that intermediate users that develop innovations have been shown to occur in the following industries: semiconductors (von Hippel, 1977), printed circuit CAD software (Urban and von Hippel, 1988), library information systems (Morrison, Roberts and von Hippel, 2000). Consumer users have been found mainly in consumer products and, somewhat surprisingly, in sports-related consumer goods, such as mountain biking (Lüthje, Herstatt and von Hippel, 2005), and kite surfing (Tietz, Morrison, Lüthje and Herstatt, 2005).

When it comes to explaining why users innovate, it is argued that they possess the distinctive knowledge and expertise necessary. For example, the development of kite surfing was possible only because of the expertise gained from years of experience of windsurfing (Franke and Shah, 2003). Indeed, in his later research, von Hippel (2005) argues that, when one compares innovations from producers with those of users, frequently those from users are distinctive because of the unique tacit knowledge they have gained from extensive use of the products (Bogers et al., 2010).

The lead-user school further contends that, whilst many users modify products for their own use, for example, computer hardware and software for industrial processes and high-end sports equipment (Haavisto, 2014), these innovations are concentrated amongst the lead users. The example of surfers is cited as an illustration: they developed an experimental surf board with foot-straps that enabled them to leverage the energy of waves to make controlled flights. Lead users are characterised as being ahead of the majority of users with respect to an important market trend and they expect to gain relatively high benefits from the solution to the needs they have encountered: '. . . lead users are users whose present strong needs will become general in a marketplace months or years in the future' (*idem.*, 107). Further, it is argued that, by focusing on working with lead users, companies can increase the probability that they will discover innovative solutions that they can leverage and sell to their other customers. For companies seeking to increase their capacity to innovate, the lead-user school argues that it provides a firm foundation for a strategy of innovating with selective customers; and that it is a much more effective basis for an innovation strategy than the more traditional technology-centred approach, where scientific exploration and technology development lead to opportunities for firms to exploit. This approach led to the growth of a whole new sport, kite-surfing: 'Clearly this had little to do with surfboard manufacturers who did not discover this innovation; rather it was innovative surfers' (Franke et al., 2006).

When it comes to technology-intensive products, it is so-called lead users that form the basis for much insight into products and also help with the diffusion process. Lead users are those who demand requirements ahead of the market and, indeed, often are involved themselves in developing product ideas because there is nothing in the market at present to meet their needs. For example, Stephan Wozniak co-founded Apple Computer with Steve Jobs in 1976 and created the Apple I and Apple II computers in the mid-1970s. He was a lead-user computer engineer, ahead of the general population. Such lead users can help to codevelop innovations and are, therefore, often early adopters of such innovations. The initial research by Eric von Hippel in the 1970s suggested that lead-users adopt an average of seven years before typical users. In a recent study Morrison et al. (2004) identified a number of characteristics of lead users:

- recognise requirements early;
- expect high level of benefits from the product;
- develop their own innovations and applications;
- perceived to be pioneering and innovative.

Shimano

Shimano product sales constitute 50 per cent of the global bicycle component market. Its products include drivetrain, brake, wheel and pedal components for road, mountain and hybrid bikes.

Shimano has consistently adopted an approach based on the introduction of innovation only at the high-end level of its products and then trickled the technology down to lower product levels as it became proven and accepted. This has helped Shimano deliver innovative new products for over 91 years. Shimano has, for many years, worked with elite athletes (i.e. lead users) to develop new product ideas. This has led to a wide variety of new product areas for the firm to exploit, such as specialist sports cycling clothing.

Source: Andrew Paterson/Alamy Images

Lead users are particularly significant for products that are using technology at the frontiers of development and those within technology-intensive industries, such as software, engineering and science. In a study of over 50 years of product innovation in the whitewater kayaking field, Hienerth et al. (2014) found users in aggregate were approximately three times more efficient at developing important kayaking product innovations than were producers in aggregate. The researchers believe this was due to 'efficiencies of scope' in problem-solving, where users benefited from higher economies of scale in product development.

Users as innovators in the virtual world

Recent research by Chandra and Leenders (2012) shows user innovators in the virtual life broadly resemble those in the real life, as reported in the literature. Their study shows that 'Second Life' as a virtual world breeds opportunities leading to entrepreneurial acts in the 'real' world as well as further opportunities in the Second Life.

Crowdsourcing for new product ideas

Using the talent of the employees within organisations is one of the most fundamental challenges facing firms. Those firms that have been able to get their talented employees to work together have often been the same firms that have developed and launched exciting products and services. Most firms know this, but making it happen is difficult. For example, employee suggestion schemes have led to new product ideas and changes to the way firms operate to bring huge cost reductions. Over the past few years, two different concepts have developed and gained popularity amongst the business community. These are open innovation and crowdsourcing. Software manufacturers have spotted an opportunity to bring these two concepts together in the form of an innovation management tool for large firms with many thousands of employees. Essentially, this software allows employees to post an idea for others to see and comment. Other features exist to allow ranking and leaderboards for ideas. The software also allows firm managers to track the development of these ideas and to add resources and recognition. One of the main advantages of such software is the opportunity it provides for employees to share ideas and engage in product-centred discussions. One of the most successful is HYPE Innovation Management, a German software product. It is, essentially, an idea capture and rating system (see www.hypeinnovation.com).

Crowdsourcing is a method of getting ideas, content, support or other types of solutions from a group of people. The term was coined by *Wired* magazine in 2005. Effectively, it is outsourcing solutions to crowds through social media. Research by Poetz and Schreier (2012) suggests that, at least under certain conditions, crowdsourcing might constitute a promising method to gather user ideas that can complement those of a firm's professionals at the idea-generation stage in NPD.

Crowdsourcing sites, such as Kickstarter and Indiegogo, allow fans to give financial support in exchange for incentives, so people can complete their projects. There are many other businesses that incorporate the idea of getting input from the masses into their business model. Applause (formerly uTest) is a technology application-testing site that enables crowd beta-testing worldwide. Local Motors brings crowd-sourcing to new vehicle innovations. Businesses around the world can build consensus, get instant product feedback and listen to and incorporate customers' input. Engaging crowds to make products better is getting easier, thanks to social media and consumers' desire to have their voices heard. Many firms provide contests to encourage participation. Four of the most common techniques are illustrated below:

1 *Ask which product customers would like produced.* This toy store needed to know which LEGO product would sell the fastest, so it set up a simple vote contest and asked its customers directly. It motivated people to vote by running a giveaway of the winning LEGO set to a contest participant.

2 *Ask which products customers prefer.* The shoe company, Crocs, for example, hosts a 'new release shoesday' contest on Facebook. It engages its fans by asking them what their favourite new shoe is that week, and fans who participate have a chance to win Croc shoes. Crocs then gains relevant consumer insights about market preferences.

3 *Ask customers to name the new product.* In 2014, Sony looked to the public to help develop a name for its new wireless speaker product. The speakers are small balls in pink, white and black. Sony posted the contest on its blog and promoted it on all of its social sites, through media and other promotional methods. Participants entered their suggested names by commenting on the blog post.

4 *Ask customers for new product variations.* Walkers Crisps (Lay's) has been hosting contests to engage the public by creating new crisp flavour ideas. And the Lay's 'Do Us a Flavour' contest is one of the most successful new product crowd-sourcing campaigns. Participants can access the contest through Facebook or their contest landing page.

Illustration 3.2

Crowdsourcing product ideas for baby products

Generating ideas for new products used to be the exclusive domain of marketers, engineers, and/or designers. Whereas some have attributed great potential to outsourcing idea generation to the 'crowd' of users (crowdsourcing), others have clearly been more sceptical. Research by Poetz and Schreier (2012) undertook a comparison of ideas actually generated by a firm's professionals with those generated by users in the course of an idea generation contest. Both professionals and users provided ideas to solve an effective and relevant problem in the consumer goods market for baby products. Executives from the underlying company evaluated all the ideas (blind to their source) in terms of key quality dimensions, including novelty, customer benefit and feasibility. The findings showed that the crowdsourcing process generated user ideas that score significantly higher in terms of novelty and customer benefit, and somewhat lower in terms of feasibility. Even more interestingly, it is found that user ideas are placed more frequently than expected amongst the very best in terms of novelty and customer benefit.

Frugal innovation and ideas from everywhere

The bottom of the pyramid is the largest, but poorest socio-economic group. In global terms, this is the three billion people who live on less than US$2.50 per day. The phrase 'bottom of the pyramid' is used in particular by people developing new models of doing business that deliberately target that demographic, often using new technology (see Innovation in action below). Thus, developing no frills products and services is not new; one only has to look at airlines, retailing and automotives. So, what is frugal innovation? In their book *Frugal Innovation*, Navi Radjou and Jaideep Prabhu (2015) argue it is more about the process of reducing the complexity and cost of a good and its production. Usually, this refers to removing non-essential features from a durable good, such as a car or phone, in order to sell it in developing countries. Designing products for such countries may also call for an increase in durability and, when selling the products, reliance on unconventional distribution channels. These are business ideas that have long been used before. However, it is the emphasis on so-called 'overlooked consumers', where firms hope large volume will offset small profit margins that may prove key. In many developing countries, rising incomes may also drive frugal innovation. Such services and products need not be of inferior quality, but must be provided cheaply (Bhatti et al., 2013).

For example, India's Mahindra & Mahindra sells lots of small tractors to US hobby farmers. This, of course, raises concerns for US tractor manufacturer John Deere. China's Haier has undercut Western competitors in a wide range of products, from air conditioners and washing machines to wine coolers. Some Western companies are turning to emerging markets first to develop their products. For example, Diagnostics for All, a Massachusetts-based start-up, developed small paper-based diagnostic tests. Interestingly, it chose to commercialise its idea first in the developing world so as to circumvent the USA's slow approval process for medical devices.

Other examples abound. The chairman of the Chinese computer-maker Lenovo argued that it is the best company in the world at balancing innovation and efficiency. By keeping costs down, it has stolen market share from its big Western rivals. Lenovo has recently ousted HP to become the world leader in desktop computers. One may argue that the Chinese firm is not an imaginative innovator like Apple, whose radical designs transform whole markets. Rather, it is able to execute design and innovation economically and be a frugal innovator.

Frugal innovation has also been applied to public service design and delivery. In India and other developing economies, creating frugal solutions to deliver improved or previously non-existent public services has given more people access to a wider range of services.

Innovation in action

Bottom of the pyramid diffusion: toilets in India

India leads the world in open defecation. Over 600 million Indians lack toilets, according to the latest census data, a crisis that contributes to disease, childhood malnutrition, loss of economic output and, as highlighted recently, violence against women.

→

For generations, most of the 750 families in Katra, in Uttar Pradesh, northern India, have lived without toilets. They have grown used to holding their bladders and bowels, being stalked by wild boars and hyenas and, during the rainy season, watching out for snakes. But, since May 2014, when two girls, 14 and 15, were found gang raped and hanged after they went to relieve themselves in the dark, Katra's residents have been gripped by a new fear.

Source: think4photop/Shutterstock.com

Sanitation is a good example of product innovations for the poor at the so-called bottom of the income pyramid. Research by Ramani et al. (2012) has examined why and how sanitation entrepreneurs are succeeding in India to diffuse toilets – an innovation for rural households, which never had access to one before. Their findings show that progressive sanitation entrepreneurs are succeeding because of their adoption of a 'market-based approach'. There are market failures stemming from the demand side, due to problems in knowledge, expression of demand and its mismatch with the perceived value of the innovation. To overcome these informational asymmetries and sluggish market demand, sanitation entrepreneurs use creative offers and pricing to ensure sustained use of toilets.

Source: http://www.theguardian.com/global-development/2014/aug/28/toilets-india-health-rural-women-safety; Ramani, S.V., SadreGhazi, S. and Duysters, G. (2012) On the diffusion of toilets as bottom of the pyramid innovation: lessons from sanitation entrepreneurs, *Technological Forecasting and Social Change*, vol. 79, no. 4, 676–87.

Innovation diffusion theories

Technological diffusion is the process by which innovations, whether they are new products, new processes or new management methods, spread within and across economies. Diffusion involves the initial adoption of a new technology by a firm (inter-firm diffusion) and the subsequent diffusion of the innovation within the firm (intra-firm diffusion), the latter being the process by which the firm's old technologies and facilities are replaced by new ones.

Innovation diffusion theories try to explain how an innovation is diffused in a social system over time; the adoption of an innovation is, therefore, a part of the wider diffusion process. Such theories tend to be more comprehensive relative to their **adoption theory** cousins. This is because they investigate the reasons for adoption at the aggregate level. Perceived innovation characteristics theory, which is a part of the innovation **diffusion theory** of Rogers (1962), is similar to adoption theories, such as the theory of reasoned action (TRA), the theory of planned behaviour (TPB) and the technology acceptance model (TAM), as it includes analysis down to the individual level. Yet, diffusion of innovation theories, in general, includes many more factors, such as the influences of psychological or personal features, technology perceptions, communication behaviour and socio-demographic attributes on diffusion or adoption process. It is worth saying at this point that the study of how and why consumers purchase goods and services falls within the arena of consumer buyer behaviour and there are lots of very good textbooks that explore this subject in great detail. The purpose of introducing some of these concepts here is to ensure the reader is aware of the important influence of this body of research on explaining how and why some new product innovations are successful and why others are not.

Everett Rogers is usually credited with introducing the concept of diffusion theory to the business community. Rogers' work was undertaken initially in developing countries where he studied the diffusion of new ideas amongst communities (Rogers, 1962). He later developed his work and applied it to new product innovations in the market and was able to illustrate different consumer categories on the basis of its relative time of adoption. Rogers (1983) stated that the adopter categorisation in relation to adoption time requires the determination of the number of adopter categories, the percentage of adopters in each category, and a method to define these categories. Rogers' (1962) adopter categorisation is based on a normal distribution curve that shows the adoption of an innovation over time on a frequency basis, which takes the form of an 'S' when plotted on a cumulative basis (see Figure 3.3). Indeed, the diffusion curve is much related to the concept of the product life cycle, which shows the level of total sales over time. The close relationship between these two concepts would be expected to the extent that sales are proportional to cumulative adoption.

In this model, Rogers (1962) classified different adopter segments in terms of their standard deviation positions from the mean time of adoption of the innovation

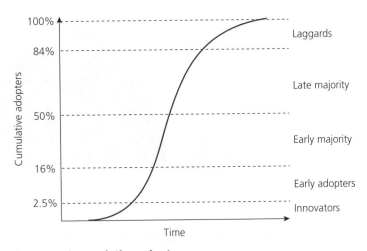

Figure 3.3 S-curve of cumulative adopters

for the entire market. In this way, he utilised the average and a normal distribution of adopters in order to group them into five categories and obtain the percentage of individuals to be included in each of these categories (see Figure 3.3). Rogers stated that innovators comprise the adopter segment, which adopts an innovation earlier than the other adopter groups. Innovators are followed by early adopters, early majority, late majority and laggards. In this context, Rogers assumed that these five diverse adopter segments differ on the basis of their demographical features, personality-related characteristics, communication behaviour and social relationships.

Rogers classifies stages in the technology life cycle by the relative percentage of customers who adopt it at each stage (Rogers, 1995). Early on are the innovators and early adopters (who are concerned with the underlying technology and its performance). Then come in succession the early majority pragmatists, the late majority conservatives and, lastly, the laggards (all of whom are more interested in solutions and convenience). In a contribution to this debate, Geoffrey Moore depicts the transition between the early adopters and early majority pragmatists as a chasm that many high-technology companies never successfully cross (see Figure 3.4) (Moore, 2004). Moore's contribution to the diffusion debate helped create new approaches for marketing in high-tech industries. His successful book *Crossing the Chasm* has proved popular for helping firms bring cutting-edge products to progressively larger markets. Clayton Christensen prefers to look at the phenomenon of technology take-up from the perspective of the level of performance required by average users (those in the early and late majority categories in Figure 3.3) (Christensen, 1997). He argues that, once a technology product meets customers' basic needs, they regard it as good enough and no longer care about the underlying technology.

Beacon products

Research by Peng and Sanderson (2014) on digital MP3 players suggests that, sometimes, a specific product model has great appeal to customers and sends a strong signal about what they want. They found that Apple's first iPod model triggered widespread appeal and that many competitors tried to emulate the original iPod

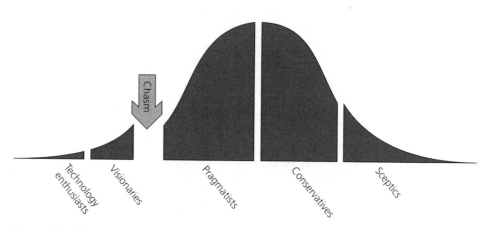

Figure 3.4 Adopter categorisation on the basis of innovativeness
Source: Adapted from Moore, G.A. (1991) *Crossing the Chasm*, Harper Business.

design, leading to convergence around its key design features. But it took the iPod/iTunes store combination, a new ecosystem for the legal download of digital music, to bridge the gap between early MP3 adopters, primarily young people, to mainstream markets. The iPod/iTunes ecosystem proved more difficult for competitors to copy and many of the firms that had pioneered the MP3 category, such as Creative, RCA and Dell, exited the industry or were relegated to small niches. By subsequently introducing new models at lower prices and expanding iTunes Store offerings, Apple effectively pre-empted competitors from gaining a share in this growing market (Peng and Sanderson; 2014).

In terms of demographical characteristics, earlier adopters, such as innovators and early adopters, are presumed to be younger, wealthier and better educated people. When personality-related characteristics are considered, the most distinguishing features of earlier adopters are that they are more eager to take risks and they hold more positive perceptions towards technology in general. Communication behaviours of earlier adopters are assumed to differ on the basis of their media usage behaviour and interpersonal communications with the rest of the consumer segments. Therefore, these people are supposed to be opinion leaders in their social relationships throughout the diffusion process.

Diffusion may also be examined from an even more macroperspective and, in some instances, it can be particularly important to do so. For example, researchers like Dekimpe et al. (2000) have investigated the global diffusion of technological innovations. In their work, they focus on issues concerning the two-stage (implementation stage and confirmation stage) nature of the global diffusion process as defined by Rogers (1983), the irregularity of a diffusion pattern due to network externalities and/or central decision makers, and the role of the installed base of older-generation technologies that an innovation replaces (Dekimpe et al., 2000: 51). As they point out, 'For most innovations, the adoption process of each country starts with the implementation stage, which is followed by the confirmation stage.' However, they point out that, for technological innovations, within-country diffusion might be instantaneous – due to network externalities (e.g. established standards) or central decision makers – and, as such, the confirmation stage for certain countries may have a zero duration. As previously discussed, a good example of this was the introduction of digital television within the UK. The UK Government, through the BBC, invested considerable sums of money to educate and inform the population about the advantages of digital television over analogue and to explain that the country will eventually stop transmitting television over analogue signals.

The mobile handset market was once highly profitable; it seems now it has become a commodity. As technologies diffuse within an economy, firms face declining marginal profits, especially in a saturating market. If this is then coupled with proliferation of competitors, over-estimation of demand and diminishing margins, those once attractive markets soon turn ugly. Hence the need for firms to continually adopt new technologies and cling on to their attractive margins: this is the fickle world of market adoption.

Pause for thought

Given that the internet, and now mobile banking, has been available for over 20 years, do you think internet banking has crossed the chasm? Is it always just a matter of time and, so long as you are patient, products will always eventually succeed?

Seasonality in innovation diffusion

Firms have recognised, for some time, how seasons affect diffusion. It appears that cosmetics are affected by the seasons, as weather conditions and emotional changes affect consumers' beauty habits and regimes and offer manufacturers the chance to capitalise with products for specific needs. The ability to forecast new product growth is especially important for innovative firms that compete in the marketplace. Today, many new products exhibit very strong seasonal behaviour, which deserve specific modelling, both for producing better forecasts in the short term and for better explaining special market dynamics and related managerial decisions (Guidolin and Guseo, 2014).

The Bass Diffusion Model

The Bass Diffusion Model was developed by Frank Bass and it contributed some mathematical ideas to Rogers' concept. Frank Bass's model consists of a simple differential equation that describes the process of how new products get adopted in a population. The basic premise of the model is that adopters can be classified as innovators or as imitators and the speed and timing of adoption depends on their degree of innovativeness and the degree of imitation amongst adopters. The Bass Model has been widely used in forecasting, especially new products' sales forecasting and technology forecasting. For example, Turk and Trkman (2012) use the Bass Diffusion Model to analyse broadband diffusion for European OECD member countries. Their research shows that, if the present trends continue, broadband services will not reach the 100 per cent penetration rate in the near future.

Adopting new products and embracing change

Diffusion is, essentially, consumer willingness to embrace change. But change can be simple and complex. These range from a change in perception to a significant change in required behaviour in order to use the product. For example, dishwasher appliances require a significant shift in the way people behave in the kitchen and their approach to using cutlery and crockery; similarly for iPods with regard to storing and collecting music. Consumers' reactions to innovative new products and their willingness to embrace them are also, of course, driven by the benefit they expect to derive from the products. For discontinuous innovations, such products, which often involve new technologies, frequently require changes in thinking and behaviour and hence require more from the consumer. Unsurprisingly, these products carry a high risk of market failure. When it comes to technology, consumers have a love–hate relationship with it and this is because of the paradoxes of technological products. For example, products such as appliances that are purchased in order to save time, often end up wasting time. In their codification of the various paradoxes discussed across the technology literature, Mick and Fournier (1998) present a typology of paradoxes of technological products. These are captured in Table 3.1. These paradoxes play an important role in shaping consumers' perceptions of innovations as well as determining their willingness to adopt new products.

In the world of mobile communications, user interface, as the interactive layer between user and information systems, has a great role in system adoption. Research

Table 3.1 Paradoxes of technological products

Paradox	Description	Illustration
Control – chaos	Technology can facilitate order and it can lead to disorder	Telephone answering machine can help record messages but leads to disorder due to uncertainty about whether the message has been received
Freedom – enslavement	Technology can provide independence and it can lead to dependence	The motorcar clearly gives independence to the driver but many drivers feel lost without it
New – obsolete	The user is provided with the latest scientific knowledge but this is soon outmoded	Computer games industry
Efficiency – inefficiency	Technology can help reduce effort and time but it can also lead to more effort and time	Increased complexity in Smart TVs has led to many wasting time in setting recordings
Fulfils needs – creates needs	Technology can help fulfil needs and it can lead to more desires	The internet has satisfied the curiosity of many but has also stimulated many desires
Assimilation – isolation	Technology can facilitate human togetherness and can lead to human separation	Email and social media help communication but, in some cases, heavy users can become isolated
Engaging – disengaging	Technology can facilitate involvement but it can also lead to disconnection	Advances in mobile phone memory means that many people no longer need or have the skills to discover the telephone number from a telephone directory

Source: Adapted from Mick and Fournier (1998).

by Basoglu et al. (2014) shows acceptance of a system can be explained as a function of perceived usefulness (PU) and perceived ease of use (PEOU).

In addition to the various trade-offs or paradoxes that affect consumers' willingness to embrace innovative products – an aspect of a new product offering that should be considered in the design stage as well as the later product launch stage – consumers develop their own ways of coping with innovations and these can impact diffusion as well. Potential customers may ignore a new technology altogether, delay obtaining the new product, attempt to try an innovative new product without the risk of outright purchase, embrace the product and master it, and so on (Carver et al., 1989; Mick and Fournier, 1998). Furthermore, in evaluating discontinuous new products, there are certain factors that are likely to come into play more than they do for less innovative products. Lack of familiarity, irrationality, user–product interaction problems, uncertainty and risk, and accordance or compatibility issues may play a decisive role in customers' evaluations of products in either the development and testing stages or once the product is introduced into a market (Veryzer, 1998a: 144). For example, during the course of one radical innovation development project, managers were struck by how irrational customers were in that they often focused on things that the product development team thought to be unimportant, and test customers ignored aspects of a prototype product that the team had expounded a great deal of effort and money on. Even though this type of irrationality may frustrate product development teams, in the domain of highly innovative products, assumptions must be checked against those who will be the final arbitrators of success (Veryzer, 1998b).

Generally, radical innovations are not easily adopted in the market. Potential adopters experience difficulties to comprehend and evaluate radical innovations due to their newness in terms of technology and benefits offered. Consequently, adoption intentions may remain low. A study by Reinders et al. (2010) shows that product bundling enhances the new product's evaluation and adoption intention, although it does not increase comprehension of the radical innovation. Thus, offering a radical innovation in a product bundle could be a fruitful strategy for companies that target customers with little or no prior knowledge of the product domain.

Recent research on the general factors related to the adoption of mobile services suggests firms still lack precise information about consumer adoption factors and their weightings. In an ideal scenario, firms would allocate their limited resources to the most important factors and draw appropriate strategies to improve the content and quality of their mobile services. Research in Taiwan with Chunghwa Telecom, a leading telecommunication company, suggests such a position remains elusive (Shieh et al. 2014).

Market adoption theories

There is a considerable amount of confusion with regard to adoption and diffusion. This is due largely to differences in definition. Most researchers in the field, however, view adoption of innovations as a process through which individuals pass from awareness to the final decision to adopt or not adopt; whereas diffusion concerns the communication over time within a wider social system. The adoption research is derived mainly from social psychology and focuses on the individual. This includes such models as the theory of reasoned action (TRA), the theory of planned behaviour (TPB) and the technology acceptance model (TAM). The diffusion of innovations theory combines both adoption and the wider societal issues derived from sociology (see Yu and Tao, 2009). As previously mentioned, the study of how and why consumers purchase goods and services falls within the arena of consumer buyer behaviour and is beyond the scope of this book.

Case study

How three students built a business that could affect world trade

This case study tells the story of how three MSc students at the Technical University of Delft in The Netherlands had an idea for a folding shipping container and went about building a business. There are many examples of university students starting businesses, but few of these have the potential to revolutionise world trade.

Almost all containers today that you see on ships, trains or on trucks are 20 ft or 40 ft in length. The reason for the massive change in both transportation and the global economy is because of this simplicity of size – a small set of standard sizes that allowed ships, trucks, receiving bays, and all of the related logistical systems to easily adapt to an industry-wide standard. Prior to standardisation, there were major inefficiencies in commercial shipping: packaging and crating

was inconsistent. But, what about empty containers? Are there ships travelling the world with containers that are empty? If so, is this a business opportunity?

Source: Pearson Education Ltd/Photodisc

Introduction

Jan, Mark and Stephan were studying for their MSc in mechanical engineering at the Technical University of Delft in The Netherlands. They had arrived late for their lecture and had been forced to sit at the front. They had cycled the short distance from their house on the other side of town and would have arrived on time if it had not been for the lifting bridge over the canal, which had to be raised for a large boat carrying steel shipping containers. This incident was to prove significant. For it was during the lecture by a professor of mechanics that the students hit upon the idea of a folding steel container. The professor was explaining that springs can, in theory, be used to lift very heavy weights, providing the springs are large enough. We are all aware of the Anglepoise lamp that uses springs to enable the movement of its steel arm and lamp. The same principle can be used to move much larger objects, providing one has much larger springs. Initially, the students thought about springs to raise and lower a bridge, but this was soon dismissed. A steel container that could be folded into a small space had many more attractions. The three students went away to experiment with their idea and conduct calculations on weight, force, stress and strain measurements. Eventually, they developed a prototype and modelled it on a computer simulation program. It worked. After much dancing around the computer lab, the three then looked at each other as if to say 'now what?' It was a good question. Should

they run and get a patent on their idea before someone else stole it? What are the benefits of a folding container? Maybe a folding container already exists? A working computer simulation is a long way from a folding 40 ft steel container. (By way of illustration you can drive a large car into one of these containers.) Would anyone be interested? And how can we make any money out of the idea? Having interesting technology is a long way from a profitable money-making business.

The first thing Jan did was to contact the Port of Rotterdam, which is only 15 km from Delft and is one of the world's busiest container ports (see Table 3.2). Eventually, he was able to speak to the Commercial Director of the Port. He explained to Jan that folding and collapsible containers have been around for many years, but they have never really worked. This is primarily because they are expensive to manufacture (usually 10 per cent more than the standard container) and bits get lost, for example the roof from one container sometimes does not fit another container, and the additional equipment required to assemble the containers all adds to the cost. The list of criticisms seemed to be very long. At the end, Jan asked, 'What about folding containers that are all in one piece, where the sides can be folded down by hand?' The Director laughed and said: 'Yeah, right, like on the Disney channel!' Jan reported back to his friends that potential customers may not believe that they could deliver such a product.

Table 3.2 Busiest container ports

	Port	Country	TEUs* (000s)	% increase from 2004
1	Singapore	Singapore	23,192	8.7
2	Hong Kong	China	22,427	2.0
3	Shanghai	China	18,084	24.2
4	Shenzhen	China	16,197	19.0
5	Busan	South Korea	11,843	3.6
6	Kaohsiung	Taiwan (Republic of China)	9,471	0.0
7	**Rotterdam**	**Netherlands**	**9,287**	**12.2**
8	Hamburg	Germany	8,088	15.5
9	Dubai	United Arab Emirates	7,619	18.5
10	Los Angeles	USA	7,485	2.2

*Twenty-foot equivalent units.

The friends faced a number of difficulties and many uncertainties. They needed advice, after all they were engineers, very clever engineers, but not experts in developing businesses. Fortunately, the university had a business incubator that helped students develop their ideas and create businesses. It would be able to help them with their patent application, but Jan, Mark and Stephan soon realised they did not know answers to simple questions, such as: Who would buy it? Who are the customers? How many containers are there in The Netherlands/ Europe/world? How much does it cost to make a container? How much does it cost to buy one? It was soon clear that many days of research lay ahead. This would have to be squeezed in between lectures and coursework.

A brief history of shipping containers

The students' research uncovered the following. During the 1960s, 1970s and 1980s the standardisation of shipping containers revolutionised global trade and has dramatically reduced the cost of transporting goods around the world. According to Marc Levinson (2006), author of *The Box: How the Shipping Container Made the World Smaller and the World Economy Bigger*, much of this revolution was down to one man – Malcolm McLean, who challenged the norm and introduced standardised, packaged shipping. More than 50 years ago, Malcom McLean, a North Carolina trucking entrepreneur, originally hatched the idea of using containers to carry cargo. He loaded 58 containers onto his ship, *Ideal X*, in Newark, New Jersey and, once the vessel reached Houston, Texas, the uncrated containers were moved directly onto trucks – and reusable rectangular boxes soon became the industry standard. What was new in the USA about McLean's innovation was the idea of using large containers that were never opened in transit between shipper and consignee and that were transferable on an intermodal basis, amongst trucks, ships and railroad cars.

Now, most students of business immediately will recognise the benefits that can flow from the introduction of a uniform standard. And history is littered with examples of industries struggling to grow until a single uniform standard is adopted, thereby signalling the end of uncertainty and the start of the adoption of the standard technology. Prior to a standard width gauge, the UK railway industry had two competing gauges and the computer industry has battled for many years over operating systems. The shipping industry was in a similar position with many different types of containers. Packaging and crating products was inconsistent and inefficient. Large numbers of people were employed in ports around the world to break bulk cargo. Frequently, separate items had to be handled individually, such as bags of sugar or flour packed next to copper tube. Today, approximately 90 per cent of non-bulk cargo worldwide moves by containers stacked on transport ships. Some 18 million containers make over 200 million trips per year. For the past 10 years, demand for cargo capacity has been growing almost 10 per cent a year.

This background research on the industry proved to be more interesting than the students first had thought and it delivered some exciting findings. Most importantly, that this was a growing industry, it had international firms with large budgets. And they had uncovered the fact that the storage of containers poses a significant problem for the shipping lines that are always on the lookout for ways to reduce this cost.

Background: containers

The students now needed to explore in detail the shipping container and how it is used. More research was required and soon they uncovered more useful information. The history of the use of purpose-built containers for trade can be traced back to the 1830s; railroads on several continents were carrying containers that could be transferred to trucks or ships, but these containers were small by today's standards. Originally used for shipping coal on and off barges, 'loose boxes' were used to containerise coal from the late 1780s. By the 1840s, iron boxes were in use as well as wooden ones. The early 1900s saw the adoption of closed container boxes designed for movement between road and rail. Towards the end of the Second World War, the US Army began using specialised containers to speed up the loading and unloading of transport ships. After the US Department of Defense standardised an 8 ft × 8 ft cross-section container in multiples of 10 ft lengths for military use, it was rapidly adopted for shipping purposes. These standards were adopted in the United Kingdom for containers and rapidly displaced the older wooden containers in the 1950s.

Containers, also known as intermodal containers or as ISO containers because the dimensions have been defined by the ISO, are the main type of equipment used in intermodal transport, particularly when one of the modes of transportation is by ship. Containers are 8 ft wide by 8 ft high. Since their introduction, there have been moves to adopt other heights. The most common lengths are 20 ft and 40 ft, although other lengths exist. They are made out of steel and can be stacked on top of each other.

Container capacity often is expressed in *twenty-foot equivalent units* (TEU or, sometimes, teu). An equivalent unit is a measure of containerised cargo capacity equal to one standard 20 ft (length) × 8 ft (width) container. The use of Imperial measurements to describe container size reflects the fact that the US Department of Defense played a major part in the development of containers. The overwhelming need to have a standard size for containers, in order that they fit all ships, cranes and trucks, and the length of time that the current container sizes have been in use, makes changing to an even, metric size impractical. Table 3.3 shows the weights and dimensions of the three most common types of container worldwide. The weights and dimensions quoted above are averages; different manufactured series of the same type of container may vary slightly in actual size and weight.

Handling containers

On ships, containers are, typically, stacked up to seven units high. When carried by rail, containers can be loaded on flatcars or in container well cars. When the container ship arrives at the container terminal (port), specialist equipment is required. The transfer from ship to land may be between ships and land vehicles, for example trains or trucks. Maritime container terminals tend to be part of a larger port, whereas inland container terminals tend to be located in or near major cities, with good rail connections to maritime container terminals.

A container crane, or gantry crane, is used at container terminals for loading and unloading shipping containers from container ships. Cranes normally transport a single container at once. However, some newer cranes have the capability to pick up up to 4 20-ft containers at once. Handling equipment is designed with intermodality in mind, assisting with transferring containers between rail, road and sea. These can include:

- Transtainer for transferring containers from sea-going vessels onto either trucks or rail wagons. A transtainer is mounted on rails with a large boom spanning the distance between the ship's cargo hold and the quay, moving parallel to the ship's side.
- Gantry cranes, also known as straddle carriers, are able to straddle rail and road vehicles allowing for quick transfer of containers. A spreader beam moves in several directions, allowing accurate positioning of the cargo.
- Reach stackers are fitted with lifting arms as well as spreader beams and lift containers to swap bodies or stack containers on top of each other.

Table 3.3 Specifications of the three most common types of container

		20′ container		40′ container		45′ high-cube container	
		Imperial	Metric	Imperial	Metric	Imperial	Metric
External dimensions	Length	20′ 0″	6.096 m	40′ 0″	12.192 m	45′ 0″	13.716 m
	Width	8′ 0″	2.438 m	8′ 0″	2.438 m	8′ 0″	2.438 m
	Height	8′ 6″	2.591 m	8′ 6″	2.591 m	9′ 6″	2.896 m
Volume		1,169 ft^3	33.1 m^3	2,385 ft^3	67.5 m^3	3,040 ft^3	86.1 m^3
Maximum gross mass		66,139 lb	30,400 kg	66,139 lb	30,400 kg	66,139 lb	30,400 kg
Empty weight		4,850 lb	2,200 kg	8,380 lb	3,800 kg	10,580 lb	4,800 kg
Net load		61,289 lb	28,200 kg	57,759 lb	26,600 kg	55,559 lb	25,600 kg

→

Container shipping companies

Informally known as 'box boats', these vessels carry the majority of the world's manufactured goods. Cargoes like metal ores, coal or wheat are carried in bulk carriers. There are large mainline vessels that ply the deep-sea routes, and then many small 'feeder' ships that supply the large ships at centralised hub ports. Most container ships are propelled by diesel engines and have crews of between 20 and 40. Container ships now carry up to 15,000 TEU. The world's largest container ship, the M/V *Emma Mærsk* has a capacity of 15,200 containers. (See Table 3.4.)

Most containers used today measure 40 ft (12 m) in length. Above a certain size, container ships do not carry their own loading gear, so loading and unloading can be done only at ports with the necessary cranes. However, smaller ships with capacities of up to 2,900 TEU are often equipped with their own cranes.

The world's oceans can be scary places in bad weather, hence the transit of containers around the world inevitably carries a considerable risk. And yet, the well-known challenging routes, such as round the Cape Horn, are not where most containers are lost. Most risks are linked to the loading and unloading of containers. The risks involved in these operations affect both the cargo being moved on to or off the ship, as well as the ship itself. Containers, due to their fairly non-descript nature and the sheer number handled in major ports, require complex organisation to ensure they are not lost, stolen or misrouted. In addition, as the containers and the cargo they contain make up the vast majority of the total weight of a cargo ship, the loading and unloading is a delicate balancing act, as it directly affects the whole ship's centre of mass. There have been some instances of poorly loaded ships capsizing at port.

It has been estimated that container ships lose over 10,000 containers at sea each year. Most go overboard on the open sea during storms but there are some examples of whole ships being lost with their cargo. When containers are dropped, they immediately become an environmental threat – termed 'marine debris'.

It is not surprising that, when the three students visited Rotterdam Container Port to discuss their idea with senior managers from the port, the managers were very enthusiastic about containers and the benefits they deliver. They explained that container cargo could be moved nearly 20 times faster than pre-container break bulk cargo. They also argued that, whilst there were increased fuel costs, due to the extra weight of the containers, labour efficiencies more than compensate. Nonetheless, for certain bulk products this makes containerisation unattractive. On railways, the capacity of the container is far from its maximum weight capacity. In some areas (mostly the USA and Canada) containers are double-stacked, but this is not usually possible in other countries.

At the end of the meeting, the Commercial Director explained to the students that, for their idea to succeed, they would need to receive the necessary certification from agencies such as Lloyds Register or

Table 3.4 Biggest shipping container companies

Top 10 container shipping companies in order of TEU capacity			
Company	**TEU capacity**	**Market share (%)**	**Number of ships**
A.P. Moller-Maersk Group	1,665,272	18.2	549
Mediterranean Shipping Company S.A.	865,890	11.7	376
CMA CGM	507,954	5.6	256
Evergreen Marine Corporation	477,911	5.2	153
Hapag-Lloyd	412,344	4.5	140
China Shipping Container Lines	346,493	3.8	111
American President Lines	331,437	3.6	99
Hanjin-Senator	328,794	3.6	145
COSCO	322,326	3.5	118
NYK Line	302,213	3.3	105

Bureau Veritas. Their approval is required regarding the seaworthiness of any marine equipment. Without such certification, no shipping company would be interested in their ideas. There seemed to be many obstacles to their business idea.

Business opportunity: moving empty containers

Containers are intended to be used constantly, being loaded with a new cargo for a new destination soon after being emptied of the previous cargo. This is not always possible and, in some cases, the cost of transporting an empty container to a place where it can be used is considered to be higher than the worth of the used container. This can result in large areas in ports and warehouses being occupied by empty containers left abandoned. The shipping industry spends a great deal of time and money in repositioning empty containers. If trade was balanced, there would be no empty containers. But trade imbalance, especially between Europe and North America with Asia, has resulted in approximately 2.5 million TEUs of empty containers stored in yards around the world with empties comprising 20–23 per cent of the movement of containers around the world. According to research conducted by International Asset Systems, the average container is idle or undergoing repositioning for over 50 per cent of its life span. The research also determined that shipping companies spend $16 billion in repositioning empties. To compensate for these costs, carriers add surcharges, ranging from $100 to $1,000 per TEU, to freight rates.

Folding containers would provide further advantages: for example, they would relieve congestion at ports. Storing empty containers takes up prime real estate. For example, the storage yards around the Port of Jersey, UK, are cluttered with an estimated 100,000 empty containers belonging to leasing companies and an additional 50,000 belonging to ocean carriers. Folding containers would be quicker to load (four at a time), resulting in faster turnaround time for ships. Energy costs would drop as well, as one trailer rather than four would transport empties. Finally, there is also a security feature to the folded container built to ISO standards. Nothing can be smuggled in a collapsed empty. It was estimated that, if 75 per cent of empty containers were folded by 2010, the result would be a yearly saving in shipping of 25 million TEUs or 50 per cent of the total volume of empty containers shipped.

Concept to product

The background research had been done. There was genuine interest from potential customers. The students now needed money to build a working scale model of the folding container. They had to prove to everyone that it would work. Moreover, the concept also had to be compatible with existing equipment for intermodal transport. That is, it would need to be exactly the same size/shape/weight, etc. It would also have to have proper sealing and locking devices and should interlock with other containers. Computer models were fine to a point, but a physical model was now required, especially if they were going to convince people to invest. With the help of the university and the Incubator, the students set about constructing a full working steel model. It was to be a 1/10th scale. So it would be 2 ft long × 0.8 ft high. Real working springs would have to be in place. The friends realised immediately that a patent drawing is theory and it did not resemble reality. Numerous fabrication and manufacturing problems had to be overcome. Eventually, after two months of experimenting with steel springs and welding equipment in the workshop, a fully working model emerged that required two people to manoeuvre the steel box. More importantly, it had taken a considerable amount of time and investment in materials and equipment. When the model was demonstrated to senior figures at the Port of Rotterdam, they were very impressed and immediately wanted to see a full-size version – a prototype. But, who would pay for a full-size prototype? It would be enormous and probably cost thousands of euros to produce.

Source: Pearson Education Ltd/Photodisc

The three students had made some significant steps forward with their business idea, but they still

→

did not have an order, let alone any sales or cash. Was this to be just a hobby, something they enjoyed, but not something that generated any cash? Would anyone pay for one of these things? The students needed money to finance the next stage, but, as well as being impoverished, they were not manufacturers!

Decision time

All three students were excited about the possibilities and the huge potential that existed. They would love to start their own business, rather than work for someone else. There were many uncertainties: money, career, what happens if they fail? As if to underline their concerns, an open page of the *Financial Times* glared at them and gave them further worries:

> **Credit crunch hits shipping as trade falls**
>
> *2009 has seen a considerable slowdown in global trade. It has left the Indian shipping industry high and dry, with the country's idle capacity set to rise from 150,000 TEUs in October 2008 to 750,000. Not surprisingly freight rates for container ships from India have also fallen by almost 80 per cent since summer 2008. The freight rates on the India–UK sector was $1,100 for a 20 ft container and this has come down to $280 to $300, and to ferry a 20 ft container unit to the Gulf is just $90 against $550 in 2007. Globally, things are similar elsewhere. In Singapore, one of the world's busiest ports, some vessels are now being used to store empty containers to save on port rentals. Port-related businesses, such as inland container ports and container freight stations, are also suffering.*

The global downturn raised further worries for the friends – maybe this was the wrong time to start a business?

Source: Levinson, M. (2006) *The Box: How the Shipping Container Made the World Smaller and the World Economy Bigger*, Princeton University Press, Princeton.

Questions

1 Would you advise the students to start this business?
2 Who are their customers going to be?
3 Who can they license the technology to?
4 Can they form any partnerships or alliances?
5 How would you enter this market?
6 What aspects of product diffusion will they need to address?
7 Use the CIM (Figure 1.9) to illustrate the innovation process in this case.
8 Is patent protection essential here? If not, why not?
9 How can the students help customers adopt the product?
10 Standardisation led to growth in container usage: what will be the effect of this non-standard folding container?

Note: This case has been written as a basis for class discussion rather than to illustrate effective or ineffective managerial or administrative behaviour. It has been prepared from a variety of sources and from observations.

Chapter summary

This chapter has explored the wider context of innovation, in particular the role of the state and the role of the market. It has shown that innovation cannot be separated from political and social processes. This includes both tangible and intangible features, including economic, social and political institutions and processes and mechanisms that facilitate the flow of knowledge between industries and firms. It has also shown the powerful influence of the market on innovation; in particular the need to consider long time frames when developing technology and innovative new products. Finally, this chapter discussed an aspect of innovation that is frequently overlooked – the pattern of consumption of the new product or new service. It is changes to the way the new product or service is consumed that all too often determine whether it will be a success or not.

Discussion questions

1 Explain how crowdsourcing is used to generate product ideas.

2 Discuss the merits and limitations of lead users as a source of innovations.

3 How does diffusion differ from adoption?

4 How does frugal innovation differ from targeting low income segments?

5 What role should marketing play in the early stages of product innovation?

6 List some of the additional factors that affect the adoption of highly innovative products.

7 Explain how market vision can help the innovation process.

8 How does the pattern of consumption influence the likely success or failure of a new product?

Key words and phrases

Market vision *89*	**Adoption theory** *99*
Lead-user theory *93*	**Diffusion theory** *99*

References

Basoglu, N., Daim, T. and Polat, E. (2014) Exploring adaptivity in service development: the case of mobile platforms, *Journal of Product Innovation Management*, vol. 31, 501–15.

Bhatti, Y.A., Khilji, S.E. and Basu, R. (2013) 'Frugal innovation', in Khilji, S. and Rowley, C. (eds) *Globalization, Change and Learning in South Asia*, Oxford, UK: Chandos Publishing.

Bogers, M., Afuah, A. and Bastian, B. (2010) Users as innovators: a review, critique, and future research directions, *Journal of Management*, vol. 36, no. 4, 857–75.

Carver, C.S., Scheier, M.F. and Weintraub, J.K. (1989) Assessing coping strategies: a theoretically based approach, *Journal of Personality and Social Psychology*, vol. 56, 267–83.

Chandra, Y. and Leenders, M.A. (2012) User innovation and entrepreneurship in the virtual world: a study of Second Life residents, *Technovation*, vol. 32, no. 7, 464–76.

Christensen, C.M. (1997) *The Innovator's Dilemma: When New Technologies Cause Great Firms to Fail*, HBS Press, Cambridge.

Dekimpe, M.G., Parker, P.M. and Sarvary, M. (2000) 'Multimarket and global diffusion', in Mahajan, V., Muller, E. and Wind, Y. (eds) *New-product Diffusion Models*, Kluwer Academic, Dordrecht, The Netherlands, 49–73.

European Innovation Scoreboard (EIS) (2010) Pro Inno Europe Paper No. 15, http://www.proinno-europe.eu/metrics.

Franke, N. and Piller, F. (2004) Value creation by toolkits for user innovation and design: the case of the watch market, *Journal of Product Innovation Management*, vol. 21, no. 6, 401–16.

Franke, N. and Shah, S. (2003) How communities support innovative activities: an exploration of assistance and sharing among end-users, *Research Policy*, vol. 32, no. 1, 157–78.

Franke, N., von Hippel, E. and Schreier, M. (2006) Finding commercially attractive user innovations: a test of lead-user theory, *Journal of Product Innovation Management*, vol. 23, no. 4, 301–15.

Guidolin, M. and Guseo, R. (2014) Modelling seasonality in innovation diffusion, *Technological Forecasting and Social Change*, vol. 86, 33–40.

Hamel, G. and Prahalad, C.K. (1994) 'Competing for the future', *Harvard Business Review*, vol. 72, no. 4, 122–8.

Haavisto, P. (2014) Observing discussion forums and product innovation – a way to create consumer value? Case heart-rate monitors, *Technovation*, vol. 34, no. 4, 215–22.

Hienerth, C., von Hippel, E. and Jensen, M.B. (2014) User community vs. producer innovation development efficiency: a first empirical study, *Research Policy*, vol. 43, no. 1, 190–201.

Jun, S.P., Yeom, J. and Son, J.K. (2014) A study of the method using search traffic to analyze new technology adoption, *Technological Forecasting and Social Change*, 81, 82–95.

King, S. (1985) 'Has marketing failed or was it never really tried?', *Journal of Marketing Management*, vol. 1, no. 1, 1–19.

Leifer, R., Colarelli O'Connor, G., Peters, L.S., Rice, M., Veryzer, R.W. and McDermott, C.M. (2000) *Radical Innovation*, HBS Press, Boston, MA.

Lüthje, C., Herstatt, C. and Von Hippel, E. (2005) User-innovators and 'local' information: the case of mountain biking, *Research Policy*, vol. 34, no. 6, 951–65.

Martin, J. (1995) Ignore your customer, *Fortune*, Vol. 1, No. 8, 121–5.

Mick, D.G. and Fournier, S. (1998) Paradoxes of technology: consumer cognizance, emotions, and coping strategies, *Journal of Consumer Research*, vol. 25, no. 9, 123–47.

Moore, G.A. (2004) *Crossing the Chasm: Marketing and Selling Technology Products to Mainstream Customers*, 2nd edn, Capstone, Oxford.

Morrison, P.D., Roberts, J.H. and Midgley, D. (2004) The nature of lead users and measurement of leading edge status, *Research Policy*, vol. 33, 351–62.

Morrison, P.D., Roberts, J.H. and von Hippel, E. (2000) Determinants of user innovation and innovation sharing in a local market, *Management Science*, vol. 46, no. 12, 1513.

Norton, J.A. and Bass, F.M. (1987) A diffusion theory model of adoption and substitution for successive generations of high technology products, *Management Science*, vol. 33, no. 9, 1069–86.

Norton, J.A. and Bass, F.M. (1992) Evolution of technological change: the law of capture, *Sloan Management Review*, vol. 33, no. 2, 66–77.

Peng, Y.N. and Sanderson, S.W. (2014) Crossing the chasm with beacon products in the portable music player industry, *Technovation*, vol. 34, no. 2, 77–92.

Poetz, M.K. and Schreier, M. (2012) The Value of Crowdsourcing: Can Users Really Compete with Professionals in Generating New Product Ideas? *Journal of Product Innovation Management*, vol. 29, 245–56.

Radjou, N. and Prabhu, J. (2015) *Frugal Innovation: How To Do More With Less*, Profile Books with *The Economist*.

Reinders, M.J., Frambach, R.T. and Schoormans, J.P.L. (2010) Using product bundling to facilitate the adoption process of radical innovations, *Journal of Product Innovation Management*, vol. 27, 1127–40.

Rogers, E.M. (1962) *Diffusion of Innovations*, Free Press, New York.

Rogers, E.M. (1983) *Diffusion of Innovations*, 3rd edn, The Free Press, New York.

Rogers, E.M. (1995) *Diffusion of Innovations*, 4th edn, The Free Press, New York.

Shah, S.K. and Tripsas, M. (2007) The accidental entrepreneur: the emergent and collective process of user entrepreneurship, *Strategic Entrepreneurship Journal*, vol. 1, no. 1–2, 123–140.

Shieh, L.F., Chang, T.H., Fu, H.P., Lin, S.W. and Chen, Y.Y. (2014) Analyzing the factors that affect the adoption of mobile services in Taiwan, *Technological Forecasting and Social Change*, vol. 87, 80–88.

Tauber, E.M. (1974) Predictive validity in consumer research, *Journal of Advertising Research*, vol. 15, no. 5, 59–64.

Tietz, R., Morrison, P.D., Luthje, C. and Herstatt, C. (2005) The process of user-innovation: a case study in a consumer goods setting, *International Journal of Product Development*, vol. 2, no. 4, 321–38.

Turk, T. and Trkman, P. (2012) Bass model estimates for broadband diffusion in European countries, *Technological Forecasting and Social Change*, vol. 79, no. 1, 85–96.

Urban, G.L. and Von Hippel, E. (1988). Lead-user analyses for the development of new industrial products, *Management Science*, vol. 34, no. 5, 569–82.

van der Panne, G., van Beers, C. and Kleinknecht, A. (2003) Success and failure of innovation: a review of the literature, *International Journal of Innovation Management*, vol. 7, no. 3, 309–38.

Veryzer, R.W. (1998a) Key factors affecting customer evaluation of discontinuous products, *Journal of Product Innovation Management*, vol. 15, no. 2, 136–50.

Veryzer, R.W. (1998b) Discontinuous innovation and the new product development process, *Journal of Product Innovation Management*, vol. 15, no. 4, 304–21.

Veryzer, R. (2003) 'Marketing and the development of innovative products', in Shavinina, L. (ed.) *International Handbook on Innovation*, Pergamon Press, Canada, 43–54.

Von Hippel, E. (1977) The dominant role of the user in semiconductor and electronic subassembly process innovation, *IEEE Transactions on Engineering Management*, 2, 60–71.

von Hippel, E. (1994) 'Sticky information' and the locus of problem solving: implications for innovation, *Management Science*, vol. 40, no. 4, 429–39.

Von Hippel, E. (2005) *Democratizing Innovation*, MIT Press, Cambridge, Mass.

Yu, C. and Tao, Y. (2009) Understanding business-level innovation technology adoption, *Technovation*, vol. 29, no. 2, 92–109.

Further reading

For a more detailed review of market adoption and technology diffusion, the following develop many of the issues raised in this chapter:

Bogers, M., Afuah, A., and Bastian, B. (2010). Users as innovators: a review, critique, and future research directions. *Journal of Management*.

Hienerth, C., and Lettl, C. (2016). Understanding the Nature and Measurement of the Lead User Construct. *Journal of Product Innovation Management*.

Herstatt, C., Schweisfurth, T., and Raasch, C. (2016). When passion meets profession: How Embedded Lead Users contribute to corporate innovation. *Revolutionizing Innovation– Users, Communities and Open Innovation. MIT Press, Cambridge*, MA.

Moore, G.A. (2004) *Crossing the Chasm: Marketing and Selling Technology Products to Mainstream Customers*, 2nd edn, Capstone, Oxford.

Rogers, E.M. (2003) *Diffusion of Innovations*, 5th edn, Free Press, New York.

Stockstrom, C.S., Goduscheit, R.C., Lüthje, C., and Jørgensen, J. H. (2016). Identifying valuable users as informants for innovation processes: Comparing the search efficiency of pyramiding and screening. *Research Policy, 45*(2), 507–516.

Trott, P., Van Der Duin, P. and Dap Hartmann (2013) Users as innovators? Exploring the limitations of user driven innovation, *Prometheus*, vol 31, 2, 125–138.

Veryzer, R. (2003) 'Marketing and the development of innovative products', in Shavinina, L. (ed.) *The International Handbook on Innovation*, Pergamon Press, Canada.

Chapter 4
Managing innovation within firms

Introduction

Virtually all innovations, certainly major technological innovations such as pharmaceutical and automobile products, occur within organisations. The management of innovation within organisations forms the focus for this chapter. The study of organisations and their management is a very broad subject and no single approach provides all the answers. The identification of those factors and issues that affect the management of innovation within organisations is addressed here. The W.L. Gore case study at the end of this chapter shows how this firm has developed an organisation culture that supports innovation and creativity. Also, Gore is a regular winner of *The Sunday Times* 'best organisation to work for' award.

Chapter contents

Learning objectives

When you have completed this chapter you will be able to:

- identify the factors organisations have to manage to achieve success in innovation;
- explain the dilemma facing all organisations concerning the need for creativity and stability;
- recognise the difficulties of managing uncertainty;
- identify the activities performed by key individuals in the management of innovation; and
- recognise the relationship between the activities performed and the organisational environment in promoting innovation.

Organisations and innovation

Chapter 1 outlined some of the difficulties in studying the field of innovation. In particular, it emphasised the need to view innovation as a management process within the context of the organisation. This was shown to be the case, especially in a modern industrialised society where innovation is increasingly viewed as an *organisational activity*. Chapters 2 and 3 offered an overview of the wider issues of innovation, in particular the economic and market factors, which ultimately will be the judge of any product or service that is launched. This chapter tackles the difficult issue of managing innovation within organisations. To do this, it is necessary to understand the patterns of interaction and behaviour that represent the organisation.

The dilemma of innovation management

Within virtually all organisations there is a fundamental tension between the need for stability and the need for creativity. On the one hand, companies require stability and static routines to accomplish daily tasks efficiently and quickly. This enables the organisation to compete today. For example, the processing of millions of cheques by banks every day or the delivery of food by multiples to their retail outlets all over the country, demands high levels of efficiency and control. On the other hand, companies also need to develop new ideas and new products to be competitive in the future. Hence they need to nurture a creative environment where ideas can be tested and developed. This poses one of the most fundamental problems for management today (see Figure 4.1).

Take any medium to large company and examine its operations and activities. From Mars to Ford and from P&G to Sony, these companies have to ensure that their products are carefully manufactured to precise specifications and that they are delivered for customers on time day after day. In this hectic, repetitive and highly organised environment, the need to squeeze out any **slack** or inefficiencies is crucial to ensure a firm's costs are lower than their competitors'. Without this emphasis on cost reductions, a firm's costs would simply spiral upwards and the firm's products and services would become uncompetitive. But we have already seen in the previous chapter that long-term economic growth is dependent on the ability of firms to make improvements to products and manufacturing processes. This means that

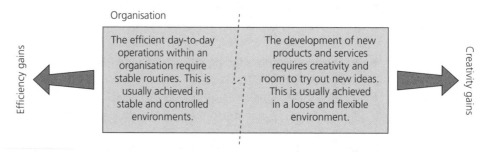

Figure 4.1 Managing the tension between the need for creativity and efficiency

firms need to somehow make room for creativity and innovation, that is, allow slack in the system.

Here, then, is the dilemma: 'The farther that any company seeks to innovate, as measured by the degrees of change from its base markets and technologies, the greater the likelihood that its innovation efforts will fail. And yet, the less that a firm seeks to innovate, across the board, the greater the likelihood that the corporation itself will fail.'

So, how do firms try to reduce costs and slack to improve competitiveness on the one hand and then try to provide slack for innovation on the other? As usual, with dilemmas, the answer is difficult and has to do with balancing activities. The firm needs to ensure there is a constant pressure to drive down costs and improve efficiency in its operations. At the same time, it needs to provide room for new product development and making improvements. The most obvious way forward is to separate production from research and development (R&D) but, whilst this usually is done, there are many improvements and innovations that arise out of the operations of the firm, as will be seen in the next chapter. Indeed, the operations of the firm provide enormous scope for innovation.

This is the fundamental tension at the heart of an enterprise's long-run survival. The basic problem confronting an organisation is to engage in sufficient exploitation to ensure its future viability. Exploitation is about efficiency, increasing productivity, control, certainty and variance reduction. Exploration is about search, discovery, autonomy, innovation and embracing variation. **Ambidexterity** is about doing both. O'Reilly and Tushman (2008) argue that efficiency and innovation need not be strategic trade-offs and highlight the substantive role of senior teams in building dynamic capabilities. In organisational terms, dynamic capabilities are at the heart of the ability of a business to be ambidextrous – to compete simultaneously in both mature and emerging markets – to explore and exploit. Ambidexterity entails not only separate structure sub-units for exploration and exploitation, but also different competencies, systems, incentives, processes and cultures – each internally aligned (O'Reilly and Tushman, 2008; Smith and Tushman, 2005). Current research is exploring how firms should dynamically reconfigure resource portfolios to leverage organisational ambidexterity for new product development (Wei et al., 2014).

Pause for thought

To resolve the innovation dilemma, why do firms not simply separate the creative side of their business from the operational side?

Innovation dilemma in low technology sectors

Research in the area of low technology intensive industries shows a dominance of incremental, mostly process-driven innovations where disruptive innovation activities are scarce. Generally, the dominant pattern of technological development in low technology intensive industries is characterised by a high path-dependency, which is continuously stabilised by incremental innovation activities. High returns on investment are generated from continuous optimisation of processes and of the existing technologies, thereby reinforcing the development paths. Smart et al. (2010) reviewed the process innovation literature and developed a model of costs associated with adoption, this included: capital costs, development costs and switching costs. This cost-minimising orientation is particularly apparent in many mature industries, such as the food and FMCG industries, where price-based competition is high. Benner and Tushman's (2002) study within the paint and photographic industries suggests that this focus can result in a shift in the balance of innovation, towards efficiency at the expense of long-term adaptation. This, in turn, creates an emphasis on exploitative activities, crowding out more significant innovations. Whilst these activities may help firms learn and adapt quickly in the short term, they were seen to inhibit a longer-term focus and lead to inertia. This creates a pressure on R&D to improve the product and production process to lower costs over time, which can, in turn, stifle more significant innovation. Thus, arguably the innovation dilemma in low-tech sectors is even worse than high tech sectors.

Dynamic capabilities

How, then, do firms escape from the innovation dilemma? The literature on organisational capabilities offers insight into the different resources and environment necessary for developing incremental and radical innovations. Incremental innovation reinforces the capabilities of established organisations, whilst radical innovation forces them to ask a new set of questions, to draw on new technical and commercial skills, and to employ new problem-solving approaches. The impact of this on the nature of innovation activities is that, as the organisation learns and increases its efficiency, subsequent innovation is increasingly incremental. Another constraint on innovation that can arise from this is a shift to simply meeting existing customer needs.

The literature on dynamic capabilities seems to offer the most likely solution for firms. It has found that every firm has a zero-level or baseline set of routines, i.e., those that serve the purpose of producing and marketing the given products and services currently in the portfolio (how we earn a living now). Some firms have dynamic capabilities, i.e., those routines that relate to the innovation of products and services, to the innovation of the production process, or to the search and attraction of new customers, etc. – dynamic capabilities implement the change of old routines with new ones. Chapter 7 explores this issue further.

Managing uncertainty

Whilst management in general involves coping with uncertainty, sometimes trying to reduce uncertainty, the *raison d'être* of managers involved in innovation is to develop something different, maybe something new. The management of the innovation process involves trying to develop the creative potential of the organisation. It involves trying to foster new ideas and generate creativity. **Managing uncertainty** is a central

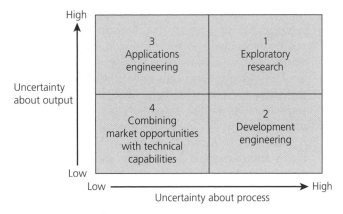

Figure 4.2 Pearson's uncertainty map

Source: Pearson, A.W. (1991) 'Managing innovation: an uncertainty reduction process', in Henry, J. and Walker, D. (eds), *Managing Innovation*, Sage/OU.

feature of managing the innovation process. This has been recognised for over 40 years within the innovation and R&D management literature (Pearson, 1983). Nonetheless, it continues to be a cause for concern for firms. At the very least, there is the uncertainty of output (including market uncertainty) – i.e., what is required – and also uncertainty of process – i.e., how to produce it. Pearson offered a helpful uncertainty matrix for managers to help them deal with different levels of uncertainty. This recognised that different environments required different management styles (see Figure 4.2).

Pearson's uncertainty map

Pearson's uncertainty map (Pearson, 1991) provides a framework for analysing and understanding uncertainty and the innovation process. The map was developed following extensive analysis of case studies of major technological innovations, including Pilkington's float glass process, 3M's Post-It Notes and Sony's Walkman. In these and other case studies, a great deal of uncertainty surrounded the project. If it involves newly developed technology, this may be uncertainty about the type of product envisaged. For example, Spencer Silver's unusual adhesive remained unexploited within 3M for five years before an application was found. Similarly, if a market opportunity has been identified, the final product idea may be fairly well-established, but much uncertainty may remain about how, exactly, the company is to develop such a product.

So, Pearson's framework divides uncertainty into two separate dimensions:

uncertainty about ends (what is the eventual target of the activity or project); and uncertainty about means (how to achieve this target).

The development of Guinness's 'In-can system' clearly highlights the problems of managing uncertainty about means. Here, several projects were unsuccessful and there were, probably, several occasions where decisions had to be taken regarding future funding. Decisions had to be made, such as whether to cancel, continue or increase funding. In these situations, because the degree of uncertainty is high, senior managers responsible for million-dollar budgets have to listen carefully to those most closely involved and those with the most information and knowledge. Further information and knowledge usually are available with the passage of time, so time is another element that needs to be considered. Indeed, it is because time is limited that decisions are required. It is clear, however, that many decisions are made with imperfect knowledge, thus there is, usually, an element of judgement involved in most decisions.

Pearson's framework, shown in Figure 4.2, addresses the nature of the uncertainty and the way it changes over time. The framework is based on the two dimensions discussed above, with uncertainty about ends on the vertical axis and uncertainty about means on the horizontal axis. These axes are then divided, giving four quadrants.

Quadrant 1

Quadrant 1 represents activities involving a high degree of uncertainty about means and ends. The ultimate target is not clearly defined and how to achieve this target is also not clear. This has been labelled **exploratory research** or blue sky research, because the work sometimes seems so far removed from reality that people liken it to working in the clouds! These activities often involve working with technology that is not fully understood and where potential products or markets have also not been identified. This is largely the domain of university research laboratories, which usually are removed from the financial and time pressures associated with industry. Some science-based organisations also support these activities, but, increasingly, it is only large organisations that have the necessary resources to fund such exploratory studies. For example, Microsoft conducts the majority of its research in Seattle, United States. Interestingly, it calls this centre a campus.

Quadrant 2

In this area, the end or target is clear. For example, a commercial opportunity may have been identified but, the means of fulfilling this has yet to be established. Companies may initiate several different projects centred around different technologies or different approaches to try to achieve the desired product. Also, additional approaches may be uncovered along the way. Hence, there is considerable uncertainty about precisely how the company will achieve its target. This type of activity often is referred to as development engineering and is an ongoing activity within manufacturing companies that are continually examining their production processes, looking for efficiencies and ways to reduce costs. A good example of a successful development in this area is the Guinness 'In-can system'. The company was clear about its target – trying to make the taste of Guinness from a can taste the same as draught Guinness. Precisely how this was to be achieved was very uncertain and many different research projects were established.

Quadrants 3 and 4 deal with situations where there is more certainty associated with how the business will achieve the target. Usually, this means that the business is working with technology it has used before.

The Guinness In-can system illustrates an output from a research environment where there is a clear objective in mind, but there is uncertainty about precisely how this is to be achieved.
Source: Chloe Johnson/Alamy

Quadrant 3

In this area, there is uncertainty regarding ends. Usually, this is associated with attempting to discover how the technology can be used most effectively. Applications engineering is the title given to this area of activity. Arguably, many new materials fall into this area. For example, the material kevlar (used in the manufacture of bullet-proof clothing) currently is being applied to a wide range of different possible product areas. Many of these may prove to be ineffective, due to costs or performance, but some new and improved products will emerge from this effort.

Quadrant 4

This area covers innovative activities where there is most certainty. In these situations, activities may be dominated by improving existing products or creating new products through the combination of a market opportunity and technical capability. With so much certainty, similar activities are likely to be undertaken by the competition. Hence, speed of development is often the key to success here. New product designs that use minimal new technology but improve, sometimes with dramatic effect, the appearance or performance of an existing product are examples of product innovations in this area. A good exponent of this is Samsung. It has demonstrated an ability to introduce new mobile phones incorporating new designs rapidly into the market, thereby maintaining its position as market leader.

Applying the uncertainty map in practice

The uncertainty map's value is partly the simplicity with which it is able to communicate a complex message, that of dealing with uncertainty, and partly its ability to identify the wide range of organisational characteristics that are associated with managing uncertainty with respect to innovation. The map conveys the important message that the management of product and process innovations is very different. Sometimes, one is clear about the nature of the target market and the type of product required. In contrast, there are occasions when little, if anything, is known about the technology being developed and how it could possibly be used. Most organisations have activities that lie between these two extremes, but such differing environments demand very different management skills and organisational environments. This leads the argument towards the vexed question of the organisational structure and culture necessary for innovation, which will be addressed in the following sections.

Quadrant 1 highlights an area of innovative activity where ideas and developments may not be recognisable immediately as possible commercial products. There are many examples of technological developments that occurred within organisations that were not recognised. In Xerox's Palo Alto laboratories, the early computer software technology was developed for computer graphical interface as far back as the early 1970s. Xerox did not recognise the possible future benefits of this research and decided not to develop the technology further. It was later exploited by Apple Computer and Microsoft in the 1980s. This raises the question of how to evaluate research in this area. Technical managers may be better able to understand the technology, but a commercial manager may be able to see a wide range of commercial opportunities. Continual informal and formal discussions are usually the best way to explore all possibilities fully, in the hope that the company will make the correct decision regarding which projects to support and which to drop. This is a problem that will be returned to in Chapter 10.

At the other extreme is Quadrant 4, where scientists often view this type of activity as merely tinkering with existing technology. However, commercial managers often get very excited because the project is in a close-to-market form with minimal technical newness.

Between these two extremes lie Quadrants 2 and 3. In the applications engineering quadrant, where the business is exploring the potential uses of known technology, management efforts centre on which markets to enter; whereas in the development engineering quadrant, special project-management skills are required to ensure that projects either deliver or are cancelled before costs escalate.

In all of the above, particular organisational environments and specialist management skills are required, depending on the type of activity being undertaken. These will be determined by the extent of uncertainty involved.

Chapters 9 and 10 examine R&D management in more detail.

Pause for thought

If most new products are minor modifications of existing products, why do firms continue with high-risk, high-cost projects?

Managing innovation projects

We now need to examine innovation projects. Henderson and Clark examined product innovations and demonstrate that product innovations are complex entities embedded in organisational capabilities, which are difficult to create and costly to

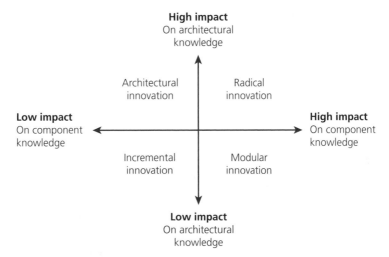

Figure 4.3 Matrix of complexity of architectural/component knowledge

Source: Henderson, R. and Clark, K. (1990) Architectural innovation: the reconfiguration of existing product technologies and the failure of established firms, *Administrative Science Quarterly*, vol. 35, no. 1. Reproduced with permission of Johnson at Cornell University.

adjust (Hannan and Freeman, 1984; Nelson and Winter, 1982). Henderson and Clark (1990) divide technological knowledge along two dimensions: *knowledge of the components* and knowledge of the linkage between them, which they called *architectural knowledge* (see Figure 4.3). In this framework, technology development could be a radical innovation, only if it revolutionises both component and **architectural knowledge**. Similarly, an incremental innovation will build upon existing component and architectural knowledge. Modular innovations will require new knowledge for one or more components, but the architectural knowledge remains unchanged. Whereas architectural innovation will have a great impact upon the linkage of components, the knowledge of single components will remain the same.

It is against the backcloth of the above discussions that theoretical indications for having more than one model for project management are clear. We need also to recognise that to develop an existing product further is not, generally, viewed by R&D managers as a high-risk activity. Indeed, these types of low-uncertainty projects are so very different from high-uncertainty R&D projects that it is evidently clear why a classification of project types is necessary. Figure 4.4 uses a two-dimensional typology of innovation projects to illustrate the range of innovation projects required to be managed. The vertical axis classifies project style and uses Coombs et al.'s (1998) classification of R&D project. The horizontal axis captures technological uncertainty. The traditional distinction within innovation management between research projects and development projects, however outmoded and inappropriate, may, nonetheless, still retain usefulness in the practical realities of the laboratory. In particular, it distinguishes between the management of projects that deliver mainly knowledge and those that deliver a physical product. There is also an emphasis (not surprisingly, within the new product development (NPD) literature) on project management models that explicitly focus on the new product development process (for example, see Cooper, 1986). This emphasis may have overlooked the need for subtly different approaches to project management for innovation management and R&D, in particular, that does not necessarily lead directly to the launch of a new product.

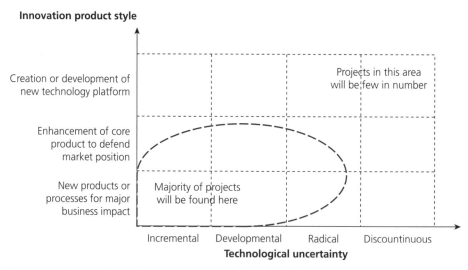

Figure 4.4 A two-dimensional typology of innovation projects

Organisational characteristics that facilitate the innovation process

The innovation process, outlined at the end of Chapter 1, identified the complex nature of innovation. It also emphasised the need to view innovation within the context of the organisation. In a recent study examining the relationship between innovation stimulus, innovation capacity and innovation performance, Prajogo and Ahmed (2006) found that there was a strong relationship between innovation stimulus and innovation capacity and a strong relationship between innovation capacity and innovation performance. Figure 4.5 illustrates this diagrammatically. The findings did not detect any direct relationship between innovation stimulus and innovation performance. The implications of this for firms are clear: if firms wish to improve innovation performance, first they need to put in place and then develop factors that stimulate innovation, such as appropriate leadership, R&D and creativity. Within such an environment, the nurturing and building of innovation capacity can then occur. Prajogo and Ahmed (2006) argue that innovation capacity is the combination of technological and human factors. In other words, having good science and laboratories is necessary but insufficient. In addition, effective intangible skills are required, such as project management, innovative experience and risk management.

Figure 4.5 Innovation stimulus, capacity and performance
Source: D.I. Prajogo and P.K. Ahmed (2006).

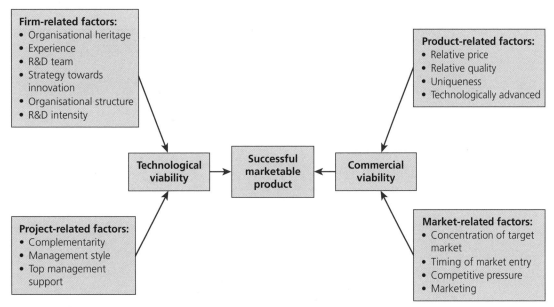

Figure 4.6 Critical factors for innovation success

Source: van der Panne et al. (2003).

Armed with this information, the challenge for firms remains immense. Putting in place the necessary stimulus and then nurturing capacity may sound straightforward, but what does this mean? A review of the innovation management literature by van der Panne et al. (2003) provides us with some of the answers. This research examined factors that contribute to success and failure of innovative projects within firms (see Figure 4.6). This major review identified a wide range of factors, but this is classified into four major groups:

1 Firm-related factors.
2 Project-related factors.
3 Product-related factors.
4 Market-related factors.

In this chapter we will concentrate on firm-related factors that affect innovative success for the firm. Other chapters in this book address the three other areas. For example, project-related factors are discussed in Chapters 10 and 17. Product-related factors are addressed in Chapters 12, 13, 14 and 15. And finally market-related factors are addressed in Chapters 3, 6, 12 and 16.

Over the past 50 years, a considerable literature has accumulated on the subject of innovation and how best to manage the process within the firm (Porter and Ketels, 2003). Within this literature, there is evidence that competitive success is dependent upon a firm's management of the innovation process (Adams et al., 2006). Yet, attempting to measure the process of innovation is a major challenge because, for practitioners and academics, it is characterised by diversity of approaches and practices. Nonetheless, for those of us attempting to understand better how innovation management can be improved, we need to know 'ingredients' and, possibly, 'recipes' that at least give us some indication of what is required and if and when we are to turn ideas into marketable products. Adams et al. (2006)

Table 4.1 Innovation management measurement areas

Framework category	Measurement area
Inputs	People Physical and financial resources Tools
Knowledge management	Idea generation Knowledge repository Information flows
Innovation strategy	Strategic orientation Strategic leadership
Organisation and culture	Culture Structure
Portfolio management	Risk/return balance Optimisation tool use
Project management	Project efficiency Tools Communications Collaborations
Commercialisation	Market research Market testing Marketing and sales

Source: Adams et al. (2006).

developed a framework of the innovation management process with illustrative measures to map the territory. This framework is shown in Table 4.1.

This framework enables managers within firms to evaluate their own innovation activities. This enables them to explore the extent to which innovation is embedded within their organisation and identify areas for improvement. Hopefully, readers of this book now recognise that innovation is not a linear process where resources are fed in at one end and at the other emerges a new product or process. Innovation requires a variety of competencies at key stages in the innovation cycle. Each of these requires its own space and time but, along with specialised skills, comes the need for coordination and management. The framework in Table 4.1 shows the wide variety of elements that need to be in place and can be measured. There are still big questions that remain regarding precisely how one measures these elements and which metric is used but, nonetheless, it provides a starting point.

The above discussions present an overview of how innovation is successfully managed within organisations. Figures 4.5 and 4.6, together with Table 4.1, provide us with a solid base of evidence from which we can develop a list of organisational characteristics that influence the innovation process. If we add to this the major findings from the studies detailed in Table 1.8, we have a useful checklist of factors that firms need to consider. Table 4.2, then, is a summary of the organisational characteristics that facilitate the innovation process. The W.L. Gore case at the end of this chapter provides an illustration of these internal organisational attributes, which contribute to innovative success, in action.

Table 4.2 Summary of the organisational characteristics that facilitate the innovation process

Organisational requirement	Characterised by
1 Growth orientation	A commitment to long-term growth rather than short-term profit
2 Organisational heritage and innovation experience	Widespread recognition of the value of innovation
3 Vigilance and external links	The ability of the organisation to be aware of its threats and opportunities
4 Commitment to technology and R&D intensity	The willingness to invest in the long-term development of technology
5 Acceptance of risks	The willingness to include risky opportunities in a balanced portfolio
6 Cross-functional cooperation and coordination within organisational structure	Mutual respect amongst individuals and a willingness to work together across functions
7 **Receptivity**	The ability to be aware of, to identify and to take effective advantage of, externally developed technology
8 Space for creativity	An ability to manage the innovation dilemma and provide room for creativity
9 Strategy towards innovation	Strategic planning and selection of technologies and markets
10 Coordination of a diverse range of skills	Developing a marketable product requires combining a wide range of specialised knowledge

Growth orientation

It is sometimes surprising to learn that not all companies' first and foremost objective is growth. Some companies are established merely to exploit a short-term opportunity. Other companies, particularly family-run ones, would like to maintain the company at its existing size. At that size, the family can manage the operation without having to employ outside help. Companies that are seeking growth are more likely to be interested in innovation than those that are not. For those companies whose objective is to grow the business, innovation provides a means to achieving growth. This does not imply that they make large profits one year then huge losses the next, but they actively plan for the long term. There are many companies that make this explicit in their annual reports, for example, Roche, Siemens, Google and Microsoft (see Dobini, 2010).

Pause for thought

If we know what organisational characteristics are required for innovation, why are not all firms innovative?

Organisational heritage and innovation experience

A firm's heritage and culture is, undisputedly, considered crucial to the firm's technological capabilities, as it fosters and encourages widespread recognition of the need to innovate. This is clearly illustrated in the extent to which groups and departments are willing to cooperate. Numerous problems arise when individuals and groups are either unwilling or reluctant to work together and share ideas. At the very least, it slows down communication and decision making and, at worst, leads to projects being abandoned due to lack of progress. Frequently, the difference between a firm succeeding or not lies not in their scientific ability or commercial knowledge but simply in the firm's internal ability to share information and knowledge. The pharmaceutical firm Pfizer is frequently cited as delivering exceptional new products, yet its R&D is not more highly regarded than other firms. In other words, it is the ability of the firm to convert technology into products that sets it apart from its competitors.

Previous experience with innovative projects is clearly conducive to the firm's technology and R&D management capabilities, as these enhance the skills that are necessary to turn technology into marketable products. Numerous advantages also flow from learning by doing and learning from failure effects.

Vigilance and external links

Vigilance requires continual external scanning, not just by senior management but also by all other members of the organisation. Part of this activity may be formalised. For example, within the marketing function the activity would form part of market research and competitor analysis. Within the research and development department scientists and engineers will spend a large amount of their time reading the scientific literature in order to keep up to date with the latest developments in their field. In other functions it may not be as formalised but it still needs to occur. Collecting valuable information is one thing, but relaying it to the necessary individuals and acting on it are two necessary, associated requirements. An open communication system will help to facilitate this. Extensive external linkages with the market, competitors, customers, suppliers and others will all contribute to the flow of information into the firm (see Kang and Kang, 2009; also see Chapter 11).

Commitment to technology and R&D intensity

Most innovative firms exhibit patience in permitting ideas to germinate and develop over time. This also needs to be accompanied by a commitment to resources in terms of intellectual input from science, technology and engineering. Those ideas that look most promising will require further investment. Without this long-term approach, it would be extremely difficult for the company to attract good scientists. Similarly, a climate that invests in technology development one year then decides to cut investment the next will alienate the same people in which the company encourages creativity. Such a disruptive environment does not foster creativity and probably will cause many creative people to search for a more suitable company with a stronger commitment to technology.

In addition, it seems almost obvious to state that a firm that invests more in R&D will increase its total innovative output. But the relationship between R&D expenditures as a percentage of sales and commercial success is less clear-cut. This will be examined in more detail in Chapter 9.

Acceptance of risks

Accepting risks does not mean a willingness to gamble. It means the willingness to consider carefully risky opportunities. It also includes the ability to make risk-assessment decisions, to take calculated risks and to include them in a balanced portfolio of projects, some of which will have a low element of risk and some a high degree of risk.

Cross-functional cooperation and coordination within organisational structure

Interdepartmental conflict is a well-documented barrier to innovation. The relationship between the marketing and R&D functions has received a great deal of attention in the research literature. This will be explored further in Chapter 17, but, generally, this is because the two groups often have very different interests. Scientists and technologists can be fascinated by new technology and may sometimes lose sight of the business objective. Similarly, the marketing function often fails to understand the technology involved in the development of a new product. Research has shown that the presence of some conflict is desirable, probably acting as a motivational force (Souder, 1987). It is the ability to confront and resolve frustration and conflict that is required. In addition, a supportive organisational structure underpinned by a robust information and communication technology system all contribute to facilitating the organisation to coordinate cross-functional cooperation (see later sections in this chapter).

Receptivity

The capability of the organisation to be aware of, identify and take effective advantage of externally developed technology is key. Most technology-based innovations involve a combination of several different technologies. It would be unusual for all the technology to be developed in-house. Indeed, businesses are witnessing an increasing number of joint ventures and alliances (see Chapter 8), often with former competitors. For example, Sony and Ericsson formed a joint venture to work on the development of mobile phone handsets (see the case study on Sony-Ericsson in Chapter 11 for more details). Previously, these two companies fought ferociously in the battle for market share in the mobile phone handset market.

Space for creativity

Whilst organisations place great emphasis on the need for efficiency, there is also a need for a certain amount of slack to allow individuals room to think, experiment, discuss ideas and be creative (Birdi, et al., 2012; Dobini, 2010; Troilo et al., 2014). In many R&D functions this issue is directly addressed by allowing scientists to spend 10–15 per cent of their time on the projects they choose. This is not always supported in other functional areas. (See also ambidexterity in the earlier section, 'The dilemma of innovation management'.)

Strategy towards innovation

An explicit strategic approach towards innovation can come in many forms, as is shown in Chapter 7. For the firm and those within it, however, it means that the firm has developed plans for the future regarding selection of markets to enter and which technologies may be appropriate for the firm. Recognising that the organisation possesses skills, technology and knowledge and that there are appropriate markets that suit these, requires careful planning, probably utilising a project portfolio approach. This will involve further long-term planning, establishing a range of projects, some of which will subsequently provide opportunities that the firm will be able to exploit. This long-term planning and investment with regard to technology and markets distinguishes such firms from their short-termism counterparts (see Dobini, 2010).

Diverse range of skills

Organisations require a combination of specialist skills and knowledge in the form of experts in, say, science, advertising or accountancy and generalist skills that facilitate cross-fertilisation of the specialist knowledge. In addition, they require individuals of a hybrid nature who are able to understand a variety of technical subjects and facilitate the transfer of knowledge within the company. Similarly, hybrid managers who have technical and commercial training are particularly useful in the area of product development (Wheelwright and Clark, 1992). It is the ability to manage this diversity of knowledge and skills effectively that lies at the heart of the innovation process. This is wonderfully illustrated below in the analysis of conducting or managing an orchestra. On the one hand, great individual musical talent is required and yet, at the same time, individuals must play as part of the team. Even the greatest business pioneers in technology cannot do it alone, as is shown in Illustration 4.1.

Business pioneers in technology

You do not have to be a young and inexperienced outsider in business to change the world in the computing and internet industries. But it certainly helps.

More than half of the industry's leading pioneers founded their companies before their 27th birthdays, from Sony's Akio Morita in 1946 (aged 25) to Mark Zuckerberg, who set up Facebook in 2004 when he was only 19, though that was still three months older than Bill Gates when he started in software.

It is not just the relative immaturity of the computer and internet worlds that accounts for this bias towards youth. It also reflects the industry's periodic upheavals, as successive waves of new technology have risen to overwhelm what came before. At such times, it is often the outsider with the different perspective who emerges on top.

Youth has been a more pronounced factor in the software and internet industries than in electronics and hardware. Thomas Watson was 40 when he joined the business machinery company that he later renamed IBM, building it into the first behemoth of the computing era, though he retired just as the first commercial mainframes hit the market. Ren Zhengfei, a former Chinese army officer, was 43 when he started Huawei, the communications equipment company.

Yet, both men created business empires that conform to another truism of the tech world: founder-led companies have tended to dominate the industry.

Only Lou Gerstner, a career manager, was not involved in the early days of the company where he made his greatest impact. But, by reviving a struggling IBM in the 1990s, he pulled off a turnaround that was unrivalled in the history of the tech industry – at least, until Steve Jobs returned to a founding Apple

Source: Zurijeta. Shutterstock/Pearson Education Ltd

and rebuilt it to become the world's most valuable company.

Whilst making hardware was the main route to riches in the industry's early days, the biggest fortunes in tech have been made by more intangible means: creating the software code or the online services on which the digital world increasingly depends.

Pause for thought

The uncertainty map tries to explain that varying levels of uncertainty create very different working environments and, hence, different management skills are necessary for each quadrant. Is it possible for firms to operate across all four quadrants?

Industrial firms are different: a classification

A brief look at companies operating in your town or area will soon inform you that industrial firms are very different. You may say that this is axiomatic. The point is, however, that, in terms of innovation and product development, it is possible to argue that some firms are users of technology and others are providers. For example, at the simplest level, most towns will have a range of housebuilding firms, agricultural firms, retail firms and many others offering services to local people. Such firms tend to be small in size, with little R&D or manufacturing capability of their own. They are classified by Pavitt (1994) as *supplier-dominated firms*. Many of them are very successful because they offer a product with a reliable service. Indeed, their strength is that they purchase technologies in the form of products and match

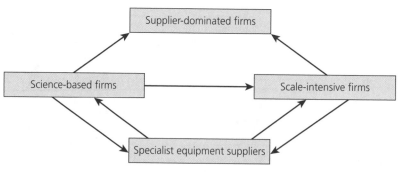

Figure 4.7 Technological linkages amongst different types of firms

Source: Pavitt, K. (1994) Sectoral patterns of technological change: towards a taxonomy and theory, *Research Policy*, vol. 13, 343–73.

these to customer needs. Such firms usually have limited, if any, product or process technology capabilities. Pavitt offers a useful classification of the different types of firms with regard to technology usage; this is shown in Figure 4.7.

At the other end of the scale are science-based firms or technology-intensive firms. These are found in the high-growth industries of the twentieth century: chemicals, pharmaceuticals, electronics, computing, etc. It is the manipulation of science and technology, usually by their own R&D departments, that has provided the foundation for the firms' growth and success. Unlike the previous classification, these firms tend to be large and would include corporations such as Bayer, Hoecht, GlaxoSmithKline, Sony and Siemens.

The third classification Pavitt refers to as scale-intensive firms, which dominate the manufacturing sector. At the heart of these firms are process technologies. It is their ability to produce high volumes at low cost that is usually their strength. They tend to have capabilities in engineering, design and manufacturing. Many science-based firms are also scale-intensive firms, so it is possible for firms to belong to more than one category. Indeed, the big chemical companies in Europe are a case in point.

Innovation in action

Miele: A €3 billion German engineering family firm

The family business was formed in 1899 and started making butter churns. Today, the firm is best known for its high-end washing machines, first introduced in 1929. Typically, they sell for £2,000 apiece. But they are built to last and many owners, including your author, will tell of machines that are still going strong after 20 years. Even Mrs Merkel, the German Chancellor, has told of her trusty family Miele washing machine when growing up as a child. Miele's sales rose by 3.8 per cent in

Source: Art Directors & TRIP/Alamy Images

2013 to €3.15 billion. The company has a 30 per cent market share of the washing machine market in Germany – much less in other European markets. It continues to manufacture in Germany and has resisted options to manufacture in cheaper labour countries (see the case study at the end of Chapter 2). Miele has resisted moving manufacturing because of the close link between its manufacturing and its R&D. It is proud of its family owned status and it enables the firm to make long-term decisions without any pressure from shareholders or stock market analysts. The firm argues that because it is a family firm this has also helped its innovation. The firm's motto is 'Immer besser', which translates to 'forever better'. This means the firm is always trying to continually improve. Currently, the firm is introducing technology into its washing machines that enables them to use power when it is at its cheapest.

The final classification is specialist equipment suppliers. This group of firms is an important source of technology for scale-intensive and science-based firms. For example, instrumentation manufacturers supply specialist measuring instruments to the chemical industry and the aerospace industry to enable these firms to measure their products and manufacturing activities accurately.

This useful classification highlights the flows of technology between the various firms. This is an important concept and is referred to in later chapters to help explain the industry life cycle in Chapter 13, the acquisition of technology in Chapter 10, the transfer of technology in Chapter 11 and strategic alliances in Chapter 8.

Organisational structures and innovation

The structure of an organisation is defined by Mintzberg (1978) as the sum total of the ways in which it divides its labour into distinct tasks and then achieves coordination amongst them. One of the problems when analysing organisational structure is recognising that different groups within an organisation behave differently and interact with different parts of the wider external environment. Hence, there is a tendency to label structure at the level of the organisation with little recognition of differences at group or department level. Nonetheless, there have been numerous useful studies exploring the link between organisational structure and innovative performance.

The seminal work by Burns and Stalker (1961) on Scottish electronic organisations looked at the impact of technical change on organisational structures and on systems of social relationships. It suggests that 'organic', flexible structures, characterised by the absence of formality and hierarchy, support innovation more effectively than do 'mechanistic' structures. The latter are characterised by long chains of command, rigid work methods, strict task differentiation, extensive procedures and a well-defined hierarchy. Many objections have been raised against this argument, most notably by Child (1973). Nevertheless, flexible rather than mechanistic organisational structures are still seen, especially within the business management literature, as necessary for successful industrial innovation. In general, an organic organisation is more adaptable, more openly

Table 4.3 Organic versus mechanistic organisational structures

Organic	Mechanistic
1 Channels of communication Open with free information flow throughout the organisation	**1 Channels of communication** Highly structured, restricted information flow
2 Operating styles Allowed to vary freely	**2 Operating styles** Must be uniform and restricted
3 Authority for decisions Based on the expertise of the individual	**3 Authority for decisions** Based on formal line management position
4 Free adaptation By the organisation to changing circumstances	**4 Reluctant adaptation** With insistence on holding fast to tried and true management principles, despite changes in business conditions
5 Emphasis on getting things done Unconstrained by formally laid out procedures	**5 Emphasis on formally laid down procedures** Reliance on tried and true management principles
6 Loose, informal control With emphasis on norm of cooperation	**6 Tight control** Through sophisticated control systems
7 Flexible on-job behaviour Permitted to be shaped by the requirements of the situation and personality of the individual doing the job	**7 Constrained on-job behaviour** Required to conform to job descriptions
8 Decision making Participation and group consensus used frequently	**8 Decision making** Superiors make decisions with minimum consultation and involvement of subordinates

Source: Slevin, D.P. and Covin, J.G. (1990) Juggling entrepreneurial style and organizational structure: how to get your act together, *Sloan Management Review*, Winter, 43–53.

communicating, more consensual and more loosely controlled. As Table 4.3 indicates, the mechanistic organisation tends to offer a less suitable environment for managing creativity and the innovation process. The subject of organisation structures is also discussed in Chapter 17 in the context of managing new product development teams.

Formalisation

Following Burns and Stalker, there have been a variety of studies examining the relationship between formalisation and innovation. There is some evidence of an inverse relationship between formalisation and innovation. That is, an increase in formalisation of procedures will result in a decrease in innovative activity. It is unclear, however, whether a decrease in procedures and rules would lead to an increase in innovation. Moreover, as was argued above, organisational planning and routines are necessary for achieving efficiencies.

Complexity

The term complexity here refers to the complexity of the organisation. In particular, it refers to the number of professional groups or diversity of specialists within the organisation. For example, a university, hospital or science-based manufacturing company would represent a complex organisation. This is because, within these organisations, there would be several professional groups. In the case of a hospital, nurses, doctors and a wide range of specialists represent the different areas of medicine. This contrasts sharply with an equally large organisation that is, for example, in the distribution industry. The management of supplying goods all over the country will be complex indeed; but it will not involve the management of a wide range of highly qualified professional groups.

Centralisation

Centralisation refers to the decision-making activity and the location of power within an organisation. The more decentralised an organisation, the fewer levels of hierarchy are usually required. This tends to lead to more responsive decision making closer to the action.

Organisational size

Size is a proxy variable for more meaningful dimensions, such as economic and organisational resources, including number of employees and scale of operation. Below a certain size, however, there is a major qualitative difference. A small business with fewer than 20 employees differs significantly in terms of resources from an organisation with 200 or 2,000 employees.

The role of the individual in the innovation process

The innovation literature has consistently acknowledged the importance of the role of the individual within the industrial technological innovation process (Boh et al. 2014; Langrish et al., 1972; Martins and Terblanche, 2003; van de Ven, 1986; Wolfe, 1994). Furthermore, a variety of key roles have developed from the literature stressing particular qualities (see Table 4.4).

Some have gone further, arguing that the innovation process is, essentially, a people process and that organisational structure, formal decision-making processes, delegation of authority and other formal aspects of a so-called well-run company are not necessary conditions for successful technological innovation. Studies have revealed that certain individuals had fulfilled a variety of roles (often informal) that had contributed to successful technological innovation.

In a study of biotechnology firms, Sheene (1991) explains that it is part of a scientist's professional obligation to keep up to date with the literature. This is achieved by extensive scanning of the literature. However, she identified feelings of guilt associated with browsing in the library by some scientists. This was, apparently, due to a fear that some senior managers might not see this as a constructive use of their time. Many other studies have also shown that the role of the individual is critical in the innovation process (Allen and Cohen, 1969; Allen, 1977; Hauschildt, 2003; Wheelwright and Clark, 1992).

Table 4.4 Key individual roles within the innovation process

Key individual	Role
Technical innovator	Expert in one or two fields. Generates new ideas and sees new and different ways of doing things. Also referred to as the 'mad scientist'.
Technical/commercial scanner	Acquires vast amounts of information from outside the organisation, often through networking. This may include market and technical information.
Boundary spanner	Similar to above, but with emphasis on personal networking and making links beyond the boundary of the firm.
Gatekeeper	Keeps informed of related developments that occur outside the organisation through journals, conferences, colleagues and other companies. Passes information on to others, finds it easy to talk to colleagues. Serves as an information resource for others in the organisation.
Product champion	Sells new ideas to others in the organisation. Acquires resources. Aggressive in championing his or her cause. Takes risks.
Project leader	Provides the team with leadership and motivation. Plans and organises the project. Ensures that administrative requirements are met. Provides necessary coordination amongst team members. Sees that the project moves forward effectively. Balances project goals with organisational needs.
Sponsor	Provides access to a power base within the organisation: a senior person. Buffers the project team from unnecessary organisational constraints. Helps the project team to get what it needs from other parts of the organisation. Provides legitimacy and organisational confidence in the project.

Source: Based on Roberts, E.B. and Fushfield, A.R. (1981) Staffing the innovative technology-based organisation, *Sloan Management Review*, Spring, 19–34.

IT systems and their impact on innovation

The impact of large IT systems on firms and the way they operate has been one of the most noticeable changes within organisations of the late 1990s and early twenty-first century. Enterprise resource planning (ERP) business software has become one of the most successful products in the world. For many firms, such as Microsoft, Owens Corning, UBS and Procter & Gamble, it has changed the way they work (Gartner, 2002). Indeed, substantial claims are made about the software's capabilities. A complete system could take several years and several hundred million dollars to deploy. The market leaders in this highly lucrative business-to-business market are SAP and Oracle. SAP has over 20,000 R/3 products installed worldwide and Oracle has installed databases in nearly every one of the world's top 500 companies. However, the impact of these systems on a firm's innovative capability is now under scrutiny. In some creative working environments, where previously autonomous and creative minds were free to explore, they are now being restricted to what is on offer via 'pull-down' menus.

ERP systems have been adopted by the majority of large private sector firms and many public sector organisations in the United Kingdom, Europe and the industrialised world in general. This growing trend towards ERP systems would not materialise unless significant advantages were to be expected from its introduction. Although there may be some isomorphic effects at work that facilitate the spread of perceived best practice and help the marketing efforts of key players in the industry to succeed, these factors on their own would not be able to explain the widespread adoption of ERP systems in the absence of real benefits.

The principal benefits that can arise from ERP systems are linked to expected gains in the efficiency and effectiveness of business processes that come about with the availability of more accurate and timely information. ERP offers integration of business functions and can reduce data collection and processing duplication efforts.

In summary, some of the potential benefits of implementing ERP systems are:

- more efficient business processes;
- reduction of costs to several business procedures;
- better coordination and cooperation between functions and different company departments;
- better management monitoring and controlling functions;
- modification and adaptation abilities accordingly to company and market requirements;
- more competitive and efficient entrance to electronic markets and electronic commerce;
- possible redesigning of ineffective business functions;
- access to globalisation and integration to the global economy;
- inventory visibility and better decision support;
- active technology for market research and media environment; and
- improving communication between partners of the channel.

Business managers of organisations with significant ERP experience suggest that ERP system introduction into an organisation amounts to a near reinvention of the organisation. ERP systems do not easily fit any organisation. ERP systems offer significant advantages, but, in order to work efficiently and effectively, they require that organisational processes be made to fit their system demands. As we will discuss below, the price to be paid for efficiency and effectiveness comes with a prescribed rigidity that may hinder innovation and creativity.

There is also a problem with the impact of ERP on the innovative climate in organisations and on the existent company operations (Johannessen et al., 2001). In short, ERP systems very often require a reconfiguration of work processes and routines. Many people, however, feel unhappy when they are asked to change established ways of doing things and they may, rightly, feel that new standardised work processes may undermine their autonomy enjoyed in current non-standardised operations. ERP systems, however, can deliver only the promised efficiency gains with a standard information set and leave no alternatives to a standardised approach. But it is not only that information processing and work routines have to be standardised; with an integrated system, everyone's performance and achievements become much more visible. Information sharing easily can be perceived as serving the purpose of tightening management control if the organisational climate has deteriorated in the ERP implementation process. If employees feel that they are losing their autonomy and that they are subjected to a culture of instant accountability, then this may have dramatic effects on their productivity and creativity and may nullify some of the potential ERP gains.

There are several ways in which ERP systems operations may have a negative impact on individual creativity. First of all, ERP systems may reduce the richness of information content when informal communication processes get increasingly replaced by standardised data exchanges made available through ERP systems. The previous section noted the role of tacit knowledge with respect to innovation and that it is embedded in social processes. If ERP becomes the key communication medium and information has to be made palatable to its data requirements, then tacit knowledge outside the system may be sidelined (Johannessen et al., 2001; Nonaka, 1991). As a consequence, explicit knowledge may get preference over tacit knowledge. But individual and group creativity is not only dependent on rich information. There are motivational factors at work as well. If ERP leads to a culture of instant control and accountability, then this may undermine the intrinsic motivation of employees and may lead to a culture where risk taking and experimentation becomes increasingly less desirable. It will always be safer to use the available ERP data than to look elsewhere for inspiration. Diligent users of the ERP system are more difficult to blame for their mistakes or lack of achievement. ERP can become a very useful legitimating tool.

More significantly, firms must recognise that ERP systems (like any database) are driven from master data, such as customer records, bill of material records (BoM), and, like other databases, are unforgiving. Get a field entry wrong and it can cause serious problems. Most likely, the internal logic of ERP systems will require large amounts of time being devoted to ensuring the correct entry is made. This is yet another example of how the IT infrastructure impacts on people's working practices. A simple example may be useful here. Consider the activities of an architect working for a major property developer in Europe. The architect develops a variety of homes for consideration and specifies the building design and materials required. Whilst, in the past, the architect may have flicked through some trade catalogues or contacted suppliers for what might be available, now all possible options available are prescribed via a pull-down menu. The advantages are clear to see: reduced time searching, order processing at the press of a few keys. But what about the impact on the creativity of the design of the building?

Unlike other IT management information systems, ERP has a dramatic impact on the way people work. Indeed, such business intelligence systems force change on an organisational structure, working practices, policies and procedures. The interdependence of the organisational components is never more clearly illuminated. Indeed, it is the knock-on effects of ERP in other aspects of the organisation, such as staff skills, budgets, performance measurement procedures, and so on, that frequently cause most angst.

The level of personal autonomy individuals have and are perceived to hold is frequently cited as one of the key people issues during the implementation of ERP systems (Sauer, 1993). There is much more emphasis on correct routines and prescribed ways of working; indeed, individual peculiar working practices have to be removed for ERP to be effective. Staff may find their daily activities dominated by highly prescriptive procedures on their computer screens. The overall perception often is one of the enterprise moving towards a more autocratic, centralised management style. There are a significant number of conflicts between the demands on the organisation of an ERP system and the necessary characteristics that have been identified within the literature for innovation to occur. For example, ERP requires discipline and aids managerial control, whereas freedom and creativity in the form of professional autonomy is continually cited as necessary for innovation to occur. Figure 4.8 provides an overview over some of the key fundamental clashes of organising principles between ERP systems requirement and the success factors of innovative organisations (Trott and Hoecht, 2004).

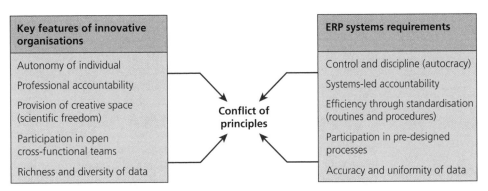

Figure 4.8 Paradox of ERP systems and innovation organisational requirements

Management tools for innovation

Many science and technology-related organisations innovate for a time, successfully exploit their innovations to gain status in their industry or field of research, then stagnate. Well-established management principles can help the leaders of an organisation sustain innovation and even recover from a period of stagnation, if they are applied correctly and vigorously. This section explores some of these principles and the relevant tools and techniques that may help leaders of firms ensure they remain leaders in their industry.

We do not have to look very far to draw up a lists of successful firms that later became less successful. Indeed, Peters and Waterman's (1982) famous study of successful firms in the 1980s that were less than successful in the 1990s is a useful reminder. Firms such as Disney, IBM, Ford, General Motors, AT&T and Philips can all be found here. If we focus on technology-intensive industries where firms are innovative for a period and then stagnate, the list may take slightly longer to compile, but it, too, provides us with a timely reminder of the need for good management and the impact that poor management can have. Firms like 3M have an impressive record of innovation. It frequently received accolades as the most innovative firm in the 1980s and 1990s, but struggled to deliver a return for its shareholders in 2000 and beyond. Pilkington Glass, similarly heralded as a world leader in glass technology as a result of its float glass process in the 1960s and 1970s, failed to follow up this technology development. It was sold in 2006 to Nipon Glass. Even Apple Inc., whilst extremely successful at present with its iPod and iPhone, struggled in the late 1980s with a series of product failures including the Pippin (a games consul) and Newton (a personal digital assistant). Most high profile of all was the dominant position once enjoyed by Nokia, only for it to fail to keep pace with Apple and Samsung.

Innovation management tools and techniques

Developing successful innovative products does not always mean using the latest patented technology. Being successful at managing innovation is rather a way of thinking and finding creative solutions within the company. With this in mind, innovation management can benefit from well-established management principles to help the leaders of an organisation sustain innovativeness and even recover from a period of stagnation, if applied correctly and vigorously. We need to look at the range of tools and techniques that have been shown to be helpful to firms as they manage the innovation process. Coombs et al. (1998) identified three major types of R&D projects and offered a template for their management. This study also identified a wide range of management tools that could be used to help facilitate the management of these projects. Ten years later, in a major review of innovation management techniques and tools, Hidalgo and Albors (2008) identified some of the most widely used innovation methodologies and tools. Together, these studies provide a comprehensive overview of innovation management tools and techniques (see Table 4.5).

There is no universal project management procedure that fits all organisations. As the previous sections have outlined, there are different types of projects (with varying levels of uncertainty) and different types of firms operating in different types of industries. This, necessarily, means a diversity of solutions is required and, thankfully, is available. It cannot be claimed that there is a closed set of developed and proven innovation management tools capable of solving all challenges faced by business. There are, however, some principles of good practice and Table 4.5 illustrates a wide range of tools and techniques. Many of these are very well known and have been used for many years, hence there is no need for an explanation of each one.

The use of these tools and techniques to improve the management of innovation within the firm cannot be considered in isolation. Firms often will use combinations of tools and techniques to ensure a particular project is successful. In addition, techniques are continually trialled, adopted and/or dropped. The benefit gained by the company depends on a combination of tools and techniques and the firm itself, and the mix of these two elements is what determines an effective outcome (see Illustration 4.2).

Illustration 4.2

The Open2-Innova8ion Tool: A software tool for rating organisational innovation performance

This publicly available web-tool has been developed to help firms evaluate their own innovation performance. It was funded by the EU Framework 7 programme. The Open2-Innova8ion Tool is an interactive, multimedia, web-based software tool for rating organisational innovation performance. It is designed for users with experience of employment in an organisation, from senior managers to all types of employees, with an interest in rating the innovation performance of their organisation. The Tool is quick and intuitive to use, and provides textual feedback, together with graphic ratings using Google meters. Feedback is based on user perceptions of organisational indicators of Innovation Enablers, Activities and Outputs to provide an overall rating of innovation performance; this can be compared with a self-rating of innovativeness. It may start some useful discussions, even if it offers few solutions (Caird et al., 2013).

Table 4.5 Innovation management tools and methodologies

Innovation management typologies	Methodologies and tools
Knowledge and technology management	Knowledge audits Knowledge mapping Technology road maps Industry foresight panels Document management IPR management
Market intelligence	Technology watch/technology search Patents analysis Business intelligence Competitor analysis Trend analysis Focus groups Customer relationship management (CRM)
Cooperation and networking	Groupware Team-building Supply chain management Industrial clustering
Human resources management	Teleworking Corporate intranets Online recruitment e-Learning Competence management
Interface management	R&D – marketing interface management Concurrent engineering
Creativity development	Brainstorming Lateral thinking TRIZ* Scamper method Mind mapping
Process improvement	Benchmarking Workflow Business process re-engineering Just in time
Innovation project management	Project management Gannt charts Project appraisal Stage-gate processes Project portfolio management
Design and product development	CAD systems Rapid prototyping Usability approaches Quality function deployment Value analysis NPD computer decision models
Business creation	Business simulation Business plan Spin-off from research to market

* This is a Russian acronym and stands for: Теория решения изобретательских задач (*Teoriya Resheniya Izobretatelskikh Zadatch*), which is a problem-solving, analysis and forecasting tool. In the English language the name is typically rendered as the Theory of Inventive Problem Solving. It was developed by the Soviet inventor and science fiction author Genrich Altshuller in the 1940s.

Source: Hidalgo and Albors (2008) and Coombs et al. (1998).

Applying the tools and guidelines

Over the past 50 years, numerous models, guidelines and tools have been developed to try to help firms achieve successful product innovation. Whilst there is debate within the literature about the detailed design and content of the models, generally the literature argues that, by following a common formalised model so that projects pass through a series of phases, an organisation will improve its level of product development (Engwall et al., 2005). What is less clear is the extent to which firms' and managers' practical actions adhere to the formalised model. Indeed, there is plenty of evidence to suggest that these models are not rigidly followed (Sauer and Lau, 1997; Werr, 1999).

Other research has found that the models serve a variety of different purposes other than that originally intended: for example, creating legitimacy, attracting support for a project, disciplining the project team and providing an illusion of a sense of control (Hodgson, 2002). It seems there is a lack of studies on the actual use of models in practice. In their study of project managers, Engwall et al. (2005) found that:

- structured development models contributed to NPD;
- they were seen as guides for action but not followed rigidly;
- models need to be applied pragmatically; and
- they provided a common language.

Analysing the range of well-established management principles that can help the leaders of an organisation sustain innovativeness and even recover from a period of stagnation is clearly necessary, but we also need to recognise that the decision to implement or use one or more of these techniques may be down to the leaders themselves. Innovation leadership is discussed either by innovation management researchers in the context of top management support or by leadership scholars under the heading of 'leadership and organisational change'. Nonetheless, the key challenges in innovation for any manager or leader are (Deschamps, 2003):

- the urge to do new things;
- the obsession to redefine customer value;
- the courage to take risks;
- an ability to manage risk;
- speed in spotting opportunities and project execution;
- a shift in focus and mindset from business optimisation to business creation.

These drivers of change could equally be used to characterise entrepreneurship (long recognised as a key factor in firm innovation) and, indeed, it is the role of the entrepreneur that is often missing from many models of innovation. Even within extremely successful companies that have had many years of innovation success, top managers have to be reminded of their responsibility to support and champion innovation leaders: those people who exercise their initiative and create change. Such people will make mistakes, but many of the tools and techniques discussed in this chapter can help firms manage risks and reduce the level of mistakes.

Innovation audit

As in financial auditing, where the purpose is to determine the health of the firm, so too can firms undertake an innovation audit. The purpose of which is to uncover

Self-assessment of your organisation's ability to facilitate innovation

	High	Low
1 Growth orientation		
2 Vigilance		
3 Commitment to technology		
4 Assemble knowledge		
5 Acceptance of risks		
6 Cross-functional cooperation		
7 Receptivity		
8 'Slack'		
9 Adaptability		
10 Diverse range of skills		

Figure 4.9 Innovation audit

areas of strength and weakness and to see how to improve the firm's performance. Many innovation tool kits have been developed over the past 30 years by government industry departments and management consultants. In the UK, NESTA continues to fund studies in this area.

A simple but, nonetheless, useful audit is shown in Figure 4.9. This uses the organisational characteristics identified in this chapter as a basis for assessing the innovation performance capability within the firm. This has been shown to provide a useful starting point for senior managers to consider how best to improve and where to invest resources.

Case study

Gore-Tex® and W.L. Gore & Associates: an innovative company and a contemporary culture

This case study explores the role of organisational management and culture within a very innovative firm, which is responsible for some very well-known products, such as the famous Gore-Tex® fabric, and, yet, few people know very much about this remarkable organisation. It is operated in a similar way to that of a cooperative or the John Lewis Partnership in the United Kingdom, where the employees are also owners. In addition, the organisation seeks to minimise management with the emphasis on action and creativity. Today, this enigmatic firm employs approximately 7,000 people in more than 45 plants and sales locations worldwide. Manufacturing operations are clustered in the United States, Germany, Scotland, Japan and China. Proprietary technologies with the versatile polymer polytetrafluoroethylene (PTFE) have resulted in numerous products for electronic signal transmission; fabric laminates; medical implants; as well as membrane, filtration, sealant and fibre technologies for a range of different industries.

→

Today, the organisation divides its products into four main groupings: medical products; fabric products; electronic products; and industrial products. Gore has approximately 650 US patents and thousands worldwide. Further details of these can be found by visiting the US Patent & Trademark office website at www.uspto.gov.

Introduction

W.L. Gore & Associates is probably best known in Europe for its Gore-Tex® product (that piece of material in your coat that keeps you dry yet allows your body to breathe), yet few people know very much about this privately owned and relatively secret company. Fewer still realise the very innovative and contemporary way the organisation is run – it seeks to have an 'unmanagement style'. Annual revenues top $3 billion. W.L. Gore is a privately held company ranking in the top 150 of the Forbes top 500 privately held companies for 2016. Indeed, W.L. Gore would rank in the Fortune 500 companies in terms of profits, market value and equity value. Given that the firm is a privately held corporation, many details of the company's operations and strategies are not widely known. Unlike publicly listed firms, it does not need to share information on such topics as marketing strategies, manufacturing processes or technology development. The company is owned primarily by its employees (known as associates) and the Gore family. W.L. Gore enterprises has more than 7,000 associates at over 45 locations around the world.

W.L. Gore & Associates was founded in 1958 in Newark, Delaware, when Bill and Vieve Gore set out to explore market opportunities for fluorocarbon polymers, especially polytetrafluoroethylene (PTFE). First developed by Bill Gore when he worked as a scientist for the Dupont Corporation. Gore could not get anyone at Dupont to invest in his new idea, so he bought the patent and went into business on his own. Within the first decade alone, W.L. Gore wire and cables landed on the moon (the firm supplied cables for the 1969 lunar missions); the company opened divisions in Scotland and Germany; and a venture partnership took root in Japan.

W.L. Gore has introduced its unique technical capabilities into hundreds of diverse products. It has defined new standards for comfort and protection for workwear and activewear (Gore-Tex®); advanced the science of regenerating tissues destroyed by disease or traumatic injuries; developed next-generation materials for printed circuit boards and fibre optics; and pioneered new methods to detect and control environmental pollution.

Gore-Tex®, a breathable fabric

In 1969, Bob Gore discovered that rapidly stretching PTFE created a very strong, microporous material (this became known as expanded PTFE, or ePTFE), which offered a range of new, desirable properties. To be effective, a waterproof fabric needs to be able to prevent moisture getting from the outside to the inside. Furthermore, a waterproof fabric must have the ability to withstand water entry in active conditions, such as walking in wind-driven rain and sitting or kneeling on a wet surface. In the case of garments for wear, especially in active conditions, perspiration is a common problem. If perspiration vapour becomes trapped inside clothing, it can condense into liquid moisture that causes dampness – and wet heat loss is 23 times faster than dry heat loss. A fabric that would enable moisture to escape and at the same time prevent moisture from entering would seem unachievable, but that is precisely what the Gore-Tex® fabric does. Raincoats incorporating the Gore-Tex® fabric were first introduced way back in 1976, hence the patent for the breathable fabric expired in 1996. However,

Source: Anthony Redpath/Getty Images

new patents are still active on improved methods of making Gore-Tex® fabric. There are now many generic versions of breathable fabric on the market. The success of the product has been witnessed largely in the 1990s as outdoor pursuits grew rapidly in popularity during this period. This led to an explosion in sales of Gore-Tex® related products, such as coats, backpacks, shoes and trousers. Indeed, clothing manufacturers who used the Gore-Tex® fabric in their garments, such as Berghaus, Karrimor and North Face, became household names, as this once esoteric specialised clothing market became mainstream.

Working within W.L. Gore Associates

The very unusual organisational structure and management sets this firm apart from its competitors. Moreover, there is some evidence to support its claim to be highly creative and innovative, as Gore–US has made all annual lists of the '100 Best Companies to Work for' in *Fortune* magazine from 1998 to 2016. Its UK firm was ranked the second best place to work in the UK in 2016 www.greatplacetowork.co.uk/. Often, it is cited as a model for effective management of innovation and the firm is proud of its heritage and how it works:

> We encourage hands-on innovation, involving those closest to a project in decision-making. Teams organize around opportunities and leaders emerge. Our founder, Bill Gore created a flat lattice organization. There are no chains of command nor pre-determined channels of communication. Instead, we communicate directly with each other and are accountable to fellow members of our multi-disciplined teams.
>
> Associates are hired for general work areas. With the guidance of their sponsors (not bosses) and a growing understanding of opportunities and team objectives, associates commit to projects that match their skills. Everyone can quickly earn the credibility to define and drive projects. Sponsors help associates chart a course in the organization that will offer personal fulfilment while maximizing their contribution to the enterprise. Leaders may be appointed, but are defined by 'followership.' More often, leaders emerge naturally by demonstrating special knowledge, skill, or experience that advances a business objective.

> Associates are committed to four basic guiding principles articulated by Bill Gore:

> freedom to encourage, help, and allow other associates to grow in knowledge, skill, and scope of fairness to each other and everyone with whom we come in contact; responsibility; the ability to make one's own commitments and keep them; and consultation with other associates before undertaking actions that could impact the reputation of the company by hitting it below the waterline.

(Gore, 2003)

Non-hierarchical corporate culture

The firm's unique structure was born out of Bill Gore's frustration with a large corporate bureaucracy; the W.L. Gore culture seeks to avoid taxing creativity with conventional hierarchy. The company encourages hands-on innovation, involving those closest to a project in decision making; hence decision making is based on knowledge rather than seniority. Teams organise around opportunities and leaders emerge based on the needs and priorities of a particular business unit. The company bases its business philosophy on the belief that, given the right environment, there is no limit to what people can accomplish.

The formula seems to have worked. In 40 years of business, W.L. Gore & Associates has developed hundreds of unique products that reflect an underlying commitment to fluoropolymer technologies. The company is passionate about innovation and has built a unique work environment to support it based on a corporate culture that encourages creativity, initiative and discovery. According to Gore:

> You won't find the trappings of a traditional corporate structure here: no rigid hierarchy, no bosses, and no predictable career ladder. Instead, you'll find direct communication, a team oriented atmosphere, and one title – associate – that's shared by everyone. It's an unusual corporate culture that contributes directly to the business' success by encouraging creativity and opportunity.

(Gore, 2003)

The last principle is meant to protect the company from inappropriate risk. Whilst employees are given wide latitude to pursue entrepreneurial opportunities, no one can initiate projects involving significant corporate financial commitments without thorough review and participation by qualified associates.

An individual starting at W.L. Gore is assigned three sponsors. A starting sponsor helps get the associate acquainted with W.L. Gore. An advocate sponsor makes sure the associate receives credit and recognition for their work and a compensation sponsor makes sure the associate is paid fairly. One person can fill all three sponsor roles. Compensation is determined by committees and relies heavily on evaluations by other associates as well as the compensation sponsor.

Employee ownership structure

The goal of Gore's highly flexible and competitive programme is to maximise freedom and fairness for each associate. The benefit plans consist of core benefits and flexible benefits. Core benefits are basic plans and services provided by Gore to all eligible associates. They include an Associate Stock Ownership Plan, holidays, profit sharing, sick pay, basic life insurance, travel accident insurance and adoption aid.

The Associate Stock Ownership Plan (ASOP) is the most valuable financial benefit. Its purpose is to provide equity ownership and, through this ownership, to provide financial security for retirement. All associates have an opportunity to participate in the growth of the company by acquiring ownership in it. Every year, W.L. Gore contributes up to 15 per cent of pay to an account that purchases W.L. Gore stock for each participating associate. W.L. Gore contributes the same percentage of pay for each associate active in the plan. An associate is eligible for this benefit after one full year of employment and qualifies for full ownership of their accounts after five years of service, when they are fully vested. Valued quarterly, W.L. Gore stock is privately held and is not traded on public markets. The ASOP, although it does not own all of the W.L. Gore shares, does own a majority of them, with the remainder owned by the Gore family.

Associates also qualify for cash profit-sharing distributions when corporate profit goals have been reached. Profit-sharing distributions typically occur an average of twice a year. In addition, each pay period associates are provided with pre-tax benefits, called flex dollars, to use for the purchase of 'flexible benefits'. These include medical plans, dental plans, long-term disability insurance, personal days, supplemental individual life insurance, family life insurance and health care or dependent care spending accounts.

Unique characteristics of ownership culture

W.L. Gore believes that, given the right environment, there is no limit to what people can accomplish. That is where the W.L. Gore lattice system comes in to play. It gives the associates the opportunity to use their own judgement, select their own projects and directly access the resources they need to be successful. Another unique aspect of the lattice system is the company's insistence that no single operating division become larger than 200 people in order to preserve the intimacy and ease of communications amongst smaller work groups. As divisions grow, they are separated into constituent parts to preserve that culture.

Discussion

This case illustrates some of the organisational characteristics that are necessary for innovation to occur. The unique organisational model seems to work for W.L. Gore. It is certainly contemporary and does seem to help to unleash creativity and to foster teamwork in an entrepreneurial environment that seeks to provide maximum freedom and support for its employees (associates). Many of the organisational characteristics are not, however, unique to W.L. Gore and there are many other firms where these characteristics can be found, such as 3M, Hewlett-Packard, Corning, Dyson, BP and Shell. It does reinforce the need for firms wishing to be innovative to adopt these characteristics (see Table 4.2).

There are several key characteristics that help make the W.L. Gore company successful, both financially and as a place to work. First, the high-quality technology and heritage of the firm that encourages an emphasis on developing superior products. Second, the use of small teams encourages direct one-on-one communication; this contributes to the ability to make timely, informed decisions and get products to market very quickly. Third, the channels of communications are very open, the lattice structure allowing all employees the freedom to meet and discuss projects, situations, concerns and share congratulations with everyone. Fourth, W.L. Gore believes that providing equity compensation to its employees establishes a sense of ownership and increased commitment amongst its employees. The ASOP programme at W.L. Gore is the majority owner of the company. Fifth, W.L. Gore provides a comprehensive set of employee benefits and is continually looking for ways to improve upon what is currently available. Sometimes, that just means re-evaluating what the employees want and need. Finally, making sure that the individual work groups do not get too large to be effective is a key element of 'right-sizing' for the company culture. This way, W.L. Gore maintains a sense of intimacy and ease of communications amongst its work groups.

Whilst the employee share ownership sounds attractive, any decrease in performance and fall in value of the shares can cause enormous resentment within the firm as they see the value of their savings decrease. And, unlike publicly listed firms, these shareholders cannot remove the managers. W.L. Gore's competitors are varied and diverse: there is no single company that competes with Gore in every product area. Firms such as Bayer, Hoecht, Corning, Dow and Du-Pont all compete in Gore's product fields: medical, fabric, industrial and electronic applications.

The business strategy pursued by W.L. Gore Asssociates has been very successful to date. However, in some of its markets, competition is beginning to emerge. Gore must decide whether it wants to become involved in and attempt to win a price war in these markets or to try to offer superior name-brand products. Alternatively, it could decide to rely on its traditional approach of utilising its R&D to develop new product applications that will enable it to enter new markets, often as the sole business offering certain product types. Gore may need to reassess its R&D activities to focus on specific and marketable new technology if it wishes to keep its position as the technological leader in many of its industries. Rather than allowing individual associates to organise and conduct their own projects, more emphasis could be placed on strategic R&D programmes where the business sees opportunities for growth to enable it to create new ventures.

Sources: Anfuso, D. (1999) 'Core values shape W.L. Gore's innovative culture', *Workforce magazine* (US), March, 48–53; Gore (2003) Extract from the W.L. Gore Associates website; Harrison, L. (2002) 'We're all the boss', *Time*, Inside Business edition, 8 April; McCall, A. (ed.) (2002) 'The firm that lets staff breathe', *The Sunday Times* (London), 24 March, '100 Best Companies to Work For', special section; Milford, M. (1996) 'A company philosophy in bricks and mortar', *New York Times*, 1 September, Sec. R, p. 5. *The Sunday Times* (2007) '100 Best Companies to Work For' supplement, 11 March.

Questions

1 Explain what happened to the Gore-Tex® brand after the patent expired. What activity can firms use to try to maintain any advantage developed during the patent protection phase?

2 List some of the wide range of products where the Gore-Tex® fabric has been applied.

3 It seems that Gore Associates is heavily oriented towards technology; what are some of the dangers of being too heavily focused on technology?

4 Cooperatives and share-ownership schemes provide many attractions and benefits, but there are also limitations; discuss these.

5 What has been the Gore strategy to achieving success in its markets? How is this strategy now being challenged?

6 Using CIM (Figure 1.9) illustrate the innovation processes within W.L. Gore.

Note: This case has been written as a basis for class discussion rather than to illustrate effective or ineffective managerial or administrative behaviour. It has been prepared from a variety of published sources, as indicated, and from observations.

Chapter summary

This chapter has helped to explain how firms can manage innovation. In particular, it explored the organisational environment and the activities performed within it that are necessary for innovation to occur. Emphasis was placed on the issue of uncertainty and how different types of projects require different types of skills.

Another key component of successful innovation management is the extent to which an organisation recognises the need for and encourages innovation. This is often easy for firms to say but it seems much more difficult for firms to do.

This chapter also examined the range of well-established management tools and methodologies that may be helpful to firms to manage innovation. In addition, several roles were identified as necessary for innovation to occur and it was stressed that often these are performed by key individuals.

Discussion questions

1 Can organisations operate across the entire spectrum of innovation activities?

2 Explain the fundamental dilemma facing organisations and the tensions it creates.

3 Discuss the impact to the firm of changes in architectural knowledge and component knowledge.

4 Explain how management tools for innovation may help a firm regain its innovative performance.

5 Explain how organisational characteristics can facilitate the innovation process.

6 Explain the key individual roles within the innovation process and the activities they perform.

Key words and phrases

Dilemma of innovation management *118*

Slack *118*

Ambidexterity *119*

Managing uncertainty *120*

Exploratory research *122*

Architectural knowledge *125*

Receptivity *129*

Gatekeeper *138*

Product champion *138*

References

Adams, R., Bessant, J. and Phelps, R. (2006) Innovation management measurement: a review, *International Journal of Management Reviews*, vol. 8, no. 1, 21–47.

Allen, T.J. (1977) *Managing the Flow of Technology*, MIT Press, Cambridge, MA.

Allen, T.J. and Cohen, W.M. (1969) Information flow in research and development laboratories, *Administrative Science Quarterly*, vol. 14, no. 1, 12–19.

Benner, M. J. and Tushman, M. (2002) Process management and technological innovation: a longitudinal study of the photography and paint industries, *Administrative Science Quarterly*, vol. 47, no. 4, 676–707.

Birdi, K., Leach, D. and Magadley, W. (2012) Evaluating the impact of TRIZ creativity training: an organizational field study, *R&D Management*, vol. 42, 315–26

Boh, W.F., Evaristo, R. and Ouderkirk, A. (2014) Balancing breadth and depth of expertise for innovation: a 3M story, *Research Policy*, vol. 43, no. 2, 349–66

Brunsson, N. (1980) The functions of project management, *Journal of Management Studies*, vol. 10, no. 2, 61–71.

Burns, T. and Stalker, G.M. (1961) *The Management of Innovation*, Tavistock, London.

Caird, S., Hallett, S. and Potter, S. (2013) The Open2-Innova8ion Tool – a software tool for rating organisational innovation performance, *Technovation*, vol. 33, no. 10, 381–5.

Child, J. (1973) Predicting and understanding organisational structure, *Administrative Science Quarterly*, vol. 18, 168–85.

Coombs, R., McMeekin, A. and Pybus, R. (1998) Toward the development of benchmarking tools for R&D project management, *R&D Management*, vol. 28, no. 3, 175–86.

Cooper, R.G. (1986) *Winning at New Products*, Addison-Wesley, Reading, MA.

Deschamps, J.P. (2003) 'Innovation and leadership', in L. Shavina (ed.) *International Handbook on Innovation*, Elsevier, Amsterdam.

Dobini, C. (2010) The relationship between an innovation orientation and competitive strategy, *International Journal of Innovation Management*, vol. 14, no. 2, 331–57.

Engwall, M., Kling, R. and Werr, A. (2005) Models in action: how management models are interpreted in new product development, *R&D Management*, vol. 35, no. 4, 427–39.

Gartner (2002) How Proctor & Gamble runs its global business on SAP, CS-15-3473, Research Note, 25 February 2000.

Hannan, M. and Freeman, J. (1984) Structural inertia and organizational change, *American Sociological Review*, vol. 49, 149–64.

Hauschildt, J. (2003) 'Promoters and champions in innovations: development of a research paradigm', in Shavinina, L. (ed.) *The International Handbook on Innovation*, Elsevier, Oxford.

Henderson, R. and Clark, K. (1990) Architectural innovation: the reconfiguration of existing product and the failure of established firms, *Administrative Science Quarterly*, vol. 35, 9–30.

Hidalgo, A. and Albors, J. (2008) Innovation management techniques and tools: a review from theory and practice, *R&D Management*, vol. 38, no. 2, 113–127.

Hodgson, D. (2002) Disciplining the professional: The case of project management. *The Journal of Management Studies*, vol. 39, no. 6, 803.

Johannessen, J., Olaisen, J. and Olsen, B. (2001) Management of tacit knowledge: the importance of tacit knowledge, the danger of information technology, and what to do about it, *Journal of Information Management*, vol. 21, no. 1, 3–20.

Kang, K. and Kang, J. (2009) How do firms source external knowledge for innovation? Analysing effects of different knowledge sourcing methods, *International Journal of Innovation Management*, vol. 13, no. 1, 1–17.

Langrish, J., Gibbons, M., Evans, W.G. and Jevons, F.R. (1972) *Wealth from Knowledge*, Macmillan, London.

Leonard-Barton, D. (1987) Implementing structured software methodologies: a case of innovation in process technology, *Interfaces,* vol. 17, no. 3, 6–17.

McCall, A. (ed.) (2002) The firm that lets staff breathe, *Sunday Times* (London), 24 March, '100 Best Companies to Work For', special section.

Martins, E.C. and Terblanche, F. (2003) Building organizational culture that stimulates creativity and innovation, *European Journal of Innovation Management*, vol. 6, no. 1, 64–74.

Mintzberg, H. (1978) Patterns in strategy formulation, *Management Science*, vol. 24, 934–48.

Nelson, R.R. and Winter, S.G. (1982) *An Evolutionary Theory of Economic Change*, Harvard University Press, Cambridge, MA.

Nonaka, I. (1991) The knowledge-creating company, *Harvard Business Review*, November–December, 96–104.

O'Reilly, C.A. and Tushman, M.L. (2008) Ambidexterity as a dynamic capability: resolving the innovators' dilemma, *Research in Organization Behavior*, vol. 28, 185–206.

Pavitt, K. (1994) Sectoral patterns of technological change: towards a taxonomy and theory, *Research Policy*, 13, 343–73.

Pearson, A.W. (1983) Planning and monitoring in research and development: a 12 year review of papers in *R&D Management*, vol. 13, no. 2, 107–16.

Pearson, A. (1991) 'Managing innovation: an uncertainty reduction process', in Henry, J. and Walker, D. (eds) *Managing Innovation*, Sage/Oxford University Press, London, 18–27.

Peters, T.J. and Waterman, R.H. (1982) *In Search of Excellence,* Harper and Row, New York.

Porter, M.E. and Ketels, C.H.M. (2003) *UK Competitiveness: Moving to the next stage*, Department of Trade and Industry, London.

Prajogo, D.I. and Ahmed, P.K. (2006) Relationships between innovation stimulus, innovation capacity and innovation performance, *R&D Management*, vol. 36, no. 5, 499–515.

Sauer, C. (1993) *Why Information Systems Fail: A Case Study Approach*, Alfred Waller, Henley-on-Thames.

Sauer, C. and Lau, C. (1997) Trying to adopt systems development methodologies – a case-based exploration of business users' interests, *Information Systems Journal*, vol. 7, 255–75.

Sheene, M.R. (1991) The boundness of technical knowledge within a company: barriers to external knowledge acquisition, paper presented at R&D Management Conference on *The Acquisition of External Knowledge*, Kiel, Germany.

Smart, A.U., Bunduchi, R. and Gerst, M. (2010) The costs of adoption of RFID technologies in supply networks, *International Journal of Operations and Production Management*, vol. 30, no. 4, 423–47.

Smith, W.K. and Tushman, M.L. (2005) Managing strategic contradictions: a top management model for managing innovation streams, *Organization Science*, vol. 16, no. 5, 522–36.

Souder, W.E. (1987) *Managing New Product Innovations*, Lexington Books, Lexington, MA.

Trott, P. and Hoecht, A. (2004) Enterprise resource planning (ERP) and its impact on innovation, *International Journal of Innovation Management*, vol. 8, no. 3, 381–98.

Troilo, G., De Luca, L.M. and Atuahene-Gima, K. (2014) More innovation with less? A strategic contingency view of slack resources, information search, and radical innovation, *Journal of Product Innovation Management*, vol. 31, 259–77.

van der Panne, G., van Beers, C. and Kleinknecht, A. (2003) Success and failure of innovation: a review of the literature, *International Journal of Innovation Management,* vol. 7, no. 3, 309–38.

van de Ven, A.H. (1986) Central problems: the management of innovation, *Management Science*, vol. 32, no. 5, 590–607.

Wei, Z., Yi, Y. and Guo, H. (2014) Organizational learning ambidexterity, strategic flexibility, and new product development, *Journal of Product Innovation Management*, vol. 31, no. 4, 832–47.

Werr, A. (1999) *The Language of Change – the roles of methods in the work of management consultants*, Economic Research Institute, Stockholm School of Economics, Stockholm.

Wheelwright, S.C. and Clark, K.B. (1992) *Revolutionising Product Development*, The Free Press, New York.

Wolfe, R.A. (1994) Organisational innovation: review and critique and suggested research directions, *Journal of Management Studies*, vol. 31, no. 3, 405–31.

Further reading

For a more detailed review of the innovation management literature, the following develop many of the issues raised in this chapter:

Boh, W.F., Evaristo, R. and Ouderkirk, A. (2014) Balancing breadth and depth of expertise for innovation: a 3M story, *Research Policy*, vol. 43, no. 2, 349–366.

Berkhout, A.J., Hartmann, D. and Trott, P. (2010) Connecting technological capabilities with market needs using a cyclic innovation model, *R&D Management*, vol. 40, no. 5, 474–90.

Caird, S., Hallett, S. and Potter, S. (2013) The Open2-Innova8ion Tool – a software tool for rating organisational innovation performance, *Technovation*, vol. 33, no. 10, 381–85.

Dobini, C. (2010) The relationship between an innovation orientation and competitive strategy, *International Journal of Innovation Management*, vol. 14, no. 2, 331–57.

Wei, Z., Yi, Y. and Guo, H. (2014) Organizational learning ambidexterity, strategic flexibility, and new product development, *Journal of Product Innovation Management*, vol. 31, no. 4, 832–47.

Chapter 5
Operations and process innovation

Introduction

Effective research and development (R&D) requires close links with the part of the organisation that produces the product (or service) – that is, operations. Many new product ideas are based on existing products and may be developed from within the production or service operations function and it is necessary, therefore, to examine the role of operations and its management when studying innovation. These innovative ideas are likely to be ideas for improvement in the process of manufacture or delivery of the product or service. A large number of these ideas may be modest and incremental rather than radical, but the combined effect of many small innovative ideas may be substantial. The case study at the end of this chapter examines a new paperboard material with unusual properties that may enable the paper packaging industry to compete with plastic packaging. It shows the role of innovation and product development within a process industry and how, in such industries, innovation occurs on the production line rather than in laboratories.

Chapter contents

Learning objectives

When you have completed this chapter you will be able to:

- recognise the importance of innovation in operations management;
- recognise the importance of sales volume in product design;
- recognise the importance of design in the process of making and delivering a product or service;
- appreciate the different relationships between product and process innovation;
- recognise that much innovation is not patentable; and
- provide an understanding of a number of approaches to design and process management.

Operations management

Most organisations provide items that are a combination of product and service elements – for example, a restaurant provides a product (the food) and a service (delivery to your table). The term operations management was coined to bring together the skills and techniques developed in the manufacturing and service sectors in order to help encourage the transfer of the best practices. In an age of global mass production and competition, it is often the service element of any purchase that gives the supplying operation its crucial competitive advantage. Innovation within the operations function is, therefore, crucial in achieving the organisation's strategic objectives.

Operations management is about the control of a conversion process from an *input* to an *output* (see Table 5.1).

This chapter considers the **design** and management of the conversion processes given in Table 5.1. A large percentage of the asset base of the organisation normally lies within these boundaries, and it is essential that the assets be used to effect, to gain an advantage in this increasingly competitive world. In particular, the degree of innovation involving these expensive assets is crucial, if the organisation is to prosper. Figure 5.1 illustrates the operation function and includes the elements of design, planning and control and improvement.

To this process (Figure 5.1) need to be added three other very important dimensions:

1 the customer who becomes part of the process, as in self-service supermarkets or in the education process taking place in tutorials;
2 information from customers (complaints or compliments), market research or government agencies (standards, laws, EU directives, etc.); and
3 the physical and business environment in which the organisation operates.

Table 5.1 Operations inputs and outputs

Organisation	Input	Processes include	By-products	Output
A car producer	Material (steel, rubber, glass)	Welding	Material waste	Cars
	People	Painting	Heat waste	Salaries
	Skills	Assembly		
	Energy			
A university	Students	Lectures	Waste paper	Graduates
	Teachers	Seminars		Academic papers
	Information	Research		
	Knowledge	Learning		
A hospital	Doctors	Medical operations	Clinical waste	Healthy patients
	Patients			
	Medicines	Radiotherapy		
	Knowledge			
A publishing company	Paper	Editing	Paper pulp	Books
	Ink	Binding	Chemical waste	Royalties
	Author's work	Printing		

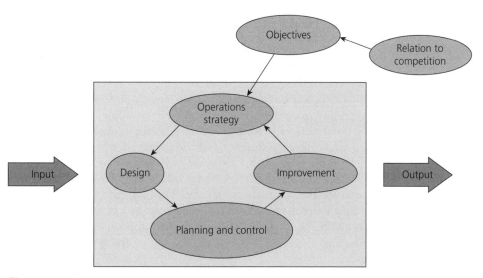

Figure 5.1 The operations manager's role

Source: Adapted from Slack, N. et al. (2004) *Operations Management,* 4th edn, © Pearson Education Limited.

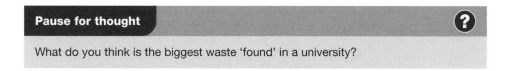

Pause for thought

What do you think is the biggest waste 'found' in a university?

The nature of design and innovation in the context of operations

Some innovations are described as 'leading edge' and are based upon work from within the R&D laboratories and may involve patent applications. Innovation (as we saw in Chapter 1) may also be a new application of an existing technique to a different situation. Something that is new and innovative to one company may be a tried and tested procedure or product to another. Also, every innovative idea may not be suitable to patent but, to those concerned, the novelty, the ingenuity, the problems associated with its introduction and the cost–benefit to the organisation may be just the same.

Although in many companies designers quite frequently make inventions, designing and inventing are different in kind. Design is usually more concerned with the process of *applying* scientific principles and inventions (Roy and Weild, 1993). Design is a compromise between the different elements that constitute the design. For example, increasing the wall thickness of a product made from steel may increase the product's strength, reliability and durability, but only with the consequential increase in product weight and cost.

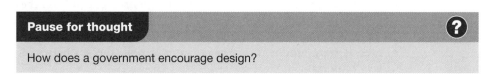

Pause for thought

How does a government encourage design?

Design requirements

The objective of design is to meet the needs and expectations of customers. Good design, therefore, starts and ends with the customer. Marketing gathers information from customers and *potential* customers to identify customer needs and expectations. Expectations differ from customer to customer – indeed, they may vary from day to day from the same customer. For example, what would constitute the design of a good university lecture will vary from one student to another. The same student also might have a different need and expectation from the lecturer after a long lunch break in the union bar. Customer expectations vary.

Working with marketing, the product and service designer then designs a specification for the product and service. This is a complex task involving complex inter-relating variables and aspects of the company's objectives. To help in the specification process, Slack et al. (2007) remark that all products and services can be considered as having three aspects (the case study at the end of this chapter illustrates this point):

- a *concept* – the expected benefits the customer is buying;
- a *package* of component products that provides those benefits defined in the concepts, i.e., what the customer actually purchases and constitutes the ingredients of the design; and
- the *process*, which defines the relationship between the component product and services by which the design fulfils its concept.

A meal in a restaurant consists of products (the food and drink) and services, such as the style of waitress service and background music. Some products or service elements are core to the operation and could not be removed without destroying the nature of the package. Other parts of the package serve to enhance the core. In a fast-food restaurant, the food and the speed of delivery are essential core elements of the package whilst the ambience and layout of the restaurant supports the core (see Illustration 5.1).

By changing the core, or adding or subtracting supporting services, organisations can provide different packages and, therefore, design very different products and services. In a fast-food restaurant, the customer may order the food at the counter (and possibly pay the bill) and stand for a moment or two until the choice is delivered in disposable containers. The service is substantially different from that purchased in an exclusive restaurant.

Another example of product design comes from Braun, a leading European manufacturer of small domestic appliances. Braun has over 60 per cent of its sales from products with less than 5 years from product launch. Given the design brief to combine together, and perform as least as well as, three specialist kitchen appliances, the designers applied 10 industrial design principles to the Braun Multimix product (see Illustration 5.2). For a similar list of design principles in the service sector, see Van Looy et al. (2003), Chapter 15.

The different examples of the design parameters considered illustrate the complexity of the process of design. The design brief depends on the market for which the product or service is created. For example, the aesthetics of a domestic water tap is not important when mounted out of sight under the kitchen sink. If, however, it were mounted in a visible application, the aesthetics of the tap would be very important.

A fast-food restaurant

The success of fast-food restaurants like McDonald's could be due to a number of factors, but amongst the most important would be the design of its operating system that ensures consistency and uniformity of its *products* and *service* in all its premises. In London, New York, Vancouver and Hong Kong, the customer will be familiar with the layout and decor and will know what food to expect. This recipe for success has been duplicated and copied by competitive organisations the world over.

The original key innovation was to have a very simple menu of just three foods and six drinks. This simplicity allowed straightforward cooking and preparation procedures that ensured consistent product quality. McDonald's was able to influence and manage its supply chain to ensure uniformity of raw material, again helping the consistency of product produced.

Fast-food restaurants often have other operational characteristics that contribute to their success. If there is a counter to queue at, it will be well away from the door – a *fast*-food restaurant would *not* want to advertise a queue. You pay for the food in advance, avoiding the need to revisit the counter.

A Burger King store manager said: 'One of the things that we're constantly looking at is, how do we prepare for our rush periods and a pre-rush period? How can we get our condiments, utensils, napkins, and all of that prepared, so that, when a lunch rush comes, you're highly efficient? You're not having to run to the back room to get supplies; they're all appropriated by the pick-up window right in your space. So those are things that you've really got to be ready for.'

Simple menu, simple procedures, standard facilities and good operations management combine to give a cost-effective operation.

Source: Adapted from Slack, N. et al. (2007) *Operations Management*, 5th edn, Pearson, London.

A design spectrum ranges from the concept designer, whose primary concern is ensuring technical excellence, to the focus of the industrial designer on manufacturability and the ease of use of the product. For example, the design team involved in the manufacture of a hi-fi set would include:

- an electronics engineer concerned with the ability of the electrical circuits to faithfully produce sound from the CD – i.e. the function of the product;
- the marketing department members who would be concerned about the look of the product, i.e. the aesthetics, the ease of use, the market price, and so on;
- an industrial engineer who will be concerned with the sales volume required; how the product is to be made and assembled, i.e. the operations tasks involved in creating the product;
- consideration of the packaging requirements for items on display for protection during transport.

In this illustration, the knowledge required by a designer in the design spectrum ranges from acoustics, electronics, mechanics, plastic processing technology and industrial engineering to ergonomics and is, therefore, so broad and complex that no one person can be professionally competent in the whole range of disciplines required. In addition to their own specific competence, the designer also needs an appreciation of the problems of other elements of the design spectrum. Managing such a diverse range of disciplines is a complex matter.

Illustration 5.2

Design principles at Braun AG

1 *Usefulness*. The product was designed with the electric motor aligned vertically with the attachments (competitive products have horizontal motors and vertical attachments requiring a more complex gearbox).

2 *Quality*. Braun designers emphasised four aspects of quality:

   (a) Versatility – the design included the full range of expected tasks required in cooking: mixing, blending, kneading and chopping.

   (b) High mechanical efficiency – providing high performance across the range of required tasks.

   (c) Safety features – to prevent contact with moving parts.

   (d) Integrating – injection moulding of the main housings into a single manufacturing tool.

3 *Ease of use*. Great emphasis was placed on the human engineering of the product to ensure ease of use and cleaning.

4 *Simplicity*. What was relevant was stressed, what was superfluous was omitted.

5 *Clarity*. The need for complex instructions was avoided. For example, inserting attach-

ments automatically set the required motor speed.

6 *Order*. All the details of the product had a logical and meaningful place.

7 *Naturalness*. The designers avoided any contrived or artificially decorative elements.

8 *Aesthetics*. Although not a primary objective, it was achieved by simplicity, attention to detail and the quest for order and naturalness.

9 *Innovation*. Braun was committed to achieving long-lasting appeal for its design so the innovations involved were carefully developed and managed.

10 *Truthfulness*. The principle that 'only honest design can be good design' was applied, avoiding any attempt to play on people's emotions and weaknesses.

This approach has been successful in producing many new products and the aesthetics of Braun's products have been recognised, with samples on display in the Museum of Modern Art in New York.

Source: Adapted from Slack, N. et al. (2007) *Operations Management*, 5th edn, Pearson, London.

Design and volumes

All the operations management functions involve making decisions – some are tactical or structured and have short-term consequences whilst others are more strategic with longer-term implications for both the operations function and the organisation as a whole. One such major decision relates to the implications of the production **volume** required.

The highly skilled eighteenth-century craftsman making furniture at the rate of a few per year is a different type of person from the individual on a twenty-first-century assembly line making furniture at a production rate of hundreds per day. As well as a different type of person, the machinery, the processing techniques used, the materials and the design will also be very different. Choosing the most appropriate and cost-effective method of manufacture is critical to the continued success of the organisation.

When a designer first has an innovative idea for a product, he may have made (possibly make himself) a model to look at and to handle in order to help develop the idea. He may want to show this model to his colleagues or potential customers. Even with all the modern technology available (CAD/CAM, etc.) the 'one-off' models are produced frequently to refine the design or to help gauge customer interest in the product (as witnessed by the concept cars seen at motor shows). At this stage in the innovation process, detailed drawings may not be required or appropriate and highly skilled and expensive personnel therefore make the product. At this stage of a product life cycle, the term used to describe the manufacturing process is the *project method of manufacture*. Projects are unique or one-off and the required disciplines and techniques involved can be found in projects of all scales, from an academic dissertation to that of building the Channel Tunnel.

To illustrate this point, consider the development of a simple product such as a toolbox. The design engineer (or innovator), after preliminary meetings with the marketing people and/or potential customers, makes a scale model of the product. In the earliest stage of this product, it is best made by the personnel, machinery and techniques involved in a *project* style of production process. The innovator or designer listens to the observations and is able to reflect on these points in the development of the design (see Figure 5.2).

The design is well received and, after minor modifications, the design team decides to have a sample batch made (using common fasteners) by the operations function to help evaluate the market. The toolbox is shown to a range of customers who are each keen to buy a large batch at a competitive price. The industrial design team recognises that, by changing the design and avoiding the need for fasteners, investing in tools to shape the individual elements of the box and welding the components together, the assembly time will be reduced and substantial costs saved. *As the required volume increases, the most appropriate method of manufacture changes.*

Another key point is that assembly skills required to produce the product have become *embedded in the process machinery* and the workers involved have become machine minders (see Illustration 5.3 on the production of blocks on HMS *Victory*). If the volume required increases even more, by having robots on the assembly line the direct labour involved is further reduced. If the product demand rises even further, it may be appropriate that the product is redesigned again and made out of a plastic material (lighter and stronger) requiring investment in a very different processing technology.

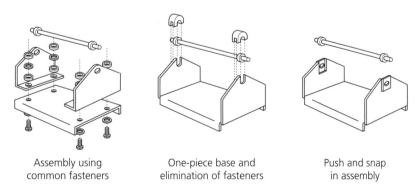

| Assembly using common fasteners | One-piece base and elimination of fasteners | Push and snap in assembly |

Figure 5.2 Design simplification

Illustration 5.3

Innovation and design in the manufacturing process

The first use of machine tools in mass production was during the Napoleonic Wars in the early 1800s. The British Navy, based in Portsmouth, had a need for 100,000 blocks (blocks house the sail ropes) per annum both to equip new ships and to provide spares. For example, HMS *Victory* alone required 900 blocks and each of these was individually carved by skilled craftsmen. Because the blocks were subject to storm, sea water, wind, ice and sun, each ship sensibly would set sail with a full set of replacements and the many suppliers just could not cope with such a high demand.

Marc Brunel (born in France in 1769) was, in 1798, dining with the British aide-de-camp in Washington, DC, a Major General Hamilton, when the conversation turned to ships and navies and to the particular problems with the manufacture of these wooden blocks. This was an opportunity to innovate in the process of manufacture and Brunel seized it. His idea was to simplify the manufacturing process into many more stages and to design specialist machines for each part of the operation of manufacture, thus enabling the large volume production of blocks.

In 1799, and with the help of an introduction from General Hamilton to Earl Spencer of Althorp, Brunel persuaded the British Navy to install the 43 Brunel-designed machine tools in a factory in the naval dockyards in Portsmouth. By 1807, the facility was providing all the needs of the Navy with only 10 unskilled men. Moreover, as the human element had been much removed from the process, the resulting blocks were far more likely to be consistent in dimensions and, therefore, of 'better' quality. The machines were still in use over 100 years later and 7 are on display in the Portsmouth Naval Museum.

HMS *Victory*

Brunel also applied the same innovative process design logic to other manufacturing problems. In 1809, he was shocked to see the damaged feet of returning war veterans that had been caused by their poorly made and fitted footwear. Therefore, he designed a set of machines that produced boots and shoes in 9 different sizes with 24 disabled soldiers manning the machines. The boots and shoes were very successful and, in 1812, the production volume was expanded to meet the Army's total requirements.

Brunel's son, Isambard Kingdom Brunel, designed and built steamships, railways and many bridges for which he is correctly revered as one of most influential engineers in British history. However, most of what we consume and take for granted is based on the innovation in the processes of manufacture of 200 years ago by men such as Marc Brunel, who introduced the concepts of mass production.

Source: www.brunelenginehouse.org.uk/people Accessed 10 April 2015; and the Portsmouth Naval Museum, United Kingdom.

Craft-based products

Some products are craft-based and only ever will be made in small volumes – for example, products from the *haute couture* fashion houses. Unique gowns are hand-made by very skilled personnel and paraded at the fashion show (a new product launch). The designs are 'copied' by other organisations and there is a rush to get copies made and supplied to the high street retailers. These copies may look similar but are usually made from different materials using different techniques and are, consequently, less costly to make and to purchase. The operations management of the supplier to the high street has to be able to respond very quickly to get the goods to the market before the fashion changes. The flexibility and speed of response of the operation is, therefore, critical to the success of the organisation. In this illustration, good marketing is also vital to avoid the end-of-season excess stocks that ambitious and unrealised sales can cause.

Pause for thought

Is the illustration concerning block manufacture for HMS *Victory* the first example of a mass production system?

Design simplification

The purpose of design is to develop things that satisfy needs and meet expectations. By making the design such that the product is easy to produce, the designer enables the operation to *consistently* deliver these features.

If the product is simple to make, the required quality management procedures will be less complex, easy to understand and, therefore, likely to be more effective. If a design is easy to make, there will be fewer rejects during the manufacturing process and less chance that a substandard product reaches the customer. Referring to the toolbox illustration (Figure 5.2), the reduction in the number of components from over 30 to fewer than 5, makes material control simpler. This, in turn, leads to simpler purchasing of components and less complex facility layouts. The same logic applies equally well in service sector applications (Brown et al., 2001; Johnston and Clark, 2001).

The application of technology and the technique of 'concurrent engineering' (where research, design and development work closely or in parallel rather than in sequence) have made important contributions to this area of management (Waller, 1999). Innovation within the manufacturing function involves searching for new ways of saving costs and is a continual process, and the closer designers work with operations and marketing personnel, the more likely the organisation is to succeed. This point is developed in the quality function deployment (QFD) section below.

It can take several years and cost millions of pounds to plan and build a major assembly facility, such as a car plant. With such a huge investment it is essential that the design of the product is 'correct' at an early stage, as errors detected later can be prohibitively expensive to rectify.

Reverse engineering

The process of duplicating an existing component, subassembly or product, without the aid of drawings, documentation or computer model is known as reverse engineering.

Reverse engineering can be viewed as the process of analysing a product to:

- identify the components and their interrelationships;
- create representations of the product in another form;
- create the physical representation of that product.

Reverse engineering is very common in such diverse fields as software engineering, entertainment, automotive, consumer products, microchips, chemicals, electronics and mechanical designs. For example, when a new design comes to market, competing manufacturers may buy one and disassemble it to learn how it was built and how it works. A chemical company may use reverse engineering to defeat a patent on a competitor's manufacturing process. In software engineering, good source code is often a **variation** of other good source code.

In some situations, designers give a shape to their ideas by using clay, plaster, wood, or foam rubber, but a CAD model is needed to enable the manufacturing of the part. Reverse engineering provides a way of creating the physical model, which is the source of information for the CAD model.

Another reason for reverse engineering is to compress product development times. In the intensely competitive global market, manufacturers are constantly seeking new ways to shorten lead-times to market a new product. Rapid product development (RPD) refers to recently developed technologies and techniques that assist manufacturers and designers in meeting the demands of reduced product development time. For example, injection-moulding companies must drastically reduce the tool and die development times. By using reverse engineering, a three-dimensional product or model can be captured quickly in digital form, remodelled, and exported for rapid prototyping/tooling or rapid manufacturing.

Reverse engineering enables the duplication of an existing part by capturing the component's physical dimensions, features and material properties. Reverse engineering is, typically, cost effective only if the items to be reverse engineered reflect a high investment or will be reproduced in large quantities. Reverse engineering of a part may be attempted, even if it is not cost effective, if the part is absolutely required and is mission-critical to a system.

Process design

The process design is based on the technology being used within the process. The metal-forming processes, the chemical processing industry, the plastic material processing and electronic assembly are all sophisticated subjects with their own literature.

In order to illustrate a feature of innovation within process design, consider one of the important elements of operations – that of the design of the layout of the facility providing the goods or service. In service-type operations, the customer may be inside and will have **visibility** of the company's operations function and the significance of layout is even more important.

If an employee spends his working day assembling automotive car seats on an assembly line, he quickly becomes expert in that area of manufacture and design.

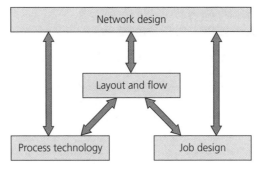

Figure 5.3 The design of processes

Most people spend the bulk of their 'awake' time involved with work and enjoy talking about their job, if the opportunity arises. In all organisations, it is the intellect of the employees that is the source of innovation and it is the role of senior managers to create an atmosphere to encourage appropriate intellectual activity, if the organisation is to prosper. We go to art galleries or concerts to be entertained and inspired and so it should be in our place of work, in order that the elusive spark of innovation is encouraged.

The importance of the working environment is also recognised in the consideration given to the planning and layout of whole business areas (Wallis, 1995) and university campuses. The Chinese have Feng Shui, which is devoted to the impact of these factors on our working and personal environment. The design of the process is linked with the technology involved in the process and is, fundamentally, linked both to the organisation and job design.

Figure 5.3 models the relationship between the elements of process design and this is as applicable to the service sector as it is to the manufacturing sector. The flow of product within a factory operation may correspond to the flow of the customer (as with an airport design) or of information (as in the headquarters of a bank). The impact on the people involved in delivering the service is clear.

The product design engineer considers the ergonomics of the product, such as a car seat (a key feature in a car purchase decision), whilst the process design engineer considers the ergonomics of a workstation on an assembly line.

In the service sector, the process design parameters of minimising the flow of information are even more critical as the customer is often within the organisation itself. Customers may be made part of the process, as in carrying their own luggage at airports or serving themselves in what is, essentially, the organisation's stock room at the supermarket. Clear signs and directions, easy-to-understand routes through the operation, understandable forms and approachable staff are all features of a well-designed service system. These are examples of *keeping things simple* – if the customer does not have to communicate with an employee to obtain the service, there is less chance for communication and quality problems. Think of and compare the children's party game of Chinese whispers with the processing of paperwork or messages through several different departments in a large organisation. At every point of information transfer there is an opportunity for the quality of the information to be degraded.

Innovation in action

Be creative about distribution

'Our consumers tell us the number one reason why they don't buy Jones Soda is because they can't find it,' says Jonathan Ricci, CEO of Jones Soda.

When Jones Soda tried to launch its range of drinks in Seattle, it found it difficult to get products into the established retail outlets, such as supermarkets and convenience stores, as these were dominated by the big soft drink brands.

Rather than give up, they looked at the other types of stores to which their target customers liked to go – snowboarding shops, tattoo parlours and music retailers – and provided them with chillers and a supply of drinks. In these retailers there was no competition, and the brand quickly built up enough sales and customer loyalty that the main distributors then wanted to get in on the action.

Source: 100 Thoughts (2010) HSBC, London.

Source: Newscast Online/Alamy Images

Process design and innovation

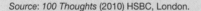

There can be few who doubt the importance of process innovation to the firm. Famous examples, such as Ford's Model T production line, Pilkington's float glass production process and SAP's Enterprise Resource Planning (ERP) systems, have shown clearly that when it comes to delivering benefits to the firm it is process innovations that can generate enormous wealth for the firm.

Given its widely acknowledged importance, process innovation has received much less attention than product innovation in the literature on innovation management. This may be because product innovations are visible, whereas process innovations frequently are invisible. Indeed, Rosenberg argued that process innovations have been subsumed into treatments of productivity and that many of the process innovations that firms make are silent, requiring little strategic decision making (Rosenberg, 1982). It is, therefore, not surprising that the following idiom often is quoted in the industry: 'Product innovations are for show whereas process innovations are for dough.' Yet, in a major review of the literature of why firms engage in process innovation, Reichstein and Salter (2006) found that product and process innovations are interdependent.

Process industries are characterised by:

- high production speed, short throughput time;
- rigid process control;

- high capital investment;
- clear determination of capacity, one routing for all products, limited volume flexibility;
- low product complexity;
- low added value;
- strong impact of changeover times;
- small number of production steps;
- limited number of products.

(Fransoo (1994) and Wallace (1998))

A good example of such an industry is the food packaging industry. These are products we handle every day as we prepare and eat food. For example, a great deal of success has been achieved by a few packaging innovations. In the beverages sector, innovations such as Tetrapak, PET bottles, and in-can systems (such as the Guinness 'In-can-system'), have achieved numerous awards, market share improvements and improved profitability for the firms involved. In all of these cases, significant investment in production process technology was required and major manufacturing changes were introduced.

Process innovations are an important source for increased productivity and they can help a firm gain competitive advantage. In the food industry, process innovations often are associated with the introduction of new plant, equipment or machinery. The introduction of a cost-reducing process often is accompanied by changes in product design and materials, whilst new products frequently require the

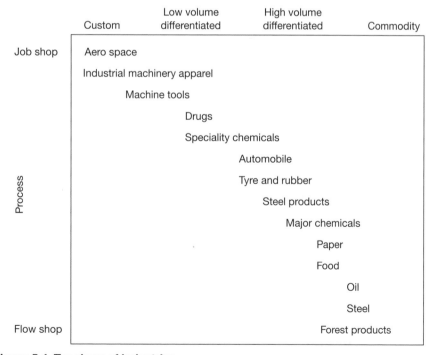

Figure 5.4 Typology of industries

Source: Taylor, S.G., Seward, S.M. and Bolander, S.F. (1981) Why the process industries are different, *Production and Inventory Management Journal*, vol. 22, no. 4, 9–24.

development of new equipment. In practice, product and process innovation are interwoven and any distinction between them is arbitrary. Yet, virtually every book on technological change has compared innovations in products with innovations in processes (Simonetti et al., 1995).

The relationship between product and process innovation

In a major review of the constructs of product and process innovations, Simonetti et al. (1995) conclude that 97 per cent of innovations incorporate product and process innovation attributes.

Process innovation can be defined as new activities introduced into a firm's production or service operations to achieve lower costs and/or produce higher quality product (Reichstein and Salter, 2006). This, then, may be why it is often regarded as the Cinderella activity compared to the more glamorous product innovation. It is true that many of its activities and improvements may go unnoticed. Changes in the production process of a cereal box that reduces costs by 10 per cent would not be noticed by end consumers; but certainly it would be noticed by the firm. In a major study examining the sources of process innovation, Reichstein and Salter (2006) found that 'the presence of R&D activities is associated with process innovation' (Reichstein and Salter, 2006: 677). Further, in industrial economics, a number of studies have attempted to theoretically model the factors that shape the propensity of firms to undertake product and process innovations. Some recent models suggest that firms will favour product innovation where there is a high level of product differentiation and competition is intense. In contrast, process innovation will be undertaken where products are less differentiated and there is less competition in the industry. Clearly, the industrial context will shape decision making and Porter's taxonomy of technology strategies illustrates this. In this framework, process innovation often is associated with the attempts of firms to achieve cost leadership in their market segment or to focus on cost reductions in the production of existing products. Table 5.2 shows a classification of product and process interdependence (Hullova, et al., 2016).

Managing the manufacturing: R&D interface in process industries

To be successful at innovation, firms need to be able to capture value from their innovative functional products and then they must be able to manufacture them in a competitive cost structure. In process industries, this is even more important and is dependent on the relationship between firms' manufacturing and innovation activities. Research by Storm et al. (2013) examined the firm's raw material innovation, innovation of process technology and product innovation. They found that process innovation provided the most likely route to achieve that highly sought-after prize of product flexibility.

Stretch: how innovation continues once investment is made

Process industries are characterised by large fixed items of capital equipment. Hence, this causes a problem for firms of how to create change once these plants are built.

Table 5.2 A classification of interdependence between product and process innovation

Classification of interdependence between product and process innovation	
Reciprocal	Both and either product or process developments lead to improvements in the other.
Pooled	Where developments in product and process activities are pooled and then a selection is made. Similar to reciprocal, except that internal decision making may prevent improvements in either product or process.
Process sequential	Where innovation is dependent on process developments. In this scenario, the process dominates.
Product sequential	Where innovation is dependent on product developments. In this scenario, the product dominates.
Amensalism	A type of symbiosis between two species where one limits the success of the other without being affected, positively or negatively, by the presence of the other. Plants are a good example. In the case of product and process innovation, a situation could exist where the presence of a dominant process or product technology could hinder developments in the other.
Unilateral	Where no relationship exists (difficult in practice) where product or process innovations take place, irrespective of the other.

According to research by Aylen (2013), stretch is the mechanism by which established plants incorporate improvements in process and product technology, and make higher output and new products as a result. Essentially stretch here means evolutionary problem solving. For example, intensity of use leads to familiar learning effects. Enhanced maintenance of the plant can also lead to improvements. Other changes can come from system-wide effects of improvements in feedstock and downstream processing. To ensure stretch occurs, research by Aylen argues that efficiency-driven production managers need to accept risky interventions in production schedules to allow continuing innovation.

Application development needs to be an institutionalised function in process industry firms. It provides a way for firms to add value to customer products. It focuses on bridging the gap between a product supplier's knowledge of the product's performance scope and the customer's knowledge of its own production process requirements. For example, KernPack is an expert in packaging machinery solutions and automation, whether it is wrapping hot cross buns, magazines or mail. The firm has over 60 years' experience with precision systems. Kern is able to offer improved products for its customers, if it knows more about how its customers use Kern machinery. Research by Lager and Storm (2013) shows that establishing long-term customer relationships is the best way to achieve application development.

Innovation in the management of the operations process

The task of all managers is to improve their operation – otherwise they are supervisors and do not justify their job title. New, innovative ways of working within the operations process to gain competitive advantage is, therefore, part of every operations manager's duties. The question often is how to start? How to **trigger** off an investigation resulting in an improvement? One approach is first to identify techniques or triggers to help this improvement process and a number of these triggers are discussed in the following sections.

An excellent starting point for all analysis is the customer. Quality performance is the key operations management responsibility and innovation to help improve quality performance is critical to all organisations.

Triggers for innovation

Gap analysis

In order to design quality products and services, it is necessary to fully understand your customers and their expectations. Assessing expectations is difficult, as customers are different from each other and change with time. Twenty-five years ago, teachers used acetates and overhead projectors in the classroom. Today's students expect a computer-generated image (for example, PowerPoint) presentation with the occasional video/CD clip to illustrate the lecture, i.e. the student expectations and requirements have increased with time.

A technique used extensively to aid understanding of the differences (or gaps) between the customer and producer view or experience of a product or service is called 'gap analysis'. Consider the example given by Figure 5.5 about a service product – a university lecture, where the same lecture is experienced by the teacher and the student. However, viewing the lecture from the student's (customer's) viewpoint is different from that of the producer (the lecturer or university).

The student's expectations are based upon the university's and the lecturer's image, experience and word of mouth exchanges. These combine and may lead to the student having a specification of what he/she expects from the lecture. The university, through its management, has a concept of what should be in the lecture (the syllabus). The lecturer takes this concept and produces his slides, handouts (hopefully simple and easy to understand) and delivers the lecture. These differences or

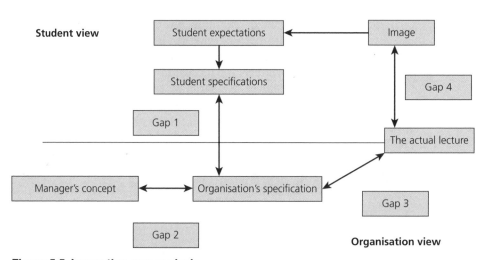

Figure 5.5 Innovation gap analysis

Source: Adapted from Slack, N. et al. (2004) *Operations Management,* 4th edn, © Pearson Education Limited.

Table 5.3 Gap analysis

Gap	Action required to ensure high perceived quality	Action by
Gap 1	Ensure consistency between internal quality specifications and the expectations of the students	Marketing course development and management
Gap 2	Ensure internal specification meets the intended design of the course	Marketing course development
Gap 3	Ensure actual lecture conforms to its internally specified quality level	The lecturing team course management
Gap 4	Ensure that promises made to the students concerning the teaching can really be delivered	Marketing

Source: Adapted from Slack, N. et al. (2007) *Operations Management*, 5th edn, © Pearson Education Limited.

gaps are shown in the figure and each is a source of dissatisfaction with the lecture from the student's or university's perspective.

These identified gaps help to show those corrective actions required in the design of the lecture or its delivery process. Table 5.3 illustrates these points.

Quality circles and process improvement teams

A quality circle is a small group of voluntary workers who meet regularly to discuss problems (not necessarily restricted to quality matters) and determine possible solutions. The **quality circle** concept was developed from the ideas of Deming, Juran and Ishikawa in the 1960s (Juran, 1995). Most people are expert in their job and appreciate this being acknowledged. Members of quality circles are given training in quality control and evaluation techniques. An idea coming from a member of the quality circle is far more likely to be adopted than an idea imposed from above. Quality circles, therefore, reflect and exploit the advantages of the human resource theories embedded in employee participation and empowerment approaches. Furthermore, the recognition by senior managers that the employees are worth listening to helps to improve the total quality ethos of the company with beneficial effects on the company and its customers.

Since their introduction it is estimated that over 10 million Japanese workers have been part of a quality circle with an average saving of several thousand US dollars (Russell and Taylor, 2003). The later term 'process improvement team' was used (amongst others) to reflect the need to look at the whole business process being considered. There has been adoption of the quality circle approach by organisations in Europe and the United States, but some argue that the cultural and adversarial differences between management and unions have inhibited the success of the approach in certain situations. However, quality circles can be a rich source of innovative solutions to problems and cost savings and patent applications may follow.

Total quality management (TQM)

Most business texts have chapters on quality from their marketing, human resources or operations perspectives. It is the concept of **total quality management** that has been amongst the most significant in its effect. First introduced by Arm and

Feigenbaum in the 1950s and then developed and refined by others (including Crosby, Deming, Ishikawa and Juran), TQM became defined as:

> *An effective system for integrating the quality development, quality maintenance and quality improvement efforts of the various groups in an organisation so to enable production and service at the most economical levels which allows for full customer satisfaction.*

(Feigenbaum, 1986: 96)

The TQM philosophy stresses the following points:

- meeting the needs and expectations of customers;
- covering all the parts of the organisation;
- everyone in the organisation is included;
- investigating all costs related to quality (internal and external);
- getting things right by designing in quality;
- developing systems and procedures that support quality improvements; and
- developing a continuous process of improvement.

Meeting expectations is difficult: as the quality level of products improves this, in turn, increases customer expectations. For example, in 1970, it was accepted that family-size cars required servicing every 3,000–6,000 miles and lasted for 60,000–70,000 miles. The automotive technical improvements now mean that a service interval of 15,000 miles and cars that last for over 100,000 miles are now the norm and are *expected*. Innovation in the ways to achieve what the customer expects in the combination of product and service provided is one way to gain sustainable advantage over your competition. The humorous and much quoted example in Illustration 5.4 shows the different approaches to quality management.

For a TQM approach to be successful, all the staff in all departments have to be involved. Quality is the responsibility of everyone and not some other manager or department. Quality and employee improvements are, therefore, inextricably linked and should be part of a continuous cycle. If a modest innovative and improvement cycle continues, by embedding the approach in the culture of the organisation, the long-term and total result may exceed that of a radical solution. The 'knowledge' of the organisation has thereby increased. No organisation has the ability to recruit and retain all the very best brains and operation managers need to recognise that they need to exploit the skills and enthusiasm of all their people. The impact of

Illustration 5.4

Different approaches to quality

IBM of Canada ordered a batch of components from a Japanese supplier and specified that the delivery should have an acceptable quality level of three defective parts per thousand. When the parts arrived, they were accompanied by a letter that expressed the supplier's bewilderment at being asked to supply defective parts as well as good ones. The letter also explained that they had found it difficult to make parts that were defective, but had done so and these were included and wrapped separately with the delivery.

Source: Adapted from Slack, N. et al. (2007) *Operations Management*, 5th edn, © Pearson Education Limited.

small, relatively easy to achieve, improvements can be very positive. Much of the improvement in the reliability of cars over the past 20 years has been attributed to a very large number of incremental improvements initiated by thousands of employees in all the car manufacturing companies and their suppliers.

TQM, with its continuous improvement, employee involvement and process ownership, has shown itself to be an effective policy in managing organisations, not least because of the enthusiastic implementation (team building). TQM is not a substitute for real leadership or a passing fad. However, if an idea generated meant that an element of the process was no longer needed and jobs were lost, what then of employee involvement? Many, if not most, employees would be unwilling to suggest losing jobs. Even in circumstances when alternative work was available to those displaced, many would be reluctant to vigorously pursue the idea. The very feeling of process ownership by the employees may *obstruct* all radical change, i.e. TQM may not support major innovation (Giaever, 1998). This problem is where management and leadership are required.

Quality function deployment (QFD)

Making design decisions concurrently rather than sequentially requires superior coordination amongst the parties involved – marketing, engineering, operations and, most importantly, the customer. **Quality function deployment (QFD)** is a structured approach to this problem that relates the *voice* of the customer to every stage of the design and the delivering process. In particular, QFD:

- promotes better understanding of customer demands;
- promotes better understanding of design interactions;
- involves operations in the process at the earliest possible moment;
- removes the traditional barriers between the departments; and
- focuses the design effort.

Also known as the 'House of Quality', the technique is regarded by some as a highly complex technique only suitable for projects in large organisations. Others see QFD as a solution to the complex problems faced by designers and deserving of the perseverance necessary. This was the case in the Japanese car component firm, Kayaba, which attempted to use the QFD systems of Toyota and initially suffered almost total failure. Kayaba went on to develop its own successful version, which it called 'Anticipatory Development' and won the company a Deming Prize for its quality achievements (Lowe and Ridgway, 2000).

The ISO 9000 approach

Many countries developed their own quality systems and standards and in 1994 these were combined to become the International Standards Organization ISO 9000 – a set of standards governing documentation of a quality programme. A qualified external examiner checks that the company complies with all the requirements specified and certifies the company. Once certified, companies are listed in a directory and this information is made available to potential customers. As many large organisations *insist* on all suppliers having the ISO quality standards, much time and effort was spent in new, innovative ways of controlling and developing processes to maintain the agreed and certified standards. Completing the certification process can be long and expensive (Krajewski and Ritzman, 2001: 267); however, compliance with ISO 9000 says nothing about the *actual quality* of the product.

In part to reflect this point, the ISO 9000 (2000)[1] was developed to include four additional principles:

- quality management should be customer-focused;
- quality performance should be measured;
- quality management should be improvement-driven;
- top management must demonstrate their commitment to maintaining and continually improving management systems.

Despite these revisions, the ISO approach is not seen as beneficial by all parties.

The EFQM excellence model

In 1988, 14 leading Western European companies formed the European Foundation for Quality Management and gave an award for the most successful application of TQM in Europe. In 1999, this idea and model was refined and developed into the *EFQM Excellence Model* that reflected the increased understanding and emphasis on customer (and market) focus and is results-oriented. The underlying idea is that *results* (people, customer, society and key performance) are achieved through a number of *enablers* (Figure 5.6) in managing and controlling the input/output transformation *processes* involved.

Performance measurement is by self-assessment, which EFQM defines as 'a comprehensive, systematic, and regular review of an organisation's activities and results referenced against a model of business excellence'. It may be easier to understand *and apply* this approach than is the case with some of the more philosophical concepts within TMQ. Furthermore, the EFQM excellence model also embeds *innovation and learning* in the performance of the organisation (Slack et al., 2007; Van Looy et al., 2003).

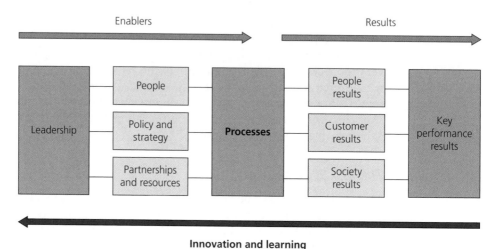

Figure 5.6 The EFQM excellence model

Source: Adapted from Slack, N. et al. (2004) *Operations Management*, 4th edn, © Pearson Education Limited.

---

[1] ISO/IEC 2000 is the first international standard for IT service management. It was developed in 2005, by ISO/IEC JTC 1/SC 7.

Pause for thought

How well does the EFQM business excellence model apply to service sector situations?

Design of the organisation and its suppliers: supply chain management

Figure 5.3 shows the relationships between network, process and job design, whilst Figure 5.7 extends this network to include suppliers and customers.

Delivering prompt, reliable products and services cost-effectively form part of most organisations' strategic plan. The term **supply chain management** describes the system of managing all the activities across company boundaries in order to drive the whole chain network towards the shared objective of satisfying the customers. Material (or information) flows through a series of operations in both directions and the principles of operations management apply.

Increasingly, organisations concentrate on their core activities and subcontract more of their support activities to their suppliers (Hoecht and Trott, 2006). In many situations, these suppliers are global and supply chain management has become a key strategic issue for many organisations.

Inclusion of suppliers in design activities is, therefore, essential. Much of the improvement in car design has been at the initiative of their suppliers. Developments, such as automatic braking and engine management systems, have come with the extensive involvement from the industrial suppliers to the automotive industry. With the involvement of suppliers in the new product development process, it has also been found that more cost-effective designs have been created (Christopher, 2004).

For a company to achieve its own quality goals it must consider the quality of the product from its suppliers and the suppliers' own quality control procedures. For

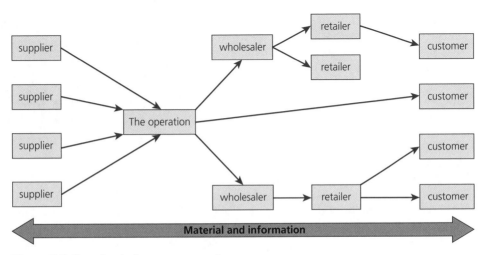

Figure 5.7 Supply chain management

example, large organisations may help their smaller suppliers with training in quality circles. Successful supply chain management is, therefore, very dependent on good network coordination mechanisms, business relationships and information technology.

McDonald's built a restaurant in Moscow. To achieve its required and expected level of quality and service, the company set up an entire supply chain for growing, processing and distributing the food to its stores. McDonald's made sure that all parties along the whole chain understood its expectations of performance and closely monitored performance (Upton, 1998).

Waste is a by-product of many processes (Table 5.1) and, by definition, costs money. Waste can take many forms – material, rejects, wasted movements, waiting time, over production, i.e. any activity that does not add value. Waste avoidance and process efficiency combine in the management principle termed 'just in time' (JIT), a definition of which is:

> *JIT aims to meet demand instantaneously, with perfect quality and no waste.*

> (Slack et al., 2007)

Japan has limited natural resources. Consequently, the Japanese were champions of waste avoidance in their processes and were amongst the first to introduce the JIT techniques and processes to their large-scale manufacturing plants in the early 1970s. Quality circles, process improvement teams, QFD and quality assurance systems were all used as triggers for many small incremental *innovative improvements*. Working in teams, continuous improvement, simplifying operations, keeping things simple, doing them well and eliminating waste in all its forms helped JIT to be extended to develop what has become known as the lean philosophy (Slack et al., 2007: 469).

Illustration 5.5

Intensive care uses Formula One techniques

The skills developed during Formula 1 pit stops are now being used to save lives at a top children's hospital. This may, at first, seem like an unlikely partnership but operational similarities exist. London's Great Ormond Street Hospital has changed the way that young patients are treated after an operation.

Like a pit stop, the hospital transfer requires quick coordination and teamwork, and this is at a time when a patient is vulnerable – after a long and difficult operation, a child must be detached from one set of tubes and lines in the operating theatre, then wheeled into the intensive care unit (ICU) and connected to another set. The receiving hospital ward has to absorb information from the surgical team about the way the patient is responding and how his or her condition can be kept stable. Previously, unlike the F1 pit stops,

Source: imageBROKER/Alamy Images

the hospital handovers tended to be chaotic, so the Great Ormond Street Hospital contacted McLaren and then Ferrari. They soon realised that their own transfer was poorly organised,

Lean innovation

Lean principles are derived from the Japanese manufacturing industry. The term was first coined by John Krafcik in his 1988 article, 'Triumph of the Lean Production System'. Lean manufacturing or lean production is a systemic method for the elimination of waste within a manufacturing process. More recently, the concept of lean innovation has been gathering interest from firms around the world.

Lean innovation embraces a philosophy of not letting perfection get in the way of progress. It leverages the Pareto principle that 20 per cent of a product's features will most likely deliver 80 per cent of the benefits sought by customers. Indeed, in many ways, software firms like Google have been practising lean innovation without realising it. Google, for many years, has released so-called 'beta' products to its consumers. For example, for many years, Google Scholar was used by many research students, even though it was not yet complete and probably contained some software errors.

A definition of lean innovation is creating a new product or process, including the work required to bring an idea or concept into a final form, with emphasis on identifying and creating the value and removing the waste of the new product development (NPD) process.

As an approach, lean innovation lends itself especially well to corporate cultures, particularly engineering ones and others strongly focused on process-improvement programmes, such as Six Sigma. It has a simple straightforward, step-by-step methodology that makes it relatively easy to explain and to implement:

- Identify the minimal viable product.
- Develop a version rapidly and test it with customers, ideally in a real-world competitive situation.
- Repeat the process until the core product is competitive or pivot to explore a new approach.

Many argue that lean innovation is very different from conventional approaches to product development in which teams expend enormous effort trying to create a perfected product without sufficient in-market customer feedback. The resulting new products are often too expensive, too complicated, too different from what customers want, and sometimes end up being too late to market.

In his book *Lean Product Management*, Greg Cohen (2011) describes lean innovation as five steps and principles:

1 *Identify customer value:* define value from the perspective of the customer.
2 *Map the value stream:* identify all steps in the value creation process and remove those steps that do not create value. Value stream analysis focuses on the flow of material and information through the system with a focus on throughput and wait times.

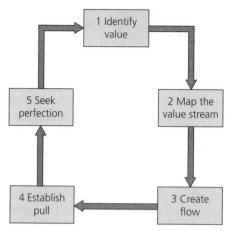

Figure 5.8 Lean innovation

Source: G. Cohen (2011) *Lean Product Management*, © 2011 The 280 Group, reproduced with permission.

3 *Create flow:* assemble value-creating steps in a tight sequence to enable value to flow quickly through the system.

4 *Establish pull:* as value starts to flow, value is pulled through the system, ideally by the customer and at the rate of customer demand ('build to order' is a pull system).

5 *Seek perfection:* repeat the previous four steps until all waste has been removed in the system. Perfection is a state that the professionals continue to approach, but never actually achieve.

Early reviews of firms that have adopted lean innovation techniques seem to show that it helps to create a better environment for learning. It helps to focus on the most important product attributes and encourages rapid cycling of trial and error. In other words, lean innovation is not a better innovation process; rather it can be a more efficient learning process. According to Tom Agan (Agan, 2014), 'We need to think of lean innovation as a process that drives more efficient learning. But to maximise success, lean innovation must be linked to practices that effectively capture these lessons and make them readily available to everyone within the organization.'

Pause for thought ❓

Can you think of anything you control that you do not measure?

Case study

Innovation on the production line

This case study examines a new paperboard material with unusual properties that may enable the paper packaging industry to compete with plastic packaging. The paper and board packaging industry is a major supplier to the food industry. It is characterised as a high-volume commodity product. This case illustrates the role of innovation and product development within a process industry and how, in such industries, innovation occurs on the production line rather than in laboratories.

Introduction

Chester Packaging is a leading supplier of cartons, labels, leaflets and specialist paper packaging. The company currently produces packaging for a range of fast-moving consumer goods brands, as well as for many pharmaceutical firms. Part of Chester Packaging's pharmaceutical packaging range is blister packs for tablets and pills. Currently, the packaging of almost all tablets/pills consists of packs made from board, plastics and foil. For the pharmaceutical industry, this method of packaging has become the dominant design, due to the assurance of the integrity provided to each tablet by the combination of these materials and the ability to print dates on the foil seal. However, with growing customer concerns about environmental issues, some firms are starting to question their reliance upon non-recyclable plastics. This, then, formed the basis for the development of Chester Packaging's Paperboard Blister Pack.

In 2012, a paper mill located in northern Italy began developing an innovative paperboard material. Whilst the material offered the same robustness and protection as traditional paperboard, it also featured a unique characteristic: it was malleable. Compared to the restrictive rigidity of its traditional counterpart, the new formable paperboard could be manipulated into a variety of dynamic shapes (see the photo) and offered the ability of increased indentations (with heights of 5 mm possible compared to 0.2 mm indention with traditional paperboard). These qualities offered a number of packaging improvements across a wide range of product categories and allowed brand owners the opportunity to make their packaging (and their brand) stand out from the competition. The development process for the formable material is much the same as those for traditional paperboard, but with two distinct differences. The first difference is the use of several thin layers of laminated paper forming the basis for the paperboard, unlike traditional paperboard that features a thicker single layer. According to the production manager: 'These layers of paper allow for the material to be manipulated during the production process to a far greater extent

than a single sheet would allow.' These layers are then agitated at a higher rate than standard paperboard, creating a unique orientation of the fibres within the material and a texture that is more corrugated. The second difference lies in the final stage of the production process: the forming of the material using roller machines. The same machines are used as those with traditional paperboard; however, the roller is engaged using differential speed patterns. This process alters the structure and orientation of the fibres further, resulting in a malleable material with up to 15 per cent more movement than the average 2 per cent found in standard paperboard.

The first firm interested in the malleable paperboard was Swedish paper producer Billerud who invested €10 million in gaining intellectual property rights for the material. These rights granted Billerud access to know-how regarding the development of the material in terms of pulping, ingredients and production processes. This allowed the company the ability to produce flat sheets of the material and prevented other firms gaining access to this know-how. The firm also invested a further €2 million to alter the structure of the fibres, further giving the material up to 20 per cent more movement than traditional paperboard. However, despite these investments, Billerud lacked market and product knowledge. After all, Billerud was a material supplier; it was unsure of product applications for the material. Moreover, with no specific target customer or application in mind, the material was, effectively, being developed blind.

Product applications of the formable paperboard material

Source: Andrei Mayatnik/Shutterstock.com

Applying the technology to possible products

Chester Packaging first received a sample of the paperboard in 2013. The possible applications for the formable board for Chester Packaging transcended product and industry boundaries and included:

- replacing existing packaging materials (i.e., environmentally unfriendly plastics);
- differentiating products from their competitors by using unique packaging in terms of materials and decoration (an eye-catching highly indented brand logo);
- improving the functionality of new or existing packaging (better shaped mouldings for chocolate boxes); and
- use in areas outside of packaging (improving the quality of Braille texts).

Such was the extent of its application, that Chester Packaging felt as though it could replace almost any packaging with this new material, and considered it to be 'one of the most significant packaging innovations in the history of the paperboard packaging industry'.

Chester Packaging initially discovered, through experimentation, that it was possible to use the material for small items of packaging, such as the blister pack. During these experiments, they also discovered that the production of small items was possible using existing production line machinery with only minor changes to the manufacturing process. This provided a considerable advantage: that the company could avoid the costs of investing in new production machinery. In July of 2013, Chester Packaging approached Billerud with an offer to purchase intellectual property rights to the formable paperboard to gain exclusivity for its packaging. This offer initially was declined, along with alternative proposals from other companies hoping to gain an exclusivity deal. Chester Packaging faced fierce competition in gaining rights to the material: gaining exclusivity for a material or technology that has so many uses was, inevitably, going to be a difficult task. Understandably, Billerud recognised the value of the material and the interest it had gained, so it wanted to take advantage of every opportunity available to it. Following 12 months of intense negotiations, the two parties reached an agreement, allowing Chester Packaging exclusive rights to the use of the material, but only for pharmaceuticals packaging. According to the marketing manager: 'The licensing agreement we arranged allowed us to use the paperboard in the packaging for our pharmaceuticals, and also to adjust and add to the original ingredients so the material would be suitable for sensitive products.'

Product development process

The product development process for a new blister pack soon ran into difficulty. The initial relatively shallow indentations created as part of the early experimental development stages were produced using the existing machine tools; more significant indentations (including deeper and larger areas), however, required new machinery with the capability to produce a much larger force to compress the board. Clearly, additional machinery costs would raise adoption barriers for potential customers. Chester Packaging's tooling partner initially was sceptical about the concept and the likelihood of success. This was because the firm had over 40 years' experience of producing polymer-based blister packs. It was wedded to the idea that only polymers could be moulded with its tooling. It was, therefore, reluctant to become involved in what it saw as a crazy idea that was unlikely to be commercially useful. It argued that the development costs were likely to be too high, especially given the unique nature of the material and the changes required to the production processes. The production manager explained: 'Margins are tight in this industry and any cost increase is usually met with derision.'

Despite these concerns, the development team at Chester Packaging was confident that the benefits the new packaging brought were so great that firms would be willing to incur these cost increases. For example, in the toothpaste market, recently the firm noticed that one of its customers had been willing to double its packaging costs in order to achieve an elaborate gloss finish to the box. After several months of codevelopment, new tooling eventually was developed to accommodate the formable paperboard at a cost of £25,000. The increased pressure required to create the larger indentations in the material demanded steel tooling to replace existing brass tooling.

Finally, the blister pack went into production. With the many benefits this innovative packaging brings, the total costs to the customer are more than double that of traditional plastic and foil packaging. Operating in an industry where decisions are so often based on costs has made adoption for the new packaging difficult. To accelerate the diffusion process, Chester Packaging is targeting leading pharmaceutical companies for the adoption of the new packaging. In addition, Chester Packaging has negotiated a further licence with Billerud, allowing it use of the material in food and drinks packaging.

Finding customers

The blister pack product category is an obvious potential customer. However, legislation is tight around pharmaceutical products and this extends to its packaging. Consequently, change tends to be slow and decision making cautious. Also, a key question facing a firm considering adopting the product is what advantage will it give me?

By targeting large pharmaceutical firms, Chester Packaging is seeking a lead user to adopt the formable board for its blister packs and, in turn, to help the technology cross the chasm and gain wider market adoption. This is the most difficult step in making the transition between a few early adopters and the large mass markets of pragmatists (Moore, 2004). To achieve this aim, Chester Packaging will need to effectively communicate the benefits of the product relative to existing packaging and to bridge the gap between technological uncertainty and market need. It will also need to demonstrate that the benefits of the new packaging outweigh the significant increase in costs compared to existing methods. The total costs of the new packaging are more than double those of traditional blister packs. This increase comes from the new materials and more complex production process, as well as the investments in licences, tooling and the inevitable new marketing communications for the new product.

Appreciating and understanding the potential product applications of a technology and uncovering whether markets will embrace these products, is critical in the innovation process. Firms in certain markets (i.e. toothpaste) appear more receptive to making

packaging investments. Chester Packaging must discover which product applications of the technology will deliver a return on its investments and efforts in the innovation process. For example, using the technology to create increased indentations (5 mm depth), a cereal box could be developed for Kellogg's, featuring the brand's signature trade-mark cockerel protruding from the pack. This would create unique packaging, differentiating Kellogg's from its competitors on the shelf. Due to the nature of the product, it may also be an application of the technology that poses fewer challenges than the blister pack.

Conclusions

This case illustrates typical risks and issues frequently experienced when making investment decisions in process industries. This is particularly true for commodity industries, such as packaging, where emphasis is placed on costs and efficiency of production. This emphasis often can lead to an emphasis on short-term decision making with innovation being sidelined.

Whilst Chester Packaging's experiments and prototyping have demonstrated the product capabilities to be superior to existing packaging, the changes required for firms in adopting the technology may be too great. Such changes go beyond those of the production processes for the firm and include consumer perceptions of the new product. Marketing communications will be required from Chester Packaging to demonstrate the superiority of the new product to potential customers and to diminish any concerns regarding product integrity for end users.

Firms need to consider how and in what ways the innovation will cause changes to its existing supply chain and whether new business relationships need to be nurtured that will help it develop the required supply chain. Furthermore, negotiating financial arrangements and agreeing costs, margins and royalty payments will help the firm achieve the right mix of partner firms to build its business model. As the present case demonstrates, such agreements and contracts take time to secure and are often overlooked in models of innovation.

Questions

1 Given that this is 'one of the most significant packaging innovations in the history of the paperboard packaging industry', what are the main problems?

2 Discuss whether the technology has benefits and what the advantages are over existing products.

3 Who benefits from this innovation and who is paying for it?

4 Discuss why this seems like a chicken and egg problem with investment depending on orders.

5 How important is exclusivity on a licence deal?

6 Examine the intellectual property concerns for potential food brand owner customers regarding whether their competitors may get access to the product.

7 It seems that firms like the product, but do not want to pay extra for it. How could this be ameliorated?

8 You are a small business, you employ 50 people and you have a turnover of £4 million. Would you invest £100,000 pounds? Would you go to the bank and borrow £100,000?

Note: This case has been written as a basis for class discussion rather than to illustrate effective or ineffective managerial or administrative behaviour. It has been prepared from a variety of published sources, as indicated, and from observations.

Chapter summary

The quality of design and management within operations is, thus, seen as an essential part of innovation management. Indeed, the process of innovation can be judged as an operations process with inputs and outputs. Often, by understanding the basics of good design by, perhaps, 'keeping things simple' and looking at your products and services as your customers receive them, will help to deliver a continual stream of new product and service improvements. Continuous redesign of the company and its products and service, listening to your customers, watching your competitors, keeping aware of inventions and emerging technologies is a daunting task. We are not just talking about *fitting* the various departments and functions together as a team, but creating a *resonance* across all the constituents of the design spectrum.

Discussion questions

1 What do you understand by *innovation* within the education sector?

2 Apply Braun's principles to your university or college.

3 Which elements of the TQM philosophy could you apply to your university or college? What might be the benefits?

4 Do you think the EFQM model of excellence could apply to your university? What might be the benefits?

5 Consider the innovation activities of the design spectrum. How much of the range would involve patents?

6 Can you think of any circumstances in which the philosophy of 'keeping things simple' would not apply?

7 'Technology changes. The laws of economics do not.' Discuss the implications and validity of this statement.

Key words and phrases

Design *156*

Volume *160*

Visibility *164*

Variation *164*

Trigger *170*

Quality circle *171*

Total quality management *171*

Quality function deployment (QFD) *173*

Supply chain management *175*

Business process re-engineering (BPR) *178*

References

Abernathy, W.J. and Utterback, J. (1978) 'Patterns of industrial innovation', in Tushman, M.L. and Moore, W.L. *Readings in the Management of Innovation*, HarperCollins, New York, 97–108.

Agan, T. (2014) *The Secret to Lean Innovation is Making Learning a Priority*, January 23, HBR.org/2014/01.

Aylen, J. (2013) Stretch: how innovation continues once investment is made, *R&D Management*, vol. 43, 271–87.

Brown, S., Blackmon, K., Cousins, P. and Maylor, H. (2001) *Operations Management*, Butterworth-Heinemann, Oxford.

Christenson, C.M. (1999) *Innovation and the General Manager*, McGraw-Hill, London.

Christopher, M. (2004) *Logistics and Supply Chain Management*, Prentice Hall, London.

Cohen, G. (2011) *Lean Product Management*, 280, Group Press.

Feigenbaum, A.V. (1986) *Total Quality Control*, McGraw-Hill, New York.

Fransoo, J.C. (1994) A typology of production control situations in process industries, *International Journal of Operations & Production Management*, vol. 14, no. 12, 47–57.

Giaever, H. (1998) Does total quality management restrain innovation?, DNV report no. 99–2036.

Hammer, M. (1990) Re-engineering work: don't automate, obliterate, *Harvard Business Review*, July/August, 104–12.

Hoecht, A. and Trott, P. (2006) Innovation risks of outsourcing, *Technovation*, vol. 26, no. 4, 672–81.

Independent (2000) Internet reforms will help case for euro, 25 March.

Johnston, R. and Clark, G. (2001) *Service Operations Management*, Prentice Hall, London.

Juran, J.M. (ed.) (1995) *A History of Managing for Quality: The Evolution, Trends, and Future Directions of Managing for Quality*, AAQ Press.

Krafcik, J.F. (1988) Triumph of the lean production system, *MIT Sloan Management Review*, vol. 30, no. 1, 41.

Krajewski, L.J. and Ritzman, L.P. (2001) *Operations Management*, Prentice Hall, London.

Lager, T. and Storm, P. (2013) Application development in process firms: adding value to customer products and production systems, *R&D Management*, vol. 43, 288–302.

Lowe, A. and Ridgway, K. (2000) UK user's guide to quality function deployment, *Engineering Management Journal*, June.

Moore, G.A. (2004) *Crossing the Chasm: Marketing and selling technology products to mainstream customers*, 2nd edn, Capstone, Oxford.

Peters, T. (1997) *The Circle of Innovation*, Hodder & Stoughton, London.

Reichstein, T. and Salter, A. (2006) Investigating the sources of process innovation among UK manufacturing firms, *Industrial and Corporate Change*, vol. 15, 653–82.

Rosenberg, N., Landau, R. and Mowery, D.C. (1992) (eds) *Technology and the Wealth of Nations*, Stanford University Press, Stanford, California, USA.

Roy, R. and Weild, D. (1993) *Product Design and Technological Innovation*, Open University Press, Milton Keynes.

Russell, R. and Taylor, B. (2003) *Operations Management*, Prentice-Hall, Englewood Cliffs, NJ.

Simonetti, R., Archibugi, D. and Evangelista, R. (1995) Product and process innovations: How are they defined? How are they quantified? *Scientometrics*, vol. 32, no. 1, 77–89.

Slack, N., Chambers, S., Harland, C., Harrison, A. and Johnson, R. (2007) *Operations Management*, 5th edn, Pearson Education Limited, London.

Storm, P., Lager, T. and Samuelsson, P. (2013) Managing the manufacturing – R&D interface in the process industries, *R&D Management*, vol. 43, 252–70.

Upton, D.M. (1998) *Designing, Managing and Improving Operations*, Prentice-Hall, Englewood Cliffs, NJ.

Van Looy, B., Gemmel, P. and Van Dierdonck, R. (2003) *Services Management*, Prentice Hall, London.

Wallace, T.F. (1998) *APICS Dictionary*, 5th edn, American Production and Inventory Control Society, Falls Church, VA.

Waller, D.L. (1999) *Operations Management – A Supply Chain Approach*, International Thomson Publishing, London.

Wallis, Z. (1995) The good the bad and the ugly – what does your office say about your company? *Facilities*, vol. 13, no. 2, 26–7.

Young, T., Brailsford, S., Connel, C., Davies, R., Harper, P. and Kelin, J. (2004) Using industrial processes to improve patient care, *British Medical Journal*, vol. 328, 162–5.

Further reading

For a more detailed review of the operations and process innovation literature, the following develop many of the issues raised in this chapter:

Barney, J.B. and Clark, D.N. (2007) *Resource-based Theory: Creating and Sustaining Competitive Advantage*, Oxford University Press, Oxford.

Chang, H. and Luo, C. (2010) Analyze innovation strategy of technical-intensive industries: scenario analysis viewpoint, *Business Strategy Series*, vol. 11, no. 5, 302–7.

Christensen, C.M. (2003) *The Innovator's Dilemma: When New Technologies Cause Great Firms to Fail*, 3rd edn, HBS Press, Cambridge, MA.

Drucker, P.F. (2002) *Managing in the Next Society*, Butterworth-Heinemann, Oxford.

HSBC (2010) *100 Thoughts*, HSBC, London.

Hullova, D, Trott, P. and Simms, C.D. (2016) Uncovering the reciprocal complementarity between product and process innovation. *Research Policy*, 45, 5, 929–940.

Reichstein, T. and Salter, A. (2006) Investigating the sources of process innovation among UK manufacturing firms, *Industrial and Corporate Change*, vol. 15, 653–82.

Chapter 6
Managing intellectual property

Introduction

Intellectual property concerns the legal rights associated with creative effort or commercial reputation. The subject matter is very wide indeed. The aim of this chapter is to introduce the area of intellectual property to the manager of business and to ensure that they are aware of the variety of ways that it can affect the management of innovation and the development of new products. The rapid advance of the internet and e-commerce has created a whole new set of problems concerning intellectual property rights. All these issues will be discussed in this chapter. Finally, the case study at the end of this chapter explains how the pharmaceutical industry uses the patent system to ensure it reaps rewards from the drugs that it develops.

Chapter contents

Learning objectives

When you have completed this chapter you will be able to:

- examine the different forms of protection available for a firm's intellectual property;
- identify the limitations of the patent system;
- explain why other firms' patents can be a valuable resource;
- identify the link between brand name and trademark;
- identify when and where the areas of copyright and registered design may be useful; and
- explain how the patent system is supposed to balance the interests of the individual and society.

Intellectual property

This chapter will explore this dynamic area of the law and illustrate why firms need to be aware of this increasingly important aspect of innovation.

If you just happen to come up with a novel idea, the simplest and cheapest course of action is to do nothing about legal protection, just keep it a secret (as with the recipe for Coca-Cola). Whilst this, in theory, may be true, in reality, many chemists and most ingredients and fragrance firms would argue that science now can detect a droplet of blood in an entire swimming pool and, to suggest that science cannot analyse a bottle of cola and uncover its ingredients, is stretching the bounds of reason. The keep-it-secret approach prevents anyone else seeing it or finding it. Indeed, the owner can take their intellectual property to their grave, safe in the knowledge that no one will inherit it. This approach is fine, unless you are seeking some form of commercial exploitation and, ultimately, a financial reward, usually in the form of royalties.

One of the dangers, of course, with trying to keep your idea a secret, is that someone else might develop an idea similar to yours and apply for legal protection and seek commercial exploitation. Independent discovery of ideas is not as surprising as one might think at first. This is because research scientists working at the forefront of science and technology often are working towards the same goal. This was the case with Thomas Edison and Joseph Swan, who independently invented the light bulb simultaneously either side of the Atlantic. Indeed, they formed a company called Ediswan to manufacture light bulbs at the end of the nineteenth century.

Table 6.1 shows an overview of the different forms of intellectual property and rights available for different areas of creativity.

The issues of intellectual property are continually with us and touch us probably more than we realise. Most students will have already confronted the issue of intellectual property, either with recording pre-recorded music or copying computer software. The author is always the owner of his or her work and the writing of an academic paper entitles the student to claim the copyright on that essay. Indeed, the submission of an academic paper to a scientific journal for publication requires the author to sign a licence for the publisher to use the intellectual property. Patenting is, probably, the most commonly recognised form of intellectual property, but it is only one of several ways to protect creative efforts. Registered designs, trademarks and copyright are other forms of intellectual property. These will be addressed in

Table 6.1 An overview of the main types of intellectual property

Type of intellectual property	Key features of this type of protection
1 Patents	Offers a 20-year monopoly
2 Copyright	Provides exclusive rights to creative individuals for the protection of their literary or artistic productions
3 Registered designs	As protected by registration, is for the outward appearance of an article and provides exclusive rights for up to 15 years
4 Registered trademarks	Is a distinctive name, mark or symbol that is identified with a company's products

the following sections. However, before you get into the details of intellectual property, read Illustration 6.1. Trevor Baylis, the inventor of the wind-up radio, argues that intellectual property theft should be regarded as a criminal offence. This illustration also discusses the long-standing issue about whether intellectual property is merely a smokescreen.

Governments have the challenge of trying to maximise economic and societal benefits. Clearly, a paradox exists because stronger patent laws with longer durations allow greater profit to the inventor, but strong and long patent protection discourages related innovation as the protection for the underlying technology becomes broader and duration is longer (see the patent paradox, Gold–berg and Linton, 2012).

Illustration 6.1

Theft of intellectual property 'should be a crime'

Trevor Baylis is angry. The inventor of the clockwork radio believes inventors and entrepreneurs are having their intellectual property (IP) stolen, whilst the Government and the courts fail to offer adequate protection.

'The theft of intellectual property should become a white-collar crime,' Baylis says.

'If I stole from you, then I would probably go to jail. But, if I were to steal your intellectual property, which potentially could be worth billions of pounds, it would only be a civil case – and, even then, most of us can't afford to pay £350 an hour for a lawyer.'

For Baylis, it is the inventor who underpins society. 'Art is pleasure, but invention is treasure. What is more important to society: a sheep in formaldehyde or a paperclip?'

It is a good question and, whilst Damien Hirst, along with other artists, musicians and writers, is protected by automatic copyright laws, the inventor – at the pre-patent application stage – has no legal recourse should someone decide to patent their idea first. Even with a patent, copyright or trademark (around a business name or brand) in place, IP theft is still extremely common. Gill Grassie, head of IP and technology at Maclay Murray & Spens, a Scottish firm of solicitors, points out that recent studies have shown the impact of counterfeiters on all industry sectors in the UK is as much as £11 billion a year. Adam Morallee, a partner in the IP Group at Mishcon de Reya, a commercial law

Source: Pearson Education Ltd/Photodisc

firm based in London, says his firm recovered more than £100 million in the last five years alone for its clients who have had their IP rights infringed.

In 2006, Japan and the USA established the Anti-Counterfeiting Trade Agreement (ACTA) to fight the growing tide of counterfeiting and piracy. Preliminary talks started that year, and it is hoped some sort of global agreement – now that the two founders have been joined by 35 other nations – can be reached later this year. However, at the UK level, patent infringement is currently a civil offence, which for some remains the best way to deal with it.

Grassie says: 'In the area of patents, it is more debatable whether infringement should be a criminal offence, as often there may be arguments regarding the validity of the patent or indeed whether there truly has been infringement in the first place.'

→

As it is a civil matter, one benefit is that you can claim for damages, notes Clive Halperin, a partner at GSC Solicitors. In addition, those seeking to protect their rights only have to prove the matter on the *balance of probabilities, rather than beyond all reasonable doubt*, as in a criminal case.

Yet, part of the problem faced by entrepreneurs and inventors is the sheer cost of registering a patent in the first place.

'The patent process is slow, expensive and time-consuming', says Stephen Streater, chief executive of Forbidden Technologies and the founder of Eidos, a video games company.

Mark Redgrave, chief executive of OpenAmplify, an online text analysis service, notes that his business has secured 14 patents over the past 8 years, but this has cost his company hundreds of thousands of pounds. Registering a patent in 8 European countries alone for 10 years can cost up to £40,000. Even if an entrepreneur can afford these costs, protecting a patent against possible infringement can simply be prohibitive. Mark England, chief executive of Sentec, a metering technology specialist, says: 'If you go to court in a patent case, then effectively you need to have £1 million in your back pocket to be able to finance the case, which of course most small companies cannot afford to do.'

This is why many entrepreneurs consider the whole issue of intellectual property as nothing more than a smokescreen.

'Intellectual property has become the genie in the lamp of the twenty-first-century business landscape; an overblown smokescreen that entrepreneurs and businesses are afraid to release for fear of idea theft,' says René Carayol, a writer and broadcaster on business and entrepreneurship.

'Yes, IP is important and, yes, people must be wary about others stealing a march on a good initiative, but this is more about trust than it is about employing high-cost IP lawyers . . . This obsession with intellectual property is stifling progress. Those that make the biggest waves are those that have the confidence to fire first, aim, then get ready.'

A simple way to overcome a lack of trust is to make sure potential colleagues or financial backers agree to sign a non-disclosure agreement. 'You've got to make sure you have one so that you have protection', says Halperin at GSC. 'Once the idea is out there, you've lost your chance.'

Indeed, when John Barrington-Carver, now director at PRAM, a Leeds-based public relations and marketing consultancy, worked with Baylis on the invention of the clockwork radio, he says his job was to keep it out of the media in general to prevent large south-east Asian electronics companies from taking the idea and throwing money at developing a successful production prototype before Baylis could protect the patent.

According to the Intellectual Property Office, the UK patents authority, there are no plans to make patent infringement into a criminal offence. Without this, Baylis believes the inventor or entrepreneur will not gain true recognition: 'We have to make society realise that the most important thing the nation has is knowledge and creativity.'

Pause for thought

Given the impressive advances made in science over the past 50 years, especially in the area of detecting substances and ingredients, scientists now claim to be able to detect one drop of blood in a swimming pool full of water. Does anyone still believe that the ingredients in Coca-Cola, for example, are secret and unknown?

Trade secrets

There are certain business activities and processes that are not patented, copyrighted or trademarked. Many businesses regard these as trade secrets. It could be special ways of working, price costings or business strategies. The most famous example is the recipe for Coca-Cola, which is not patented. This is because Coca-Cola did not want to reveal the recipe to its competitors. Unfortunately, the law covering intellectual property is less clear about the term *trade secret*. Indeed, Bainbridge (1996) argues that there is no satisfactory legal definition of the term.

An introduction to patents

Foreign applications for Chinese patents have been growing by over 30 per cent a year. With foreign companies more deeply engaged with the Chinese economy, returns from protecting their intellectual property in China have increased. This has been driven by domestic Chinese firms' ability to imitate foreign technology and competition between foreign firms in the Chinese market: such competitive threats create an urgency for protecting intellectual property (Hu, 2010). Illustration 6.2 dramatically illustrates the importance of patents to the business world. A patent is a contract between an individual or organisation and the state. The rationale behind the granting of a temporary monopoly by the state is to encourage creativity and

Illustration 6.2

Apple sues Samsung for ripping off designs and features

In 2014, Apple sued Samsung for damages of $2 billion, claiming infringement of five patents by Samsung devices sold in the USA, including Galaxy smartphones and tablets. Samsung is claiming infringement of two of its patents by the iPhone and iPad. One of the issues is whether the patents involved are overly broad patents that allow companies to block competition – something governments try hard to avoid.

The latest Apple–Samsung case will be tried less than two years after a federal jury found the South Korean firm was infringing on Apple patents. Samsung was ordered to pay $929 million, but has been allowed to continue selling products using the technology after the judge denied Apple a sales injunction pending appeal. Judge Koh ruled then that there was no clear evidence that the specific patents that Samsung had been found to infringe actually drove sales.

Samsung countered that it has broken technological barriers with its own ultra-slim, lightweight phones. Indeed, Samsung attorneys wrote, 'Apple has copied many of Samsung's innovations in its Apple iPhone, iPod and iPad products.'

Each side has 25 hours of court time to put their case and rebut the other side's.

If Apple prevails, the costs to Samsung could reach $2 billion. Apple's costs, if it lost, are expected to be about $6 million.

Experts agree that the problem, in cases like this, is that each smartphone has thousands of patented ideas in it; Apple is challenging just five. Equally, a high proportion of those patents are, typically, licensed for fractions of a penny per device.

innovation within an economy. By the individual or organisation disclosing in the patent sufficient detail of the invention, the state will confer the legal right to stop others benefiting from the invention (Derwent, 1998). The state, however, has no obligation to prevent others benefiting from it. This is the responsibility of the individual or organisation who is granted the patent. And herein lies a major criticism of the patent system. The costs of defending a patent against infringement can be high indeed. This point is explored later.

The UK Patent Office was set up in 1852 to act as the United Kingdom's sole office for the granting of patents of invention. From 2 April 2007, the UK Patent Office changed its name to the UK Intellectual Property Office. This is to reflect that patents now represent only part of its activities along with Registered Designs and Trademarks. The origins of the patent system stretch back a further 400 years. The word patent comes from the practice of monarchs in the Middle Ages (500–1500) conferring rights and privileges by means of 'open letters', that is, documents on which the royal seal was not broken when they were opened. This is distinct from 'closed letters' that were not intended for public view. Open letters were intended for display and inspection by any interested party. The language of government in medieval England was Latin and the Latin for open letters is *litterae patentes*. As English slowly took over from Latin as the official language, the documents became known as 'letters patent' and, later, just 'patents'.

- *Monopoly for 20 years.* Patents are granted to individuals and organisations that can lay claim to a new product or manufacturing process or to an improvement of an existing product or process that was not previously known. The granting of a patent gives the 'patentee' a monopoly to make, use or sell the invention for a fixed period of time, which, in Europe and the United States, is 20 years from the date the patent application was first filed. In return for this monopoly, the patentee pays a fee to cover the costs of processing the patent and, more importantly, publicly discloses details of the invention.
- *Annual fees required.* The idea must be new and not an obvious extension of what is already known. A patent lasts up to 20 years in the United Kingdom and Europe, but heavy annual renewal fees have to be paid to keep it in force.
- *Patent agents.* The role of a patent agent combines scientific or engineering knowledge with legal knowledge and expertise and it is a specialised field of work. Many large companies have in-house patent agents who prepare patents for the company's scientists. They may also search patent databases around the world on behalf of the company's scientists.

The earliest known English patent of invention was granted to John of Utynam in 1449. The patent gave Utynam a 20-year monopoly for a method of making stained glass that previously had not been known in England. For a patent to benefit from legal protection it must meet strict criteria:

- novelty;
- inventive step; and
- industrial application.

Novelty

The Patent Act 1977, section 2(1), stipulates that 'an invention shall be taken to be new if it does not form part of the state of the art'. A state of the art is defined as all matter, in other words, publications, written or oral or even anticipation (see *Windsurfing International Inc. v. Tabur Marine (GB) Ltd* below), will render a patent invalid.

Inventive step

Section 3 of the Patent Act 1977 states that 'an invention shall be taken to involve an inventive step if it is not obvious to a person skilled in the art'. In the United States, the term 'non-obvious' is used as a requirement for patentability. Although the basic principle is roughly the same, the assessment of the inventive step and non-obviousness varies from one country to another. A set of rules regarding the approach taken by the United Kingdom courts was laid out by the Court of Appeal in *Windsurfing International Inc. v. Tabur Marine (GB) Ltd* [1985] RPC 59, in determining the requirements for inventive step:

1 identifying the inventive concept embodied in the patent;
2 imputing to a normally skilled, but unimaginative, addressee what was common general knowledge in the art at the priority date;
3 identifying the differences, if any, between the matter cited and the alleged invention; and
4 deciding whether those differences, viewed without any knowledge of the alleged invention, constituted steps that would have been obvious to the skilled man or whether they required any degree of invention.

Industrial applications

Under the Patent Act, an invention shall be taken to be capable of industrial application if it can be a machine, product or process. Penicillin was a discovery that was not patentable but the process of isolating and storing penicillin clearly had industrial applications and, thus, was patentable.

Pause for thought

If states and governments, in particular, are determined to outlaw monopolistic practices in industry and commerce, why do they offer a 20-year monopoly for a patent?

Exclusions from patents

Discoveries (as opposed to inventions), scientific theory and mathematical processes are not patentable under the Patent Act 1988. Similarly, literary artistic works and designs are covered by other forms of intellectual property, such as trademarks, copyright and registered designs.

The patenting of life

The rapid scientific developments in the field of biology, medical science and biotechnology has fuelled intense debates about the morality of patenting life forms. Until very recently, there was a significant difference between the US patent system, which enabled the granting of patents on certain life forms, and the European patent system, which did not. Essentially, the US system adopted a far more liberal approach to the patenting of life. This difference was illustrated in the 'Harvard oncomouse' case (Patent No. 4,581,847). The Harvard Medical School had its request for a European patent refused because the mouse was a natural living life form and, hence, unpatentable. This European approach had serious implications for the European biotechnology industry. In particular, because the R&D efforts of the biotechnology industry could not be protected, there was a danger that capital, in the form of intellectual and financial, could flow from Europe to the United States, where protection was available. The other side of the argument is equally compelling: the granting to a company of a patent on certain genes may restrict other companies' ability to work with those genes. On 27 November 1997, the European Union agreed to Directive 95/0350(COD) and COM(97)446, which permits the granting of patents on certain life forms. This had a particular significance in the area of gene technology.

The subject of cloning a new life form from existing cells stirs the emotions of many. When Dolly, the first large mammal to be created from cells taken from other sheep, was announced, it generated enormous controversy and publicity. This was especially so for the group of scientists from the Roslin Institute, a publicly funded institute, and PPL Therapeutics, a biotechnology company that developed Dolly. The debate about the ethics of the science continues and related to this is the intellectual property of the gene technology involved. It raises the issue of whether the patent developed all those years ago is suitable for this type of industry or the twenty-first century in general.

In 1998, the European Union harmonised patent law to give European scientists and investors the chance to make one application for one big market, rather than separate applications to member states. It also gave European entrepreneurs the right to patent genes or life. In the past few years, the biotechnology firms have been making numerous patent applications for genes or partial human gene sequences. This, of course, leads to the argument that human genes are being turned into intellectual property and licensed to the highest bidders. The key question is, will this property then be made widely available to help the hungry, the sick and the desperate? Or will a few rich firms profit from many years of publicly funded science and exploit the poor and vulnerable? These are clearly difficult ethical questions that you may wish to debate amongst yourselves, but at the heart of this is patent law. This is illustrated in the case study at the end of this chapter. The purpose of any patent system is to strike a balance between the interests of the inventor and the wider public. At present, many believe that US patent law is too heavily biased towards the needs of inventors and investors and does not take into account the poor and developing countries of the world.

Innovation in action

A final year student, a patent and a £7 million business

Starting a business in your final year at university does not sound like a good idea, but for Sara Davies it was an inspired decision. Sara describes herself as someone from a working class background who went to a local comprehensive and not a high achiever, but someone who works hard.

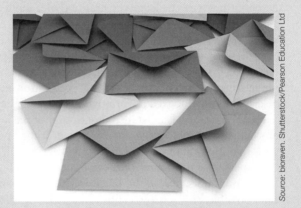

Source: bioraven. Shutterstock/Pearson Education Ltd

The business idea grew from her experience on her internship year. She worked for a small Durham business that produced handmade cards and their sales came from TV sales channels. These channels are full of arts and crafts products. Sarah noticed an opportunity to generate money. She struck a deal early on with the station Ideal World and now has six presenters working for her business. It is a great route to market. Eight years later, Crafter's Companion, which has its headquarters in County Durham, employs 40 people in Britain and 20 in California. Sales reached £7 million in 2014, £5.7 million of that in Britain.

She was in her final year at York University when she set up Crafter's Companion, selling products to hobbyists who make their own cards and envelopes. Her first product was the Enveloper, a device for making envelopes that are made to measure. In just three months, she sold 30,000 at £14.99 apiece. People loved making cards, but envelopes came in only a few sizes. So, she designed the Enveloper and asked a local carpenter to make up a prototype. Davies had a problem, however, and that was no money to pay the carpenter. She approached the TV channel, pitched and got an order. She explained to the carpenter that she would be paid in 45 days and that he would be paid in 46. She made £100,000 profit in three months.

Davies also recognised there was considerable competition and that she needed to keep ahead of her competitors. She hired software developers to develop software that enabled coloured paper and envelopes to be printed out from a CD-Rom. She

→

has been able to licence this and generate income. The US west coast is the biggest craft market and, in 2011, Davies acquired Sunday International, a small Californian art and design company with eight staff.

Davies has had to defend her design for the Enveloper five times in court. Good lawyers are important and expensive. Ensuring her product was patented has proved to be a wise decision. Even though defending it required money.

The configuration of a patent

For a patent to be granted, its contents need to be made public so that others can be given the opportunity to challenge the granting of a monopoly. There is a formal registering and indexing system to enable patents to be accessed easily by the public. For this reason, patents follow a very formal specification. Details concerning country of origin, filing date, personal details of applicant, etc., are accompanied by an internationally agreed numbering system for easy identification. The two most important sources of information relating to a patent are the patent specification and the *patent abstract*. Both of these are classified and indexed in various ways to facilitate search.

The specification is a detailed description of the invention and must disclose enough information to enable someone else to repeat the invention. This part of the document needs to be precise and methodical. It will also usually contain references to other scientific papers. The remainder of the specification will contain claims. These are to define the breadth and scope of the invention. A patent agent will try to write the broadest claim possible, as a narrow claim can restrict the patent's application and competitors will try to argue that, for example, a particular invention applies only to one particular method. Indeed, competitors will scrutinise these claims to test their validity.

The patent abstract is a short statement printed on the front page of the patent specification, which identifies the technical subject of the invention and the advance that it represents. Abstracts usually are accompanied by a drawing. In addition, these abstracts are published in weekly information booklets.

It is now possible to obtain a patent from the European Patent Office for the whole of Europe, and this can be granted in a particular country or several countries. The concept of a world patent, however, is a distant realisation. The next section explores some of the major differences between the two dominant world patent systems.

Patent harmonisation: first to file and first to invent

Most industrialised countries offer some form of patent protection to companies operating within their borders. However, whilst some countries have adequate protection, others do not. Moreover, different countries are members of different conventions and some adopt different systems. The European and the US patent systems have many similarities, for example a monopoly is granted for 20 years under both systems. There is, however, one key difference. In the United States the patent goes to the researcher who can prove they were the first to invent it, not – as in Europe – to the first to file for a patent.

The implications of this are many and varied, but there are two key points that managers need to consider.

1 In Europe, a patent is invalid if the inventor has published the novel information before filing for patent protection. In the United States, there are some provisions that allow inventors to talk first and file later.
2 In Europe, patent applications are published whilst pending. This allows the chance to see what monopoly an inventor is claiming and object to the Patent Office if there are grounds to contest validity. In the United States, the situation is quite different – applications remain secret until granted.

The issue of patent harmonisation has a long history. The Paris Convention for the Protection of Industrial Property was signed in 1883 and, since then, it has received many amendments. At present, its membership includes 114 countries. European countries have a degree of patent harmonisation provided by the European Patent Convention (EPC) administered by the European Patent Office.

The sheer size of the US market and its dominance in many technology-intensive industries means that this difference in the patent systems has received, and continues to receive, a great deal of attention from various industry and government departments in Europe and the United States.

Some famous patent cases

- *1880: Ediswan.* It is rare that identical inventions should come about at the same time. But that is what happened with the electric light bulb, which was patented almost simultaneously on either side of the Atlantic by Thomas Edison and Joseph Swan. To avoid patent litigation, the two business interests combined in England to produce lamps under the name of Ediswan, which is still registered as a trademark.
- *1930: Whittle's jet engine.* Whilst Frank Whittle was granted a patent for his jet engine, his employer, the RAF, was unable to get the invention to work efficiently and could not manufacture it on an industrial scale. It was left to the US firms of McDonnell Douglas and Pratt & Witney to exploit the commercial benefits from the patents.
- *1943: Penicillin.* Alexander Fleming discovered penicillin in 1928 and 13 years later, on 14 October 1941, researchers at Oxford University filed Patent No. 13242. The complete specification was accepted on 16 April 1943 (see Illustration 6.3).

Illustration 6.3

BTG

Penicillin was discovered in a London hospital by Alexander Fleming in 1928. It was to take another 12 years (1940) before a team working at Oxford University discovered a method of isolating and storing the drug. However, as a result of the Second World War, which drained Britain of much of its financial resources, Britain did not have the capability to develop large-scale fermentation of the bacteria. Help was sought from the United States and the success of the technology is well known.

→

The UK Government was concerned that it gave away valuable technology. By way of a response to this, following the end of the Second World War, it established the National Research Development Corporation (NRDC) in 1948 to protect the intellectual property rights of inventors' efforts that had been funded by the public sector. For example, this included research conducted in universities, hospitals and national laboratories.

From its very beginning, the NRDC soon began generating funds. Oxford University developed a second generation of antibiotics called cephalosporins. They were patented worldwide and the royalties secured the financial base of the NRDC for many years.

The NRDC changed its name to the British Technology Group (BTG) and has continued to be successful in arranging and defending patents for many university professors. In 1994, BTG became an independent public limited company.

Historically, BTG was involved only in UK intellectual property issues, but its activities have expanded. It was recently involved in litigation with the US Pentagon for patent infringement on the Hovercraft, as well as another case concerning Johnson and Johnson, the US healthcare group. BTG was so successful in this case that Johnson & Johnson asked BTG to manage a portfolio of nearly 100 inventions to try to generate royalties.

In 2015, BTG plc mostly earns revenues from speciality pharmaceutical and interventional medicine product sales and on royalties from partnered products.

Patents in practice

There are many industrialists and small business managers who have little faith in the patent system. They believe, usually as a result of first-hand experience, that the patent system is designed primarily for those large multinational corporations that have the finances to defend and protect any patents granted to them. The problem is that applying and securing a patent is only the beginning of what is usually an expensive journey. For example, every time you suspect a company may be infringing your patent, you will have to incur legal expenses to protect your intellectual property. Moreover, there are some examples of large corporations spending many years and millions of dollars in legal fees battling in the courts over alleged patent infringement. One of the most well-known cases was *Apple Computer Inc.* v. *Microsoft*, where Apple alleged that Microsoft had copied its Windows operating system. The case lasted for many years and cost each company many millions of dollars in legal fees.

Many smaller firms view the patent system with dread and fear. Indeed, only 10 per cent of the UK patents are granted to small firms. Yet, small firms represent 99 per cent of companies.

Fees to file a UK patent at the UK IPO are £30 for the examination and £100 for the initial search to be made within 12 months of applying. The substantive examination needs to be made within 18 months of filing and that fee is £70. On the fourth anniversary of the filing date, the patent must be renewed and every year after that. The fees for renewing in the fifth year are £50. It then goes up every year until the 20th year, which costs £400.

In theory, it sounds straightforward: £225 to apply for a UK patent. In practice, however, companies should be considering £1,000–£1,500 to obtain a UK patent.

Furthermore, protection in a reasonable number of countries is more likely to cost £10,000. Illustration 6.1 highlights many of the limitations of the patent system.

In some industries, it seems the rules of intellectual property may need to change. Some have argued that reforming the intellectual property law may help to stimulate more innovation and that a growing part of the economy (e.g. services, information technology) is only weakly protected under current intellectual property law. One possible way to encourage innovation is by extending coverage to these products and broadening legal protection to cover new product ideas for a short period. Small companies and individual entrepreneurs would benefit most from this broader but shorter protection.

Expiry of a patent and patent extensions

There is much written on the subject of patent application and the benefits to be gained from such a 20-year monopoly. There is, however, much less written about the subject of the effects of patent expiry. In other words, what happens when the patent protecting your product expires? A glance at the pharmaceutical industry reveals an interesting picture. Illustration 6.4 shows the reality for a firm when its patent expires.

For any firm operating in this science-intensive industry, the whole process of developing a product is based around the ability to protect the eventual product through the use of patents. Without the prospect of a 20-year monopoly to exploit many years of research and millions of dollars of investment, companies would be less inclined to engage in new product development. On expiry of a patent, competitors are able to use the technology, which hitherto had been protected, to develop their own product. Such products are referred to as generic drugs (a generic sold on its chemical composition). When a generic drug is launched, the effect on a branded drug which has just come off-patent can be considerable. For example, when two major cardiovascular drugs – Plavix and Coversyl – came off-patent in 2011, spending by the NHS on these drug treatments fell significantly. In 2008, the NHS spent £53,000 on Plavix and, in 2012, this fell to £7,000. Similarly, for Coversyl, spending fell from £35,000 in 2008 to £3,000 in 2012. The same trend is expected when Pfizer's Lipitor patent expires in 2016 (see Figure 6.1). Remarkably, market share falls of 85 per cent are typical (Nakamoto and Pilling, 2004). A generic drug is cheap to produce as no extensive research and development costs are incurred and pharmaceutical drugs are relatively easy to copy. It is, in effect, a chemical process. The principal forms of defence available to manufacturers are brand development and further research.

Illustration 6.4

FDA gives approval for generic versions of Eli Lilly's Prozac

Prozac, with 40 million users, accounted for a quarter of Eli Lilly's $10.8 billion in sales and more than a third of its $3 billion profit. With Prozac's US patent set to expire, however, Lilly will no longer be protected from cheaper generics. Within weeks, the company could see two-thirds of its global market for Prozac, and much of its profit, vanish.

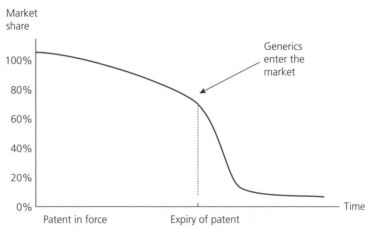

Figure 6.1 **The effect on its market share of a drug coming off-patent**

Pause for thought

If you obtain a patent for an invention and pay all the necessary fees, what happens if one day you see your invention in a shop window? Can you call in at the local police station and report it? Who will pay to bring a case against the retailer and manufacturer?

Developing a brand requires long-term development. Pharmaceutical companies with a product protected by patents usually will have between 10 and 20 years to develop a brand and brand loyalty, the aim being that, even when the product goes off-patent, customers will continue to ask for the branded drug as opposed to the generic drug. In practice, companies adopt a combination of aggressive marketing to develop the brand and technical research on existing drugs to improve the product still further and file for additional patents to protect the new and improved versions of the product.

Patent extensions

Patent extensions are known in Europe as Supplementary Protection Certificates, usually abbreviated to SPC. They were introduced in Europe in the mid-1990s to compensate patent owners for regulatory delays in approving their pharmaceuticals and agrochemicals. The approvals sometimes took so long that the patent had reached the end of its 20-year life, thus opening the invention to all comers, before the inventor had had much chance to commercialise it.

The SPC was designed to provide a level playing field for all pharmaceuticals/agrochemicals patent owners that had suffered regulatory delay exceeding 5 years, to restore to them an effective 15-year term of protection. The SPC takes effect at the instant of patent expiry, and then lasts for the length of time by which regulatory approval exceeded five years. Each SPC, therefore, has its own fixed duration, but, to protect the public, the maximum duration is five years' effect.

The United States achieves a similar result by a different route, namely by directly extending the lifetime of those individual patents where the applicant can show regulatory delay in getting the product on to the market. Japan has been considering legislation to achieve broadly similar results.

Every month of patent extension can mean hundreds of millions of dollars in additional revenues for blockbuster products. A number of companies, including Bristol Myers Squibb, AstraZeneca, GlaxoSmithKline and Schering-Plough have been accused of using such tactics to boost profits. However, a Federal Trade Commission report found only eight instances of suspect patent extensions between 1992 and 2000 (Bowe and Griffith, 2002).

The use of patents in innovation management

Patent offices for each country house millions of patents. In the United Kingdom, there are over two million British patents and all this information is available to the public. Each publication, because of the legal requirement that details of patents be disclosed, is a valuable source of technological knowledge. Indeed, the information provision activities of the Patent Office have increased in their function. For example, scientists working in a particular field often will search patent databases to see how the problems they face have been tackled in the past. They will also use previous patents to identify how their current area of work fits in with those areas of science and technology that have been developed and patented previously. Very often, patents can provide a valuable source of inspiration.

In addition, many firms also use the patent publication register to find out what their competitors are doing. For example, a search of the worldwide patent databases may reveal that your major competitor has filed a series of patents in an area of technology that you had not considered previously. Armed with prior knowledge of the industry and the technology, it may be possible to uncover the research direction in which your competitor is heading, or even the type of product line that it is considering developing. All this industrial intelligence can help research teams and companies to develop and modify their own strategy or to pursue a different approach to a problem.

Patent trolls

Patent trolls have many faces, since the media uses this expression in various ways. In pejorative usage, a patent troll is a person or company that attempts to enforce patent rights against accused infringers far beyond the patent's actual value or contribution to the prior art. Patent trolls often do not manufacture products or supply services based upon the patents in question. According to Fischer and Henkel (2014), the troll business model is based around purchasing patents that are more likely to be infringed, harder to substitute and robust to legal challenges. In its worst form, a patent troll obtains patents being sold at auctions by bankrupt companies attempting to liquidate their assets or by doing just enough research to prove they had the idea first. However, Research by Pohlmann and Opitz (2013) reveals that a patent troll as such has no distinct shape or appearance. They find negative but also positive effects of the troll business on incentives to innovate. They assess the troll business and its effects and suggest the nature of troll behaviour to be:

- a practice to enforce IP rights, enabling repayments for earlier innovation investments;
- a strategy that may create costs to affected industries.

Do patents hinder or encourage innovation?

According to Professor William Haseltine, the rush for patents did not hamper AIDS research. In the 1980s, he worked for a team that deciphered the DNA of the HIV virus, worked out the sequences of its genes and discovered some of the proteins those genes made. His name is on more than a dozen patents on the AIDS virus, but the patents are held by the cancer institute he then worked for at the Harvard Medical School. He makes a very strong case in favour of the patent system for fostering innovation. Indeed, he thinks the patents speeded up the assault on the virus itself.

> There is, however, another school of thought. The front page of The Economist, in August 2015, argued that the patent system has created a parasitic ecology of trolls and defensive patent-holders, who aim to block innovation, or at least to stand in its way unless they can grab a share of the spoils. An early study found that newcomers to the semiconductor business had to buy licences from incumbents for as much as $200m. Patents should spur bursts of innovation; instead, they are used to lock in incumbents' advantages.
>
> (The Economist (2015) Time to fix patents, 8 August, p. 3)

Strong words indeed. Andrew Brown (2007) put forward similar arguments many years earlier: so called sub-marine patents – those that surface only after the technologies they protect have come into wide use – are obviously dangerous. But even ordinary, open, honest patents now function as a brake on innovation. He uses the illustration of the French company Alcatel suing Microsoft for infringing its patents on the MP3 compression scheme. This, he argues, is an example of firms abusing intellectual property law. The patents arising from the MP3 technology joint venture (between Bell Labs, US telephone company, and the Fraunhofer Institute, Germany), were thought by everyone to belong to the German Research Organisation, which duly licensed them and made a reasonable amount of money from this. Microsoft, for example, paid $16 million to incorporate MP3 support into Windows Media Player. But, when Alcatel bought the remains of Bell Labs, now known as Lucent Technologies, it behaved as any modern company would, and tried to squeeze maximum value from the patents it had acquired. It asserted that these covered some of the MP3 technology that everyone assumed Fraunhofer owned, and sued two PC companies – Dell and Gateway – for selling computers equipped to play MP3s. Microsoft promised to fight the suit on their behalf and so the case came eventually to court.

Table 6.2 shows the reasons why firms patent. It is clear from this that most firms use the patent system to prevent other firms copying their technology and blocking. Blocking here refers to owners of a patent preventing others from using the technology. It is this area that is a growing concern for firms and governments around the world. For the aim of the patent system is to encourage innovation and, yet, there is increasing evidence that it is now being used to prevent other firms developing technology.

Table 6.2 Reasons why firms patent

	Products %	Processes %
Prevent copying	96	78
Patent blocking	82	64
Prevent suits	59	47
Use in negotiations	48	37
Enhance reputation	48	34
Licensing revenue	28	23
Measure performance	6	5

Source: Cohen, W.M. (2002) *Patents: Their Effectiveness and Role*, Carnegie Mellon University & National Bureau of Economic Research. With permission from Wesley Cohen.

The European Federal Trade Commission (EFTC) (2006) investigated the role of patents to see whether the balance between protection for the intellectual property owners and stimulating innovation had now shifted too much in favour of protection. Their investigation revealed that patents can indeed impair competition, innovation and the economy. In particular, the EFTC found that there was an increasing use of patent thickets in software and internet-related industries. A patent thicket is a form of defensive patenting where firms unnecessarily increase the number of patents to increase complexity. This forces competing companies to divert resources from original R&D into paying to use the patents of other firms. Patent thickets make it more difficult to commercialise new products and raise uncertainty and investment risks for follow-on firms. Specifically, patents deter innovation by:

- denying follow-on innovators access to necessary technologies (EULA);
- increasing entry barriers;
- the expense required to avoid patent infringement;
- the issuance of questionable patents.

This view was confirmed in 2007 when the Commission accused Microsoft of demanding excessive royalties from companies wishing to license technical information about its Windows operating system. The EU fined Microsoft €800 million.

One radical answer would be to abolish patents altogether. This, to many, seems to be a step too far and would allow a free for all where the powerful are able to steal intellectual property from the weak (see Illustration 6.7 about the use of prizes as an alternative to patents). The problem at present is that it is the powerful who are exploiting the system.

The case study at the end of this chapter examines whether the pharmaceutical industry is generating supra industry profits as a result of the patent system.

Alternatives to patenting

The previous discussions would seem to suggest that firms consider patenting to be a useful appropriation mechanism. Yet, when studies are compared, it seems that the value of patents as an appropriation mechanism remains questionable. For example, Cohen et al. (2000) found that in only 26.67 per cent of product innovations and

23.33 per cent of process innovations were patents considered an effective appropriation mechanism in the semiconductor industry. It seems that there are two other appropriation mechanisms that are considered superior by semiconductor firms, namely secrecy and lead time or first mover advantage. Research shows that there are a number of reasons why large companies in the semiconductor industry patent, and that these reasons are mostly strategic. For example, small firms in the semiconductor industry use patents in order to acquire venture capital and prefer secrecy as an appropriation mechanism over patents.

Similarly, the benefits of owning a patent have changed from protection of innovation to a number of strategic uses. An important benefit of a patent is the freedom to operate that it allows. In the semiconductor industry, freedom to operate is an important issue, because a lot of the innovations overlap. This is why the large semiconductor firms cross-license patents and allow competition to use each other's patents (Grindley and Teece, 1997). A strong patent portfolio provides firms with a strong negotiation position. If firms do not provide the freedom to operate, they can block. Patenting with the intention to block competition is quite common and, in the semiconductor industry, 75 per cent of the participants declared blocking a reason to patent (Cohen et al., 2000). In a study of German firms, Blind et al. (2009) find clear evidence that a company's patenting strategies are related to the characteristics of its patent portfolios. For example, companies using patents as bartering chips in collaborations receive fewer oppositions to their patents. Patents are, sometimes, also used as an indicator of value to an external party, through the promise of income or as a signal of innovative and protected capability. In the semiconductor industry, small firms have indicated that a reason to patent is to attract venture capital.

A number of alternative strategies to patents (see Table 6.3) have been developed by companies, where they felt other forms of intellectual property protection were

Table 6.3 Alternative strategies to patenting

Alternatives to patents	Definition
Secrecy	Relatively easy, no legal protection.
Accumulated tacit knowledge	Acquired through experience, it is an asset that is difficult to imitate.
Lead time	Market share and profits need to be secured quickly.
After-sales service	Market share acquired by the lead-time advantages can be sustained through after-sales service. If a better and cheaper product is introduced, especially in business-to-business, customer loyalty can disappear very quickly.
Learning curve	Prior knowledge has made the process more efficient.
Complementary assets	Additional useful, extra products are offered to make the original product more desirable.
Product complexity	Helps avoid imitation by increasing product complexity. The semiconductor industry is a good example of this, because expensive devices are needed to reverse engineer semiconductor products.
Standards	A highly effective (but risky) way of getting large returns on the investment in R&D. Winners can take the whole market and losers get nothing.
Branding	Branding is an important way to appropriate returns from innovation; it can also create customer loyalty.

better suited to their needs (Leiponen and Byma, 2009). Recent research by Thomä and Bizer (2013) reveal that, for many innovative small firms, the key question is not whether to use intellectual property rights (IPRs) or not, but whether to protect their innovations from imitation at all. In a study of small German firms, they found that secrecy and lead-time advantages over competitors are often combined with IPRs. Yet, a number of small firms use complexity of design as a substitute to patent protection. The relevance of each appropriation mode depends on such factors as the degree of innovativeness, the type of innovator, the general market environment and industry sector.

Trademarks

Trademarks have particular importance to the world of business. For many companies, especially in the less technology-intensive industries where the use of patents is limited, trademarks offer one of the few methods of differentiating a company's products. The example of Coca-Cola is a case in point. Trademarks are closely associated with business image, goodwill and reputation. Indeed, many trademarks have become synonymous with particular products: Mars and chocolate confectionery, Hoover and vacuum cleaners and Nestlé and coffee. The public rely on many trademarks as indicating quality, value for money and origin of goods. Significant changes have been made to trademark law in the United Kingdom. The Trade Marks Act 1994 replaced the Trade Marks Act 1938, which was widely recognised as being out of touch with business practices today. The United Kingdom now complies with the EC directive on the approximation of the laws of member states relating to trademarks and ratified the Madrid Convention for the international registration of trademarks. The law relating to trademarks is complex indeed. For example, what is a trademark? The following section offers a brief introduction to some of the key considerations for product and business managers.

Section 1(1) of the Trade Marks Act 1994 defines a trademark as:

being any sign capable of being represented graphically which is capable of distinguishing goods or services of one undertaking from those of other undertakings.

This can include, for example, Apple Computers, the Apple logo and Macintosh, all of which are registered trademarks. Some of the first trademarks were used by gold- and silversmiths to mark their own work. The first registered trademark, No. 1, was issued to Bass in 1890 for their red triangle mark for pale ale. Illustration 6.5 on the Mr Men offers an example of the effective and successful use of trademarks.

There are certain restrictions and principles with the use of trademarks. In particular, a trademark should:

- satisfy the requirements of section 1(1);
- be distinctive;
- not be deceptive; and
- not cause confusion with previous trademarks.

Illustration 6.5

Mr Hargreaves and the Mr Men

Each one of the Mr Men characters is trade-marked. The Mr Men books have sold a stagger-ing 100 million copies in no fewer than 30 countries. They are nearly 40 years old. They were the invention of Roger Hargreaves, a shrewd Sussex-based advertising copywriter, who saw in the books a way of quitting the rat race and enjoy-ing the prosperity he craved. His dream paid off. His first book, *Mr Tickle*, became an instant suc-cess and five more quickly followed. Within three years, Hargreaves had sold a million copies and, ultimately, became so wealthy he moved to Guernsey as a tax exile. But, in 1988, the dream came to an abrupt end when he suffered a stroke whilst walking down to breakfast. He was taken to hospital, but died later that day, aged just 53.

That could have been the end of the Mr Men, but Hargreaves' eldest son, Adam, valiantly stepped into the breach. On the face of it, he was not the most obvious candidate. He was 25, working as a dairyman and stockman and, throughout his teens, had studiously ignored his father's day job, finding the whole thing acutely embarrassing. Despite his substantial real estate, Adam, now 46, seems untainted by wealth or success. In fact, he is as unshowy as they come – affable, modest and self-effacing. Adam believes the secret of their appeal lies in the Mr Men's uni-versal personality traits. And then there's the col-lectability factor, which is something children are always going to enjoy.

In 2004, Adam and his family made the deci-sion to sell the intellectual property rights of the Mr Men to the entertainment group Chorion, for a cool £24 million. 'The sale of the likes of Thomas the Tank Engine to multi-national cor-porations had made us aware that there was a big market for property rights and many of our rivals were now getting a huge amount of investment that we had no hope of matching', he says. 'Our business was happily ticking along, but there were limits to what we could achieve from our small office in Sussex. We knew that a much larger company with marketing skills, investment opportunities and contacts could open up the worldwide market much more effectively.' He had few qualms about the sale. Though it was a difficult wrench for his mother, he knew that his father would have approved. Roger Hargreaves' commercial nous was also evident in the way that he and his agent seized on the potential of licens-ing in the mid-Seventies, following in the foot-steps of Disney. They licensed everything and anything. And the beauty of the Mr Men was that they could be associated with an enormous range of products – from Mr Messy baby bibs to Mr Grumpy slippers for Father's Day. All of which now deliver profits to Chorion.

Source: http://www.sussexlife.co.uk/people/celebrity-interviews/interview_with_adam_hargreaves_mr_men_illustrator_and_writer_1_1636359.

Satisfy the requirements of section 1(1)

The much wider definition of a trademark offered by the 1994 Act opened the possibility of all sorts of marks that previously would not have been registrable. Sounds, smells and containers could now be registered. A number of perfume manufacturers have applied to register their perfumes as trademarks. Coca-Cola and Unilever have applied to regis-ter their containers for Coca-Cola and Domestos respectively. In 2010, Lego failed to get its plastic eight-stud brick trademarked. The European Court of Justice ruled that a three-dimensional image of Lego's eight-stud bricks did not qualify for a trademark because the blocks served a functional purpose. The case centred on an EU ruling that shapes used for a technical result did not qualify for a trademark (Farrell, 2010).

Be distinctive

A trademark should be distinctive in itself. In general, this means that it should not describe in any way the product or service to which it relates. Usually, words that are considered generic or descriptive are not trademarked. In addition, it should not use non-distinctive expressions that other traders might reasonably wish to use in the course of a trade. For example, to attempt to register the word 'beef' as a trademark for a range of foods would not be possible, since other traders reasonably would want to use the word in the course of their trade. It would, however, be acceptable to use beef in association with a range of clothing because this would be considered distinctive. Laudatory terms are not allowed, for example the word 'heavenly' for a range of cosmetics would not be possible, since it is a laudatory term. In 2015, the European Council published proposals to recast the Trade Marks Directive to further align registration procedures in the EU and to make them more accessible and efficient for businesses in terms of lower costs, increased speed, more predictability and greater legal certainty. Importantly, there are also proposals to provide more effective trademark protection against counterfeits. The extent of the changes is evident from the increase from 19 articles to 57 in the Trade Marks Directive. Illustration 6.6 shows an example of a trademark infringement involving Gucci.

Not be deceptive

A trademark should also not attempt to deceive the customer. For example, to attempt to register Orlwoola, as happened in 1900, as an artificial fibre would not be possible, since the very word could persuade people to believe the material was made of wool.

Illustration 6.6

Gucci loses trademark infringement case against Guess in France

Gucci has been accusing Guess of trademark violations for years and the Court of Paris reached a decision in the matter that had already been addressed in Italian and US courts.

In February 2015, the French court ruled in Guess's favour, finding no trademark infringement, no counterfeiting and no unfair competition between the luxury Italian label and the American mall brand. Gucci's request for €55 million in damages was denied and, instead, the company was ordered to pay Guess €30,000. The court also nullified Gucci's trademark of three of its 'G' logos. In a statement, a representative for Gucci responded, saying the company strongly disagreed with the verdict and 'will certainly and immediately bring an appeal against the decision'.

Source: Directphoto Collection/Alamy Images

Not cause confusion

Finally, a trade or service mark will not be registered if it could be confused with the trademark of a similar product that has already been registered. For example, 'Velva-Glo' was refused as a trademark for paints because it was judged to be too near the word 'Vel-Glo', which was already registered.

Brand names

Increasingly the link between the **brand name** and the **trademark** is becoming closer and stronger. The literature tends to separate the two, with brands remaining in the sphere of marketing and trademarks within the sphere of law. In terms of a property right that is exploitable, however, brand names and trademarks are cousins. They both serve to facilitate identity and origin. That origin, in turn, indicates a certain level of quality, as reflected in the goods. Indeed, it is worthy of note that many brands have been registered as trademarks.

Like other capital assets owned by a firm, such as manufacturing equipment or land, a brand can also be considered an asset, and a valuable one at that. 'Brand equity' is the term used to describe the value of a brand name. Accountants and marketers differ in their definitions and there have been a variety of approaches to define the term:

- the total value of a brand as a separable asset – when it is sold or included on a balance sheet;
- a measure of the strength of consumers' attachment to a brand; and
- a description of the associations and beliefs the consumer has about the brand.

Brand equity creates value for both customers and the firm. The customers clearly can use brand names as simplifying heuristics for processing large amounts of information. The brand can also give customers confidence in the purchasing situation. Firms benefit enormously from having strong brand names. Investment in a brand name can be leveraged through brand extensions and increased distributions. High brand equity often allows higher prices to be charged; hence it is a significant competitive advantage.

A firm may decide to purchase a brand from another company rather than to develop a brand itself. Indeed, this may be less expensive and less risky. IKEA, for example, purchased the Habitat brand. Habitat had a strong UK presence in the furniture and household products market and enabled IKEA to increase its presence in the UK furniture market.

Using brands to protect intellectual property

Product managers, product designers and R&D managers all recognise that, despite their best efforts, sometimes the success of a product can be dependent on the brand. In the cigarette market, for example, over 70 per cent of consumers are loyal to a particular brand (Badenhausen, 1995) and this makes entry to this market very difficult. Brands help buyers to identify specific products that they like and reduce the time required to purchase the product. Without brands, product selection would be random and maybe more rational, based on price, value and content of the product. Certainly, it would force consumers to select more carefully. If all the products in a store had the same plain white packaging, but information was made available on ingredients, contents and details of the manufacturing process, consumers would spend an enormous amount of time shopping. Brands symbolise a certain quality level and this can be transferred to other product items. For example, Unilever extended the Timotei shampoo name to skincare products. This clearly enabled the company to develop a new range of products and use the benefits of brand recognition of Timotei.

An area of branding that is growing rapidly is that of the licensing of trademarks. Using a licensing agreement, a company may permit approved manufacturers to use its trademark on other products for a licensing fee. Royalties may be as low as 2 per cent of wholesale revenues or as high as 10 per cent. The licensee is responsible for all manufacturing and marketing and bears the cost if the product fails. Today, the licensing business is a huge growth industry. The All England Tennis and Croquet Club licenses its brand to a small group of companies each year. During the summer those companies use the association with Wimbledon to promote their products. Products such as Robinsons soft drinks, Wedgwood pottery, Slazenger sports goods and Coca-Cola have all signed licence agreements with the All England Club. For an organisation like the All England Club, the advantages are obvious: increased revenue and, to a lesser extent, increased promotion of the tournament. To other firms, like JCB, Jaguar Cars and Harley-Davidson, all of whom license their trademarks to clothing manufacturers, it clearly provides increased revenues, but also raises opportunities for diversification. The major disadvantages are a lack of control over the products, which could harm the perception and image of the brand. The All England Club, for example, has numerous committee meetings to consider very carefully the type of organisation and product that will bear its trademark.

Exploiting new opportunities

Product and brand managers must continually be vigilant about changes in the competitive market. This will help to realise new development opportunities for the brand. Some companies have developed reputations for exploiting the latest technology developments; indeed, some of these firms are responsible for the breakthroughs. The following list of examples illustrates how pioneering firms have exploited opportunities and developed their brands:

- *New technology*. Microsoft and HP are examples of firms that over the past 30 years have continually exploited new technology. There brands are associated with leading edge technology.
- *New positioning*. Dell computers and Uber uncovered and developed unique positions for themselves in the market. Dell was one of the pioneers of bespoke personal computers and continued to build on this position. Similarly Uber has become a world leader in linking drivers of cars with people who need transportation.
- *New distribution*. Amazon developed new channels of distribution for their products and services. Amazon was a pioneer of on-line retailing and has exploited this position.

Frequently, rival firms will develop **generic products** and services to rival the brand. Nowhere is this more apparent than in the pharmaceutical industry, as the previous section illustrated. One of the key issues for brand managers is whether the brand can sustain its strong market position in the face of such competition. It is possible to defend a brand through effective marketing communications, but this is rarely enough. Usually, the brand will need to innovate in one or more of the areas listed above. Some brands have failed to innovate and have then struggled in the face of fierce competition. One example is the Kellogg's brand. Over the past 10 years, Kellogg's has seen its share of the cereal market gradually decline in the face of strong competition from store brands. Critics of Kellogg's argue that its brand managers have failed to innovate and develop the brand.

Pause for thought

Intellectual property does not just lie in physical products, it can also reside in services and ways of operating. What role does the brand play in service-based industries, such as airlines?

Brands, trademarks and the internet

Nowhere is the subject of trademarks and brands more closely intertwined than on the internet. Individuals and firms are linked up and identified through domain names. These are, essentially, an address, comprising four numbers, such as 131.22.45.06. The numbers indicate the network (131), an internet protocol address (22 and 45) and a local address (06). Numeric addresses, however, are difficult to remember. Internet authorities assigned and designated an alphanumeric designation and mnemonic, which affords the consumer user-friendly information with regard to identity and source – the domain name (for example, microsoft.com and ports.ac.uk).

It can be seen, then, that domain names act as internet addresses. They serve as the electronic or automated equivalent to a telephone directory, allowing web browsers to look up their intended hits directly or via a search engine, such as Alta Vista. One may argue at this point that domain names act as electronic brand names. Moreover, the characteristics of a domain name and a trademark are considerable. A recent US judgment has pronounced that domain names are protectable property rights in much the same way as a trademark.

Duration of registration, infringement and passing off

Under the Trade Marks Act 1994, the registration of a trademark is for a period of 10 years from the date of registration, which may be renewed indefinitely for further 10-year periods. Once accepted and registered, trademarks are considered to be an item of personal property.

The fact that a trademark is registered does not mean that one cannot use the mark at all. In the case of *Bravado Merchandising Services Ltd* v. *Mainstream*

Publishing Ltd, the respondent published a book about the pop group Wet Wet Wet under the title *A Sweet Little Mystery – Wet Wet Wet – The Inside Story*. Wet Wet Wet was a registered trademark and the proprietor brought an injunction against the use of the name. The court decided that the trademark had not been infringed because the respondent was using the mark as an indication of the main characteristic of the artefact which, in this instance, was a book about the pop group (Bainbridge, 1996).

Where a business uses a trademark that is similar to another or takes unfair advantage of or is detrimental to another trademark, infringement will have occurred. This introduces the area of passing off and is the common law form of trademark law. Passing off concerns the areas of goodwill and reputation of the trademark. In *Consorzio de Prosciutto di Parma* v. *Marks & Spencer plc* (1991) Lord Justice Norse identified the ingredients of a passing off action as being composed of:

- the goodwill of the plaintiff;
- the misrepresentation made by the defendant; and
- consequential damage.

Registered designs

A new product may be created that is not sufficiently novel or does not contain an inventive step so as to satisfy the exacting requirements for the granting of a patent. This was the situation faced by Britain's textile manufacturers in the early nineteenth century. They would create new textile designs, but these would be copied later by foreign competitors. The Design Registry was set up in the early 1800s in response to growing demands from Britain's textile manufacturers for statutory protection for the designs of their products. Today, designs that are applied to articles may be protected by design law. There are two systems of design law in the United Kingdom. One is similar to that used for patent law and requires registration; the other system of design protection is design right and is provided along copyright lines. There is a large area of overlap between the two systems.

The registered designs system is intended for those designs proposed to have some form of aesthetic appeal. For example, electrical appliances, toys and some forms of packaging have all been registered.

A design as protected by registration is the *outward appearance of an article*. Only the appearance given by its actual shape, configuration, pattern or ornament can be protected, not any underlying idea. The registered design lasts for a maximum of 15 years. Initially, the proprietor is granted the exclusive right to a design for a fixed term of five years. This can be renewed for up to five further five-year terms.

To be registered, a design must first be new at the date an application for its registration is filed. In general, a design is considered to be new, if it has not been published in the United Kingdom (i.e. made available or disclosed to the public in any way whatsoever) and if, when compared with any other published design, the differences make a materially different appeal to the eye. For example, if a company designed a new kettle that was very different from any other kettle, the company could register the design. This would prevent other kettle manufacturers from simply copying the design. Clearly, the kettle does not offer any advantage in terms of use, hence a patent cannot be obtained, but a good design is also worth protecting.

Copyright

This area of the law on intellectual property rights has changed significantly over the past few years, mainly because it now covers computer software. Computer software manufacturers are particularly concerned about the illegal copying of their programs. The music industry has also battled with this same problem for many years. It is common knowledge that this was an exceptionally difficult area of law to enforce and new technology may, at last, provide copyright holders with an advantage. The impact of this may be to hinder creativity in the long term (see Illustration 6.7).

For the author of creative material to obtain copyright protection, it must be in a tangible form so that it can be communicated or reproduced. It must also be the author's own work and thus the product of his or her skill or judgement. Concepts, principles, processes or discoveries are not valid for copyright protection until they are put in a tangible form, such as written or drawn. It is the particular way that an

Illustration 6.7

Intellectual property laws can prevent access to knowledge and thereby hinder innovation

Let us examine the growing view that intellectual property laws may be hindering creativity and innovation. Let us take the field of copyright, for example. In Shakespeare's time, there was no protection for copyright at all. Today's copyright laws would have suffocated much Elizabethan creativity. The length of copyright – 50 years – seems excessive. The vast majority of income from books and music comes immediately after publication (with the exception of a tiny number of very successful artists). The key issue here, of course, is monopolisation. Monopolies can lead to higher prices and lower output and the costs can be especially high when monopoly power is abused. What is more, the hoped-for benefit of enhanced innovation does not always materialise. Let us not forget the most important input into research is knowledge, and IP sometimes makes this less accessible. This is especially true when patents take what was previously in the public domain and 'privatise' it. The patents granted on

Basmati rice and on the healing properties of turmeric are good examples. Furthermore, as Stiglitz argues (2006) 'conflicting patent claims make profitable innovation more difficult. Indeed, a century ago, a conflict over patents between the Wright brothers and rival aviation pioneer Glenn Curtis so stifled the development of the airplane that the US government had to step in to resolve the issue'.

Patents are not the only way of stimulating innovation. For example, the Royal Society of Arts has long advocated the use of prizes. The alternative of awarding prizes would be more efficient and more equitable. It would provide strong incentives for research, but without the inefficiencies associated with monopolisation.

Source: Trott, P. and Hoecht, A. (2010) How should firms deal with counterfeiting: a review of the success conditions of anti-counterfeiting strategies, Internal Report, University of Portsmouth Business School, No. 12. Reprinted with permission. Stiglitz, J.E. (2006) Innovation: a better way than patents, *New Scientist*, Sept., p. 20.

idea is presented that is valid for copyright. This particular point, that ideas cannot be copyrighted, often causes confusion. If someone has written an article, you cannot simply rephrase it or change some of the words and claim it as your own. You are, however, entitled to read an article, digest it, take the ideas from that article together with other sources and weave them into your own material without any copyright problems. In most instances, common sense should provide the answer.

Copyright is recognised by the symbol © and gives legal rights to creators of certain kinds of material, so that they can control the various ways in which their work may be exploited. Copyright protection is automatic and there is no registration or other formality.

Copyright may subsist in any of nine descriptions of work and these are grouped into three categories:

1 original literary, dramatic, musical and artistic works;
2 sound recordings, films, broadcasts and cable programmes; and
3 the typographical arrangement or layout of a published edition.

Each of these categories has more detailed definitions. For example, films in category 2 include videograms; and 'artistic work' in category 1 includes photographs and computer-generated work.

The duration of copyright protection varies, according to the description of the work. In the United Kingdom, for literary, dramatic, musical and artistic works, copyright expires 70 years after the death of the author, in other cases 50 years after the calendar year in which it was first published. The period was for 75 years in the United States (but is now 50 years for all works created after 1978), but this issue is currently causing a great deal of concern for one of the most well-known organisations in the world (see Illustration 6.8).

Illustration 6.8

Mickey Mouse is now past 75 and was to be out of copyright

This issue of copyright is currently causing great concern for one of the most famous organisations in the world and certainly the most famous cartoon character. In the USA copyright lasts for 75 years (for creations prior to 1978) and Mickey Mouse in 2003 was 75 years old. At this point, the first Mickey Mouse cartoon was to be publicly available for use by anyone. *Plane Crazy* was released in May 1928 and was to slip from the Disney empire in 2003. In the autumn of 1928 Disney released *Steam Boat Willie*, the world's first synchronised talking cartoon and soon after Disney copyrighted the film.

At first glimpse one may be tempted to have some sympathy for the Disney organisation. However, Walt Disney wisely registered Mickey

Source: Getty Images/Condé Nast Archive

Mouse as a trademark, recognising from an early date that Mickey Mouse had value far beyond the screen. Hence, the use by others of the character on numerous products produces large licensing revenues for the Disney Corporation.

The Disney Corporation managed to secure a twenty-year extension from Congress under the 1998 Copyright law.

Source: James Langton, *Sunday Telegraph*, 15 February 1998; *Financial Times*, 10 January 2002.

Remedy against infringement

There are some forms of **infringement** of a commercial nature, such as dealing with infringing copies that carry criminal penalties. Indeed, HM Customs has powers to seize infringing printed material. Also a civil action can be brought by the plaintiff for one or more of the following:

- damages;
- injunction; and
- accounts.

Damages

The owner of the copyright can bring a civil case and ask the court for damages, which can be expected to be calculated on the basis of compensation for the actual loss suffered.

Injunction

An injunction is an order of the court that prohibits a person making infringing copies of a work of copyright.

Accounts

This is a useful alternative for the plaintiff in that it enables access to the profits made from the infringement of copyright. This is useful, especially if the amount is likely to exceed that which might be expected from an award of damages.

Counterfeit goods and IP

The production and sale of counterfeit products is big business in the international economy. The value of counterfeit products marketed annually in the world is estimated to be over $1 trillion. Counterfeiters are serving a market as willing to buy their illicit wares as they are to sell them. Nowhere is this more evident than in China (Hung, 2003; Naim, 2005). The massive expansion of the Chinese economy has led to a huge increase in foreign direct investment (FDI) and international technology transfer (ITT) and has brought the issue of intellectual property to the fore. The extent of product counterfeiting operations in China is astounding; estimates range from 10 per cent to 20 per cent of all consumer goods manufactured in the country. The Quality Brands Protection Committee (QBPC), for example, an anti-piracy body under the auspices of the China Association of Enterprises with Foreign Investment, claims that government statistics show that counterfeit products outnumber genuine products in the Chinese market by 2:1. Indeed, in a review of the intellectual property system in China, Yang and Clarke (2004) concluded that the emerging IP system requires improvements in legislation, administration and enforcement, in order to create a secure IP environment in line with the international standard. Enforcement efforts are made even more futile by popular acceptance of piracy in China. Rising incomes have created an enthusiasm for foreign goods and brands, but Chinese consumers have become so accustomed to cheap, pirated goods that they are unwilling to pay full prices for the real thing. It almost seems like imitation in modern China is a way of life.

Many argue that authentic manufacturers have contributed to the problem of counterfeiting due to their unyielding self-interest of pursuing lowest possible manufacturing cost (McDonald and Roberts, 1994; Tom et al., 1998). Even in the face of increased counterfeiting, these firms have continued to seek production opportunities in developing countries where counterfeiting is a known problem. It may be that, given the short-term gains of lower production costs, firms may be either lacking in risk management or even willing to risk the loss of intellectual property with its potential long-term damage of loss of competitive advantage for the sake of short-term gains. If this is the case, then the risk of losing intellectual property is the cost of doing business in China (Naim, 2005). Recent research by Schmiele (2013), analysing German firms with innovation activities in China, revealed that firms with international R&D activities are increasing their chances of losing technological knowledge to their local competitors abroad. The research illustrated three different types of IP infringements from abroad:

- the usage of firms' technical inventions;
- product piracy; and
- copying of corporate names and designs.

Furthermore, the effectiveness of the current approaches towards counterfeiting is questionable. Indeed, in fast moving technology-intensive industries, legal remedies tend to be too slow and too costly for regulating complex technological developments and their associated intellectual property and ownership rights (Deakin and Wilkinson, 1998; Liebeskind and Oliver, 1998). Furthermore, Thurow has argued that the whole approach to the defence of the intellectual property rights is simplistic because it applies the same rule to all types of products in all types of industries. He argues that, for example, the 'Third World's need to get low-cost pharmaceuticals is not equivalent to its need for low-cost CDs. Any system that treats such needs equally, as our current system does, is neither a good nor a viable system' (Thurow, 1997; Vaidhyanathan, 2001). This view is shared by other economists (e.g. Sachs, 1999). Moreover, we should acknowledge that society seems content with a system that provides protection only for rich owners. It was more than 25 years ago that the Advisory Council for Applied Research and Development (ACARD, 1980) in the United Kingdom noted that, if society wanted to treat intellectual property like tangible property, the state would prosecute alleged offenders at public expense. Since this time, little has changed and it remains that, if intellectual property is stolen, responsibility generally rests with the owner to prosecute.*

Pause for thought

Who owns the copyright on your essays that you write? What can you do if you find sections of one of your essays in a newspaper or in a book?

Case study

Pricing, patents and profits in the pharmaceutical industry

This case study explains how the pharmaceutical industry uses the patent system to ensure it reaps rewards from the drugs that it develops. Increasingly, however, there is alarm at the high costs of these drugs to the underdeveloped world, especially against a backcloth of malaria and AIDS epidemics in Southern Africa. Whilst the pharmaceutical industry has responded with several concessions, the case against the industry is that it enjoys a privileged position, partly due to the patent system.

Introduction

There is a story about a pharmaceutical executive on a tour of the US National Mint who inquired how much it cost to produce each dollar bill. On hearing the answer, the man smiled. Making pills, it seemed, was even more profitable than printing money. Whether true or not, the three most profitable businesses in the world are reputed to be narcotics, prostitution and ethical pharmaceuticals. Studies by Oxfam showing the scale of the AIDS problem in Southern Africa has brought the pharma companies into the spotlight. The allegation is that these companies exploit the poor in the developing world. With a median 35 per cent return on equity, pharmaceuticals is far and away the world's most profitable major

industry. With profits of more than $6 billion, pharma companies, such as Pfizer and GlaxoSmithKline, dwarf the likes of Unilever, Siemens or Coca-Cola. Yet, every year in the developing world, millions of people die from diseases, such as malaria and tuberculosis, which the rich developed world has eradicated. Table 6.4 shows the scale of the problem.

In the past, the pharmaceutical industry has maintained that many of the drugs that could benefit the

Table 6.4 The scale of the AIDS epidemic in Southern Africa (% of adult population infected)

Botswana	23.0
Lesotho	23.3
Malawi	10.0
Mozambique	11.3
Namibia	13.4
South Africa	17.3
Swaziland	26.0
Zambia	12.5
Zimbabwe	14.9

Source: UNICEF (2015) http://www.unicef.org/esaro/5482_HIV_AIDS.html.

---

* UK IP law does contain some criminal provisions (e.g. S 92 TM Act 1994, and S 107 Copyright Patents and Designs Act 1988). Some European countries have criminal provisions relating to patent infringement as well, though that is less common. Nonetheless, the target of criminal law relating to IP is usually deliberate counterfeiters rather than inadvertent infringers or those who might legitimately argue they are not infringing. See the *National Intellectual Property (IP) Enforcement Report* (2005), 1–139.

suffering in the underdeveloped world are expensive and have taken years to research and develop. The only way the pharmaceutical industry can claw back its expenditure on research and development is by patenting their drugs, thereby providing them with a 20-year monopoly in which to generate sales and profits. The social contract underlying the patents system is based on an agreement that in return for such investment – and for publishing through patents the details of the research results – a company is entitled to an exclusive right to the sale of the resulting product for a limited period of time: 20 years.

The case against the pharmaceutical industry

Most drug prices bear no relation to the very small cost of production because the industry has a contract with society, enshrined in the patent system. For a limited period (usually 10 years not allowing for clinical trials, etc.), pharmaceutical companies charge monopoly prices for patented medicines. In return, they invest huge amounts of research dollars in pursuit of the next innovation.

At a time when the AIDS epidemic appears to have stabilised in most advanced countries, thanks largely to the use of sophisticated drugs, the disease is continuing to spread at an ever more alarming rate through developing countries (see Table 6.4). With only 5 per cent of the world's population, Eastern and Southern Africa is home to half the world's population living with HIV. Today, the region continues to be the epicentre of the HIV/AIDS epidemic.

Yet those countries now suffering the most from the disease are also those least able to afford the drugs necessary to control it. The issue, of course, challenges the whole patenting system.

It is not just the underdeveloped countries that are experiencing difficulties with intellectual property laws and medicine. A 30-year-old London woman contacted Bristol-Myers Squibb, a US pharmaceutical company, begging help to obtain Taxol. This drug could have controlled her breast cancer, but her National Health Service region did not prescribe it because of its exorbitant cost. There is no patent on Taxol, as the US Government discovered it. But Bristol-Myers Squibb, because it performed minor work calculating dosage levels, holds the intellectual property rights on dose-related data, even though the data originally was collected by the Government.

Ultimately, the company was shamed into offering her free medicine, if she moved to the United States. However, doctors concluded that the offer was probably too late.

The developing countries are demanding changes. They argue that patent laws should be relaxed, allowing, for example, either for their own companies to produce cheaper generic versions of the expensive anti-AIDS drugs, or for the import of such generic copies from other countries. The Indian company Cipla offered to make a combination of AIDS drugs available at about one-third of the price being asked by companies in developing countries. This price is already less than those in the West. If ever there was a good example of profiteering, here it is. Worst of all, it seems to be profiteering at the expense of the poor. The charge of unethical behaviour seems to be ringing loudly. But for how long will the legal systems and courts in the world tolerate thousands of deaths before one of them decides enough is enough? The pharmaceutical industry is aware of the strength of public opinion and the mounting pressure it is under and has made significant concessions, including cutting the price of many of its drugs to the developing world. Will this, however, be enough? The whole industry, it seems, is now under pressure to justify the prices it charges for its drugs. If it fails to convince governments, it may see the introduction of legislation and price controls.

In the UK, the purchase of drugs is the responsibility of the National Institute for Health and Care Excellence (NICE). It frequently has to make difficult decisions. For example, in 2015, cancer charities criticised the decision by the NHS treatment watchdog to reject an innovative new drug to treat ovarian cancer on the grounds of cost. NICE said, in a draft guidance, it was disappointed that it must turn down olaparib (Lynparza), but the price tag of more than £49,000 a year was considerably higher than its ceiling of £20,000 to £30,000. When tests to assess patient suitability for the drug are included, the price rises higher still.

The case for the pharmaceutical industry

The pharmaceutical industry can claim that it has been responsible for helping to rid many parts of the world of dreadful diseases. It is able to claim that the enormous sums of money that it spends each year on research and development is possible only because

→

of the patent system. Any change in the system will put at risk the billions of dollars that are spent on research into heart disease, cancer and other killers. This is usually enough for most governments and others to back away from this very powerful industry. Not surprisingly, the drugs industry is appalled at the prospect of price controls. Sidney Taurel, chief executive of the US drugs company Eli Lilly, has warned, 'If we kill free markets around the world, we'll kill innovation.'

The industry clearly has a unique structure and differs markedly from many others, but whether there is evidence for supra-normal profits is questionable. Professor Sachs, director of the Center for International Development at Harvard University, argues that, if price controls were introduced, companies simply would scale back their investments in research. This is often seen by many as a 'threat' that the industry uses against governments. Once again, there is limited evidence to suggest this necessarily would happen. Sachs suggests, 'This is an extremely sophisticated, high cost, risky business with very long lead-in times and an extremely high regulatory hurdle.' He continues, 'My sense is that every rich country that has said, "You're making too much money" and has tried to control prices, has lost the R&D edge.'

The pharmaceutical industry has a powerful voice. It is a large employer, invests large sums of money in science and technology and is, without doubt, an industry that will grow in this century. Most governments would like to have a thriving pharmaceutical industry and, hence, try to help and not hinder their efforts. Moreover, there are thousands of people in the developed world whose lives are being saved and extended by new sophisticated drugs that are being developed every month. The industry has many advocates and supporters.

Price cuts

Britain's biggest drugs company, GlaxoSmithKline, has reduced the cost to the developing world of drugs for treating malaria, diarrhoea and infectious diseases. Merck and Bristol-Myers Squibb, two of the world's largest drugs companies, had already announced that they were supplying AIDS drugs at cost price or less to all developing countries. Bristol-Myers Squibb also announced that it would not be enforcing its patent rights in Southern Africa.

The field of pricing pharmaceutical products is complicated because, in most countries, prices are determined by what governments, the main buyers in the industry, are prepared to pay. The same pill made by the same company may cost half in Canada of what it does in the United States. In Mexico, it may cost still less. Such differential pricing is fundamental to the pharmaceutical industry. Because consumers are not paying for raw materials, but rather for intellectual property, drug companies charge what they can get away with and governments pay what they deem affordable. The United States, however, is the exception, as here prices are determined on the open market.

Conclusions

It is the unique structure of the industry and the patent system that is at the crux of the problem. Europe, the United States and Japan account for virtually all the profits of the pharmaceutical companies. In most other markets, profits are driven down by the power and price sensitivity of customers. But, in pharmaceuticals, neither the patient who consumes the drugs nor the doctor who prescribes them is price sensitive. Customers for medicines are not price sensitive because they do not pay for them. In Europe it is the taxpayer who foots the bill.

Whereas most companies have profits capped by aggressive industry buyers, the pharmaceutical firms have to negotiate only with civil servants and, when taxpayers' money is available, commercial disciplines frequently disappear. But, even in the United States where a free market exists, the pharmaceutical companies are able to charge even higher prices. Once again, this is because the pharmaceutical companies frequently are selling to private health insurers. Many US employers offer health insurance as part of the employment package.

Competition is another key force that drives down prices in most industries. In electronics – an industry even more innovative than pharmaceuticals – excess profits from a new product soon disappear as competitors bring out copies. But, in the pharmaceutical business, it is the patent system that ensures high profits continue for an average of 10 years. The consequence of this ability to negotiate very high prices and the absence of competitive threat is that the giant pharmaceuticals have no incentive to compete on price. It also helps to explain why the pharma companies have been unwilling to sell cheap medicines to the poor in Africa and Asia. The real worry is that dropping prices to the developing world would undermine the enormous margins being received in Europe and the United States. Buyers would soon be reimporting medicines at a fraction of the official price, which may be the case soon in the United States.

The industry's justification for its high prices and patent monopolies is that it encourages innovation, but to what extent is this true? In most other industries it is intense competition and a fight to survive and win market share that drives forward innovation. Without new and better products, companies such as Hewlett-Packard and Canon know they will not maintain growth and market share. As we have seen in Chapters 1, 2, 3 and 4, innovation is dependent on a collection of factors and the patent system alone cannot stimulate innovation. It is necessary, but not sufficient.

The industry's most popular argument to defend the patent system is that it has unusually high cost structures due to the enormous sums of money it has to invest in science and technology. Increasingly, however, the industry is spending more on marketing existing products than it is on developing new ones. Analysts argue that marketing costs are now typically almost double the R&D spend. GlaxoSmithKline, for example, has 10,000 scientists but 40,000 salespeople! Even this well-rehearsed argument is now beginning to sound hollow.

The pharmaceutical industry has enjoyed 60 years of substantial growth and substantial profits and many people have benefited. The patent system is intended to balance the interests of the individual and society; increasing numbers of people are questioning this balance. The pharmaceutical companies need to consider every step carefully for they, surely, do not want to become the unacceptable face of globalisation.

Sources: Doyle, P. (2001) AIDS and the pharmaceutical industry, *The Guardian*, 10 March; Meikle, J. (2003) NHS seeks £30m from drug firms in price fixing claim, *The Guardian*, 23 December, 6; Goldenberg and Linton (2012).

Questions

1 Explain how the pricing of drugs contributes to the acquisition of supra-normal profits in the pharmaceutical industry.

2 It is because drugs are absolutely essential to life that the pharmaceutical industry is able to justify large profits. Discuss the merits of this argument. Consider also that bread and milk companies do not make huge profits.

3 Explain why drugs are not price-sensitive.

4 Explain why the patent system may not be working as originally intended.

5 Use CIM (Figure 1.9) to illustrate the innovation process in this case.

6 Nobel Prize winning economist Joseph Stiglitz argues that prizes rather than patents could stimulate scientific competition. Explain how this might work.

Chapter summary

This chapter has explored the area of intellectual property and the different forms of protection available to a firm. This is a dynamic area of business. The operation of trademark law throughout the European Union is now controversial, as is the area of patents. It seems that the pharmaceutical industry is preparing itself for significant changes. This chapter also made it clear that the patent system has fierce critics, largely due to the associated costs involved with defending a patent against infringement. The patent system, however, was also highlighted as a valuable source of technological knowledge that is used by many companies.

Discussion questions

1 Explain why many research organisations are against the patenting of life forms.

2 Explain why theft of intellectual property should be a crime.

3 Explain why discoveries are not patentable.

4 Discuss some of the limitations of the patent system.

5 Is the pharmaceutical industry the unacceptable face of globalisation (consider the anti-capitalist demonstrations of recent years)?

6 Discuss why Lego wanted to trademark its block.

7 Explain, with the use of examples, when it would be appropriate to use trademarks and copyright to protect a firm's intellectual property.

Key words and phrases

Patent *190*

Copyright *190*

Registered design *190*

Patent extension *202*

Brand name *210*

Trademark *210*

Brands to protect intellectual property *210*

Generic products *212*

Infringement of intellectual property *216*

References

ACARD (1980) *Exploiting Invention*, report to the Prime Minister, London, December.

Badenhausen, K. (1995) Brands: the management factor, *Financial World*, 1 August, 50–69.

Bainbridge, D.I. (1996) *Intellectual Property*, 3rd edn, Financial Times Pitman Publishing, London.

Blind, K., Cremers, K. and Mueller, E. (2009) The influence of strategic patenting on companies' patent portfolios, *Research Policy*, vol. 38, no. 2, 428–36.

Bowe, C. and Griffith, V. (2002) Proposal on patents set to hit revenues, *Financial Times*, 22 October.

Brown, A. (2007) Beware the backwards-looking patents that can stifle innovation, *The Guardian*, 1 March, www.guardian.co.uk/technology.

Cohen, W.M., Nelson, R.R. and Walsh, J.P. (2000) *Protecting their Intellectual Assets: Appropriability Conditions and Why U.S. Manufacturing Firms Patent (or not)*, Working Paper 7552, Cambridge National Bureau of Economic Research (available at www.nber.org/papers/w7552).

Court of Appeal (1985) Reports of Patent, Design and Trade Mark Cases (RPC), No. 59.

Deakin, S. and Wilkinson, F. (1998) 'Contract law and the earning of inter-organisational trust', in Lane, C. and Bachmann, R. (eds) *Trust Within and Between Organisations: Conceptual Issues and Empirical Applications*, Oxford University Press, Oxford, 146–72.

Derwent (1998) Derwent World Patents Index, Derwent Scientific and Patent Information: www.Derwent.com.

Economist, The (2015) Time to fix patients, 8 August, 3.

European Federal Trade Commission (2006). See European Union (2006).

European Union (2006) *European Innovation Scoreboard: Comparative analysis of innovation performance*, Brussels. Accessed 3 February 2007 from European Union website: www.proinno-europe.eu/doc/EIS2006_final.pdf.

Farrell, S. (2010) Just another brick in the wall: Lego's bid to trademark blocks fails in court, *Daily Telegraph*, Business Section, 15 September, 2.

Fischer, T., & Henkel, J. (2012) Patent trolls on markets for technology – an empirical analysis of NPEs' patent acquisitions, *Research Policy*, vol. 41, no. 9, 1519–33.

Goldenberg, D. H. and Linton, J. D. (2012) The patent paradox – new insights through decision support using compound options, *Technological forecasting and social change*, 79(1), 180–185.

Grindley, P.C. and Teece, D.J. (1997) Managing intellectual capital: licensing and cross-licensing in semiconductors and electronics, *California Management Review*, vol. 39, no. 2, 1–34.

Hu, A.G. (2010) Propensity to patent, competition and China's foreign patenting surge, *Research Policy*, vol. 39, no. 7, 985–93.

Hung, C.L. (2003) The business of product counterfeiting in China and the post-WTO member-ship environment, *Asia Pacific Business Review*, vol. 10, no. 1, 58–77.

Leiponen, A. and Byma, J. (2009) If you cannot block, you better run: small firms, cooperative innovation, and appropriation strategies, *Research Policy*, vol. 38, no. 9, 1478–88.

Liebeskind, J. and Oliver, A. (1998) 'From handshake to contract: intellectual property, trust and the social structure of academic research', in Lane, C. and Bachmann, R. (eds) *Trust Within and Between Organisations: Conceptual Issues and Empirical Applications*, Oxford University Press, Oxford, 118–45.

McDonald, G.M. and Roberts, C. (1994) Product piracy: the problem will not go away, *Journal of Product & Brand Management*, vol. 3, no. 4, 55–65.

Naim, M. (2005) *Illicit*, William Heinemann, London.

Nakamoto, M. and Pilling, D. (2004) Tough tasks ahead at Takeda, *Financial Times*, 23 August.

National Intellectual Property Enforcement Report (2005) The Patent Office, London (www.ipo.gov.uk).

Pohlmann, T. and Opitz, M. (2013) Typology of the patent troll business, *R&D Management*, vol. 43, 103–20.

Sachs, J. (1999) Helping the world's poorest, *The Economist*, 14 August, 16–22.

Schmiele, A. (2013). Intellectual property infringements due to R&D abroad? A comparative analysis between firms with international and domestic innovation activities. *Research Policy*, vol. 42, no. 8, 1482–95.

Thomä, J. and Bizer, K. (2013) To protect or not to protect? Modes of appropriability in the small enterprise sector, *Research Policy*, vol. 42, no 1, 35–49.

Thurow, L.C. (1997) Needed: a new system of intellectual property rights, *Harvard Business Review*, vol. 75, 95–103.

Tom, G., Garibaldi, B., Zeng, Y. and Pilcher, J. (1998) Consumer demand for counterfeit goods, *Psychology and Marketing*, vol. 15, no. 5, 405–21.

Vaidhyanathan, S. (2001) *Copyrights and Copywrongs*, New York University Press, New York.

Yang, D. and Clarke, P. (2004) Review of the current intellectual property system in China, *International Journal of Technology Transfer and Commercialisation*, vol. 3, no. 1, 12–37.

Further reading

For a more detailed review of the intellectual property literature, the following develop many of the issues raised in this chapter:

Borg, E.A. (2001) Knowledge, information and intellectual property: implications for marketing relationships, *Technovation*, vol. 21, 515–24.

The Economist (2015) Time to fix patents, 8 August, 3.

The Economist (2000) The knowledge monopolies: patent wars, 8 April, 95–9.

Goldenberg, D. H., & Linton, J. D. (2012). The patent paradox–New insights through decision support using compound options. *Technological forecasting and social change* 79(1), 180–185.

Naim, M. (2005) *Illicit*, William Heinemann, London.

Part Two
Turning technology into business

New technologies are transforming markets, businesses and society at an ever-increasing rate. Businesses need, somehow, to manage their way through this new terrain. Given that virtually all firms are established to generate funds for their owners, one of the fundamental issues for them to address is how to transform technology into profits. In this second part of the book, we turn our attention to this key issue in innovation: knowledge and technology. Chapter 7 looks at how firms accumulate knowledge and utilise this to develop business opportunities. It is these opportunities that are at the heart of new product ideas. To profit from these technologies, however, firms need to offer products that are a lower price or different from their competitors; for long-term success they need to ensure what they offer is not easily copied by others.

A firm's capabilities lie not just within but also outside the linkages and networks that it has established over time – Chapter 8 examines the subject of strategic alliances. It is not only large international companies that are using alliances to develop products and technology; small innovative companies also recognise the potential benefits of working with others.

Chapter 9 examines how companies manage research and development (R&D). It details the main activities performed by R&D departments and how these can influence the development of new products. Chapter 10 explores the challenges faced by R&D managers as they wrestle with project selection and evaluation. Important questions are raised concerning when to stop pouring money into struggling research projects. The extent to which a company can acquire technology developed outside the organisation via technology transfer is studied in Chapter 11.

Chapter 7
Managing organisational knowledge

Introduction

The ability of firms to identify technological opportunities and exploit them is one of the most fundamental features that determines successful from unsuccessful firms. But technology by itself will not lead to success. Firms must be able to convert intellect, knowledge and technology into things that customers want. The ability to use its assets to perform value-creating activities can lead to the development of firm-specific competencies. These competencies provide firms with the ability to generate profits from their technology assets. This chapter examines the role of competencies and how these determine the innovative potential of firms.

The case study at the end of this chapter explores how the cork industry is responding to the challenge from synthetic plastic closures in the wine industry. It seems the cork industry had not recognised the significant changes taking place in the wine industry to which it acts as a supplier.

Chapter contents

Learning objectives

When you have completed this chapter you will be able to:

- explain the significance of technology trajectories for firms investing in technology;
- recognise the importance of firm-specific competencies in generating long-term profits;
- provide an understanding of the role of an organisation's knowledge base in determining innovative capability;
- provide an understanding of the concept of the learning organisation;
- recognise the importance of technical and commercial capabilities in innovation management; and
- recognise a variety of different innovation strategies.

The Battle of Trafalgar

The Battle of Trafalgar in 1805 may not seem like an appropriate place to begin the study of strategy and technological innovation. It does, however, provide an interesting historical example of how strategy (in this case military strategy) often is linked to new technological developments.

The Battle of Trafalgar in 1805 was influenced by technology.
Source: Mary Evans Picture Library

For those who are unable to recall their eighteenth- and nineteenth-century maritime history, Nelson defeated the French and Spanish fleets in the Battle of Trafalgar. Today, Nelson's ship, HMS *Victory*, stands in a dry dock in Portsmouth Harbour (see p. 162). The Battle was fought off the south-west coast of Spain and the sailing ships of the day were armed with cannons that used gunpowder to launch cannon balls at the enemy's ships, the aim being to hole the ship so that it would, ultimately, sink. Failure to achieve this would either result in being 'holed' oneself or being invaded by the enemy's crew, if they were able to get alongside.

Nelson's fleet, whilst composed of fewer vessels, had a crucial strategic advantage. It possessed a simple but important piece of technology that, arguably, was instrumental in securing victory. The Spanish and French Armadas were armed with cannons, but theirs were fired by lighting a short fuse that burned and then ignited the gunpowder. There were several limitations to this ignition process. First, the fuse would not always burn and, second, valuable time was being wasted whilst waiting for it to burn. Nelson's ships, on the other hand, had overcome this limitation through the development of a simple hammer-action ignition system that ignited the gunpowder. The firing process involved placing a cannon ball in the cannon and rolling it into position, with its nose poking through the aperture in the side of the ship. A cord would be pulled to trigger the hammer action and ignite the gunpowder, causing an explosion that would force the cannon ball out towards the target. Nelson's ships were able to load and fire several cannon balls whilst the enemy's fleet was waiting for fuses to burn.

Technology trajectories

The Battle of Trafalgar provides a useful illustration of the pivotal role of technology in competition. Nowhere is this more evident than in the world of business. Firms with superior technology have delivered spectacular financial rewards to their owners: Intel's microprocessors, Samsung's mobile telephones and Pfizer's Viagra, to name only a few. But, as we have seen in Chapter 1, technology alone cannot deliver victory; technology, however, coupled with a market opportunity and the necessary organisational skills to deliver the product to the market, will help significantly.

In Admiral Nelson's case, the choice of where to deploy technological effort was far more limited than that open to firms today. Large firms and, to a lesser extent, small firms have a bewildering array of opportunities to exploit, especially when they have products operating in many markets across several industries. As one would expect, those given responsibility for charting the direction of the firm, the leaders, will have views on where the firm should be heading, but the technology capability of the firm frequently dictates what is possible and what can or cannot be achieved in a given time frame. In other words, a firm's opportunities are constrained by its current position and current knowledge base, i.e. it is path-dependent. For example, many firms may marvel at the huge profits generated by Apple's iPhone, but few firms are in a position to develop a similar or superior product. Only those operating in related industries will be in a position to respond and, even then, the possible entrants will be limited to those who have prior knowledge of the related fields of technology, determined by its range of research projects. Acquiring knowledge about technology takes time, involves people and experiments and requires learning. To exploit technological opportunities, a firm needs to be on the 'technology escalator'. As we will see later in this chapter, firms cannot move easily from one path of knowledge and learning to another. The choices available to the firm in terms of future direction are dependent on its own capabilities, that is, the firm's level of technology, skills developed, intellectual property, managerial processes and its routines. Furthermore, the choices made by any firm must take place in a changing environment, characterised by changing levels of technology, changing market conditions and changing societal demands. Teece and Pisano (1994) refer to this concept as the **dynamic capabilities** of firms.

Pause for thought

If technology trajectories are determined by a firm's past, how can it change trajectories and get on another one?

The acquisition of firm-specific knowledge

Arguing for knowledge and the need to acquire it is a bit like arguing for peace or education. Few can argue against such a laudable aim. But it is not any knowledge that is required, it is firm-specific knowledge; knowledge that is useful and applicable. Otherwise reading the telephone directory would constitute acquiring knowledge, but this clearly has limited benefits. For example, 3M often is cited as having **core competencies** in coatings and adhesives, hence one would expect the firm to have a wide range of research projects related to these technologies. This, then, is the key: how do firms know what knowledge to acquire and when do they know when they have acquired it? This is clearly dependent on the firm's prior knowledge and introduces the notion of absorptive capacity. This refers to a firm's ability to acquire and utilise new knowledge. This notion is explored further in the chapters on R&D management and technology acquisition.

The resource-based perspective

The impact and influence of the development over the past 30 years of the resource-based perspective within strategic management has been considerable. This is not just in terms of philosophical management debate but also within the boardrooms of firms. For example, such questions as 'What are our key resources?' and 'How can we diversify using our core competencies?' are now not uncommon. This is a significant shift away from questions such as 'What is our corporate mission?' and 'What business are we in?' There has been a reorientation in the way firms consider strategic decision making from, to put it crudely, an external analysis of the environment and aligning the firm to it, to an internal analysis and aligning the firm's resources to the external environment. This later approach is referred to as a resource-based perspective (RBP). The perspective is dependent on two basic principles:

- There are differences between firms based upon the way they manage resources and how they exploit them (Nelson, 1991).
- These differences are relatively stable.

If the RBP is dependent on these two key principles, then a key question arises, which is: how does one identify these differences that determine the success of a firm? It is the detail that is significant here. Here, by differences, we mean strengths and it is around this concept of strengths that so much of the debate has taken place.

Strengths have been interpreted as resources, capabilities and competencies (Barney, 1991; Wernerfelt, 1984). Hamel and Prahalad (1994) developed the idea of core competence for a very specific type of resource. Indeed, they developed three tests that they argue can be used to identify core competencies, namely 'customer value', 'competitor differentiation' and 'extendibility'. Yet, despite the widespread acknowledgement of the salience of core competencies for acquiring and sustaining a competitive position, the notion of core competencies has remained largely amorphous (Onyeiwu, 2003).

It is Jay Barney (1991) that is considered by many to have made a significant contribution to the debate on the RBP when he argued that there can be heterogeneity of firm level differences amongst firms that allow some of them to sustain competitive advantage. Therefore, he emphasised strategic choice, where responsibility lies with the firm's management to identify, develop and deploy resources to maximise returns. Further, he proposed that above industry average rents can be earned from resources when they are: valuable, rare, imperfectly imitable and non-substitutable (so-called VRIN attributes).

A key issue for debate within the literature has been over what form resources take. It is now widely accepted that resources include tangible ones, such as patents, properties and proprietary technologies and intangible resources, such as relationships and trust built up over time (Galbreath and Galvin, 2004). It is this wider interpretation of the concept of resources and, in particular, the recognition that resources include information, knowledge and skills that has further developed the concept of RBP.

Significantly, the idea that firms develop firm-specific routines as they conduct their business differentiated the concept of RBP from the more static SWOT (strengths, weaknesses, opportunities and threats) framework. Teece et al. (1997) put forward the idea that firms develop dynamic capabilities that are difficult to replicate and it is this that makes firms different. This seems to chime well with the ideas of the founding mother of the RBP, Edith Penrose (1959), who suggested that it is resources that enable firms to create services or flows.

Dynamic competence-based theory of the firm

The *dynamic competence-based theory of the firm* sees both the external and internal environments as dynamic: the external environment is constantly changing as different players manoeuvre themselves and a company's internal environment is also evolving. The management of this internal process of change, together with an understanding of the changes in the external environment, offers a more realistic explanation of the challenges facing senior management. In addition, firms are seen as different (Nelson, 1991) and hence compete on the basis of competencies and capabilities (Cohen and Levinthal, 1990; Hamel and Prahalad, 1994; Pavitt, 1990. This literature presents a related theoretical view that centres around an organisation's ability to develop specific capabilities. These capabilities tend to be dependent on the organisation's incremental and cumulative historical activities. In other words, a company's ability to compete in the future is dependent on its past activities. This view of an organisation's heritage is developed by Cohen and Levinthal (1990) in the context of the management of research and development. In their research, they developed the notion of 'absorptive capacity'.

They see R&D expenditure as an investment in an organisation's absorptive capacity. They argue that an organisation's ability to evaluate and utilise external knowledge is related to its *prior knowledge* and expertise and that this prior knowledge is, in turn, driven by prior R&D investment. The issue of an organisation's capacity to acquire knowledge was also addressed by Nelson and Winter, who emphasised the importance of 'innovative routines'.

They argue that the practised routines that are built into the organisation define a set of competencies that the organisation is capable of doing confidently. These routines are referred to as an organisation's core capabilities. It is important to note that the notion of routines here does not necessarily imply a mechanistic,

A useful example of tacit knowledge is tying a shoelace. Virtually everyone knows how to tie a shoelace. However, it is extremely difficult to explain to someone in diagrams, words or speech how to perform this task. Hence, tacit knowledge may be described as knowledge that is acquired but difficult to explain to others.

Figure 7.1

bureaucratic organisational form (see Chapter 4). The potential for controversy is resolved by Teece (1986), who distinguishes between 'static routines', which refer to the capability to replicate previously performed tasks, and 'dynamic routines', which enable a firm to develop new competencies. Indeed, dynamic organisational routines are very often those activities that are not easily identifiable and may be dominated by tacit knowledge (see Figure 7.1).

The point here is that, over long periods, organisations build up a body of knowledge and skills through experience and learning-by-doing. In addition to these internal organisational processes, the *external linkages* that a company has developed over time and the investment in this network of relationships (generated from its past activities) form a distinctive competitive capability. Moreover, this can be transformed into competitive advantage when added to additional distinctive capabilities, such as technological ability and marketing knowledge (Casper and Whitley, 2003).

Dynamic competences enable innovation

Every firm has a baseline set of routines that enable it to serve the purpose of producing and marketing the given products and services currently in the portfolio. Some firms have dynamic capabilities that relate to the innovation of products and services, to the innovation of the production process, or to the search and attraction of new customer segments. This enables many firms to adapt and evolve. There is, then, a further level of capabilities, so-called dynamic capabilities that relate to the innovation of the way innovation is pursued. These are highly creative 'reconfigurations' of thinking and methods for innovating. Examples would include: Dyson's development of the bagless vacuum cleaner, Pfizer's Viagra or Tesla's electric sports car. In all of these cases, it is clear that considerable investments and policies were needed to promote the advance of cumulative knowledge, diffuse technological solutions within the firm and focus on visible, urgent and frequent problems.

Any firm typically follows a 'technology development path' – that is cumulative, path-dependent and often quite binding. That is, the firm becomes increasingly good at doing what it did in the past. It benefits from economies of scale and acquires experience. This relates to the innovation dilemma in Chapter 4. Thus, it may perfect what it is very good at whilst, simultaneously, it may be unable to

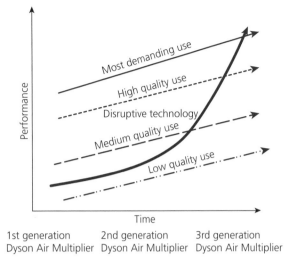

1st generation   2nd generation   3rd generation
Dyson Air Multiplier Dyson Air Multiplier Dyson Air Multiplier

Figure 7.2 How dynamic competencies help a firm adapt to disruptive technologies?

reconfigure its bundle of routines, especially when a new technology comes along. This concept is captured in Figure 7.2. It shows what happens when a disruptive technology emerges. This can be applied to any industry sector. For illustration, we will select the domestic air fan sector. This is a mature technology, hence here are many firms producing low price fans (low quality use on figure). There is another large group of firms producing medium quality use products. Typically, these use the same technology but have quieter motors and the materials used may be of a higher quality. There is also a 'high quality use' sector of firms providing air fans to more demanding customers who have specific requirements, such as very low noise or very light weight or high performance needs. Finally, there is a sector of the industry that produces fans required in the most demanding uses. These firms may use different technologies. Usually, the volumes are low and the product specifications are high.

This industry was stable and mature and had been using the same technology for almost 100 years. Things changed because, in 2009, Dyson Appliances developed the Dyson Air Multiplier. It did not appear to have any visible blades. Because of the unique technology, which utilises inducement and entrainment, it was able to provide air flow that did not buffet the air. In terms of performance, it was initially noisy and had limited power, hence it begins life towards the bottom of the performance vertical scale. The second generation product was much quieter and it incorporates superior digital motors, hence the technology moves up the performance scale. Over time, this technology, which has required enormous investment in new technologies, could yet disrupt the whole industry.

Developing firm-specific competencies

The ability of firms to identify technological opportunities and exploit them is one of the most fundamental features that determines successful from unsuccessful firms. Increasingly, economists are using the notion that firms possess discrete

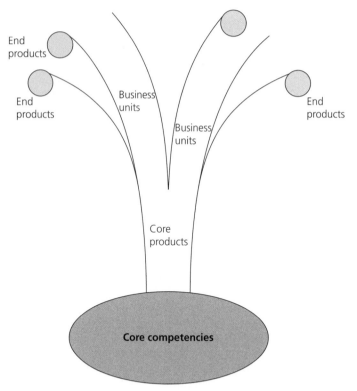

Figure 7.3 Core competencies

Source: Adapted from Hamel, G. and Prahalad, C.K. (1990) The core competence of the corporation, *Harvard Business Review*, May/June, 79–91.

sets of capabilities or competencies as a way of explaining why firms are different and how firms change over time. Hamel and Prahalad (1994) use the metaphor of the tree to show the linkages between core competencies and end products. They suggest that a firm's core competencies are comparable to the roots of a tree, with the core products representing the trunk and business units smaller branches and final end products being flowers, leaves and fruit (see Figure 7.3). Technology in itself does not mean success; firms must be able to convert intellect, knowledge and technology into things that customers want. This ability is referred to as a firm's competencies: *the ability to use its assets to perform value-creating activities*. This frequently means integrating several assets, such as: product technology and distribution; product technology and marketing effort; and distribution and marketing.

Competencies and profits

According to Hamel and Prahalad, a firm's ability to generate profits from its technology assets depends on the level of protection it has over these assets and the extent to which firms are able to imitate these competencies. For example, are competencies at the periphery or the centre of a firm's long-term success? If they

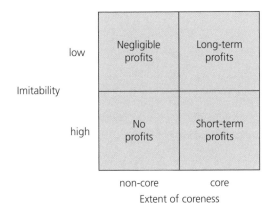

Figure 7.4 Core competencies, imitability and profits

Source: Afuah, A. (2003) *Innovation Management: Strategies, Implementation and Profit*, p. 53, Fig. 3.5, Oxford University Press Inc., New York.

are at the centre and difficult for firms to imitate, then long-term profits are assured, e.g. Honda and its ability to produce performance engines. Over the past 50 years, few firms have been able to imitate Honda's success in developing engines. The following are examples of other firms that have been cited as having core competencies that are difficult to replicate:

● Intel's ability to develop microprocessors that exploit its copyrighted microcode;
● Coca-Cola's ability to develop products for which people are willing to pay a premium;
● Honda's ability to produce high quality and performance engines; and
● 3M's ability to develop a wide range of products from coatings to adhesives.

These firms can be placed in the uppermost right-hand quadrant of the matrix in Figure 7.4. These firms have been able to generate long-term profits based on their core competencies and few firms have been able to imitate their activities. If a competence is non-core and imitability is high, then one may not be able to make profits from it, all else being equal. If it is non-core, but imitable, the firm may be able to make some negligible profits from it. If, however, the competence is core, but easily imitated, the firm can make profits, but these are likely to be temporary, as competitors will soon imitate.

Technology development and effort required

Foster (1986) and Abernathy and Utterback (1978) argue that the rate of technological advance is dependent on the amount of effort put into the development of the technology. As was pointed out in Chapter 1, with President Kennedy's pledge to get a man on the moon, if unlimited resources are made available, as in the Kennedy example, there may well be very few limits. Under normal circumstances, however, technological progress starts off slowly, then increases rapidly and, finally, diminishes as the physical limits of the technology are approached. This is diagrammatically referred to as an S-curve. Slow progress at the start equates to a horizontal line, rapid progress as knowledge is acquired equates to a vertical line and slow progress towards

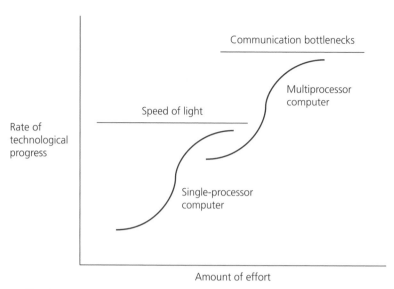

Figure 7.5 Technology life cycles and S-curves

the end equates to a horizontal line. It is usually at this point that a new technology replaces the existing one; indeed, it is necessary, if advances are to continue. Figure 7.5 illustrates the development of supercomputers.

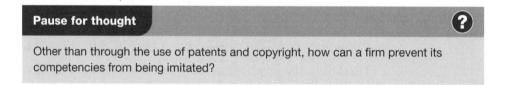

Pause for thought ❓

Other than through the use of patents and copyright, how can a firm prevent its competencies from being imitated?

The knowledge base of an organisation

Many organisations have shown sustained corporate success over many years. This does not mean only unbroken periods of growth or profit, but also combinations of growth and decline that, together, represent sustained development and advancement. Research by Pavitt et al. (1991: 82), writing on innovative success, led them to remark:

> *Large innovating firms in the twentieth century have shown resilience and longevity, in spite of successive waves of radical innovations that have called into question their established skills and procedures . . . Such institutional continuity in the face of technological discontinuity cannot be explained simply by the rise and fall of either talented individual entrepreneurs or of groups with specific technical skills. The continuing ability to absorb and mobilise new skills and opportunities has to be explained in other terms.*

Pavitt et al. (1991) identify a number of properties of innovative activities in large firms. They place a great deal of emphasis on the concept of firm-specific competencies that take time to develop and are costly to initiate. Key features of these competencies are the ability to convert technical competencies into effective innovation and the generation of effective *organisational learning*. The observations made earlier suggest a need to analyse organisational knowledge and the processes involved in realising that knowledge, rather than analysing organisational structure. If we can uncover the internal processes that determine a company's response to a given technology, this may help to explain the longevity of large innovating companies.

But what is meant by organisational knowledge? One may be tempted to think that the collective talents and knowledge of all the individuals within an organisation would represent its knowledge base. It is certainly the case that one individual within an organisation, especially within a large organisation, rarely sees or fully understands how the entire organisation functions. Senior managers in many large corporations have frequently said, with some amusement, when addressing large gatherings, that they do not understand how the organisation operates! The following quote is typical:

> *I am constantly being surprised as I travel around the many different parts of this organisation; while I know that we are in the car production business I am constantly amazed at the wide range of activities that we perform and how we do what we do. We regularly convert our raw materials of steel and many different component parts into fine automobiles, and then get them all over the world all within a matter of days. It's amazing and difficult to explain how we do it.*
>
> (Senior executive from a US car producer)

This statement highlights the notion that *an organisation itself can seem to have knowledge*. That is, no one individual, even those people charting the course of the company, actually fully understands how all the internal activities and processes come together and function collectively. This concept of the organisation retaining knowledge is developed by Willman (1991: 2), who argues that 'the organisation itself, rather than the individuals who pass through it, retains and generates innovative capacity, even though individuals may be identified who propagate learning'.

The whole can be more than the sum of the parts

It is important to recognise that the knowledge base of an organisation is not simply the sum of individuals' knowledge bases. If this were the case, and knowledge was only held at the individual level, then an organisation's expertise and acquired abilities would change simply by employee turnover. The wealth of experience built up by an organisation through its operations clearly is not lost when employees leave. The employment of new workers and the retirement of old workers does not equate to changing the skills of a firm. Figure 7.6 attempts to show how a collective knowledge base is larger than the sum of individual knowledge bases. (See also Illustration 7.1.)

Organisational heritage

Organisational knowledge is distinctive to the firm. That is, it is not widely available to other firms. Hence, the more descriptive term **organisational heritage**. It is true that technical knowledge, in the form of patents, or commercial knowledge, in the form of unique channels of distribution, although used by an organisation, are available to

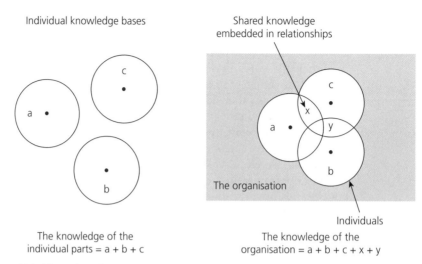

Figure 7.6 **How the whole can be viewed as more than the sum of the parts**

other firms. However, organisational knowledge includes these and more. For example, a vehicle manufacturer may use a wide variety of technologies and patents. This knowledge will not necessarily be unique to the organisation, that is other companies will be aware of this technology. But the development and manufacture of the vehicle will lead to the accumulation of skills and competencies that will be unique to the organisation. Hence, it is the individual ways in which the technology is applied that lead to organisation-specific knowledge.

To explore the above example further, groups or teams of people will develop specific skills required in the manufacture of a product. Over time, the knowledge, skills and processes will form part of the organisation's routines, which it is able to perform repeatedly. Individuals may leave the organisation and take their understanding to other organisations. But, even if large groups of people leave, it is likely that understanding will have been shared with others in the organisation and it will have been recorded in designs or production planning records for use by others.

When the performance of the organisation is greater than the abilities of individuals

Organisational knowledge represents internal systems, routines, shared understanding and practices (see Figure 7.7). In the past, it was loosely described as part of an organisation's culture, along with anything else that could not be explained fully. Organisational knowledge, however, represents a distinctive part of the much broader concept of organisational culture.

There are several tangible representations of this knowledge, such as minutes of meetings, research notebooks, databanks of customers, operating procedures, manufacturing quality control measures, as well as less tangible representations, such as tried and tested ways of operating. Nelson and Winter argue that such learning-by-doing is captured in organisational routines. It is evident that the knowledge base of an organisation will be greater, in most cases, than the

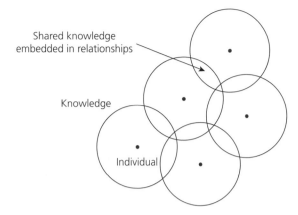

Figure 7.7 Knowledge embedded in relationships

sum total of the individual knowledge bases within it. Willman (1991) argues that this is because knowledge is also embedded in social and organisational relationships (see Figure 7.7). A popular illustration and example of this phenomenon is team work. In football leagues around the world, frequently a team will perform beyond what the individual talents of the players would suggest. There may be many explanations for this, including exceptional coaching, training and simply hard work.

Characterising the knowledge base of the organisation

Discussions concerning the knowledge base of an organisation tend to focus on R&D activities and other technical activities. However, an organisation's ability to develop new products that meet current market needs, to manufacture these products using the appropriate methods and to respond promptly to technological developments, clearly involves more than technical capabilities. Nelson (1991) has argued that, in industries where technological innovation is important, firms need more than a set of core capabilities in R&D:

> *These capabilities will be defined and constrained by the skills, experience, and knowledge of the personnel in the R&D department, the nature of the extant teams and procedures for forming new ones, the character of the decision making processes, the links between R&D and production and marketing, etc.*
>
> (Nelson, 1991: 66)

The wide range of skills mentioned by Nelson implies that the commonly held view of an organisation's knowledge base comprising only technical matters is too narrow. This is supported by Adler and Shenhar (1990), who suggest that an organisation's knowledge base is made up of several dimensions. The following five dimensions can be considered (see Figure 7.8):

- *Individual assets* – the skills and knowledge of the individuals that form the organisation. It is the application of these that influences corporate success.
- *Technological assets* – the most immediately visible elements of the technological base, the set of reproducible capabilities in *product*, *process* and *support areas*.

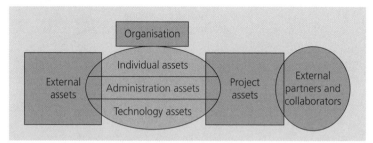

External environment

Figure 7.8 The knowledge base of an organisation

Technological assets can be more or less reliably reproduced; the other elements are, by contrast, fundamentally relational, which makes them much more difficult to replicate.

- *Administration assets* – the resources that enable the business to develop and deploy individual and technological assets. These are, specifically, the skill profile of employees and managers, the *routines*, *procedures* and *systems* for getting things done, the organisational structure, the strategies that guide action and the culture that shapes shared assumptions and values.
- *External assets* – the relations that the firm establishes with current and potential allies, rivals, suppliers, customers, political actors and local communities, e.g. joint ventures, distribution channels, etc.
- *Projects* – the means by which technological, organisational and external assets are both deployed and transformed. Projects should be considered as part of the knowledge base in so far as the organisation's *modus operandi* is a learned behavioural pattern that can contribute to or detract from technological and business performance.

Innovation in action

Smoking cessation products and dominant designs

Economic theory predicts that policies that discourage the consumption of a particular good will induce innovation in a socially desirable substitute. For example, carbon emission taxes on vehicles has led to improvements in the carbon emissions of vehicles generally. However, the literature on technology trajectories emphasises the possibility of innovation waves associated with the identification of new dominant designs. New research by Werfel and Jaffe (2013) on the invention of new smoking cessation products finds that an increase in cigarette tax levels had no discernible impact on the industry-wide rate of invention in smoking cessation products. However, they do find evidence consistent with the emergence of dominant designs having substantial positive innovation effects. They estimate that the introduction of the nicotine gum and patch increased the overall rate of patenting activity in smoking cessation products by 60–75 per cent, subject to a 10 per cent rate of decay.

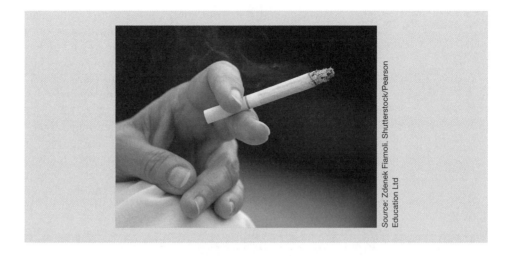

Source: Zdenek Fiamoli. Shutterstock/Pearson Education Ltd

This more realistic assessment of an organisation's knowledge base shows how the various components of an organisation are interrelated. The inclusion of external networks is an important point. The formal and informal links an organisation has developed, often over many years, are a valuable asset. Pennings and Harianto (1992) include history of technological networking within the organisational skills necessary for innovation. At this point, one may argue that it would be more appropriate to consider an organisation's knowledge base rather than select individual parts for analysis, which may be compared to trying to establish a racing car's performance by only analysing the engine. There are clearly other factors that will also have a dramatic impact on the car's performance.

The suggestion that an organisation's knowledge base is also time-dependent, that the acquisition of knowledge takes place over many years, introduces the notion of organisational heritage, discussed above. If we accept the notion of organisational knowledge, this leads to the question of whether it is possible for organisations to learn.

The learning organisation

The concept of the **learning organisation** has received an unprecedented level of attention in management literature. A special edition of *Organisational Science* was dedicated to the subject and it has received the attention of mainstream economics. The emphasis of much of the early literature on this subject was on the history of the organisation, and the strong influence of an organisation's previous activities and learning on its future activities. That is, the future activities of an organisation are strongly influenced by its previous activities and what it has learned (Pavitt et al., 1991; Tidd, 2000).

Unfortunately, the term organisational learning has been applied to so many different aspects of corporate management, from human resources management to technology management strategies, that it has become a particularly vague concept. At its heart, however, is the simple notion that successful companies have an ability to acquire knowledge and skills and apply these effectively, in much the same way as human beings learn. Arguably, companies that have been successful over a long period clearly have demonstrated a capacity to learn. Cynics have argued that this is just another management fad with a new label for what successful organisations have been doing for many years. However, according to Chris Argyris (1977), organisations can be extremely bad at learning. Indeed, he suggests that it is possible for organisations to lose the benefits of experience and revert to old habits. It is necessary to engage in double-loop rather than single-loop learning, argues Argyris, since the second loop reinforces understanding. At its most simple level, single-loop learning would be the adoption of a new set of rules to improve quality, productivity, etc. Double-loop learning occurs when those sets of rules are continually questioned, altered and updated in line with experience gained and the changing environment.

Innovation, competition and further innovation

Chapters 1–4 illustrated how innovation occurs within the firm and indicated the important knowledge flows and linkages beyond the boundary of the firm. The launch of an innovative new product into the market, however, usually is only the beginning of technology progress. At the industry level, the introduction of a new technology will cause a reaction: competitors will respond to this new product, hence technological progress depends on factors other than those internal to the firm. We need to consider the role of competition. Product innovation, process innovation, competitive environment and organisational structure all interact and are closely linked together. Abernathy and Utterback (1978) argued there were three phases in an innovation's life cycle: fluid, transitional and specific (see Table 7.1 and Figure 7.9). The first phase they call the *fluid phase*, where technological and market

Table 7.1 Phases of innovation and technology development

	Innovation phase		
Variable	**Fluid**	**Battle for dominant design**	**Commoditisation**
Innovation	Product changes/radical innovations	Major process changes, architectural innovations	Incremental innovations, improvements in quality
Product	Many different designs, customisation	Less differentiation due to mass production	Heavy standardisation in product designs
Competitors	Many small firms, no direct competition	Many, but declining after the emergence of a dominant design	Few, classic oligopoly
Organisation	Entrepreneurial, organic structure	More formal structure with task groups	Traditional hierarchical organisation
Threats	Old technology, new entrants	Imitators and successful product breakthroughs	New technologies and firms bringing disrupting innovations
Process	Flexible and inefficient	More rigid, changes occur in large steps	Efficient, capital intensive and rigid

Source: Abernathy and Utterback (1978), © 1978 from MIT Sloan Management Review/Massachusetts Institute of Technology, all rights reserved, distributed by Tribune Content Agency.

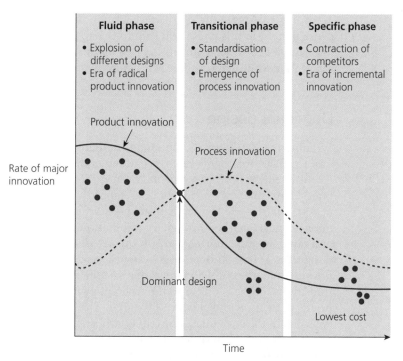

Figure 7.9 Abernathy and Utterback's three phases of innovation

Source: Utterback (1994), © 1994 from MIT Sloan Management Review/Massachusetts Institute of Technology, all rights reserved, distributed by Tribune Content Agency.

uncertainties prevail, and a large experimental game occurs in the marketplace. In this phase of uncertainty, the manufacturing process relies on craftsmanship and highly skilled labour and general-purpose equipment: there is almost no process innovation and the many small firms competing will base their advantage on differentiated product features. Competition tends not to be as fierce as in later phases because companies have no clear idea about potential applications for the innovation, or in which direction the market might grow. There is low bargaining power from suppliers, since no specialised materials are used in the production. The major threats come from the old technology itself and from new entrants, if the innovation was radical and competence-destroying. Abernathy and Utterback argued that, frequently, a firm will try to outmanoeuvre the competitors and establish its product as the 'dominant design' (something Apple Inc. achieved with the iPod, but failed to achieve with the Apple Mac); this strategy will involve agreements with distributors and marketing investments (such as brand development) to affect customers' perceptions. Alternatively, the firm can try to take control of complementary assets and wait for the appearance of the dominate design; then, once the standard becomes clear, it will try to secure most of the profits, basing its competitive advantage on distribution channels, supplier contracts, complementary technologies, value-added services, etc.

The passage of time sees further technological development as producers start to learn more about the technology application and about customers' needs, and some standardisation will emerge (this is when standards battles occur, such as that for VCRs and computer operating systems). Usually, by this time, the acceptance of the innovation starts to increase and the market starts growing; these are signals that, according to Abernathy and Utterback, mark the *transitional phase*. The convergence pattern in this phase will lead to the appearance of a dominant design, which 'has features to which competitors and innovators must adhere if they hope to command significant market share following' (Utterback, 1994).

Dominant design

Winning the battle for the **dominant design** is desirable because it will enable the firm to collect monopoly rents, providing imitation can be limited, possibly with the use of intellectual property rights. Even if the standard is 'open', the developer can build complementary products or enhanced versions faster, possibly establishing a new standard in the future. (Samsung has achieved remarkable success in the mobile phone handset market through a combination of reverse engineering, product design and rapid manufacture.) Microsoft managed to establish Windows as the dominant design for graphical operating systems, largely because of its previous dominant position with the MS-DOS operating system. The threat of new entrants during the transitional phase is linked to the technology involved in the innovation: if it is proprietary, then incumbents are favoured. Firms in this phase will use strategies to consolidate their product positioning and start increasing production capacity and process innovation in order to face the next phase: the *specific phase*. Competition now shifts from differentiation to product performance and costs. Companies now have a clear picture of market segments and will, therefore, concentrate on serving specific customers. Manufacturing will use highly specialised equipment with the ability to produce the product on a large scale, hence highly skilled labour becomes less important. Since there is commoditisation taking place, the bargaining power of both suppliers and customers will increase. Competition becomes more intense and the market moves towards an oligopoly. As a consequence, incumbents are able to secure their position through supplier relations, distribution channels and other complementary assets that will create entry barriers to new entrants. Lastly, Tushman and Rosenkopf (1992) argued that, the more complex the technology, the more intrusion from sociopolitical factors during the evolution of the technology. This is clearly evidenced in the current development of electric powered automobiles where legislation and political decision making are influencing the shape and size of the future market (see Figure 7.10).

Table 7.1 captures and summarises the Abernathy and Utterback model, which attempts to illustrate the linkages between technology development and its impact upon products and processes, to market dynamics and competition, and to organisational structure and strategic decisions within companies.

How firms cope with radical and incremental innovation

In the analysis in Table 7.1, one of the key dimensions that requires further attention is that of the innovation itself and, in particular, the technology. For it is the level of newness and corresponding changes caused by this that will shape strategic decision making for the firm. Much of the debate in this area has centred on the incremental-radical product dichotomy. Radical and incremental innovations have such different competitive consequences because they require quite different organisational capabilities.

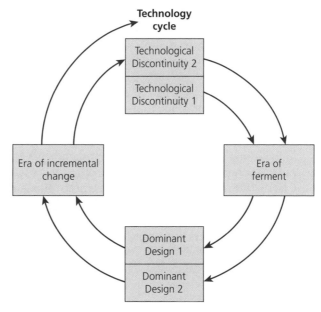

Figure 7.10 Tushman and Rosenkopf's technology cycle

Source: Tushman and Rosenkopf (1992), © Elsevier, 1992.

Organisational capabilities are difficult to create and costly to adjust (Hannan and Freeman, 1984. Incremental innovation reinforces the capabilities of established organisations, whilst radical innovation forces them to ask a new set of questions, to draw on new technical and commercial skills, and to employ new problem-solving approaches (Burns and Stalker, 1961; Ettlie et al., 1984; Hage, 1980). There are two dimensions that we can use to separate an incremental from a radical innovation:

- The first is an internal dimension, based on the knowledge and resources involved. An incremental innovation will build upon existing knowledge and resources within the firm, leading to the enhancement of its competencies. Whereas a radical innovation will require completely new knowledge and/or resources and may, therefore, destroy many of the existing competencies.
- The second dimension is external. It differentiates the innovation based on the technological changes and the impact upon the market competitiveness. An incremental innovation will involve modest technological changes and the existing products in the market will remain competitive. A radical innovation will, instead, involve large technological advancements, rendering the existing products uncompetitive and, eventually, obsolete.

The radical-incremental conceptual framework clearly suggests that incumbents will be in a better position if the innovation is incremental, since they can use existing knowledge and resources to leverage the whole process. New entrants, on the other hand, will have a large advantage if the innovation is radical because they will not need to change their knowledge background. Furthermore, incumbents struggle to deal with radical innovation both because they operate under a 'managerial mindset' constraint and because, strategically, they have less of an incentive to invest in the innovation if it will cannibalise their existing products. Kodak illustrates this well. The company dominated the photography market over many years and, throughout this extended period, all the incremental innovations solidified its leadership. As soon as the market experienced a radical innovation – the entrance of digital technology – Kodak struggled to defend its position against the new entrants. The new technology required different knowledge, resources and mindsets.

This pattern of innovation is typical in mature industries. However, in some of the newly established industries, such as software and mobile phones, there have been cases where new entrants managed to displace incumbents with incremental innovations and other cases where incumbents kept their leadership exploiting a radical innovation. An explanation for this was put forward by Henderson and Clark (1990), who argued that some innovations might appear incremental at first sight, yet this may not be the case, especially in technology-intensive industries with broad technology bases. In such circumstances, it is necessary to analyse how the innovation impacts on the technological knowledge required to develop new products and, consequently, to introduce innovations. Henderson and Clark (1990) divide technological knowledge along two new dimensions: *knowledge of the components* and knowledge of the linkage between them, which they called *architectural knowledge* (see Figure 4.3). In this framework, technology development could be a radical innovation, only if it revolutionises both component and architectural knowledge. Similarly, an incremental innovation will build upon existing component and architectural knowledge. Modular innovations will require new knowledge for one or more components, but the architectural knowledge remains unchanged. Whereas architectural innovation will have a great impact upon the linkage of components, the knowledge of single components will remain the same. For example, the technology architecture of portable computers is significantly different from the architecture of desktop computers. The portability dimension introduces new design constraints and demands architectural innovation; in particular, the need to minimise the size of all components and also their energy consumption. These tighter design constraints posed by the new architecture illustrate the relationship and differences between component innovation and architectural innovation.

The above discussions reveal that, when technology development is viewed through a wider lens, it can be seen as a complex system containing elements that function interdependently. The complexity is expressed by the matrix of interdependencies between elements in complex systems called a system's architecture (see Figure 4.3). Companies, therefore, must be careful in distinguishing between incremental and architectural or modular innovations because the competencies and strategies required to exploit one might not suit perfectly the other, if at all. Canon was able to invade Xerox's market because it developed the right architectural knowledge required to redesign the photocopier machine with smaller dimensions. Within this wider systems view, if we also consider the role of the consumer and, in particular, the extent of change required in the consumption of the product, we can see that some innovations cause disruption (forces consumers to alter the way they consume and use the product, such as MP3 players) and others sustain because they improve the performance of existing products along the dimensions that mainstream customers value. Significantly, Christensen (1997) argued that disruptive innovations frequently will have characteristics that traditional customer segments may not want, at least initially. Furthermore, they may appear as cheaper, simpler and even with inferior quality, if compared to existing products, but some marginal or new segment will value them.

Creative destruction – incumbents and new entrants

The creative destruction of existing industries as a consequence of discontinuous technological and disruptive technologies, such as digital music, is a key challenge for any innovation manager. Established arguments hold that incumbents are seriously challenged only by 'competence-destroying' or 'disruptive' innovations, which make their existing knowledge base or business models obsolete and leave them vulnerable to attacks from new entrants – as was the case when Apple disrupted the music industry with the introduction of the iPod and iTunes. Others argue that this view overestimates the ability of new entrants to destroy and disrupt established industries and underestimates the capacity of incumbents to perceive the potential of new technologies and integrate them with existing capabilities. Research by Bergek et al. (2013) put forward the notion of 'creative accumulation' as a way of conceptualising the innovating capacity of the incumbents that appear to master such turbulence. They show that creative accumulation requires firms to handle a triple challenge of simultaneously:

- fine-tuning and evolving existing technologies at a rapid pace;
- acquiring and developing new technologies and resources; and
- integrating novel and existing knowledge into superior products and solutions.

Recently, in a survey of 212 Chinese firms, Su et al. (2013) found that knowledge creation capability and absorptive capacity have a synergistic effect on product innovativeness.

Illustration 7.1

Joining up the dots to deliver 'corporate memory'

Source: Getty Images/Stock Illustration Source

'If only Unilever knew what Unilever knows', went the old lament. And you can substitute the name of almost any other company into that last sentence.

It was this lingering sense of unconnectedness, of dots not being joined up, that led to the emergence of 'knowledge management' as a business discipline two decades ago. It was based on the idea that all sorts of valuable information – about customers' preferences or what employees knew – was simply disappearing into the cracks that separated teams and business units. People within their silos could not or would not share knowledge.

Maybe knowledge management (KM) was too drab a label to hold people's attention. 'KM' soon fell prey to the curse of the management fad. It was talked about, popularised, then forgotten. Today, too few companies can be confident that their employees share the knowledge and information that they need. Do their people know what they know?

→

Smart knowledge management involves spotting useful patterns in the data that you have. Leaders should reward 'pattern recognisers'. They should also 'stress the importance of passing on items of value to others'. The best example of this is Pfizer's Viagra. The case study at the end of Chapter 9 illustrates how a few people spotted the pattern of side-effects within healthy volunteers.

Managers need more than gut instinct and past experience to help them make good decisions. This means firms have to invest in turning information into knowledge (see Chapter 11 on technology transfer).

Developing innovation strategies

The innovation framework outlined in Chapter 1 emphasises the interaction that any firm has with the external environment, both in terms of markets and science and technology. The developments taking place in these external environments will continue largely independent of the individual firm. Any firm's ability to survive is dependent on its capability to adapt to this changing environment. This suggests that a firm has a range of options open to it. A company will attempt to look ahead and try to ensure that it is prepared for possible forthcoming changes and, in some instances, a firm can modify world science and technology. But, mostly, the future is unknown – some firms will prosper; others will not. In virtually all areas of business it is not always clear who are the players in the innovation race. Very often, contenders will emerge from the most unexpected places. Furthermore, companies often find themselves in a race without knowing where the starting and finishing lines are! Even when some of these are known, companies often start out with the aim of becoming a leader and end up being a follower (Pavitt et al., 1991).

The development of new products and processes has enabled many firms to continue to grow. However, there is a wide range of alternative strategies that they may follow, depending on their resources, their heritage, their capabilities and their aspirations. Collectively, these factors should contribute to the direction that the corporate strategy takes. Unfortunately, technology is rarely an explicit element of a firm's corporate strategy. This is so, even in science- and technology-intensive firms. Very often, along with manufacturing, technology is the missing element in the corporate strategy. Until very recently, technological competencies were not viewed as an integral part of the strategic planning process. They were seen as things to be acquired, if required. As was discussed earlier, scientific knowledge cannot be bought like a can of tomatoes, off the shelf. By definition (see Chapter 1), technology is embedded in products and processes and, whilst it is possible to acquire a patent, for example, this does not necessarily mean that the company will also possess the technological capability to develop products and processes from that patent. This has been an expensive lesson learned by many international chemical companies that have acquired licences from other chemical companies to develop a chemical process, only to experience enormous difficulties in producing the product. In one particular case, the company abandoned the plant, having already sunk several million pounds into the project.

The innovation policy pursued, cuts a wide path across functions such as manufacturing, finance, marketing, R&D and personnel, hence the importance attached to its consideration. The four broad innovation strategies commonly

Table 7.2 Throughout the twentieth century 'late entrants' have been surpassing pioneers

Product	Pioneer(s)	Imitator/Later Entrant(s)	Comments
35 mm Cameras	Leica (1925) Contrax (1932) Exacta (1936)	Canon (1934) Nikon (1946) Nikon SLR (1959)	The pioneer was the technology and market leader for decades until the Japanese copied German technology, improved upon it, and lowered prices. The pioneer then failed to react and ended up as an incidental player.
CAT Scanners (Computer Axial Tomography)	EMI (1972)	Pfizer (1974) Technicare (1975) GE (1976) Johnson & Johnson (1978)	The pioneer had no experience in the medical equipment industry. Copycats ignored the patents and drove the pioneer out of business with marketing distribution and financial advantages, as well as extensive industry experience.
Ballpoint pens	Reynolds (1945) Eversharp (1946)	Parker 'Jotter' (1954) Bic (1960)	The pioneers disappeared when the fad first ended in the late 1940s. Parker entered eight years later. Bic entered last and sold pens as cheap disposables.
MRI (Magnetic Resonance Imaging)	Fonar (1978)	Johnson & Johnson's Technicare (1981) General Electric (1982)	The tiny pioneer faced the huge medical equipment suppliers, which easily expanded into MRI. The pioneer could not hope to match their tremendous market power.
Personal computers	MITS Altair 8800 (1975) Apple II (1977) Radio Shack (1977)	IBM-PC (1981) Compaq (1982) Dell (1984) Gateway (1985)	The pioneers created computers for hobbyists, but, when the market turned to business uses, IBM entered and quickly dominated, using its reputation and its marketing and distribution skills. The cloners then copied IBM's standard and sold at lower prices.
VCRs	Ampex (1956) CBS-EVR (1970) Sony U-matic (1971) Catrivision (1972) Sony Betamax (1975)	JVC-VHS (1976) RCA Selectra Vision (1977) made by Matsushita	The pioneer focused on selling to broadcasters whilst Sony pursued the home market for more than a decade. Financial problems killed the pioneer. Sony Betamax was the first successful home VCR, but was quickly supplanted by VHS, a late follower, which recorded for twice as long.
Word-processing software	Wordstar (1979)	WordPerfect (1982) Microsoft Word (1983)	The pioneer was stuck with an obsolete standard when it failed to update. When it did update, Wordstar abandoned loyal users, offered no technical support and fought internally. The follower took advantage.

found in technology-intensive firms (Freeman, 1982; Maidique and Patch, 1988) are discussed below. These are not mutually exclusive or collectively exhaustive. A wide spectrum of other strategies is logically possible; indeed, very often a firm adopts a balanced portfolio approach with a range of products. It is worth remembering, as Table 7.2 shows, that late entrants surpass pioneers.

Leader/offensive

The strategy here centres on the advantages to be gained from a monopoly, in this case a monopoly of the technology. The aim is to try to ensure that the product is launched into the market before the competition. This should enable the company either to adopt a price-skimming policy, or to adopt a penetration policy based on gaining a high market share. Such a strategy demands a significant R&D activity and usually is accompanied by substantial marketing resources to enable the company to promote the new product. This may also involve an element of education about the new product, for example Toyota's Prius and Apple's iPad.

Fast follower/defensive

This strategy also requires a substantial technology base in order that the company may develop improved versions of the original, improved in terms of lower cost, different design, additional features, etc. The company needs to be agile in manufacturing, design and development and marketing. This will enable it to respond quickly to those companies that are first into the market. In the mobile phone market, Alcatel, Sagem and others are able to get new mobile phone handsets into the market quickly. None of these firms competes with Samsung, Apple and Sony in terms of innovative technology, but they have, nonetheless, delivered profits and a return for their investors. Without any in-house R&D, their response would have been much slower, as this would have involved substantially more learning and understanding of the technology.

Very often, both the first two strategies are followed by a company, especially when it is operating in fierce competition with a rival. Sometimes, one is first to the market with a product development, only to find oneself following one's rival with the next product development. This is commonly referred to as healthy competition and is a phenomenon that governments try to propagate.

Cost minimisation/imitative

This strategy is based on being a low-cost producer and success is dependent on achieving economies of scale in manufacture. The company requires exceptional skills and capabilities in production and process engineering. This clearly is similar to the defensive strategy, in that it involves following another company, except that the technology base usually is not as well developed as for the above two strategies. Technology often is licensed from other companies. However, it is still possible to be extremely successful and even be a market leader in terms of market share. Arguably, HP has achieved this position in the PC market. Originally, its PCs were IBM clones, but were sold at a cheaper price and are of a superior quality to many of the other competitors.

This is a strategy that has been employed very effectively by the rapidly developing Asian economies. With lower labour costs, these economies have offered companies the opportunity to imitate existing products at lower prices, helping them enter and gain a foothold in a market, for example footwear or electronics. From this position, it is then possible to incorporate design improvements to existing products.

Market segmentation specialist/traditional

This strategy is based on meeting the precise requirements of a particular market segment or niche. Large-scale manufacture usually is not required and the products tend to be characterised by few product changes. Often, they are referred to as traditional products. Indeed, some companies promote their products by stressing the absence of any change, for example Scottish whisky manufacturers.

A technology strategy provides a link between innovation strategy and business strategy

For each of the strategies discussed above, there are implications in terms of the capabilities required. When it comes to operationalising the process of innovation, this invariably involves considering the technology position of the firm. Hence, the implementation of an innovation strategy usually is achieved through the management of technology.

Many decisions regarding the choice of innovation strategy will depend on the technology position of the firm with respect to its competitors. This will be based largely on the heritage of the organisation. In addition, the resource implications also need to be considered. For example, a manufacturer of electric lawnmowers wishing to adopt an innovation leadership strategy would require a high level of competence in existing technologies, such as electric motors, blade technology and injection moulding, relative to the competition, as well as an awareness of the application of new technologies, such as new lightweight materials and alternative power supplies. Adopting a follower strategy, in contrast, would require more emphasis on development engineering and manufacture.

In terms of resource expenditure, whilst the figures themselves may be very similar, it is where the money is spent that will differ considerably, with the leader strategy involving more internal R&D expenditure and the follower strategy involving more emphasis on design or manufacturing. This area of **technology strategy** and the management of technology is explored in more detail in Chapters 9, 10 and 11.

Case study

The cork industry, the wine industry and the need for closure

Introduction

This case study explores the use of cork as a way of sealing wine in a bottle; referred to as a closure in the wine industry. This 400-year-old industry, with all its associated working practices, has continued largely unaffected by technology changes in almost all other industries – until, that is, the 1990s when synthetic plastic closures were used by some wine producers instead of natural cork. With a requirement of over 17 billion wine bottle closures a year, the cork industry could, arguably, afford a little competition, but it seems the cork industry had not recognised the significant

changes taking place in the wine industry to which it acts as a supplier (Cole, 2006). The wine industry was experiencing a revolution where new producers from Australia, California and Chile had new and different requirements. In a matter of a few years, the industry had changed completely.

The cork industry

The Portuguese cork industry is facing an environmental and economic disaster as wine makers and large grocery chains defect from natural cork closures to modern synthetic closures, such as rubber or plastic.

→

Source: The Picture Pantry/Alamy Images

Portugal supplies more than half of the world's cork and has been experiencing a slow move away from cork since the mid-1990s. More recently, the trickle has turned into a flood, as changes in the wine industry and buying behaviours contribute to the rise in demand for modern closures. The cork industry accounts for nearly 3 per cent of Portugal's GDP. Its cork forests, and workers, are under threat from innovation in one of the oldest industries in the world. For hundreds of years, cork was the accepted method of closure for bottles, especially wine, but a wide range of closures for bottles have existed for many years, including screw caps and resealable plastic caps.

Few in the wine industry believed that vineyards, bottlers and wine drinkers would ever wish to use anything other than natural cork. However, the wine industry has changed significantly over the past 20 years. The historical dominant producers of Europe – France, Germany, Italy and Spain – are being challenged by new wine producers, such as California, Australia, New Zealand, South Africa, Chile, etc. Moreover, these new producers have developed international wine brands, such as Jacobs Creek and Blossom Hill, which fundamentally have changed the wine market. This is because the international brands have demanded a consistent product that has little variation. This is in complete contrast to the traditional wine products that have always had a degree of variety, dependent on the grape, the climate and production. Furthermore, the buyers of wine were changing, too – the supermarket chains, such as Tesco, Sainsbury, Carrefour, Wal-Mart, had become the biggest buyers and they now have enormous power in the industry and are able to offer wine producers access to millions of consumers and, correspondingly, millions of sales of bottled wine.

Cork is harvested exclusively from the cork oak, found predominantly in the Mediterranean region. Though the tree can flourish in many climates, the conditions that favour commercial use are fairly narrow. The major cork-producing nations are listed in Table 7.3. Cork is harvested in a steady cycle that promotes healthy growth to the tree over its expected lifespan of over 200 years. Typically, virgin cork is not removed from saplings until the 25th year, and reproduction cork (the first cycle) may not be extracted for another 9–12 years. Cork suitable for wine stoppers is not harvested until the following 9- to 12-year cycle, so farmers have invested over 40 years before natural wine corks are produced.

Table 7.3 Cork production, 2015

Country	Forest area Hectares	% of world's forest area	Production Tons (000)	% of world's production
Portugal	725,000	33	175	52
Spain	510,000	23	110	32
Italy	225,000	10	20	6
Morocco	198,000	9	15	4
Algeria	460,000	21	6	2
Tunisia	60,000	3	9	3
France	22,000	1	5	1
TOTAL	2,200,000	100	340	100

The cork forests, owing to the mutual efforts of the European Union (EU) and various environmental groups, is expected to increase, due to the active efforts to protect existing forests and sponsorship of significant new plantings. Cork bark is removed from trees in spring or summer. At this time of year, the cork comes away easily from the trunk because the tree is growing and the new, tender cork cells being generated break easily. Harvest difficulties occur if the process is not carried out when the tree is in full growth. To keep the trees in good productive health, there are laws that regulate the harvest of cork oaks. In Portugal, trees are harvested every 9 years and on the island of Sardinia (Italy) the harvest occurs every 12 years. (Numbers are painted on to the bark to keep track of when a tree was stripped.) Therefore, harvest forecasting is based on 9- or 12-year cycles, i.e. projections for the 2016 Portuguese cork harvest are based on the kilos harvested in 2007. It is in the forests where the management of cork quality begins.

Cork production has shown significant expansion in recent years – reflecting the impact of approximately 120,000 hectares of highly productive, new cork forests in Spain and Portugal (see Table 7.3).

Applications of natural cork

Cork is used in a wide variety of products – from construction materials to gaskets and, most importantly, as a stopper for wines. The cork industry employs an estimated 30,000 workers in a variety of jobs. Wine corks are the most visible and most profitable of the many products derived from cork. They account for approximately 15 per cent of total production by weight and two-thirds of cork revenues. The wine industry is by far the most important customer of the cork industry, the dominant cork producer being Amorim. More than 13 billion wine bottle closures are needed each year and the market is growing.

The wine industry

Wine consumption in the UK has grown dramatically over the past 20 years and this has been the case in the USA, too. The UK wine market is expected to grow in value by 6.1 per cent to £13.14 billion by 2018, with volume growth forecast to pick up again in 2017, according to a market report by Key Note. The USA remains the world's biggest market for all colours of wines. Wine has continued to be the drink of choice for increasing numbers of younger people in the USA.

China has become the leading market in the world for red wine. Over the past five years it has seen an increase of 136 per cent. The colour red is considered lucky in China and is also affiliated with the Communist Government, whilst white is associated with death and is seen predominantly at funerals.

Wine has become a fixture on the weekly grocery list of UK consumers, alongside bread and eggs. This has meant that the UK multiples (Tesco, Sainsbury's, M&S, Morrisons, ASDA) have become some of the largest buyers of wine in the world. With this buying power has come the ability to make demands on suppliers. In particular, a homogeneous product free from fault. The world of wine has changed considerably over the last couple of decades and, whilst many of the changes have been for the better, some are giving cause for concern. One area of considerable change is the growth in branded wines or so-called 'modern' wine by traditionalists.

According to the traditionalists, wine may be divided simply into two categories: the first is a commodity, that is grapes are grown, crushed and made into wine, which is then sold cheaply and consumed uncritically. In this case, as long as the quality is adequate and the price is right, consumers are not too worried about the source. This first category accounts for the majority of wine across the world. This is the 'modern' approach to wine production and distribution. The second type of wine is 'traditional' wine that is purchased and consumed not because of low price, but because of interest. This interest stems from the fact that there exists a diversity of wine types that are each able to express elements of their cultural and geographical origins in the finished product. Crucial here is the importance of the starting material – the grapes. Unlike lager or whisky, where the agricultural input (wheat or barley) is minimal and the human input is dominant, this kind of winemaking is best viewed as a process of stewardship rather than one of manufacturing.

The diversity of wine is vast. Not only are hundreds of different grape varieties in relatively common use, but there are also the complex influences of soil types, climate, viticulture (the study and production of grapes) and winemaking practices. There is also a rich traditional heritage in the more established wine-producing countries, whereby cultural and viticultural influences collude to produce a variety of wine classifications (appellations in France), that is, geographical areas where grapes for certain wines were grown.

Table 7.4 Modern and traditional wine

Branded (modern)	Estate (traditional)
• volume of production is managed • typically made from bought-in grapes • often 'international' in style, lacking a sense of place • usually defined by winemaking style • made to a style and to fit a price point • because production is limited only by the supply of suitable purchased grapes, these wines often are widely available • heavily marketed • lack diversity	• made from grapes grown in one vineyard or several neighbouring vineyards • vineyards supplying the grapes usually are owned by the company making the wine or are supplied by growers on long-term contracts • limited production, subject to vintage variation • typically display regional influences or a 'sense of place' • availability is sometimes a problem because of the limited production • marketing is often minimal • hugely diverse

According to the traditionalists, it is this diversity that makes wine so interesting. They argue that, divorced from its geographical origins, wine is only marginally more interesting than fruit juice, lager or gin. And you do not get people naming either of these three beverage types as one of their interests or hobbies.

These two genres of wine have coexisted quite happily and there is no reason that they cannot continue to do so, sitting side-by-side on the shelf. They serve different functions and are consumed in different situations, often by different groups of consumers. These two genres may also be labelled 'branded' and 'estate bottled' (see Table 7.4).

The modern retailing environment

The traditionalists argue that estate bottled wine does not sit well with the modern retail environment (see Figure 7.11). They argue that, because wine is an agricultural product, not a manufactured one in the eyes of the big retailer, this is a bad thing. The way the modern multi-outlet branded/franchised shop is configured, continuity of supply and economies of scale are hugely important. This is not something the traditional wine producers, most notably in France, have been willing to embrace. It is the diversity within wine that the traditionalists want to celebrate: vintage variation – at times a frustrating reality, but one that adds an extra level of interest – and typically the limited production of each producer means that wine is not an easy product to deal with. Usually, it comes in small parcels and the production level changes each year. Modern retailing, however, is big business. To survive in the modern retailing environment, you need to be big, highly visible and have lots of outlets.

Effective marketing in this modern environment is an expensive business and you can only really make use of it if you are a big player. This automatically rules out almost all estate wines, leaving the market open to the international brands. Figure 7.11 illustrates the power and influence within the supply chain of wine.

The illusion of choice

Supermarkets and other multiple outlets do not like dealing with the diversity and complexity of wine, but they are quite attached to the 'idea' of diversity. So, typically, they will stock hundreds of different lines, giving the consumer the impression of a broad portfolio of wines. The problem here is that this diversity is actually an illusory one. The wines are, almost always, industrially produced, in large quantities and to a formula. For example, you may have in your minds the romantic notion that all wine is discovered by a dedicated wine hound who has trekked across remote parts of the world stopping at cellar after cellar searching out a wine that will give your tastebuds a treat. The truth is very different. Most wine purchased by the supermarkets today is led by financial motives, which are driven by cost sheets and market forecasts.

Remember also that wines that appear on recipe cards or in magazines have been paid for. Waitrose charges suppliers a nominal fee of £300 for a mention in its *Wine List* magazine (Moore, 2007). According to the traditionalists, whilst customers now experience far less risk of picking a bad bottle, they also have far less chance of picking a wine that is at all interesting. Traditionalists argue that, whilst high quality is desirable, a uniformity of style is disastrous. They maintain that branded wines, with their

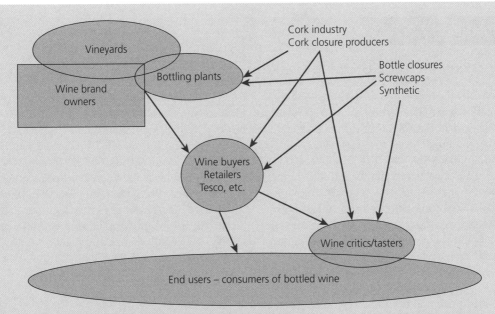

Figure 7.11 Power and influence in the supply chain of wine

manufactured, processed character and lack of connection with the soil, hinders complete choice and diversity. Worst of all, they argue, their growing dominance of the marketplace threatens the very existence of the traditional article: estate wines.

Wine bottle closures

Cork has been used as a closure for bottles for hundreds of years. Indeed, one might reasonably ask why it has survived so long. It is partly because it is a natural product that breathes, which is a quality required for some wines. For most wine drinkers, the pop of the cork from the bottle is an intrinsic part of the wine drinking experience and they love it. Wine producers, on the other hand, view natural corks with deep suspicion, due largely to the rogue chemical 2-4-6 trichloranisole (TCA, a compound created by the interplay of a cork-borne fungus, the chlorine used to sanitise wine corks and plant phenols), often referred to as cork taint that makes wine taste anything from slightly muted to very mouldy. Although it is harmless if swallowed by humans, TCA imparts a musty, wet cardboard smell and taste to the wine it affects. TCA is detectable in wine at concentrations as low as four parts per trillion and, although some wine drinkers are more sensitive to it than others, the taste and smell of a 'corked' wine are as unforgettable as the disappointment a sommelier

(trained wine professional) or host feels upon the discovery of a tainted bottle. The wine industry argues that this had risen to an unacceptable level. Estimates of this level vary wildly, as do different people's sensitivity to and awareness of TCA. The cork industry quotes less than 2 per cent. Some wine producers claim it is as high as 15 per cent. Whatever the precise figure, wine producers are deeply worried that a significant proportion of their customers experience a substandard form of the liquid they originally put in the bottle. And they are almost more worried by a light incidence of TCA that simply flattens the aroma and fruit of their wines than by TCA at its most obvious, virtually undrinkable extreme. In the first case, the consumer probably will think, wrongly, that the fault lies with the wine rather than the cork. The cork industry has been working hard to introduce new techniques that minimise the incidence of TCA taint in their products, and to demonstrate that TCA can arise not just from corks but other sources, such as wooden pallets. Because of all this uncertainty, wine producers have been seeking alternative bottle stoppers, or closures, with much lower or minimal risks of TCA taint, and closure manufacturers have identified this business opportunity that demands more than 13 billion wine bottle closures and is a growing market. But they risk alienating their customers who love cork or at least the 'pop' of the closure.

Illustration 7.2

Breaking into the UK wine market

Consider the lot of a wine producer looking to break into the UK market. With 75 per cent of wine sales in the UK going through supermarkets, you might want to target them first. So, you approach the supermarket buyers. If you are from a relatively unfashionable country like Portugal, probably you will be talking to a 22-year-old junior buyer fresh out of college who has, perhaps, two slots to fill at a £3.99–4.99 price point. They want serious volumes, a fresh, fruity style and the cheaper the better. If you are from Australia, you may have better luck, but the volumes required will be huge and the price points will be very keen. Even at the higher price points, the continuity of supply and volume issues favour the branders very heavily. If you are selling wine from recognised appellations, such as Chablis or St Emilion, then the buyers will be looking for the best Chablis at the entry-level price point for this wine, effectively ruling out the estate wines here also. A supermarket would much rather have a vaguely palatable Chablis at £5.99 – which will fly out of the door – than a really good one at £8.99. That is life . . . it is hard.

Source: Wine Anorak.com, 2006.

It is wider changes in the wine industry that have led to innovation in wine bottle closures and suitable remedial activity in the natural cork industry itself, even though this problem/opportunity has been obvious to all in the wine business for at least 15 years. The first generation of alternatives to natural cork were synthetic copies of the real thing, cylinders of various oil-industry-derived materials, 'plastic corks' which, though improved, can still be difficult to get out of a bottle neck, and even more difficult to put back in. They retain natural cork's disadvantage of needing a special tool to extract them. In 1999, the synthetic cork was dealt a significant blow by the Australian Wine Research Institute (regarded by the industry as the most important impartial research project) comparing the technical performance of different closures. This showed that synthetic corks started to let in dangerous amounts of oxygen after about 18 months, which means they are really suitable only for the most basic wines for early consumption.

In terms of costs, synthetic was initially more expensive than natural cork, but fierce competition between different manufacturers and economies of scale have brought synthetic cork prices down; rising oil prices have put pressure on this but, generally, a plastic cork costs considerably less than a natural one – well under 3p each, when a good quality cork can cost easily more than 10p. Cork and synthetic require a foil capsule over the top, which costs 0.8p. Synthetic corks have several more big drawbacks, such as they are non-biodegradable, unlike natural cork. Furthermore, the ecosystem of southern Portugal depends on our continuing to buy natural corks – an argument that is questionable, given that the cork forests of Alentejo were planted expressly for the cork industry.

Screwcaps

Both natural and synthetic are cheaper than the next most obvious alternative, screwcaps, which currently are the favourite closure for many a wine technician (anyone who has to open a lot of bottles), although the special bottles needed for screwcaps are expected to become cheaper as screwcaps become more common – and there is no need to pay for a foil capsule over a screwcap.

Unlike synthetic corks, screwcaps are extremely good at keeping wine's enemy, oxygen, out of the bottle – almost too good, in fact. It is becoming increasingly clear that screwcaps are associated with the opposite of oxidation: reduction, which can suppress wine's all-important aroma and even imbue it with a downright nasty one. This problem particularly affects Sauvignon Blanc, a grape that tends naturally to reduction, but not Riesling.

For the moment, these two grapes are those most frequently found under screwcap, because their bright, aromatic, unoaked wines have so far seemed to respond best to this particular seal.

In New Zealand and Australia, an estimated 30 per cent of all wines, red and white, are already bottled under screwcaps, which are gradually spreading throughout the northern hemisphere. But the jury is still out on the effect of screwcaps on oaked whites and reds, which actually may need more oxygen during the ageing process than screwcaps allow.

Globally, cork has a total market share of 40 per cent and screwcap 60 per cent locally but this changes for reds retailing for over 30 euros a bottle – 60 per cent bottled under cork. It would seem that no single closure works for every wine on the market.

But not all consumers are as thrilled by screwcaps as producers. They still carry the stigma of being associated with cheap wines and spirits – and, unlike the natural cork, they involve precious little theatre of cork screw and pop. Furthermore, screwcap application requires the installation of a completely new set of machinery from the old cork insertion kit. This has discouraged many smaller producers from adopting the screwcap, or Stelvin as it is known in many markets after the market leader. It has also made plastic corks seem a much more attractive alternative.

In Australia and New Zealand, there is near total acceptance that the screwcap is the preferable closure. In the UK, they are now commonplace in mass market wines; UK wine bottlers report that the proportion of all wine they stopper with a screwcap has risen to 85 per cent in the past three years. But, in much of mainland Europe, and certainly in the USA, there is still considerable consumer resistance to this innovation.

More innovative alternatives now include the Vinolok, a glass stopper reminiscent of an old-fashioned pharmacy, currently being trialled in Germany; Gardner Technologies' MetaCork, a US stopper that can be screwed off but is lined with a natural cork for resealing; and, more recently, from Australia, the Zork, a plastic, peel-off stopper that, so far, seems good at keeping oxygen out and also provides the vital 'pop' when being extracted (see Illustration 7.3).

Zork has the disadvantage for producers of being a relatively late arrival on the scene and, initially at least, being more expensive than any other closure. But it is extremely easy to use and may well find favour with consumers because of what the manufacturers describe as 'the sex appeal of the cork'.

The cork industry fights back

The cork industry has launched its own offensive against synthetic closures. First, the cork industry via the Cork Quality Council (CQC) is sponsoring ongoing research into the relationships between TCA, cork and bottled wine. The following research was carried out in 2010 by ETS Laboratories. It involves the use of chemical tests to quantify TCA content in individual corks and in cork harvests. The results have shown several interesting characteristics of TCA in cork soaks (cork soaking is the process prior to putting the cork in the bottle). It has also demonstrated a direct relationship between the level of TCA found in a cork soak and TCA that is transmitted to bottled wine. Testing has proven to be quicker, more sensitive and accurate than previous analysis available to the industry. The procedure offers an immediate improvement in cork quality control procedures involving screening manufactured corks. Further value is seen in other research projects designed to eliminate TCA prior to the completion of cork manufacture. The chemical test is now being used by CQC member companies to supplement sensory analysis of incoming cork shipments.

Illustration 7.3

ZORK®

According to its manufacturer, ZORK® is a revolutionary wine closure product that combines the benefits of cork and screwcap. The company humorously suggests that ZORK® is Australian for cork. Similar to synthetic and screwcap closures, ZORK® offers the winemaker a competitively priced, quality-controlled consistent barrier to oxygen that will not taint the wine or scalp its flavour. Unlike synthetic, however, it is made from durable, food-grade polymers and is fully recyclable.

ZORK®, developed and manufactured in Adelaide, South Australia, seals like a screw-cap and pops like a cork. The ZORK® snaps on to a standard cork mouth wine bottle and, after simple, low-cost modification, can be applied at high speed using industry-standard capping equipment.

The ZORK® closure consists of three parts; a robust outer cap that provides a tamper-evident clamp that locks on to the European CETIE band of a standard cork mouth bottle, an inner metal foil that provides an oxygen barrier similar to a screwcap, and an inner plunger that creates the 'pop' on extraction and reseals after use. The closure is easy to remove by hand and simple to reseal.

To open the bottle, peel the seal to remove the tamper-evident tab. The closure can then be pulled out like a cork, and pop! After pouring, the bottle can be resealed by pushing it back in. According to the advertising copy: ZORK® delivers a superior technical seal but retains the sense of celebration associated with traditional closures.

No corkscrew, no crumbling, no cork taint, no worries.

Second, cork manufacturers have invested $200 million in the past five years in new plants and supply chain integration, says APCOR (Association of Portuguese Cork Producers). The industry passed a self-regulatory code in 2000 to standardise manufacturing practices. Over 200 Portuguese cork makers have been certified. Cork producers have also vertically integrated their distribution channels. For example, Amorin Cork, the largest producer of natural corks, has taken over supply and distribution lines it once contracted out.

Marketing the benefits of cork

Third, in 2003, the Portuguese Government and APCOR members launched a 12-month $6.5 million marketing campaign to turn consumers against synthetic closures (Almond, 2003). One of the tactics has been to stress the dangers of switching to synthetic and the environmental disasters that could result. Another has been to gain support from wildlife groups to stress their concerns to wildlife if the cork forests are lost. In 2004, WWF, the conservation group, urged wine drinkers to avoid bottles sealed with plastic corks or screwtops. It said that falling demand for traditional corks was threatening the habitat of the Iberian lynx, the world's rarest big cat. The latest figures from the IUCN, the World Conservation Union, show that there are only 156 lynx left, prompting the IUCN to upgrade its status to 'critically endangered' (Bugalho et al. 2011).

A slightly more sophisticated tactic has been to focus on the consumer. For example, surveys show that wine drinkers dislike synthetic closures, long associated with cheap wine. Yet, the synthetic market share is growing, mainly from medium-end wines from 'new world' markets: Argentina, Chile and Australia. Synthetics account for 7–8 per cent of a worldwide market of an estimated 17 billion bottle stoppers, growing at a rate of 10–30 per cent a year, according to US-based Supreme Corq, the largest synthetic cork maker. The challenge for the cork industry is to try to nurture the consumers' love of natural cork.

The use by some wine brands of the flanged bottle (roll top rim) first introduced in 1999 to try to convey a premium product, is now being replaced by the standard shaped bottle. This is partly in response to consumer research that reveals that premium quality is no longer associated with the flanged bottle, largely because the design became almost universal amongst the international wine brands. A similar argument could be made with the use of screwcaps, where there may be a consumer backlash because people may associate screwcaps with mass market wines, which would result in enormous damage to the premium labels (Almond, 2003).

Conclusions

This case study has explored some of the issues surrounding changes in the wine industry and their impact on one of the world's oldest industries – cork wine closures. The issues stir strong emotions and there are powerful lobby groups at work trying to influence consumers and government officials.

Environmentalists say that undercutting demand for natural cork will render cork forests less profitable and spark an ecological and economic disaster. Such arguments, whilst they play well with certain consumer groups, are hard to sustain when many of the forests have been planted specifically to harvest cork.

It seems the switch to screwcap has been made for the benefit of the wine, not just the image or for reduced costs. The cork industry's response has been to invest in research to address the issue of cork taint and to increase promotional campaigns about the benefits of cork. This, however, largely has been through the use of fear, arguing that the cork forests of Portugal will be lost, along with all the associated wildlife if the move from cork as a closure continues and to suggest that consumers will reject wine from a screwcap bottle. The evidence for this last claim is not there, certainly in many parts of the world.

According to wine industry figures, faults attributable to the use of cork as a seal run between 3–7 per cent, depending on who you ask; this is high and would be labelled a disaster in any other industry, especially for food and beverage. It is particularly so when there are ways the industry can directly address the issue, by looking at alternative seals, as they are now doing. The decision to change closure, however, has to include consideration of costs and consumer preference. At present, a plastic cork costs considerably less than a natural one. With regard to consumer preference, this is more difficult to gauge. In some countries, most notably Australia and New Zealand, consumers, it seems, have readily embraced the screwcap. Indeed, the corkscrew is rapidly becoming

redundant in both countries. When even Kay Brothers of McLaren Vale, the dusty old winery that has hardly changed since the eponymous brothers bought it in 1890, is using screwcaps exclusively, the time for a cork revival may be too late.

According to the cork industry, more than one in two wineries are considering using the screwcap. However, many in the industry will continue to use natural cork for higher-priced bottles largely, they say, because of cork's ability to facilitate the proper aging of wine and overall consumer acceptance. The new synthetic corks have succeeded in getting the natural cork producers to take quality control far more seriously and, as a result, the quality of cork closures has improved. But many wine makers and retailers remain unimpressed and argue that the cork industry has not yet eliminated cork taint.

Whilst the battle over closures rages, the so-called traditionalists argue that the wine industry is merely exploiting profits in the short term by producing large volumes of homogenised wine and that this may harm the wine industry in the long term because consumers will grow bored with the uniformity of style.

Source: Almond, M. (2003) The cork industry spins out the fear factor, FT.com, 23 March; Bugalho, M., Caldeira, M., Pereira, J., Aronson, J. and Pausas, J. (2011) Mediterranean cork oak savannas require human use to sustain biodiversity and ecosystem services, *Frontiers in Ecology and the Environment*, vol. 9, no. 5, 278–86. Cole, E. (2006) Americans set to overtake French in wine consumption, *Decanter*, vol. 8, no. 4; Houlder, V. (2002) Wildlife body takes a pop at plastic corks, *Financial Times*, 27 December; Moore, V. (2007) The great wine rip-off, *The Guardian*, G2, 5 April, 4–7; Randolph, N. (2002) Cork industry fights off taint, *Financial Times*, Commodities and Agriculture, 27 August; Robinson, J. (2004) A question of closure, FT.com, 11 June http://winemag.co.za/cork-vs-screwcap-2014/.

Questions

1 To what extent is the cork industry guilty of complacency and a lack of innovation?

2 If consumers love corks, why are the producers not providing what their customers want?

3 Is it wine quality or costs that have driven producers to synthetic?

4 How could technology forecasting have helped the cork industry?

5 What level of R&D investment would be required to help the industry diversify and develop new opportunities for its materials?

6 What portfolio of R&D projects would you establish for the cork industry?

7 What role have the wine buyers (end users and others in the supply chain) played in contributing to the fall in demand for cork as a closure?

8 Use the CIM (Figure 1.9) to illustrate the innovation process in this case.

9 In terms of closures, what are the disadvantages that the cork industry needs to address and what are the advantages that it could promote?

10 Will the cork industry have to concede defeat to the Zork?

Chapter summary

This chapter examined how business strategy affects the management of innovation. In so doing, it introduced the notion of an organisation's knowledge base and how this links strategy and innovation. The heritage of a business was also shown to form a significant part of its knowledge base. Moreover, a firm's knowledge base largely determines its ability to innovate and certainly has a large influence on the selection of any innovation strategy.

Discussion questions

1 Explain the role played by core competencies in a firm's strategic planning.

2 What is meant by the technology escalator in the concept of technology trajectories?

3 Explain why a business's heritage needs to be considered in planning future strategy.

4 Try to plot two firms in each of the quadrants on the profit–competency matrix (Figure 7.4).

5 Explain the difference between individual knowledge and organisational knowledge and show how an organisation's knowledge can be greater than the sum of individual knowledge bases.

6 How would you compare the knowledge bases of two organisations?

7 How can late entrants win the innovation race?

Key words and phrases

Technology trajectories *229*

Dynamic capabilities *229*

Core competency *230*

Knowledge base of
  an organisation *236*

Organisational heritage *237*

Learning organisation *241*

Dominant design *244*

Degree of innovativeness *248*

Technology strategy *251*

References

Abernathy, W.J. and Utterback, J. (1978) Patterns of industrial innovation, *Technology Review*, vol. 80, no. 7, 40–7.

Adler, P.S. and Shenhar, A. (1990) Adapting your technological base: the organizational challenge, *Sloan Management Review*, Autumn, 25–37.

Argyris, C. (1977) Double loop learning in organizations, *Harvard Business Review*, September/October, 55.

Barney, J. (1991) Firm resources and sustained competitive advantage, *Journal of Management*, vol. 17, 99–120.

Bergek, A., Berggren, C., Magnusson, T. and Hobday, M. (2013) Technological discontinuities and the challenge for incumbent firms: destruction, disruption or creative accumulation? *Research Policy*, vol. 42, no. 6, 1210–24.

Burns, T. and Stalker, G.M. (1961) *The Management of Innovation*, Tavistock, London.

Casper, S. and Whitley, R. (2003) Managing competencies in entrepreneurial technology firms: a comparative institutional analysis of Germany, Sweden and the UK, *Research Policy*, vol. 33, 89–106.

Cohen, W.M. and Levinthal, D.A. (1990) A new perspective on learning and innovation, *Administrative Science Quarterly*, vol. 35, no. 1, 128–52.

Christensen, C.M. (1997) *The Innovator's Dilemma: When New Technologies Cause Great Firms to Fail*, Harvard Business School Press, Boston, MA.

Dosi, G. (1982) Technical paradigms and technological trajectories: a suggested interpretation of the determinants and directions of technical change, *Research Policy*, vol. 11, no. 3, 147–62.

Ettlie, J.E., Bridges, W.P. and O'Keefe, R.D. (1984) Organization strategy and structural differences for radical versus incremental innovation, *Management Science*, vol. 30, 682–95.

Foster, R. (1986) *Innovation: The Attacker's Advantage*, New York: Summit Books.

Freeman, C. (1982) *The Economics of Industrial Innovation*, 2nd edn, Frances Pinter, London.

Galbreath, J. and Galvin, P. (2004) Which resources matter? A fine-grained test of the resource-based view of the firm, Academy of Management Best Paper Proceedings, p. L1–6, 6p; (AN 13863763), August, New Orleans, LA.

Hage, J. (1980) *Theories of organizations*, Wiley, New York.

Hamel, G. and Prahalad, C.K. (1994) Competing for the future, *Harvard Business Review*, vol. 72, no. 4, 122–8.

Hannan, M. and Freeman, J. (1984) Structural inertia and organizational change, *American Sociological Review*, vol. 49, 149–64.

Henderson, R. and Clark, K. (1990) Architectural innovation: the reconfiguration of existing product and the failure of established firms, *Administrative Science Quarterly*, vol. 35, 9–30.

Maidique, M. and Patch, P. (1988) 'Corporate strategy and technology policy', in Tushman, M.L. and Moore, W.L. (eds) *Readings in the Management of Innovation*, HarperCollins, New York.

Nelson, R.R. (1991) Why do firms differ, and how does it matter? *Strategic Management Journal*, vol. 12, no. 1, 61–74.

Onyeiwu, S. (2003) Some determinants of core competencies: evidence from a binary-logit analysis, *Technology Analysis and Strategic Management*, vol. 15, no. 1, 43–63.

Pavitt, K. (1990) What we know about the strategic management of technology, *California Management Review*, vol. 32, no. 3, 17–26.

Pavitt, K., Robson, M. and Townsend, J. (1991) Technological accumulation, diversification and organisation in UK companies, 1945–1983, *Management Science*, vol. 35, no. 1, 81–99.

Pennings, J.M. and Harianto, F. (1992) Technological networking and innovation implementation, *Organisational Science*, vol. 3, no. 3, 356–82.

Penrose, E.T. (1959) *The Theory of the Firm*, John Wiley, New York.

Su, Z., Ahlstrom, D., Li, J. and Cheng, D. (2013) Knowledge creation capability, absorptive capacity, and product innovativeness, *R&D Management*, vol. 43, 473–85.

Teece, D. (1986) Profiting from technological innovation: implications for integration, collaboration, licensing and public policy, *Research Policy*, vol. 15, 285–305.

Teece, D.J. and Pisano, G. (1994) The dynamic capabilities of firms: an introduction, *Industrial and Corporate Change*, vol. 3, no. 3, 537–56.

Teece, D.J., Pisano, G. and Shuen, A. (1997) Dynamic capabilities and strategic management, *Strategic Management Journal*, vol. 18, no. 7, 509–33.

Tidd, J. (2000) *From Knowledge Management to Strategic Competence: Measuring Technological Market and Organisational Innovation*, Imperial College Press, London.

Tushman, M.L. and Rosenkopf, L. (1992) Organizational determinants of technological change: toward a sociology of technological evolution, *Research in Organizational Behavior*, vol. 14, 311–47.

Utterback, J.M. (1994) *Mastering the Dynamics of Innovation: How Companies Can Seize Opportunities in the Face of Technological Change*, Harvard Business School Press, Boston, MA.

Werfel, S.H. and Jaffe, A.B. (2013) Induced innovation and technology trajectory: evidence from smoking cessation products, *Research Policy*, vol. 42, no. 1 15–22.

Wernerfelt, B. (1984) A resource based view of the firm, *Strategic Management Journal*, vol. 5, no. 2, 171–80.

Willman, P. (1991) Bureaucracy, innovation and appropriability, paper given at ESRC Industrial Economics Study Group Conference, London Business School, November 22.

Further reading

For a more detailed review of the knowledge management literature, the following develop many of the issues raised in this chapter:

Argyris, C. (1977) Double loop learning in organizations, *Harvard Business Review*, September/October, 55.

Frow, P., Nenonen, S., Payne, A., and Storbacka, K. (2015). Managing Co-creation Design: A Strategic Approach to Innovation. *British Journal of Management*, 26(3), 463–483.

Gibbert, M. (2006) Generalizing about uniqueness: an essay on an apparent paradox in the resource-based view, *Journal of Management Inquiry*, vol. 15, no. 2, 124–34.

Kay, J. (1996) Oh Professor Porter, whatever did you do? *Financial Times*, 10 May, 17.

Morris, M., Schindehutte, M., Richardson, J., and Allen, J. (2015). Is the business model a useful strategic concept? Conceptual, theoretical, and empirical insights. *Journal of Small Business Strategy*, *17*(1), 27–50.

Newbert, S.L. (2007) Empirical research on the resource-based view of the firm: an assessment and suggestions for future research, *Strategic Management Journal*, vol. 28, 121–46.

Chapter 8
Strategic alliances and networks

Introduction

In strategic alliances firms cooperate out of mutual need and share the risks to reach a common objective. Strategic alliances provide access to resources that are greater than any single firm could buy. This can greatly improve its ability to create new products, bring in new technologies, penetrate other markets and reach the scale necessary to survive in world markets.

Collaboration with other firms, however, can take many forms. Virtually all firms have networks of suppliers and, in some cases, this can form part of a firm's competitive advantage.

The case study at the end of this chapter explores the development of high-definition video and the format war between Sony's Blu-ray and Toshiba's HD-DVD. The influence of strategic alliances in this war clearly is evident.

Chapter contents

Learning objectives

When you have completed this chapter you will be able to:

- recognise the reasons for the increasing use of strategic alliances;
- recognise the role of embedded technology in strategic alliances;
- provide an understanding of the risks and limitations of strategic alliances;
- explain how the role of trust is fundamental in strategic alliances;
- examine the different forms an alliance can take;
- explain how the prisoner's dilemma game can be used to analyse the behaviour of firms in strategic alliances; and
- identify the factors that affect the success of an alliance.

Defining strategic alliances

Faced with new levels of competition, many companies, including competitors, are sharing their resources and expertise to develop new products, achieve economies of scale and gain access to new technology and markets. Many have argued that these strategic alliances are the competitive weapon of the next century. A strategic alliance is a contractual agreement amongst organisations to combine their efforts and resources to meet a common goal. It is, however, possible to have a strategic alliance without a contractual agreement, hence a more accurate definition would be:

> *A strategic alliance is an agreement between two or more partners to share knowledge or resources, which could be beneficial to all parties involved.*

One of the major factors that prevents many firms from achieving their technical objectives and, therefore, their strategic objectives, is the lack of resources. For technology research and development (R&D), the insufficient resources are usually capital and technical 'critical mass'. The cost of building and sustaining the necessary technical expertise and specialised equipment is rising dramatically. Even for the largest corporations, leadership in some market segments that they have traditionally dominated cannot be maintained because they lack sufficient technical capabilities to adapt to fast-paced market dynamics.

In the past, strategic alliances were perceived as an option reserved only for large international firms. Intensified competition, shortening product life cycles and soaring R&D costs mean that strategic alliances are an attractive strategy for the future. It is now accepted that strategic alliances provide an opportunity for large and small high-technology companies to expand into new markets by sharing skills and resources. It is beneficial for both parties, since it allows large firms to access the subset of expertise and resources that they desire in the smaller firm, whilst the smaller company is given access to its larger partner's massive capital and organisational resources.

For many firms, the thought of sharing ideas and technology, in particular, with another company is precisely what they have been trying to avoid doing since their conception. It is a total lack of trust that lies at the heart of their unwillingness to engage in any form of cooperation. The element of trust is highlighted through the use of the **prisoner's dilemma**.

Technology partnerships between, and in some cases amongst, organisations are becoming more important and prevalent. As the costs, including risk associated with R&D efforts, continue to increase, no company can remain a 'technology island' and stay competitive. Illustration 8.1 shows that Silicon Valley is home to some of the world's fastest growing tech firms. Many of the firms collaborate on technology projects.

The term strategic alliance is used to cover a wide range of cooperative arrangements. The different forms of strategic alliances will be explored later in this chapter.

Illustration 8.1

Silicon Valley – the best example of an innovation network

Silicon Valley is a leading hub and start-up eco-system for high-tech innovation and development, accounting for one-third of all of the venture capital investment in the United States. Silicon Valley is located in the southern San Francisco Bay Area. Significantly, it is home to hundreds of start-up and global technology companies, with Google, Apple and Facebook amongst the most prominent (see Figure 8.1). The word 'Valley' refers to the Santa Clara Valley, where the region traditionally has been centred, which includes the city of San Jose and surrounding cities and towns. The word 'Silicon' originally referred to the large number of silicon chip innovators and manufacturers in the region. Stanford University is also located close by

and has a large postgraduate population. Many of its graduates take up positions in the region with large and small firms; many have started their own business. The term 'Silicon Valley' eventually came to refer to all high-tech businesses in the area. It was in Silicon Valley that the silicon-based integrated circuit, thed microprocessor, and the microcomputer, amongst other key technologies, were developed.

And what about other Silicon Valleys? It seems that, across Europe, there are many other clusters forming in the regions circling around London/ Cambridge, Paris, Amsterdam and Munich. Any of these could develop into a thriving innovation centre. Time will tell.

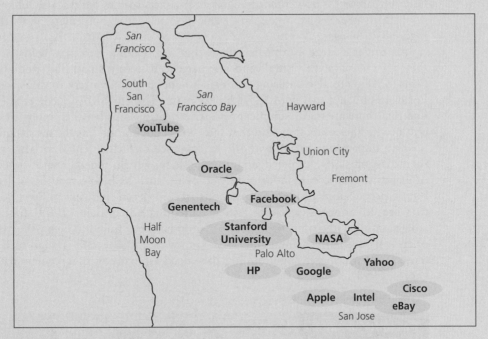

Figure 8.1 Silicon Valley

The fall of the go-it-alone strategy and the rise of the octopus strategy

Businesses are beginning to broaden their view of their business environment from the traditional *go-it-alone* perspective of individual firms competing against each other. The formation of strategic alliances means that strategic power often resides in sets of firms acting together. The development of mobile phones, treatments for viruses such as AIDS, aircraft manufacture and motor cars are all dominated by global competitive battles between groups of firms. For example, the success of the European Airbus strategic alliance has been phenomenal. Formed in 1969 as a **joint venture** between the German firm MBB and the French firm Aerospatiale, it was later joined by CASA of Spain and British Aerospace of the United Kingdom. The Airbus A300 range of civilian aircraft achieved great success, securing large orders for aircraft ahead of its major rival Boeing.

The so-called octopus strategy (Vyas et al., 1995) gets its name from the long tentacles of the eponymous creature. Firms often develop alliances with a wide range of companies. Car making may be one of the world's most competitive big industries, but rival producers have always been ready to cooperate on expensive new technologies and products when the cost or risk of going it alone was too high. The hunt for partners is now intensifying as automakers seek to build scale, cut costs and pool efforts in areas like small cars, vehicle electrification and emerging markets, as Figure 8.2 shows.

It is not just large established firms that are rushing into new fields in which they are comparatively small and inexperienced. Many small and medium-sized firms (SMEs) are also entering strategic alliances with a variety of different firms. For example, in a survey of 137 Chinese manufacturing SMEs, Zeng et al. (2010) find that there are many significant positive relationships between inter-firm cooperation. Furthermore, they find that inter-firm cooperation has the most significant positive impact on the innovation performance of SMEs. They are able to offer their existing skills, knowledge and technology, which, together with other areas of expertise, can create 'hybrid' technologies, such as bioelectronics, or by combining process and product innovations from different industries. Even competitors are collaborating. Ritala and Hurmelinna-Laukkanen (2009) found that collaborating with competitors (coopetition) has been found to be an effective way of creating both incremental and radical innovations, especially in high-tech industries. Firms are increasingly finding they need an array of complementary assets (Teece, 1998).

Pause for thought

Many small firms are reluctant to engage in any form of sharing information and knowledge, because they believe other firms may steal their valuable information and customers. Maybe there are some firms that should not engage in alliances?

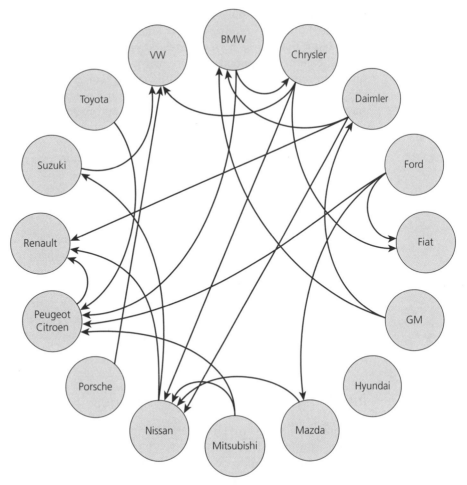

Figure 8.2 The tangled web of alliances between car manufacturers
Source: FT.com, 4 May 2010.

Complementary capabilities and embedded technologies

The example of Silicon Valley above illustrates that even firms with a long and impressive heritage to defend see technology as the main determinant of competitive success. As a result, they increasingly realise they need access to new technology. Moreover, they also realise they cannot develop it all themselves. Acquiring technology from outside using technology transfer (the subject of technology transfer is explored in much more detail in Chapter 11) and forming alliances with others is now regarded as the way forward.

Many large established firms, such as Sony, IBM and HP, have developed global brands and sophisticated distribution infrastructures, but these are of limited value in the computer hardware industry without a constant stream of new products and technologies. Hence, these firms have developed extensive linkages or networks around the world. Hamel (1991) argues that this is necessary because, historically, regions of the world have developed skills and competencies in certain areas. For example, European countries have a long history of developing science-based inventions, but suffer from a poor understanding of markets and frequently fail to capture the full commercial potential from their inventions. US firms have demonstrated an ability to generate significant profits from market innovations, but then do not make the continual improvements in cost and quality, whereas Japanese and Asian firms have extensive skills in the areas of quality and production efficiencies. Given this global spread of expertise, firms consequently have developed linkages with a wide variety of firms all over the world.

The mechanisms of patents, **licensing** and technology transfer agreements help to create an efficient market for technology, but, as we have seen in earlier chapters, technology usually is embedded with experience, know-how and tacit knowledge. Hence, alliances allow not only for exchange of technology but also for the exchange of skills and know-how often referred to as competencies. For example, General Motors used its joint venture with Toyota to learn about 'lean' manufacturing practices. Similarly Thompson, the French consumer electronics group, relied on its alliance with JVC, from Japan, to learn to mass produce the micromechanic subsystem key to successful videocassette recorder production (Doz and Hamel, 1997). The embedded nature of new technologies has forced firms to view technologies as competencies (clearly, some technologies will be more embedded than others). This has resulted in an increasing number of alliances, whereas previously a technology licensing or purchase agreement may have been used.

Interfirm knowledge-sharing routines

The only way to ensure effective learning for both parties is to build knowledge-sharing routines. This will involve sharing information, know-how and skills. Information can readily be shared via hard copy and electronic data transfer, but

Innovation in action

Creativity comes in small packages

Looking at the logo designed for the London 2012 Olympics, the Australian founders of Design-Crowd.com were frustrated. It had been produced by a major agency for a large budget, but they believed they knew dozens of people who could do better, but were never given the opportunity.

It was a familiar refrain from the design community. There's a world of creativity out there, and yet large companies restrict themselves to a 'preferred suppliers' list of the largest design agencies. Spurred by this thought, Design-Crowd created a website to enable large companies and small businesses to get ideas and designs from thousands of freelance designers or smaller agencies around the world. The client specifies its requirements for the design and the amount it will pay for the winning design. It then receives dozens, or even hundreds, of submissions from different designers and can pick its favourite.

Source: HSBC (2010) *100 Thoughts*, HSBC, London.

know-how and skills are much more difficult, as we have seen in Chapter 7. Nonetheless, it is possible and many firms rely on individuals spending time within other firms, either on secondment for a set time or through exchanges of staff. It is the interpersonal interaction that facilitates the transfer of tacit knowledge. Design and manufacturing alliances, such as those established by Nike, are very effective at knowledge-sharing routines and hence become more innovative than their competitors. This, then, becomes a powerful competitive advantage that is extremely difficult to replicate and copy and may give a firm an advantage for many years. Moreover, it is an advantage that a firm may possess that does not require costly patent protection and avoids the risk of copycat branding.

Forms of strategic alliance

Strategic alliances can occur *intra-industry* or *inter-industry*. For example, the three major US automobile manufacturers have formed an alliance to develop technology for an electric car. This is an example of an *intra-industry alliance* and is in response to US legislation requiring a certain percentage of US cars to be gasoline-free by 2020. The UK pharmaceutical giant GlaxoSmithKline has established many *inter-industry* alliances with a wide range of firms from a variety of industries; it includes companies such as Matsushita, Canon, Fuji and Apple.

Furthermore, alliances can range from a simple handshake agreement to mergers, from licensing to equity joint ventures. Moreover, they can involve a customer, a supplier or even a competitor. Research on collaborative activity has been hindered by a wide variety of different definitions. There are eight generic types of strategic alliance:

● licensing;
● supplier relations;
● outsourcing;
● joint venture;
● collaboration (non-joint ventures);
● R&D consortia;
● industry clusters; and
● innovation networks.

Licensing

Licensing is a relatively common and well-established method of acquiring technology. It may not involve extended relationships between firms but, increasingly, licensing another firm's technology often is the beginning of a form of collaboration. Usually, there is an element of learning required by the licensee and, frequently, the licensor will perform the role of 'teacher'. Whilst there are clearly advantages of licensing, such as speed of entry to different technologies and reduced cost of technology development, there are also potential problems, particularly the neglect of internal technology development. In the videocassette recording (VCR) industry, JVC licensed its VHS recording technology to many firms, including Sharp, Sanyo and Thompson. This clearly enabled these firms to enter the new growth industry of the time. But these firms also continued to develop their own technologies in other fields. Sharp, in particular, built on JVC's technology and developed additional features for its range of videocassette recorders.

Supplier relations

Many firms have established close working relations with their suppliers and, without realising it, may have formed an informal alliance. Usually, these are based on cost-benefits to a supplier. For example:

- lower production costs that might be achieved if a supplier modifies a component so that it 'fits' more easily into the company's product;
- reduced R&D expenses, based on information from a supplier about the use of its product in the customer's application;
- improved material flow brought about by reduced inventories, due to changes in delivery frequency and lot sizes; and
- reduced administration costs through more integrated information systems.

At its simplest level, one may consider a sole-trader electrician, who over time builds a relationship with his equipment supplier, usually a wholesaler. This can be regarded as simply a 'good customer' relationship, where a supplier will provide additional discounts and services for a good customer, such as obtaining unusual equipment requests, making special deliveries, holding additional stock, etc. The next level may involve a closer working relationship where a supplier becomes more involved in the firm's business and they share experience, expertise, knowledge and investment, such as developing a new product. For example, the French electronics firm Thompson originally supplied radiocassette players to the car manufacturer Citroën. This relationship developed further when Citroën asked Thompson if it could help with the development of radio controls on the steering wheel. This led to an alliance in the development of new products. Many manufacturing firms are, increasingly, entering into long-term relationships with their component suppliers. Often, such agreements are for a fixed term, say five years, with the option of renewal thereafter. British Aerospace adopts this approach when negotiating component suppliers for its aircraft. Such five-year agreements may also include details of pricing, where British Aerospace will expect the price of the component to fall over time as the supplier benefits from economies of scale and manufacturing experience.

Today, firms are linked by cyber space via information technology systems, software and networks. Research by Williams (2014) suggests many firms exist within cyber supply chains without recognising the risks to itself.

Outsourcing

Outsourcing refers to the delegation of non-core operations from internal provision or production to an external entity specialising in the management of that operation. The decision to outsource often is made in the interests of lowering firm costs, redirecting or conserving energy directed at the competencies of a particular business, or to make more efficient use of worldwide labour, capital, technology and resources

(Huang, 2014). A good illustration of this is the outsourcing of IT services to specialist providers and of telephone call centres by the financial services industry.

Outsourcing involves transferring or sharing management control and/or decision making of a business function to an outside supplier, which involves a degree of two-way information exchange, coordination and trust between the outsourcer and its client. Such a relationship between two economic entities is qualitatively different from traditional relationships between buyer and seller of services. This is because the two parties involved in an 'outsourcing' relationship dynamically integrate and share management control of the labour process rather than enter into contracting relationships where both entities remain separate in the coordination of the production of goods and services. Consequently, there is a great deal of debate concerning the benefits and costs of the practice. The Apple case study at the end of Chapter 1 and the Innocent case study at the end of Chapter 14 illustrate this debate.

Joint venture

A joint venture usually is a separate legal entity with the partners to the alliance normally being equity shareholders. With a joint venture, the costs and possible benefits from an R&D research project would be shared. Usually, they are established for a specific project and will cease on its completion. For example, Sony-Ericsson was a joint venture between Ericsson of Sweden and Sony of Japan. It was established to set design manufacture and distribute mobile phones. Previously, both firms had been unsuccessful in the handset market. The intention of establishing a joint venture is, generally, to enable the organisation to 'stand alone'. Illustration 8.2 shows how the Corning Corporation has, for many years, followed a strategy of developing a range of joint ventures based on its technologies.

Collaboration (non-joint ventures)

The absence of a legal entity means that such arrangements tend to be more flexible. This provides the opportunity to extend the cooperation over time, if so desired. Frequently, these occur in many supplier relationships, but they also take place beyond supplier relations. Many university departments work closely with local firms on a wide variety of research projects where there is a common interest. For example, a local firm may be using a carbon-fibre material in manufacturing. The local university chemistry department may have an interest in the properties and performance of the material. Cooperation between the parties may produce benefits for both. Such **collaboration** is frequently extended and maintained for many years (see Illustration 11.2).

R&D consortia

A consortium describes the situation where a number of firms come together to undertake what often is a large-scale activity. The rationale for joining an **R&D consortium** includes sharing the cost and risk of research, pooling scarce expertise and equipment, performing pre-competitive research and setting standards (see 'Forms of external R&D' in Chapter 10 for a more detailed explanation of this form of strategic alliance).

The Corning Corporation

Corning is unique amongst major corporations in deriving the majority of its turnover from joint ventures and alliances. The company has a long and impressive heritage: as a specialist glass manufacturer it had its own R&D laboratory as far back as 1908. In the 1930s, it began combining its technologies with other firms in other industries, giving it access to a wide variety of growth markets. An alliance with PPG gave it access to the flat glass building market; an alliance with Owens provided access to the glass fibres market and an alliance with Dow Chemicals provided it with an opportunity to enter the silicon products market (recent lawsuits in the United States from people whose silicon breast implants were unsuccessful have forced the Dow–Corning alliance to close). Corning now has a network of strategic alliances based on a range of different technologies. These alliances now deliver revenue in excess of its own turnover.

In addition, Corning has established a separate division to further develop alliances with firms in the fibres and photonics technologies. Corning Innovation Ventures was established to provide Corning Incorporated with insight and visibility into new technologies and to build future customer partnerships. Corning's unique access to the market and technologies provides partners with guidance to help build and execute a better business plan. The Innovation Ventures team brings together a unique background of technical and marketing skills with 38 years of combined

Source: Pearson Education Ltd/Digital Stock

fibre optic and photonic experience within the market leader in optical communications.

In particular, Corning plans to form partnerships with large or small entrepreneurial firms. Such firms may wish to partner with Corning because it is the leader in the optical layer of telecommunications. By utilising its 1,600 scientists, engineers and five major research facilities dedicated to photonic research, any entrepreneur partners are guaranteed access to a wealth of knowledge and experience in photonics and optical fibre. Through the firm's vast network of marketing experience across all its optical product lines, and its extensive customer base at the OEM and carrier level, partners are also granted access to the insight, marketing and commercial experience that has led the firm to its market leadership position.

Source: www.corning.com/innovationventures, Corning Incorporated.

Industry clusters

Michael Porter (1998) identified a number of very successful **industry clusters**. Clusters are geographic concentrations of interconnected companies, specialised suppliers, service providers and associated institutions in a particular field that are present in a nation or region. It is their geographical closeness that distinguishes them from innovation networks. Clusters arise because they increase the productivity with which companies can compete. The development and upgrading of clusters is an important agenda for governments, companies and other institutions. Cluster development initiatives are an important new direction in economic policy, building on earlier efforts in macroeconomic stabilisation, privatisation, market opening and reducing the costs of doing business.

Porter explains how clusters pose a paradox. In theory, location should no longer be a source of competitive advantage. Open global markets, rapid transportation and high-speed communications should allow any company to source anything from any place at any time. But, in practice, location remains central to competition. Today's economic map of the world is characterised by what Porter calls clusters: critical masses in one place of linked industries and institutions – from suppliers to universities to government agencies – that enjoy unusual competitive success in a particular field. The most famous examples are found in Silicon Valley and Hollywood, but clusters dot the world's landscape. Porter explains how clusters affect competition in three broad ways: first, by increasing the productivity of companies based in the area; second, by driving the direction and pace of innovation; and third, by stimulating the formation of new businesses within the cluster. Geographic, cultural and institutional proximity provides companies with special access, closer relationships, better information, powerful incentives and other advantages that are difficult to tap from a distance. The more complex, knowledge-based and dynamic the world economy becomes, the more this is true. Competitive advantage lies increasingly in local things – knowledge, relationships and motivation – that distant rivals cannot replicate.

Low technology industry rely on networks for innovation

The food industry traditionally has experienced very low levels of investment in R&D, yet has delivered both product and process innovation over a sustained period. In such environments, innovation can be explained through learning by doing and the use of networks of interactions and extensive tacit knowledge. Research by Jensen et al. (2007) characterised a learning by 'Doing, Using and Interacting' (DUI) mode of innovation where extensive on-the-job problem solving occurs and where firms interact and share experiences. More recently, Fitjar and Rodriguez-Pose (2013) developed a classification of DUI firm interactions in a study of firm level innovation in the food industry in Norway. They found that 'firms which engage in collaboration with external agents tend to be more innovative than firms that rely on their own resources for innovation' (Fitjar and Rodriguez-Pose, 2013: 137).

Innovation networks

The use of the term network has become increasingly popular. To many, it is the new form of organisation offering a sort of 'virtual organisation'. Terms such as web or cluster are also used to describe this or a similar phenomenon. Others believe them to be nothing more than a new label for a firm's range of supplier and market relationships. For example, brand management firms like Nike are frequently regarded as network firms. This is because Nike essentially owns and manages the brand and relies on an established network of relationships to produce and distribute its products. It does not own all the manufacturing plant used to manufacture its shoes or all the retail outlets in which its products are sold. It undertakes research, design and development, but has a network of manufacturers in Asia, India and

Table 8.1 Assembling the component parts to make an iPhone

Company	Country	Part
1 Samsung	Korea	CPU video processing chips
2 Infineon	Singapore	Baseband communications hardware
3 Primax Electronics	Taiwan	Digital camera modules
4 Foxconn International	Taiwan	Internal circuitry
5 Entery Industrial	Taiwan	Connectors
6 Cambridge Silicon	Taiwan	Bluetooth chip sets
7 Umicron Tech.	Taiwan	Printed circuit boards
8 Catcher Technology	Taiwan	Stainless metal casings
9 Broadcom	USA	Touchscreen controllers
10 Marvell	USA	802.11 specific parts
11 Apple	Shenzhen China	Assembly; stocks; packs; ships

South America. Similarly, it has a network of distributors in all the countries in which it operates. Table 8.1 shows the supplier network used by Apple to assemble the iPhone.

There is little consensus in literature about precisely what an **innovation network** is or, indeed, when an innovation network is said to exist, but there is some agreement that a network is more than a series of supplier and customer relationships (Levén et al., 2014). Some networks have been described as federated in that a set of loosely affiliated firms work relatively autonomously but, nonetheless, engage in mutual monitoring and control of one another (Day and Schoemaker, 2000). Other networks can be viewed more as a temporary web, in which firms coalesce around one firm or a business opportunity. For example, following most natural disasters around the world, a collection of organisations, including emergency services, government departments, charities and volunteer organisations, quickly work together as a network to tackle the immediate problems. Other networks are sometimes referred to as strategic partnerships and usually evolve from long-standing supplier relationships.

Through repeated dealings, trust and personal relationships evolve. For example, firms with an established track record in supplying materials, components, etc. to Apple may well find themselves becoming involved in additional activities such as concept testing and product development. This may also include universities, government agencies and competitors.

The United Kingdom's so-called 'Motorsport Valley', a 100-mile area across southern England centred on Oxford and stretching between Cambridge and Poole, is an interesting example of a loose network or web of firms working within Formula One motorsport. It has a geographic clustering of companies in related industries, a strong focus on innovation and many small flexible manufacturing firms (see Illustration 8.3). The point at which a large cluster of firms becomes classified as a 'science park' is a moot point (see Chapter 11 for more on science parks). But, in this particular example, unlike Silicon Valley that represents a cluster of firms operating in computer hardware and software industries, the focus of Motorsport Valley is on one market – Formula One motorsport.

Illustration 8.3

Lewis Hamilton, McClaren, Red Bull and the rest make the UK's Motorsport Valley a world leader

Motorsport Valley is a 100-mile area across southern England centred on Oxford and stretching between Cambridge and Poole; it has many of the features of regionalised, flexible production seen as vital to economic growth in advanced economies (à la Silicon Valley, California). These include a geographical clustering of companies in the same sector; high rates of company formation; a strong focus on innovation; emphasis on exports; and flexibility of products and production processes.

With an annual turnover of £6 billion, and supporting over 38,000 jobs, motor sport and performance engineering is one of the UK's industrial success stories. The motorsport industry is also a best practice example of how creativity, engineering, manufacturing and support services can be combined to produce world-class radical innovations that have an impact well beyond motor racing. Carbon fibre wheelchairs, non-slip boots, hi-tech fishing line and the influence of pit-stop crews on the efficient transferral of patients from the operating theatre to intensive care, are all innovations that have their origins in the motorsport industry.

There is virtually no other industry in which the need for continual innovation and change is greater than in racing car construction and that what they see as a surprising degree of flexibility of response at managerial and employee levels plays a large part in the industry's success in the UK.

The competition between the teams helps create a fierce battle for supremacy. Motor sport involves a continuous striving for products and processes to give the winning edge, with knowledge transfer core to the process. Their proximity, within the Valley and at race meetings, also allows the transmission of knowledge through gossip, which plays a much more important role than most realise.

That component suppliers typically work for several teams is seen as beneficial because of the rapid rate of innovation. As long as a team knows it can keep ahead of its rivals, it is not viewed as a problem if the ideas eventually get transferred throughout the industry. An individual team probably has more to gain than lose through the skills that components suppliers learn by servicing a number of different racing car companies.

Source: Delbridge, R. and Mariotti, F. (2009) Racing for radical innovation: How motorsport companies harness network diversity for discontinuous innovation, Advanced Institute of Management Research, London.

Source: Crash Media Group/Alamy Images

The 'virtual company'

More recently, the idea of a **virtual company** has begun to emerge. This is where every aspect of the business is outsourced and run by unknown suppliers. Illustration 8.4 shows how the pharmaceutical industry is making progress in this radical way of running a business. However, there clearly are aspects of control that may be lost in such organisations. Other aspects, such as intellectual property, skills and know-how may also be lost, if everything is outsourced. Illustration 8.4 gives the chilling warning of the business opportunities that may be lost when activities are outsourced. When IBM launched its first PC in 1981, it outsourced the development of the operating system to a small firm called Microsoft!

Illustration 8.4

The virtual organisation

Many business commentators allege that the business organisation of the future will be virtual. But precise definitions of what it means to be a virtual organisation are hard to find. A virtual company resembles a normal traditional company in its inputs and its outputs. It differs in the way in which it adds value during the journey in between.

The virtual organisation has an almost infinite variety of structures, all of them fluid and changing. Most of them need virtually no employees. A New York insurance company was started once from scratch by someone whose overriding aim was to employ nobody but himself. The UK's Virgin Group briefly held 5 per cent of the British cola market with just 5 employees. This was achieved by tightly focusing on the company's core competence: its marketing. Everything else, from the production of the drink to the distribution of it, was done by someone else.

The virtual organisation has few physical assets, reflecting the fact that adding value is becoming more dependent on (mobile) knowledge and less dependent on (immobile) plant and machinery. The case study at the end of Chapter 13 illustrates how Innocent has built a business with few physical assets. Hollywood often is cited as a template for the virtual organisation. The way that films have been made since the industry freed itself from the studio system (where everyone was a full-time employee) has been virtual.

A number of freelancers, from actors to directors via set builders and publicity agents, come together with a common purpose: to make a film, to tell a story on celluloid. Then they go their separate ways and another (unrelated) bunch of people (with a similar set of skills) comes together to make another film. And so it goes on, very productively.

Linked to the idea of the virtual organisation is the idea of the virtual office, a place where space is not allocated uniquely to individual employees. People work as and when they need to, wherever space is available. This practice is commonly referred to as hot-desking. The virtual office has the advantage of providing a different vista every day. But it makes it difficult to form close relationships with colleagues.

The process of defining the virtual organisation is a gradual one. As companies withdraw more and more into their core competencies, so they become more virtual. The virtual organisation is able to leverage this core into almost any industrial sector. Thus it can be in the pensions business and the railway business at the same time (as is the Virgin organisation in the UK). Then it can rapidly desert any one of those businesses, and equally rapidly move into something completely different by establishing strategic alliances with organisations that have the essential skills that it lacks. It can do this anywhere in the world.

Table 8.2 Reasons for entering a strategic alliance

Reasons	Examples
1 Improved access to capital and new business	European Airbus to enable companies to compete with Boeing and MacDonnell Douglas
2 Greater technical critical mass	Alliance (LG Philips) between Philips of The Netherlands and LG Electronics of Korea. Provides access to Philips' technology and lower manufacturing costs in Korea
3 Shared risk and liability	Sony-Ericsson, a joint venture between two electronics firms to try to dominate mobile phone handset market
4 Better relationships with strategic partners	European Airbus
5 Technology transfer benefits	Customer–supplier alliances, e.g. VW and Bosch
6 Reduce R&D costs	GEC and Siemens 60/40 share of telecommunications joint venture: GPT
7 Use of distribution skills	Pixar and Disney; Waitrose and Ocado
8 Access to marketing strengths	NMB, Japan and Intel; NMB has access to Intel's marketing
9 Access to technology	Ericsson gained access to Sony's multimedia technology for third-generation mobile phones
10 Standardisation	Sony licensed their Blu-ray technology to other manufacturers to help secure industry standard over Toshiba's HD DVD
11 By-product utilisation	GlaxoSmithKline and Matsushita, Canon, Fuji
12 Management skills	J Sainsbury and Bank of Scotland; Sainsbury accessed financial skills

Sources: Littler, D. A. (1993) 'Roles and rewards of collaboration', in Tidd, J., Besant, J. and Pault, K. (eds) (2001) *Managing Innovation*, Wiley, Chichester, p. 51; Chan, P.S. and Heide, D. (1993) Strategic alliances in technology: key competitive weapon, *Advanced Management Journal*, vol. 58, no. 4, 9–18; Harney, A. (2001) Ambitious expansion loses its shine: analysts change their tune about Sony's dreams and begin to count the costs of the new mobile phone alliance with Ericsson, *Financial Times*, 2 October; Budden, R. (2003) Sony-Ericsson seeks success with new phones, FT.com, 3 March.

Motives for establishing an alliance

Frequently, alliances will have multiple objectives. For example, an alliance may seek to access technology, gain greater technical critical mass and share the risk of future technology development. The European Airbus is a good example of an alliance that has multiple objectives. Table 8.2 lists the most common reasons cited for entering a strategic alliance. Research in this area has shown continually that strategic business alliances will achieve a sustainable competitive advantage only if they involve learning and knowledge transfer (see Figure 11.6).

The process of forming a successful strategic alliance

The formation of a strategic alliance is a three-step process (see Figure 8.3). It begins with the selection of the right partner. Clearly, this will depend on what is required and the motivation for the strategic alliance. Usually, this is followed by negotiations based

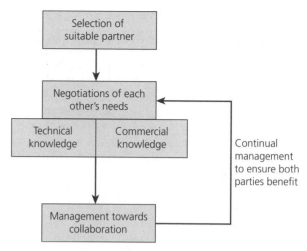

Figure 8.3 The process of forming a strategic alliance

on each partner's needs. The third and final stage is the management towards collaboration. This last step encompasses a wide range of activities, including joint goalsetting and conflict resolution. Moreover, this last stage needs constant work to keep the relationship sound. Aside from collaborative management, the success of a business alliance depends on the existence of mutual need and the ability to work together, despite differences in organisational culture. The passage of time usually helps firms learn from one another. Recent research by Wang and Hsu (2014) finds that relationship learning contributes significantly to both exploratory and exploitative innovations.

Negotiating a licensing deal

The most common form of alliance is the well-established licensing agreement. Licensing deals are just that – a deal struck between two parties. There is not a correct deal or an incorrect one, simply an agreement where two parties agree to do business that usually will result in benefits for both. For example, the licensing deal struck between Bill Gates and his tiny Microsoft company and the mighty IBM in the 1980s is regarded by many as the one single act of genius that Gates made that helped to launch Microsoft. Similarly, the licensing deal struck by J.K. Rowling's agent and the publisher where the author held on to the film rights was another decision of inspired brilliance.

Since most people engaged in deal making are involved in multiple deals at the same time, important aspects can be forgotten or overlooked at any time and for any deal. The following is an inexhaustive list that provides an insight into the areas that need to be agreed upon. Most firms that are involved in licensing will ensure they have people in such positions that are well-educated and experienced in dealing with the scientific, legal and business arenas, all at the same time. After all, as experienced negotiators will testify, there is only one thing more expensive than a patent agent and that is a bad patent agent. Simple mistakes can be costly. And what is crucial to one party may not be to the other.

Terms for the agreement

Each licence will have its own specific set of definitions and clear definitions will add great clarity to a licence. All other appropriate terms should be listed and defined. For example, if dealing with a company, is it the company and all its affiliates? All of its subsidiaries? Or only the parent company? Products/processes licensed should be specifically defined as 'Licensed Products' or 'Licensed Processes'. If only certain types of inventions are covered, these need to be referred to as 'Inventions', including the patent number and/or patent application number that is being licensed. The agreement must also specify whether know-how is included.

Licensee, sales, net sales, profit, territory, field, patents, patent rights, intellectual property and non-profit are examples of other relatively common terms, and there are many more. Once defined, these terms usually will appear throughout the rest of the contract.

Rights granted

The agreement should also include which intellectual property rights the licence is given under: patent right only or know-how right only or both, and exclusive right, coexclusive with the licensor, or non-exclusive. The licence agreement should also specify the term of the exclusivity and/or non-exclusivity and whether such a right is irrevocable; and if there is a right to grant sub-licences.

Licence restrictions

Either of the parties may also wish to include licensee restrictions concerning the industry or market, territory, prior licensee's rights and the commercial rights retained by the licensor.

Improvements

The agreement needs to address any improvements made and/or patented (by whom and paid for by whom) during the term of the licence by either the licensor or licensee and what obligations are present in the deal as to whether or not to include future technology under the present licence or to have future technology fall under the reservation of rights to the licensor.

Consideration (monetary value)

The consideration is relatively involved and can be cut back, if equity is not part of the payment for the licence. Royalty, milestone payments, type of currency, determining rate of exchange and equity-ownership issues all need to be considered, as this can result in substantial differences in payments. The issue of minimum annual payments is particularly important in the case of an exclusive licence.

Reports and auditing of accounts

The issue of establishing the level of royalties can be tricky. Firms rely on the licensor to inform them of the actual level of sales achieved. Hence, royalties based on any measure tied to a product's sales needs to be paid to the licensor, accompanied by a report stating how the royalty was calculated. The agreement should also specify how often and when these reports (and royalties) are due. Additionally, the right of the licensor to audit the books that generate these reports can be a part of the licence agreement.

Representations/warranties

Certain basic representations and warranties need to be given by each party to the other, such as the ability to enter into the agreement, the validity of the intellectual property and a standard warranty disclaimer.

Infringement

The agreement needs to address issues associated with infringement, such as: if the IP is infringed by third parties, how such an infringement will be handled and, if there is a recovery for the infringement, how that will be divided between the licensor and licensee.

Confidentiality

A confidentiality, or non-disclosure, agreement usually will have been signed prior to the licensee agreement to enable exploration of terms of business, etc. This should remain effective during the term of the license agreement.

Arbitration

In the case of a major disagreement about the terms of an agreement, parties may wish to take the issue to arbitration. Arbitration can be carried out in many different ways and it is easier to specify in the agreement the rules to be used for arbitration, before there is an issue to arbitrate. A trade body or other independent organisation could perform this role. This should help avoid expensive legal costs.

Termination

Areas to consider include: the right of either party to end the agreement for no reason at all; the rights of the party that has performed when confronted with a party that refuses to perform; material breach issues; and length of notification of breaching activity and time given to the breaching party to cure the breach before losing rights and/or being charged penalties. Issues dealing with the natural expiration of the licence should be considered, as well. What happens to the know-how (if any) upon the expiration of all patents? And what are the confidentiality provisions?

Risks and limitations with strategic alliances

So far we have addressed only the potential benefits to be gained from strategic alliances. However, a strategic alliance also has a downside. It can lead to competition rather than cooperation, to loss of competitive knowledge, to conflicts resulting from incompatible cultures and objectives, and to reduced management control. A study of almost 900 joint ventures found that less than half were mutually agreed to have been successful by all partners (Dacin et al., 1997; Harrigan, 1986; Spekman et al., 1996). Illustration 8.5 shows how, after more than 10 successful years together, Sony and Ericsson decided to end the joint venture.

The literature on the subject of technological cooperation presents a confusing picture. There is evidence to suggest that strategic alliances may harm a firm's ability to innovate. Arias (1995) argues that inter-firm networking may result not only in desired outcomes but also in negative consequences. The creation of closely structured networks of relationships may produce increased complexity, loss of autonomy and information asymmetry. These hazards may, ultimately, lead to a decreased ability to innovate and participate in technological change.

To avoid these problems, management should anticipate business risks related to partnering, carefully assess their partners, conduct comprehensive resource planning and allocation of resources to the network and develop and foster social networks. All parties should also ensure that the motives for participating are positive, that the networks are as formidable as the alliances within them and that there is a perception of equal contribution and benefits from the parties. Lastly, there should be communication, data sharing, goals and objectives.

The level and nature of the integration appears to be a crucial factor. In some cases, the alliance is very tight indeed. For example, Motoman, a robotic systems supplier, and Stillwater Technologies, a tooling and machining company, share the same facility for their offices and manufacturing and their computer and communications systems are linked (Sheridan, 1997). For other firms, a loose alliance is far more comfortable.

Illustration 8.5

Sony and Ericsson end joint venture

Sony has spent more than £1 billion to take full control of its handset manufacturing joint venture, Sony Ericsson.

Sony Ericsson was created in 2001 from two companies that were struggling in the handset business. For a while, the joint venture was profitable, but the advent of Apple's iPhone, and then of cheap handsets running Google's Android software, destroyed its high-end market share.

Sony has been developing its answer to iTunes, the Sony Entertainment Network, which streams Sony-produced films, games and music to devices, including its Bravia TV sets, PCs and PlayStation consoles. Sony has all the elements, it delivers more entertainment than anybody – it produces billions of discs, many movies, millions of devices, and the PlayStation Network has 90 million members. Tying this together presents an opportunity for Sony to compete with Apple, Google and Microsoft.

For Ericsson, the payment means that it can exit the mobile phone business effectively without ties, and focus on building mobile and wireless networks, where its expertise lies.

Insourcing helps Brompton Bicycle's profits rise

Brompton Bicycle is the London-based company that makes folding bicycles familiar to health-conscious business people. It is led by Will Butler-Adams, 34. Brompton Bicycle has 120 suppliers, three-quarters of them in the UK. Some 70 per cent of its output is exported to countries including Japan, Spain, Germany, South Korea and the US. The bicycles sell for £550 to £1,000. Butler-Adams came to the company in 2004 from the chemicals industry.

Each bike contains 1,200 parts, 70 per cent of which are unique to its bicycles and which have been designed by Brompton. In 2005, it made three-quarters of the parts and outsourced the rest; now the proportion is more like the other way around. The change has increased efficiency and enabled it to make more bikes in the same amount of space.

In 2014, sales reached £28 million, with profits of £3.4 million. It was on course to hit sales of £30 million in 2015. Brompton now has 230 people and was on course to make 50,000 bikes in 2015. It sells to 44 countries around the world and 80 per cent of its folders are exported.

The company was founded in 1978 by Andrew Ritchie, a former Cambridge University engineering graduate, who remains technical director and a large shareholder, but has recently relinquished the top job in the company to the younger man.

Source: Moules, J. (2010) How to keep your best people happy in the saddle, *Financial Times*, 25 October.

Research in the area of failure of alliances identifies seven different reasons (Duysters et al., 1999; Vyas et al., 1995):

1. Failure to understand and adapt to new style of management required for the alliance.
2. Failure to learn and understand the cultural differences between the organisations.
3. Lack of commitment to succeed.
4. Strategic goal divergence.
5. Insufficient trust.
6. Operational and or geographical overlaps.
7. Unrealistic expectations.

The formation of strategic alliances by definition fosters cooperation rather than competition. Ensuring competition remains is a major implication of strategic alliances.

The respective government departments of trade and commerce around the world need to be vigilant of the extent to which firms that cooperate are also capable of manipulating the price of products.

There is, of course, another way: **insourcing**. Illustration 8.6 shows how Brompton Cycles has brought manufacturing back in house and profits have increased.

The role of trust in strategic alliances

The business and management literature and accepted management thinking are predominantly optimistic in their belief that there is much to gain from strategic alliances and collaborative technology development. This optimism remains largely robust, despite substantial failures of high-profile alliances highlighting the difficulties and limitations of such strategic alliances (see Bleeke and Ernst, 1992; Porter, 1987).

According to the strategic management literature, firms with a global presence – in particular those operating in technology-intensive sectors – are, increasingly, reliant on collaborative technology development. They can no longer continue to rely on the use of traditional means to protect their 'secrets', such as internalisation and legal controls, because they need to become more 'outward-looking' and therefore more receptive in their technology development strategy. By its very nature, collaborative technology development means that sharing knowledge and 'openness' is a precondition for successful organisational learning. Openness and free exchange of information, however, make companies more vulnerable to risks of information leakage. It is in this specific context that the problem of trust emerges most clearly in collaborative technology development. In order to reap the benefits from collaborative technology development, companies or, more precisely, research managers need to be able to trust their partners (Hollis, 1998).

The concept of trust

All forms of collaboration involve an element of risk and require substantial amounts of trust and control. It is the leakage of sensitive information to competitors that is of most concern to firms. Innovative applied research often develops out of the collaboration of firms and research institutions, where this is initiated with the help of previous academic contacts of key players in firms and universities. In this case, the selection of, and decision to trust, a partner typically is made on the basis of prior professional and or social knowledge (Liebeskind and Oliver, 1998). For example, scientists working at one large firm will have graduated from university with friends who took up similar positions in other large firms. Hence, every scientist will have a small network of scientists largely as a result of university. Firms recognise that all their scientists operate within networks and expect them to exercise their professional judgement. Usually, personal knowledge and the desire to protect one's professional reputation are sufficient safeguards to justify a limited-scale disclosure of sensitive information. If the initial collaboration is successful, the scale of collaboration can be increased incrementally and higher levels of mutual trust will be reached (Lewicki and Bunker, 1996).

Trust is not the same as confidence. For example, supporters of football teams are confident that their team will work hard and win some games over the course of the season, but they trust their players, manager and club that, collectively, the organisation will try to win and that results are not 'fixed' through corruption. Both confidence and trust are based on expectations about the future, but trust entails the exposure to the risk of opportunistic behaviour by others. One can say that an agent exhibits trust when he or she has no reason to believe that the trusted other will exploit this opportunity (Giddens, 1990; Humphrey and Schmitz, 1998).

It is important to keep in mind that trust is practised and exercised between individuals, even if they represent an organisation. Trust is a personal judgement and carries an emotional as well as a cognitive dimension. Whilst trust at the system level is similar to confidence – as there is no choice but to trust the currency to store value – trust in an institution or organisation depends on personal experience with individuals representing the organisation at its contact points (Giddens, 1990). This does not mean that the institutional dimension should be underestimated.

Table 8.3 Types of trust

Type of trust	Characteristics
Process	Where trust is tied to past or expected exchange, such as reputation or gift exchange
Personal	Where trust is tied to a person, depending on family background, religion or ethnicity
Institutional	Where trust is tied to formal structures, depending on individual or firm specific attributes
Competence trust	Confidence in the other's ability to perform properly
Contractual trust	Honouring the accepted rules of exchange
Goodwill trust	Mutual expectations of open commitment to each other beyond contractual obligations

Trust, then, exists at the individual and organisational levels and research has attempted to distinguish different levels and sources of trust (Hoecht and Trott, 1999; Sako, 1992). The bases of trust in alliances are identified in Table 8.3.

The sources of trust production are not mutually exclusive and often work in conjunction. For instance, whilst membership of an ethnic group (personal-based trust) can be a vital initial advantage for setting up a business, or having studied at a particular university for finding 'open doors', this will not be enough to sustain trust over time. Trust can be initiated as personal trust, but it will have to be 'earned' before long (Humphrey and Schmitz, 1998). Similarly, bestowing trust on to a person or an institution does not mean that methods of limiting the damage from potential 'betrayal' cannot be used. Contractual safeguards, access to legal redress and institutional assurances can have a very positive effect on collaborative business relations, as Lane and Bachmann (1996) have shown in their comparison of the role of trust in UK and German supplier relations.

In the context of collaborative R&D, institutional sources of trust production will, however, be of limited use only. It is clearly not possible to rely on institutional-based trust and legal safeguards for the protection of intangible, pre-competitive knowledge against misuse (Sitkin and Roth, 1993). Even if such safeguards were workable, the necessity to incorporate each little step along the development path of a collaborative research project into a contractual arrangement would cause enormous delays and, hence, endanger its very success. The level of trust needed here is the one labelled 'goodwill trust' by Sako (1992), where the mutual commitment goes beyond honouring what is explicitly agreed and the trustee can be trusted to exercise the highest level of discretion, to take beneficial initiatives and to refrain from taking unfair advantage, even if such opportunities arise (Hoecht and Trott, 1999).

Innovation risks in strategic outsourcing

Outsourcing originally was confined to peripheral business functions and motivated mainly by a cost-saving logic, but has now developed into a routine strategic management move that affects not only peripheral functions, but also the heart of the competitive core of organisations. At the same time, there is a move from traditional outsourcing with one or a small number of key partners and long-term contracts to

Table 8.4 Main risks identified in the literature

Main negative outcomes	Main references
1 Dependence on the supplier	Alexander and Young (1996); Aubert et al. (1998)
2 Hidden costs	Alexander and Young (1996); Aubert et al. (1998); Barthelemy (2001); Earl (1996); Lacity and Hirschheim (1993)
3 Loss of competencies	Alexander and Young (1996); Aubert et al. (1998); Bettis et al. (1992); Doig et al. (2001); Khosrowpour et al. (1995); Martisons (1993); Quinn and Hilmer (1994)
4 Service provider's lack of necessary capabilities	Aubert et al. (1998); Earl (1996); Kaplan (2002)
5 Social risk	Barthelemy and Geyer (2000); Lacity and Hirschheim (1993)
6 Inefficient management	Lynch (2002); Wang and Regan (2003)
7 Information leakage	Hoecht and Trott (2006)

Source: Adapted from Quélin, B. and Duhamel, F. (2003) Bringing together strategic outsourcing and corporate strategy: outsourcing motives and risks, *European Management Journal*, vol. 21, no. 5, 647–61.

strategic outsourcing with multiple partners and short-term contracts. Such a strategy is not without risks. Indeed, the literature has identified many risks and limitations with outsourcing (see Table 8.4). One in particular needs to be considered carefully here. This risk is related closely to the more general issue of information leakage that arises when business organisations collaborate in order to gain access to knowledge and expertise that they cannot develop on their own. Hoecht and Trott (1999) have demonstrated that there is a trade-off between access to cutting-edge knowledge via collaborative research and technology development in knowledge-intensive industries and the risk of losing commercially sensitive knowledge to competitors. This risk, they argue, cannot be controlled by traditional management approaches and legal contracting alone, but requires the operation of social control and, in particular, the development of trust to be contained.

Strategic outsourcing goes beyond traditional outsourcing in the sense that competitive advantages are being sought through opening up all business functions, including the core competencies, which should provide competitive advantage to whoever can provide the perceived best solution, internal or external (Quélin and Duhamel, 2003). In contrast to traditional outsourcing, there are no protective boundaries around core activities, in the hope that the organisations can maximise their innovative capacity by being an active part of a networked economy. This means that, rather than having exclusive arrangements with one or very few service providers over long periods of time, which will be expected to offer tailor-made solutions, strategic sourcing arrangements will be with multiple partners over short periods of time (Da Rold, 2001) and with very little protection of internal core competency functions against outsiders.

There is a certain paradox inherent in this approach: a very high level of trust is required for such relationships, as the risks involved are substantial, whilst, at the same time, the conditions for building trust are undermined by a shorter-term orientation with less commitment compared to traditional outsourcing relationships. The risks are significantly higher than with traditional outsourcing: not only is the risk of leakage of commercially sensitive information significantly increased when firms cooperate with multiple partners, but also the very core of the competitive advantage, in terms of knowledge, expertise and capabilities, will be made dependent on outsiders. There is a danger that the organisations pursuing strategic sourcing may even lose the absorptive capacity required to recognise and exploit new opportunities by themselves.

Information leakage and levelling out of expertise

The reliance on outside providers can be problematic, not only because key areas of expertise may be lost gradually to the outsourcing organisation, but also because outside providers may not have the desired leading edge expertise over the long term (Earl, 1996) or may spread their expertise amongst many clients so that it degrades from 'best in world' to mere industry standard. The problem of information leakage lies at the heart of this dilemma. Companies want exclusivity in their relationships with their service providers, but consultants who work with many clients are unlikely not to be influenced and not to spread the best practice they acquire when working with different client firms. Detailed legal contracts may offer short-term solutions, as they can protect tangible outcomes from specific projects undertaken, but not every innovation-related project outcome is tangible and can be defined clearly in legal contracts. Also, consultants are clearly expected to work at the cutting edge of their professional expertise for all of their clients.

By entertaining more than one relationship with external service providers itself, the individual buyer firm will have less certainty than before in its exclusive relationships, but at least it would also have the chance to benefit from the more widely shared industry best practice, spread amongst its competitors by the service providers. The effect might be a levelling out of core skill advantages within the industry, benefiting the industry overall, but eroding the competitive advantage of some of its members. From the point of view of the individual firm, then, the question is how it can maintain a commitment to secrecy and confidentiality from multiple service provider firms whilst sharing in the benefits of best practice in the industry.

As a consequence of the problem of 'levelling out' of leading edge expertise, the innovation impact of outsourcing is not limited to the issue of core competencies and the need of companies to retain at least the absorptive capacity to exploit innovations that have been developed by outside service providers. There is also the problematic assumption that service providers are always able to infuse best practice into the company. In a traditional outsourcing relationship, a long-term commitment is entered into that 'locks' a company to a service provider for the length of the service contract. The ability to infuse best industry practice may not only depend on the relative competence of the provider, but the service providers may also be restricted in their ability to pass on best practices by confidentiality agreements with previous and other current clients. A significant dilemma emerges: individual firms have a reasoned case against competitors gaining the fruits of their investment and innovation efforts, whilst, at the same time, the majority of companies choose outsourcing not least in the hope of gaining such advantages from other firms. This dilemma is left mainly to the service providers and the individual consultants they employ to resolve. It is, however, a very important issue from an organisational innovation perspective. We will see below that this issue becomes even more pressing when companies and industries move away from traditional long-term outsourcing relationships with single service providers to strategic outsourcing, i.e. to much more open, short-term relationships with multiple suppliers involving all business processes.

Eating you alive from the toes up

There are innovation risks associated with outsourcing. The next section examines some of these risks. Within virtually every industrial sector, firms are under pressure continually from their shareholders, customers and employees to deliver more profits, to cut costs and to deliver improved products and services. Over the past two decades, firms have turned to outsourcing in an attempt to deliver in these areas. This began with outsourcing periphery activities, such as catering and cleaning, but increased to include maintenance and IT infrastructure. For manufacturing firms, the idea of outsourcing to China and India was attractive because of the low labour costs. Some of these firms proved to be so very effective at the manufacturing that they also took on distribution of products. A good example of this is in the personal computer (PC) industry. Since 1976, Acer has been building PCs for others, including Dell, IBM and Hewlett Packard. This has helped drive the growth of Taiwan's IT industry. With over 25 years of experience in manufacture and assembly, Acer is regarded as an expert and leader in its field. It decided to develop its own brand of PC, the Acer brand, which competes with the very same firms for which it builds PCs. In 2015, Acer was the sixth-largest personal computer vendor in the world.

Many firms believe that many activities can be outsourced, but that their creative knowledge development should be retained. However, even in the R&D and new product development arenas, some firms have turned outside for help to:

- obtain additional expertise;
- put together additional resources;
- reduce development costs;
- reduce time to market;
- develop new areas of competencies.

The risk here, of course, is that, once a firm outsources its R&D and new product development (NPD), one is left wondering what it does do. The answer from such a firm is that it owns the brand and will develop and invest in the brand. The danger here, of course, is that the firm doing the outsourcing may well decide that it, too, can develop a brand and so, eventually, does everything. The outsourcing firm slowly has eaten the client firm from the toes up, and finally consumed it.

The use of game theory to analyse strategic alliances

Research using game theory has suggested that some alliance structures are inherently more likely than others to be associated with a high opportunity to cheat, high behavioural uncertainty and poor stability, longevity and performance. Parkhe (1993) argues that maintaining robust cooperation in inter-firm strategic alliances poses special problems. The study by Parkhe looked at 111 inter-firm alliances. The findings suggested the need for a greater focus on game-theoretic structural dimensions and institutional responses to perceived opportunism in the study of voluntary inter-firm cooperation.

The development of the VCR industry is littered with strategic alliances formed by various businesses to try to help ensure they gain access to the relevant technology. Unfortunately, not all the alliances were successful. Sony embarked on several strategic alliances with competitors in an attempt to try to make its Betamax technology the industry standard. When JVC, Toshiba and others refused, the alliance existed in name only (Baden-Fuller and Pitt, 1996). There are many other examples of alliances failing – some soon after inception, others after a long and successful relationship.

The issue of trust is a critical element in any strategic alliance. By its very nature, an alliance, like a marriage, is dependent on all parties working together so that the total outcome is greater than any one party can achieve on its own. It is important to note that trust usually is established over a long period of time, in much the same way as courtship prior to marriage involves understanding one another and building confidence in the relationship. In order to lose trust, however, one must have gained it in the first place. A more serious proposition is that firms may enter a strategic alliance with a lack of trust in the other party. The issue of trust is the underlying theme of the prisoner's dilemma, which is discussed in the next section.

Game theory and the prisoner's dilemma

The prisoner's dilemma: this is probably the most well-known of the games from game theory. Most of us can put ourselves readily in the shoes of the prisoner behind bars, as he wrestles with the dilemma of which answer to give in order to achieve the best outcome.

Source: Lou Oates. Shutterstock/Pearson Education Ltd

The extent to which two companies are going to cooperate is a key question for any strategic alliance. This question can be examined using the prisoner's dilemma. It graphically highlights the options facing companies when they embark on a strategic alliance. It illustrates that cooperation is the mutually advantageous strategy but that non-cooperation provides high-risk opportunities to both parties.

The basic form of this game is known as the prisoner's dilemma and gets its name from the following scenario. Suppose two criminals are arrested for drug dealing. The local police chief arrests them both and takes them to the cells for interrogation. They are placed in separate cells and face fierce questioning. The police chief, however, does not have sufficient evidence to gain a conviction. The chief asks Detective Holmes to offer a deal to both criminals. If either confesses, he will receive a minimal sentence for becoming an informer and helping the police. If neither confesses, they will both receive a sentence based upon some other lesser charge for which the police chief does have evidence. If they both confess, the court will take this cooperation

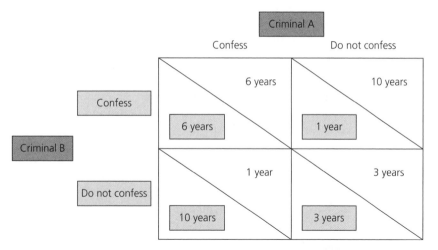

Figure 8.4 Prisoner's dilemma

into account and probably will pass a lighter sentence on both. The game matrix is represented in Figure 8.4, with the relevant years of sentence to be expected.

Both criminals A and B have a dominant strategy. No matter what the other does, both are better off, if they confess. The option of 'do not confess' carries with it the risk of spending 10 years in prison. The maximum sentence for confessing is six years with a possibility of only a year. Given this pay-off matrix, both criminals should confess. This is the classic form of the prisoner's dilemma.

It has a close relative, which is the repeated game. This is a more realistic interpretation of reality, as few business relationships are one-off events. For example, BMW competes with Volkswagen in a variety of markets now and, most likely, in the future. With the knowledge that one is to repeat any game played, the options are likely to be different. To return to the criminals locked up in prison: if they both realise that squealing on a fellow-prisoner may bring with it some form of revenge, such as death, from the prisoner's friends, the range of outcomes changes significantly. The dominant solution is now to play, do not confess. Figure 8.5 shows the repeated game matrix.

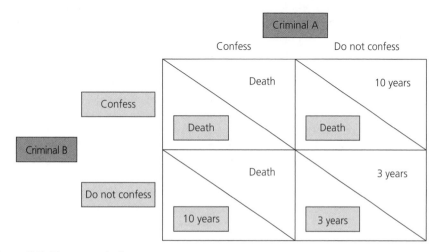

Figure 8.5 The repeated game

Use of alliances in implementing technology strategy

As we have seen, alliances often are pursued as ways to explore new applications, new technologies or both. By their very nature, they confront uncertainty and knowledge asymmetry between the partners. Consequently, there are many calls for full explicit agreements with plans to be signed in advance of any collaboration, especially by accountants and lawyers. Yet this can prevent and hinder collaboration because of the lack of familiarity between the partners. What is often required is a more informal approach to enable both parties to learn from each other. Moreover, the collaboration and learning often evolves over time as the parties begin to understand one another better. The benefits can be great indeed, but the costs often are not fully visible. There are significant hidden costs, such as management time and energy.

Pause for thought

Many analysts argue that strategic alliances are like marriages. But does this mean many of them will end in tears? Is it possible to have a happy ending?

Case study

And the winner is Sony's Blu-ray – the high-definition DVD format war

Christopher Simms and Paul Trott

This case study explores the development of high-definition video and the format war between Sony's Blu-ray and Toshiba's HD DVD. A format war describes competition between mutually incompatible proprietary formats that compete for the same market, typically for data storage devices and recording formats for electronic media. A useful historical example of one of the first format wars was between railway width gauges in the United Kingdom during the Industrial Revolution of the early 1800s. Isambard Kingdom Brunel developed a 2.1 m width gauge for his Great Western Railway because it offered greater stability and capacity at high speed. Whilst George Stephenson developed a 1.44 m width gauge for the first mainline railway, the Liverpool to Manchester Railway; the de facto standard for the colliery railways where Stephenson had worked. Needless to say, the narrower 1.44 m gauge won simply because

more of this track had been laid, but trains today could be travelling much faster, if the wider gauge had been adopted.

The story of the VCR, Betamax, DVD, HD DVD and Blu-ray

Blu-ray Disc (popularly known simply as Blu-ray) is an optical disc storage medium designed to supersede the standard DVD format. Its main uses are for storing high-definition video, PlayStation 3 video games and other data. Blu-ray Disc was developed by the Blu-ray Disc Association, a group representing makers of consumer electronics, computer hardware and motion pictures. The discs have the same physical dimensions as standard DVDs and CDs. The name *Blu-ray Disc* derives from the 'blue laser' used to read the disc. Whilst a standard DVD uses a 650 nanometer (nm) red laser, Blu-ray Disc uses a shorter wavelength 405 nm laser, and allows for over five times more data storage on single-layer and over 10 times

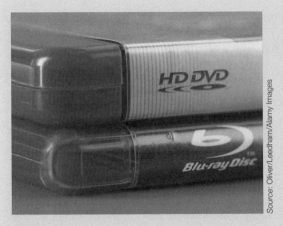

Source: Oliver/Leedham/Alamy Images

on double-layer Blu-ray Disc than a standard DVD. During the high-definition optical disc format war, Blu-ray Disc competed with the HD DVD format. Toshiba, the main company that supported HD DVD, conceded defeat in February 2008, and the format war came to an end. In late 2009, Toshiba released its own Blu-ray Disc player. The two formats have been battling for the growing high-definition share of the £12.3 billion a year global home DVD market. High-definition DVDs offer improved visuals and sound, but also make it harder for content to be illegally copied and pirated. It is a sweet victory for the Sony-backed Blu-ray format. Sony's technically superior Betamax video format lost out to JVC-backed VHS when those formats went head to head in the 1980s.

The story of film and broadcast recording technology for home use dates back to the mid-twentieth century. When television first took off in the 1950s, the only means of preserving video footage was through kinescope, a process in which a special motion picture camera photographed a television monitor. Kinescope film took hours to develop and made for poor quality and was useful only for the broadcasters themselves. The electronics industry saw opportunities to develop recording technologies and a race developed to create a standard format for doing this. This race continues today.

Overview of the development of the VCR industry

Invented in 1956, the VCR had a lifespan of around 50 years and revolutionised the film industry,

changed television-watching habits, triggered the first 'format wars' and raised new copyright questions, establishing jurisprudence on fair use.

The big electronic companies of the 1950s raced to develop a technology for home recording and playback during the 1950s, seeing a significant opportunity and market gap, and therefore they started working on recorders that used magnetic tape. The first player launched was developed by the Ampex Corporation: however, the world's first magnetic tape video recorder, the VRX-1000 (which was launched in April 1956), had a price tag of $50,000 and expensive rotating heads that had to be changed every few hundred hours. This, therefore, made it an unviable consumer item, although it was popular with television networks.

Many companies abandoned their research and followed Ampex's lead. RCA pooled patents with Ampex and licensed in the Ampex technology. The new goal for the firms in the industry was to develop a video machine for home use. It had to be solid, low-cost and easy to operate. Sony released a first home model in 1964, followed by Ampex and RCA in 1965. Whilst these machines, and those that followed over the next 10–15 years, were much less expensive than the VRX-1000, they remained beyond the means of the average consumer, and were bought primarily by wealthy customers, businesses and schools. But there was still strong competition to develop a consumer format.

The competition between the companies attempting to develop a consumer format led to the release of three different, mutually incompatible VCR formats: Sony's Betamax in 1975, JVC's VHS in 1976 and the Philips V2000 in 1978. Two of these would come head-to-head in the 1980s in what became known as the First Format War. Before the technology battle could begin, however, the consumer electronics industry had to find an answer to a more pressing problem: content. Where would it come from? What would people watch on their VCRs? At this stage, the industry regarded the VCR's television recording feature as a bonus option of little utility to the average home user: why, they asked, would anyone want to record a TV show and watch it later? They thought movie videos would provide an answer to the content problem, but the movie industry itself was convinced this idea was not to its advantage.

→

Copyright issues for the VCR

Home video sent the movie industry into a spin. Television had already stolen a big part of its market, and it saw the VCR as a massive new threat. Copyright, the film industry argued, was at stake. Did not the mere recording of a television show constitute an infringement of the copyright owner's rights over reproduction? The studios took the issue to court. In 1976, the year after Sony's release of the Betamax VCR, Universal City Studios and the Walt Disney Company sued Sony, seeking to have the VCR impounded as a tool of piracy.

New communications technology – then as now – has always challenged previous assumptions and jurisprudence in the area of copyright. The first court decision in 1979 went against the studios, ruling that use of the VCR for non-commercial recording was legal. The studios appealed and the decision was overturned in 1981. Sony then took the case to the US Supreme Court, who finally ruled that home recording of television programmes for later viewing constituted 'fair use'. An important factor in the Court's reasoning was that 'time-shifting' – i.e. recording a programme to watch at another time – did not represent any substantial harm to the copyright holder, nor did it diminish the market for the product.

By then, the VCR had become a popular consumer product and, contrary to their fears, the film studios found themselves to be major beneficiaries of the technology as the sale and rental of film videos began generating huge new revenue streams. In 1986 alone, home video revenues added more than $100 million of pure profit to Disney's bottom line. The television stations, on the other hand, having found that the 'useless' recording option was a big hit with viewers, faced a different problem. They had to find new ways to keep their advertisers happy now that viewers could fast-forward through the commercial breaks.

Setting the standard: VHS v. Betamax

Meanwhile, the format war between VHS and Betamax was under way. When Sony released Betamax, it was confident of the superiority of its technology and assumed that the other companies would abandon their formats and accept Betamax as the industry-wide technical standard. It was wrong. On its home turf in Japan, JVC refused to comply and went to market with its VHS format. In the European market, Philips did not play along either, but technical problems were to take Philips out of the fight almost before it began.

From where Sony stood, the only clear advantage of the VHS format was its longer recording time. So, Sony doubled the Betamax recording time and JVC followed suit. This continued until recording times were no longer an issue for potential customers, and marketing overtook superior technology as the key to the battle.

Betamax was, arguably, a superior technology (although debate on this continues today, and many argue that the difference in quality was relevant only really to those using the machines commercially); Beta SP was still used by professional videographers until relatively recently. But what Betamax really needed was market share. Morita (Sony's CEO) blames Betamax's eventual defeat on insufficient licensing. Despite the fact that it was the better product, Betamax never achieved a large enough presence to create consumer preference. VHS had gravity and won the battle.

The two companies were on a par for several years, until JVC's VHS format pulled ahead. This was due, in part, to JVC's broader licensing policy. Counting on increased royalties to make money on its VHS machines, JVC licensed the technology to big consumer electronics companies like Zenith and RCA (a company with significant presence in the United States at the time). As a result, VHS machines became more abundant on the market and prices fell, increasing their consumer appeal.

At about the same time, in the early 1980s, video rental shops started springing up on every street corner. Early on, the video shop owners recognised that they would have to make VCRs available for cheap rental to attract a larger client base. The high-quality Betamax machines were more expensive, harder to repair, and the first models were compatible only with certain television sets. So, VHS became the obvious choice for the rental shops. Another factor that influenced the outcome is the adult entertainment industry (porn). The size of this industry is enormous and the porn studios' decision to use VHS may also have influenced the outcome. This combined effect of greater availability of machines and increased availability of content on VHS eventually squeezed out Betamax.

Technology development, of course, did not stand still. By 2003, DVD sales had overtaken those of the VCR, signalling the dying days of magnetic tape. Video rental shops, sensitive to market trends, switched to DVD, accelerating the demise of the VCR, eventually leading to a sharp demise in sales of video recorders (VHS). The DVD had advantages in terms of quality, although it lacked the same flexibility and ease of recording that were the case for the VHS format. Today, few VCRs are sold (and it is very difficult to find players, with most retailers having stopped selling such machines), and the format is close to being obsolete.

An ongoing issue that rumbles on in the background of the format wars is the issue of copyright. It continues to be a key influence in firm's strategic decision making towards the new formats of streaming and download-able media, as well as the HD disk formats.

The development of DVD

The development of the Laserdisc by Philips in 1969 yielded many of the technologies Sony carried over and utilised when it partnered with Philips to jointly cre-ate the CD in 1979. In the early 1990s, these two com-panies then worked closely together again to develop a new high-density disc called the MultiMedia Compact Disc (MMCD was the original name), but their format was eventually more or less abandoned in favour of Toshiba's competing Super Density Disc (SD), which had the vast majority of backers at the time, such as Hitachi, Matsushita (Panasonic), Mitsubishi, Pioneer, Thomson and Time Warner. The two factions cut a deal, brokered by IBM president Lou Gerstner, on a new format: DVD. Toshiba wound up on top after the dust settled in 1995–6, and Sony and Philips, who were not cut in on the standard (and royalties) nearly as much as they would have liked, immediately started work on a next generation system. The Professional Disc for DATA (aka PDD or ProDATA), which was based on an optical disc system Sony had already been developing alongside the existing project, even-tually would become the Blu-ray disc. Toshiba, not to be outdone by Philips and Sony, also started work on a new generation system: the Advanced Optical Disc, which eventually evolved into the HD DVD.

Blu-ray DVD v. HD DVD

After 35 years of optical audio/video disc develop-ment, history seems to have repeated itself with the launch of the two competing formats of HD DVD and Blu-ray DVD, with both factions attempt-ing to beat one another in order to 'reap the rewards'. The Blu-ray and HD DVD formats were both launched in the early twentieth century, with each format having been developed by competing electronics companies. Sony, alongside Royal Philips Electronics, developed the Blu-ray format, whilst HD DVD was developed by Toshiba, along-side Hitachi.

In 2005, what could be described as 'ongoing peace talks' between the Blu-ray and HD DVD camps, finally dissolved after many attempts to develop a compromise of the next-generation format. This meant that the two companies would have to compete head to head to become the standard for the next generation of video recording and reproduc-tion for the living room.

The two formats are incompatible with one another, despite using lasers of the same type. HD DVD discs also have a different surface layer (the clear plastic layer on the surface of the data, which is the bit you get fingerprints and scratches on) from Blu-ray discs. HD DVD uses a 0.6 mm-thick surface layer, the same as DVD, while Blu-ray has a much smaller 0.1 mm layer to help enable the laser to focus. Herein lie the issues associated with the higher cost of Blu-ray discs. This thinner surface layer is what makes the discs more costly: because Blu-ray discs do not share the same surface layer thickness of DVDs, costly production facilities must be modified or replaced in order to produce the discs. A special hard coating must also be applied to Blu-ray discs, so their surface is sufficiently resilient enough to protect the data a mere 0.1 mm beneath – this also drives the cost up. Blu-ray, therefore, unlike HD DVD, requires a hard coating on its discs because data is 0.5 mm closer to the surface. The polymer coating it uses, called Durabis, was devel-oped by TDK and is supposedly extremely resilient and fingerprint resistant. The added benefit of keep-ing the data layer closer to the surface, however, is more room for extra layers. This increased cost, which would more than likely lead to increased prices to the consumer, was an issue that would threaten the potential success of the Blu-ray, although the format does hold more data (as shown in Table 8.5).

→

Table 8.5 DVD performance details

Capacity			
Blu-ray		**HD DVD**	
ROM single layer	23.3/25GB	Single layer	15GB
ROM dual layer	46.6/50GB	Dual layer	30GB
RW single layer	23.3/25/27GB	–	–
RW dual layer	46.6/50/54GB	–	–
Highest test	100GB	Highest test	45GB
Theoretical limit	200GB	Theoretical limit	60GB

Film studio support

Not only did each format have to compete to establish itself as superior in the eyes of the consumer, there was also a separate battle to be won with the film studios in order to secure eventual success. Table 8.6 shows the different studios and their initial support of each format.

It is also worth noting that, in the years prior to the launch of these formats, and immediately afterwards, Sony acquired a number of film studios. Sony was also rumoured to be paying some studios large sums to take on and stick with its format.

A much more difficult factor to unravel is the list of networks (formal and informal) that each group of firms developed. In some cases, it was clear, with firms listing associate members of each board. Once again, Blu-ray had a longer list of members and interested parties. It seemed Sony had learnt from its mistakes with VCR and it was not going to make the same mistake again (see Table 8.7).

Whilst the mainstream film studios play a key role in determining the relative success of each format, perhaps as important as the big media conglomerates may be the adult entertainment industry. Most industry analysts agree that US pornographers' decision to adopt the cheap convenient VHS – rather than rival Betamax – when the two systems were introduced in the 1970s, killed off Betamax, and sales of pornographic films drove the adoption of video recorders. It may have been Sony's failure to license Betamax that led to its demise, but the adult entertainment industry probably also contributed to its demise. Dario Betti, an analyst at London-based digital media consultancy Ovum, says: 'Like it or not,

Table 8.6 Studios supporting HD DVD and Blu-ray

Studios (film and game) listed as supporting members	
Blu-ray	**HD DVD**
20th Century Fox	Buena Vista Home Entertainment
Buena Vista Home Entertainment	New Line Cinema
Electronic Arts	Paramount Pictures
MGM Studios	The Walt Disney Company
Paramount Pictures	Universal Studios
Sony Pictures Entertainment	Warner Bros.
The Walt Disney Company	
Vivendi Universal Games	
Warner Bros.	

Table 8.7 Interlinkages and networks between firms

Companies listed as members of the board or managing members	
Blu-ray	**HD DVD**
Apple Computer Corp.	Memory-Tech Corporation
Dell, Inc.	NEC Corporation
Hewlett Packard Company	Sanyo Electric Co.
Hitachi, Ltd	
LG Electronics Inc.	
Mitsubishi Electric Corporation	
Panasonic (Matsushita Electric)	
Pioneer Corporation	
Royal Philips Electronics	
Samsung Electronics Co., Ltd	
Sharp Corporation	
Sony Corporation	
TDK Corporation	
Thomson	
20th Century Fox	
Walt Disney Pictures and Television	

pornography drives each new, convenient visual technology.' Few may be willing to admit it, but sex sells, and there is certainly a case that more convenient nudity (and the pornographers' preferred choice between HD DVD and Blu-ray) will play some role in determining which of the two formats is, ultimately, successful.

The Sony PlayStation

The first Blu-ray player launched by Sony (the primary developer of the Blu-ray format) was actually the PlayStation 3 (PS3), which featured the ability to play Blu-ray disks. This gave Sony something of an upper hand for some time, because its PlayStation 3 games console has a built-in Blu-ray player. Sony had, therefore, sold more than 10 million Blu-ray units, whilst only about 1 million HD-DVD players have been sold, mostly in Japan.

The PlayStation 3 originally was launched at a price of around £500, the first 'pure' Blu-ray player was launched later at a price of around £800.

Obviously, in comparison to the PlayStation, this player lacked a number of features, particularly the ability to play games. Interestingly, one of the earliest machines to play HD DVD was also a games console, the Xbox 360, which was Microsoft's primary competitor against the PlayStation (and priced around £200 cheaper). Both of these consoles were notably more expensive than Nintendo's Wii, which was attracting much attention around this time. Despite the high technological performance of both the PlayStation and Xbox, Nintendo was, at that time, able to gain a majority share in the market (and this is also despite the PlayStation's ability to play Blu-ray disks).

Discussion: the winner and the future

Sony's decision to incorporate Blu-ray playback into the PS3 is thought to have been a decisive factor in the format emerging victorious. Ultimately, the Blu-ray format won the war to become the next generation of HD player. Another factor that has been linked

→

to this is the 'Wal-Mart effect' – after an announcement from the US retailer that it would sell only Blu-ray films and players. This retailer has massive power in the US market. With Sony's victory, however, comes another battle: film downloads. Music downloading destroyed the CD industry; the same may happen in DVD. Why would people go out to the shops to buy discs when they can buy high-definition films straight away online? What does this suggestion say for the future of Blu-ray?

Interestingly, despite Apple giving its backing to the Blu-ray format, it has yet to produce a single computer with a Blu-ray drive. Instead, Apple seems to be concentrating on films delivered across the internet, through iTunes and the new Apple TV, rather than on physical discs. So, although Blu-ray has won this battle, it may not have won the war. As home internet speeds become faster and consumers get used to video on-demand services, the film market could undergo a similar change to the music sector, with films downloaded rather than physically bought. Enter a new format war of online video . . .

When Google released the high-quality WebM video format royalty-free to the world, digital video publishers were faced with a conundrum: support the guaranteed royalty-free but slightly lower-quality WebM standard, or the sharper but potentially more expensive H.264 industry standard? The industry divided amongst the WebM camp, the

H.264 supporters and the true neutrals of the browser world:

- WebM support only: Mozilla Firefox;
- H.264 support only: Microsoft internet Explorer and Apple Safari;
- both: Google Chrome and Opera.

In 2010, the MPEG LA technology licensing body announced that the H.264 standard would join WebM on the royalty-free side of the fence until the end of time or until the standard becomes obsolete, whichever comes first. This makes Google's $133 million buyout of On 2 Technologies seem like a waste of money – that is where the technology for WebM came from, and now there is really no need to provide a royalty-free alternative to the prevailing standard. But few believe that H.264 would be free today, if Google had not made that investment.

H.264 is not *entirely* free, even now. Free use extends only to services that are free to end users, such as Google's YouTube. Apple will still have to pay licence fees for the videos it sells through iTunes. But, part of that payment goes back into Apple's own pockets – the company is a long-time backer of and patent contributor to the H.264 standard. Other major beneficiaries of the H.264 licence fee include Microsoft, Cisco Systems and Dolby Laboratories. Keeping the standard relevant and revenue-producing is important to these firms, whilst Google is not part of the consortium and so has little incentive to support H.264.

Questions

1. What does this case tell us about whether or not it is the best technology and/or being first in the market that determines the winner of these product format battles?

2. Illustrate some other business sectors where different formats coexist and some where a single format is preferred.

3. Use the CIM (Figure 1.9) to illustrate the innovation process in this case.

4. Why was the PlayStation the first Blu-ray player and, subsequently, when Blu-ray players were launched, why did the PlayStation remain cheaper? Consider possible reasons for this.

5. What additional factors helped Blu-ray win the battle? What role did licensing and networks play in the relative success of each format?

6. What related industries contributed to the format war and how did they influence its outcome?

7. With the increasing popularity and use of downloading films, what influence will the DVD format winner play in this related battle?

8. What are the implications for innovation strategy, R&D expenditure and marketing for firms engaged in or likely to be engaged in a format war?

9. List the key factors that seem to determine the eventual winner in industry format wars. Divide these into primary and secondary factors.

Chapter summary

This chapter has explored the role of strategic alliances and how firms are increasingly recognising that alliances provide access to resources that are greater than any single firm could buy. The main purpose was to highlight their growing importance within the world of business. This is further reinforced by the concept of industry clusters and networks. In some knowledge-intensive industries, such as the film industry, the role of alliances has been further developed. In these network industries, loose alliances are formed to undertake a project and, when the project is finished, the organisation ceases to exist. Linked to the issue of cooperation is the question of intellectual property and, in particular, the potential problem of information leakage. Many firms are understandably reticent about entering any form of collaboration, for they fear losing the small advantage that they perceive they have over their competitors. Trust is frequently at the centre of any decision on whether a firm enters an alliance and, usually, trust has to be established over a period of time before firms agree to enter an alliance.

Discussion questions

1 Explain why the car industry seems to have so many strategic alliances.

2 What is meant by 'levelling out of knowledge'? How can firms prevent this happening when engaging in strategic alliances?

3 Considering the case study, discuss some of the wider strategic reasons why firms may wish to enter a strategic alliance.

4 Apple seems to have many strategic alliances and supplier relations. Discuss the extent to which these contribute to its success.

5 Explain some of the risks involved with all strategic alliances.

6 Explain why the repeated game of the prisoner's dilemma is considered to be more useful in predicting behaviour.

Key words and phrases

Prisoner's dilemma *266*

Joint venture *268*

Licensing *270*

Outsourcing *272*

Collaboration *273*

R&D consortia *273*

Industry clusters *274*

Innovation networks *276*

Virtual company *278*

Insourcing *284*

The concept of trust *285*

References

Alexander, M. and Young, D. (1996) Outsourcing: where's the value? *Long Range Planning*, vol. 29, no. 5, 728–30.

Arias, J.T.G. (1995) Do networks really foster innovation? *Management Decision*, vol. 33, no. 9, 52–7.

Aubert, B.A., Patry, M. and Rivard, S. (1998) Assessing the risk of IT outsourcing, Working Paper, 98s-16, May, Cirano, Montreal.

Baden-Fuller, C. and Pitt, M. (eds) (1996) *Strategic Innovation*, Routledge, London.

Barthelemy, J. (2001) The hidden costs of IT outsourcing, *Sloan Management Review*, vol. 42, no. 3, 60–9.

Barthelemy, J. and Geyer, D. (2000) IT outsourcing: findings from an empirical survey in France and Germany, *European Management Journal*, vol. 19, no. 2, 195–202.

Bettis, R., Bradley, S. and Hamel, G. (1992) Outsourcing and industrial decline, *Academy of Management Executive*, vol. 6, no. 1, 7–22.

Bleeke, J. and Ernst, D. (1992) *Collaborating to Compete*, John Wiley, New York.

Da Rold, C. (2001) 'Buying commodity/access services instead of outsourcing', Gartner Group, Research Note, June.

Dacin, M.T., Hitt, M.A. and Levitas, E. (1997) Selecting partners for successful international alliances, *Journal of World Business*, vol. 32, no. 1, 321–45.

Day, G.S. and Schoemaker, P.J.H. (2000) *Wharton on Managing Emerging Technologies*, John Wiley, New York.

Doig, S.J., Ritter, R.C., Speckhals, K. and Woolson, D. (2001) Has outsourcing gone too far? *McKinsey Quarterly*, vol. 4, 24–37.

Doz, Y. and Hamel, G. (1997) 'The use of alliances in implementing technology strategies', in Tashman, M.L. and Anderson, P. (eds) *Managing Strategic Innovation and Change: A Collection of Readings*, Oxford University Press, New York.

Duysters, G., Kok, G. and Vaandrager, M. (1999) Crafting successful strategic technology partnerships, *R&D Management*, vol. 29, no. 4, 343–51.

Earl, M. (1996) The risks of outsourcing IT, *Sloan Management Review*, Spring, 26–32.

Fitjar, R.D. and Rodríguez-Pose, A. (2013) Firm collaboration and modes of innovation in Norway, *Research Policy*, 42(1), 128–138.

Giddens, A. (1990) *The Consequences of Modernity*, Oxford University Press, Oxford.

Gulati, R. (1995) Does familiarity breed trust? The implications of repeated ties for contractual choice in alliances, *Academy of Management Journal*, vol. 38, no. 1, 85–112.

Hamel, G. (1991) Competition for competence and inter-partner learning within international strategic alliances, *Strategic Management Journal*, vol. 12, no. 1, 83–103.

Harrigan, K.R. (1986) *Managing for Joint Venture Success*, Lexington Books, Lexington, MA.

Hoecht, A. and Trott, P. (1999) Trust, risk and control in the management of collaborative technology development, *International Journal of Innovation Management*, vol. 3, no. 3, 257–70.

Hoecht, A. and Trott, P. (2006) Innovation risks of strategic outsourcing, *Technovation*, vol. 26, no. 4, 672–81.

Hollis, M. (1998) *Trust Within Reason*, Cambridge University Press, Cambridge.

Huang, S. K. (2014). The emergence of the outsourcing market and product technological performance, *Technological Forecasting and Social Change*, 82, 132–139.

Humphrey, J. and Schmitz, H. (1998) Trust in inter-firm relations in developing and transition economies, *Journal of Development Studies*, vol. 34, no. 4, 32–61.

Jensen M.B., Johnson, B., Lorenz, E., Lundvall, B.A. (2007) Forms of knowledge and modes of innovation, *Research Policy*, vol. 36, no. 5, 680–93.

Kaplan, J. (2002) Partners in outsourcing, *Network World*, vol. 19, no. 11, 41.

Kaufman, A., Wood, C.H. and Theyel, G. (2000) Collaboration and technology linkages: a strategic supplier typology, *Strategic Management Journal*, vol. 21, 649–63.

Khosrowpour, M., Subramanian, G. and Gunterman, J. (1995) 'Outsourcing organizational benefits and potential problems', in Khosrowpour, M. (ed.) *Managing Information Technology Investments with Outsourcing*, Idea Group Publishing, London, 244–68.

Lacity, M. and Hirschheim, R. (1993) *Information Systems Outsourcing: Myths, Metaphors and Realities*, John Wiley, Chichester.

Lane, C. and Bachmann, R. (1996) The social construction of trust: supplier relations in Britain and Germany, *Organisation Studies*, vol. 17, no. 3, 365–95.

Levén, P., Holmström, J. and Mathiassen, L. (2014) Managing research and innovation networks: evidence from a government sponsored cross-industry program, *Research Policy*, vol. 43, no. 1, 156–68.

Lewicki, R.J. and Bunker, B.B. (1996) 'Developing and maintaining trust in work relationships', in Kramer, R. and Tyler, T. (eds) *Trust in Organisations*, Sage, London, 114–39.

Liebeskind, J. and Oliver, A. (1998) 'From handshake to contract: intellectual property, trust and the social structure of academic research', in Lane, C. and Bachmann, R. (eds) *Trust Within and Between Organisations: Conceptual Issues and Empirical Applications*, Oxford University Press, Oxford, 118–45.

Lynch, C. (2002) Price vs value: the outsourcing conundrum, *Logistics Management and Distribution Report*, vol. 41, no. 2, 35.

Martisons, M. (1993) Outsourcing information systems: a strategic partnership with risks, *Long Range Planning*, vol. 26, no. 3, 18–25.

Nelson, R.R. and Winter, S. (1982) *An Evolutionary Theory of Economic Change*, Harvard University Press, Boston, MA.

Parkhe, A. (1993) Strategic alliance structuring: a game theoretic and transaction cost examination of interfirm cooperation, *Academy of Management Journal*, August, vol. 36, no. 4, 794.

Porter, M.E. (1987) From competitive advantage to corporate strategy, *Harvard Business Review*, May–June, 43–59.

Porter, M.E. (1998) Clusters and the new economics of competition, *Harvard Business Review*, November–December, 10–24.

Quélin, B. and Duhamel, F. (2003) Bringing together strategic outsourcing and corporate strategy: outsourcing motives and risks, *European Management Journal*, vol. 21, no. 5, 647–61.

Quinn, J. and Hilmer, F. (1994) Strategic outsourcing, *Sloan Management Review*, Summer, 43–55.

Ritala, P. and Hurmelinna-Laukkanen, P. (2009) What's in it for me? Creating and appropriating value in innovation-related competition, *Technovation*, vol. 29, no. 12, 819–28.

Sako, M. (1992) *Prices, Quality and Trust: Inter-firm Relations in Britain and Japan*, Cambridge University Press, Cambridge.

Sheridan, J. (1997) An alliance built on trust, *Industry Week*, vol. 246, no. 6, 67.

Sitkin, S. and Roth, N. (1993) Explaining the limited effectiveness of legalistic 'remedies' for trust/distrust, *Organization Science*, vol. 4, 367–92.

Spekman, R.E., Lynn, A.I., MacAvoy, T.C. and Forbes, I. (1996) Creating strategic alliances which endure, *Long Range Planning*, vol. 29, no. 3, 122–47.

Teece, D. (1998) Capturing value from knowledge assets: the new economy, markets for know-how and intangible assets, *California Management Review*, vol. 40, no. 3, 55–79.

Vyas, N.M., Shelburn, W.L. and Rogers, D.C. (1995) An analysis of strategic alliances: forms, functions and framework, *Journal of Business and Industrial Marketing*, Summer, vol. 10, no. 3, 47.

Wang, C.H. and Hsu, L.C. (2014) Building exploration and exploitation in the high-tech industry: the role of relationship learning, *Technological Forecasting and Social Change*, vol. 81, 331–40.

Wang, C. and Regan, A.C. (2003) Risks and reduction measures in logistics outsourcing, TRB Annual Meeting.

Williams, C. (2014) Security in the cyber supply chain: Is it achievable in a complex, inter-conected world? *Technovation*, vol. 34, no. 7, 382–4.

Zeng, S.X., Xie, X.M. and Tam, C.M. (2010) Relationship between cooperation networks and innovation performance of SMEs, *Technovation*, vol. 30, no. 3, 181–94.

Zucker, L. (1986) Production of trust: institutional sources of economic structure, 1840–1920, *Research in Organisational Behaviour*, vol. 8, 53–111.

Further reading

For a more detailed review of the strategic alliances and innovation networks literature, the following develop many of the issues raised in this chapter:

Ahuja, G. (2000) Collaboration networks, structural holes, and innovation: a longitudinal study, *Administrative Science Quarterly*, vol. 45, 425–55.

Brusoni, S., Prencipe, A. and Pavitt, K. (2001) Knowledge specialization, organizational coupling, and the boundaries of the firm: why do firms know more than they make? *Administrative Science Quarterly*, vol. 46, 597–621.

Deeds, D.L., DeCarolis, D. and Coombs, J. (2000) Dynamic capabilities and new product development in high technology ventures: an empirical analysis of new biotechnology firms, *Journal of Business Venturing*, vol. 15, no. 3, 211–29.

Faulkner, D. (1995) *Co-operating to Compete*, McGraw-Hill International, Maidenhead.

Mason, G., Beltram, J. and Paul, J. (2004) External knowledge sourcing in different national settings: a comparison of electronics establishments in Britain and France, *Research Policy*, vol. 33, no. 1, 53–72.

Ritala, P. and Hurmelinna-Laukkanen, P. (2009) What's in it for me? Creating and appropriating value in innovation-related competition, *Technovation*, vol. 29, no. 12, 819–28.

Williams, C. (2014) Security in the cyber supply chain: Is it achievable in a complex, interconnected world? *Technovation*, vol. 34, no. 7, 382–4.

Zeng, S.X., Xie, X.M. and Tam, C.M. (2010) Relationship between cooperation networks and innovation performance of SMEs, *Technovation*, vol. 30, no. 3, 181–94.

Chapter 9
Management of research and development

Introduction

This chapter shows how R&D is managed, as there remains a strong belief that R&D departments are freewheeling places of artistic disorder. Yet, in the large industrialised firm where R&D is institutionalised, it is fully recognised that invention and creativity emerge from the routine of R&D, and innovation follows under management instruction and control. This is not merely understood, but also a requirement. For, when firms such as Siemens spend annually in excess of $5 billion on R&D, their shareholders would rightly expect that this investment is closely managed and its activities monitored. Moreover, a decent return on these R&D investments is expected. At the end of this chapter is a case study telling the story of the development of Viagra. This helps to illustrate the prominent role given to R&D in technology-intensive industries. But it also shows the key role played by marketing in helping to make the product successful.

Chapter contents

Learning objectives

When you have completed this chapter you will be able to:

- recognise that R&D management is context dependent; the development of a new engine for an aircraft, for example, may take 10 years and involve many different component suppliers; the development of a new domestic cleaning product, however, may take only a few months;

- recognise that the R&D function incorporates several very different activities;

- explain that formal management techniques are an essential part of good R&D management; and

- recognise that investment in R&D must be looked at in the same way as any other investment in the business – the benefits it produces must exceed the costs.

What is research and development?

To many, especially academics, the term research will mean the systematic approach to the discovery of new knowledge. Universities usually do not develop products – unless one considers teaching material as the product of the research. In industry, however, research is a much more generic term and can involve both new science and the use of old science to produce a new product. It is sometimes difficult to determine when research ends and development begins. It is probably more realistic to view industrial R&D as a continuum with scientific knowledge and concepts at one end and physical products at the other. Along this continuum it is possible to place the various R&D activities (see Figure 9.1). Later in this chapter we discuss the variety of R&D activities usually found within a large R&D department.

Technology is a commonly used word and, yet, is not fully understood by all those who use it. Hickman (1990) offers a comprehensive classification of technology, used to describe both products and processes. Roussel et al. (1991) define technology as the application of knowledge to achieve a practical result. More recently, the term know-how has been used in management literature to describe a company's knowledge base, which includes its R&D capability.

Research and development has, traditionally, been regarded by academics and industry alike as the management of scientific *research* and the *development* of new products; this was soon abbreviated to R&D. Twiss (1992: 2) offers a widely accepted definition:

> *R&D is the purposeful and systematic use of scientific knowledge to improve man's lot even though some of its manifestations do not meet with universal approval.*

The recent debates about scientific cloning of animal cells are a good example of what Twiss means by the results of R&D often delivering controversial outcomes. A more contemporary definition is offered by Roussel et al. (1991), who define the concept as:

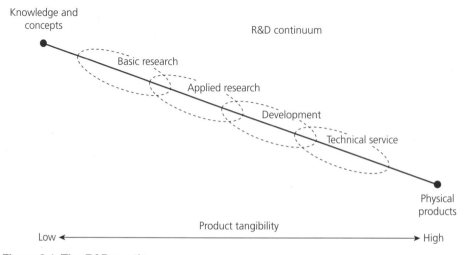

Figure 9.1 The R&D continuum

To develop new knowledge and apply scientific or engineering knowledge to connect the knowledge in one field to that in others.

This definition reflects the more recent view that scientific knowledge is expanding so rapidly that it is extremely difficult for one company to remain abreast of all the technologies that it needs for its products. Companies pull together scientific knowledge from a wide variety of sources. For example, the manufacture of a personal computer will require technology from several different streams, including microprocessor technology, visual display technology and software technology. It would be almost impossible for a company to be a technology leader in all of these fields.

The traditional view of R&D

After the Second World War, research and development played an important role in providing firms with competitive advantage. Technical developments in industries such as chemicals, electronics, automotive and pharmaceuticals led to the development of many new products, which produced rapid growth. For a while, it seemed that technology was capable of almost anything. The traditional view of R&D has, therefore, been overcoming genuine technological problems, which subsequently leads to business opportunities and a competitive advantage over one's competitors.

President Kennedy's special address to the US Congress in 1961, in which he spoke of 'putting a man on the moon before the decade was out', captured the popular opinion of that time. Many believed anything was possible through technology. This notion helps to explain one of the major areas of difficulty with R&D. Traditionally, it has been viewed as a linear process, moving from research to engineering and then manufacture. It was US economists and policy makers after the Second World War who were largely responsible for the linear model of science and innovation. This was because statisticians had to measure research spending and this led to the categorisation of science and research (see also Vannevar Bush's *Science: The Endless Frontier* (1945)). That R&D was viewed as an overhead item was reinforced by Kennedy who pledged to spend 'whatever it costs' and, indeed, enormous financial resources were directed towards the project. But this was a unique situation without the usual economic or market forces at play. Nevertheless, industry adopted a similar approach to that used by the space programme. Vast amounts of money were poured into R&D programmes in the belief that then the interesting technology generated could be incorporated into products. In many instances, this is exactly what happened, but there were also many examples of exciting technology developed purely because it was interesting, without any consideration of the competitive market in which the business operated. Hence, many business leaders began to question the value of R&D.

R&D management and the industrial context

As will become clear, there is no single best way to manage R&D. There is no prescription, no computer model that will ensure its success. Each company and every competitive environment is unique and in its own state of change. R&D needs to be

---

Illustration 9.1

Industrial R&D has a long history

Many of Europe's largest chemical companies have a long history of funding industrial research. After the end of the First World War, several reports were written examining the scope and nature of industrial research in German chemical companies. The following extract is taken from one of these reports:

One of the most striking features in the works visited is the application in the broadest sense of science to chemical industry. This is naturally very

prominent in the triumvirate of the Bayer, Farbwerke Hoechst and the BASF, but it is equally noticeable in many of the smaller undertakings. The lavish and apparently unstinted monetary outlay on laboratories, libraries and technical staff implies implicit confidence on the part of the leaders of the industry in the ability to repay with interest heavy initial expenditure.

Source: ABCM (1919) 'Report of the British Chemical Mission on Chemical Factories in the Occupied Area of Germany'.

---

managed according to the specific heritage and resources of the company in its competitive industry. Whilst the management of R&D in the aircraft industry is very different from the textile industry, there are, nonetheless, certain factors and elements that are common to all aspects of R&D management, almost irrespective of the industry. This chapter will draw on examples from across several different industries. This will help to highlight differences as well as identify commonalities in the management of R&D. Illustration 9.1, taken from a 1919 visit to the occupied territories of Germany, emphasises the very long history of industrial R&D.

At the beginning of this book, we discussed one of the most fundamental dilemmas facing all companies: the need to provide an environment that fosters creativity and an inquisitive approach whilst, at the same time, providing a stable environment that enables the business to be managed in an efficient and systematic way. Somehow, businesses have to square this circle. Nowhere is this more apparent than in the management of research and development. For it is here that people need to question the accepted ways of working and challenge accepted wisdom.

One may be tempted to think that research, by definition, is uncertain, based around exploring things that are unknown. It cannot, therefore, be managed and organisations should not try to do so. There is, however, overwhelming evidence to suggest that industrial technological research can, indeed, be managed and that most of those organisations that spend large amounts of money on R&D, such as Volkswagen, IBM, Sony, Siemens and Astra-Zeneca, do so extremely well (see Table 9.1). This table of Europe's leading firms in terms of R&D expenditure is part of the EU's annual R&D Scoreboard.

Large organisations with more resources can clearly afford to invest more in R&D than their smaller counterparts. Therefore, in order to present a more realistic comparison than that derived from raw sums invested, R&D expenditure frequently is expressed as:

$$\text{R\&D as \% of sales} = (\text{R\&D expenditure} \div \text{total sales income} = 100\%)$$

This not only allows comparisons to be made between small and large firms, but also gives a more realistic picture of R&D intensity within the organisation. Across

Table 9.1 Europe's R&D expenditure league (2013)

Rank	Company	R&D spend (£M)	R&D as a % of sales	Industrial sector
1	Volkswagen Germany	11,743.0	6.0	Engineering, vehicles
2	Novartis Switzerland	7,173.5	117.1	Pharmaceuticals
3	Roche Switzerland	7,076.2	18.6	Pharmaceuticals
4	Daimler Germany	5,379.0	4.6	Electronic and electrical equipment
5	BMW Germany	4,792.0	6.3	Engineering, vehicles
6	Sanofi-Aventis France	4,757.0	14.4	Pharmaceuticals
7	Robert Bosch Germany	4,653.0	10.1	Electronic and electrical equipment
8	Siemens Germany	4,556.0	6.0	Engineering
9	GlaxoSmithKline UK	4,154.3	13.1	Pharmaceuticals
10	Airbus The Netherlands	3,581.0	6.0	Aerospace
11	Ericsson Sweden	3,484.8	13.6	Electronic and electrical equipment
12	BMW Germany	2,448.00	5.1	Engineering, vehicles
13	Ericsson Sweden	2,401.68	11.9	Telecommunications
14	Nokia Finland	3,456.0	14.7	Electronics
15	Fiat Italy	3,362.0	3.9	Engineering, vehicles
16	Bayer Germany	3,259.0	8.1	Chemicals
17	AstraZeneca UK	3,202.8	17.2	Pharmaceuticals
18	Boehringer Ingelheim Germany	2,743.0	19.5	Pharmaceuticals
19	Alcatel Lucent France	2,374.0	16.4	Engineering
20	SAP Germany	2,282.0	13.6	Software

Source: http://iri.jrc.ec.europa.eu/research/scoreboard_2015.htm, © European Union, 1995–2016.

Table 9.2 R&D expenditure across industry sectors

Industry sector	R&D expenditure as % of sales
Pharmaceuticals and biotechnology	15.8
Software and computer services	7.4
Fixed line telecommunications	5.1
Technical hardware equipment	5.1
Aerospace and defence	4.2
Automotive and parts	4.1
Electronic and electrical equipment	3.9
Food production	1.7
Banks	1.5
Oil and gas	0.5

Source: www.innovation.gov.uk/rd_scoreboard (2015).

industry sectors there are great differences in expenditure. Table 9.2 shows typical levels of R&D expenditure across different industry sectors. Some industries are technology intensive with relatively high levels of R&D expenditure. The Dyson case study at the end of Chapter 16 shows that, even in those industries not normally associated with R&D, the benefits of successful R&D can be large indeed.

The fact that some of the largest and most successful companies in the world spend enormous sums of money on R&D should not be taken as a sign that they have mastered the process. It is important to acknowledge that R&D management, like innovation itself, is part art and part science. Industry may not be able to identify and hire technological geniuses like Faraday, Pasteur or Bell, but many companies would argue that they already employ geniuses who, year after year, develop new patents and new products that will contribute to the future prosperity of the organisation. These same companies would also argue that they cannot justify spending several millions of dollars, pounds or euros purely on the basis of chance and good fortune. This would, clearly, be unacceptable, not least to shareholders. So, whilst companies appreciate that there is a certain amount of serendipity, there are also formal management techniques that, over the years, have been learnt, refined and practised and that now are a necessary part of good R&D management.

R&D investment and company success

The Strategy& (PricewaterhouseCooper's strategy consulting business) 2014 Global Innovation 1000 Study (www.strategyand.pwc.com, 2015), which analyses R&D investment at the 1,000 biggest-spending public companies in the world, found that R&D spend rose by only 1.4 per cent, well below the 10-year average growth rate of 5.5 per cent. Apple, Google and Amazon are still seen as the most innovative companies, as identified by survey respondents, but are not, necessarily, the ones spending the most on their R&D – indicating, once again, that it is not how much companies spend on research and development that determines success – what really matters is how those R&D funds are invested in capabilities, talent, process and tools.

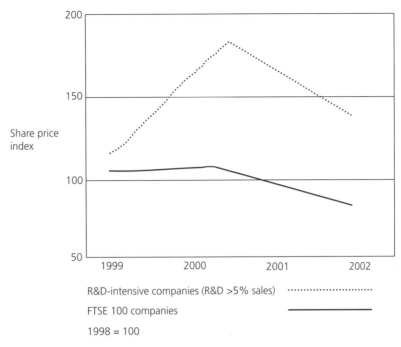

R&D-intensive companies (R&D >5% sales) ·······························

FTSE 100 companies ————————

1998 = 100

Figure 9.2 Comparison of share price performance of R&D-intensive firms and the FTSE 100 firms

R&D expenditure now consumes a significant proportion of a firm's funds across all industry sectors. This is, principally, because companies realise that new products can provide a huge competitive advantage. Yet, comparing national strengths in science and technology is a hazardous exercise, bedevilled by incompatible definitions. Whilst it is relatively easy to measure inputs, it is far harder to measure outputs in terms of quality. Figure 9.2 shows a comparison of share price performance of R&D-intensive firms and the FTSE 100 firms. Clearly, the performance of a firm's share price is not, necessarily, a true guide of performance; it is, nonetheless, one output. What is worthy of note is that the number of R&D-intensive firms is increasing. Also, in a study of the German manufacturing industry, Lang (2009) examined the long-term relationship between domestic R&D, knowledge stock and productivity dynamics. He found that 50 per cent of the effects of R&D on the knowledge stock appear within four years.

It is now widely recognised that competition can appear from virtually anywhere in the world. Countries formerly viewed as receptacles for the outputs of factories across Europe are now supplying products themselves. Mexico, Brazil, Malaysia, China and India now supply a wide range of products to Europe, including car components, computer hardware and clothing. Globalisation provides opportunities for companies but it also brings increased competition. The introduction of new products provides a clear basis on which to compete, with those companies that are able to develop and introduce new and improved products having a distinct advantage.

Firms are also uneasy about R&D or, to be more accurate, a lack of R&D. Ever since 1982, when ICI completed a study into the effects of stopping product innovation, companies have viewed innovation and R&D investment with some anxiety. They fear that, should they stop investment in R&D, and product innovation in particular, the consequences would be severe. The results of the study showed that profits would decline very slowly for around 15 years, before falling very sharply. It is worthy of note that, if a similar study were to be undertaken today, it is almost certain that the 15-year figure would be halved to approximately 8. The ICI study also posed another important question. How long, it wondered, would it take for profits to recover if, after the 15 years, the company magically resumed its product innovation at three times its previous rate? The study revealed that it would take another 25 years for profit to recover to the level achieved before the product innovation programme was stopped (Weild, 1986).

These findings reflect the conventional wisdom that dominated thinking in this field for most of the twentieth century. That is, most companies assume that R&D investment is a good thing; like education, in general, it is, surely, a worthy investment. In the 1980s, there was great interest in the concept of technology transfer and the belief that companies could buy in any technological expertise they required. Later research highlighted the folly of such arguments (Cohen and Levinthal, 1990; Quintas et al., 1992) and the business community has returned to a view that, fundamentally, R&D investment is beneficial. The difficulty lies in where, precisely, to invest; which projects and technology to invest in; and when to stop pouring money into a project that looks likely to fail but could yet deliver enormous profits.

Many international companies, including Unilever, BT and BAE Systems, have conducted numerous studies attempting to justify R&D expenditure. This has not been easy because there is no satisfactory method for measuring R&D output. Many studies have used the number of patents published as a guide. This is mainly because it is quantifiable rather than being a valid measure. It is, however, quality not quantity of output that is clearly important. It is worthy of note that most companies would like to be able to correlate R&D expenditure with profitability. Edwin Mansfield (1991) undertook a major study exploring the relationship between R&D expenditure and economic growth and productivity. He concluded:

although the results are subject to considerable error, they establish certain broad conclusions. In particular, existing econometric studies do provide reasonably conclusive evidence that R&D has a significant effect on the rate of productivity increase in the industries and time periods studied.

Furthermore, a study by Geroski et al. (1993) did reveal a positive relationship between R&D expenditure and *long-term growth*. This is reinforced by the 2006 R&D scoreboard, which concludes that:

R&D is a major investment contributing to company success along with other factors like excellent operations and good strategic choices. There are well-established links between R&D growth and intensity and sales growth, wealth creation efficiency and market value.

This raises an important point. R&D expenditure should be viewed as a long-term investment. It may even reduce short-term profitability. Company accountants increasingly question the need for large sums to be invested in an activity that shows no obvious and certainly no rapid return. Many argue that public money should be used for 'pure research' where there is no clear application. Its outputs could then be taken and used by industry to generate wealth. However, the UK Government's recent initiatives to couple science to the creation of wealth, through

Illustration 9.2

R&D tax incentives

In many countries in the world, including Canada, the USA and the UK, governments provide tax incentives (in the form of tax credits and/or refund) to businesses to support R&D. These programmes were introduced first in Canada in the 1980s. It is intended to encourage businesses of all sizes – particularly small and start-up firms – to conduct R&D that will lead to new, improved or technologically advanced products or processes. R&D expenditures (already deducted against revenue) may qualify for investment tax credits (i.e. a reduction in income taxes payable), cash refunds or both. Qualified expenditures may include wages, materials, machinery, equipment and some overheads.

Source: Pearson Education Ltd/Nick Rowe/Photodisc

such programmes as Technology Foresight, seems to suggest that even public money is being directed towards **applied research**. Illustration 9.2 shows how governments encourage firms to invest in R&D.

This raises the issue of evaluating R&D. Whilst few, if any, of the companies listed in Table 9.1 would question the value of R&D, this does not preclude the need for evaluation. How much money should companies invest in R&D? How much should be used for applied research and how much for pure research? These questions will be addressed later in this chapter and also in Chapter 10.

Pause for thought

A company generates $1 million profit. How can the R&D director convince the other directors to invest this money in R&D? The sales director will make a strong case that more sales staff will lead to more sales. And the IT director will explain that more investment in IT will help to reduce costs and improve efficiency!

Classifying R&D

Traditionally, industrial research has focused on a variety of research activities performed *within* the organisation. This practice was modelled on the research undertaken within universities during the early part of the twentieth century. This was seen as public research financed by public money for the public good. In other words, research undertaken within universities was performed in the pursuit of new

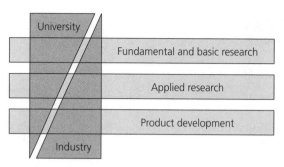

Figure 9.3 Classification of areas of research emphasis in industry and university

knowledge. Its results were available publicly and the commercial exploitation of this knowledge largely was disregarded. For example, Fleming's discovery of penicillin initially was not patented. Industrial research, on the other hand, was intended specifically for the benefit of the company funding the research. Industry's purpose was to grow and make profits and this was to be achieved through the development of new products and new businesses. Hence, industry's expectations of its own research expanded to include the development of knowledge into products (see Figure 9.3).

Illustration 9.3

2014 EU R&D Scoreboard

Highlights

- In 2013, the world's top 2,500 R&D investors, which account for about 90 per cent of global industrial R&D, continued to increase their investment in R&D (4.9 per cent), well above the growth of net sales (2.8 per cent). The 633 EU companies amongst the top world 2,500 R&D investors show an annual R&D investment growth rate of 2.6 per cent, well below the world average. This is accompanied by a decrease in sales (–2.0 per cent) and operating profits (–6.6 per cent).

- The EU-based carmaker Volkswagen leads the global ranking for the second consecutive year, showing again a remarkable increase of R&D investment in 2013 (23.4 per cent, up to €11.7 billion). Second continues to be Samsung, showing a very impressive R&D increase of 25.4 per cent.

- An examination of *Scoreboard* company patent portfolios shows that the patents to R&D ratios

are very much sector-specific. This is combined with a wide variation within sectors, determined by the individual technological profiles of companies and their degree of specialisation. The pharmaceutical sector, one of the most technologically concentrated, is a good example, with some companies focused purely on pharmaceuticals but others specialised in medical technologies (Johnson & Johnson) or chemistry (Bayer) and some with substantial patenting activity in biotechnology (Roche).

- EU companies in the automobile sector, accounting for one quarter of the total R&D invested by the EU-633 *Scoreboard* companies, continued to increase significantly their R&D investments in 2013 (6.2 per cent). This reflects the good performance of automobile companies based in Germany (9.7 per cent) that account for three-quarters of this sector's R&D in the EU.

Source: Hernandez et al. (2015), © European Union, 1995–2016.

Over the years, industrial research and development increasingly has been guided by the aims of its financiers via its business strategy and, to a lesser extent, by the pursuit of knowledge. The main activities of industrial R&D have included the following:

- discovering and developing new technologies;
- improving understanding of the technology in existing products;
- improving and strengthening understanding of technologies used in manufacturing; and
- understanding research results from universities and other research institutions.

The management of R&D can be viewed as two sides of the same coin. On the one side, there are research activities, often referred to as fundamental or **basic research** and, on the other side, usually the development of products. Many industries make a clear distinction between research and development and some companies even suggest that they leave all research to universities, engaging only in development. Figure 9.3 shows the areas of research emphasis in industry and universities. In between the discovery of new knowledge and new scientific principles (so-called fundamental research) and the development of products for commercial gain (so-called development) is the significant activity of transforming scientific principles into technologies that can be applied to products (see CSI case study at the end of Chapter 10). This activity is called applied research. The development of the videocassette recorder (VCR) shows how, over a period of almost 30 years, industry worked with existing scientific principles to develop a product with commercial potential.

The operations that make up R&D

Figure 9.1 illustrated the R&D operations commonly found in almost every major research and development department. They may have different labels but, within Siemens, BMW and Shell, such operations are well-documented. In smaller organisations, the activities are less diverse and may include only a few of these operations. This section explains what activities one would expect to find within each type of R&D operation. To help put these activities in context, Figure 10.6 shows how they relate to the product life cycle framework.

Basic research

This activity involves work of a general nature intended to apply to a broad range of uses or to new knowledge about an area. It is also referred to as fundamental science and usually is conducted only in the laboratories of universities and large organisations. Outputs from this activity will result in scientific papers for journals. Some findings will be developed further to produce new technologies. New scientific discoveries, such as antibiotics in the 1940s, belong to this research category.

Curiosity-driven basic research

The case study at the end of Chapter 10 shows the development of genetic fingerprinting. Alec Jeffreys, a British geneticist, along with many other scientific groups, has argued how curiosity-driven research, unfettered by the market, has led to important

Source: Trinity Mirror/Mirrorpix/Alamy Images

developments in the interest of society, such as his genetic fingerprinting. Albert Einstein probably sums this up best with his famous quote: 'I have no special talents. I am only passionately curious.' The important point here, of course, is that the model of innovation being advocated is science-focused with virtually no concern for the market. Whereas applied research is full of directions, priorities and time frames. Alec Jeffreys argues such an approach tends to direct scientists towards establishing and solving obvious problems. But, as far as the firm is concerned, the research must deliver a return for the shareholders and this usually will involve a need for new products and new services.

Applied research

This activity involves the use of existing scientific principles for the solution of a particular problem. It is sometimes referred to as the application of science. It may lead to new technologies and include the development of patents. It is from this activity that many new products emerge. This form of research typically is conducted by large companies and university departments. The development of the Dyson vacuum cleaner involved applying the science of centrifugal forces first explained by Newton. Centrifugal forces spin dirt out of the air stream in two stages (or cyclones), with air speeds of up to 924 miles an hour. This technology led to the development of several patents.

Development

This activity is similar to applied research in that it involves the use of known scientific principles, but differs in that the activities centre on products. Usually, the activity will involve overcoming a technical problem associated with a new product. It may also involve various exploratory studies to try to improve a product's performance. To continue with the Dyson vacuum cleaner example, the prototype product underwent many modifications and enhancements before a commercial product finally was developed. For example, the company has launched a cylinder model to complement its upright model.

Technical service

Technical service focuses on providing a service to existing products and processes. Frequently, this involves cost and performance improvements to existing products, processes or systems. For example, in the bulk chemical industry it means ensuring that production processes are functioning effectively and efficiently. This category of R&D activity also would include design changes to products to lower the manufacturing costs. For Dyson Appliances, extensive efforts will be employed in this area to reduce the cost of manufacturing its vacuum cleaner, leading to increased profit margins for the company.

R&D management and its link with business strategy

Planning decisions are directed towards the future, which is why strategy often is considered to be as much an art as a science. Predicting the future is extremely difficult and there are many factors to consider: economic, social, political, technological, natural disasters, etc. The R&D function also has to make some assessment of the future in order to perform effectively. Thus, senior R&D managers have to build into their planning process a conscious view of the future. However imprecise, this will include:

- environmental forecasts;
- comparative technological cost-effectiveness;
- risk; and
- capability analysis.

Environmental forecasts

These are, primarily, concerned with changes in technology that will occur in the future. But this cannot be considered in isolation and other factors, such as economic, social and political factors, also have to be considered.

- Who will be our competitors in 5 or 10 years' time?
- What technologies do we need to understand to avoid technological surprises?
- What will be the new competitive technologies and businesses?

Comparative technological cost-effectiveness

It is argued that technologies have life cycles and that, after a period, further research produces negligible benefit. When this stage is reached, a new branch of technology is likely to offer far more promising rewards. This may require a significant shift in resources. Today, for example, many car manufacturers are increasing their research efforts in electrical power technology.

Risk

The culture of the organisation and its attitude to risk will influence decision making. Usually, risk is spread over a portfolio of projects and will include some exploratory high-risk projects and some developmental low-risk ones. Planning cannot remove risk, but it can help to ensure that decisions are reached using a process of rational analysis.

Capability analysis

It is fairly obvious to state, but companies have to consider their own strengths and weaknesses. This analysis should help them ensure that they have the necessary capabilities for the future.

Integration of R&D

The management of research and development needs to be fully integrated with the strategic management process of the business. This will enhance and support the products that marketing and sales offer and provide the company with a technical body of knowledge that can be used for future development. Too many businesses fail to integrate the management of research and technology fully into the overall business strategy process (Adler et al., 1992). A report by the European Industrial Research Management Association (EIRMA, 1985) recognises R&D as having three distinct areas, each requiring investment: R&D for existing businesses, R&D for new businesses and R&D for exploratory research (see Figure 9.4).

These three strategic areas can be broken down into operational activities.

Defend, support and expand existing businesses

The defence of existing businesses essentially means maintaining a business's current position, that is keeping up with the competition and ensuring that products do not become outdated and ensuring that existing products can compete. For example, the newspaper industry has seen numerous technological changes dramatically alter the way it produces newspapers. In particular, the introduction of desktop publishing and other related computer software has provided increased flexibility in manufacturing operations as well as reducing production costs.

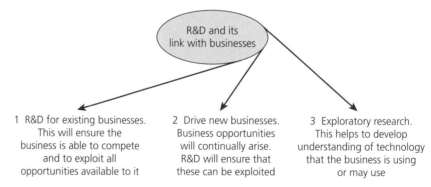

Figure 9.4 The strategic role of R&D as viewed by the business

Source: EIRMA (1985) 'Evaluation of R&D output: working group report, 29', European Industrial Research Management Association, Paris; Roussel, P.A., Saad, K.N. and Erickson, T.S. (1991) *Third Generation R&D*, Harvard Business School Press, Boston, MA.

Drive new businesses

Either through identification of market opportunities or development of technology, new business opportunities will be presented continually to managers. Sometimes, the best decision is to continue with current activities. However, there will be times when a business takes the decision to start a new business. This may be an extension of existing business activities, but sometimes it may be for a totally new product. For example, Motorola initially was a microprocessor manufacturer and it was able to use this technology to develop new businesses, such as mobile handsets.

Broaden and deepen technological capability

The third area is more medium- to long-term strategy. It involves the continual accumulation of knowledge, not only in highly specialised areas where the company is currently operating, but also in areas that may prove to be of importance to the business in the future. For example, Microsoft initially concentrated its efforts on computer-programming technologies. The company now requires knowledge in a wide variety of technologies, including telecommunications, media (music, film and television), sound technology, etc.

Strategic pressures on R&D

The R&D process has changed over the years, moving from a technology-centred model to a more interaction-focused view (Nobelius, 2004). Nobelius describes the R&D process and the five generations it has been through (see Table 9.3).

In technology-intensive industries, much of the technological resources consumed by a particular business are in the form of engineering and development (often called

Table 9.3 Description of five generations of the R&D process

R&D generations	Context	Process characteristics
First generation	Black hole demand (1950 to mid-1960s)	*R&D as ivory tower*, technology-push oriented, seen as an overhead cost, having little or no interaction with the rest of the company or overall strategy. Focus on scientific breakthroughs.
Second generation	Market shares battle (mid-1960s to early 1970s)	*R&D as business*, market-pull oriented, and strategy-driven from the business side, all under the umbrella of project management and the internal customer concept.
Third generation	Rationalisation efforts (mid-1970s to mid-1980s)	*R&D as portfolio*, moving away from individual projects view, and with linkages to both business and corporate strategies. Risk-reward and similar methods guide the overall investments.
Fourth generation	Time-based struggle (early 1980s to mid-1990s)	*R&D as integrative activity*, learning from and with customers, moving away from a product focus to a total concept focus, where activities are conducted in parallel by cross-functional teams.
Filth generation	Systems integration (mid-1990s onward)	*R&D as network*, focusing on collaboration within a wider system – involving competitors, suppliers, distributors, etc. The ability to control product development speed is imperative, separating R from D.

Source: Nobelius, D. (2004) Towards the sixth generation of R&D management, *International Journal of Project Management*, vol. 22, 369–75.

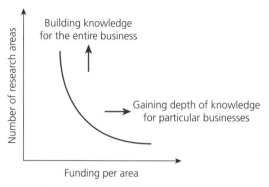

Figure 9.5 Strategic pressures on R&D

Source: Adapted from Mitchell, G.R. (1988) 'Options for the strategic management of technology', UNESCO Technology Management, Interscience Enterprises Ltd, Geneva.

technical service). These resources can be spread over a wide range of technical activities and technologies. In addition, a firm will have a number of specific areas of technology in which it concentrates resources and builds a technological competence. As one would expect, there is a significant difference between possessing general technical service skills and possessing scientific competence in a particular area. The building and development of technological knowledge competencies take time and demand a large amount of research activity.

There is a trade-off between concentrating resources in the pursuit of a strategic knowledge competence and spreading them over a wider area to allow for the building of a general knowledge base. Figure 9.5 shows the demands on technical resources. The growth of scientific and technological areas of interest to the firm (in particular the research department) pressurises research management to fund a wider number of areas, represented by the upward curve. The need for strategic positioning forces the decision to focus resources and build strategic knowledge competencies, represented by the downward curve. In practice, most businesses settle for an uneasy balance between the two sets of pressures.

The technology portfolio

From an R&D perspective, the company's technology base can be categorised as follows:

- core technologies;
- complementary technologies;
- peripheral technologies; and
- emerging technologies.

Core technologies

The core technology usually is central to all or most of the company's products. Expertise in this area also may dominate the laboratories of the R&D department as well as strategic thinking. For example, in the photocopying industry, photographic technologies are core.

Complementary technologies

Complementary technologies are additional technology that is essential in product development. For example, microprocessors are becoming essential in many products and industries. For the photocopying industry, there are several complementary technologies, including microprocessor technology and paper-handling technology, which enables the lifting, turning, folding and stapling of paper.

Peripheral technologies

Peripheral technology is defined as technology that is not necessarily incorporated into the product but whose application contributes to the business. Computer software often falls into this category. The photocopying industry increasingly is using software to add features and benefits to its products, such as security.

Emerging technologies

These are new to the company but may have a long-term significance for its products. In the photocopying industry, telecommunications technologies may soon be incorporated as standard features of the product.

Innovation in action

The fastest growing exports sales of 2014 from 80-year-old technology

Cobalt Light Systems was ranked number 1 in *The Sunday Times* SME Export Track. This lists SMEs with export sales. The business was formed in 2008. The technology was developed at the Rutherford Appleton Laboratory (RAL) in the UK. Cobalt's Chief Scientific Officer developed the laser technology that identifies the chemical composition of materials in sealed and opaque packages. The technology comes from basic scientific principles, which are 80 years old: Raman spectroscopy. When a beam of light hits a material, a small number of photons interact with its molecules and either gain or lose energy – the Raman effect. Every material produces slightly different energy changes, so by measuring this 'scattering' effect it is possible to identify the substance being tested.

Source: Keypix/Alamy Images

→

Initially, the firm was unsure how to use the technology, but it soon came across a need in the form of airport security. This technology enables airports to scan the contents of drinks bottles, etc. The firm has sold its technology to Amsterdam Airport Schiphol, Paris Charles de Gaulle Airport and others.

Source: *The Sunday Times* SME Export Track, 17 May 2015.

The difficulty of managing capital-intensive production plants in a dynamic environment

Many manufacturing operations involve the careful management of multi-million-pound production plants. Such businesses have a slightly different set of factors to consider than a company operating the manufacturing plant for, say, shoes, which is labour- rather than technology-intensive. Hundreds of millions of pounds are invested in a new chemical plant and options open to it, in terms of changes in products, are limited. This is because a production plant is built to produce one chemical product. Moreover, the scrapping of an existing plant and the building of a new one may cost in excess of £300 million. There are few companies in the world that continually could build, scrap and rebuild chemical plants in response to the demands of the market and make a profit from such actions. Hence, companies operating process plants cannot respond *completely* to market needs.

This particular dilemma faced by companies with large investments in production technology is overlooked frequently by those far removed from the production floor. Young marketing graduates may feel that a company should be able to halt production of one product in order to switch to the production of another offering better prospects. The effect of such a decision may be to bankrupt the company! The chemical industry increasingly is developing smaller, more flexible plants rather than the large, single-purpose plants that have been common since the turn of the twentieth century.

In some industries where investment lies less in the technology and more in the human resources, changes to a production plant are possible.

Pause for thought

With products incorporating technologies from increasingly diverse fields, is it realistic to continue to believe that firms can continue to be world leaders in all these areas? Maybe they can rely on their suppliers to conduct all the necessary R&D?

Which business to support and how?

It is well understood that technological developments can lead to improved products and processes, reduced costs and, ultimately, better commercial performance and competitive advantage. The ability to capitalise on technological developments and profit from the business opportunities that may, subsequently, arise requires a business to be in an appropriate strategic position. That is, it must possess the capability to understand and use the technological developments to its own advantage.

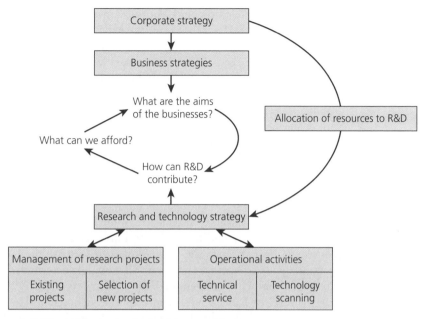

Figure 9.6 The R&D strategic decision-making process

This requires some form of anticipation of future technological developments and also strategic business planning. Technological forecasting and planning are fraught with uncertainty. Figure 9.6 illustrates the iterative and continual process involved in the management of research and technology.

The effect of corporate strategy usually is most noticeable in the selection of R&D projects. For example, a corporate decision by Unilever to strengthen its position in the luxury perfume business may lead to the cancellation of several research projects, with more emphasis being placed on buying brands like Calvin Klein. Ideally, a system is required that links R&D decision making with corporate strategy decision making. However, it is common in R&D departments to make decisions on a project-by-project basis in which individual projects are assessed on their own merits, independent of the organisation. This is partly because the expertise required is concentrated in the R&D department and partly due to scientists' fascination with science itself. This used to be the case in many large organisations with centralised laboratories. Such a decision-making process, however, is valid only when funds are unlimited and this is rarely the case. In practice, funds are restricted and projects compete with each other for continued funding for future years. Not all projects can receive funding and, in industrial R&D laboratories, projects are cancelled week after week, frequently to the annoyance of those involved.

The flow diagram in Figure 9.6 highlights the need for integration of corporate and R&D strategy. The process of corporate planning involves the systematic examination of a wide variety of factors. The aim is to produce a statement of company objectives and how they are to be achieved. Essentially, a number of questions need to be considered:

- What might the company do?
- What can the company do?
- What should the company do?

This leads to the development of business strategies. At the base of the diagram are the inputs from R&D activities, in particular existing R&D projects and potential projects that may be selected for funding. The organisation must ask itself repeatedly: what are the needs of the businesses? What should R&D be doing? What can R&D do? This process is neither a bottom–up nor a top–down process. What is required is continual dialogue between senior management and R&D management.

While it is tempting to say that technology influences the competitive performance of all businesses, in reality some businesses are more heavily influenced than others. In many mature and established industries, the cost of raw materials is much more of an influence on the competitive performance of the business than are technology developments. For example, the price paid for commodities like coffee, cocoa and sugar can influence profits in many food industries dramatically. Similarly, in the chemical industry, the competitive position of petroleum-based plastics is determined by the price paid for the raw material, oil. Consequently, some businesses, especially those operating in mature industries, would be unable to influence their competitive position through technology alone. Even if the business was to increase the level of R&D investment substantially, its competitive position still would be determined by raw material prices.

Several attempts have been made by industry to quantify this factor when considering the level of R&D investment required. Scholefield (1993) developed a model using the concept of **technology leverage**. This is the extent of influence that a business's technology and technology base has on its competitive position. In general, technology leverage will be low when the influence of raw material and distribution costs and economic growth is high. High-volume, bulk commodity products would fall within this scenario.

Technology leverage and R&D strategies

The state of a business in terms of its markets, products and capabilities will determine largely the amount of research effort to be undertaken. Research by Scholefield (1993) suggests that there are, essentially, two forms of activity for a R&D department, growth and maintenance. Within these two groups, it is possible to conduct significantly different types of activity. Hence, these categories can be subdivided into the four groups depicted in Figure 9.7.

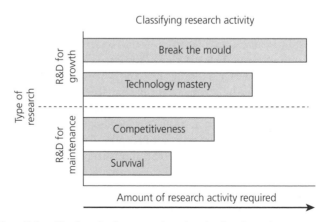

Figure 9.7 Classifying the level of research using technology leverage

A business's expenditure on research activity normally would be reviewed annually or quarterly. The model is used as a guide to establish whether a business's research activity is appropriate for its position. Experience has shown that, without such a guide, research activity can drift over time, resulting in too much or too little activity appropriate for the business. The model provides the facility for business and research managers to monitor research activity. In practice, this involves continual analysis, adjustment and realignment. For example, each quarter, a business's executive would meet and discuss quarterly results. During these meetings, its strategic position could be reclassified, according to performance and external environmental factors. That is, a business's category may change from, say, 3 to 4 or from 2 to 1.

Survival

This type of activity is conducted if the decision has been made to exit the business. In such circumstances, the role of the R&D department is to ensure its interim survival against technological mishaps to process or product. This would be a reactive problem-solving role and may be termed 'survival research'.

Competitive

If the intention is to sustain the business, then the role of research is to maintain the relative competitive technological position by making improvements to both product and process. For example, in the automotive industry, most manufacturers have invested heavily in their own processes and vehicle build-qualities have improved dramatically; so much so, that reliability, although still improving, is almost taken for granted by car buyers. The process technologies involved have become widely accepted and used. However, if any one manufacturer allowed its process technologies to fall behind those of its competitors, it would, almost certainly, provide an advantage to them. The amount of research activity required to maintain a high-technology leverage position, however, will be significantly greater than that required to maintain a low-technology leverage position. Thus, it seems reasonable to split this category in two: competitive (low-technology leverage) and competitive (high-technology leverage).

Technology mastery

Incremental growth of a business in a strong position involves improving the product and process relative to the competition. This clearly will involve a level of research activity greater than the competitive position outlined above. It will involve keeping abreast of all technological developments that may affect the business's products or processes. Hence, a much higher level of R&D expenditure will be required.

Break the mould

If the aim is to create a technological advantage, then a much higher order of novelty and creativity is required. Following such a strategy will involve developing new patentable technology and may involve a higher level of basic scientific research.

Strengths and limitations of this approach

The model attempts to introduce some theory into what is often an arbitrary competition for research activity. It provides a framework within which discussions may take place. In practice, the model is used to check decisions made by research and business managers, as opposed to being used for dictating decisions. In addition, it includes a technological perspective for classifying a business's strategic position. Many strategic management tools, whilst paying lip service to the importance of technology, fail to accommodate a technological perspective in the decision-making process. There is an over-emphasis on the financial or marketing perspective (Ansoff, 1968; BCG, 1972; Porter, 1985).

It also shows how the role of strategic technology management and a business's selected growth strategy can influence the business climate within which managers operate. For example, if a strategic decision is taken to exit a business, this clearly will have a profound influence on the nature of activities. One would expect the activities of a business operating in a climate of growth to be different from those of one operating in a climate of decline.

Allocation of funds to R&D

Unlike many other business activities, successful R&D cannot be managed on an annual budgetary basis. It requires a much longer-term approach, enabling knowledge to be acquired and built up over time. Often, this leads to tensions with other functions that are planning projects and activities. Nonetheless, as was explained earlier in this chapter, R&D has to be linked to the business strategy.

It is unusual for unlimited funds to be available, hence business functions usually compete with other departments for funds. Marketing will, no doubt, present a very good case why extra money should be spent on new marketing campaigns; the IT department will request more funds for more equipment and valuable training for everyone; and the sales department will, almost certainly, ask for more salespeople to boost sales. It is a difficult circle to square. A great deal depends on the culture of the organisation and the industry within which it is operating (see Chapters 4 and 7). 3M, for example, spends proportionally large sums on R&D, many say too much, especially when one considers its more recent performance (see the case study at the end of Chapter 17). Other companies spend very little on R&D but huge amounts on sales and marketing. This is the case for the financial services industry. So, one of the most difficult decisions facing senior management is how much to spend on R&D. Many companies now report R&D expenditure in their annual reports. However, whilst it is now relatively easy to establish, for example, that Volkswagen spent 6 per cent of sales on R&D in 2014, exactly how the company arrived at this figure is less clear.

Achieving a well-balanced innovation portfolio is an often advocated goal for R&D managers, but guidelines on how to achieve this are scarce in innovation and management literature. Research by Bauer and Leker (2013) investigated the effects that balancing R&D budget allocation between exploratory and exploitative innovation activities has on new product performance. They found that new product performance is enhanced through the simultaneous pursuit of exploratory and exploitative innovation activities (i.e., they are complementary), which holds true for product and process innovation alike. They also found that, in process innovation, exploration requires more funding to achieve maximum performance when compared to product innovation.

Setting the R&D budget

In practice, establishing the R&D budget for a business is influenced by short-term performance fluctuations and availability of funds, which is, in turn, influenced by the setting of annual budgets. Additionally, budgets are also influenced by the long-term strategic technological needs of the business. It is extremely difficult to establish a basis for the allocation of funds that will be acceptable to all parties. A number of different approaches are used by different companies (see below). In practice, businesses use a combination of these methods. In addition, managerial judgement and negotiation often will play a significant role. The portfolio management approach, outlined earlier in this chapter, enables profits from today's successful businesses to be invested into what the company hopes will become the profitable businesses of tomorrow. Many businesses also invest in basic research. This is research that is perceived to be of interest to the company as a whole and of benefit to the organisation in the long term.

There are several key factors that need to be considered when allocating funds to R&D:

- expenditure by competitors;
- company's long-term growth objectives;
- the need for stability; and
- distortions introduced by large projects.

The following six approaches can be used for allocating funds to R&D.

Inter-firm comparisons

Whilst R&D expenditure varies greatly between industries, within similar industries there is often some similarity. It is possible to establish reasonably accurately a competitor's R&D expenditure, the number of research personnel employed, etc. By analysing the research expenditure of its competitors, a business is able to establish an appropriate figure for its own research effort. Table 9.4 would suggest that a company trying to establish its R&D budget should consider spending between 14 and 17 per cent of sales on R&D.

Table 9.4 Comparison of R&D expenditure within the European pharmaceutical industry

Company	R&D expenditure as % of sales
Roche (Switzerland)	18.6
Astra-Zeneca (UK)	17.2
Novartis (Switzerland)	17.1
Sanofi-Aventis (France)	14.4
GlaxoSmithKline (UK)	13.1

Source: Hernandez et al. (2015), © European Union, 1995–2016.

A fixed relationship to turnover

R&D expenditure can be based on a constant percentage. Turnover normally provides a reasonably stable figure that grows in line with the size of the company. As an example of this method, a company has decided to spend 2 per cent of its annual turnover on R&D. If its turnover is £10 million, then its annual R&D expenditure would be £200,000. A criticism of this method is that it uses past figures for future investments.

A fixed relationship to profits

Fixing R&D expenditure to profits is highly undesirable. It implies that R&D is a luxury that can be afforded only when the company generates profits. This method completely ignores the role of R&D as an investment and the likely future benefits that will follow. Often, in fact, poor profits can be turned around with new products.

Reference to previous levels of expenditure

In the absence of any criteria for measurement, a starting point for discussions is likely to be the previous year's expenditure plus an allowance for inflation. In spite of its crudeness, this method is used often in conjunction with one or more of the other methods, especially during negotiations with other functional managers.

Costing of an agreed programme

An R&D manager is concerned with managing research projects, so the allocation of funds for each individual project may seem attractive. This allows him or her to add together the requirements for certain projects and arrive at a figure. Invariably, the total will exceed what the department is likely to receive. Negotiations are then likely to ensue, focusing on which projects to cut completely or on which to reduce expenditure.

Internal customer–contractor relationship

In some large multinational companies, the individual business units may pay for research carried out on their behalf by the R&D function. In addition, there is usually some provision for building the knowledge base of the whole organisation. For example, each business manager within the German chemical giant, Bayer, manages his or her own R&D budget, but each business must also contribute 10–12 per cent for long-term research. Shell operates a similar programme.

The role of low technology intensive firms and industries in modern economies is complex and frequently misunderstood. This is partly due to Hatzichronoglou's (1997) widely used revision of the OECD classification of sectors and products which only refers to high technology (defined as spending more than five per cent of revenues on research and development). This has contributed to an unfortunate tendency to understate the importance of technological change outside such R&D-intensive fields. Clearly low and medium technology firms do invest in R&D, but less as a percentage of revenues. Significantly, however, they invest in production processes that have impact across the sector. For example, in process industries, development activities take place within a production line or plant environment rather than in at an R&D centre or design office. This means there are no prototypes, rather the plant is run and outputs tested. This is fundamentally different from other industries. It is experimental by nature with emphasis on manipulating the plant to deliver the required outcome. In the food industry suppliers of raw materials are key contributors during the early design and concept creation phases of process development. Indeed, much of the activity is iterative trial-and-error to reduce uncertainty (Frishammar et al., 2013). Furthermore, an orientation toward cost minimisation is particularly apparent in this type of industry where price-based competition is high. This results in an emphasis on minimising costs and improving production efficiency within NPD.

Level of R&D expenditure

Lord Lever's famous quote about advertising expenditure could be applied equally to R&D investment: 'Half the money I spend on advertising is wasted, the problem is I don't know which half.' Scientists and technologists would, rightly, argue that, even if the return on investment is not a profitable product, the investment in knowledge is not wasted. Without getting drawn into a philosophical debate on the acquisition of knowledge, the point is that an evaluation of a financial investment in R&D should be subject to the same criteria as evaluations of other investments made by the organisation. However, herein lies the difficulty. There are many short-term returns from an R&D investment, as was made clear above, but there is also a longer-term return. Often, technological expertise is built up over many years through many consecutive short-term research projects. It is extremely difficult to apportion the profit to all contributing functions from a product developed over a period of several years. There is also considerable merit in the argument that without the R&D investment there would not have been a product at all. This subject has received a great deal of attention over the past four decades (Cordero, 1990; Mansfield et al., 1972; McGrath and Romeri, 1994; Meyer-Krahmer, 1984; Williams, 1969).

The R&D manager is under the same pressures as the senior management team. They have to ensure that the business has opportunities to exploit for future growth. In reality, a few successful projects usually are sufficient to justify the investment.

Virtually all R&D managers are responsible for a portfolio of projects. The aim is to try to select those that will be successful and drop those that will not be. The Viagra case study at the end of this chapter highlights the difficulty of project selection. Sometimes, it is the project least likely to succeed that turns out to be the next Post-it Notes business. One of the most dramatic examples of the high level of uncertainty involved in R&D project evaluations is demonstrated in the Viagra case study below.

Financial forecasts made at the time of R&D project selection are subject to gross errors, either because the development costs turn out to be much higher (rather than lower) or the financial benefits derived from the project are higher or lower than originally forecast. Such forecasts are clearly of limited value. Nonetheless, some form of financial analysis cannot be avoided. It will certainly be demanded by senior management. Analyses that are unrealistic and have no credibility within the organisation are of limited value. This area of decision making is dominated by personal experience and historical case studies that the company has experienced.

A variety of quantitative and qualitative measurements have been developed to try to help business managers tackle the problem of project selection. It remains, however, a combination of uncertain science and experience. Chapter 10 explores how businesses attempt to evaluate R&D projects in terms of whether to continue funding or to drop the project.

The long and difficult 13-year journey to the marketplace for Pfizer's Viagra

Introduction

There are many stories that have emerged over the years concerning Pfizer's product Viagra. Some of these are true, but many are simply fictional stories developed to try to reinforce a particular argument. One of the most common is that Viagra was the result of luck. This case study explores the long 13-year journey from laboratory to the marketplace and looks at some of the key challenges faced by Pfizer; most notably, project evaluation considerations, when the available market research evidence suggests a small market for the product, and product launch considerations, when impotence is such an unpopular topic that it is almost impossible for advertisers to refer to it without alienating the very consumer base they are trying to reach.

What is Viagra?

Pfizer's Viagra is now part of business folklore in terms of an example of a successful new product. Viagra is now one of the most recognised brands in the world; it has become a social icon with annual sales in excess of $1.7 billion in 2012 and $2 billion in 2015. And it has transformed Pfizer from a medium-sized pharmaceutical firm into the world's leader. Yet, Viagra was almost dismissed during clinical trials as interesting, but not clinically or financially significant. It is true that Viagra was something of an accidental discovery. Scientists testing an angina drug found that, as a side effect, it seemed to cure impotence in many patients. It did not take long for Pfizer to decide to focus on its unexpected benefit and to develop the product further as an anti-impotence drug. The drug was licensed by the US FDA (Food and Drugs Administration) and launched in the USA in April 1998, amidst a huge fanfare of serious and not so serious media hype. At the time, many news organisations used attention-grabbing headlines, often stretching the product's capabilities, such as how Viagra could enhance sexual performance. In the first month, 570,000 new prescriptions for Viagra were issued, generating $100 million in revenue. One aspect of the story that frequently seems to get highlighted is that this product was due to serendipity or luck. Whilst this may be true for a very small part of the story, as this case shows, the vast majority of the product's success was due to effective management, excellent research and development and very clever marketing.

Unfortunately, the serendipity aspect of the Viagra case overshadows the ground-breaking science involved (the Nobel Prize for physiology was awarded to scientists involved in the related research for Viagra) and the effective management by Pfizer of the new product development process. Moreover, this story reinforces in the minds of the public that science and research are dependent on luck. This is misleading at best and, at worst, dangerous. According to some journalists, Viagra owes its existence to serendipity. They argue it started its life as a potential treatment for angina and was being tested in clinical trials. As an angina treatment, it was pretty useless, but then the researchers began to get reports of some unexpected side effects and, hence, Viagra was born. This, of course, is not only incomplete but is misleading. Of course, it would be naive to think that the complexities of scientific research will always be relayed accurately to a mass audience but, for medicine and science to be portrayed as scientists playing around in the laboratories in the hope that something will drop from their test tubes, is, quite simply, untrue. If science is not careful, Viagra will end up like the discovery of penicillin and, therefore, antibiotics: that it was all down to luck. Few people realise that, whilst Alexander Fleming discovered penicillin in 1928, it took another *20 years* for scientists Howard Florey and Ernst Chain to develop a method of producing a product that could be used by patients for treatment in the form of antibiotics that we know today.

The true story of Viagra is more complex and illustrates that the research project team had to fight hard for the huge investment that was required to develop the compound into a product. Indeed, it was almost not developed at all. Gill Samuels was director of science policy at the Pfizer Central Research Site, Sandwich, Kent, and was one of the key developers of Viagra. She was awarded a CBE for services to bioscience in the Queen's 2002 birthday honours list. She recalls some of the problems:

Even in the early stages when it was known that we were doing trials in the UK we had patients writing in wanting to participate, and we have had some wonderful letters from patients who participated in those trials. Even before Viagra was launched in the US [in April 1998] we realised that it had a very profound effect. The question was how many of those men who did have erectile dysfunction would actually want to receive treatment for it? It was very, very difficult to predict the absolute numbers. There is no doubt about it that the media interest in Viagra raised the awareness of erectile dysfunction, and probably encouraged men who had the problem, but did nothing about it, to contact their doctor.

(BBC.co.uk, 2006)

From angina to Viagra

To develop this one successful medicine, scientists screened over 1,500 compounds and spent an estimated £600 million (at today's prices). Furthermore, it took 13 years (1985–98) to bring Viagra from conception to production. This level of investment is sometimes needed for research, development and to prove that the new medicine is safe and effective. Table 9.5 illustrates the stages from initial concept to final product.

Viagra started life as a medicine intended to treat angina pectoris. Alfred Nobel – an explosives manufacturer from Norway – suffered from angina (angina is defined as brief attacks of chest pain due to insufficient oxygenation of heart muscles). In 1890, he was prescribed nitro-glycerine (called *trinitrin*) to relieve the pain of angina attacks. It is still used today. Over 100 years later, the work of Robert Furchgott, Louis Ignarro and Ferid Murad showed that nitric oxide (NO) was an important signalling molecule in the cardiovascular system. It is released from nerve endings and cells lining the walls of blood vessels. The effect is to make the blood vessel relax or dilate. It is also involved in the prevention of blood clots. In 1998,

they received the Nobel Prize for Physiology. The Nobel Prizes were set up by the same Alfred Nobel who had been treated with nitro-glycerine. Building on this knowledge, research by other groups is being undertaken to develop new medicines that moderate the actions of nitric oxide for the treatment of cardiovascular and other disorders (Pfizer, 2005).

Dilating arteries

Researchers started by trying to understand the process of vasodilation (what makes the arteries dilate). They decided to target the action of the new medicine on to the enzyme PDE (*Phosphodiesterase*). This enzyme breaks down the signalling molecule cGMP, which causes vasodilation. By preventing the breakdown of cGMP, the new medicine would increase vasodilation. Enzymes have a very specific shape. Viagra fits into the active site and blocks it. This prevents the PDE from breaking down the cGMP, which then stays in the blood and continues to cause vasodilation. The first step to developing the new medicine was to isolate and characterise the PDE enzyme (later called PDE-5). Once the PDE had been isolated, researchers could use it to find out the optimum conditions in which it works and also do tests to find efficient inhibitors. This enables molecules to be modified and designed to affect the enzyme.

Clinical trials

In 1991, following six years of laboratory research, a clinical trial was undertaken in Wales for a compound known as UK-92.480. The findings from the trial on healthy volunteers revealed disappointing results. The data on blood pressure, heart rate and blood flow were discouraging. The R&D project was in trouble. Some patients reported side effects of episodes of indigestion, some of aches in legs and some reported penile erections. This final point was listed merely as an observation by the clinicians involved in the study, at that moment no one said 'wow' or 'great'. Indeed, the decision to undertake trials into erectile dysfunction was not an obvious one. This was partly because the prevailing view at the time was that most erectile dysfunction was psychological and not treatable with drugs. Few people believed it was possible to produce an erection with an injection of drugs. Men, particularly older men who are more likely to suffer from impotence, were treated as if it

$\rightarrow$

Table 9.5 The main stages in the development of Viagra

1985	Initial concept	In 1985, scientists at Pfizer decided to develop a medicine to treat heart failure and hypertension. They were looking for a medicine that would vasodilate, or 'open', arteries, lower blood pressure and reduce strain on the heart. They chose to target the medicine to act on an enzyme found in the wall of blood vessels.
1986–90	Research and development starts	Between 1986 and 1990, hundreds of possible medicines were synthesised and tested in laboratory experiments. The most promising compound was given the code name UK-92.480. It showed properties that suggested it would be a good medicine to treat angina. Research was redirected to look at this heart disorder. The medicine was later called Sildenafil and finally renamed Viagra (Sildenafil citrate).
1991	Volunteer trials	In 1991, healthy volunteers took part in clinical trials to test the safety of Viagra and how the body metabolised the compound. These showed that it was safe. In trials over 10 days, the healthy volunteers reported some unexpected side effects. Male volunteers reported more frequent erections after taking the angina medicine!
1992	Erectile dysfunction	Following the unusual side effects seen in the volunteer trials, researchers switched to looking into using Viagra to treat erectile dysfunction (ED). This serious condition causes psychological and emotional problems that affect many families. Research into using Viagra to treat angina continued but the medicine did not prove powerful enough to be really useful.
1993–6	ED clinical trials start	'Double-blind, placebo controlled' clinical trials started in 1993 to test how well Viagra treated patients with erectile dysfunction. To make the trials a fair test, neither the patients nor their doctors knew if they were receiving the medicine or an inactive placebo. Viagra proved to be a great success.
1997	Licence application	All medicines need to be licensed by the medical authorities before they can be prescribed by doctors. To achieve this, trials must show it is safe and effective. Approval usually takes about 12 months but in the case of Viagra it received its licence in only 6 months.
1998	Licence approval	Viagra was given a licence. It could be used in the treatment of erectile dysfunction in 1998. In its first three months, there were 2.9 million prescriptions for the medicine.

Source: Pfizer.com.

was their fault, that it was all in the mind and that they should try to accept their sex life was more or less over.

In any large research laboratory, there will be hundreds and, sometimes, thousands of research projects being undertaken at any one time. Each project has to give regular reports on progress to senior R&D managers, who continually have to decide with which projects to continue investment and which to stop and which new projects to start. In 1991, the leader for the Viagra project had to report on progress and the results were disappointing. Essentially, the medicine was not effective in treating angina. The senior R&D managers were preparing to drop the angina R&D project due to its disappointing results. It was also considering dropping all studies on the compound, even as a possible drug for erectile dysfunction. This was partly because it was not clear that it would have a clinical use. Not all the healthy volunteers had reported erections. Moreover, how would Pfizer be able to conduct trials for such a condition? Furthermore, the market for such a drug was not clear. At that time, survey results revealed only 1 in 20 million men suffered from erectile dysfunction; hence, even if a medicine could be developed, the market would be very small. The R&D team involved in the project eventually managed to gain two years of funding to develop the drug and undertake clinical trials.

One needs to be aware that, at the time, Pfizer had many drugs under consideration for the treatment of many other conditions, such as colonic cancer, diabetes, asthma, etc. These markets were well-known and understood. The business case for all of these projects and others could be made easily. Accurate predictions could be made on the number of people who suffered from asthma and what customers would be willing to pay for such drugs. It was not possible to draw up an accurate business case for Viagra due to the uncertainties of the market and the condition. There simply was not a similar drug on the market with which to make a comparison. This made it an even more difficult decision for R&D managers at Pfizer. Fortunately, in 1992 the go ahead was given to provide funds for the continuation of clinical trials into erectile dysfunction (ED). But another problem now faced the team: how to conduct clinical trials in this very sensitive area. Would the team be able to find people willing to participate and discuss their experiences? Fortunately, the team did not experience any major difficulty in recruiting volunteers. Whilst it was true that large parts of the population did not feel comfortable in participating, sufficient numbers of people were willing to take part, not least those suffering from ED. The pharmaceutical industry is aware that, despite advances in technology and scientific know-how, the odds of a drug candidate's success has not shifted in the past 20 years. Of 12 molecules that Pfizer classes to be its best bets – those drugs that have made it to the verge of clinical testing – only 1 will make it to market (Michaels, 2001).

Product and market evaluation: decision time!

In 1996, following successful clinical trials, the clinical success of the drug and obtaining patent protection did not seem to be in doubt, but that alone is not enough to proceed with the huge investment required to take the drug to market. Major uncertainties remained, especially with the business case:

- What is the size of the market? How many people suffer from ED?
- Could the market be bigger?
- Can we make the market bigger?
- The market for ED is not developed; can it be developed and how?
- Is it a growing market?
- Is there an existing customer base (i.e. current sufferers)?

- Is the potential big enough to warrant the investment?
- Does it support our short-term and long-term plans for the business?

We sometimes need reminding that virtually all businesses are established to make a profit for their investors; hence, most decisions centre on finance. What is the investment and what is the likely return? This decision was no exception. The business case for Viagra certainly was interesting but there were many risks, not least would the product sell and how would Pfizer be able to market the product to a public that, in the USA, at least, was known to be conservative and prudish about talking about impotence and sex? The likelihood of a television commercial going out at 8 pm on ABC or NBC promoting the virtues of Viagra in overcoming impotence was simply unimaginable in the mid-1990s. Hence, there were risks in terms of the size of the market and, even if the market proved to be as big as Pfizer hoped, how would it be able to communicate with this market and promote the product?

Is there a viable marketing plan?

The drug cannot be purchased over the counter; hence men would have to get a prescription from their physician. The challenge for Pfizer, then, was to encourage men to go to their doctor and ask for treatment. This poses a significant challenge. The marketing campaign would need to focus on education and raising awareness of the condition. Impotence, however, is such an unpopular topic that it is almost impossible for advertisers to refer to it without alienating the very consumer base they are trying to reach. The audience would need reprogramming. Whilst sex sells, it was important to numb the audience and society with educating material: an audience made up of sensitive males with problems that are often highlighted as the butt of many jokes. The consumer had to be reprogrammed to look at the situation in a new light. In order to do this, a large amount of money had to be there for the product launch and the subsequent advertising that ties to it.

After much debate and discussion, Pfizer decided to attempt to create a sense of pride in the consumer through the opposite sex's testimonials of newly found happiness and through mainstream sports stars that epitomise the definition of manliness. The Viagra ads eventually selected by Pfizer tried to break

→

through men's reluctance to address the issue by using celebrity spokesmen who embody respectability (politician Bob Dole); athleticism (NASCAR driver Mark Martin, Brazilian footballer Pele and Texas Rangers baseball player Rafael Palmeiro); and virility (Hugh Hefner). Altogether, Pfizer spent more than $100 million on endorsements, television advertising, online marketing and sports event sponsorship. The celebrities encouraged men to fix the problem – as they would fix a headache with Aspirin. The campaign earned Viagra brand-name recognition approaching that of Coca-Cola and has led to a saturation of Viagra jokes and spam emails.

Some analysts argue Pfizer made a critical error by selecting Bob Dole as its advertising spokesperson. Dole, in his 70s, was clearly the market for Viagra, but he was not the target. The target is the 50-year-old married man who is having trouble, but is terrified of asking his doctor. Positioning the product for older men tells younger men that Viagra was not for them. Viagra would have been wiser choosing younger, more macho-looking men to help remove the stigma of ED and make younger men feel more comfortable talking about the problem and product. Today, you do see much younger male models in the Viagra ads.

Launch

At the launch, the priority for Pfizer was to retain control over the brand image, ensuring that it was positioned as Pfizer wanted it to be and that accurate information was given to the public. A campaign estimated to be costing tens of millions of dollars on consumer-orientated advertising in popular magazines, such as *Time*, *Life* and *Newsweek*, was undertaken. The enormous level of pre-launch publicity that Viagra had generated was not, necessarily, a good thing. The publicity was out of Pfizer's control, meaning that it could be inaccurate and/or damaging to the brand image. The thousands of jokes made about the brand could well have had a negative effect, making patients embarrassed about owning up to an impotence problem and asking for the drug. Pfizer waited until the worst of the publicity had died down before launching its campaign to make sure that its message was heard properly and that the drug was taken more seriously. This, along with all the media hype, had led to a rapid take-up after its introduction.

Source: Pearson Education Ltd/Photodisc.

Sales continued to grow as the product was launched progressively on worldwide markets. In 1998, total sales had reached $776 million, $1,016 million by 1999 and $1,344 million by 2000, representing over 5 per cent of human drug sales for Pfizer. The 2000 Annual Report proclaimed that more than 300 million Viagra tablets had been prescribed for more than 10 million men in more than 100 countries: Viagra had become a worldwide brand in a very short period of time.

All the US publicity was heard in Europe and made the European market a little more difficult to enter. When Viagra eventually was licensed in Europe late in 1998, the UK health minister pronounced that Viagra would not be made available on the National Health Service (NHS). This had a lot to do with NHS priorities: impotence is not high on the list, apparently, and there were fears about the cost to the NHS if all the hype produced the same sort of level of demand as in the USA. There were fears that it would cost the NHS £1 billion per year if it was available on demand. Although some relaxation has subsequently taken place, and doctors are allowed more say in prescribing the drug, it is still not readily available on prescription. Impotence in itself is not enough for free treatment – it must be caused by specific medical conditions, such as diabetes.

Viagra's advertising campaigns were never the key to its success, however. Because of its unique clinical function, Viagra became an immediate cultural point for all issues relating to virility, male sexuality and aging, and through this continual popular referencing, much more than the effects of its $100 million advertising budget, Viagra has achieved a level of brand recognition that is reserved only for superstar drugs like Tylenol and Prozac. Indeed, Viagra continues to be a constant source of office jokes and comments for late night talk show hosts. More than simply spreading the word on what Viagra is, the enormous street and media buzz that Viagra has inspired has established Viagra's image overwhelmingly in terms of power and efficacy as the remedy for impotence.

Competition

The greatest challenge to Viagra came when Pfizer lost some of its patent protection. The main, or active, ingredient in Viagra is sildenafil, and potential competitors Eli Lilly and Icos Corporation challenged the legitimacy of the original patent issued in 1993. The court ruled that the knowledge on which it had been based was already in the public domain in 1993 and that the patent was now restricting research by other companies. Other companies would now be able to sell drugs that treat impotence by blocking PDE-5, a chemical, although Pfizer retains a patent on the active ingredient in Viagra – meaning that direct copies of the drug itself will not be permitted. In January 2002, the Court of Appeal (UK) had agreed with an earlier High Court ruling that knowledge covered by the Pfizer patent on the 'PDE-5 inhibitor' was already in the public domain. Similarly, in 2004, Pfizer faced increased competition in China after Beijing overturned its domestic patent for the main ingredient in Viagra. Although the molecular structure of Viagra was still protected, the main active ingredient was now open to competitors. The first serious challenge came from Uprima after it received its European licence in 2001. Its makers, Abbott Laboratories, based in Illinois, USA, claimed it worked more quickly than Viagra, with fewer side effects and cost less than £5 for both low and high dosage tablets. Quick action can help spontaneity, unlike Viagra, which has to be taken at least an hour before sex.

Pfizer continued with its legal battles as it attempted to prevent competitors copying key elements of the drug. GlaxoSmithKline, the Anglo-American group, and its German partner Bayer were relying on Vardenafil to revive their flagging share prices (Firn and Tait, 2002). Critics argued that Pfizer's goal was simply to delay competitive entry for Viagra as long as possible and, if the patent actu-

ally were to stick, that simply would be additional profits.

In 2003, the competition for Viagra increased noticeably when Viagra came third in the first independent comparison with its two new competitors. According to the research, 45 per cent of the 150 men involved in the trial preferred Eli Lilly's Cialis, while 30 per cent voted for Levitra, jointly marketed by GlaxoSmithKline and Bayer. The findings are likely to play an important part in the fierce marketing battle between the four pharmaceutical groups over treatments for impotence. Pfizer said the research was not scientifically rigorous (Dyer, 2003).

The challenge for the competitors is different from that faced by Pfizer. Viagra is already a well-known remedy for impotence in the popular imagination; alternative drugs are fighting an uphill battle against the power of the Viagra brand. The marketing challenge that faced the makers of Cialis and Levitra is that they would have to re-establish the problem of impotence – a problem that many consumers see as already having been solved by Viagra – in order to offer their products as a cure. But, because Viagra already exists, Levitra and Cialis would have to rely on advertising to increase their market share and, since ED appears to be a distasteful topic, advertisers decided to concentrate on enhancing ED's image, rather than its products' image. Cialis differentiates itself from both Viagra and Levitra by offering a 36-hour window of efficacy. This beats Viagra's and Levitra's four- to eight-hour period and allows Cialis to focus its advertising on timing rather than performance. All three advertising campaigns ultimately suggest the discomfort, shame, embarrassment and fear that surround sex in general, and the lack of any compassionate, humane, truthful discourse on sexual dysfunctions in our culture. Sex appears as a paranoid game where invisible spectators cheer winners and boo losers.

Conclusions

By virtually all measures, this product has been universally successful for Pfizer, transforming it from a large pharmaceutical firm into the world's leading pharmaceutical firm. The actual market for this type of drug is now known to be far greater than the original market research data had revealed. This is a cautionary tale of the need sometimes to encourage innovation and support scientific freedom in the face of evidence to stop the project.

Viagra was the first-mover and first-prover in this category. However, Viagra has not been quick to respond to competitive scientific advancements in erectile dysfunction drugs. It takes Viagra anywhere from 30 minutes to an hour to work but Levitra, launched in 2001, improves upon that by working in 16 minutes. And Cialis, also launched in 2001, improves upon Levitra by being able to last up to 36 hours. Indeed, competitors argue Pfizer has already conceded defeat by introducing a loyalty programme, which they argue is not about building a long-term relationship with their patients, as Pfizer's marketing director says. Rather, they see it as a scheme by Pfizer to get the most out of the Viagra brand and it will continue to lose market share to better, more effective options from Levitra and Cialis. The erectile dysfunction market grew 3.5 per cent from 2003 to be worth $1.95 billion in 2005 and is almost entirely composed of sales from the three brands: Viagra (sildenafil), Cialis (tadalafil) and Levitra (vardenafil). Table 9.6 reveals the continued dominance of Viagra.

One aspect of this case study that is seldom discussed is the extent to which Pfizer has benefited from raising disease awareness. A lot of money can be made from healthy people who believe they are sick. Pharmaceutical companies are able to sponsor diseases and promote them to prescribers and consumers, a practice sometimes known as 'disease mongering' (i.e. widening the boundaries of treatable illness in order to expand markets for those who sell and deliver treatments). Within many disease categories, informal alliances have emerged, comprising drug company staff, doctors and consumer groups. Ostensibly engaged in raising public awareness about under-diagnosed and under-treated problems, these alliances tend to promote a view of their particular condition as widespread, serious and treatable.

Table 9.6 Sales of impotence drugs

Impotence drug: brand	Sales (2015)
Levitra (vardenafil)	$0.3 bn
Viagra (sildenafil)	$1.38 bn (43%)
Cialis (tadalafil)	$0.5 bn

Because these 'disease awareness' campaigns are commonly linked to companies' marketing strategies, they operate to expand markets for new pharmaceutical products. Alternative approaches – emphasising the self-limiting or relatively benign natural history of a problem, or the importance of personal coping strategies – often are played down or ignored. As the late medical writer Lynn Payer observed, disease mongers 'gnaw away at our self-confidence' (Payer, 1992). For example, a double-page advertisement in the Sydney *Morning Herald*'s *Weekend Magazine* told Australians that 39 per cent of men who visit general practitioners have ED. The 39 per cent claim in the advertisement was referenced to an abstract of a survey finding. However, another Australian study, not cited in the advertisement, estimated that erection problems affected only 3 per cent of men in their 40s and 64 per cent of men in their 70s. The advertisement's fine print cited a host organisation, Impotence Australia, but did not mention that the advertisement was funded by Pfizer (Moynihan et al., 2002). The key concern with 'disease mongering' is the invisible and unregulated attempts to change public perceptions about health and illness to widen markets for new drugs.

Source: Dyer, G. (2003) Pfizer hits back at results of research on Viagra, *Financial Times*, 17 November; Firn, D. and Tait, N. (2002) Pfizer loses legal battle to protect Viagra patent, *Financial Times*, 18 June; Michaels, A. (2001) Pfizer R&D unable to sustain group growth rate, *Financial Times*, 12 September; Moynihan, R., Heath, I. and Henry, D. (2002) Selling sickness: the pharmaceutical industry and disease mongering, *BMJ*, 13 April, vol. 324, no. 7342, 886–91; Payer, L. (1992) *Disease-mongers*, John Wiley, New York; Pfizer (2005) www.Pfizer.com.

Questions

1 Was Viagra the result of serendipity or is this journalistic licence to help sell a story, where the real story is a complex one of difficult decisions full of risks?

2 Explain why it was so necessary to ensure marketing was involved in the early stages of this new product development project.

3 Explain how, despite the enormous resources of Pfizer, a lack of available information made the evaluation of the new product proposal so very difficult.

4 Explain how the Viagra case needs to be viewed as a successful example of excellent applied science but also an excellent example of good marketing.

5 How can Pfizer manage the threat posed to Viagra by new entrants to the market?

6 How has Pfizer helped create a market for Viagra and thereby contributed to disease mongering?

Chapter summary

This chapter has introduced the substantial subject of R&D management and some of the challenges that it presents. Emphasis has been placed on highlighting the wide range of different activities undertaken by most R&D functions. Formal management techniques were shown to be an essential part of good R&D management. Companies are unable to justify spending millions of dollars purely on the basis of chance and good fortune. The issue of investment in R&D and industry comparisons was another area of discussion.

The link between R&D and the strategic management activities of the business was also discussed in some detail. This presents its own set of challenges in terms of deciding in which areas to invest and what type of R&D investment to follow. Most companies try to manage a balance of activities, but it is important to be aware of the nature of the pressures placed on management.

Discussion questions

1 Discuss whether R&D should be viewed just like any other expenditure and, hence, should deliver a positive return for the investor.

2 Explain why R&D functions often are thought as freewheeling places of disorder, yet, in reality, R&D is routine and follows many procedures.

3 Explain how two firms, A and B, in the same industry, investing the same in R&D as a percentage of sales, can perform so differently. Firm A delivers three new patents and two new successful products; whereas firm B fails to deliver anything.

4 Consider a firm of your choice. Examine what its level of expenditure on R&D could be. What should it be? And what is its actual expenditure?

5 Use CIM (Figure 1.9) to illustrate the innovation process in the Viagra study.

6 Firms investing in R&D in the many countries in the world receive tax credits. How can countries encourage further R&D investment?

7 Describe a balanced portfolio of R&D projects for Nokia. This should incorporate its technology portfolio.

8 What are the advantages and disadvantages from cutting R&D in a downturn?

Key words and phrases

R&D as a percentage of sales *308*

Applied research *313*

Basic research *315*

Technical service *317*

Technology portfolio *320*

Core technologies *320*

Complementary technologies *321*

Peripheral technologies *321*

Emerging technologies *321*

Technology leverage *324*

References

Adler, P.S., McDonald, D.W. and MacDonald, F. (1992) Strategic management of technical functions, *Sloan Management Review*, Winter, 19–37.

Ansoff, H.I. (1968) *Corporate Strategy*, Penguin, Harmondsworth.

Bauer, M. and Leker, J. (2013) Exploration and exploitation in product and process innovation in the chemical industry, *R&D Management*, vol. 43, 196–212.

BCG (1972) *Perspectives on Experience*, Boston Consulting Group, Boston, MA.

Bush, V. (1945) *Science: The Endless Frontier*, A Report to the President.

Cohen, W.M. and Levinthal, D.A. (1990) A new perspective on learning and innovation, *Administrative Science Quarterly*, vol. 35, no. 1, 128–52.

Cordero, R. (1990) The measurement of innovation performance in the firm: an overview, *Research Policy*, vol. 19, no. 2, 10–21.

Dyer, G. (2003) Pfizer hits back at results of research on Viagra, *Financial Times*, 17 November.

EIRMA (1985) Evaluation of R&D output: working group report, 29, European Industrial Research Management Association, Paris.

Firn, D. and Tait, N. (2002) Pfizer loses legal battle to protect Viagra patent, *Financial Times*, 18 June.

Geroski, P., Machin, S. and van Reenen, J. (1993) The profitability of innovating forms, *Rand Journal of Economics*, vol. 24, 198–211.

Hatzichronoglou, T., *Revision of the High: Technology Sector and Product Classification*, STI Working Papers 1997/2, OCDE, Paris, 1997.

Hernández, H., Tübke, A., Hervás, F., Vezzani, A., Dosso, M., Amoroso, S. and Grassano, N. (2015) *EU R&D Scoreboard:*, The 2014 EU Industrial R&D Investment Scoreboard, The European Commission.

Hickman, L.A. (1990) *Technology*, McGraw-Hill, Maidenhead.

Independent (1992) R&D Scoreboard, 10 June, 20.

Lang, G. (2009) Measuring the returns of R&D – An empirical study of the German manufacturing sector over 45 years, *Research Policy*, vol. 38, no. 9, 1438–45.

Mansfield, E. (1991) Social returns from R&D: findings, methods and limitations, *Research, Technology Management*, November/December, 24.

Mansfield, E., Rapoport, J., Schnee, J., Wagner, S. and Hamburger, M. (1972) *Research and Innovation in the Modern Corporation*, Macmillan, London.

McGrath, M.E. and Romeri, M.N. (1994) The R&D effectiveness index, *Journal of Product Innovation Management*, vol. 23, no. 2, 213–20.

Meyer-Krahmer, F. (1984) Recent results in measuring innovation output, *Research Policy*, vol. 13, no. 3, 12–24.

Michaels, A. (2001) Pfizer R&D unable to sustain group growth rate, *Financial Times*, 12 September.

Mitchell, G.R. (1988) Options for the strategic management of technology, *UNESCO Technology Management*, Interscience Enterprises Ltd, Geneva.

Moynihan, R., Heath, I. and Henry, D. (2002) Selling sickness: the pharmaceutical industry and disease mongering, *BMJ*, 13 April, vol. 324, no. 7342, 886–91.

Nobelius, D. (2004) Towards the sixth generation of R&D management, *International Journal of Project Management*, vol. 22, 369–75.

Payer, L. (1992) *Disease-mongers*, John Wiley, New York.

Pfizer (2005) www.Pfizer.com.

Porter, M.E. (1985) *Competitive Advantage: Creating and Sustaining Competitive Advantage*, Free Press, New York.

Quintas, P., Weild, D. and Massey, M. (1992) Academic–industry links and innovation: questioning the science park model, *Technovation*, vol. 12, no. 3, 161–75.

Roussel, P.A., Saad, K.N. and Erickson, T.S. (1991) *Third Generation R&D*, Harvard Business School Press, Boston, MA.

Scholefield, J.H. (1993) The development of a R&D planning model at ICI, *R&D Management*, vol. 23, no. 4, 20–30.

Twiss, B. (1992) *Managing Technological Innovation*, 4th edn, Financial Times Pitman Publishing, London.

Weild, D. (1986) 'Organisational strategies and practices for innovation', in Roy, R. and Weild, D. (eds) *Product Design and Technological Innovation*, Open University Press, Milton Keynes.

Williams, D.J. (1969) A study of the decision model for R&D project selection, *Operational Research Quarterly*, vol. 20.

Further reading

For a more detailed review of the R&D management literature, the following develop many of the issues raised in this chapter:

Bush, Vannevar (1945) *Science: The Endless Frontier*, A Report to the President.

Dhewanto, W., and Sohal, A.S. (2015). The relationship between organisational orientation and research and development/technology commercialisation performance. *R&D Management*, 45(4), 339–360.

Hernández, H, Tübke, A., Hervás, F., Vezzani, A., Dosso, M., Amoroso, S. and Grassano, N. (2015) *EU R&D Scoreboard*, The 2014 EU Industrial R&D Investment Scoreboard, The European commission.

Howells, J. (2008) New Directions in R&D: Current and Prospective Challenges, *R&D Management*, vol. 38, Issue 3, pp. 241–52.

Trott, P. and Hartmann, D. (2009) Old wine in new bottles, *International Journal of Innovation Management*, vol. 13, no. 4, 1–22.

Vannevar Bush's *Science: The Endless Frontier* (1945)

Von Hippel, E. (2005) *Democratizing Innovation*, MIT Press, Boston, MA.

Xu, Q., Chen, J., Xie, Z., Liu, J., Zheng, G. and Wang, Y. (2007) Total Innovation Management: a novel paradigm of innovation management in the 21st century, *Journal of Technology Transfer*, vol. 32, 9–25.

Chapter 10
Managing R&D projects

Introduction

The past 20 years have witnessed enormous changes in the way companies manage their technological resources and, in particular, research and development. Within industrial R&D, the effect is a shift in emphasis from an internal to an external focus. Contract R&D, R&D consortia and strategic alliances and joint ventures now form a large part of R&D management activities.

The need to provide scientific freedom and still achieve an effective return from any R&D investment, however, remains one of the most fundamental areas of R&D management. The use of formal planning techniques for R&D is viewed by many as a paradox: the introduction of any planning mechanism would, surely, stifle creativity and innovation. And yet, R&D departments do not have unlimited funds, so there has to be some planning and control. This chapter explores the problems and difficulties of managing R&D projects within organisations.

The case study at the end of this chapter explores the phenomenon of *CSI: Crime Scene Investigation*. It has been one of television's greatest success stories of all time and is a huge hit all over the world. Yet, few people recognise that it was a UK scientist – Alec Jeffreys – who, driven by curiosity, uncovered a technique for DNA fingerprinting.

Chapter contents

Learning objectives

When you have completed this chapter you will be able to:

- recognise the changing nature of R&D management;
- recognise the factors that influence the decision whether to undertake internal or external R&D;
- recognise the value of providing scientific freedom;
- examine the link with the product innovation process;
- recognise the significance of evaluating R&D projects; and
- explain how prior knowledge affects a firm's ability to acquire externally developed technology.

Successful technology management

Organisations that manage products and technologies and have been built on a strong research and development base are looking constantly for opportunities to diversify horizontally into new product markets. Their strategic management activities seek to mobilise complementary assets to successfully enter those markets. For example, Apple's knowledge of manufacturing small hand-held music players (iPods) enabled it to move into the manufacture of mobile phones. Similarly, in production-based technologies, key opportunities lie in the technological advances that can be applied to products and production systems, enabling diversification vertically into a wider range of production inputs. The injection-moulding process has had many adaptations, enabling its use in an increasing range of manufacturing techniques. However, companies do not have a completely free choice about the way they manage their technologies (Pavitt, 1990: 346):

> In many areas it is not clear before the event who is in the innovation race, where the starting and finishing lines are, and what the race is all about. Even when all these things are clear, companies often start out wishing to be a leader and end up being a follower!

There are two key technology risks that technology managers have to evaluate. First, 'appropriability risks' reflect the ease with which competitors can imitate innovations (see Chapter 7). They are, typically, managed through patent and copyright protection or through controlling complementary assets (such as branding, distribution, specialised services, etc.), as discussed by Teece (1986). In the pharmaceutical industry, for example, patent protection is relatively effective because minor changes in the structure of therapeutic drugs can have major consequences for their operation in the human body. As a result, drug discovery firms are able to specialise in highly risky activities without needing to develop complementary assets to protect their innovations.

The second risk is 'competence destruction'. This reflects the volatility and uncertainty of technical development that vary greatly between technologies, both in terms of the technological trajectories (see Chapter 7) being followed and market acceptance. Where technological uncertainty is high, it is difficult to predict which investments and skills will be effective and firms have to be able to change direction at short notice. Consequently, the managers of firms attempting to develop radically discontinuous innovations are faced with the need to attract and motivate expert staff to work on complex problems when unpredictable outcomes may involve redundancy and/or organisational failure.

These two kinds of technology risk tend to be inversely related. Investments in developing highly uncertain technologies usually are undertaken when appropriability risks are limited (e.g. intellectual property protection is available, such as pharamaceuticals and software), whilst firms developing innovations that are more open to such risks tend to focus on more cumulative and predictable technologies (e.g. food industry and other fast-moving consumer goods (FMCG) areas). Companies racing to produce highly radical, discontinuous innovations have to be flexible in their use of key resources, such as highly expert technologists, and in changing direction, whilst those developing more imitable technologies have to develop complementary competencies (branding, distribution) and integrate them through organisational routines. By making innovations more customer-specific and bundling additional services with them, such companies increase their organisational specificity and limit the ease with which they can be imitated (e.g. Coca-Cola, Unilever). However, these kinds of entrepreneurial technology firms are more organisationally complex than radically innovative companies and have to develop stronger coordinating organisational capabilities (Casper and Whitley, 2004; Mason et al., 2004).

The above discussions reveal the weaknesses in some of the commonly accepted views of technology strategy promoted by many business schools and management consultants. It is not helpful to the organisation to try to predetermine whether its technology strategy should be to lead or to follow, to develop a product or a process. Technology cannot be developed to order or acquired to fill a position in a matrix. It can be successful only if it is fully integrated into the company's business. This means that the company needs a range of complementary assets in other areas, such as marketing and distribution, in order to exploit its technology successfully. Developing these skills and capabilities and integrating them into the company takes time. Often, these characteristics will be determined by the company's size, its previous activities and its accumulated competencies. However, it is these latter factors and not the company's strategy that will determine whether it will successfully exploit its technology.

As virtually all practitioners realise, there is no easy formula for success. In a review of the literature on technology management, Pavitt (1990) identified the following necessary ingredients for successful technology management:

- the capacity to orchestrate and integrate functional and specialist groups for the implementation of innovations;
- continuous questioning of the appropriateness of existing divisional markets, missions and skills for the exploitation of technological opportunities; and
- a willingness to take a long-term view of technological accumulation within the firm.

Innovation in action

Be transparent

A problem that online retailers face, as opposed to their bricks and mortar counterparts, is that customers cannot touch and feel exactly what they are buying.

This gap is compounded in industries like floristry where, despite tempting brochure shots, florists often cannot guarantee exactly what they are sending because of variations in availability. The resulting 'transparency gap' creates nervousness in customers. This, in turn, presents opportunity.

New Zealand-based florists Roses are Red have addressed this by sending customers a digital photograph of the exact bouquet they have sent. And, if customers are not completely happy with it, they can have a full replacement.

Source: WENN Ltd/Alamy Images

Source: HSBC (2010) 100 Thoughts, HSBC, London.

The changing nature of R&D management

R&D activities have changed dramatically since 1950. The past 20 years have witnessed enormous changes in the way companies manage their technological resources and, in particular, their research and development. There are numerous factors that have contributed to these changes (see Illustration 10.1). The key factors are:

- *Technology explosion.* It is estimated that 90 per cent of our present technical knowledge has been generated during the past 60 years.
- *Shortening of the technology cycle.* The technology cycle includes scientific and technological developments prior to the traditional product life cycle. These cycles

---

Illustration 10.1

Finding new drugs is harder and more expensive, especially clinical trials

The world's drugs companies are coming to terms with a difficult conundrum in research and development: despite huge advances in technology and scientific know-how, R&D productivity seems to have stalled.

The large pharmaceuticals companies' amazing growth in the 1980s and 90s was fuelled by a series of drugs that they turned into blockbusters.

There have been considerable technical and scientific advances, most notably in biotechnology, genomics and related fields. But everyone seems to have underestimated how long it will take for the greater knowledge to result in medicines.

Greater understanding of our genetic make-up is also leading to ideas for drugs that can correct DNA deficiencies before they have caused damage or, more precisely, identify people at risk from certain conditions.

However, these advances are recent and all target the start of the R&D process. Even without any unexpected obstacles, companies would take a few years yet to turn them into a flow of drugs at the other end of the pipeline.

But there are unexpected obstacles. The first is poisonous – or toxicological – side effects. As we learn more about the body's biochemistry, we can strive to test better what pathways a drug will disrupt aside from those that it was intended to. After a drug candidate is successful in its toxicology trials, it still has to be tested in humans – the trials are increasingly subject to criticism, with medical journals warning that the promise of big financial rewards is compromising independence. And with companies and regulators more mindful of side effects, clinical trials are becoming larger and taking longer, another reason why R&D costs are rising.

A high percentage of new drug candidates fail to reach the market during clinical trials, and these failures imply massive financial losses for the pharmaceutical companies. Clinical trials have distinctive characteristics and additional complexity compared with the late stages of product development in many other industrial sectors.

Research by Buonansegna et al. (2014) identified seven critical management issues causing failures in clinical trials:

1. chaotic and slow patient recruitment;
2. lack of experience in choosing and monitoring partners;
3. lack of feasibility of the study protocol;
4. low quality of the registered data;
5. too high incidence of serious adverse events and severe incidents;
6. unmanageable level of portfolio complexity; and
7. incorrect assessment of the market potential or returns.

Source: A. Michaels (2001) Quick-hit chemistry becomes elusive, Financial Times, 12 September. Reprinted with permission. Buonansegna, E., Salomo, S., Maier, A. M. and Li-Ying, J. (2014) Pharmaceutical new product development: why do clinical trials fail? R&D Management, vol. 44, 189–202.

have been slowly shortening, forcing companies to focus their efforts on product development. For example, the market life of production cars has decreased from approximately 10 years in the 1960s to approximately 6 years in the 2000s. In some cases, a particular model may be restyled after only three years.

- **Globalisation of technology.** East Asian countries have demonstrated an ability to acquire and assimilate technology into new products. This has resulted in a substantial increase in technology transfer in the form of licensing and strategic alliances.

In addition, the following specific changes are facing R&D managers today:

- the increasingly distributed and open nature of networked research and innovation;
- the growth of externally sourced R&D (and, as a consequence, the relative decline in internally generated R&D) within firms;
- overcoming barriers towards the increased productivity and effectiveness of R&D;
- the continued globalisation of R&D, particularly in terms of its spread and reach, associated with R&D offshoring;
- the relative shift from manufacturing-centred R&D towards more service-orientated R&D;
- R&D projects are being managed with the aid of more continuous feedback and information evaluation from stakeholders and sponsors – thereby strengthening the joint role of R&D performers and their clients.

(Howells (2008); Brzustowski et al. (2010))

Figure 9.3 showed the traditional areas of research activity for universities and industry. University emphasis has been on discovering new knowledge, with industry exploiting these discoveries in the form of products. The past decade has seen a significant increase in collaborative research, with industry sponsoring science departments in universities and engaging in staff exchanges with university departments.

The effect of these macro-factors is a shift in emphasis within industrial R&D from an internal to an external focus. Traditionally, R&D management, particularly in Western technology-based companies, has been management of internal R&D. It could be argued that one of the most noticeable features of Japanese companies since the Second World War has been their ability successfully to acquire and utilise technology from other companies around the world. However, the external acquisition of technology exposes technology managers to new responsibilities. Although this implies that acquiring technology from outside the organisation is something new, this is clearly not the case, as the long history of licensing agreements will show. However, the importance now placed on technology acquisition by technology-based companies reveals a departure from a focus on internal R&D and an acknowledgement that internal R&D is now only one of many technology development options available. The technology base of a company is viewed as an asset; it represents the technological capability of that company. The different acquisition strategies available involve varying degrees of organisational and managerial integration. For example, internal R&D is viewed as the most integrated technology-acquisition strategy with technology scanning the least integrated strategy.

There are numerous ways of acquiring external technology (see Figure 10.1). Significantly, we should not overlook the many forms of informal linkages, alliances

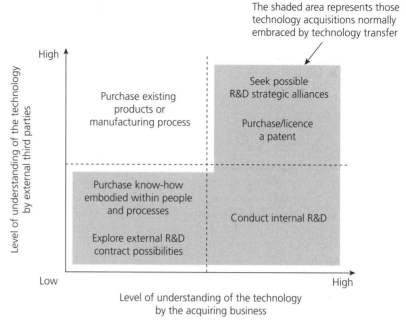

Figure 10.1 Acquisition of external technology/knowledge matrix

and industry associations that are known to exist and that often result in extensive transfer of knowledge and technology. Numerous stories abound of R&D scientists and managers meeting at conferences and a few months later signing a collaborative agreement to work together.

The wide range of activities now being expected from R&D departments and the demands being placed on them are becoming ever more complex. Particular emphasis is being placed on a company's linkages with other organiaations (West and Bogers, 2014). Networking is now regarded as an effective method of knowledge acquisition and learning. It is argued that the ability to network in order to acquire and exploit external knowledge enables the firm to enter new areas of technological development. The following areas now explicitly require involvement from the R&D department:

● Industry has expanded its support of university research and established numerous collaborations with university departments (Abelson, 1995).
● Industry has increased the number of technological collaborations. R&D personnel are being involved increasingly in technology audits of potential collaborators.
● Research and development personnel increasingly are accompanying sales staff on visits to customers and component suppliers to discuss technical problems and possible product developments.
● The acquisition and divestment of technology-based businesses have led to a further expansion of the role of R&D. Input increasingly is required in the form of an assessment of the value of the technology to the business.
● A dramatic rise in the use of project management as organisations shift to provide customer-driven results (Englund and Graham, 1999).

● The expansion of industrial agreements, usually in the form of licensing, contract work and consultancy, has resulted in a new area of work for R&D. The rapid growth in knowledge-intensive service firms is clear evidence of this (Berkhout et al., 2010).

The focus of these new areas of work is on external knowledge acquisition and assimilation. This is forcing many companies to reassess the way they manage their R&D. In addition, this increased portfolio of activities requires a different range of skills from the individuals involved. The traditional role of a research scientist as a world expert in a particular field, who uses a convergent, narrow-focus approach to uncover new and cheaper ways of producing chemicals and products, is being replaced by researchers who have additional attributes. These include an ability to interact with a wide variety of external organisations, thereby increasing awareness of specific customer needs, market changes, the activities of competitors and the larger environment. Historically, R&D staff faced alternative definitions of career success and reward in career paths, either involving increasing administrative responsibility and a path into managerial hierarchy or one involving increasing prestige as technical specialists. This dual-ladder career structure looks more and more out of place in today's varied and rapidly changing R&D environment.

Organising industrial R&D

The increasing emphasis on knowledge acquisition and assimilation is forcing companies to look for ways to improve their effectiveness in this area. Given the growing use of external sources of technology, the R&D manager now has to determine which form of R&D is most appropriate for the organisation. This is particularly difficult, as much depends on how much investment is made. Research by Hagedoorn and Wang (2012) illustrates that internal R&D and external R&D (R&D alliances or R&D acquisitions) are complementary innovation activities at higher levels of in-house R&D investments, whereas at lower levels, internal and external R&D turn out to be substitutive strategic options. Figure 10.2 shows the many guises of R&D.

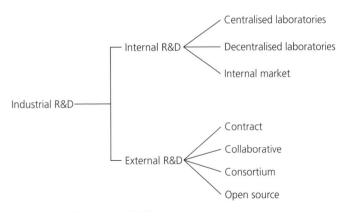

Figure 10.2 Organising industrial R&D

Centralised laboratories

The main advantage with **centralised laboratories** is critical mass. The idea is that far more can be achieved when scientists work together than when they work alone. Those firms trying to achieve technological leadership often centralise their R&D. There is also the possibility that synergy can result, with technologies from different businesses being employed in different unrelated businesses. 3M argues that it gains synergies between businesses resulting in internal technology transfer by having a centralised R&D laboratory.

Decentralised laboratories

The main advantage of **decentralised laboratories**, i.e. decentralising the R&D function, is to reinforce the link with the business, its products and its markets. It is argued that with a large, centralised R&D effort, it is often too removed from where the technology is eventually applied. By providing each business or division with its own R&D effort, it is argued that this fosters improved communication and product development. However, the weakness of this closer link is that it can lead to an emphasis on short-term development only.

Internal R&D market

An internal market structure for R&D essentially involves establishing a functional cost centre, where each business pays for any R&D services required. This raises the issue of whether a business is also able to use external R&D services, say from a university. The extent to which this erodes the knowledge base of the organisation, however, is debatable. The limitations of this approach are similar to those for decentralised R&D laboratories.

The acquisition of external technology

So far in this book, we have concentrated on viewing R&D as an activity performed internally by the business. It is necessary, however, to understand that R&D is not, necessarily, an internal organisational activity. R&D, like any other business function, say marketing or production, can, in theory, be contracted out and performed by a third party. The previous section highlighted the increasing use of collaborations and strategic alliances to acquire technology (the role of strategic alliances was discussed in detail in Chapter 8). The extent to which it is possible for an organisation to acquire externally developed technology is uncertain and is discussed in Chapters 7 and 11. Nonetheless, many businesses establish research contracts with organisations, such as universities, to undertake specific research projects.

There is a significant difference between acquiring externally developed technology and external R&D. This difference lies in the level of understanding of the technology involved, often referred to as prior knowledge. To illustrate, the purchase of new computer software will lead to the acquisition of new technology. This is an option available to virtually all businesses, irrespective of their prior knowledge of the technology. However, developing an R&D strategic alliance or an external R&D contract with a third party requires a high level of prior knowledge of the technology concerned. Similarly, the level of prior knowledge of the external third party also influences the choice of method to acquire the technology concerned (Mason et al., 2004).

The matrix in Figure 10.1 offers an insight into the issue of technology acquisition. Whilst the matrix is an oversimplification of a complex subject, it does, nonetheless, help to classify the wide range of acquisition options available to companies, from purchasing technology 'off the shelf' to conducting internal R&D. The horizontal axis refers to the level of prior knowledge of the business acquiring the technology. The vertical axis refers to the level of prior knowledge of external third parties.

As was explained in Chapter 4, there are many companies that conduct little, if any, R&D, yet are associated with a wide variety of technology-intensive products. For example, low-tech sectors, such as the food industry. This is particularly the case for supplier-dominated and scale-intensive firms (Pavitt, 1984). Many such companies assemble component parts purchased from other manufacturers and sell the final product stamped with their own brand. Some companies do not even assemble; they simply place their own brand on the purchased product (often called re-badging). In these cases, the company concerned usually has commercial and marketing strengths, such as service quality and distribution skills. This is similar to own-branding in the grocery market.

The subject of technology transfer is discussed in detail in Chapter 11. It is, nonetheless, worth pointing out here that technology transfer usually embraces the activities in the shaded area on the matrix. It is not normally used to describe, say, the purchase of new computer software. Technology transfer is defined as:

> *The process of promoting technical innovation through the transfer of ideas, knowledge, devices and artefacts from leading edge companies, R&D organisations and academic research to more general and effective application in industry and commerce.*
>
> (Seaton and Cordey-Hayes, 1993: 46)

Level of control of technology required

In acquiring externally developed technology, a business must also consider the extent of control over the technology that it requires. For example, if a research project shows promising results that could lead to the development of a new radical technology with many new product opportunities, it is likely that the business would want to keep such research under close control and, thus, internal. On the other hand, a project with specific technical problems requiring expertise in an area of technology beyond the scope of the business may be suited ideally to a research contract with a university department. Figure 10.3 shows a classification of technology acquisition methods. You will see that they are classified according to the degree of integration with the organisation.

The particular stage of development of the research, or its position in the technology life cycle, will heavily influence the level of control required. For example, is the research at an early stage without any particular product idea in mind (pre-competitive) or is it near completion and shortly to be incorporated in a new product launch (competitive)? Clearly, competitive research will require careful monitoring to ensure that maximum competitive advantage can be secured.

There may also be occasions when the company does not have the in-house expertise to undertake the research. In this case, some form of external R&D will be

Maximum organisational integration

Degree of organisational integration

Internal R&D within the organisation

Acquisition of firms with technology, including part ownership and contractual obligations

Joint ventures, underpinned by formal contracts; this will include joint R&D projects

Technology cooperation, including those arrangements that do not necessarily involve a formal contract

Purchase of technology, including contract R&D, the purchase of licences and sponsored research at universities

Open source R&D (co-producers of R&D)

Technology scanning, including formal and informal methods of acquiring technological know-how

Minimal organisational integration

Figure 10.3 Technology acquisition: how much control of the technology is required?

necessary. A word of caution. Research by Lin et al. (2012) examining interfirm R&D alliances, suggested R&D alliances should be regarded as a complement to, rather than a substitute for, a firm's internal R&D.

Forms of external R&D

Contract R&D

In those situations where the business has a low level of understanding of the technology (bottom left-hand corner of technology acquisition matrix), contracting the R&D out to a third party often is suitable. University research departments have a long history of operating in this area. However, the use of commercial research organisations is expanding rapidly, especially in the field of biotechnology. R&D service firms are highly innovative knowledge-intensive businesses and offer R&D contracts that allow firms to de-risk the uncertain process of early technology development and to meet customer's needs (Probert et al., 2013). This method of R&D is also used in urgent situations, when setting up internal research teams would be too slow.

R&D strategic alliances and joint ventures

This area of management was explored in Chapter 8. At this point, it is necessary only to be aware of the key advantages and disadvantages of using strategic alliances. This is a generic term for all forms of cooperation, both formal and informal, including joint ventures. With a joint venture, the costs and possible benefits from an R&D research project would be shared. They are usually established for a specific project and will cease on its completion. For example, Sony and Ericsson formed a joint venture to develop mobile phone handsets. The advantages are usually obvious. In this example, both companies (who were former competitors) were able to share their expertise and reduce the inevitable costs and risks associated with any R&D project. The disadvantages are that either company could inadvertently pass knowledge to the other and receive little in return. It is for this reason alone that many companies still refuse to enter into any form of strategic alliance. It can be usefully explained using game theory principles and, in particular, the prisoner's dilemma (see Chapter 8).

R&D consortia

In this context, **R&D consortia** are separate from the large-scale technology consortia often found in the Far East. In Japan *keiretsus* (literally meaning societies of business) consist of 20–50 companies, usually centred around a trading company and involving component suppliers, distributors and final product producers, all interwoven through shareholdings and trading arrangements. In South Korea, *chaebols* are similar to *keiretsus*, except that they are financed by the government rather than by banks or a trading company and, usually, the company links are based on family ties (Sakakibara, 2002). Such types of business groups are based on common membership and collaborate over a long period of time.

The use of R&D consortia has increased substantially over the past 10 years in both the United States and Europe. The European Union offers a number of programmes to encourage R&D cooperation across the Union. One of the most successful, and certainly high-profile, cases is SEMTECH, a consortium of 14 US semiconductor manufacturers. In 1980, nine out of the top 10 silicon chip makers were from the United States. By 1990, five out of the top six were Japanese. SEMTECH was established to try to help the US chip manufacturers. It had substantial funding from the US Defense Department, with the aim of creating a viable semiconductor manufacturing equipment and materials industry, thus ensuring that domestic chip producers would not be dependent on Japanese equipment sources. SEMTECH has played a major role in developing successive generations of chip-making technology. By 1995, the US semiconductor industry had experienced a dramatic increase in its share of the world market (Corey, 1997).

Inspired by R&D consortia in advanced countries, Taiwan and the Chinese mainland have sought to develop the cooperative R&D mechanism in their own distinctive contexts. R&D consortia in Taiwan and Public Technological Platforms (PTPs) in the Chinese mainland have unique structural characteristics with their common catch-up goals and have been developing in different ways reflecting the relationships and interaction between academia, industry and government.

One of the potential weaknesses of this concept is the potential for reducing competition. The European Union and the US Government spend a great deal of time and money trying to detect those organisations operating a cartel. Harsh penalties usually are enforced on any offending organisation. R&D consortia are closely monitored and have to be registered.

The main advantages of this approach are the ability to reduce costs and risks, the ability to access technologies and to influence industry standards on new technology (the experience of the VCR industry and the computer-operating system industry have shown the potential dangers in having competing industry standards). The main disadvantages are similar to those for joint ventures, in that one party may not be able to gain any technological benefit from the consortia.

Open source R&D

The term 'open source' is taken from the more familiar open source software development, which has resulted in many 'free to use' software applications, including web browsers, word processing and email. More recently, it has been applied to R&D: distributed or 'open source innovation' in which customers (or anyone else for that matter) are the co-producers of the products and services they consume. Illustration 10.2 shows how Procter & Gamble has used the principles (Chesbrough and Bogers, 2014).

Open source has also been transferred to other areas ranging from an open source encyclopedia – Wikipedia – and collaborative industrial design, such as Think-Cycle to open source aeroplane design, cola recipes, film scripts and beer. The latter was developed with the help of some self-appointed beer aficionados (found on the internet) who created everything from the name of the beer to its packaging and advertising. But, perhaps the biggest opportunity for open source innovation lies within the pharmaceutical industry. One of the problems with traditional pharmaceutical R&D is that the patent system effectively blocks outside insights or enhancements to a particular discovery or invention. It also means that there is little or no incentive to develop drugs aimed at people (or countries) with little or no money to spend.

How can open source principles be adopted by commercial organisations? In some ways, open source can be thought of as a suggestion box scheme – albeit one

Illustration 10.2

Procter & Gamble's open sourced R&D: Connect & Develop

Most companies are still clinging to the internal innovation model, built on the idea that their innovation must, principally, reside within their own organisation. This does tend to induce an obsession about secrecy. Not surprisingly, this approach limits both the quantity and quality of ideas, so companies have started to search for new ways of developing new ideas. By 2000, it was clear to Procter & Gamble (P&G) that its invent-it-ourselves model was not capable of sustaining high levels of top-line growth. The explosion of new technologies was putting ever more pressure on its innovation budgets. According to P&G, 'Our R&D productivity had levelled off, and our innovation success rate had stagnated at about 35 per cent. Squeezed by nimble competitors, flattening sales, lacklustre new launches and falling income, P&G had to do something.'

P&G turned to an open source approach. The company has an objective to generate 50 per cent of new product ideas from outside the company. P&G's Collaborative Planning, Forecasting and Replenishment process (CPFR) is a collaborative and transparent process that allows P&G's customers and suppliers to improve its supply chain. Another example is P&G's use of the virtual technology market, yet2.com. P&G lists every one of its thousands of patents on yet2.com in the hope that it will facilitate connections and ideas from the outside.

Procter & Gamble launched a new line of Pringles potato crisps in 2004 with pictures and words – trivia questions, animal facts, jokes – printed on each crisp. They were an immediate hit. P&G says: 'In the old days, it might have taken us two years to bring this product to market, and we would have shouldered all of the investment and risk internally. But by applying a fundamentally new approach to innovation, we were able to accelerate Pringles Prints from concept to launch in less than a year and at a fraction of what it would have otherwise cost.'

Source: Chesbrough and Bogers (2014); Chesbrough and Crowther (2006).

with a giant transparent box. A topic is posted on a website, and anyone from industry experts to members of the public can contribute to the solution. Everything is transparent in the sense that all ideas are shared and discussed in public. In some instances, people will do this for nothing, whilst in others they will, ultimately, have to be paid in some way.

Some detractors argue that **open source R&D** is little more than giant focus groups, but there are big differences. The first is sheer scale. Focus groups rarely involve more than a hundred people. Open source can involve thousands and still turn things around faster than more traditional approaches. Second, focus groups usually ask people to react to ideas. Open source asks people for solutions and allows ideas to build cumulatively. Third, focus groups rely on a representative sample of people who are 'ordinary' and, by definition, uninterested. Open source relies on people who are articulate, passionate and enthusiastic.

Pause for thought

Open source R&D feels a bit like firms undertaking R&D for free with help from anyone willing to contribute. I can see how it works with software because you end up with free software, but firms like Procter & Gamble have to sell their products; they cannot give them away.

Effective R&D management

Managers of R&D have to try to develop systems and procedures that will enhance the probability of success. To outside observers, the research and development process may seem like a random procedure in which inspired scientists, working around the clock, come up with major breakthroughs late at night. It is true that R&D is a high-risk activity, but the process is much less random than it first appears. Over the past 40 years, there has been extensive research in R&D management and there is an academic journal dedicated to the subject (*R&D Management*). This research has revealed the presence of certain factors in many successful R&D projects and their absence in many failed projects. Table 10.1 summarises these factors.

Effective R&D management can make a considerable impact on the performance of a company. Illustration 10.3 shows how, over a period of 100 years, R&D has led to many different applications of a drug.

Managing scientific freedom

The idea of applying formal planning techniques to R&D is viewed by many as a paradox. The popular view is that research, by definition, is concerned with uncovering new things and discovering something that previously was unknown. To try to introduce any form of planning would, surely, stifle creativity and innovation. This leads to one of the most fundamental management dilemmas facing senior managers: how to encourage creativity and, at the same time, improve efficiency. This dilemma

Table 10.1 Organisational characteristics that facilitate the innovation process and the management of R&D

R&D requirement	Characterised by
1 Growth orientation	A commitment to long-term growth rather than short-term profit
2 Organisational heritage and innovation experience	Widespread recognition of the value of innovation
3 Vigilance and external links	The ability of the organisation to be aware of its technology threats and opportunities
4 Commitment to technology and R&D intensity	The willingness to invest in the long-term development of technology
5 Acceptance of risks	The willingness to include risky opportunities in a balanced portfolio
6 Cross-functional cooperation and coordination within organisational structure	Mutual respect amongst individuals and a willingness to work together across functions
7 Receptivity	The ability to be aware of, to identify and to take effective advantage of externally developed technology
8 Space for creativity	An ability to manage the innovation dilemma and provide room for creativity
9 Strategy towards innovation	Strategic planning and selection of technologies and markets
10 Coordination of a diverse range of skills	Developing a marketable product requires combining a wide range of specialised knowledge
11 Project management	Good project management skills and systems
12 Market orientation	An awareness of the needs and changing nature of the market

Illustration 10.3

The continued development of aspirin

Research published in 2014 suggests that an aspirin a day could dramatically cut people's chances of getting and dying from common cancers. A research team led by Professor Jack Cuzick, head of the centre for cancer prevention at Queen Mary University of London, concluded that people between 50 and 65 should consider regularly taking the 75 mg low-dosage tablets.

Through continued research and development, new uses are continually being found for one of the oldest pharmaceutical products – aspirin. Aspirin was first introduced to the market more than 100 years ago in 1897. It was research into salicin, a compound that is found naturally on willow bark, by Bayer, a large German chemical manufacturer, that led to the development of aspirin as we know it today.

The drug was first used as a treatment for arthritis sufferers. Pharmacologist John Vane received the Nobel Prize for Chemistry for uncovering how aspirin relieved arthritis. He showed that prostaglandins are released by the body when cells are injured, triggering the symptoms of inflammation, swelling and pain. Aspirin halts the production of these prostaglandins, hence its effectiveness in treating arthritis.

Aspirin has been shown to have a number of additional effects:

- It acts as an analgesic to ease pain.
- It acts as an anti-inflammatory to control inflammation.
- It acts as an antipyretic to reduce fever.
- By thinning the blood, it helps to reduce the danger of blood vessels clotting, thereby helping to prevent strokes and heart attacks.
- It has also been shown to help reduce colonic cancer.
- It is currently being used in the treatment of Alzheimer's disease.

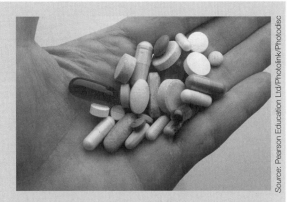

Source: Pearson Education Ltd/Photolink/Photodisc

Source: Boseley, S. (2014) Aspirin a day could dramatically cut cancer risk, says biggest study yet, *The Guardian*, 6 August, http://www.theguardian.com/science/2014/aug/06/aspirin-could-dramtically-cut-cancer-risk-say-scientists-biggest-study-yet.

was tackled at a generic level in Chapter 4 so, to avoid repetition, we will address the problem from an R&D perspective.

R&D managers will argue that the technologist's and scientist's spirit of enquiry must be given room and freedom to exercise (**scientific freedom**). Without the freedom to work on projects that may not appear of immediate benefit to the company, the laboratory may become conservative and uncreative (see the CSI case study at the end of this chapter). Furthermore, it may be difficult to attract and retain the best scientists, if they are not allowed to pursue those areas that are of interest to them. There are many disputes between research and technology managers and other senior functional managers concerning the extent of time that scientists and research teams should be able to allocate for personal research programmes.

However, R&D managers are realistic: they recognise that few companies, if any, are going to invest large sums of money solely as an act of faith. There are many formal management techniques that are employed to help to improve the effectiveness and productivity of R&D without necessarily destroying the possibility of serendipity.

Virtually all companies accept that a certain amount of time should be made available for scientific enquiry (after all, there are many examples of such research producing profitable outcomes). The issue is, *how much time?* One approach, adopted by many technology-intensive companies, such as Siemens, 3M, Ericsson and Nokia, is to consider that a company that invests heavily in R&D is, in reality, managing two types of R&D project. This can best be shown schematically, as in Figure 10.4, which is an extension of Figure 9.6, and shows a variety of project outcomes, which are explained below in Table 10.2.

The R&D projects are divided into two separate groups. The first group is by far the largest, usually accounting for 90 per cent of the R&D budget. It is established in response to requests from the various businesses and supports and maintains the corporate objectives. In Figure 10.4 these projects are labelled A, B and C. The second group of projects are those generated by the scientists themselves, usually as a result of personal interest in the technology. These are labelled S1 to S5. These projects will be generating technology of a commercial value but free from the constraints of corporate

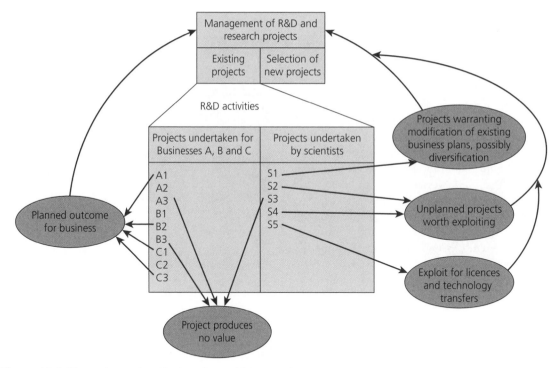

Figure 10.4 Managing scientific freedom within an R&D function

Table 10.2 Research project outcomes

Research project	Outcome	Action
A1, B2, C1 and C3	Planned outcome for the business	Research project produces desired results for business to incorporate into products
A3, B3 and S3	Project produces no immediate commercial value	Results of project will be examined by other research groups to see if the findings can be used; knowledge remains with R&D
S1	Project warrants changing existing business strategy	In exceptional circumstances, the findings from a research project can be so unusual and promising that they warrant a change in business strategy to accommodate possible new product ideas
S5	License technology to third party	When the research results produce interesting technology that is beyond exploitation by the business, it may be possible to generate income from licensing the technology to a third party
S2 and S4	Unplanned projects worth exploiting further	The findings from these personal research projects are so interesting that they require further funding and possible inclusion in business research
A2, B1 and C2	Projects lead to further research projects undertaken by scientists	The findings in themselves are of limited commercial value but stimulate further research projects

objectives. This latter group of research projects is financed by funds that are allocated at the discretion of the R&D manager or, more usually, an R&D committee or team. Very often, these funds represent about 10 per cent of the total R&D budget. This group of research projects has a variety of labels in industry, including blue-sky research, special projects and personal research. Virtually all major technology-intensive companies accommodate a certain amount of time for individuals to pursue their own research projects. Typically, about 10 per cent of a scientist's time will be spent on autonomous research projects.

It is possible to view R&D managers as managing two business activities. The primary activity supports the various businesses and the corporate objectives and the other supports a technology business, involved in generating technology of a commercial value that is unrelated to the corporate objectives.

Skunk works

Technology-intensive companies recognise that, if they are to attract and retain the best scientists, they have to offer scientific freedom. Moreover, experience has shown that scientists will covertly undertake these projects, if autonomy is not provided. There are many examples of exciting technology and successful products that were initiated by scientists operating in a covert manner. In the United States, such research projects are referred to as **skunk works** (see Illustration 10.4 for an explanation of its origin).

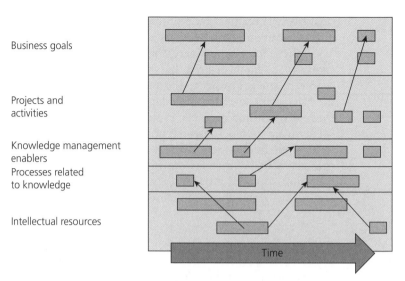

Business goals

Projects and
activities

Knowledge management
enablers
Processes related
to knowledge

Intellectual resources

Time

Figure 10.5 Technology road map with links to business goals

Technology roadmapping

Technology roadmaps were developed originally by Motorola in the 1970s to align the development of their products and their supporting technologies. A technology roadmap is, essentially, a plan that matches short-term and long-term goals with specific technology solutions to help meet those goals (Carvalho et al., 2013).

The concept has evolved into a methodology to help firms and managers align investments in technology and the new development of capabilities, so that they are able to fully exploit market needs. This is a tool that brings important support to the innovation manager, letting them define the firm's technological evolution in advance (Tierney et al., 2013).

A technology roadmap (TRM) has three major uses. It helps reach a consensus about a set of needs and the technologies required to satisfy those needs; it provides a mechanism to help forecast technology developments; and it provides a framework to help plan and coordinate technology developments.

Figure 10.5 shows the links between the future business goals and the technology and intellectual capital required to achieve these goals. When constructing TRM managers, must take into account:

● current technologies in the firm, which are included or serve as a base for other products, or are part of previous innovation plans;
● technologies intended to be developed in the medium and long term;
● technologies able to be developed by external providers of technology.

The link with the product innovation process

Chapters 7, 8 and 9 have all emphasised the accumulation of knowledge as a key part of the R&D process and the process of developing new products. The link between R&D and new product development often is overlooked or frequently they are treated

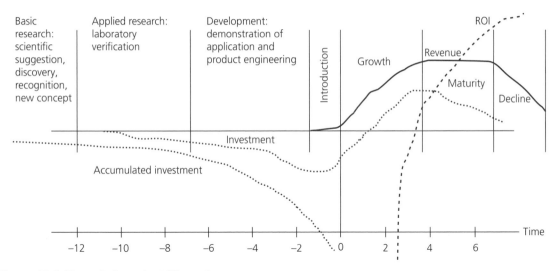

Figure 10.6 Extended product life cycle

as separate subjects. In practice, the two activities are interlinked. This can be shown simply by looking at the **extended product life cycle**. This well-known conceptual framework purports to capture some of the stages in a product's life from launch to final withdrawal. What is seldom shown is the series of activities prior to the first stage, *introduction*. For some products, most notably aircraft or pharmaceuticals, the lead time prior to launch can be 10 or even 15 years. Figure 10.6 shows the extended product life cycle with some of the key R&D activities incorporated. Mapped on top are the investment and expenditure curves showing the scale of upfront money required in some industries, most notably those with long lead times, as previously discussed.

Studies of new product development have demonstrated the value of effective interaction between research and development and manufacturing, but service operations often are overlooked, despite their growing importance. In complex product development projects, Olausson and Berggren (2012) show that it is necessary to create the conditions for integrated knowledge-based approaches across functions, which involve the generation and sharing of new knowledge.

Many of the models of new product development (NPD) emphasise the link to the R&D department. In particular, the network model of NPD, shown in Figure 14.14 (in Chapter 14), emphasises this continual interaction throughout the development of the product. Knowledge is accumulated over time as an idea for a product is transformed into a research project. The R&D function will be consulted continually on virtually all aspects of the product, including:

- design;
- manufacturing;
- choice of materials to be used;
- required shelf life;
- effects of transportation;
- packaging;
- intellectual property rights; and
- product safety, etc.

It is important to bear in mind that an investment in R&D to develop an existing product further is not, generally, viewed by product managers as a high-risk activity. The following quote from the brand manager of the makers of one of the leading washing detergents in Europe reflects a commonly held view:

> *We know we can improve the product, our scientists can always improve the product. In fact the launch date for our new improved shampoo has been set but the research is still on-going! The only doubt is the extent of the improvement that our scientists will make.*

A similar example could be drawn from the software industry, which is synonymous with new, improved versions of its software. The key point here is the way R&D investment is viewed. For many firms with years of experience in the management of R&D, an output is expected from their investment in R&D; the only doubt is the detail. Given this perspective on R&D, the following section analyses the range of effects that R&D investment can have on a product's profitability.

The effect of R&D investment on products

Analysis of the products that a company manages will reveal that these contribute in different ways to the overall profit and growth of the company. It is important to recognise that R&D activities can influence this profit contribution in several ways.

Development of existing products

The life cycle of most products lasts for several years. There are some products, especially in the food industry, that seem to have an eternal life cycle. Cadbury's Milk Tray and Coca-Cola are two examples of products that have been on the market for over 100 years. In virtually all other industry sectors, however, a product's market share will fall slowly as competitors compete on price and product improvements (see Chapter 14). R&D's role is to extend the life of the product by continually searching for product improvements. The two most common approaches to extend the life of a product are capturing a larger market share and improving profit margins through lowering production costs. For example, the performance of zinc-carbon batteries has improved greatly due to the threat of alkaline batteries like Duracell. This has helped to improve the market share for alkaline batteries. Similarly, personal computer manufacturers, such as Dell, Apple, Hewlett-Packard and IBM, are continually lowering their production costs in order to ensure that their products compete successfully in the PC market.

Early introduction of a new product

Many companies strive to be technological leaders in their industry. Their aim is to introduce innovative products into the market before the competition to gain a competitive advantage. In some industries, such as pharmaceuticals, this approach is very successful. In other sectors, being first to market does not always ensure success (see the section on Market entry in Chapter 13).

Late introduction of a new product

Deliberately postponing entry into a new market until it has been shown by competitors to be valid reduces the risk and costs. This was the approach used by Amstrad in the European mobile phone market. Furthermore, by deliberately slowing down product launches into the market, it is possible to maximise profits. For example, software companies have been very successful in launching improved versions and upgrades every six to nine months.

Long-term projects

Looking further into the future, R&D departments will also be developing products that the public do not yet realise they require. This area also includes starting new initiatives and new areas of research. Technology-intensive companies such as Siemens, Microsoft, Airbus and 3M will be working on products for 2015 and beyond.

Evaluating R&D projects

As was discussed in the above section ('The link with the product innovation process'), virtually all large technology-intensive firms will have many more ideas than it would wish to fund as research projects; the problem, as usual, is limited resources. Inevitably, choices have to be made about which ideas to support and convert to a funded project and which to drop. There have been many studies on this common problem faced by R&D managers (see Carbonell-Foulquie et al., 2003; Cooper, 2001; Farrukh et al., 2000). The subject of **evaluating R&D projects** is analysed from a marketing perspective in the final chapter of this book on evaluating new product ideas. An R&D perspective is now taken in the following section.

Deciding which projects to select for further resources will, inevitably, result in dropping others. Typically, for every 60 technical ideas considered, approximately 12 will receive funding for further evaluation. Of these, about six will receive further funding for design and development; half of these will be developed into prototypes and may even go for market testing. But only two will remain for product launch and, in most cases, only one of these is successful (Babcock, 1996). Figure 10.7 illustrates the dropout rate of project ideas. Dropping an R&D project is, theatrically, referred to as 'killing a project'. Unsurprisingly, it causes considerable anxiety amongst those involved, especially when one's fellow scientists have been involved with the project for many months or, in some cases, years. Evaluating research projects, then, is a critical issue.

Evaluation criteria

The evaluation criteria used by businesses varies considerably from industry to industry. There is a considerable body of research devoted to this single area of evaluating research projects. This is not surprising, given the long list of famous cases illustrating how many firms rejected projects that later turned into extremely successful products. To this list we must now add that the world's best-selling human drug – Pfizer's Viagra – was almost dropped because of the market research findings (see Illustration 10.5).

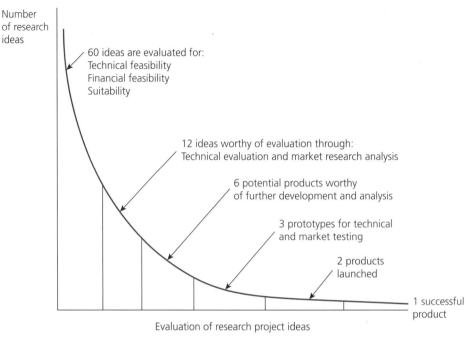

Figure 10.7 **Drop-out rates for R&D projects**

Source: Adapted from Babcock, D.L. (1996) *Managing Engineering Technology: An Introduction to Management for Engineers*, 2nd edn, Prentice Hall, Inc. © 1996, adapted by permission of Pearson Education, Inc., Upper Saddle River, NJ.

Illustration 10.5

Pfizer's Viagra almost slipped away!

Pfizer's Viagra is now part of business folklore in terms of an example of a successful new product. Viagra is now one of the most recognised brands in the world; it has become a social icon with sales in excess of $1.7 billion in 2015 and $2 billion in 2012. And it has transformed Pfizer from a medium-sized pharmaceutical firm into the world's leader. However, Viagra was almost dismissed during clinical trials as interesting, but not clinically or financially significant. (See also the case study at the end of Chapter 9.)

The discovery of Viagra was unintended in that it fell out of clinical trials for a new drug being developed for the treatment of angina (angina is defined as brief attacks of chest pain due to insufficient oxygenation of heart muscles). In 1992, following seven years of research, a clinical trial was undertaken in Wales for a compound known as UK-92.480. The findings from the trial on healthy volunteers revealed disappointing results. The data on blood pressure, heart rate and blood flow were discouraging. The R&D project was in trouble. Some patients reported side effects of episodes of indigestion, some of aches in legs and some reported penile erections. This final point was listed merely as an observation; at that moment no one said 'wow' or 'great'. Indeed, the decision to undertake trials into erectile dysfunction was not an obvious one. This was partly because the prevailing view at the time was that most erectile dysfunction was psychological and not treatable with drugs. Few people believed it was possible to produce an erection with an injection of drugs. Pfizer was preparing to drop the angina R&D project due to its disappointing results. It was also considering dropping all studies on the compound, even as a possible drug for erectile dysfunction. This was partly because it was not clear that it would have a clinical use. Not all the healthy volunteers had reported erections. How would Pfizer be able to conduct trials for such a condition? Moreover, the market for such a drug was not clear. At that time, survey results revealed only 1 in 20 million men suffered from erectile dysfunction; hence, even if a medicine could be developed, the market would be very small. The R&D team involved in the project managed to gain two years of funding to develop the drug and undertake clinical trials. The rest is, as they say, history. Moreover, the actual market for this type of drug is now known to be far greater than the data had revealed. This is a cautionary tale of the need sometimes to encourage innovation and support scientific freedom in the face of evidence to stop the project.

Source: Extracts from www.pfizer.com.

We will look at the range of techniques and methods used by firms later, but it is important to recognise that, whilst many firms may state publicly that they adopt quantitative weighted scoring models or specially adapted software to evaluate all project ideas, inevitably, as with so many business decisions, there is an element of judgement. After all, that is what managers are in a position to do – make decisions based on their experience and expertise. This is confirmed by a study of R&D decision making in the electronic sensors industry by Liddle (2004). He argues that managers continue to rely on rules of thumb and heuristics for the evaluation of research projects:

I just think it's a smell test. Does it sound too good to be true? Does it sound truly incremental to what we're doing? Is it something that sounds worthy of the investment of more time? Extract from an interview with an R&D manager.

(Liddle, 2004: 60)

Whether businesses used formal evaluation models or more informal methods, most will involve some or all of the checklist items shown in Table 10.3. This can be developed further using a weighted checklist or scoring model in which each factor is scored on a scale. A relative weight reflecting the importance of that factor is used as a multiple and the weighted scores for all factors are added.

The new product development literature offers a plethora of screening and decision-making methods and techniques aimed at assisting managers in making this difficult evaluation. Cooper (2001) identifies three broad categories of screening methods:

1 benefit measurement models;
2 economic models; and
3 portfolio selection models.

Benefit measurement models

Benefit measurement models usually are derived from a group of well-informed and experienced managers identifying variables such as those listed in Table 10.3, and then making subjective assessments of projects. Frequently, these variables are brought together in the form of a quantitative or qualitative model that will provide the organisation with a value with which to make comparisons of projects. These models are usually: mathematical, scoring, decision-trees (Holger, 2002).

Financial/economic models

Financial and economic models are the most popular project selection tool. This may not be surprising, given that firms are established to make money; however,

Table 10.3 R&D project evaluation criteria

Criteria	Typical questions
1 Technical	Do we have experience of the technology? Do we have the skills and facilities? What is the probability of technical success?
2 Research direction and balance	What is its compatibility with research goals? What is its balance of risk in project portfolio?
3 Competitive rationale	How does this project compare relative to the competition? Is it necessary to defend an existing business? Is the product likely to be superior?
4 Patentability	Can we get patent protection? What will be the implication for defensive research?
5 Stability of the market	How stable is the technology? Is the market developed? Is there an industry standard?
6 Integration and synergy	What is the level of integration of this project relative to other products and raw materials? Will it stand alone?
7 Market	What is the size of the market? Is it a growing market? Is there an existing customer base? Is the potential big enough to warrant the resource?
8 Channel fit	Do we have existing customers who might be interested, or do we have to find new customers?
9 Manufacturing	Can we use existing resources? Will we require new equipment, skills, etc.?
10 Financial	What is the expected investment required and rate of return?
11 Strategic fit	Does it support our short-term and long-term plans for the business?
12 Partners	Who can we partner with to develop the technology? Who can we partner with to help access market? Who can we partner with to help with manufacturing?

Source: Adapted from Seiler, R.E. (1965) *Improving the Effectiveness of Research and Development: Special Report to Management*, McGraw-Hill Book Company, New York.

this type of model generally is accepted as having considerable limitations. This is partly because of the emphasis on financial formulas and their inherent short-term bias. Another limitation of financial models is limited accurate future financial data, which inevitably leads to inaccurate estimates of future revenues, etc.

Portfolio selection models

Portfolio models attempt to find those ideas that 'fit' with the business strategy and attempt to balance the product portfolio. They consider a business's entire set of projects rather than viewing new research projects in isolation. The dimension of balance can be:

- *Newness* – how new is the product likely to be? A radically different product, product improvement, repositioning, etc. (see Chapter 14).
- *Time of introduction* – is the new product portfolio going to deliver a constant stream or will it be a case of feast and then famine?
- *Markets* – are the different markets and business areas of the company receiving resources proportionate to their size and importance?

Portfolio models use a hierarchy of criteria or factors to evaluate projects. Figure 10.8 shows an example of a portfolio model. The first level of criteria identifies probability of technical success, probability of commercial success, reward, business strategic fit, strategic leverage, and performance. These are broken down further in the next level. These lower level criteria are also called attributes and are connected to the alternative. Each project is scored against the scale or metric assigned to the lower level criterion. In this example, four projects are being managed by the R&D Portfolio Manager. They are 1) a new product; 2) a derivative

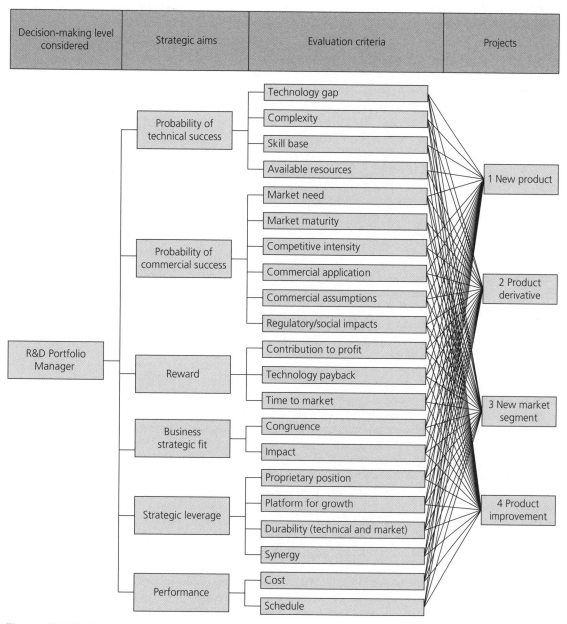

Decision-making level considered	Strategic aims	Evaluation criteria	Projects

Figure 10.8 Project evaluation scoring software

of an existing product; 3) a new market segment product, which is attempting to carve out a new market niche; and 4) a simple way of improving an existing product item.

Such models are incorporated in software applications and these allow for tailoring of the software to suit the industry and the firm. For example, relative weights need to be assigned to the criteria on each level of the hierarchy. Every decision involves trade-offs. In the end, the decision means that one element is being traded off for another.

Case study

CSI and genetic fingerprinting

The US drama *CSI: Crime Scene Investigation* (*CSI*) has been one of television's greatest success stories of all time. It is a huge hit all over the world. The show's popularity owes a great deal to the writers and actors who bring the stories to life. But another intriguing element is the cutting-edge technology used by the crime lab in trying to solve crimes. Collecting and analysing DNA evidence tops the list of the lab's forensic toolkit, and its ubiquity in shows like *CSI* and the UK's *Silent Witness* and *Waking the Dead* has increased public awareness to the point that many jurors in real-world courtrooms expect to see DNA evidence presented – whether a case calls for it or not. Indeed, such television programmes as *CSI* have come in for fierce criticism from police chiefs and prosecutors who argue that they portray an inaccurate image of how police solve crimes. There have, however, been some positive outcomes of the so-called 'CSI effect' and that is the bringing of science to a mass audience and encouraging interest in science amongst children.

The extraordinary growth in the business of DNA fingerprinting has been matched only by the mass appeal of the *CSI* television shows. In just a few years, the industry has grown into a 20 billion dollar technology-intensive colossus. But where and when did this all begin? This case study shows how a UK scientist, Alec Jeffreys, driven by curiosity, uncovered a technique for DNA fingerprinting. First, we need to look at the background to this development.

Background

In 1865, Gregor Mendel hypothesised that the phenomenon of the inheritance of certain characteristics is due to transferable elements – the gene. Hence, we

Source: Pearson Education Ltd

have Genetics as the study of Inheritance. In 1869, a Swiss biochemist, Friedrich Miescher, was the first to isolate nucleic acids, the molecular substrates of the genetic code. As time went on, more people contributed to our understanding of DNA and inheritance. However, the next major breakthrough came in 1953, when James Watson and Francis Crick discovered the structure of DNA and were able to demonstrate how genetic information encoded in DNA could be passed on from generation to generation. Since the discovery of the structure of DNA in 1953, knowledge of the composition and organisation of the genetic material has accumulated at an astonishing pace. By the early 1980s, it had become clear that most human DNA shows very little variation from one person to another. The small percentage that does vary presents enormous potential for fruitful study. The techniques that make it possible to identify a suspect using his or her unique genetic blueprint have been around only since 1985. That is when UK scientist Alec Jeffreys first demonstrated the use of DNA in a criminal investigation. Since then, DNA evidence has played a bigger and bigger role in many nations' criminal justice systems. It has been used to prove that suspects were involved in crimes and to free people who were wrongly convicted. At the heart of DNA evidence is the biological molecule itself, which serves as an instruction manual and blueprint for everything in your body. A DNA molecule is a long, twisting chain known as a double helix. Whilst the majority of DNA does not differ from human to human, some 3 million base pairs of DNA (about 0.10 per cent of your entire genome) vary from person to person. In other words, 99.9 per cent of human DNA sequences are the same for everyone, but 0.01 per cent are different enough to tell one person from another. In human cells, DNA is tightly wrapped into 23 pairs of chromosomes. One member of each chromosomal pair comes from your mother, and the other comes from your father. Unless you have an identical twin, your DNA is unique to you. This is what makes DNA evidence so valuable in investigations – it is almost impossible for someone else to have DNA that is identical to yours.

Alec Jeffreys and the development of genetic fingerprinting

In 1984, during routine experiments in his laboratory at Leicester University, Alec Jeffreys realised that the X-ray film image he was studying revealed differences and similarities in his technician's family's DNA. He was later to establish that each individual has their own unique genetic profile and how this could be revealed. Working in the laboratory, Jeffreys recalls, he and his technician simply were following their noses. They had 'absolutely no idea' of the applications that would result from the discovery they stumbled upon. 'I have never approached an experiment with a desire to solve a practical problem', he observes, pinning down his moment of discovery to precisely 9.05 am on Monday 10 September 1984. 'My forensic thoughts at 8.55 on that morning were precisely zero; they simply were not there. The technology comes first and then the applications, not the

other way around, and you see this over and over again' (*Times Higher Education*, 2009).

Interestingly, another laboratory had come up with similar patterns a year previously and binned them because it was not what they wanted. The research laboratory at the University of Leicester was funded by the Lister Institute, a medical charity research organisation that employed Jeffreys as a research fellow. The Lister Institute filed for a patent in 1984 and, in November 1984, Jeffreys discussed his findings in public for the first time at a meeting of geneticists in London. The giant chemical company ICI eventually bought the patent from the Lister Institute. In 1987, ICI formed a company called Cellmark Diagnostics, specifically to exploit the technology commercially. Jeffreys helped commercialise and popularise the science by coining the inspired phrase genetic fingerprinting and for seeing the forensic implications. Cellmark developed the technology and numerous product applications for it. Over the next 20 years, it was extremely successful and profitable. Moreover, it has been the forensic science laboratories around the world that have embraced, adopted and further developed this technology.

Curiosity-driven basic research

Jeffreys, along with many other scientific groups, has argued, in terms of many examples, how curiosity-driven research has led to important developments in the interest of society. They argue that basic research is the seed corn of the technological harvest that sustains modern society. Lasers, nuclear magnetic resonance, semiconductors, nanostructures and medical cyclotrons, all subjects of great technological and medical importance, originated in basic physical research. Albert Einstein probably sums this up best with his famous quote: 'I have no special talents. I am only passionately curious.'

The important point here, of course, is that the model of innovation being advocated is science-focused with virtually no concern for the market: the so-called technology push approach. And it is true that progress in research often is made through simple curiosity. Researchers often find different, sometimes greater, riches than the ones they are seeking. For example, the tetrafluoroethylene cylinder that gave rise to Teflon was meant to be used in the preparation of new refrigerants. And the anti-AIDS drug AZT was designed as a remedy for cancer.

→

369

Frequently, the investigators were interested in some natural phenomenon, sometimes evident, sometimes conjectured, sometimes predicted by theory.

What is significant here is that the road from fundamental discovery to practical application is often quite long, ranging from about 10 years in the example of Nylon to some 80 years in the case of liquid crystals. The role of basic research, then, is to fill the well of knowledge so that this can be tapped for new technology and new products. Of course, few would argue against more research, but there is the small question of who is going to pay. Often, it falls to national governments. But elected governments have short time horizons; hence they are interested in a tighter linkage between basic research and national goals.

Firms and their shareholders have even shorter time horizons and it is almost unrealistic to expect firms to put their hands in their pockets to fund research over such long periods of time. But we need to recognise that basic research will continue to provide a stream of ideas and discoveries that will, eventually, be translated into new products.

Applying the science to develop products and services

To get someone's DNA profile, you do not need to sequence their entire hereditary information or genome. The profiling system in use in Britain looks at 11 very small regions of DNA – about one millionth of the total. One of these tells you the person's gender; the other ten are short tandem repeats (STRs). In lots of places in our so-called 'junk' DNA there are repeating patterns of short sequences of base pairs. The number of times each short sequence is repeated varies from person to person, though within a limited range of, say, 10 to 25. However, the chances of two unrelated individuals having exactly the same number of repeats in all 10 regions used for DNA profiling are one in a billion.

The very first case that utilised DNA fingerprinting was *Sarba* v. *The Home Office* (1985), an immigration case where it was necessary to prove the direct biological relationship between Christianna Sarba and her son Andrew. By comparing Christianna's DNA sample against that of Andrew's and his three legally recognised siblings, a direct biological relationship was shown beyond a doubt. The Ghanian boy was allowed to stay in the country. This captured the public's sympathy and imagination. It was

science helping an individual challenge authority. From that moment, Jeffreys entered the realm of celebrity science. The university's switchboard was jammed with calls from people asking him to do tests. One Sunday morning, as he was pruning roses in his front garden, a car drew up and out stepped a lawyer and an immigrant family, begging him to take blood samples. They had driven all the way from London, having heard about DNA fingerprinting. But he was not a licensed phlebotomist and, therefore, could not agree. (Phlebotomy is the act of drawing blood either for testing or transfusion. It is a skill employed by physicians and many professionals in allied health fields.)

The first forensic application of DNA profiling again caught the public mood after two girls were raped and murdered in the Enderby area of Leicestershire, UK. A man had confessed to one murder but not the other and the police thought genetic profiling might prove him guilty of both. When, against all expectations, he was found innocent of both; the hunt was on to find a genetic profile from the male population of the area that matched samples taken from the two victims. Colin Pitchfork was eventually convicted – after being heard boasting that he had persuaded a friend to give a sample on his behalf. Jeffreys was relieved – not just because a killer had been trapped, but because, if the operation had failed, the public's perception of forensic DNA as an effective tool would have been shattered. It is worthy of note that genetic fingerprinting has not made Jeffreys a fortune. He lives modestly in Leicester with his wife Sue, whom he met when they were teenagers, and they have a cottage overlooking a surfing beach in Cornwall.

DNA profiling and the UK Forensic Science Service (FSS)

DNA profiling was further developed and fine-tuned by Jeffreys and his team in 1985, with the term DNA Fingerprinting being retained for the initial test that compares many small parts of DNA simultaneously. By focusing on just a few of these highly variable parts of DNA, profiling made the system more sensitive, more reproducible and amenable to computer databasing, and soon became the standard forensic DNA system used in criminal case work and paternity testing worldwide.

The development of DNA amplification opened up new approaches to forensic DNA testing. It allowed automation, greatly increased sensitivity and a move to alternative marker systems. DNA profiling was also further developed by the UK Forensic Science Service in the 1990s, allowing the launch of the UK National DNA Database (NDNAD) in 1995. With highly automated and sophisticated equipment, modern-day DNA profiling can process hundreds of samples each day. The current system developed for the NDNAD, gives a discrimination power of one in over a billion. Under British law, anyone arrested has their DNA profile stored on a database (whether or not they are convicted), which now contains the DNA information of over five million people.

The UK FSS can trace its roots back to the 1930s, but it was after the Second World War that forensic science was more widely recognised for its value in crime detection, both by the police and the general public. The Home Office put in place a network of regional laboratories. Changes in the law also changed the profile of the service. DNA profiling is the most significant development yet in forensic science and it was the Forensic Science Service that pioneered the development and implementation of DNA profiling technologies. Almost 10 years after its initial discovery, Mitochondrial DNA (mtDNA) profiling was developed for use on old and degraded material. In 1999, the industry was privatised and the UK FSS had competition from the private sector. LGC Forensics is a major player in the industry and handles a lot of work for the UK police forces. Formerly the state-owned Laboratory of the Government Chemist, LGC Ltd was sold off by the Government for £5 million in 1996. In February 2010, LGC was valued at £257 million. It has grown in other ways, too, since privatisation: staff numbers have increased from 270 to more than 1,500.

The FSS designed and built a dedicated unit, to establish the world's first DNA database to permit mouth and hair samples to be taken without consent from individuals who are charged, sported for or convicted of an offence. The database now contains more than 4 million samples, a volume that is increasing by around 40,000 to 50,000 new samples every month. Today in the UK, the national criminal database has had a remarkable impact on criminal investigation. Seventy per cent of all forensic tests done in Britain are DNA tests. If you get a crime scene DNA sample and put it on the database, the odds are that you will find your suspect straight away. It is the most powerful criminal investigation tool there is. The following shows how (Jones, 2010):

In June 2008, a 19-year-old man from Nottingham was arrested for careless and inconsiderate driving. The police took his photograph, his fingerprints and a swab from the inside of his cheek to get his DNA profile. A few months after the DNA profile of the 19-year-old careless driver was uploaded to the database, it was flagged as a close, but not perfect, match to the profile of the probable killer of Colette Aram. Aram was 16 years old when she was abducted, raped and strangled on 30 October 1983 – five years before the careless driver was born! Twenty thousand people were interviewed in the course of the investigation, but the killer was not found. In October 2008, on the 25th anniversary of the murder, Nottinghamshire police announced they had new evidence, derived using the latest forensic DNA analysis techniques. They also had the killer's DNA profile. But it did not match any of the four million profiles on the database. A new tactic was called for. The database was searched again, this time for 'near misses': profiles similar enough to the killer's that they could belong to a member of his family. The DNA of the 300 closest (male) hits was then re-examined, this time looking at markers on the Y-chromosome: as all the DNA on this is passed from father to son, it is a very good indicator of familial relationships between men. The markers on the 19-year-old careless driver's Y-chromosome came up as a match for the killer's. His father and two uncles were arrested in April 2009. The careless driver's father, Paul Hutchinson, a 51-year-old newspaper delivery agent, was charged with Colette Aram's murder. He pleaded guilty and, on 25 January 2010, was sentenced to life imprisonment.

Collecting DNA evidence and the CSI effect

Standard turnaround times – from crime scene exhibit to DNA profile – have gone down from three months to three weeks to three days. When necessary, analysis can be done in a matter of hours. It has also become possible to generate profiles from ever smaller or more degraded DNA samples. A lot of the material that is analysed comes in as swabs taken by police investigators and scene of crime officers, but finding and removing the human tissue from objects is not always straightforward. The objects in question are frequently

→

things such as cigarette ends, gloves, hats, drink cans, but sometimes there are larger objects, too. Different objects present different challenges: a cigarette end is likely to have plenty of DNA on it, but it may come from more than one person, if the cigarette has been shared, and chemicals in the paper or filter can interfere with the profiling process. There is also the potential difficulty of linking the cigarette to the crime in court. Just because the suspect smoked a cigarette found at the crime scene does not mean he committed the crime, or that he was even there: the cigarette could have been brought along on someone's shoe. So, the condition of the cigarette end has to be documented: does it look freshly stubbed out, or is it dirty and flattened? A blood-stained hammer may be easier to link to the crime, but getting the DNA profile of the last person to have wielded it presents a whole new set of problems. This raises another issue, which is time and quality of examinations. Detecting evidence is often linked to available time; so, if somebody has got all day to look at an item, then they are more likely to find something than someone who spends only an hour analysing it. This has nothing to do with technology, but simple procedure and professionalism.

For many years, fingerprints were the gold standard for linking suspects to a crime scene. Today, the gold standard is DNA evidence because DNA can be collected from virtually anywhere. Even a criminal wearing gloves may, unwittingly, leave behind trace amounts of biological material. It could be a hair, saliva, blood, semen, skin, sweat, mucus or earwax. All it takes is a few cells to obtain enough DNA information to identify a suspect with near certainty.

For this reason, law enforcement officials take unusual care at crime scenes. Police officers and detectives often work closely with laboratory personnel or evidence collection technicians to make sure evidence is not contaminated. This involves wearing gloves and using disposable instruments, which can be discarded after collecting each sample. When investigators find a piece of evidence, they place it in a paper bag or envelope, not in a plastic bag. This is important because plastic bags retain moisture, which can damage DNA. Direct sunlight and warmer conditions may also damage DNA.

The *CSI* series is known for its unusual camera angles, editing techniques, hi-tech gadgets, detailed technical discussion and graphic portrayal of bullet trajectories, blood spray patterns, organ damage, meth-

ods of evidence recovery (e.g. fingerprints from the inside of latex gloves) and crime reconstructions. This technique of shooting extreme close-ups, normally with explanatory commentary from one of the characters, is referred to in the media as the 'CSI shot'. Many episodes feature lengthy scenes in which experiments, tests or other technical work is portrayed in detail, usually with minimal sound effects and accompanying music. The CSI effect suggests that the television programme and its spin-offs, which wildly exaggerate and glorify forensic science, affect the public and, in turn, affect trials either by (a) burdening the prosecution by creating greater expectations about forensic science than can be delivered or (b) burdening the defence by creating exaggerated faith in the capabilities and reliability of the forensic sciences.

Another criticism of the show is the depiction of police procedure, which some consider to be decidedly lacking in realism. For instance, the show's characters not only investigate crime scenes ('process', as their real-world counterparts do), but they also conduct raids, engage in suspect pursuit and arrest, interrogate suspects and solve cases, areas that fall under the responsibility of uniformed officers and detectives, not CSI personnel.

Some police and district attorneys have criticised the show for giving members of the public an inaccurate perception of how police solve crimes. Victims and their families are coming to expect instant answers from showcased techniques, such as DNA analysis and fingerprinting, when, in real life, processing such evidence can take days or even weeks. District attorneys suggest that the conviction rate in cases with little physical evidence has decreased, due largely to the influence of *CSI* on jury members. However, it is not all negative; recruitment and training programmes have seen a massive increase in applicants, with a far wider range of people now interested in something previously regarded as a scientific backwater.

What often goes unmentioned is the long tedious process from physical evidence to convicted criminal. The physical evidence itself is only part of the equation. The ultimate goal is the conviction of the perpetrator of the crime. So, whilst the CSI hero scrapes off the dried blood without smearing any prints, lifts several hairs without disturbing any trace evidence and smashes through a wall in the living room, he is also considering all of the necessary steps to preserve the evidence in its current form, what the laboratory can do with this evidence in order to reconstruct the crime or identify the criminal, and the legal issues involved in making sure this evidence is admissible in court.

Conclusions

This case has shown the impact of DNA fingerprinting on the world and the forensic world in particular. It has been considerable; helped in no small way by the success of the *CSI* television series. And, yet, the story of the scientist who uncovered DNA fingerprinting is largely unknown. But, this is not unusual and, indeed, arguably is the norm for most scientific advancements. Scientific development itself rarely produces fame or fortune. It is the application of this science that usually leads to fortune and, to a lesser extent, fame.

The success, however, of DNA fingerprinting has led to problems in the world of prosecution and a phenomenon known as the prosecutor's fallacy. The fallacy here is the idea that, as the DNA profile generated from stains found at a crime scene matches the suspect's DNA profile, and as there is only a one in a billion chance of it also matching someone else's profile, then there is a one in a billion chance that the suspect is innocent. But DNA evidence simply cannot, on its own, tell you whether or not someone is guilty. The prosecutor's fallacy stems, in general, from a misunderstanding of how statistics work. In the case of DNA, however, it may be exacerbated by an almost mystical belief in the molecules' power to solve all identification and criminal investigation problems.

This case also provides an insight into the debate on the extent of curiosity-driven research. Sir Alec Jeffreys argues the importance of continuing to allow researchers to conduct 'unfettered, fundamental, curiosity-driven' research that has led to some of the most important discoveries, including his own. Firms with large R&D budgets may be able to fund some basic research but, with its long time horizons, much of the funding for basic research will remain in the hands of national governments. Applied research, with its eye on the market and potential applications of the technology, is very different from curiosity-driven research. Such research is full of directions, priorities and time frames. Jeffreys argues such an approach tends to direct scientists towards establishing and solving obvious problems. This may be true but, as far as the firm is concerned, the research must deliver a return for the shareholders and usually this will involve new products and services.

Another issue that the case raises is whether scientists today are exploited by the system. For example, compare Alec Jeffreys with James Watt. While Jeffreys was responsible for developing DNA fingerprinting – it belonged to the Lister Institute who paid for the research – and it was ICI (now Astra-Zeneca) who made it into a kit that the police and forensic science service could use. The large profits from the discovery of genetic fingerprinting do not go to the scientist who discovered it, they go to Astra-Zeneca, and the many other firms that followed. James Watt, on the other hand, financed his own laboratory at Glasgow University out of the profits he made selling steam engines to coal owners. He made a fortune in the eighteenth century, one that enabled him to maintain his independence as a scientist. Not all scientists today are able to maintain their independence and many seek funding from industry for their research.

Sources: Times Higher Education (2009) The small scientist, 3 September; Jones, T. (2010) The rise of DNA analysis in crime solving, *The Guardian*, 10 April, Weekend, 24.

Questions

1 What are the benefits of undirected research (curiosity-driven research)?

2 Should firms undertake undirected or curiosity-driven research or should all research be linked to products and businesses?

3 Show how this case illustrates the power and influence of radical innovation and incremental innovation.

4 Given the contribution to society that DNA fingerprinting has made, why is Alec Jeffreys not a household name?

5 Explain why the adoption of technology in this case seems to have happened very quickly.

6 Discuss how this case illustrates benefits and limitations of the public understanding of science.

7 Discuss the impact of the CSI phenomenon.

8 Explain the prosecutor's fallacy and why it is a problem.

Note: This case study has been written as a basis for class discussion rather than to illustrate effective or ineffective managerial or administrative behaviour. It has been prepared from a variety of published sources, as indicated, and from observations.

Pause for thought

Would you participate in a clinical trial? If not, what would encourage you to participate: money, limiting risk, a trial whose results may help a friend's suffering?

Chapter summary

This chapter has focused on the key activities of R&D management. It has shown that these have changed significantly over the past few decades. Emphasis traditionally has been placed on internal R&D, but now there is an increase in the use of external R&D. This presents another set of challenges. In particular, when acquiring externally developed technology, a business must also consider the extent of control that it requires over the technology. The need to provide scientific freedom for R&D personnel and the benefits that this brings were also considered.

R&D plays a considerable role in the product innovation process. Indeed, often there is continual interaction with R&D throughout the development of the product. Finally, the chapter considered the various ways of funding the R&D activity. The approach adopted will significantly affect the way R&D is perceived within and outside the company.

Discussion questions

1 Explain how Dyson Appliances Ltd could exploit externally sourced R&D.

2 Examine the degree of control required by a firm over its technology portfolio. Are there certain components or technologies that should remain in-house?

3 Discuss the benefits and limitations of open source R&D.

4 What is meant by scientific freedom and why is it important? How would you react to a Skunk works in your firm?

5 Discuss the relative shift from manufacturing-centred R&D towards more service-orientated R&D.

6 Explain why many product managers do not view an investment in R&D as a high-risk activity. Indeed, for some it seems they are certain of a positive result.

7 Explain the product development process in the pharmaceutical industry.

Key words and phrases

References

Abelson, P.H. (1995) Science and technology policy, *Science*, vol. 267, no. 27, 1247.

Babcock, D.L. (1996) *Managing Engineering Technology: An Introduction to Management for Engineers*, 2nd edn, Prentice Hall, London.

Berkhout, A.J., Hartmann, D. and Trott, P. (2010) Connecting technological capabilities with market needs using a cyclic innovation model, *R&D Management*, vol. 40, no. 5, 474–90.

Buonansegna, E., Salomo, S., Maier, A. M. and Li-Ying, J. (2014), Pharmaceutical new product development: why do clinical trials fail? *R&D Management*, vol. 44, 189–202.

Brzustowski, T., Butler, J., Leung, F., Linton, J.D. and Smith, J. (2010) Emerging and new approaches to R&D management: selected papers from The R&D Management Conference 2008, Ottawa, *R&D Management*, vol. 40, 1–3.

Carvalho, M., Fleury, A. and Lopes, A. P. (2013) An overview of the literature on technology roadmapping (TRM): contributions and trends, *Technological Forecasting and Social Change*, vol. 80, no. 7, 1418–37.

Carbonell-Foulquie, P., Munuera-Aleman, J.L. and Rodriquez-Escudero, A.I. (2003) Criteria employed for go/no-go decisions when developing successful highly innovative products, *Industrial Marketing Management*, June.

Casper, S. and Whitley, R. (2004) Managing competences in entrepreneurial technology firms: a comparative institutional analysis of Germany, Sweden and the UK, *Research Policy*, vol. 33, no. 1, 89–106.

Chesbrough, H. and Bogers, M. (2014) Explicating open innovation: clarifying an emerging paradigm for understanding innovation, *New Frontiers in Open Innovation*, Oxford: Oxford University Press, 3–28.

Chesbrough, H. and Crowther, A.K. (2006) Beyond high tech: early adopters of open innovation in other industries, *R&D Management*, vol. 36, no. 3, 229–36.

Cooper, R.G. (2001) *Winning at New Products*, 3rd edn, Perseus Publishing, Cambridge, MA.

Corey, E.R. (1997) *Technology Fountainheads: The Management Challenge of R&D Consortia*, Ziff-Davis/Harvard Business School Press, Boston, MA.

Englund, R.L. and Graham, R.J. (1999) From experience: linking projects to strategy, *Journal of Product Innovation Management*, vol. 16, 52–64.

Farrukh, C., Phaal, R., Probert, D., Gregory, M. and Wright, J. (2000) Developing a process for the relative valuation of R&D programmes, *R&D Management*, vol. 30, no. 1, 43–53.

Hagedoorn, J. and Wang, N. (2012) Is there complementarity or substitutability between internal and external R&D strategies? *Research Policy*, vol. 41, no. 6, 1072–83.

Holger, E. (2002) Success factors of new product development: a review of the empirical literature, *International Journal of Management Reviews*, vol. 4, no. 1, 1–40.

Howells, J. (2008) New directions in R&D: current and prospective challenges, *R&D Management*, vol. 38, no. 3, 241–52.

Liddle, D. (2004) R&D Project Selection at Danahar, MBA Dissertation, University of Portsmouth.

Lin, C., Wu, Y.J., Chang, C., Wang, W. and Lee, C.Y. (2012) The alliance innovation performance of R&D alliances – the absorptive capacity perspective. *Technovation*, vol. 32, no. 5, 282–92.

Mason, G., Beltramo, J.P. and Paul, J.-J. (2004) External knowledge sourcing in different national settings: a comparison of electronics establishments in Britain and France, *Research Policy*, vol. 33, no. 1, 53–72.

Olausson, D. and Berggren, C. (2012) Managing asymmetries in information flows and interaction between R&D, manufacturing, and service in complex product development, *R&D Management*, vol. 42, 342–57.

Pavitt, K. (1984) Sectoral patterns of technological change: towards a taxonomy and theory, *Research Policy*, vol. 13, 343–73.

Pavitt, K. (1990) What we know about the strategic management of technology, *California Management Review*, Spring, 17–26.

Probert, J., Connell, D. and Mina, A. (2013) R&D service firms: the hidden engine of the high-tech economy? *Research Policy*, vol. 42, no. 6, 1274–85.

Sakakibara, M. (2002) Formation of R&D consortia: industry and company effects, *Strategic Management Journal*, vol. 23, 1033–50.

Seaton, R.A.F. and Cordey-Hayes, M. (1993) The development and application of interactive models of technology transfer, *Technovation*, vol. 13, no. 1, 45–53.

Teece, D. (1986) Profiting from technological innovation: implications for integration, collaboration, licensing, and public policy, *Research Policy*, vol. 15, 285–305.

Tierney, R., Hermina, W. and Walsh, S. (2013), The pharmaceutical technology landscape: a new form of technology roadmapping, *Technological Forecasting and Social Change*, vol. 80, no. 2, 194–211.

West, J. and Bogers, M. (2014) Leveraging external sources of innovation: a review of research on open innovation, *Journal of Product Innovation Management*, vol. 31, no. 4, 814–31.

Further reading

For a more detailed review of the R&D management literature, the following develop many of the issues raised in this chapter:

HSBC (2010) *100 Thoughts*, HSBC, London.

Lakemond, N., Berggren, C. and van Weele, A. (2006) Coordinating supplier involvement in product development projects: a differentiated coordination typology, *R&D Management*, vol. 36, no. 1, 55–66.

Lichtenthaler, U. and Ernst, H. (2006) Attitudes to externally organising knowledge management tasks: a review, reconsideration and extension of the NIH syndrome, *R&D Management*, vol. 36, no. 4, 367–86.

Oliveira, M.G., Rozenfeld, H., Phaal, R., and Probert, D. (2015). Decision making at the front end of innovation: the hidden influence of knowledge and decision criteria. *R&D Management*, 45(2), 161–180.

Phillips, W., Lamming, R., Bessant, J. and Noke, H. (2006) Discontinuous innovation and supply relationships: strategic dalliances, *R&D Management*, vol. 36, no. 4, 451–61.

Tsai, K.-H. and Wang, J.-C. (2007) Inward technology licensing and firm performance: a longitudinal study, *R&D Management*, vol. 37, no. 2, 151–60.

Chapter 11
Open innovation and technology transfer

Introduction

Information is central to the operation of firms. It is the stimulus for knowledge, know-how, skills and expertise and is one of the key drivers of the innovation process. Most firms are involved with a two-way flow of knowledge wrapped up as technology in the form of a product or process. Those companies that spend the most on R&D are also some of the biggest licensors of technology; and dynamic, innovative firms are likely to buy in more technology than their static counterparts. This chapter examines the complex subject of technology transfer, increasingly being referred to as knowledge transfer. It explores its role in the innovation process and its influence on organisational learning. The case study at the end of this chapter illustrates how new products arise following the transfer of technology from electronic sensors to disposable nappies.

Chapter contents

Learning objectives

When you have completed this chapter you will be able to:

- recognise the importance of the concept of technology/knowledge transfer with respect to innovation management;

- provide a summary of the process of technology/knowledge transfer;

- examine the various models of technology transfer;

- assess the importance of internal organisational factors and how they affect inward technology transfer;

- explain why a 'receptive' environment is necessary for technology transfer;

- identify the different barriers to technology transfer; and

- recognise how tacit knowledge links technology transfer and innovation.

Background

The industrialised world has seen a shift from labour- and capital-intensive industries to knowledge- and technology-based economies. As competition has increased in markets throughout the world, technology has emerged as a significant business factor and a primary commodity. Knowledge, transformed into know-how or technology has become a major asset within companies. Technology is vital for a business to remain competitive. In rapidly evolving markets, such as electronics and bio-technology, new products based on new technology are essential. Even in mature markets, new technology is necessary to remain competitive on cost and quality.

In the 1960s, 70s and 80s, many businesses favoured the internal development of technology. But today, with the increasing technological content of many products, many organisations consider internal development too uncertain, too expensive and too slow for the rapid technological changes that are occurring in the market. These drawbacks can be traced to a more fundamental cause – the increasing complexity of technologies and the increasing range of technologies found within products. This has led to a shortening of product life cycles with replacement technologies rapidly succeeding others. The rising costs of conducting R&D have forced many organisations to look for research partners. In addition, companies are finding it increasingly difficult to sustain R&D capability over all areas of their business as the complexity of these areas increases. Internal R&D increasingly is focused on core competencies (see Prahalad and Hamel, 1990). R&D in all other business activities is covered progressively by collaborations, partnerships and strategic alliances. Whilst the activity is not new – Alfred Marshal noted the extensive linkages between firms in his work in 1919 (CEST, 1991) – the extent of collaboration appears to be on the increase. Hagedoorn (1990), for example, has shown a marked rise in the amount of collaboration between firms during the 1980s and 90s.

Many large firms operate in several technology fields and often are referred to as multi-technology corporations (MTC). It is extremely difficult and expensive for such corporations to be technological leaders in every technology within their scope. More and more companies are looking for outside sources of either basic technology to shorten product development time or applied technology to avoid the costs and delay of research and development. In addition, avoiding reinventing the wheel appears to be high on the list of corporate objectives. Previously, there was one well-known exception to this and that was where a competitor was undertaking similar research. Under these circumstances, duplication of research was regarded as inevitable and, thus, acceptable. However, numerous recent technological collaborations between known competitors, for example IBM and Apple, General Motors and BMW, would suggest that even this exception is becoming less acceptable to industry.

The search for acquisition and exploitation of developed technology is clearly of interest to virtually all sectors of industry, but it is of particular interest to R&D-intensive or science-based industries. A US Government study on technology transfer stated: 'Corporations trade in technology in world markets just as they do in other goods and services' (DFI International, 1998: 93).

The dominant economic perspective

It was in the 1980s that governments around the world began to recognise the potential opportunities that technology transfer could bring. This was based on a simple economic theory. Technology that has already been produced, and hence paid for by someone else, could be used and exploited by other companies to generate revenue and, thereby, economic growth for the economy (see Figure 11.1).

It was with this theory in mind that governments began encouraging companies to be involved in technology transfer. They set up a whole variety of programmes trying to utilise technology that had been developed for the defence or space industries (see subsequent section 'Models of technology transfer'). They also encouraged companies to work together to see if they could share technology for the common good. Furthermore, since 1980, the transfer of technology from universities to private industry has become big business, particularly in the United States. For example, during 2003, technology transfer revenues were approximately $1.3 billion and, more importantly, the economic benefits that flowed from the technologies that were transferred into the private sector were estimated to have exceeded $41 billion in value. Technology transfer, as a university enterprise, only came into existence with the passage of the Bayh-Doyle Act or University and Small Business Patent Procedures Act in 1980. The Bayh-Doyle legislation (sponsored by two senators, Birch Bayh of Indiana and Robert Doyle of Kansas) created an emerging industry by transferring ownership for any intellectual property that was developed with federal research funding to the developing institution. This transfer of ownership allowed universities the right to license or sell their intellectual property rights to industry for further development and profitable commercialisation. Thus, this legislation cleared the way for technology transfer to become a factor both in driving the US economy and contributing to the greater social good. Twenty-five years later, universities have become increasingly adept at developing and transferring their technology.

The alleged panacea for industry's problems did not materialise. Looking back, some still argue that it was a commendable theory, it just did not seem to work in practice. Others argue that the theory was flawed and would never work in practice (Seaton and Cordey-Hayes, 1993); this is discussed later in the section on 'Limitations and barriers to technology transfer'. There were, however, many benefits that emerged from the energetic interest in technology transfer. One of them was the realisation that successful collaboration and joint ventures could be achieved, even with competitors.

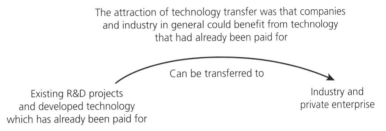

The attraction of technology transfer was that companies and industry in general could benefit from technology that had already been paid for

Can be transferred to

Existing R&D projects and developed technology which has already been paid for

Industry and private enterprise

Figure 11.1 The economic perspective of technology transfer

> ### Pause for thought
>
> Whilst it may be possible, in theory, to buy technology with little prior knowledge of it, surely it would be extremely difficult to exploit it without prior knowledge?

Open innovation

It should now be clear that the need for external linkages and connectivity is a major factor influencing the management of innovation. Furthermore, Chesbrough (2006) argued that the process of innovation has shifted even further from one of closed systems, internal to the firm, to a new mode of open systems involving a range of players distributed up and down the supply chain (see Figure 11.2). This seems to be supported by the increasing application of network theory into more and more areas of business management (Parkhe et al., 2006).

This chapter illustrates the strong link within the innovation process between the external environment of the firm and the internal environment of the firm. It examines and explores knowledge flows within the innovation process. It illustrates how the 'open innovation' paradigm builds on previous research and is presented as opportunities for the management of innovation. It confirms that accessing and utilising these flows of knowledge is a fundamental part of the innovation process. The process of accessing and transferring technology, then, is becoming increasingly crucial within innovation and new product development. In a study of 203 laboratories of Japanese firms located in Japan, the findings revealed how an open innovation policy can contribute to the laboratory's R&D performance by facilitating external collaborations by the laboratories (Asakawa et al., 2010).

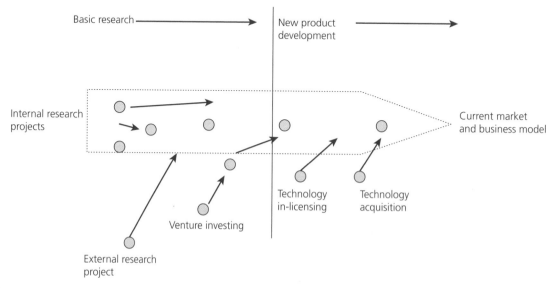

Figure 11.2 Chesbrough's open innovation approach

Table 11.1 Contrasting 'closed innovation' principles and 'open innovation' principles

Closed innovation principles	Open innovation principles
The smart people in our field work for us.	Not all of the smart people work for us so we must find and tap into the knowledge and expertise of bright individuals outside our company.
To profit from R&D, we must discover, develop, produce and ship it ourselves.	External R&D can create significant value; internal R&D is needed to claim some portion of that value.
If we discover it ourselves, we will get it to market first.	We don't have to originate the research in order to profit from it.
If we are the first to commercialise an innovation, we will win.	Building a better business model is better than getting to market first.
If we create the most and best ideas in the industry, we will win.	If we make the best use of internal and external ideas, we will win.
We should control our intellectual property (IP) so that our competitors do not profit from our ideas.	We should profit from others' use of our IP, and we should buy others' IP whenever it advances our own business model.

Source: Chesbrough, H. (2003) *Open Innovation: The New Imperative for Creating and Profiting from Technology*, HBS Press, Boston, MA.

Chesbrough (2003) presents six notions that lie behind the so-called closed model of innovation (see Table 11.1). However, whilst the dichotomy between closed innovation and open innovation may be true, in theory, it does not really exist in industry today. Unmistakably, Chesbrough has been very successful in popularising the notion of technology transfer and the need to share and exchange knowledge. Indeed, it seems that, in using a business strategy perspective, the open innovation concept may have reached new audiences (e.g., CEOs of technology-intensive companies) that, for so many years, the innovation and R&D literatures failed to reach. The fact that large multinational companies, such as Procter & Gamble and Philips, have incorporated the principles of open innovation and facilitate conferences and publications on the subject deserves admiration and praise. In essence, it has created real-life laboratories (playgrounds) in which the mechanisms of open innovation can be studied in great detail (see, for example, Hacievliyagil, 2007 and Hacievliyagil et al., 2008).

Open innovation is currently one of the most debated topics in management literature. There are many unanswered questions: how relevant is it to firms? And how should firms implement open innovation in practice (Chiaroni et al., 2009; West et al., 2014)? Furthermore, the open innovation paradigm is not without its critics. Whilst Chesbrough (2003, 2006) acknowledges the rich source of antecedents to the 'open innovation paradigm', there may be many scholars of R&D management and innovation management who would argue that this so-called paradigm represents little more than the repackaging and representation of concepts and findings presented over the past 30 years (see Trott and Hartmann, 2009). Dahlander and Gann (2010) reviewed a wide range of studies on the topic of open innovation and concluded that openness seems to manifest itself in two inbound processes: sourcing and acquiring technology, and two outbound processes, revealing and selling technology. This suggests that, fundamentally, the activities being undertaken by firms have changed little.

The paradox of openness

To innovate, firms often need to draw from, and collaborate with, a large number of actors from outside their organisation. At the same time, firms need also to be focused on capturing the returns from their innovative ideas. This gives rise to a paradox of openness – the creation of innovations often requires openness, but the commercialisation of innovations requires protection. Indeed, intellectual property lawyers frequently express concern when employees begin discussing the firm's technology with potential collaborators. The outcome of collaborative agreements depends on the effectiveness of the governance structure. Mutual commitment and trust, together with other relational and environmental characteristics, can deal with such uncertainty. Valuation of the licenses or agreements that are used to transfer technology is a very delicate, but crucial, issue in R&D collaborations (Laursen and Salter, 2014). This raises the issue of whether different types of open innovation governance are suitable in different situations (Felin and Zenger, 2014). Technological progress in an industry is enabled by the collective R&D efforts of suppliers, users and research organisations. The pattern of this R&D collaboration changes over time and there is a corresponding change in the opportunities and challenges confronting industry participants. The global semiconductor manufacturing industry from 1990 to 2010 illustrates experienced exponential technological progress that was fuelled by the deep ultraviolet (DUV) manufacturing technology. The types of interactions amongst suppliers, users and research organisations change as they collectively push the technology envelope forward (Kapoor and McGrath, 2014).

More recently, West and Bogers (2014) reviewed the literature on open innovation and found that, whilst there is plenty of research on access to technology and innovation, little is known about integrating and commercialising these innovations. This has been the fundamental problem with attempts at technology transfer over the past 40 years.

Introduction to technology transfer

The concept of **technology transfer** is not new. In the thirteenth century, Marco Polo helped introduce to the Western world Chinese inventions, such as the compass, papermaking, printing and the use of coal for fuel. In more recent years, the concept has generated an enormous amount of debate. Many argue that it was a change in US law that led to the surge of interest in the subject. The passage of the landmark National Cooperative Research Act (NCRA) of 1984 officially made cooperation on pre-competitive research legal. This, plus the Bayh-Doyle Act in 1980, certainly helped raise the profile of the concept of technology transfer (Werner, 1991).

> *Technology Transfer is the application of technology to a new use or user. It is the process by which technology developed for one purpose is employed either in a different application or by a new user. The activity principally involves the increased utilisation of the existing science/technology base in new areas of application as opposed to its expansion by means of further research and development.*
>
> (Langrish et al., 1982)

One of the main problems of research into technology transfer is that, over the years, the term has been used to describe almost any movement of technology from one place to another, to the ridiculous point where the purchase of a car could be classified as an example of technology transfer. It is true that the technology in question may take a variety of forms – it may be a product, a process, a piece of equipment, technical knowledge or expertise or merely a way of doing things. Further, technology transfer involves the movement of ideas, knowledge and information from one context to another. However, it is in the context of innovation that technology transfer is most appropriate and needs to be considered. Hence, technology transfer is defined as:

> *The process of promoting technical innovation through the transfer of ideas, knowledge, devices and artefacts from leading edge companies, R&D organisations and academic research to more general and effective application in industry and commerce.*
>
> (Seaton and Cordey-Hayes, 1993: 46)

Information transfer and knowledge transfer

It was suggested at the beginning of this chapter that information is central to the operation of firms and that it is the stimulus for knowledge, know-how, skills and expertise. Figure 11.3 helps distinguish information from knowledge and know-how, according to its context. It is argued that it is the industrial context that transforms knowledge into action, in the form of projects and activities. It is only when information is used by individuals or organisations that it becomes knowledge, albeit tacit knowledge. The application of this knowledge then leads to actions and skills (projects, processes, products, etc.). Consider Illustration 11.1.

Pause for thought

The famous Delft blue and white pottery in Holland developed in the sixteenth century and was copied from the original Chinese blue and white pottery. Similarly, the UK Wedgwood pottery developed in the nineteenth century was an imitation of the Delftware. Is this technology transfer or illicit copying?

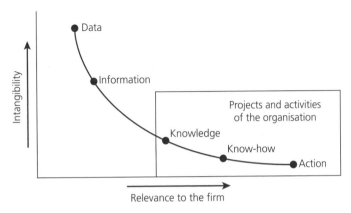

Figure 11.3 The tangibility of knowledge

Source: Adapted from Cooley, M. (1987) *Architect or Bee? The Human Price of Technology*, Hogarth Press, London. Used by permission of the Random House Group Limited and with kind permission from Professor M. Cooley.

Pilkington, information and knowledge

Materials have different melting points; for example, glass is molten at 1,500°C whereas tin is molten at 180°C. On its own, this is information that can be found in most metallurgy books. Provide an industrial context and the information is transformed into knowledge, know-how and expertise.

Pilkington pioneered the manufacturing process of 'float glass'. This, essentially, involves heating sand to 1,500°C and forcing it out through rollers and over a pool of molten tin to cool prior to being cut to size. This patented process is used universally now by every glass manufacturer in the world. Pilkington developed the process in the 1950s and 60s and then licensed it to every glass manufacturer worldwide. For an entire year, however, the pilot plant had produced nothing but scrap glass. After many operating difficulties, production engineers eventually succeeded in getting the process to work. The company made so much money out of licensing the process that it was able to purchase what was, at that time, the largest glass manufacturer in the world.

Source: Pearson Education Ltd/Image Source Ltd

Models of technology transfer

A wide variety of models of technology transfer have been used over the years, particularly in the past 20 years. The following section examines some of these models and offers examples of their application.

Licensing

Essentially, **licensing** involves the technology owner receiving a licence fee in return for access to the technology. Very often, the technology in question will be protected by patents. The details of each licensing agreement will vary considerably. Sometimes, the licensor will help the licensee in all aspects of development and final use of the technology. In other cases, the amount of involvement is minimal.

Mutual self-interest is the common dominator behind most licensing contracts, as it is in other business contracts. Licensing is the act of granting another business permission to use your intellectual property. This could be a manufacturing process that is protected by patents or a product or service that is protected by a trademark or copyright. Licensing is the main income generator for the British Technology

Group (BTG), a FTSE 250 listed company. It helps businesses and universities generate income from their intellectual property through the licensing of technology to third parties.

Licences to competitors constitute a high percentage of all licences extended; Microsoft's Windows-operating system is a case in point. These normally arise out of a desire on the part of the competitor to be free of any patent infringement in its development product features or technology. They are also due to the owner of the patent seeking financial gain from the technology.

The licensee must be careful to evaluate the need for and the benefits likely to accrue from the technology before making the commitment to pay. Technology that is only marginally useful, or that may be superseded quickly by new developments in the field, may not be worth a multi-million-dollar licensing agreement. Many companies with sufficient R&D resources believe that patents can be legally breached through creative use of technology.

Other reasons for licensing are to:

- avoid or settle patent infringement issues;
- diversify and grow through the addition of new products;
- improve the design and quality of existing products;
- obtain improved production or processing technology;
- ensure freedom of action in the company's own R&D programme (patents held by other companies may inhibit R&D activities);
- save R&D expense and delay;
- eliminate the uncertainty and risk involved in developing alternative processes and technology;
- accommodate customer needs or wishes; and
- qualify for government and other desirable contracts.

A word of caution. Research by Wang and Yin (2014) shows that, whilst many firms find inward technology licensing (ITL), as a means to access external technological knowledge, an effective and relatively inexpensive way for new product development (NPD), subsequent NPD performance has not yet been found. Indeed, they find that a firm's absorptive capacity and the knowledge endowment in the region where the licensee firm operates determines NPD performance.

Science park model

Science parks are a phenomenon that originated in the United States. The idea is to develop an industrial area or district close to an established centre of excellence, often a university. The underlying rationale is that academic scientists will have the opportunity to take laboratory ideas and develop them into real products. In addition, technology- or science-based companies can set up close to the university so that they can utilise its knowledge base. In the United States, where science parks have existed for 40 years, the achievements have been difficult to quantify. Examples are Stanford University and Silicon Valley, a collection of companies with research activities in electronics, and the 'research triangle' in North Carolina, which has several universities at its core. In the United Kingdom, one of the first science parks to be established was the Cambridge Science Park. Over the past 20 years, this has grown into a large industrial area and has attracted many successful science-based companies, such as Microsoft. Many other universities have also set up their own science parks, such as Southampton, Warwick and Cranfield. It is worth noting that the science park notion separates the innovation process: the R&D is conducted at the science park, but manufacturing is done elsewhere (see Diez-Vial and Montoro-Sanchez, 2014). Business parks, however, combine all activities.

Intermediary agency model

These come in a variety of forms and range from Regional Technology Centres (RTC) to university technology transfer managers. Their role, however, is the same: they act as the intermediary between companies seeking and companies offering technology.

Directory model

During the explosion of interest in technology transfer during the 1980s, many new companies sprang up in an attempt to exploit interest in the subject. Companies, such as Derwent World Patents, Technology Exchange, NIMTECH and Technology Catalysts, offered directories listing technology that was available for licence. Some universities in the United States also produced directories of technology available from the university's own research laboratories. (For example, The Derwent World Patents Index (DWPI) is a database containing patent applications and grants from 44 of the world's patent issuing authorities.)

Knowledge Transfer Partnership model

Previously called 'the teaching company scheme', this UK Research Council-funded programme aims to transfer technology between universities and small companies. This is achieved through postgraduate training. Students registering for a two-year MSc at a university are linked to a local company-based research project. The student studies part time for two years with the university, say two days a week, and the other three days are spent at the company working on the project. The university provides support to the student and offers other expertise to the company. These programmes continue to be very successful and have an impressive 30-year track record (see Illustration 11.2).

Ferret model

The ferret model was used first by Defence Technology Enterprises (DTE). DTE resulted from a joint initiative between the UK Ministry of Defence (MOD) and a consortium of companies experienced in encouraging, exploiting and financing new technology. The *raison d'être* of DTE was to provide access to MOD technology and generate commercial revenue. This was achieved through the use of so-called 'ferrets', qualified scientists and engineers who would ferret around for interesting defence technology that could have wider commercial opportunities. The company ceased trading in 1989.

Illustration 11.2

Cult carmaker Morgan links with universities to generate success

Morgan Motor Company, the centenarian British car manufacturer, has defied the difficulties of the global automobile industry with record sales of its cult sporty convertibles.

Turnover, 60 per cent of which comes from exports, is expected to hit a new high of £28.6 million for 2010. Unlike its larger peers, Morgan only makes cars that people have ordered, pre-selling build slots and taking sizeable deposits to secure commitment from customers. For those buying a Morgan, this means a wait of up to a year for their set of wheels, but the business model has protected Morgan from the risk of masses of unsold stock that have become the bane of its much larger peers. It is a point not missed by Charles Morgan, managing director and grandson of the company's founder: 'Our approach might not be fashionable, but we don't have a situation like some of the other companies in our industry where they have a workforce twice as big as they want', he says. 'We have never gone for volume.'

Morgan is planning to add a couple of extra positions to the 165-person workforce at its factory in the idyllic surroundings of the Malvern Hills. This will help the company raise production to a new high of 850 cars a year. Little seems to have changed on the production line since the company first started making cars there in 1909, with chassis still assembled on wooden blocks and moved by hand around the building. However, Mr Morgan notes that the method of production is not what slows down delivery. 'A lot of the things you put into a luxury car have a three- or five-month order time', he says.

The one thing Morgan orders in advance is its engines from BMW. And it is under the bonnet that Morgan has strived to match the best in the world.

Each Morgan is also fitted with the latest generation ABS braking system, providing stopping times that are better than a Ferrari, according to Bosch, its supplier. Morgan also collaborates with a number of UK universities and is one of the most successful beneficiaries of the government's Knowledge Transfer Partnership, aimed at linking academic innovation with industry. Its AeroMax and SuperSports lines are the world's first super-formed aluminium cars, making them at least 20 per cent lighter than their rivals.

'With the AeroMax we have started to attract a completely different sort of customer', Mr Morgan says. 'We are still selling the little four-door £26,500 sports car to the guy who has just retired and always promised himself a Morgan, but we are also finding people who want a second car down at the villa in France.'

Morgan plans to build on its success with an electric car, whose on-board power generation provides a range of 1,000 miles, due for launch in 2012. It has also started taking orders for its EvaGT, a four-seater sports saloon that was shown for the first time at the Pebble Beach Concours d'Elégance in California this month.

'What we aim to do is to produce a traditional British sports car without the unreliability', Mr Morgan says.

Hiring skilled employees

One of the oldest methods of technology transfer, and one of the most effective according to many research managers, is hiring people with the necessary skills and knowledge. For R&D managers who wish to establish a range of research projects in an area of technology where the company has limited knowledge or experience, this is one of the fastest methods of gaining the necessary technology. People are recruited either from other organisations, including competitors, or from university research departments that have relevant expertise. These people will bring to the organisation their own knowledge and the ways of working and methods used by their previous organisation – some of which may be replicable, others may not. The role of individual and **organisational learning** is explored towards the end of this chapter.

Technology transfer units

In the 1980s, the US Federal Labs and other research-based organisations, including universities, established industrial liaison units and technology transfer units to bring in technology from outside and/or to find partners to help exploit in-house developments. In the United States, academia has always been subject to financial pressures to generate funds. In Europe, however, universities traditionally have relied on government to fund their needs. With an ever-decreasing pool of resources, universities have recognised the potential benefits from exploiting in-house technology. This also has led to the growth in science parks. Technology transfer units use elements of the intermediary and licensing models.

One of the most successful examples of this approach is the British Technology Group (BTG), a state-owned corporation that was set up to commercialise as much state-funded research as possible, including that undertaken by universities. It was previously known as the National Research Development Corporation. It became so successful and profitable that, in 1993, BTG was sold to private investors and it is now operating as a successful public limited company (see Illustration 6.3).

Research clubs

This is a UK Department of Trade and Industry (DTI) funded programme that tries to bring companies together with common interests, in particular research areas. Some conduct collaborative research, others exchange information, knowledge and/ or experience. This approach adopts the science park model of technology transfer. One of the most successful clubs is the M62 Sensors and Instrumentation Research Club, so called because it originated from a group of companies along the M62 motorway in the north-west of England.

European Space Agency (ESA)

The ESA offers access to space research in virtually all fields of science and technology. This is achieved using a combination of three models: the intermediary agency model, the directory model and the ferret model.

Consultancy

This area has experienced rapid growth from a non-existent base in the early 1980s to a multi-billion-dollar industry today. Although it is management consultancy groups that receive a great deal of attention from the business sections of the quality press, it is the lesser-known technology consultants that have been used and continue to be used by many science-based organisations. Very often, they were formerly employed in a research capacity within a large organisation. After developing their knowledge and skills in a particular area of science, they offer their unique skills to the wider industry. R&D research groups within large organisations often will contact several consultants prior to establishing a research project in a particular field related to the consultant's area of expertise. Consultants are able to offer help, advice and useful contacts to get the research project off to a flying start. Frequently, they will remain part of the research group during the early years of the project. This is a very popular method of technology transfer and, essentially, adopts the hiring skilled employees model.

Limitations and barriers to technology transfer

The management of technology transfer has not been entirely straightforward, as is demonstrated in the range of technology transfer mechanisms that have been developed over the last 20 years or so. Research into technology transfer suggests that this is because emphasis has been on providing information about access to technology. Whilst the provision of technical ideas is a necessary part of technology transfer, it is only one component of a more complex process.

Figure 11.4 views technology transfer and inward technology transfer as a series of complex interactive processes as opposed to a simple decision process. It breaks down the transfer process into a series of subprocesses. The initial framework was developed following a study of the role of intermediaries in the technology transfer process. A mismatch was identified between the needs of potential innovators and the activities of information-centred technology transfer intermediaries. This deficiency was illuminated through the use of the conceptual framework: Accessibility–Mobility–**Receptivity** (AMR). The research revealed that, whilst much effort appeared to have been directed at providing access to technology, little effort had been aimed at understanding the needs of organisations acquiring technology developed outside the organisation.

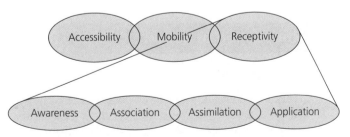

Figure 11.4 Conceptual framework of technology transfer and inward technology transfer

An organisation's overall ability to be aware of, to identify and to take effective advantage of technology is referred to as 'receptivity'. Figure 11.4 breaks down the receptivity element into four further components. This has provided a useful theoretical framework from which to analyse the notion of technology and knowledge transfer.

Subsequent research has uncovered the nature of some of the internal processes of inward technology transfer and has provided an insight into how they affect an organisation's ability to capture, assimilate and apply technology to commercial ends (Trott and Cordey-Hayes, 1996). Research by Macdonald (1992) identified the difficulty of applying other people's technology and the need for this technology to be in such a form that the organisation can reap some benefit. This highlights the importance of viewing technology development as a combination of knowledge, skills and organisations (all embodied in 'organisational know-how') rather than the economist's view of technology as an artefact to be bought and sold. Chapter 7 portrayed the notion of assimilation as an internal knowledge accumulation process, which offers an explanation of how organisations are able to use, manipulate and retain knowledge.

NIH syndrome

One of the best-known barriers to technology transfer is the not-invented-here (NIH) **syndrome**. This is defined as the tendency of a project group of stable composition to believe that it possesses the monopoly of knowledge in its field, leading it to reject new ideas from outsiders to the likely detriment of its performance (Katz and Allen, 1988). It is general folklore amongst R&D professionals that groups of scientists and engineers who have worked together for many years will begin to believe that no one else can know or understand the area in which they are working better than they do. In some cases, this attitude can spread across the whole R&D function, so that the effect is a refusal to accept any new ideas from outside. This syndrome has been so widely discussed since it was first uncovered that, like many diseases, it has been virtually wiped out. R&D managers still need to be vigilant to ensure that it does not recur (Lichtenthaler and Ernst, 2006).

The next section addresses the issue of receptivity and, in particular, how an organisation's own internal activities affect its ability to transfer technology successfully.

Innovation in action

Think small

Persuading wine drinkers to be adventurous and try more high-end wines has, traditionally, been hard. Tentative consumers tend to stick to wines at the £5 mark and only pay more for a limited number of the most famous brands.

A French start-up, WineSide, has come up with an alternative. They offer a variety of 6 cl sealed glass tubes sold individually or in boxes through retailers and their website. These packs encourage novice wine enthusiasts to sample GrandCru wines and gain confidence – without breaking the bank.

WineSide also markets its tubes to restaurants in 10 cl sizes. This allows restaurants to offer high quality wine by the glass without having to open a whole bottle.

Source: HSBC (2010) *100 Thoughts*, HSBC, London.

Absorptive capacity: developing a receptive environment for technology transfer

As was shown above, many of the traditional technology transfer mechanisms concentrate on providing access to technology, with little effort directed towards understanding the needs of organisations acquiring externally developed technology. The early literature on inward technology transfer centred on the ability of organisations to access technological knowledge (Gruber and Marquis, 1969) and their subsequent ability to disseminate this information effectively. Allen's work in the 1960s on the role of gatekeepers within organisations exemplifies this (see Allen, 1966, 1977; Allen and Cohen, 1969).

The notion of receptivity advocated by Seaton and Cordey-Hayes (1993) suggests that there are certain characteristics whose presence is necessary for inward technology transfer to occur. In a similar vein, but within an R&D context, Cohen and Levinthal (1990) put forward the notion of 'absorptive capacity'. In their study of the US manufacturing sector, they reconceptualise the traditional role of R&D investment as merely a factor aimed at creating specific innovations. They see R&D expenditure as an investment in an organisation's absorptive capacity and argue that an organisation's ability to evaluate and utilise external knowledge is related to its prior knowledge and expertise and that this prior knowledge is, in turn, driven by prior R&D investment. Absorptive capacity has, since, become one of the most influential concepts within innovation management (Enkel and Heil, 2014).

Absorptive capacity often is touted as being important for the success of open innovation. Yet, different absorptive capacities may be required for inbound versus outbound open innovation. In a study of how multiple firms participated in the development of a groundbreaking anti-influenza drug, Newey (2010) found that firms needed to develop both supplier- and customer-types of absorptive capacity. Inbound open innovation involved customer absorptive capacity and outbound innovation required supplier absorptive capacity. In each case, absorptive capacity needed to be leveraged differently.

Whilst research has produced ample evidence showing that absorptive capacity affects innovation and organisational performance outcomes, we still know little about why some organisations possess greater absorptive capacity than others (Hurmelinna-Laukkanen and Olander, 2014). According to a recent study of absorptive capacity in 218 inter-organisational projects in the German engineering industry, it emerges as an unintended consequence from organisational boundary spanners' activities (Ebers and Maurer, 2014).

Inward technology transfer will be successful only if an organisation has not only the ability to acquire but also the ability effectively to assimilate and apply ideas, knowledge, devices and artefacts. Organisations will respond to technological opportunity only in terms of their own perceptions of its benefits and costs and in relation to their own needs and technical, organisational and human resources. The process view of inward technology transfer, therefore, is concerned with creating or raising the capability for innovation. This requires an organisation and the individuals within it to have the capability to:

- search and scan for information that is new to the organisation (awareness);
- recognise the potential benefit of this information by associating it with internal organisational needs and capabilities;
- communicate these business opportunities to and assimilate them within the organisation; and
- apply them for competitive advantage.

These processes are captured in the following stages: awareness, association, assimilation and application. This four-stage conceptual framework (4A) is used to explore the processes involved in inward technology transfer (see Table 11.2).

Table 11.2 4A conceptual framework of technology transfer

Activity	Process
Awareness	Describes the processes by which an organisation scans for and discovers what information on technology is available
Association	Describes the processes by which an organisation recognises the value of this technology (ideas) for the organisation
Assimilation	Describes the processes by which the organisation communicates these ideas within the organisation and creates genuine business opportunities
Application	Describes the processes by which the organisation applies this technology for competitive advantage

Linking external technology to internal capabilities

The process of searching for and acquiring technical information is a necessary activity for organisations in order to maintain their knowledge base (see Johnson and Jones, 1957). This can be achieved effectively by scanning the technological environment, either through the scientific literature or through interactions with other people (often called networking). Thus, innovation within firms is a process of know-how accumulation, based on a complementary mix of in-house R&D and R&D performed elsewhere, obtained via the process of technology scanning.

Organisations that do not possess boundary-spanning individuals (scanning) will be restricted in the degree to which the organisation becomes aware of and assesses the relevance of innovations in the first place. Ebers and Maurer have shown that absorptive capacity emerges as an unintended consequence from organisational boundary spanners' activities (Ebers and Maurer, 2014). In a study of biotechnology firms, Fabrizo (2009) found the enhanced access to university research enjoyed by firms that engage in basic research and collaborate with university scientists leads to superior searches for new inventions and provides advantages in terms of both the timing and quality of search outcomes (see also Kang and Kang, 2009).

Given the importance of an awareness of external information and the role of technological **scanning and networking**, awareness is seen as the necessary first stage in the inward technology transfer process.

In order for an organisation to search and scan effectively for technology that will match its business opportunities, it needs to have a thorough understanding of its internal organisational capabilities. This can be achieved effectively via internal scanning and networking, which will enable it to become familiar with its internal activities. The coupling of internal technology scanning with external technology scanning activities can be seen in Figure 11.5.

External scanning without a full understanding of the organisation's capabilities and future requirements is likely to produce much 'noise' along with the 'signal'. 'Tuned scanning', achieved through the internal assimilation of an organisation's

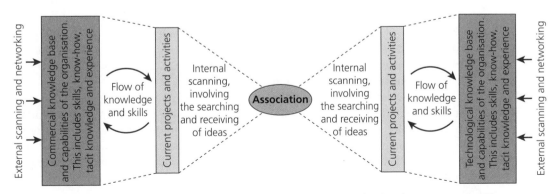

Figure 11.5 A conceptual framework for the development of genuine business opportunities

activities, as opposed to 'untuned scanning', will produce a higher 'signal-to-noise' ratio (Trott and Cordey-Hayes, 1996).

Inward technology transfer, however, involves more than identifying interesting technology; it is necessary to match technology with a market need in order to produce a potential opportunity for the business. The scanning process needs to incorporate commercial scanning as well as technology scanning so that technological opportunities may be matched with market needs (see Figure 11.5).

Such levels of awareness increase the probability of individuals being able to develop and create associations on behalf of the organisation between an internal opportunity and an external opportunity. This process of association is the second stage in inward technology transfer.

Chapter 7 emphasised the importance of recognising that the knowledge base of an organisation is not simply the sum of the individual knowledge bases. Nelson and Winter (1982) argue that such learning by doing is captured in organisational routines. It is these internal activities undertaken by an organisation that form the third stage in the process, assimilation.

Managing the inward transfer of technology

The final stage in the inward technology transfer process is the application of the business opportunity for competitive advantage. This is the stage where the organisation brings about commercial benefit from the launch of a new product or an improved product or manufacturing process. In science-based organisations, a combination of credibility and respect, coupled with extensive informal and formal communications amongst individuals within the organisation, facilitates this process (referred to as an internal knowledge accumulation process). This is not to disregard totally the presence of external influences.

Even in science-based industries, few companies are able to offer their researchers total scientific freedom, untouched by the demands of the market. R&D programmes are, therefore, focused on the business aspirations of the company and its future markets. Usually, these are set out using the most applicable technology. There is not a constant need for new ideas in technologies beyond these programmes – there are clearly resource limits on R&D departments. Inevitably, there will be crisis points, where the competition brings out something involving new technology. At these times, there is usually full management commitment and money invariably is made available to bring in new technology quickly to respond to the competition. Here the inward technology transfer processes generally works well, due to total commitment from all levels within the organisation.

Where technology is introduced on a more routine basis, a decision has to be made about spending money on a prototype or a demonstrator. The assimilation phase usually is dominated by who will put up the money to try out the new technology. This raises the question: what is the business need and who has the budget to address it and, moreover, do they have any money that can be diverted from something they are already doing to implement this new technology?

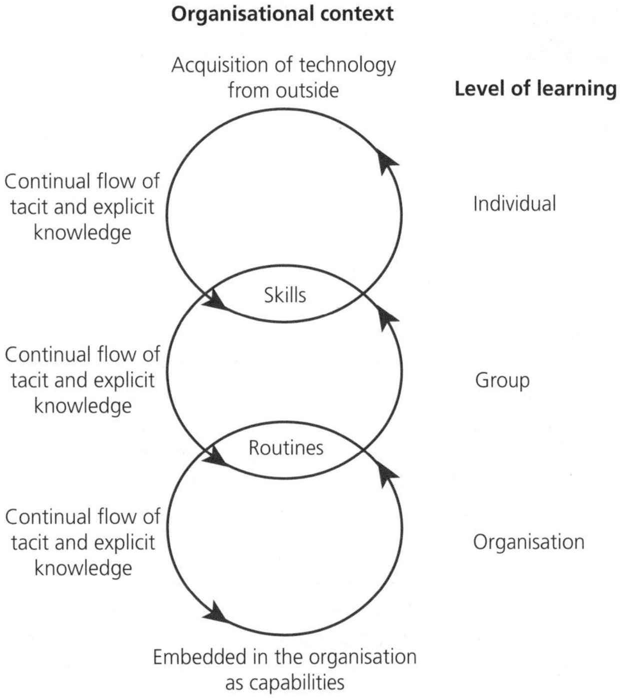

Organisational context

Acquisition of technology
from outside

Level of learning

Continual flow of
tacit and explicit
knowledge

Skills

Individual

Continual flow of
tacit and explicit
knowledge

Routines

Group

Continual flow of
tacit and explicit
knowledge

Organisation

Embedded in the organisation
as capabilities

Figure 11.6 Interlinking systems of knowledge-transfer relationships

Technology transfer and organisational learning

Organisational know-how is captured in routines, such as particular ways of working. The relationship between knowledge transfer between individuals and groups and the whole organisation may be expressed as two interlinked systems, as in Figure 11.6.

In order for inward technology transfer to take place, members of the organisation must show an awareness of and a receptivity towards knowledge acquisition. Individual learning involves the continual search for new information of potential benefit to the organisation. This frequently challenges existing procedures.

In order for the organisation to learn, the knowledge must be assimilated into the core routines of the organisation. That is, the knowledge becomes embedded in skills and know-how. The way in which the learning cycles link together is illustrated in Figure 11.6. In the manner of double-loop learning, the individual and organisational cycles are interrelated and interdependent (Argyris and Schon, 1978). The learning process forms a loop, transferring knowledge from individual into the group. The process of assimilation and adoption of this new knowledge within the inner cycle moves the knowledge into the wider environment and thus into the loop of organisational learning.

Case study

How developments in electronic sensors create destruction in the disposable nappy industry

This case study illustrates how a mature, well-established industry is undergoing radical changes as new technology is used to develop improved performance products. Sales of disposable nappies have benefited from the practice of people replacing nappies at regular intervals rather than only when they need changing. The result, of course, is increased sales as well as increased environmental concerns about disposal of millions of nappies. Falling costs of electronic sensors have created an opportunity for a moisture sensor to be incorporated into the disposable nappy that indicates accurately when a nappy should be changed. This delivers reduced costs, reduced waste and improved care.

Introduction

A meeting is taking place at Paper Products Ltd, one of the world's largest consumer goods companies. It has been called by Thomas Williams, Marketing Manager. At the meeting with him are Margaret Spilling, Brand Manager for the company's nappy brand and Dr Henry Walker, R&D Manager for Paper Products.

'So what are we going to do about this patent?' said Thomas. 'And, more importantly, what am I going to say to the MD when I meet with him next month to discuss our quarterly performance and outlook? I don't want to look like a complete fool when

he says: "What about this new nappy with sensors from your major competitor?"'

'I agree. This could be the beginning of the end of our very lucrative business,' said Margaret Spilling, Brand Manager for 'Contented', Paper Product's nappy brand and the world's leading nappy brand. Their eyes were fixed upon Dr Henry Walker, R&D Manager for Paper Products. This meeting had been called by Thomas following an email from Henry, informing him about a new patent application that one of Thomas' Patent Agents had passed to him.

'It wouldn't have been so bad if this patent was from a small start-up in Amsterdam or Cambridge,' said Margaret. 'But it's from our number one competitor: ConsumerGlobal. I am amazed that we didn't know about this. I thought we knew exactly what ConsumerGlobal were up to even before they knew what they did?'

'I am surprised that you are all so surprised,' said Henry. 'This is not the first patent application for a nappy with a sensor for detecting wetness. If you have a look at the patent databases, you will see many more from all sorts of companies. Look, here is a list of some recent patents in this area.' Henry showed them Table 11.3.

'Well, this is the first time I have heard about it,' said Thomas.

'I have only been here six months, Thomas, so I can't comment on what went on before, but I would have thought that you should have received regular updates from the R&D Manager on such matters.'

'Well, I didn't, but I am glad we appointed you, Henry,' said Thomas. 'Now go and use all those university degrees that you have and tell us what we should do now to ensure that we all have jobs this time next year!'

The R&D Manager for Paper Products took his colleagues through a number of options, which included doing nothing, embracing the technology into their own products through licencing and intensive applied R&D to see if they could invent around the patent.

Source: Bart_J. Shutterstock/Pearson Education Ltd

Table 11.3 Patent search results for nappies and sensors

	Citing patent	Issue date	Original assignee	Title
1	USD326423	26 May 1992	Breitkopf Norbert	Moisture sensing alarm for a nappy
2	US5389093	14 Feb. 1995	Knobbe, Martens, Olson & Bear, LLP	Wetness indicating nappy
3	US5468236	21 Nov. 1995	Kimberly-Clark Corporation	Disposable absorbent product incorporating chemically reactive substance
4	US5760694	2 June 1998	Knox Security Engineering Corporation	Moisture detecting devices such as for nappies and nappies having such devices
5	US5838240	17 Nov. 1998	Johnson Research & Development Company, Inc.	Wet nappy detector
6	US6603403	5 Aug. 2003	Kimberly-Clark Worldwide, Inc.	Remote, wetness signalling system
7	US7250547	31 July 2007	RF Technologies, Inc.	Wetness monitoring system
8	US7956754	7 June 2011	Kimberly-Clark Worldwide, Inc.	Connection mechanisms in absorbent articles for body fluid signalling devices

'What remains unclear,' he said, 'is whether anyone would want to buy the product. The cost of it may be so high that few would be willing to pay for it.'

'Look,' said Margaret. 'I am disappointed that it's not us with this patent, rather than our major competitor. There is a chance that ConsumerGlobal is currently planning a massive advertising campaign to launch this new moisture sensor nappy and steal 20 or 30 per cent of our business. If that happens, I don't think any of us will be in a job. We will have been caught asleep at the wheel. This is serious.'

'Yes, I agree,' said Thomas. 'But there is also another issue we need to consider. Not only are we likely to lose business to our number one competitor, but surely we are all likely to be selling fewer nappies if this product succeeds.'

'How do you mean?' said Henry.

'Well, people will no longer be changing clean nappies for clean nappies. They will now only change them when they are wet or dirty. So sales will be much lower.'

'Which begs the question,' said Margaret, 'of why ConsumerGlobal is launching this product in the first place. If they know it will result in less cash for them?'

'Unless, of course, they have developed a business plan,' said Thomas. 'Which takes account of

fewer sales of nappies but with a larger margin on the new electronic nappy that may offset the decrease in volume.'

'OK,' said Thomas. 'This is what we do. Henry, do as much as you can in the next month. Investigate this technology. Put together a small team and spend the next four weeks on this project and nothing else. Margaret, can you do as much market research as is possible in the next four weeks? Find out who would buy this and what they would be willing to pay. Let's meet again here in four weeks. We will then need to decide what to do.'

The world nappy market

Research indicates that between 3,700 and 4,200 nappies are used during the entire life of a baby. This is based on an average of four nappies per day, although there are many regions of the world that use fewer nappies than Europe/USA. China and Russia are good examples, as they are, probably, the very best at toilet training. They are able to achieve this goal before the age of 20 months, instead of the 33 or more required in Europe/USA. The rest of the world is somewhere in the middle. A good estimate for the total global potential market for baby nappies in the world is to add the total number of babies between the ages of 0 to 2.5 years and multiply by 4.2 nappies per day and a total of 365 days per year. The number 4.2 may seem small, but you have to take into account that it is the average over the whole life of the baby and not the typical consumption in the first 12 months. For example, babies use more nappies per day when they are small and far fewer when they grow older. In 2005, there were 321 million babies in the world with ages in the range of 0 to 2.5. This means the world requires 15,600 nappies per second, if every single baby used disposable nappies. This is a very lucrative business, when you consider that a weekly pack of nappies costs approximately €10.00. The two leading brands of nappies in the world maintain a healthy 75 per cent market share between them. Procter & Gamble owns the Pampers brand and Unilever owns the Huggies brand. Over the past 30 years, these companies have invested huge sums of money into their brands and this has helped them grow the market. Industry analysts argue that they were successful in different ways. For example, Pampers sold the best nappy money could buy, whilst Huggies sold the concept of a 'Good Mother'. Marketing experts have suggested that Huggies built a brand and Pampers built a great category.

Private label nappies

The idea behind private label products is to follow the market leaders as closely as possible, at a lower cost. In the baby nappy market, private labels are continuing to produce ever more sophisticated products and are becoming more of a threat to the big brands like Pampers and Huggies. For example, World Hygenic Products (WHP) manufactures, markets and sells private label baby nappies, training pants and youth pants for the majority of the largest food and drug retailers. The company says corporate branded products, also known as private label or store brands, offer consumers better value, with great quality and significant savings over national brands. On average, the company says it is possible to spend up to £2,000 or more on disposable nappies and training pants per child and, with its products, consumers can save 25 per cent by switching to private label brands without sacrificing product quality and performance.

The ageing population

The one other significant market segment that consumes nappies is the elderly. Whilst population aging is a global phenomenon, the Asian-Pacific region is expected to see a particularly drastic demographic change over the next few decades (according to the United Nations Economic and Social Commission for Asia and the Pacific). The number of elderly persons in the region – already home to more than half of the world's population aged 60 and over – is expected to triple to more than 1.2 billion by 2050, when one in four people in the region will be over 60 years old. Other parts of Asia, such as China, Taiwan, Hong Kong, South Korea and Singapore, are also anticipating a surge in the percentage of elderly citizens. In China, people over the age of 60 now account for 13.3 per cent of the country's population of 1.34 billion, up from 10.3 per cent in 2000. The rapid aging of Asia's population creates challenges for governments and societies. It also creates new opportunities for businesses serving the needs of the elderly and their carers. Across Asia, large corporations and entrepreneurs in various industries are racing to come up with new products and services for the elderly, whilst health-care related businesses are seeing soaring demand. Amongst various fields of health care for the elderly, nursing homes represent one of the fastest-growing sectors.

Four weeks later: meeting to discuss nappy sensor business opportunity

Thomas turned to his team and said: 'I keep six honest serving-men; they taught me all I knew. Their names are What and Why and When; And How and Where and Who. From *The Elephant's Child* by Rudyard Kipling.'

'Very good, Thomas, you should be on the stage,' said Henry.

Thomas ignored the jibe and said: 'So, are you two going to tell me all I need to know about nappies and sensors? Are we going to have to start making nappies with in-built sensors? How much will they cost to produce? How much can we sell them for? Will we still have jobs in a few weeks?'

Margaret stood up and began: 'As usual, we uncovered some typical reactions from the laggards and those who seem to be against any form of change. Things like an association problem in that the baby will associate a siren sound with peeing?' There was laughter all around. 'Some people suggested a flashing LED rather than a siren. We also uncovered a few more ideas, such as the use of a negative sound may be of use in the nappy around potty training time. And the possibility of a sensor in a potty that has a positive sound. Whilst this was useful, we have some specific findings from our mainstream consumers on the nappy sensor concept. Market research reveals that mothers would not pay more for a nappy with a sensor. They just say they change them when they have to: "The smell tells me when it's time to change". Anyway, some mothers like changing the nappy. It gives them quality time with their baby. After all, that's what one of the world's leading brands has spent millions convincing mothers: that they are being a good mother when they change the nappy. It is purely a male-orientated perspective that nappy changing is unpleasant.'

'At last,' added Margaret. 'So, now you know, your male understanding of the world is limited and it means that, alone, you may be unable to recognise some business opportunities.'

Thomas stepped in: 'Joking aside, this is an important point and shows the need for a joint male and female perspective in our decision making.'

'Maybe,' said Margaret. 'It also seems to show that there isn't much interest or demand from mothers for such a product. So, we don't need to start looking for new jobs. Our research revealed that a product launched in this category will have limited appeal because of the combination of high initial cost of the product and we will be up against the inertia of many years of the constant message that: loving mothers change nappies. We would now have to promote the idea that loving mothers don't change nappies!'

Thomas leaned back and put his hands behind his head: 'Interesting. So, we conclude that, despite the good technology and a potentially new product that could deliver genuine performance benefits, market entry is precluded due to the installed base effect of 20 years of advertising propaganda.'

'Their advertising has created an entry barrier,' said Margaret.

'All this jargon is beginning to sound like a business studies seminar,' said Henry. 'Can we turn to the technology?'

The technology

Henry stood up and began: 'First, as I thought, this technology is not new. Many different firms have secured patents in the field of sensors and nappies. Some of these firms are, indeed, our competitors but, it seems, for whatever reason, they did not develop the technology or a new product. If you have a look at the Table on the slide, you can see some of the details.' (See Table 11.3.)

'It could have been a cost issue,' said Margaret. 'And maybe now that the costs of sensors have fallen the product is now viable?'

'Possibly,' said Henry. 'But I think there are other things we need to consider. Let's look at the technology a bit more closely. Using low-cost moisture sensing technology it is now possible to produce a disposable nappy with an in-built sensor. A small clip-on sensor device attached to the nappy detects moisture through special carbon ink prints on the nappy's inner surface and sends the information wirelessly to PCs and mobile phones. The clip-on device isn't disposable. The most recent technology can detect wetness at three different levels, eliminating the need for repeated checks of nappies just to see whether they need to be replaced. And this is the key to unlocking the business opportunity. A technology that informs you that a nappy is wet has limited appeal. Indeed, parents can do this themselves. The utility of this product lies not in the simple moisture sensor, but in the technology that enables it to detect different levels of moisture. It is this sensitivity that makes it so attractive to customers and the adult market, in particular. To be informed that a nappy is wet is useful. To be informed when a nappy is wet and then very wet is much more useful. This could be the innovative step forward. If you combine this with a mobile device or PC, a product concept begins to emerge that enables the user to monitor several nappies at once, as this figure [Figure 11.7 below] shows.'

The team studied the table and questioned Henry about the system developed for nursing and care homes.

→

Nappy patient monitoring system		
Patient room no:	Moisture indicator	Display on monitor
1	Dry	○
2	Saturated	◗◗◗
3	Wet	◗
4	Dry	○
5	Saturated	◗◗◗
6	Wet	◗
7	Very wet	◗◗

Figure 11.7 A nappy patient moisture monitoring system

Henry continued, "Each disposable nappy costs €1.20 or less, but customers also need to purchase or lease the wireless system, including the clip-on devices. This limits its appeal to certain customers and also makes it even less attractive for the baby market. Indeed, I think the manufacturing and product costs rules out the nappy sensor for the baby market segment.'

A new business opportunity

It is only when you bring together the market research evidence and the technology product details that the true business opportunity emerges. Indeed, the size of the prize looks big indeed! Whilst first one may have thought of the baby nappy market, this is not where we should be looking. It is the elderly nappy market that provides the best business opportunity. Already, in Asia, it is this area that is providing many new business opportunities. Within the market of hospitals and nursing homes, some technology entrepreneurs are focusing on products and services they could sell to these health-care institutions. More specifically, due to the rapid aging population problem, the demand for professional elderly nursing services is rising fast. It is this demand for new services that gives rise to a new business opportunity.

For a nursing home with 100 beds, for example, a system could be purchased or leased, enabling nursing homes to upgrade their services and charge a premium.

Potential strategic alliances

Thomas said: 'As you know, with all our new product proposals, we have to show that we have considered potential partners. So, with this in mind, what have you uncovered?'

Margaret replied: 'Yes, Thomas, we have done this. We looked at sensor manufacturers. But these have become commodity products and their unit price is falling almost daily. I don't think there is much scope here for a meaningful alliance where we can build a brand for both parties or where we can benefit from a sensor brand. I suppose our only option would be Siemens? Given our objective of mass market products and not niche, the range of partners is limited. Another possibility is to partner with health care providers, but these tend to be local or regional at best. If there was a national nursing home chain for the elderly, this could be worth exploring. If we want to build a global brand, I'm not sure this would be a good move. Probably an area worth exploring would be one of the global pharmaceutical firms, such as Pfizer or GlaxoSmithKline. As you know, however, the difficulty with these is that we currently compete in beauty, hair care and skin care with these firms. So this, again, could prove difficult.'

'Thanks, Margaret,' said Thomas. 'This is still useful for me to take to the board.'

Conclusions

Thomas addressed his team again: 'This is great news, guys. You have done amazing work. I will take this proposal to the new ventures board and propose a €10 million investment for the next two years to launch this new business. It is exactly what this company has been trying to do. That is, move into more money.'

Henry replied: 'Let's see what the board says.'

lucrative service-based businesses. This is just such a business. Wish me luck.'

As Thomas left the room with a spring in his step, Margaret turned to Henry and said, 'I don't know about this idea. I think the competition is fierce. There are lots of small technology-based businesses in Korea and China. I am not sure I would invest my own

Questions

1 Explain why baby nappy producers, such as P&G and Unilever, may have dismissed this product idea? And then explain why this may have been short sighted?

2 Sketch the range of business models available and their advantages.

3 What changes in the external environment has led to this new business opportunity?

4 Use the cyclic model of innovation to show how key decisions led to this innovation.

5 What potential strategic alliances should the business explore?

6 Was the team correct to dismiss the baby nappy market so readily?

7 Discuss the different types of services that can be developed around the core technology concept.

8 Explain why you would or would not invest €10,000 of your own money in this new business?

Chapter summary

Technology transfer has a significant impact on the management of innovation. The process is concerned with facilitating and promoting innovation. The increasing use of strategic alliances means that its importance is set to increase. This chapter has introduced the subject of technology transfer and examined various models of the process. Most models of technology transfer emphasise access to technology rather than trying to understand the receptivity issues of the receiving organisation. The case study showed how effective technology transfer can be in contributing to a firm's success in very competitive conditions.

Discussion questions

1 How does technology transfer differ from simply purchasing technology?

2 Explain the limitations of many of the models of technology transfer.

3 Explain how a firm's internal activities affect its ability to acquire external technology.

4 What opportunities does 'open innovation' offer to the R&D function?

5 To what extent is open innovation 'old wine in new bottles'?

6 Explain why any technology transferred to an organisation needs to be embedded into its core routines.

7 Explain how firms can improve their absorptive capacity.

Key words and phrases

Open innovation *382*

Technology transfer *384*

Knowledge transfer *385*

Licensing *386*

Organisational learning *390*

Receptivity *391*

NIH syndrome *392*

Scanning and networking *395*

References

Allen, T.J. (1966) Performance of communication channels in the transfer of technology, *Industrial Management Review*, vol. 8, 87–98.

Allen, T.J. (1977) *Managing the Flow of Technology*, MIT Press, Cambridge, MA.

Allen, T.J. and Cohen, W.M. (1969) Information flow in research and development laboratories, *Administrative Science Quarterly*, vol. 14, no. 1, 12–19.

Argyrs, C. and Schon, D.A. (1978) *Organisational Learning*, Addison-Wesley, Reading, MA.

Asakawa, K., Nakamura, H. and Sawada, N. (2010) Firms' open innovation policies, laboratories' external collaborations, and laboratories' R&D performance, *R&D Management*, vol. 40, 109–23.

Centre for Exploitation of Science and Technology (CEST) (1991) *The Management of Technological Collaboration*, March, Manchester.

Chiaroni, D., Chiesa, V. and Frattini, F. (2009) The Open Innovation Journey: How firms dynamically implement the emerging innovation management paradigm, *Technovation*, vol. 30, no. 3, 34–43.

Chesbrough, H. (2003) *Open Innovation: The New Imperative from Creating and Profiting from Technology*, HBS Press, Boston, MA.

Chesbrough, H. (2006) 'Open innovation: a new paradigm for understanding industrial innovation', in Chesbrough, H., Vanhaverbeke, W. and West, J. (eds) *Open Innovation: Researching a New Paradigm*, Oxford University Press, Oxford, 1–12.

Cohen, W.M. and Levinthal, D.A. (1990) A new perspective on learning and innovation, *Administrative Science Quarterly*, vol. 35, no. 1, 128–52.

Dahlander, L. and Gann, D. (2010) How open is innovation? *Research Policy*, vol. 39, no. 6, 699–709.

DFI International (1998) Short- and long-term implications of technology transfer, *China Technology Transfer Report*, DTI International, London, 93–8.

Diez-Vial, I. and Montoro-Sanchez, A. (2014) Linkages with universities and innovation: an application in a science park, *Academy of Management Proceedings*, vol. 2014, no. 1, p. 13856, Academy of Management.

Ebers, M. and Maurer, I. (2014) Connections count: how relational embeddedness and relational empowerment foster absorptive capacity, *Research Policy*, vol. 43, no. 2, 318–32.

Enkel, E. and Heil, S. (2014) Preparing for distant collaboration: Antecedents to potential absorptive capacity in cross-industry innovation, *Technovation*, vol. 34, no. 4, 242–60.

Fabrizio, K. (2009) Absorptive capacity and the search for innovation, *Research Policy*, vol. 38, no. 2, 255–67.

Felin, T. and Zenger, T.R. (2014) Closed or open innovation? Problem solving and the governance choice, *Research Policy*, vol. 43, no. 5, 914–25.

Gruber, W.H. and Marquis, D.G. (1969) *Factors in the Transfer of Technology*, MIT Press, Cambridge, MA.

Hacievliyagil, N.K. (2007) The Impact of Open Innovation on Technology Transfers at Philips and DSM, M.Sc. Thesis, Faculty of Technology, Policy & Management, Delft University of Technology.

Hacievliyagil, N.K., Auger, J.-F., Maisonneuve, Y. and Hartmann, D. (2008) The position of virtual knowledge brokers in the core process of open innovation, *International Journal of Knowledge, Technology and Society*, vol. 3, no. 5, 47–60.

Hagedoorn, J. (1990) Organisational modes of inter-firm co-operation and technology transfer, *Technovation*, vol. 10, no. 1, 17–30.

Hurmelinna-Laukkanen, P. and Olander, H. (2014) Coping with rivals' absorptive capacity in innovation activities, *Technovation*, vol. 34, no. 1, 3–11.

Johnson, S.C. and Jones, C. (1957) How to organise for new products, *Harvard Business Review*, May–June, vol. 35, 49–62.

Kang, K. and Kang, J. (2009) How do firms source external knowledge for innovation? Analysing effects of different knowledge sourcing methods, *International Journal of Innovation Management*, vol. 13, no. 1, 1–17.

Kapoor, R. and McGrath, P.J. (2014) Unmasking the interplay between technology evolution and R&D collaboration: evidence from the global semiconductor manufacturing industry, 1990–2010, *Research Policy*, vol. 43, no. 3, 555–69.

Katz, R. and Allen, T. (1988) 'Investigating the NIH syndrome: a look at the performance, tenure and communication patterns of 50 R&D project groups', in Tushman, W.L. and Moore, M.L. (eds) *Readings in the Management of Innovation*, HarperCollins, New York.

Langrish, J., Evans, W.G. and Jerans, F.R. (1982) *Wealth from Knowledge*, Macmillan, London.

Laursen, K. and Salter, A.J. (2014) The paradox of openness: appropriability, external search and collaboration, *Research Policy*, vol. 43, no. 5, 867–78.

Lichtenthaler, U. and Ernst, H. (2006) Attitudes to externally organising knowledge management tasks: a review, reconsideration and extension of the NIH syndrome, *R&D Management*, vol. 36, no. 4, 367–86.

Macdonald, S. (1992) Formal collaboration and informal information flow, *International Journal of Technology Management*, Special Issue on Strengthening Corporate and National Competitiveness through Technology, vol. 7, nos. 1/2/3, 49–60.

Nelson, R.R. and Winter, S. (1982) *An Evolutionary Theory of Economic Change*, Harvard University Press, Boston, MA.

Newey, L. (2010) Wearing different hats: how absorptive capacity differs in Open Innovation, *International Journal of Innovation Management*, vol. 14, no. 4, 703–31.

Parkhe, A., Wasserman, S. and Ralstan, D. (2006) New frontiers in network theory development, *Academy of Management Review*, vol. 31, no. 3, 560–8.

Prahalad, G. and Hamel, C.K. (1990) The core competence of the corporation, *Harvard Business Review*, vol. 68, no. 3, 79–91.

Seaton, R.A.F. and Cordey-Hayes, M. (1993) The development and application of interactive models of technology transfer, *Technovation*, vol. 13, no. 1, 45–53.

Trott, P. and Cordey-Hayes, M. (1996) Developing a 'receptive' environment for inward technology transfer: a case study of the chemical industry, *R&D Management*, vol. 26, no. 1, 83–92.

Trott, P. and Hartmann, D. (2009) Old wine in new bottles, *International Journal of Innovation Management,* vol. 13, no. 4, 1–22.

Wang, Y. and Li-Ying, J. (2014) When does inward technology licensing facilitate firms' NPD performance? A contingency perspective, *Technovation*, vol. 34, no. 1, 44–53.

Werner, J. (1991) Can collaborative research work? Success could spawn 'collateral benefits' for all industries, *Industry Week*, vol. 240, no. 13, 47.

West, J. and Bogers, M. (2014) Leveraging External Sources of Innovation: A Review of Research on Open Innovation, *Journal of Product Innovation Management*, vol. 31, 814–31.

West, J., Salter, A., Vanhaverbeke, W. and Chesbrough, H. (2014) Open innovation: the next decade, *Research Policy*, vol. 43, no. 5, 805–11.

Further reading

For a more detailed review of the technology transfer literature, the following develop many of the issues raised in this chapter:

Ebers, M. and Maurer, I. (2014) Connections count: how relational embeddedness and relational empowerment foster absorptive capacity, *Research Policy*, vol. 43, no. 2, 318–32.

Enkel, E. and Heil, S. (2014) Preparing for distant collaboration: antecedents to potential absorptive capacity in cross-industry innovation, *Technovation*, vol. 34, no. 4, 242–60.

Felin, T. and Zenger, T.R. (2014) Closed or open innovation? Problem solving and the governance choice' *Research Policy*, vol. 43, no. 5, 914–25.

Kang, K. and Kang, J. (2009) How do firms source external knowledge for innovation? Analysing effects of different knowledge sourcing methods, *International Journal of Innovation Management*, vol. 13, no. 1, 1–17.

Laursen, K. and Salter, A.J. (2014) The paradox of openness: appropriability, external search and collaboration, *Research Policy*, vol. 43, no. 5, 867–78.

Newey, L. (2010) Wearing different hats: how absorptive capacity differs in Open Innovation, *International Journal of Innovation Management*, vol. 14, no. 4, 703–31.

West, J., Salter, A., Vanhaverbeke, W. and Chesbrough, H. (2014) Open innovation: the next decade, *Research Policy*, vol. 43, no. 5, 805–811.

Part Three
New product development

This final part addresses the most important part for the business: making money from the developed technology by developing products and services that people want to buy. It reviews and summarises the nature and techniques of new product development. It looks at the process of developing new products and examines many of the new product management issues faced by companies.

Chapter 12 examines business models and illustrates how new business models can be developed around new technology to challenge existing dominant business models in an industry. Product and brand strategy is the subject of Chapter 13; it addresses the positioning of the product and the importance of brand strategy on the success of any new product. In particular, it examines the influences on product planning decisions and the role of marketing management. All of these heavily influence any decision to develop new products.

Our understanding of the new product innovation process has improved significantly in the past 30 years. During this period, numerous models have been developed to help explain the process. These are examined in Chapter 14. Many of these models identify the role of market research to be significant in developing successful new products. We turn from products to services in Chapter 15 and examine the development of new services. The role of market research is addressed again in Chapter 16, but this time it explores whether there are times when market research may hinder the development of new products.

Chapter 17 moves from the conceptual to the operational level and analyses the particular challenges faced by the new product manager. Taking a practitioner viewpoint, it investigates the activities that need to be undertaken and how companies organise the process. Emphasis is placed on the role of the new product team and the chapter closes with a look at 3M, the innovating machine.

Chapter 12
Business models

Introduction

Business models fundamentally are linked with technological innovation. They are used to describe and classify businesses, especially in an entrepreneurial setting, but they are also used by managers inside companies to explore possibilities for future development. Well-known business models can operate as 'recipes' for creative managers. This chapter shows that a business model is an abstract representation of an organisation, be it conceptual, textual and/or graphical, of all core interrelated architectural, cooperational and financial arrangements, designed and developed by an organisation presently and in the future, as well as all core products and/or services the organisation offers, or will offer, based on these arrangements that are needed to achieve its strategic goals and objectives. The case study at the end of this chapter tells the story of how a firm developed a new tooth whitening product and the different business models possible to make money.

Chapter contents

Learning objectives

When you have completed this chapter you will be able to:

- understand how enterprises create value by applying business model thinking;
- understand strategic differentiation and the link between innovation and positioning;
- recognise different levels and perspectives of value;
- formulate and further refine a customer-centred value proposition; and
- recognise how to generate value from the licensing business model.

This chapter explores how businesses intend to make money from their technology. This may seem like an obvious question with an equally obvious answer, but it should not be overlooked, for there is much room for creativity for the entrepreneur. For example, it may be that the business believes it has developed a better product than the existing products in the market. It will, therefore, simply offer its product at a competitive price relative to the competition. But, this would overlook other possibilities for the business. Are there opportunities for leasing rather than simply selling? Can the business adopt a landlord business model? Famous examples abound where new business models have been developed by start-ups that challenge existing dominant business models in an industry. Table 12.1 shows a wide range of new services that have been created that also led to the creation of new business models. These range from eBay to Facebook. Figure 12.1 shows the eBay business model. Clearly, this model is dependent on a stable technology platform but, at its heart, is a simple transaction fee revenue model.

Business models are, fundamentally, linked with technological innovation, yet the business model construct is, essentially, separable from technology. According to Baden-Fuller and Haefliger (2013), business models mediate the link between technology and firm performance. Developing the right technology is a matter of a business model decision regarding openness and user engagement.

Table 12.1 A range of new services that also create new business models

Company	Industry sector	New service/new business model
eBay	Online auction	A new way of buying and selling through a community of individual users
Ryanair	Airline	A new way of consuming air travel with no-frills service and emphasis on economy
Netflix	Online movie and TV series rental	A monthly subscription service providing members with fast and easy access to movies and television programmes
Amazon	Retailer	A new way to buy goods – online retailer
Napster; iTunes	Music retailer	A new way to buy and download music
Google/Bing	Internet search engine	A fast way to search for information on the internet
PartyGaming	Online gambling, e.g. poker	Gambling and gaming from the comfort of your own home
Twitter/Facebook	Social networking	A community of users online who can chat and share music, images, news from their own home
YouTube	Online video and film archive	A community of users sharing home-made video clips plus recorded favourite clips from movies

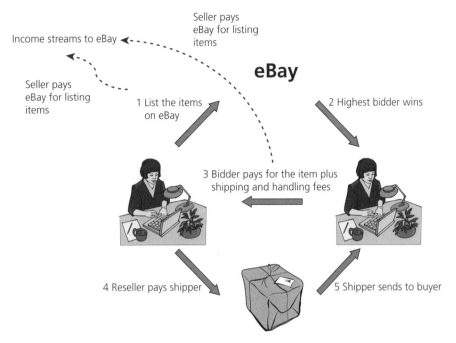

Figure 12.1 An overview of the eBay business model

What is a business model?

A **business model** describes the value an organisation offers to its customers. It illustrates the capabilities and resources required to create, market and deliver this value and to generate profitable, sustainable revenue streams. It is the revenue stream that is key here. Where is the money going to come from and how much of it will the business be able to retain? It includes considering issues like margins, allocation of profits to those within the supply chain. For example, Apple is extremely profitable partly because its margins on its products are so much higher than its competitors. So, there is a key question that needs to be addressed: How will this business make money?

To answer this question, it is necessary to address a series of additional questions, such as:

- Who is the target customer?
- What customer problem or challenge does the business solve?
- What value does it deliver?
- How does it reach, acquire and keep customers?
- How does it define and differentiate its offering?
- How does it generate revenue?
- What is the cost structure?
- What is the profit margin?

In principle, a business model does not matter to customers; it is important to the company and the organisation of its business. The business model determines the

Table 12.2 Parts of the business model

Parts of the business model
1 **Value proposition** A description of the customer problem, the product that addresses the problem and the value of the product from the customer's perspective
2 **Market segment** The group of customers to target; sometimes the potential of an innovation is unlocked only when a different market segment is targeted
3 **Value chain structure** The firm's position and activities in the value chain and how the firm will capture part of the value that it creates in the chain
4 **Revenue generation and margins** How revenue is generated (sales, leasing, subscription, support, etc.), the cost structure and target profit margins
5 **Position in value network** Identification of competitors, partners and any network effects that can be utilised to deliver more value to the customer
6 **Competitive strategy** How the company will attempt to develop a sustainable competitive advantage, for example by means of a cost, differentiation or niche strategy

Sources: Chesbrough and Rosenbloom, 2002; Shafer et al., 2005; Watson, 2005.

external relationships with suppliers, customers and partners. However, it is focused primarily on the company's business processes. Table 12.2 explains the different component parts of a business model.

In a seminal article in *Long Range Planning* (a leading international journal for the field of strategic management), Professor David Teece argued that whatever the business enterprise, it either explicitly or implicitly employs a particular business model that describes the design or architecture of the value creation, delivery and capture mechanisms it employs. This provides a useful definition of a business model (see Teece, 2010).

The business model is the key factor that leads to success in start-ups. It provides the starting point that allows a company to maximise its profits – the sooner the business model is in place, the easier it will be for the start-up to obtain support and funding. Investors will be seeking to ensure that the model is scalable. This will help reassure them that the business can grow exponentially. Investors must be able to envisage a start-up's business model (from an organisational and process perspective) as the company grows.

Many of the business models that we see today are influenced by Michael Porter's **Value Chain** (Primary and Support activities) (Porter, 1980). To these key activities are added additional operational flows, such as: plan, create demand, produce, sale/fulfil order (satisfy demand), charge, bill and accrue revenue and the after-sales service (and reverse supply chain). There are many other key activities and factors that are not mentioned, even though they may be more important than items identified. For example, the enterprise interacts with many stakeholders in such fields as technology, labour and capital markets. It is also affected by such external factors as regulatory, competitors and new entrants. In the brewing industry, for example, a change in the excise applied to beer can dramatically alter revenues and profits. Indeed, some UK brewers are now producing low alcohol beers of less than 3 per cent alcohol by volume because the excise is half that for higher strength beer (*Economist*, February 2012).

There are many different styles of business model. There is also a wide variety of frameworks available to help firms develop their own business model

(Spieth et al. 2014). All business models are representations of an architecture because they consist of both *functions* in *flows* in interconnection. Business models typically exhibit a rather abstract process taxonomy that may not align well to the enterprise structure, end flows and existing systems. As such, these models have limited practical value for the business owner or manager. (For further explanation on this see Mason and Leek, 2008; Patzelt et al., 2008; Richardson, 2008; Shafer et al., 2005; Zott and Amit, 2007.)

The business model and the business plan

The terms business model and business plan are similar but they are different. A business plan is a detailed document, typically 50 to 100 pages, with a lot of financial projections. To set up a new business and apply for a loan, the lending institution will demand a business plan. The lender wants to assess whether its customers will be able to repay the loan. A business model is much less detailed. A business model describes the specific way the business expects to make money. It should be on one page and it would be more clearly shown as a diagram. The business model itself is a single concept.

The concept of a business model is most useful for a new business (which explains the predominance of ecommerce-related references in recent years), and it is essential for a new business to establish a positive feedback loop. For example, word of mouth has to be effective and customers have to recommend other customers. Without that kind of acceleration, a business will never get off the ground. As many owners of websites found, in the early years of the worldwide web (mid-1990s), their original business model did not work and the business soon failed: a classic example of that was boo.com. Other businesses found that their customers adapted the products for a use that the businesses had not expected. This suggests that, when a business model is developed, it should be flexible and easily modified, should financial growth not meet expectations. It is, therefore, useful for the business model to include methods for its own evaluation. If a model is displayed as a series of 'boxes and arrows', the boxes represent activities, the arrows represent causal links between the boxes, and the strength of each link can be measured – or at least estimated. To help firms develop a business model, the following guidelines may help. The business model should contain:

- a graphical representation (usually in the form of a flow chart);
- a list of activities, on the part of both the business owner and potential customers;
- a likely sequence for those activities (which may later be altered in the light of customer behaviour); and
- a set of indicators or metrics for measuring the linkage between the activities.

Figure 12.2 illustrates a simple flow diagram that captures a series of activities that shows how a technology-based start-up uses its technical expertise and entrepreneurial skills to develop a product or service that is made available to the market. Revenues are then used to reinvest into the company and to further reinforce the firm's advantage.

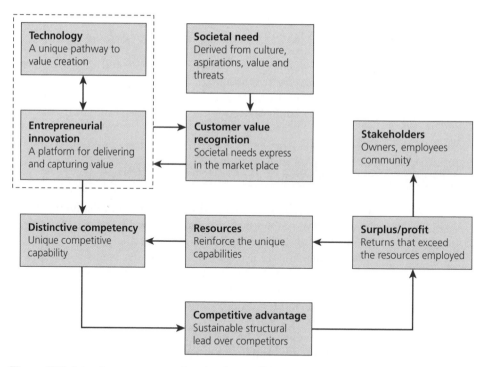

Figure 12.2 A business process showing how a firm uses its resources to create value

The range of business models

Clearly, there is a wide range of different **business models** applicable across all industries. A useful classification is provided by Weill and Vitale (2001) (see Table 12.3). This shows 16 different business models, including models such as human trafficking, which clearly is illegal. It is worthy of note that those firms that innovate on a business-model level are able to experience greater growth rates than companies that focus on innovation in products and operations. For example, the list of firms in Table 12.1 shows a range of different industry sectors in which these firms were able to develop new business models. Johnson et al. (2008) illustrates how firms can reinvent business models. There are several methods that start-ups can use to create an innovative business model, including:

- **revenue/pricing model:** change how revenue is generated through new value propositions and new pricing models (to take advantage of economies of scale). This was the Ryanair approach to developing no-frills air travel.
- **enterprise model:** specialise and configure the business to deliver greater value by rethinking what is done in-house and through collaboration. For example, Innocent Drinks was able to compete with industry giants such as Coca-Cola and others by outsourcing production and distribution, and also through building effective relationships with retailers.
- **industry model:** redefine an existing industry, move into a new industry or create a new industry. Better Place is doing this with its electric vehicle infrastructure. It

Table 12.3 The 16 detailed business model archetypes

Basic business model archetype	What type of asset is involved?			
	Financial	**Physical**	**Intangible**	**Human**
Creator	1 Entrepreneur (serial entrepreneurs)	2 Manufacturer (VW automobiles)	3 Inventor (Trevor Bayliss)	4 Human creator (illegal)
Distributor	5 Financial trader (investment banks)	6 Wholesaler/retailer (Tesco, Amazon)	7 IP trader (Logicalis)	8 Human distributor (illegal)
Landlord	9 Financial landlord (banks, insurance companies)	10 Physical landlord (hotel, car rental)	11 Intellectual landlord (publisher, brand manager)	12 Contractor (Federal Express, management consultancy)
Broker	13 Financial broker (insurance brokers)	14 Physical broker (eBay; estate agents)	15 IP broker (3i)	16 HR broker (employment agent)

Sources: Trott (2011) and Weill and Vitale (2001), © 2005 from MIT Sloan Management Review/Massachusetts Institute of Technology, all rights reserved, distributed by Tribune Content Agency.

has developed a complete national electric vehicle infrastructure for Israel and has plans for Denmark and Australia.

The sixteen business model archetypes

1. Entrepreneur (serial entrepreneur)

This first type of business model is based around the concept of entrepreneurs creating businesses and generating wealth. Such so-called serial entrepreneurs continuously come up with new ideas and start new businesses without necessarily staying with the business. One of the best known serial entrepreneurs is Sean Parker who cofounded the file-sharing computer service Napster and served as the first president of the social networking website Facebook.

2. Manufacturer

This business model is one of the simplest and most well-known. It involves creating physical products such as cars and mobile phones. Increasingly, manufacturers of physical products incorporate services within and around the product. The business model involves taking physical assets and assembling them to add value. Frequently this will include elements of the next archetype – inventor/creator.

3. Inventor/creator

With this business model individuals create or design products that can then be sold to generate money. So a simple example could be the clockwork radio designed by Trevor Bayliss or the British company ARM that designs computer chips. ARM Holdings plc (ARM) is a British multinational semiconductor and software design company. It is considered to be market dominant in the field of processors for mobile phones and tablet computers. Processors based on designs licensed from ARM, or designed by licensees of one of the ARM instruction set architectures, are used in all classes of computing devices such as microcontrollers in embedded systems – including real-time safety systems (cars' ABS).

4. Human creator

Given that the asset in this case is human any business model based around this concept is illegal. Science fiction stories have been written about the future where human beings are designed and created to meet requirements. The nearest existing similarity would be the so-called designer baby. This is the result of genetic screening or genetic modification. Embryos may be screened prior to implantation, or possibly gene therapy techniques could be used to create desired traits in a child. At present this is only done to avoid serious diseases being passed on to children.

5. Financial trader

This covers those activities involved in distributing finance. So investment banking is a good example here. An investment bank is a financial institution that assists individuals, corporations and governments in raising financial capital by underwriting or acting as the client's agent in the issuance of securities. An investment bank may also assist companies involved in mergers and acquisitions (M&A).

6. Wholesaler/retailer

Wholesaling is the sale of goods to anyone other than a standard consumer. It usually involves the resale (sale without transformation) of new and used goods to retailers, or involves acting as an agent or broker in buying merchandise, or selling merchandise. Wholesalers frequently physically assemble, sort and grade goods in large lots, then break bulk and repack and redistribute in smaller amounts. It is the task of retailers to make these products available to consumers; usually trying to offer the widest possible choice. Supermarkets play the role of wholesaler and retailer.

7. IP trader

Buying and selling intellectual property is not very different from buying and selling other goods. Usually the IP is in the form of a patent which can be licensed. Some IP trading companies specialise in the commercialisation of university intellectual property rights, such as IP group.

8. Human distributor

Such business models are illegal but exist. Human trafficking is the trade of humans, most commonly for the purpose of sexual slavery, forced labour or commercial sexual exploitation for the trafficker or others. Human trafficking is a crime against the person because of the violation of the victim's rights of movement through coercion and because of their commercial exploitation.

9. Financial landlord

Here the asset is money that is looked after by the landlord and used to generate more money. Banks collect money from consumers and then use it to lend to others. So a large part of retail banking is distributing money to consumers. Indeed, retail banking is also known as consumer banking. It is the provision of services by a bank to individual consumers, rather than to companies, corporations or other banks. Services offered include savings and transactional accounts, mortgages, personal loans, debit cards and credit cards. All of which are used to generate money.

10. Physical landlord

This is a well known business model where the physical asset is used to generate income. Hotels rent out rooms, car hire firms rent out cars. The essential model is the same.

11. Intellectual landlord

A good example of an intellectual landlord is a publisher. A publisher does not create the literature or music and does not own it. This belongs to the author. Publishing is the process of production and dissemination of literature, music or information – the activity of making information available to the general public. The scope of publishing has expanded to include electronic resources such as the electronic versions of books and periodicals, as well as websites, blogs, video game publishers.

12. Contractor

A contractor is an individual and possibly a tradesman, employed by the client on the advice of a specialist or the client him/herself if acting as the manager. A contractor is responsible for the overall coordination of a project. Management consultants are often hired to perform particular projects and will be contracted so to do. A contractor may hire specialist subcontractors to perform all or portions of the work.

13. Financial broker

General insurance brokering is carried out today by many types of authorised organisations including traditional high street brokers and telephone or web-based firms. Peer-to-peer lending is the practice of lending money to individuals or businesses through online services that match lenders directly with borrowers. Since the peer-to-peer lending companies offering these services operate entirely online, they can run with lower overheads and provide the service more cheaply than traditional financial institutions.

Financial brokering is being threatened by price comparison websites such as moneysupermarket.com. These sites use a vertical search engine that shoppers use to filter and compare products based on price, features and other criteria.

14. Physical broker

A broker is an independent agent used extensively in some industries. A broker's prime responsibility is to bring sellers and buyers together and thus a broker is the intermediary facilitator between a buyer and a seller. Estate agents perform this role in the property market. As we saw earlier, eBay has been successful in providing a market place for buyers and sellers of almost anything.

15. IP broker

An intellectual property broker mediates between the buyer and seller of intellectual property (IP) and may manage the many steps in the process of creating a deal with regard to the purchase, sale, license or marketing of intellectual property assets. This may include patents, trademarks or inventions (prototypes). An expert in this field is 3i Group plc, a multinational private equity and venture capital company. Because there is not a well defined market around the buying and selling of patents or other IP assets, if an inventor or patent owner wants to generate income from their asset, an intellectual property broker can help by serving to connect the inventor or patent owner with one or more interested buyers.

16. HR broker

An employment agency is an organisation that matches employers to employees. In all developed countries, there is a publicly funded employment agency and multiple private businesses which act as employment agencies.

Redefining the business: challenging your mental models and conventional wisdom

New business models such as those developed by Ryanair or Facebook were created by challenging existing and conventional wisdom. The following series of questions may help you come up with new models:

- What are the main industry assumptions, when it comes to pricing, customers, products and services offered, delivery, etc.?
- Does the industry have a product-centric, customer-centric, or rather competency-centric approach? What would a change in approach entail?
- Do you let yourself be constrained by the assets and capabilities you possess?
- Are you trying to use the assets you have and simply leverage them, or are you continuously striving to build new assets?
- How many of your competitors do already posses the same or similar assets?
- Which of your assets are truly unique and cannot be imitated or substituted easily by others?
- Do companies without these assets face a cost disadvantage in obtaining them?
- Which assets would you build if you started anew?

Revenue models

Revenue models often are mistaken for business models. However, revenue models are concerned specifically with the pricing element of the business model. It concerns establishing a price for the product and clearly will be dependent on reliable market intelligence. The 'bait and hook' revenue model is a good example of how firms can set a low price for part of their product to ensure that future substantial revenues are established (see Illustration 12.1). This model was clearly extremely successful for Gillette and Kodak. A wide range of revenue models are evident within online businesses. Table 12.4 illustrates five different such revenue models.

Table 12.4 Online revenue models

Type of revenue model	Approach	Examples
Advertising	Customers pay to be visible on your site/web pages	Google and Yahoo
Subscription	Customers pay a regular fee for access to information, content	*Economist*, adult porn sites
Transaction fee	Customers pay a commission fee for using your services	eBay, lastminute.com
Retail	Customers pay for goods similar to high street retailer	Amazon
Affiliate	Customers pay if you send traffic to their sites	Google

Illustration 12.1

The bait and hook revenue model

The *bait and hook* business model is also referred to as the 'tied products business model'. It involves offering a basic product at a very low cost, sometimes at a loss (the 'bait'), then charging compensatory recurring amounts for refills or associated products or services (the 'hook'). Examples include: razor (bait) and blades (hook); cell phones (bait) and air time (hook); computer printers (bait) and ink cartridge refills (hook); and cameras (bait) and film (hook). An interesting variant of this model is Adobe, a software developer that gives away its document reader free of charge, but charges several hundred euros for its document writer.

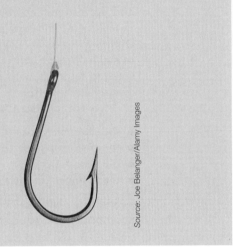

Source: Joe Belanger/Alamy Images

For a useful overview of developing business models, see Johnson et al. (2008) 'Reinventing your business model'.

Enterprise models

Enterprise models focus on redefining the internal and external boundaries of the organisation to create a new business model. This includes moving up or down the value chain, leveraging a network of partners or outsourcing non-core activities. In some cases, this requires migrating up the value chain, like Samsung with chips for cell phones, or moving down the value chain, like Apple with virtual (iTunes) and physical storefronts. Another option is for companies to find ways to leverage a network of partners that increases the effectiveness and efficiency of production, offering, distribution and sales. For example, Enterprise Car Rental has developed a network of insurance companies and car dealerships that help with sales and referrals. So, businesses have to look along their value chain and ask themselves: should I make this, collaborate with another company or outsource it? Do these choices create sustained value for us?

Industry models

New industry models are rare. When one emerges, it creates much publicity and disruption. Examples include Google creating a new industry around search and Uber completely disrupting the taxi industry with its workforce of part-time drivers. Essentially, they redefine the industry value chain. So, often, they are the result of a new enterprise model being more widely adopted by an industry. Ryanair's enterprise model led to the emergence of the low-cost industry model, now used by many competing firms.

The parts of the business model

A company's strategy defines the company's target market segment and customers, and determines the **value proposition** for the customer's business. The business model focuses on how a start-up captures some of the value for itself (i.e. how the company makes money). It determines the viability of the company. The business model focuses on coordinating internal and external processes to determine how the start-up interacts with partners, distribution channels and customers (Dubosson-Torbay et al., 2002).

According to Alex Osterwalder, there are four key aspects to any business model:

- the offering;
- the customer side;
- the infrastructure;
- the finances.

Start-up ventures need to consider each of these in turn and build their business model accordingly. Figure 12.3 illustrates the **business model framework**

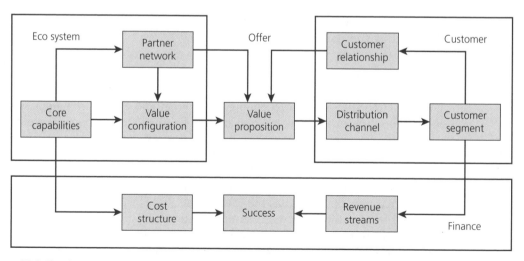

Figure 12.3 Business model framework

Source: Adapted from Osterwalder (2004).

and shows how each part interrelates. The business model describes, as a system, how the components of the business (i.e. organisational strategy, business processes) fit together to produce a profit. It answers the key question for investors: How does this business work? The answer to the question consists of two parts:

1 It includes a description of the efforts that generate sales, which produce revenue. The value proposition is delivered to the target customer through a distribution channel. The flow and update of the value proposition is influenced by the relationship capital created through the company's marketing activities. Clearly, Mozilla has developed a unique value proposition through its development of open source software. It receives donations from satisfied users as well as income from other sites to which it sends traffic from its Firefox internet browser.

2 It includes a description of the value-generating parts that make up the cost structure. A company's value proposition is created through the application of its key functions and abilities, through a configuration of operational activities that includes inputs and interaction with partners. A simple example is Toyota and its web of suppliers with whom Toyota work closely to ensure incredible quality and reliability within its vehicles.

The offering

The value proposition is the central piece that illustrates how the business plans to bind the supply side with the demand side. Value must always be considered from the buyer's perspective. Any functional, emotional or self-expressive value will vary, depending on the customer's specific situation. Understanding the customer's role (i.e., economic buyer, technical buyer, end user) as well as where the customer belongs on the technology adoption lifecycle (TALC) is critical when developing a value proposition. For the customer to consider buying a product, its value proposition must be superior to: 1) the competition; and 2) doing nothing. It must set it apart from the competition and focus on its product's unique benefits. The value proposition also requires an understanding of what your customers are trying to achieve through their strategy and actions (see Mason and Leek, 2008; Shafer et al., 2005; Richardson, 2008).

The value proposition statement consists of several key components:

● what is on offer and how is it offered to customers;
● what type of, and how much, value or benefit is associated with the offering (e.g., cost savings, time savings, revenue increase, customer/employee satisfaction);
● how the value is generated;
● why it is different from anything else on the market.

The customer side

● *Target market segment:* Defining the value proposition leads naturally into a discussion about who is the target market segment and what characterises the ideal customer. Specifically, it should have a clear understanding of the target customer's motivation to buy.

- *Customer relationships:* The business needs to consider the kind of relationship it wants to have with each customer segment. Does the offering lend itself to a more transactional, one-off relationship, or will it be an ongoing relationship that should be organised with some sort of subscription or ongoing contract? Is repeat buying important for its success?
- *Distribution channels:* Keep in mind that the offering, in combination with the relationship the business would like to have with its target customer, has strong implications for the choice of distribution channel. The trade-off is usually about balancing the complexity of the solution with the complexity of the marketing.

The infrastructure

- *Core capabilities:* List the business's core capabilities: the assets that it brings to the table when creating the offering. These include skills, patents, assets and expertise that make it unique and can be leveraged. Some of the strengths identified in a SWOT analysis can be considered a core capability.
- *Partners and allies:* Building the offering may involve third parties and suppliers who have key capabilities to complement it. Understanding how to integrate these in the offering and the processes is critical.
- *Value configuration:* Describe how all the components together create the product and serve customers. Explain the most important activities and processes needed to implement the business model, including critical tasks and timelines, the people and skills required, and the organisation's core processes.

The finances

- *Revenue streams:* Evaluate the streams through which the business will earn revenues from value-creating and customer-facing activities. Is it possible to price the product in such a way that optimises the volume?
- *Cost structure:* Calculate the costs that will be incurred to run the business model as determined by its infrastructure (above). Does the cost structure offer a reasonable profit?

Examining the finances at the end of the process allows the business to ensure that it has a balanced business model that produces value for its customers and profits for its shareholders at the same time.

Innovation in action

Blackcircles.com, a new business model

Mike Welch left school at 16, eager to make money. He started by fitting tyres at a garage, earning £50 a week. After six months he was made redundant. He then went into wholesaling tyres, but they made him redundant, too. With little option, he decided to make money for himself. In 1997, a £500 grant from the Prince's Trust for a computer helped him set up an online business selling tyres wholesale over the internet. In the evenings, he did shifts at Tesco. Looking back, he believes the site was ahead of its time. Nobody else was doing it. The formula seemed right, but he could not scale it up because he did not have the money. He never made any money from the idea so, in 1999, he was lured by Kwik Fit to become its head of ecommerce. He lasted two years before leaving to set up Blackcircles.com, whose website today sells tyres of all sizes and works with about 1,400 garages that fit them.

At its headquarters in Peebles, in the Scottish Borders, Welch employs 55 staff. The business had sales in excess of £30 million in 2013. In the beginning, he ordered a copy of every *Yellow Pages* in the UK and contacted each garage to ask if they wanted to join the Blackcircles network.

In 2011, the former Tesco chief executive, Sir Terry Leahy, backed the business. Leahy and three others invested £400,000. He later became a non-executive director. Blackcircles now has eight shareholders, including Leahy. Welch owns 35 per cent.

In 2015, Welch sold Blackcircles to French giant Michelin in a deal worth £50 million. This will net Welch approximately £17 million.

Source: Mark Fagelson/Alamy images

Another mapping approach comes from the concept of 'component business modelling'. IBM has been an early leader in this area, and has filed patents on the method. Figure 12.4 shows a visual depiction of IBM's view of a component business model. This modelling approach provides a practical way to experiment with alternative business models, by enabling firms to simulate various possibilities before committing to specific investments. It also provides the opportunity to visualise the processes underlying a business model. Thus, theoretical considerations of configuring elements of a business model here can become far more concrete (Chesbrough, 2010).

	Business Administration	New Business Development	Relationship Management	Servicing and Sales	Product Fulfillment	Financial Control and Accounting
Direct	Business Planning	Sector Planning	Account Planning	Sales Planning	Fulfilment Planning	Portfolio Planning
Control	Business Unit Tracking	Sector Management	Relationship Management	Sales Management	Fulfilment Planning	Compliance Reconciliation
	Staff Appraisals	Product Management	Credit Assessment			
Execute	Staff Administration	Product Delivery	Credit Administration	Sales	Product Fulfilment	Customer Accounts
	Product Administration	Marketing Campaigns		Customer Dialogue	Document Management	General Ledger
				Contact Routing		

Figure 12.4 Visual depiction of IBM's view of a component business model
Source: Chesbrough (2010), copyright 2010, with permission from Elsevier.

The business model dilemma of technology shifts

In 2001, Apple introduced the iPod with the iTunes store, revolutionising the music industry, creating a new market and transforming the company. But Apple was not the first to bring digital music players to market. Indeed, many people may still have a Creative MP3 player, which was market leader prior to the iPod. There were many other MP3 players on the market. So, why did the iPod succeed so spectacularly? The answer is that Apple developed a new business model – it made downloading digital music easy and convenient. It built a business model that combined hardware, software and service. This technology shift proved lethal to others in the music industry. Technology shifts are lethal to many manufacturing companies. Previous research indicates that this is not purely a problem of technological innovation, but is also closely related to the inertia of business models and business model innovation. Research by Tongur and Engwall (2014) shows that potential technology shift constitutes a business model dilemma for firms leading in the existing technology. They show why technology shifts are so difficult to master and that managing technology shifts does not require either technology or service innovation in order to create a viable business model, but instead a compound of both – as the Apple iPod case illustrates. Illustration 12.2 shows how technology shifts in the newspaper industry is having huge impact.

Illustration 12.2

The newspaper industry and the digital revolution: what business model to use?

The technology for producing and supplying journalistic content has changed dramatically. Whilst digitalisation, along with socio-cultural and technological changes, threatened the established newspaper business models, simultaneously it offered various opportunities to establish new business models, not least for quality journalism, which is crucial to a vital democracy.

Newspaper owners insist they are adapting their business models to make money online. The past 10 years have seen some titles disappear completely, whilst the rest deal with a new reality – a readership with the ability to find everything they need at the touch of a button. Newspapers are not giving up on their traditional formats, partly because they still have not quite figured out how to cope with this migration from offline to online and how to make a profit from it.

The shift of news consumption from traditional media to online news media is rapidly changing the media landscape. The news magazine *Der Spiegel* was able to reach a 1,000 per cent increase in e-paper sales in 2015 compared with sales in 2007. In addition to this, the Hamburg-based magazine was a pioneer in the digital news market: *Spiegel Online* (SPON) was launched as far back as 1994. Starting with selected articles from the print magazine, the editors anticipated only several months later that online readers are more interested in consuming unique content. Hence, the online division and the print magazine quickly began to work as separate operations. After providing free content to its users for more than 20 years, SPON is opting for a subscription-only solution.

A debate rages in the newspaper industry over the question of whether papers should charge for their content online or, as most papers now do, give it away for free in hopes of reaping faster overall revenue growth through internet advertising. Newspapers are taking a look at the option of charging readers – whether through subscriptions or article-by-article 'micro-payments' – for the content on their websites. For example, *The Huffington Post* integrates copyrighted content with its own original content. Online platforms, such as blogs, are readily able to take copyrighted content, whether news stories, magazine articles or pictures, and then republish that content on their own site without paying a licence or crediting the original pro-

Source: Andrew Holt/Alamy Images

ducer. Readers then opt to visit the blogs instead of the content of producers' websites, thereby depriving the content producers of the full return on their investment.

At *The New York Times* (NYT), editors spend hours each day discussing what to put on page one of the paper, with much less discussion about digital distribution. Since the NYT newsroom runs to the print edition's timetable, many articles go up online in the evening, whereas more people browse for news in the morning. Nearly 60 per cent of those reading NYT articles now do so on smartphones and tablets, often receiving them via Twitter, Facebook and other social networks, search engines and apps. That means fewer of them encounter the full package of reading that editors so painstakingly put together. Traffic to the NYT's home page has fallen by half from its peak in 2011; only a third of readers of NYT articles ever visit it. This makes it a lot harder to persuade them to consume a broader range of the paper's content, and to charge them for it.

Source: Rothmann, W. and Koch, J. (2014) Creativity in strategic lock-ins: The newspaper industry and the digital revolution, *Technological Forecasting and Social Change*, vol. 83, 66–83.

Considerations in designing a business model

Switching costs

The time, effort or money a customer has to spend to switch from one product or service provider to another is called **switching costs**. The higher the switching costs, the likelier a customer is to stick to one provider rather than to leave for the products or services of a competitor. Apple's introduction of the iPod in 2001 is also a great example of designing switching costs into a business model. Steve Jobs heralded his new product with the catchphrase 'thousand songs in a pocket'. Well, that was more than a product innovation focusing on storage. It was a business model strategy to get customers to copy all their music into iTunes and their iPod, which would make it more difficult for them to switch to competing digital music players. In a time when little more than brand preferences were preventing people from switching from one player to another, this was a smart move and laid the foundation for Apple's subsequent stronghold on music and later innovations.

Scalability

Scalability describes how easy it is to expand a business model without equally increasing its cost base. Consultancy is a well-understood business model and can be attractive and lucrative for techno start-ups, but it suffers from limits on scalability. Of course, software- and web-based business models are naturally more scalable than those based on bricks and mortar but, even amongst digital business models, there are large differences. An impressive example of scalability is Facebook. With only a few thousand engineers, it creates value for hundreds of millions of users. Only a few other companies in the world have such a ratio of users per employee. A company that has pushed the limits even further is the social gaming company Zynga. By building games like FarmVille or CityVille on the back of Facebook, the world's largest social network, they could benefit from Facebook's reach (and scale) without having to build it themselves.

A company that quickly learned its lessons regarding scalability was peer-to-peer communication company Skype. Its customer relationship collapsed under the weight of large numbers, when it was signing up ten thousands of users per day. It had to adapt its business model quickly to become more scalable.

Recurring revenues

Recurring revenues are best explained through a simple example. When a newspaper earns revenues from the sales at a news stand, they are transactional, whilst revenues from a subscription are recurring. Recurring revenues have two major advantages. First, the costs of sales incur only once for repetitive revenues. Second, with recurring revenues the business will have a better idea of how much it will earn in the future.

A nice example of recurring revenues is Red Hat, which provides open source software and support to enterprises based on a continuous subscription basis. In this model, clients do not pay for new software versions, because it is continuously updated. In the world of software as a service, these types of subscriptions are now the norm. This contrasts with Microsoft, which sells most of its software in the form of licences for every major release.

However, there is another aspect to recurring revenues, which are additional revenues generated from initial sales. This is the 'bait and hook' revenue model. For example, when you buy a printer, you continue to spend on cartridges or, when you buy a game console, you will continue to spend on games. This revenue model has not gone unnoticed by large corporations such as Apple; whilst Apple still earns most of its revenues from hardware sales, the recurring revenues from content and apps is steadily growing.

Cashflow

Specifically, the more the business can earn before spending, the better. Dell pioneered this model in the computer hardware manufacturing industry. By assembling on order after selling directly they managed to escape the terrible inventory depreciation costs of the hardware industry. Its impressive results showed how powerful it is to earn before spending.

Getting others to do the work

This is probably one of the least publicised weapons of mass destruction in business model design. What could be more powerful than getting others to do the work whilst you earn the money? For example, IKEA gets us to assemble the furniture we buy from them. We do the work. They save money in transportation costs and storage costs. Similarly, eBay gets us to do the work of posting details of the items we want to sell and then they get paid for any sale. Another more obvious example is open source software, where firms generate cash from a community of users developing the software.

Protecting the business from competitors

A great business model can provide a longer-term protection from competition than just a great product. An elaborate supply chain network, such as those developed by Toyota, offers it additional protection from competitors. Furthermore, Apple's main competitive advantage arises more from its powerful business model than purely from its innovative products. It is easier for Samsung, for instance, to copy the iPhone than to build an ecosystem like Apple's App Store, which caters to developers and users alike and hosts hundreds of thousands of applications.

Changing the cost structure

Cutting costs is a long practised sport in business. Some business models, however, go beyond cost cutting by creating value based on a totally different cost structure. This is what Ryanair did with its no frills airline. The newspaper industry has also changed the cost structure of its industry by making content available online and making people pay for access via a subscription charge. In addition, many daily newspapers are now given away free, with advertising paying for the production costs. Another example is Skype. It provides calls and communication almost like a conventional telecom company, but for free or for a very low cost. It can do this because its business model has a very different cost structure. In fact, Skype's model is based on the economics of a software company, whilst a telecom provider's model is based on the economics of a network company. The former's costs are mainly people; whilst the latter's cost include huge capital expenditures in infrastructure.

Intellectual property is an asset

Intellectual property (IP) is a company asset and should be treated and managed as such. Owning and acquiring IP will not overcome poor business strategy and make a company successful. There are many examples of firms with exciting technology that failed to profit from it. Classic cases, such as the EMI scanner (MRI), are told to business students. This technology was developed by EMI, but it failed to develop a business model to exploit it. The licensing business model is well-understood and well-known, but the variety of ways the licensing arrangement is organised is almost limitless.

IP is a broad concept and includes many different intangibles, such as patents (inventions), copyright (works of authorship, software, drawings, etc.) know-how (e.g. expertise, skilled craftsmanship, training capability, understanding of how something works), trade secrets (a protected formula or method), trademarks (logos, distinctive names), industrial design (the unique external appearance) and semiconductor mask works (the physical design of semiconductor circuits).

The technology licence and business relationships

Although not immediately apparent when reading an impressive looking licence agreement, it is quickly realised and understood by all businesses that, with a licence, must come other very practical agreements that will help both parties succeed. Let us take an example. Red Software Company decides to collaborate with Blue Software Company to develop a new computer game provisionally labelled Galaxywars. This will involve collaborating R&D activities. So, they sign a technology licence that gives each company rights to use each other's technology (software). In addition, they need to negotiate an R&D agreement to specify the terms of the collaboration. That is, length of time, level of investment required, resources that each company will have to make available, etc. Furthermore, what happens to all the outputs from the collaboration? Red Software Company may be able to utilise some of the outputs in its own range of computer games whereas Blue Software Company may be unable to use any of the outputs. Also, who is going to manufacture, market and distribute Galaxywars? An IP licence is interrelated to many other agreements.

Continual adaptation of the business model

Developing a business model is all well and good, but sustained success comes from changing it and continually adapting it. Companies that manage to create value over extended periods of time successfully shape, adapt and renew their business models to fuel such value creation. One only has to consider General Electric, IBM or Apple and one quickly realises that the business model of these firms that is in place today is very different from the one in place 10 or 20 years ago. Achtenhagen et al. (2013) identify three critical capabilities to achieve this:

- an orientation towards experimenting with and exploiting new business opportunities;
- a balanced use of resources;
- coherence between leadership, culture and employee commitment.

The licensing business model

A licence is a consent by the owner to the use of IP in exchange for money or something else of value (May, 2006). The owner of a licence is known as the licensor and the purchaser and user of the licence is known as the licensee.

Technology-based start-up ventures inevitably involve scientists and inventors who are interested in seeing their research or inventions commercialised for use. They are, usually, however, equally also interested in the intellectual challenge of the research. In such cases, licensing a technology idea might make good sense. Licensing allows technology producers to generate cash from their innovations by licensing them to other companies so that they may be integrated into an end product.

Licensing is most commonly applied to innovations that involve sophisticated technology protected by intellectual property (IP) agreements. The innovation itself may not be a complete product and may need to be integrated into a broader offering in order to create value for the end user. For example, the Blu-ray case study at the end of Chapter 8 illustrates how licensing can be used to secure dominance in an industry.

It is worthy of note and consideration for the start-up that technology-based licensing agreements rely on relatively intimate and long-term relationships with customers. This is because all parties must exchange certain (confidential) information and because the fundamental economics of a licensing arrangement are long-term in nature. The idea that business negotiations over licensing deals are won and lost through good and bad negotiations is overstated. There is a mutual interest in both parties surviving and thriving, hence most technology-based licensing deals are beneficial for both parties.

Bear in mind, however, it is possible that a potentially attractive licensing agreement can result in very poor results for a start-up. Such a situation could occur, for example, if a start-up signs an exclusive licence with a partner in order to secure a royalty stream. But then actions do not live up to the promises because, for example, the partner does not invest sufficiently in marketing or developing the technology. In these situations, sales and income levels will be low. This could, in turn, prevent the company from moving forward with other more productive partnerships. An alternative solution might be a licensing agreement that clearly accounts for the above situation. See the 'Payments' section later in this chapter.

Income from licensing

Licensing income usually involves a fee paid upfront to the inventor through a signed licensing agreement between the parties. These agreements also may include milestone payments that become due as the technology or innovation is commercialised and/or a royalty fee set at a percentage of the revenue or earnings from the eventual sale of products or services. The amount of the fee upfront, milestone payments and royalties are negotiated between the parties and generally reflect the effort and stage of commercialisation. In other words, the more developed a product or service, the higher the proceeds tend to be.

There exist a number of organisations interested in licensing innovative technology and inventions that complement their existing products and services for a specific purpose or market. The organisation that licenses the technology usually assumes all responsibility for subsequent costs of developing, marketing, selling and distributing the product or service.

Marketing issues related to the licensing model

The goal of marketing technology for licensing is to drive a deep understanding of the potential applications of the innovation amongst key industry insiders. Successful marketing for technology licensing focuses on creating visibility for the technology through industry presentations, establishing a presence in academic and industry journals, authoring whitepapers and otherwise evangelising the innovation. For example, the pharmaceutical industry uses academic conferences to promote awareness of new drugs. Frequently, news organisations will select articles from key academic journals that have newsworthy stories (see Illustration 12.3).

Illustration 12.3

Drug trial results suggest help for cancer patients

The findings from recent clinical trials provide hope for cancer patients suffering with leukemia. The exciting treatment involves genetically engineered T cells which seem to help destroy leukemia cells. Scientists report that some of the patients have now been cancer free for more than one year.

This research project was undertaken at the University of Pennsylvania. It involves developing genetically engineered 'T cells' taken from patients. These are later reintroduced to the patient whereupon they have been shown to attack and destroy cancer cells. The trial was undertaken in advanced cases of leukemia. The researchers reported that two of the three patients have shown positive responses to the treatment and have now been free from cancer for over a year.

Financial and strategic implications

Licensing revenues can be structured in different ways, with upfront payments by the licensee or with payments that are revenue-dependent. In order to license successfully, a company will require the funding necessary to develop their technology to the point where it becomes a suitable add-on to the offering of its licensee partner. If the licensed product is a tangible item, costs are the most important metric to monitor. Royalty fees may accompany licensing revenue on a per-unit-sale basis, or the parties may use some other transparent means of measuring usage of the licensed technology. For example, an important consideration in structuring licensing agreements is the portion of income derived from licensing revenue versus that deriving from royalties. Royalty revenue is dependent on the selling ability of the party integrating the licensed technology, and the size of the addressable market for the end product.

Strategically, licensing may run the risk of exposing IP to the party integrating the technology into their products. It is, therefore, important to ensure that patents are defensible and that other IP is protected.

Costs and benefits of the licensing model

Licensing works well in situations where developing an entire product independently is not feasible. The trade-off is that, since the offering comprises only one element of a complete product, it may hinder the development of a strong company profile, unless an 'Intel Inside' co-branding option is available. It is not uncommon for very successful firms to go unrecognised by the public. ARM, a leading chip producer from the UK, is the world's second largest developer of computer chips. Its microprocessors are found in all Apple iPhones and almost all smartphones. Yet, few people have heard of the company.

Within a licence agreement, the royalty rate may be interlinked with other factors, most notably minimum royalty commitments and decreased **royalty rates**, once certain volumes are reached. Minimum royalties are often a commitment for some form of exclusivity or access to the brand in a market. Decreasing royalty rates could be used to incentivise the licensee to achieve higher volumes as the unit cost of branded products then becomes less.

Licence agreements usually include a number of other considerations such as:

- definition of the brand being licensed;
- definition of the sales to which the royalty percentage is to be applied;
- a restriction of the use of the brand to specific products, channels and territories;
- a specific time period, say three years;
- brand use and authorisation procedures. This is to ensure that the use of the brand by the licensee is consistent with that of the brand owner;
- commitments by licensee to brand marketing. This can also be a percentage of sales or a fixed amount;
- other legal rights and obligations, such as necessary records and returns and access to audit each other's accounts.

These factors will also influence, to a greater or lesser extent, the royalty rate. If a licensee agrees, for example, to contribute to brand marketing, then the royalty rate might be reduced to compensate for this.

Table 12.5 Typical royalty rate in technology sectors

Industry	Royalty rate					
	0–2%	2–5%	5–10%	10–15%	15–20%	20–25%
Aerospace	50%	50%				
Chemical	16.5%	58.1%	24.3%	0.8%	0.4%	
Computer	62.5%	31.3%	6.3%			
Electronics		50%	25%	25%		
Healthcare	3.3%	51.7%	45%			
Pharmaceuticals	23.6%	32.1%	29.3%	12.5%	1.1%	0.7%
Telecom	40%	37.3%	23.6%			

Source: Parr (2007), republished with permission of Wiley, permission conveyed through Copyright Clearance Center, Inc.

Table 12.5 illustrates the wide range of royalty rates that exist across a broad range of different industries. The rates differ for a variety of reasons, including historical working practices. Usually, however, there is a link to typical length of time the licensor can earn income before the technology is superseded or becomes obsolete. Other influences can be the level of upfront R&D costs and volume of sales (few units of aircraft are sold compared to units of gaming software). In Table 12.5 we can see that the aerospace industry seems very conservative paying royalty rates of up to 5 per cent. Electronics, on the other hand, looks more lucrative with 25 per cent of royalties achieving a rate of between 10–15 per cent.

Other strategic uses of licensing

A start-up business may consider licensing a technology or the right to use a technology in a specific field or geographic area as a means to obtain funding for its core product.

Life science companies, particularly those developing therapeutic products, generally use licensing as a sales and marketing strategy for their products due to the very significant costs of development and clinical trials, as well as the eventual marketing, sale and distribution of the product.

Licensing a technology may also be used as a way to create an exit for a business, if it becomes clear that the business cannot fund the marketing, sales and distribution of the product from existing resources and additional financing is not available. Generally in 'stalled or failed' technology businesses that have been backed with equity investment, the shareholders will request that management or a third party attempt to license or sell the technology in an effort to provide some return on investment to shareholders. Illustration 12.4 shows the power of licensing.

Illustration 12.4

The infamous IBM-Microsoft MS-DOS licensing deal

Development of Microsoft Disk Operating System (MSDOS) began in October 1980, when IBM began searching the market for an operating system for the yet-to-be-introduced IBM Personal

Computer. IBM originally had intended to use a simple system developed by respected firm: Digital Research. IBM then talked to a small company called Microsoft. Microsoft was a language vendor. Bill Gates and Paul Allen had written Microsoft BASIC and were selling it on punched tape or disk to early PC hobbyists. Prior to this, the company's original name and goal was Traf-O-Data, making car counters for highway departments.

Microsoft had no real operating system to sell, but quickly made a deal to license Seattle Computer Products' 86-DOS operating system, which had been written by Tim Paterson earlier in 1980 for use on that company's line of 8086 computers: 86-DOS (also called QDOS, for Quick and Dirty Operating System). Fortunately for Microsoft, Digital Research was showing no

hurry in introducing its operating system. Paterson's DOS 1.0 was approximately 4000 lines of assembler source. This code was quickly polished up and presented to IBM for evaluation. IBM found itself left with Microsoft's offering of 'Microsoft Disk Operating System 1.0'. An agreement was reached between the two, and IBM agreed to accept 86-DOS as the main operating system for its new PC. Microsoft purchased all rights to 86-DOS in July 1981, from Seattle Computer products and 'IBM Personal Computer DOS 1.0' was ready for the introduction of the IBM PC in October 1981. IBM subjected the operating system to an extensive quality-assurance program, reportedly found well over 300 bugs, and decided to rewrite the programs. This is why PC-DOS is copyrighted by both IBM and Microsoft.

Case study

Developing a new product for the teeth whitening market

Nestled alongside the Olympic Park in the heart of Munich's industrial district, to the north of the city, sits Munich Gases: a German industrial gas company with a long history of supplying gases and liquids to firms across Europe. Its product range is dominated by liquid oxygen, which it supplies to health-care markets and carbon dioxide, which it supplies to the drinks and beverages industry. With a market capitalisation of €10 billion, Munich Gases is one of the industry leaders. It also has a proud history of successful R&D, which has helped to maintain its dominant position over the past 80 years. This case study tells the story of how Munich Gases uncovered a multi-billion dollar market opportunity for whitening teeth and explored how best to exploit it.

A portfolio of R&D projects

Munich Gases employs almost 48,000 employees working in more than 100 countries worldwide. In the

2009 financial year, it achieved sales of €11.211 billion. The strategy of the group is geared towards 'sustainable earnings-based growth and focuses on the expansion of its international business with new forward-looking products and services'. Munich Gases offers a wide range of compressed and liquefied gases as well as chemicals and it is, therefore, an important and reliable partner for a huge variety of industries. Its products are used, for example, in the energy sector, in steel production, chemical processing, environmental protection and welding, as well as in food processing, glass production and electronics. It is also investing in the expansion of its fast-growing health care business, i.e. medical gases, and it is a leading global player in the development of environmentally friendly hydrogen technology. It has an annual R&D budget of €100 million. Recently, it faced the decision of whether to invest 10 per cent of this budget in a single project – teeth whitening.

→

Amongst over 100 R&D projects running within Munich Gases' R&D department was one that was exploring applications for the use of plasma as a cleaning agent. Plasma is the fourth matter. Matter can be solid, liquid, a gas or a fourth type, plasma, which is actually the most common in the universe. Plasma is an ionised gas capable of conducting electricity and absorbing energy from an electrical supply. Manmade plasma is, generally, created in a low-pressure environment. (Lightning and the aurora borealis are naturally occurring examples of plasma.) When a gas absorbs electrical energy, its temperature increases, causing the ions to vibrate faster and 'scrub' a surface. Plasma has been used for many years to clean surfaces, for example, in semiconductor processing, plasma cleaning is commonly used to prepare a wafer surface prior to wire bonding. Removing contamination (flux) strengthens the bond adhesion, which helps extend device reliability and longevity. Plasma, therefore, is an effective way to clean without using hazardous solvents. Since 2011, a research team at Munich Gases has been exploring the viability of incorporating plasma for cleaning and whitening teeth.

Artificial plasmas can be created when energy is added to a gas, perhaps using an electrical field or a laser. The resulting matter can behave differently when it comes into contact with other particles. Whilst many artificially created plasmas are extremely hot – for example, the flame on an arc welder – advances in recent years have allowed the creation of much cooler plasmas. This, in turn, has opened the possibility of using them on the human body, where they could offer a very precise way of targeting tiny areas. In this case, the properties of the plasma are harmful to bacteria, without affecting the surrounding tissue.

This project at Munich Gases was quickly established, following the uncovering of a patent submitted by the University of Southern California (USC) in 2009, which claimed scientists at the USC had used plasma to sterilise teeth and one of the side-effects was a whitening of the teeth. When Munich Gases uncovered and read it, they were so intrigued by the patent and its possibilities that they quickly established a team of researchers to explore whether the idea could be a viable business opportunity. The team was given 12 months and a budget of €1 million.

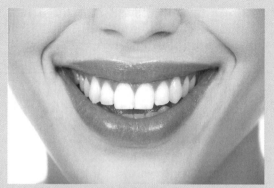

Source: kurhan. Shutterstock/Pearson Education Ltd

The plasma teeth cleaning project

Twelve months had now passed and it was time for the research project to report its findings to a panel of senior management. The panel wanted to know whether this technology would be of interest to Munich Gases. The project had caused much discussion amongst the R&D personnel – some believing that the company was mad to spend €1 million on a crazy idea, and others simply curious as to whether plasma could, indeed, work.

The project leader Thomas Wolfgang presented the findings. He explained that, when thinking of plasma, the first thing that comes to mind is temperature. Most people know, and all scientists should know, that high temperatures are required to turn gas into this state. He finished his introduction by suggesting that the findings after 12 months confirmed that it is possible to use plasma to clean teeth. The panel were fascinated, they all smiled, full of excitement and anticipation. Wolfgang began to explain some basic principles about how plasma cleaning uses ion excitation as a cleaning process. He explained that, when a gas absorbs electrical energy, its temperature increases, causing the ions to vibrate faster. In an inert gas, such as argon, the excited ions can bombard a surface ('sandblast') and remove a small amount of material. In the case of an active gas, such as oxygen, ion bombardment as well as chemical reactions occur. As a result, organic compounds and residues volatilise and are removed.

Wolfgang went on to explain that his team recently had created a new plasma laboratory instrument, which uses the matter to destroy bacterial bio-films on teeth, the main cause of them turning yellow. The micro-organisms also contribute to bad breath. He explained that it may be described as a tiny, plasma blowtorch that breaks apart the sticky bonds that holds plaque to a tooth. However, unlike the hot plasma at the centre of stars and lightning bolts, this plasma torch is no warmer than room temperature. At present, his research team had only used the torch to sterilise a tooth during a root canal but, according to Wolfgang, they already had some more exciting uses in mind. He showed the board a short film of some of the experiments. The laboratory instrument resembled a tiny purple blowtorch, with a pencil-sized jet of plasma coming out of it. Remarkably, it had the ability to annihilate bacteria with outstanding efficiency. In a study, experts show that bacteria tend to come together in a slimy matrix, which boosts their ability to resist attackers. However, the new instrument renders any kind of matrix completely useless to the micro-organisms and destroys them. In one experiment, bacterial colonies grown in the root canal of an extracted human tooth fell prey to the plasma tool so fast that, when the team analysed the surface of the canal using scanning electron microscopes, they found a near pristine surface. Heat sensors placed on the tooth also revealed that its temperature rose by only about five degrees during a ten-minute test fire with the plasma tool, which means that it remains well within tolerable pain limits for humans.

Wolfgang explained that there were real and perceived health risks; and these were considerably different. Given that this method was using essentially cold plasma, the risks were minimal. But, he acknowledged that the association of heat with plasma is so strong that there may be a negative reaction to the product, based on ignorance or lack of knowledge. Either way, this was a problem that would have to be addressed. It may mean that a part of the marketing communication budget will need to cover education.

Wolfgang saved his compelling arguments and convincing slides until last. This was a series of slides of teeth. The teeth were from pigs. As it was not possible to use or even get access to the teeth of humans, Wolfgang had to test the product on the nearest substitute, which was pigs' teeth. The slides revealed some dramatic changes in colour following exposure to the plasma. Discoloured yellow teeth noticeably changed to a shade of white. Wolfgang had to explain that white, like any other colour, has hundreds of different shades, including cream, off-white, ivory, brilliant white, etc., all of which are natural shades of teeth that can be found amongst the population of human beings.

Table 12.6 Project analysis

Progress of project	% of analysis complete
Market overview Market study Expert interviews Internal interviews Customer view	90
Intellectual property IP review Patent filing IP strategy	60
Regulatory Regulatory review Regulatory plan	100
Technology/risk assessment Assessment and mitigation Efficacy tests Risk plan	60
Product development Laboratory prototype Initial concepts/designs/proposition	95
Route to market Conceptualisation and road map Partners Value proposal	70

The meeting had to consider whether to invest €10 million in this project. Such a decision would, of course, be at the expense of other projects not being funded. Munich Gases considered a commonly used framework for evaluating R&D projects. This was made up of six key areas, indicating how much of the analysis was complete (see Table 12.6).

Market overview for plaque, periodontal (gum) disease and whitening

Wolfgang put up a slide showing the competitive space for a variety of products and techniques currently available and used by people to combat periodontal disease (see Figure 12.5). It seemed there was a clear need for an effective, simple cleaning product. For example, people were aware of the benefits of flossing, but few people actually regularly flossed their teeth because of the difficulty. Currently, there is a clear trade-off between ease of use and efficacy. Thus, things easy to use are not very effective. It was, however, the issue of teeth whitening that seemed to

→

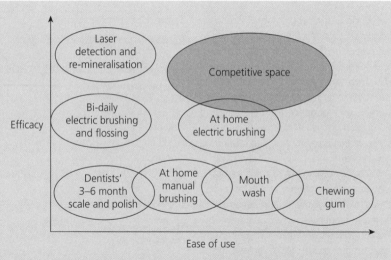

Figure 12.5 Competitor map: prevention and therapy of periodontal disease

be grabbing most people's attention. Several members of the panel were amazed at the possibility that plasma could actually whiten teeth. And it was specifically this benefit that the marketing manager believed was of most interest. He argued that whitening was a growing and lucrative market. He also argued that there were few, if any, easy to use effective whitening products available. The dentist present confirmed that the most commonly used effective whitening was a bleach-based process, where users essentially bathed their teeth in a solution of bleach for a couple of hours a day. Products in this category typically were of the format of a plastic tray that is held around the teeth to ensure the solution/gel is in contact with the teeth.

The Marketing Manager was Thomas Haas. He gave some details of the world toothpaste market. First, he put up a slide showing how the market has a number of specific segments including: regular toothpaste, anti-caries toothpaste, children's toothpaste, desensitising toothpaste, gum protection toothpaste, multi-benefit toothpaste, tartar control toothpaste, whitening toothpaste and others. He then went on to explain that toothpaste is one of the most dynamic segments of the oral care market:

The frequency of product launches in existing segments of the market contributes to continuous evolution of the toothpaste market. Increase in sales of oral hygiene products in major markets worldwide has largely resulted from growing awareness of hygiene and product innovation. New advancements have led to the launch of a variety of high-priced, value-added multifunctional products in several oral care categories such as toothpastes and toothbrushes. Whitening toothpastes and products offering multiple functions are driving growth in the dentifrices segment. Currently, for major toothpastes, averting tooth decay is not sufficient, which usually guarantee benefits such as fresher breath, healthier gums and whiter teeth. Technological advancements in recent years have altered the toothpaste segment to one that offers additional benefits besides just fighting cavities to customers. This made manufacturers roll out products with a lot of additional features that were not available previously.

He cautioned that entry into this market or related markets would be difficult, given the extent of competitors and the fact that some of these firms are multinational firms with huge power, such as Colgate-Palmolive, GlaxoSmithKline, Henkel AG & Co., Johnson & Johnson, Procter & Gamble and Unilever.

Thomas then went on to argue that this power also presents opportunities, especially when it comes to licensing technology. Powerful brand management firms with international brands to defend are always looking for opportunities to steal a march on their competitors. Exclusive access to a unique technology would provide such an opportunity. This made all the panel smile.

Thomas then gave the panel an example of a small company of three employees based in Maine, USA, that developed a new product in the teeth cleaning market. The company launched the product in a few Wal-mart stores in the USA. Sales were impressive. Immediately, Procter & Gamble took an interest and approached the company with an offer. After several months of negotiation, the small company agreed to sell the business for a staggering $165 million up-front with an 'earn-out' payment in three years, based on a formula pegged to financial results. The up-front payment alone was nearly four times annual sales of $43 million. The deal required the three employees to work at developing the business inside P&G for three years.

Consumer market or professional market

Discussions continued for another hour with a wide variety of views being expressed. The dental scientists felt more research was required to prove and fully explain precisely how the plasma was whitening teeth. Some of the business development managers felt that teeth whitening was a fad and that the product should be marketed specifically as a cleaning tool. There was one key issue that dominated the discussion towards the end of the meeting and that centred on whether to target the professional market, i.e. dentists, or the consumer market with a simple-to-use micro cylinder product. Such cylinders were incorporated commonly into pen-type torches, and were used in soldering in the jewellery industry.

In many ways, the professional market would be easier to reach and Munich Gases could work with a few lead users to develop the most appropriate product. Such a product would use much larger cylinders of plasma, as these would be in a regulated market used by professional dentists in their surgeries only.

The head of R&D tried to summarise the arguments:

Look, both options are feasible. It seems to me that we need to examine the type of business model that we wish to build. The professional market offers less risk, we could also build in an annual service to the product. This may include replacement parts and filters, for example. It also offers the opportunity for repair and maintenance and an after sales service. We could also license the product to dentists without them necessarily having to pay upfront. This all sounds very attractive. On the other hand, the consumer market

does offer the potential for big riches. We all know the margins and mark-ups available on consumer products. I mean, hundreds of per cent. Also, we have the possibility of designing in replacement cartridges and following the Gillette razor model or the ink jet cartridge model. This is where the original product is sold at a minimal price, but where complimentary products, such as cartridges, are sold with significant margins. The major profits lie in the replacement cartridges.

Smiles emerged all around the table. This was beginning to look like an opportunity to print money – lots of it.

Marcus Leitz was the Head of R&D. He explained that ink jet printer manufacturers have gone to extensive efforts to make sure that their printers are incompatible with lower cost after-market ink cartridges and cartridge refilling. This is because the printers often are sold at or below cost to generate sales of proprietary cartridges, which will generate profits for the company over the life of the equipment. Indeed, this business model is so successful that it has become known as the razor-cartridge business model.

The licensing option

There was another option that the panel had to consider. This was simply licensing the technology without forming a business. A technology licensing agreement grants a licensee the right to utilise specific technologies, patents, software, know-how or product designs. In a typical technology licence agreement, a running royalty fee based on licensed product sales revenue is paid to the licensor on a periodic basis. Stephan Boch was Licensing Manager for Munich Gases and had an impressive track record of securing some very profitable licensing deals for Munich Gases. Unsurprisingly, he was enthusiastic about the licensing option. He explained how licensing would allow Munich Gases to gain revenue from its plasma technology by licensing it to other companies so that it may be integrated into an end product. He said that the success of the model rested on secure intellectual property protection, which he said Munich Gases had. This option would allow Munich Gases to exit at this stage of the development without any further additional costs. The innovation itself clearly was not yet a complete product and would need to be integrated into a product to be of value for

→

the end user (consumer or professional). Members of the panel were now interested in this option.

Stephan went on to explain that this was not a short-term solution; this would be a long-term agreement because all parties must exchange certain (confidential) information. Boch argued that any licensing arrangement can be structured in different ways, with upfront payments by the licensee or with payments that are revenue-dependent. In this case, Munich Gases could argue for funding to develop the technology to the point where it becomes a suitable add-on to the offering of its licensee partner. Royalty fees may accompany licensing revenue on a per-unit-sale basis, or the parties may use some other transparent means of measuring usage of the licensed technology. An important consideration in structuring licensing agreements is the portion of income derived from licensing revenue versus that deriving from royalties. Royalty revenue is dependent on the selling ability of the party integrating the licensed technology, and the size of the addressable market for the end-product.

The R&D Manager was critical:

My understanding is that licensing works well in situations where developing an entire product independently is not feasible. But, in our case it is feasible. The trade-off is that, since the product comprises only one element of a complete prod-

uct, it may hinder the development of a strong company profile for Munich Gases, unless a co-branding option is available.

The room fell silent. The temperature in the room was rising and making a decision was not going to be easy. Some people were going be angry and upset if the decision went against them.

Maria Klaus was Marketing Manager for Munich Gases. She had a different view of how the project should develop:

I see things differently from Stephan. I think we can build a business around this technology. The consumer product offers the potential for big rewards. I can vision a hand-held small plasma toothbrush in bathrooms all over Europe; a product that is in addition to their existing toothbrush that the whole family can use to whiten and clean their teeth. We could build a brand that becomes synonomous with clean teeth. The business could extend the brand into other markets and become the market leader. Equally, the professional product also offers another route to a successful business. This offers less financial reward but, significantly for Munich Gases, this is less risky and less costly but, nonetheless, could raise huge profits for us, especially in the after-sales services.

Illustration 12.5

Selecting a business model

1 **Value proposition** – a description of the customer problem, the product that addresses the problem, and the value of the product from the customer's perspective.

2 **Market segment** – the group of customers to target, sometimes the potential of an innovation is unlocked only when a different market segment is targeted.

3 **Value chain structure** – the firm's position and activities in the value chain and how the firm will capture part of the value that it creates in the chain.

4 **Revenue generation and margins** – how revenue is generated (sales, leasing, subscription,

support, etc.), the cost structure, and target profit margins.

5 **Position in value network** – identification of competitors, partners and any network effects that can be utilised to deliver more value to the customer.

6 **Competitive strategy** – how the company will attempt to develop a sustainable competitive advantage, for example, by means of a cost, differentiation, or niche strategy.

Source: Chesbrough, H. and Rosenbloom, R.S. (2002) The role of the business model in capturing value from innovation: evidence from Xerox Corporation's technology spin-off companies, *Industrial and Corporate Change*, vol. 11, no. 3, 529–55.

Maria went on to explain that, in her view, it was the business model that they constructed and selected that would, ultimately, influence the outcome of discussions. She put up a slide that identified six components of any business model (see the box above 'Selecting a business model'). A long discussion ensued about what type of business model would be desirable. Her second slide showed the theoretical options that could be constructed (see Table 12.3 earlier in the chapter). There were 16 business models, but there were three categories that were applicable for this business. Munich Gases can be classified as a creator and there were three types of assets involved: entrepreneur; manufacturer and inventor.

Decision time

The R&D Manager was chairing the meeting and, after two hours, he decided to bring the panel members back to focus on the decision that was in front of them. 'We need a decision today,' he explained. 'The board will want to know our recommendation.

They will back our decision and release the €10 million, but we need to be clear and unambiguous, we cannot say we think "a" is right, but it could be "b".'

Yes or no to an investment of €10 million? And which particular product, market and business model?

This case raises many questions and not all the information is available to answer them. Nonetheless, decisions have to be taken on the best available information at a given point in time. It is always possible to delay the decision until all the information you require is available, but this may cost the business in terms of losing a position of advantage to a competitor who decides to enter the market.

Source: Weill, P., Malone, T.W., D'Urso, V.T., Herman, G. and Woerner, S. (2005) *Do Some Business Models Perform Better than Others? A Study of the 1000 Largest US Firms*, Sloan School of Management, Massachusetts Institute of Technology, Working Paper No. 226.

Questions

1 Should Munich Gases invest €10 million in this new product project?

2 What other factors may yet decide the fate of this project?

3 Which market should Munich Gases select: the consumer product market or professional/business market?

4 Sketch out five different possible business models. Of these, determine which is the most profitable and which is most likely to succeed.

5 How will the powerful toothpaste brand owners react?

6 Should Munich Gases secure an entry into the market with one of Europe's leading multiples (e.g. Lidl, Tesco, Carrefour, Aldi)?

7 Should Munich Gases secure the endorsement of one of Europe's leading toothpaste brands (e.g. Aquafresh, Signal, Macleans) before entering the market?

8 How can the firm reassure uneasy consumers about the safety of plasma in their mouths?

Chapter summary

This chapter showed the importance of developing a clear business model for the enterprise. It is a simple powerful tool to remind entrepreneurs how their ideas will make money. It shows that business models are, fundamentally, linked with technological innovation, yet the business model construct is, essentially, separable from technology. More importantly, developing the right technology is a matter of a business model decision regarding openness and user engagement. The licensing business model is common for technology-based ventures and all aspects of licensing was considered.

Discussion questions

1 For start-ups, the need to scale up can be costly; discuss how business model design can help overcome this.

2 Selling a product is great, but generating recurring revenues is better. Discuss the value in developing a 'cell phone monthly subscription' business model.

3 Discuss the problems facing the newspaper industry and the options open to it to make money.

4 Is it possible to receive payment before incurring expenditure?

5 Why are switching costs useful to consider in the design of a business model?

6 Is it possible to limit the threat of competition within your business model?

Key words and phrases

Business model *413*	Business model framework *422*
Value chain *414*	Switching costs *428*
Revenue model *416*	Scalability *428*
Enterprise model *416*	Recurring revenue *428*
Industry model *416*	Licensing model *432*
Value proposition *422*	Royalty rates *434*

References

Achtenhagen, L., Melin, L. and Naldi, L. (2013) Dynamics of business models – strategizing, critical capabilities and activities for sustained value creation, *Long Range Planning*, vol. 46, 427–42.

Baden-Fuller, C. and Haefliger, S. (2013) Business models and technological innovation, *Long Range Planning*, vol. 46, 419–26.

Chesbrough, H. and Rosenbloom, R.S. (2002) The role of the business model in capturing value from innovation: evidence from Xerox Corporation's technology spin-off companies, *Industrial and Corporate Change*, vol. 11, no. 3, 529–55.

Chesbrough, H. (2010) Business model innovation: opportunities and barriers, *Long Range Planning*, vol. 43, 354–63.

Dubosson-Torbay, M., Osterwalder, A. and Pigneur, Y. (2002) E-business model design, classification and measurements, *Thunderbird International Business Review*, vol. 44, no. 1, 5–23.

Economist, The (2012) Brewer's Droop: In Britain, February.

Johnson, M.W., Christensen, C.M. and Kagermann, H. (2008) Reinventing your business model, *Harvard Business Review*, vol. 86, no. 12, 51–9.

Mason, K. and Leek, S. (2008) Learning to build a supply network: an exploration of dynamic business models, *Journal of Management Studies*, vol. 45, no. 4, 774–99.

May, C. (2006), The world intellectual property organization, *New Political Economy*, vol. 11, no. 3, 435–45.

Osterwalder, A. (2004) *The business model ontology: a proposition in a design science approach*, These Présentée à l'Ecole des Hautes Etudes Commerciales de l'Université de Lausanne.

Parr, R.L. (2007) *Royalty Rates for Licensing Intellectual Property*, John Wiley and Sons, Inc., Hoboken, NJ.

Patzelt, H., zu Knyphausen-Aufseß, D. and Nikol, P. (2008) Top management teams, business models, and performance of biotechnology ventures: an upper echelon perspective, *British Journal of Management*, vol. 19, 205–21.

Porter, M.E. (1980) *Competitive Strategy: Techniques for Analyzing Industries and Competitors*, Free Press, New York.

Richardson, J. (2008) The business model: an integrative framework for strategy execution, *Strategic Change*, vol. 17, nos 5–6, 133–44.

Rothmann, W. and Koch, J. (2014) Creativity in strategic lock-ins: the newspaper industry and the digital revolution, *Technological Forecasting and Social Change*, vol. 83, 66–83.

Shafer, S.M., Smith, H.J. and Linder, J.C. (2005) The power of business models, *Business Horizons*, vol. 48, no. 3, 199–207.

Spieth, P., Schneckenberg, D. and Ricart, J.E. (2014) Business model innovation – state of the art and future challenges for the field, *R&D Management*, vol. 44, no. 3, 237–47.

Teece, D. (2010) Business models, business strategy and innovation, *Long Range Planning*, vol. 43, nos 2–3, 172–94.

Tongur, S. and Engwall, M. (2014) The business model dilemma of technology shifts, *Technovation*, vol. 34, no. 9, 525–35.

Watson, D. (2005) *Business Models*, Harriman House Ltd, Petersfield.

Weill, P. and Vitale, M.R. (2001) *Place to Space: Migrating to Ebusiness Models*, Harvard Business School Press, Boston, MA.

Zott, C. and Amit, R. (2007) Business model design and the performance of entrepreneurial firms, *Organization Science*, vol. 18, no. 2, 181–99.

Further reading

For a more detailed review of the business models literature, the following develop many of the issues raised in this chapter:

Achtenhagen, L., Melin, L. and Naldi, L. (2013) Dynamics of business models – strategizing, critical capabilities and activities for sustained value creation, *Long Range Planning*, vol. 46, 427–42.

Baden-Fuller, C. and Haefliger, S. (2013) Business models and technological innovation, *Long Range Planning*, vol. 46, 419–26.

Hu, B. (2014). Linking business models with technological innovation performance through organizational learning. *European Management Journal*, *32*(4), 587–595.

Spieth, P., Schneckenberg, D. and Ricart, J.E. (2014) Business model innovation – state of the art and future challenges for the field, *R&D Management*, vol. 44, no. 3, 237–47.

Tongur, S. and Engwall, M. (2014) The business model dilemma of technology shifts, *Technovation*, vol. 34, no. 9, 525–35.

Chapter 13
Product and brand strategy

Introduction

The products developed by an organisation provide the means for it to generate income. But there are many factors to consider in order to maximise the product's chance of success in competitive environments. For many technology-intensive firms, their approach is based on exploiting technological innovation in a rapidly changing market. Research by Talay et al. (2014) suggests that a firm's ability to keep up with the competition in the innovation arms race is the most significant driver of survival in the market in the automotive industry. Other firms, especially those involved in fast-moving consumer goods (FMCG), will be more focused on meeting and supplying products to meet the rapidly changing needs of their customers. All firms have to consider the market in which they are competing, the nature of the competition and how their capabilities will enable their products to be successful. The positioning of the product and the brand strategy selected are of particular importance and also reflect the subject of this chapter. The case study at the end of this chapter tells the story of how an innovative new umbrella challenged the dominance of the existing product.

Chapter contents

Learning objectives

When you have completed this chapter you will be able to:

- explain how product strategies contribute to a firm's performance;

- recognise that new products serve a variety of purposes, depending upon what is seen to be the strategic imperative;

- examine the concept of platforms in new product development;

- assess the importance of brand strategy in product development;

- explain how differentiation and positioning contribute to a product's success in the market place; and

- recognise the importance of marketing research for the effective development of new products.

Capabilities, networks and platforms

The company's core capabilities, and those that it can develop or acquire, bound what it can accomplish. However, a broader view brings in the notion of distinctive capabilities. This is wider than technical or operations competence. These broader capabilities include an organisation's 'architecture' and this embraces the network of relationships within, or around, the firm. These relationships might cover customers, suppliers, distributors or other firms engaged in related activities. This leads to the perspective that product development, and the competitive rivalry of which it is usually a part, can sometimes be better understood as undertaken by networks of partnerships and alliances rather than by individual, isolated producers (Delbridge and Mariotti, 2009).

Chapter 8 introduced the concept of networks and explained that their composition can vary widely. In some high-technology industries, a horizontal alliance of competitors or firms might dominate and, perhaps, they form a consortium for the research and development of a technology. For example, Kodak, Fujifilm, Minolta, Nikon and Canon were allied in the development of the Advanced Photo System. In other industries, it might be a vertical arrangement between suppliers, manufacturers, distributors and, possibly even, customers. It can be a formal agreement, a loose collection of understandings or a system 'managed' by a powerful member.

Saying this of capabilities leads to complications. If networks are competing, rather than individual firms, then the activities across the network need to be co-ordinated. Sometimes, it is the manufacturer that is dominant and leads and controls the network, as in the motor industry. Sometimes, it is a distributor that takes the lead and initiates new product categories, as in food retailing. On occasion, a large customer can dominate, show the need for a new product and encourage suppliers to innovate, as in the health service or defence industries. How effectively this leadership and coordination are undertaken influences substantially what products are developed and how they are developed. Another consideration is that the network members may have a collection of varied motives for being party to the relationship. Through time, they may come to stress other motives that may result in their becoming less interested in the network's aims and less willing to cooperate. The network leader, therefore, needs to spend some time monitoring motives and encouraging, or inducing, full cooperation between all network members. If the network is established for the development of a technology, then the partners have other sets of problems once the technology is available. How do they share the results and how do they each go on to establish distinctive, competitive products?

Choosing appropriate partners for the network and keeping them focused are important attributes for network leadership. Developing and refining the network's innovative ability is crucial, and this is not restricted to technical innovation because innovation in business processes and in distribution can also have a large impact.

Capabilities change. Without continuous attention they can become ineffectual or redundant, as the technology or the market requirement moves on. Alternatively, capabilities may be enhanced through internal development, through external acquisition and through the bringing together of new partnerships and alliances so that the network's capability is deeper or wider. Most capabilities thrive through continuity: through continuous incremental enhancement around a technology or a set of related technologies. This is in keeping with the idea of organisational heritage introduced in Chapters 1 and 4. Recent research by Henard and McFadyen (2012) shows the need for persistent investment in NPD to achieve performance impact.

Innovation in action

Language Connect

Iwona Stepien travelled to London from Poland in 1996 with £100 and the hope she would improve her English. Stepien studied linguistics and is fluent in Russian and German. For a year, she worked as a waitress and did translations in market research. It was at this time that she realised how much these companies require language to function. With only £500, she fired off emails and called potential clients offering to translate documents, shunning brochures and business cards to save money.

In 2003, she founded Language Connect, which provides translation services and cultural marketing strategies to blue-chip companies. The business is based in Bermondsey, southeast London, and had sales of £5.3 million in 2013 and profits in excess of £800,000. Language Connect now has offices in New York, Munich, Melbourne and Istanbul, with 80 staff, 80 per cent of whom are women. Stepien's team recently completed a £1 million project for the US publisher Marvel Comics, translating 30 million words into 12 languages. Other clients include market research giant TNS Global and retailers Karen Millen and Ted Baker. The business provides a 24-hour service to help companies go global. The business is not simply about translating languages, it is about interpreting cultures.

Product platforms

Emphasis upon continuity in the development of capabilities is also consistent with the idea of an evolving **product platform** that a 'product family' shares. The car industry is the classic example of this idea, where several individual models may share the same basic frame, suspension and transmission. The Sony Walkman gives another illustration, with its 160 variations and 4 major technical innovations between 1980 and 1990, all of which were based upon the initial platform. Black & Decker rationalised its hundreds of products into a set of product families, with consequent economies throughout the chain from procurement to distribution and after-sales service. In all these cases, the evolution of the product platform, along with the evolution of the requisite capabilities, is central to the product development strategy.

This notion may have originated in engineering, but it can be applied widely. Mobile phone handsets, food, cosmetics, clothing and furniture manufacturers can be seen to have product platforms and families. Johnson & Johnson and its development of the Acuvue disposable contact lenses provides another example. Many people needing vision correction did not wear traditional hard or soft contact lenses because of the discomfort and the cleaning requirements. Acuvue uses high quality soft contact lenses sold at a sufficiently low price to allow disposal after a week, without cleaning. This distinctive advantage, which clearly was relevant to many consumers, led to the successful launch that defined a new market segment. The original product became the basic platform for continuing innovation that is leading to other new offerings in Johnson & Johnson's vision care product family.

Sometimes, entirely new platforms and entirely new capabilities are required. Step changes in the product or manufacturing technology, in the customer need or in what the competition offers, and how it offers it, can demand radical rather than incremental

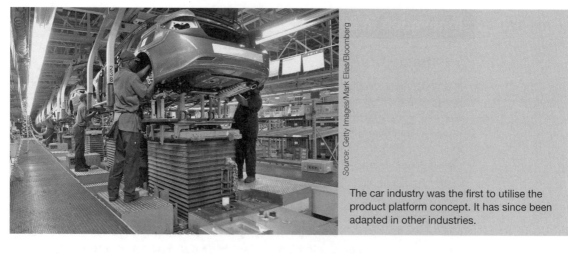

The car industry was the first to utilise the product platform concept. It has since been adapted in other industries.

change. The risk is all the more if that means the adoption of new technologies, outside the firm's traditional arena (Gawer, 2014; Gawer and Cusumano, 2014).

If we return to the car industry, we see that, today, products are developed from multiple brand product platforms. Furthermore, products of different brands are developed from inter-firm platform projects. For example, Figure 13.1 shows the Volkswagen Audi Group (VAG) inter-firm product platform development. This shows the one platform supporting several different brands with very different strategic objectives. When the car industry began using product platforms, the objective was to obtain commonality and benefits of scale within the company boundary. The basic idea was to differentiate all the components visible to the customer whilst, at the same time, sharing components and production processes across product models (Mohr et al., 2010;

Figure 13.1 VAG inter-firm product platform development

Nestlé Azera: a new top for a new product

Nestlé has made incremental improvements to the packaging of its Azera coffee brand. Whilst the distinctive metal cans were performing well, the Azera marketeers were keen to further enhance the branding and to improve merchandising via better on-shelf stacking. Robinson Plastic Packaging proposed a new overcap that features a prominent Azera logo and a functional stacking ring. The dedicated tool has also been designed specially to allow a range of other branding options for the same cap.

Wheelwright and Clark, 1992). Some 20 years later, however, the application of the product platform concept is causing concern for many industry analysts, who believe the search for commonality has gone too far at the expense of brand distinctiveness. The illustration in Figure 13.1 shows how the product platform operates across a wide variety of models/brands with different strategies and significant price gaps between the models/brands. According to Muffatto and Rovedo (2000) and Mohr et al. (2010), the benefits gained through using product platforms are:

- reduced cost of production;
- shared components between models;
- reduced R&D lead times;
- reduced systemic complexity;
- better learning across projects; and
- improved ability to update products.

When used across firms and models, there are many challenges presented. In practice, it is difficult to achieve optimum or best solution. Inevitably, compromises are sought between engineers and designers from the different brands, resulting in decisions that are not in the interest of either brand. Moreover, with inter-firm product platforms, some of the sought-after gains, such as shared components between models and reduced complexity, were not achievable because of the constraint of factory sequencing or architectural structure of the brand.

Illustration 13.2 shows how Microsoft has struggled to compete with Apple because it has had too many devices operating on slightly different platforms that require developers to write slightly different code.

Product planning

The product planning process takes place before substantial resources are applied to a project. Product planning considers the range of projects that a firm might pursue and over what time frame. It is closely linked to the broader business strategy of the firm and addresses such questions as:

- What product development projects will be undertaken?
- What is the mix of the portfolio of projects (discontinuous new products; platform products; derivative products)?
- What is the timing and sequence of the projects?

Illustration 13.2

Can Microsoft compete with Apple and Android for Apps?

For the first time ever, Windows 10 will also be a free upgrade for Windows 7, Windows 8.1 and Windows Phone 8.1 users, at least for the first year. Microsoft has taken a cue out of Apple's book, which has been giving out OS X and iOS upgrades for free, to ensure that users do not have to shell out money for an OS. Google offers its Android platform for free, too. Needless to say, this change is about charging for value-added services and access to apps, and not for operating systems, just like its competitors.

Microsoft previously tried to compete with its Windows Phone OS and Windows RT for tablet. However, having different OS was not welcomed. The company finally has decided to bring seamless integration across its platforms. Unity across operating systems is something that Apple and Google have been going on about for some time and Microsoft also clearly believes that this is the way forward.

Microsoft's decision to make available Office apps for other platforms like Android and iOS was necessary and it has become a cornerstone of its strategy to improve market share. Soon, Android and iOS users could download Microsoft Office apps for free, without the need for an Office 365 subscription.

Office 365 is Microsoft's cloud-based email and productivity suite. In the business world, Office 365 has surged ahead of Google and is dominating future enterprise deployment plans. This is partly because employees like the Outlook email program, and they get that same Outlook look and feel with Office 365. It

Source: Alamy Images/Pixellover RM9

is also because of fierce competition in the cloud world and Microsoft is offering organisations around the world financial incentives to move to its Office 365 and its cloud-based email suite. In the cloud world, companies pay only for the actual resources they use, like minutes of computing time, bytes of storage, usage of add-on apps and services, and so on. Firms prefer this and are ditching traditional software and computers at a rapid rate so they can rent their tech via cloud computing. Google, Microsoft, Apple and Amazon are all trying to sign up customers for their own cloud offerings before their competitors pinch them. They are trying to grab their share of a market that will grow to in excess of $150 billion by 2020.

The product planning activity clearly requires substantial input from research and development (R&D). It is this link to the technology portfolio of the firm that is so important and needs careful management (see Chapters 9 and 10). Deriving a set of products that customers perceive as useful and worth buying may be fortuitous but, more often, it is the result of deliberate, systematic endeavour. Organisations choose to compete in one or more product markets using a specified range of technologies (the technology portfolio). They seek to have a set of balanced capabilities that will enable them to match market opportunities by developing attractive market offerings, which customers perceive as conveying valuable benefits. How well they accomplish this, compared with competitors, is a major determinant of success.

The product plan identifies the portfolio of products to be developed by the organisation. The planning process considers product development opportunities from many sources, including marketing, R&D, customers, current product teams and competitor analysis. Usually, large firms will have more opportunities than resources to fund and the key question facing product planners is which projects to fund.

The product plan is regularly updated to reflect the changing competitive environment. Indeed, a surprise new product launch by a competitor frequently results in a major change to a firm's product plan. This was the case for Hoover when it responded quickly to Dyson's bagless vacuum cleaner. Product planning decisions generally involve senior management of the firm and form part of the ongoing strategy process. When considering product development opportunities, they are classified usually as four types:

- *New product platforms*. This type of project involves a major development effort to create a new family of products based on a new, common platform. From an R&D perspective, this would be seen as developing a new core technology. The new platform would be used to help existing products compete. An example of this would be Kodak's move into digital photography.
- *Derivatives of existing platforms*. Projects of this type develop an existing platform usually to ensure existing products are updated. This will either provide them with an advantage over the competition or make sure they can compete with the competition. Honda has been extremely successful in utilising its product platform of small petrol engines and applying this technology to a wide variety of market applications from lawn mowers to motorcycles and from outboard motors for boats to chainsaws.
- *Incremental improvements to existing products*. These projects may involve only adding or modifying features of existing products to keep the product line current and competitive. Frequently, this may be improving the packaging or reducing the manufacturing cost of producing the product or changing the design slightly. Whilst such changes may seem small, often they can have significant impact on sales. The change from see-through cellophane to foil packaging by Walker's made a huge impact on sales.
- *Fundamentally new products (discontinuous products)*. These projects involve radically different product or production technologies and may help to take the firm into new and unfamiliar markets. Such projects are inherently more risky but may help to secure the long-term future of the firm. This was the case for W.L. Gore & Associates following the development of its breathable fabric 'Gore-Tex'. This new technology has enabled the firm to enter new fabric-based markets. Previously, its portfolio of products covered the areas of medical, electronic and industrial.

Pause for thought

How do product platforms differ from umbrella brands, such as Nestlé or Kellogg's?

Product strategy

In a review of best practice in *New Product Development*, Kahn et al. (2012) found that managers should emphasise strategy when undertaking new product development (NPD) efforts and consider the fit of their projects with this strategy. New product strategy is part of a web of strategies. It is linked to, and its objectives are derived from, marketing strategy, technology strategy and the overall corporate strategy. These other strategies provide the role, the context, the impetus and the definition of the scope of new product strategy.

Competitive strategy

New products are not needed just because they are new products. They are required because they serve a customer need and an organisation need. The organisation need will be articulated in the organisation's strategy and there might be comments about striving to lead in the technology, or to be the key innovator, in its mission statement. However, much new product development is not concerned with new-to-the-world innovations and this is, partly, because many companies are followers and not leaders in their technology. NPD for a follower can be very different from NPD for a leader. New products perform different roles at different times for different companies. They serve a variety of purposes, depending upon what is seen to be the strategic imperative.

Competitive strategy may drive new product planning on a short-term or long-term basis. In the shorter term, a defensive posture may suggest that product variants are needed to shore up a declining market share, which is, perhaps, attributed to a competitor's aggressive new product activities. A reactive strategy could entail filling out product lines with different product sizes or added features that may be intended to deter a new entrant to the market, by not leaving unattended small market segments to be used as an entry point by the new competitor. Such minor product changes could also be employed to secure distributors' loyalty, because they are then able to carry a full range of the product and so be less inclined to stock rival offerings. Imitative products may be brought out, copying competitors, for similar reasons. In these kinds of situations, where the new product is a minor modification, however new the advertising proclaims it to be, it is unlikely that the full, classic NPD process would be engaged. There may be little or no research and market testing may be restricted to determining acceptable price levels or to choosing between alternative advertising messages.

In the longer run, competitive strategy may seek a more profound contribution from new products. A strategy may look for new product categories to be developed, within the same or a related technology or in a new technology area. These new products may appeal to the organisation's traditional customer base or seek new customer segments. This more radical product development would, more likely, be subject to thorough marketing and technical research, development and testing.

New products can also perform a learning function for the organisation. The development of a pioneering new product platform may, at first, be tentative and several alternative concepts for new platforms may be investigated simultaneously. Uncertainties surround such ventures because the new platform may require the development of costly new competencies whilst, simultaneously, the nature and the scale of the market opportunity are illusory. The firm may need to develop both new knowledge and new skills in technical, operations and marketing areas. The adequacy of the search for, and the acquisition of, these new skills and knowledge will mark out the leaders.

Product portfolios

Another set of strategic considerations concerns the overall portfolio of products. Analysing the organisation's total collection of products by viewing it as a portfolio, as in an investment portfolio, may give fresh insights. This approach was initiated by the share–growth matrix, or Boston Matrix, which used market share and market growth as dimensions against which to plot the positions of products. A typology was derived with high and low values for each of the two dimensions so that the four quadrants could be contrasted. For example, products classified as high share/ high growth could be contrasted with those deemed to be low share/low growth. Prospects could also be investigated by comparing where products are positioned presently, where they might be in the future with no change in strategy, and compared with some desired positions. Analyses of this kind might suggest some strategic issues. A clustering of the portfolio in one quadrant might be viewed as unbalanced, and an absence of any products in the two high-growth quadrants might be thought unhealthy.

Such a simple depiction has attracted controversy and alternative models have been suggested, using multi-factor dimensions that are composites of variables, such as business strength and market attractiveness. Most of the derivations still employ two dimensions because they can be displayed with ease, but more complex and, some say, more realistic, models are multi-dimensional. All these models share a similar aim: to give the strategist an overview that could reveal current or potential problems or opportunities in the product strategy.

This portfolio approach might also be applied to the product families and the platforms upon which they are built, although the selection of appropriate variables to describe the space can be a problem. Thought might be given to the extent to which a wide range of words might be usefully employed to indicate the dimensions, such as: robust, innovative, sophisticated, flexible, generic, evolving, traditional. For example, using relative sophistication (ranging from very sophisticated to unsophisticated) and flexibility (from very flexible to very inflexible) as descriptors of two dimensions might show the majority of product platforms to be unsophisticated and inflexible, with possibly one isolated platform that is sophisticated and flexible. Without qualification, that probably means little and it leads to no great revelation. Being unsophisticated is not, necessarily, a bad thing; it may be just what the customer needs. Regarding the other dimension, a very flexible product platform is not, necessarily, a good thing; it may result in too many compromises that lead to products that are not specialised enough for customer applications. Several such 'mapping' exercises might be tried using different descriptors. A supplementary analysis might trace connections between platforms, any spin-off from them and, in addition, bring in a time dimension.

Nothing conclusive can be expected from these analyses: they are probing and investigative. The process of taking this broader view of the portfolio draws

attention to issues that, with deeper analysis, could be significant. It is this identification of issues that can be critical and can be creative. It can flout any fixation
with norms and conventions, which can flourish readily within organisations,
and it can underline the point that approaches to product strategy development
must be original if they are to lead to distinctive new market offerings.

The competitive environment

The external environment constrains what can be done, for example within the
bounds of current understanding of a technology. Sometimes, the external environment dictates what must be done, for example following the introduction of a new
piece of legislation protecting an aspect of the natural environment. It can present
possibilities and opportunities, such as a breakthrough in an enabling technology or
the new affluence of consumers that allows them to be prepared to pay more for
products in a particular category. The external circumstances can also pose threats
and problems, as when a competitor introduces a significant product advance, or
when another rival closes access to materials or to distributors, through its acquisition of companies in those activities.

Close analysis of the present situation in the market is fundamental, along with
speculations about how it might progress and because of the potential importance
of external events and conditions some type of environmental monitoring, in a strategic sense, has become a key exercise in strategy search. Assessments of the present
situation can be extended to conjectures about future environments and, in some
industries, such as aerospace or pharmaceuticals, this may require a very long-term
view. A range of alternative future scenarios may be built around these conjectures,
indicating guesses about what the organisation sees to be the aspects of its environment carrying the most stress. These speculations might deal with some of the
following issues.

1 Estimates would be needed about the way the technology will change, and this
  could be more or less rigorous. It could involve some brainstorming within the
  organisation and it could seek various forms of external advice from government
  agencies, research centres, consultants and universities.
2 Estimates might also be made about how the industry competitive structure may
  alter. Are the same competitors likely to be contending in the market in the
  future? Are there any indications that any are preparing some kind of strategic
  shift? Will any withdraw or reduce their activities within the industry? Will there
  be changes in how companies compete and the positioning they seek in the market? Will there be any new entrants from other industries or from other countries? Unexpected arrivals in the industry, especially if they are well-funded,
  well-managed and they come with a significant innovation, can be particularly
  troublesome. That was the case when Mars entered the ice cream business and
  quickly secured a significant market share.
3 Another area of concern could be how any regulatory framework may evolve and
  this could include the extent to which it would limit activities in the future or
  open new possibilities.
4 Customer needs may be a further area in which to speculate. Will they become
  more demanding and require better materials and better performance in the

products they use? Will they perceive some emerging technology as a substitute? Will they have new kinds of needs and will there be new kinds of customers?

Taking various combinations of these factors could yield a series of scenarios and the investigation of the implications for the organisation of each of them could indicate important issues requiring attention. Such future scenarios may throw up attractive or unattractive situations and the organisation may then attempt to do what it can to prepare itself, and to do what it can to increase the likelihood of the former while inhibiting the latter. This will help to shape ideas about the potential role for new products and the scope of the problems and opportunities that they are intended to address.

Differentiation and positioning

Product strategy will express how the organisation seeks to differentiate itself, and distance itself, from its competitors and it will be the bedrock of its market positioning. It is axiomatic that for new products to be successful in the market they need to be perceived to be beneficial by prospective buyers. The benefit needs to stand out, to be distinctive and attractive. This distinction needs to be relevant to buyers and it needs to be seen to be relevant by them. It is pointless being distinctive in a way that consumers believe to be irrelevant or incomprehensible. This point is illustrated in the case study at the end of this chapter.

Differentiation

Broadly, the **product differentiation** sought by competitors could be based upon cost, with a value-for-money proposition, or it could be based upon superior quality, which might encompass better materials, better performance, new features, uncommon availability or better service. A useful perspective on product differentiation is provided by Levitt's idea of product augmentation (Levitt, 1986). He suggests that there are four levels on which products can be considered:

1 *The core product* comprises the essential basics needed to compete in a product market; a car needs wheels, transmission, engine and a rudimentary chassis.
2 *The expected product* adds in what customers have become accustomed to as normal in the product market; for a car this would be a reasonably comfortable interior and a range of accessories.
3 *The augmented product* offers features, services or benefits that go beyond normal expectations.
4 *The potential product* would include all the features and services that could be envisaged as beneficial to customers.

An interesting implication of this categorisation is that it can demonstrate that the position is dynamic because customer expectations change. In the example of the car, where would air conditioning be placed in these categories? Until recently, it would have been an augmentation for mass-market vehicles, but it has now become a standard expectation in new cars. Competition drives up consumer expectations. One rival introduces something new and, if it meets customer acceptance, other rivals follow. In consequence, augmentations become expectations and this ratchet effect means there is no equilibrium until the full potential has been realised. Even then, changes to the technology, or to another technology, might release an entirely new kind of potential, so that the process continues.

Another implication is that, as firms migrate upwards in this process, they leave market opportunities for others to exploit. There may be niche markets left for 'unbundled' products or services making low-cost, basic offers with no frills. Airlines are an example.

The choice of differentiation strategy is pivotal. It reaches back to core capabilities and it reaches forward to positioning strategy. The differentiation will not be effective, unless it is rooted firmly in the organisation's capabilities or in the capabilities of the network delivering the new product. Similarly, the positioning of the product in the market needs to be built upon, and needs to be consistent with, the differentiation strategy (see Figure 13.2).

Product positioning

Product positioning refers to the perceptions customers have about the product. It is a relative term that describes customer perceptions of the product's position in the market relative to rival products. It is founded upon understanding how customers discriminate between alternative products and it considers the factors customers use in making judgements or choices between products in the market being investigated. These are referred to as the customer's evaluative criteria and they may be the product's physical attributes, but they can include customer assessments about whom the product is meant for, when, where and how it is used and aspects of the brand's 'personality' (e.g. innovative, functional, old-fashioned, exclusive, frivolous, fun).

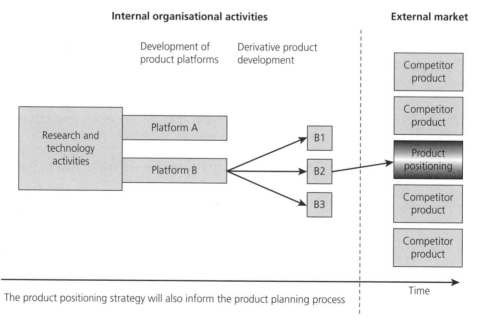

Figure 13.2 Platform development creates the architecture for a family of products

Positioning studies begin with determining a relevant set of products. The criterion for inclusion is that they must be perceived by customers to be choice alternatives. Then a list of determinant attributes is generated; that is a list of attributes that are salient or the most important to customers in discriminating between the alternatives. With this framework, customers' perceptions and preferences are then collected. This could be by survey using a structured questionnaire. Respondents would be asked to scale their feelings about each product on each attribute. They could also be asked their preferred level for each attribute. The output can be portrayed in a diagram (sometimes called a brand map or a perceptual map) showing the locations of each product against the attributes (the dimensions) and relative to the preferred level (the ideal point). This is most readily understood if the analysis is restricted to two dimensions. For example, for a food product the dimensions might be nourishment and calory count and respondents could rate all the brands they know in the category from high to low on these. Some brands may be seen to be highly nourishing with a high calory count and some not so nourishing with a low calory count. Illustrations can be found in Moore and Pessemier (1993) and in Mohr et al. (2010).

Such a study would show the proximity of, or the distance between, the perceived positions of the products considered. This might show the positions to be crowded in one area or well-spaced. If an ideal point, that is the customers' preferred position, is introduced, then the relative distance of each product from this ideal can be measured. If these relative distances accord reasonably with the relative market shares of the products, then it could be assumed that the dimensions chosen are a fair representation of the way customers choose in this market. Generally, it would be expected that the higher market shares would be won by products nearer to the ideal point.

Customers may be far from unanimous about these perceptions and preferences. If the observations were widely scattered, then further research would be needed to understand how customers make their evaluations and, perhaps, other dimensions might be tried. If there were several clusters of preferences, each in a different part of the map, this might indicate different market segments. In the food example above, there could be one group preferring a very nourishing product with a low calory count and another group wanting something nourishing with a high calory count. Mapping product positions against these two ideal points might, then, reveal one segment to be well served with many products, but an opening for a new product near the other ideal point where there may be no major existing brands.

Positioning strategy depends upon the choice of an appropriate base. This base must be relevant and important to customers and related to how they make choices in that product field. It should also attempt to distance the brand from the positions of rivals. Typically, bases include: product feature, benefits, use occasion, user category, against another product or by dissociation from all the other products, parentage (. . . because of where it comes from), manufacture (. . . because of how it is made) and endorsement (. . . because people you respect say it is good).

Selecting an appropriate positioning can make the difference between success and failure. It determines what the organisation tells the market about the product, whom it tells and how it tells it. Motorcycle producers take various positions. Piaggio's Vespa scooter is aimed at young riders and, latterly, at women. Suzuki is also now targeting women as a distinctive segment. Some of the most expensive machines are now aimed at older men with a revived interest in motorcycling and higher discretionary income. For most products, there may be a host of features, benefits and applications; few, if

Table 13.1 A comparison of the product specifications of two of P&G's successful brands

	Sure®	Secret®
Price	$2.98	$2.98
Weight	1.7 oz	1.7 oz
Ingredients	Aluminium Zirconium Trichlorohydrex Gly Cyclomethicone Dimethicone Polyethylene Silica Propylene Carbonate	Aluminium Zirconium Trichlorohydrex Gly Cyclomethicone Dimethicone Polyethylene
Patent no.	5,069,897 5,000,356	5,069,897 5,000,356

any, products have a single feature, a singular benefit and one narrow application. Choosing from amongst the possibilities can lead to creative and unique solutions and, consequently, to a highly differentiated strategy. For example, Procter & Gamble (P&G) positions two identical products, in terms of specification, very differently (see Table 13.1). 'Sure' is targeted in the USA at young males between 18 and 25, whilst 'Secret' is targeted at young females between 12 and 24. The brands clearly have different packaging and marketing communications to reflect their target market and positioning. This simple example illustrates the significance of positioning in modern marketing, especially in FMCG. Positioning can also result in costly mistakes with products being positioned in strange ways that consumers neither understand nor find credible. As the market grows and matures, it may become necessary to consider repositioning. The original differentiation could become less effective as competitors crowd in or as new types of buyers with different expectations adopt the product. A repositioning exercise could focus upon some reformulation of the product, some change to the image projected, a realignment of the segments targeted or a change to the distribution channels employed.

Competing with other products

One factor differentiates great companies from the others and that is the products they sell. Product design, thus, plays a key part. Research funded by the Dutch Ministry of Economic Affairs and led by the Industrial Design Engineering faculty at Delft University of Technology, *Products That Last*, is about finding successful business models and design strategies to create value for companies and consumers through longer-lasting products, whilst minimising the consumption of resources (see Table 13.2).

As products compete with one another, they are thus compared with one another. This leads to selection criteria and buyer behaviour. The latter is a subject and a textbook in its own right and beyond the scope of this book. It is necessary to note, however, that most models of buyer behaviour recognise two kinds of factors – objective and subjective. Objective factors may or may not be tangible but they must

Table 13.2 Product design strategies

Product strategy	Firm	How?
Classic life-long model	Miele washing machines	Primary revenue stream from sales of high-grade products (e.g. the German company Miele's washing machines) with a long useful life.
The gap-exploiter model	ECCO shoes	Exploits 'lifetime value gaps' or leftover value in product systems. Main revenue stream from selling products, parts and services based on the mixed product life of components (e.g. printer cartridges outlasting the ink they contain, shoes lasting longer than their soles).
The hybrid model	Océ-Canon printers	A combination of a durable product and short-lived consumables (e.g. Océ-Canon, printers and copiers). Main revenue stream from repeat sales of the fast-cycling consumables.
The access model	Greenwheels	Provides product access rather than ownership (e.g. the Dutch company Greenwheels, offering carsharing). Main revenue stream from payments for product access.
The performance model	Rolls-Royce	Delivers product performance rather than the product itself (e.g. hours of thrust in a Rolls-Royce, Power-by-the-Hour jet engines). Primary revenue stream from payments for performance delivered.

be quantifiable and measurable. By contrast, subjective factors are intangible and are influenced by attitudes, beliefs, experience and associations that the decision maker holds towards the product. If we leave the subjective criteria to the behavioural sciences and turn our attention to the objective criteria, it soon becomes clear that, to discriminate between products, a performance criteria is required. Many of us would recognise such a list of factors, for we have probably drawn up such a list when going to purchase a personal computer or a car. For the most part, however, such performance criteria do not play a large part in our buying decisions. In industrial markets, the reverse is the case and such criteria are the norm. Indeed, in many instances, buyers will forward their performance criteria to a list of suppliers and await a quote detailing price, warranties, delivery, etc. Table 13.3 shows typical product performance criteria commonly used by buyers in assessing a product.

Table 13.3 Product performance criteria

Product performance factors	
1 Performance in operation	10 Ease of maintenance
2 Reliability	11 Parts availability and cost
3 Sale price	12 Attractive appearance/shape
4 Efficient delivery	13 Flexibility and adaptability in use
5 Technical sophistication	14 Advertising and promotion
6 Quality of after-sales service	15 Operator comfort
7 Durability	16 Design
8 Ease of use	17 Environmental impact
9 Safety in use	

Source: *Product Strategy and Management*, Prentice Hall (Baker, M. and Hart, S. 1989), © Pearson Education Ltd.

Objective product characteristics enable firms to be grouped together so that the whole economy may be classified. The Standard Industrial Classification (SIC) Manual was first published in the United States in 1945. SIC codes now form part of an international system, making it possible to make precise comparisons between products and services between countries.

Pause for thought

To what extent is it possible to have several different **product strategies** within the same firm?

Many products may appear objectively similar, such as washing machines. This group of products are often made to a standard size (typically 600 mm wide; 500 mm depth and 1,000 mm high). Other performance criteria, such as load capacity and spin speed, can all be compared; but subjective information is supplied to the customer via branding. The process of branding can take many forms and is not restricted to physical products. Moreover, successful brands are not easily copied. For example, Dyson did not file for patents in the United States, yet, through branding, has been able to offer a unique product to consumers that competitors have struggled to imitate.

Managing brands

To many, especially the cynical, the word brand is associated with a collection of gimmicks and a lot of advertising to convince the public to buy one manufacturer's product rather than another's. To others, brands are simply products with brand names or logos. This is partly correct, but there is more to a brand than simply advertising. Even after a huge advertising expenditure, a firm would have very few customers if the product in question was faulty or of poor quality. Brands are commonly described in literature as a multiple-level pyramid, with basic physical attributes forming the base, upon which rests the tangible benefits, the emotional benefits, the brand personality characteristics, with the soul or core of the brand at its apex. Moreover, it is not just the marketing function that contributes to the brand, as Illustration 13.3 shows.

A successful brand combines an effective product, distinctive identity and added values, as perceived by customers. For some brands that have been managed effectively, this can translate into a life of over 100 years, and over 200 years in some cases. Table 13.4 illustrates just how long some of the most well-known brands have been with us.

Brands and blind product tests

There has been substantial research on the subject of whether consumers are able to recognise brands that they buy frequently from intrinsic attributes alone (taste or smell). The results reveal that, from cigarettes to peanut butter and from cola to

Illustration 13.3

The role of brand in the mobile app world

Mobile users typically download many apps, but use only a few regularly. You have to have an app that users are motivated to download and use, such as the BBC Weather App. In an article Sunil Gupta wrote for *Harvard Business Review*, he describes five app strategies that can get your brand in the top 10 of apps used. His strategies correspond with basic motivations to use an app, such as:

- *Add convenience.* Airlines have apps that allow customers to check in and to monitor flight status. ESPN's app lets sports fans check scores.
- *Offer unique value.* Tesco in South Korea allows customers with smartphones to order products from photos in train stations. Nike has Nike+, which works with a chip in runners' shoes to monitor speed, distance and more.
- *Provide social value.* Social gifting apps allow users to send gift cards. The Swedish start-up Wrapp allows people to give their Facebook friends promotional gift cards available from 100 major retailers.
- *Offer incentives.* In Brazil, Coca-Cola allowed consumers to hold their phones up

to a simulated red Coke machine at venues, such as beach-front kiosks, to get 20 megabytes of free data credits, whilst an image of a Coke bottle fills up the screen.

- *Entertain.* Smartphone users spend more than 40 per cent of their app time playing games. Red Bull has several mobile gaming apps, such as Red Bull Kart Fighter that has had approximately two million downloads.

According to Ernest Dichter (2010), people talk about brands only when they are stimulated by product involvement (share the experience), self-involvement (gain attention and credibility), other involvement (help others) or message involvement (share an entertaining or informative message). There needs to be a practical customer motivation to engage in social media or respond to an app. It will not happen when the point is to sell a brand or firm.

Source: Gupta, S. (2013) For mobile devices, think apps, not ads, *Harvard Business Review*, vol. 91, no. 2, March. Schwarzkopf, S. and Gries, R. (eds) (2010) *Ernest Dichter and Motivation Research: New Perspectives on the Making of Post-War Consumer Culture*, pp. 3–38, Palgrave Macmillan, London.

Table 13.4 Market introduction of brands

Twining	1706	Adidas	1920
Schweppes	1798	Volvo	1926
Levis	1850	Durex	1929
Heineken	1864	Mars	1932
Agfa	1873	McDonald's	1937
Coca-Cola	1886	Playboy	1953
Philips	1891	Benetton	1965
Pepsi-Cola	1898	Nike	1972
Persil	1907	Body Shop	1976
Nivea	1911	Swatch	1982
Boeing	1916	Eternity	1988

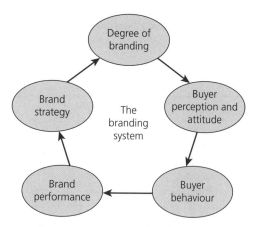

Figure 13.3 Branding system

beer, subjects are not capable of recognising their usual brand (Riezebos, 2003). Given these findings, one might ask why consumers continue to pay a premium for particular brands when they cannot taste the difference. Illustration 13.3 discusses the role of brand value.

Branding is based on random utility theory, where customers form preferences based on their perception of attributes. Decisions are then made upon these preferences with customers selecting the product with highest expected value or utility. This overview of the branding system is captured in Figure 13.3, with the degree of branding affecting buyer perception and attitudes, buyer behaviour and brand financial performance and, thereby, affecting branding strategy.

The brand manager and the firm have to decide the extent to which they wish to invest in their brand and thereby develop it. Such considerations will involve all aspects of the marketing mix and, in turn, obviously will affect buyer perception. Then, buyers will consider the benefits and values that are being promoted and make choices. In the case study at the end of the chapter, the firm could use brand endorsement to launch the product. These choices will affect the returns to the firm and will determine investment decisions for the future of the brand. This is the subject of brand strategy, which we turn to now.

Brand strategy

Brand strategy is the spearhead of the organisation's competitive intentions. It carries the company or product name into the market and shows how it is positioning itself to compete. It involves choices between having no brand name at all, so that the product is sold as a commodity, and the attempt to develop a distinctive brand name with a distinctive set of associations and expectations. In the latter case, there are further options. The product could be sold to another party for them to place their trademark or branding on it or, alternatively, the complete product, or major components, could be bought in and then company-branded. There are more choices with the brand name itself. Should the company have a single brand for all its products, such as Kellogg's, or a range of apparently unconnected brands, such as Procter

& Gamble? Should it establish a corporate brand as an umbrella with a series of sub-brands under the umbrella, such as Ford? Or should it have a mixed brand strategy with elements of all these approaches?

On one level, such consideration might appear to be quite trivial. What is in a name? Think about chocolate confectionery. If Cadbury decides to launch a new chocolate bar with no Cadbury identification, then would market acceptance be achieved? Will consumers trust it? Will they take the risk and make a first purchase? In any event, probably they would not be given the chance to buy because it would not gain sufficient acceptance by distributors. It might achieve limited distribution, but it may take a great deal of time to reach full national, let alone international, distribution.

The brand name itself is really a summary; it can stand for a great deal more. It can represent the sum of what people know about the product and its usefulness, quality and availability. It can be surrounded with associations, negative or positive, about how it can be used, where it can be used and the occasions on which it is used. It can be symbolic and loaded with imagery about the kinds of people who use the brand. For some well-known brands, the few letters in their names can be triggers to wide-ranging perceptions. Focus groups can talk for hours with just the prompt of a few brand names.

It is not just in consumer markets that this power of the brand name is apparent. Inspection of any trade magazine reveals its prevalence in all kinds of markets, and component makers now also attempt to ensure that their brand is evident in advertising and packaging.

Pause for thought

The Consumers' Association produces the magazine *Which.* This conducts regular independent product performance tests on a variety of consumer products. Why is this objective evaluation of a wide range of consumer products not always referred to when consumers make purchases of a durable good?

Given the significance of brands, it is surprising that so many firms make careless mistakes with regard to their brands. According to Helen Rubenstein (1996), many firms do not recognise how their departments affect the delivery of the brand. Figure 13.4 helps to show how brands interact with different parts of the organisation: it shows **internal and external brand contracts**. At the centre of this wheel is the finance department, as it is guided by the chief executive, who sets financial targets and determines the business objectives. Clearly the finance department has a significant impact on the brand development, in particular the degree of investment in brand development.

Brand extensions

A **brand extension** is the use of an established brand name on a new product in the same product field or in a related field. The brand name might also be stretched to an unrelated product field. A simple brand extension would be when a new or

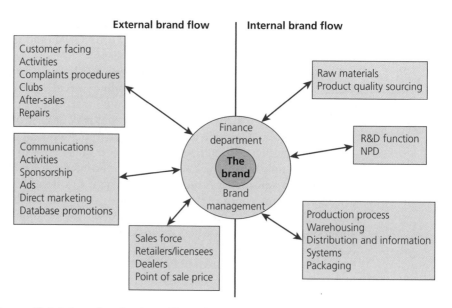

External brand flow | **Internal brand flow**

Customer facing
Activities
Complaints procedures
Clubs
After-sales
Repairs

Communications
Activities
Sponsorship
Ads
Direct marketing
Database promotions

Sales force
Retailers/licensees
Dealers
Point of sale price

Finance
department

The brand

Brand
management

Raw materials
Product quality sourcing

R&D function
NPD

Production process
Warehousing
Distribution and information
Systems
Packaging

Figure 13.4 Internal and external brand contacts

Source: Rubenstein, H. (1996) Brand first management, *Journal of Marketing Management*, vol. 12, 269–80.

unconventional size is brought out, so that the original brand name is given a prefix (e.g. Giant, Jumbo, Fun) or, for some technical products, this could be a new alpha-numeric code. Operating within the same product field, but attempting to attract a new market segment, the extension might have a modified design and there could be added words to the brand name, indicating for whom it is intended, such as men or women. Daily newspapers extended publication to Sunday and have branded sections, all carrying the original brand name in some way. In the case of an extension to a business computer package, it could specify a new application type in the branding.

More radical extensions occur when the brand is stretched or carried into un-related product fields. Some newspapers, such as *The Daily Telegraph*, started direct marketing operations selling their own brand of clothing. Several fashion houses, such as Boss and Calvin Klein, place their brand name wide and far across a range of luxury goods. Wilkinson Sword sells razors and gardening tools under the same brand. Canon markets cameras and copiers. Philips uses its brand name in diverse electrical and electronic industries. And the Virgin brand name is carried on an air-line, a railway, a cola, a retail chain and in insurance.

The rationale behind a brand extension strategy is to take advantage of potential carry-over effects from the original brand. If the original is both well-known and well-regarded, then probably it has a pool of goodwill amongst consumers and dis-tributors. The extension would be planned to dip into that pool. Three kinds of carry-over effects may be relevant:

1 *Expertise*. If the original had established and maintained itself, probably over a fairly long period, as the best available for that application or usage, then it is likely to have accrued a reputation for high-level competence in its field. Users may feel very comfortable and assured in making repeat buys. This may have been pro-moted actively and the company may have sought to have itself perceived to be the

acknowledged consultant in its area. An extension that was complementary to the original, and of the same quality, would have its introduction eased, owing to a halo-effect. Consumers would know the name already and would have positive expectations, and they may believe that the company that they trusted would not bring out a poor new product. The extension benefits from a trusting relationship established by the original.

2 *Prestige*. Some brands have enviable images and some consumers may believe that these images confer status on those that use them. Some brands benefit from particular kinds of associations and symbolism and they may have become, for some people, the only acceptable product to have in some situations. This does not apply just to consumer markets; organisational buyers can sometimes be just as subjective.

3 *Access*. A well-established original may have developed and held good access to the best suppliers and to the best distributors. An extension would capitalise upon these relationships and it may have a better reception to its initial launch than a new brand that had no reputation.

But brand extensions can also be problematic. The connection with the original brand can be strained and the carry-over effects diminished or eliminated. Bic was famous for its ballpoint pens. Its extension to disposable lighters worked because people still saw them as consistent with the original in being inexpensive, disposable, functional products. But its extension into perfumes failed. Guinness withdrew its Guinness Bitter and once it did try an apparently contradictory idea with a new version of its original stout called Guinness Light.

In some markets, brand extensions are added that contribute little and, at times, they can be harmful to the original. They can clutter the market and confuse the consumers. A series of lacklustre extensions, and no really new product development, can undermine the credibility of the company amongst distributors, customers and city analysts. For a closer look at brand extensions and brand stretching, Illustration 13.4.

Illustration 13.4

Old brands, new brands and stretching brands

The top 10 branded items bought in UK grocers have been around, on average, for 70 years, as Table 13.5 shows.

In this list of successful and relatively old products (8 out of 10 are 50 years old), it seems to suggest that being first into the market is an advantage. However, the challenge for the brand manager is how to remain appealing whilst maintaining your heritage. It may be a little bit like growing up and getting older: a few grey hairs can add dignity but, if you do not take care of yourself, you can easily look old and tired.

Multinational brand management firms, like Procter & Gamble, Unilever and Beiersdorf, know only too well that many grocery products fail, hence they recognise the value tied up in existing brands; especially those with a long heritage.

Marketing professionals have long recognised that strong brand names that deliver high sales and profits have the potential to create new product categories. But, the risks involved are high and

→

Table 13.5 Top 10 grocery products/years

Brand	Years in market
1 Coca-Cola	106
2 Warburtons	22
3 Walkers Crisps	58
4 Cadbury Dairy Milk	101
5 Hovis	116
6 Nescafé Instant	68
7 Andrex toilet tissue	64
8 Kingsmill	16
9 Robinsons	69
10 Lucozade	77

Source: Nielsen.

brand stretching exercises can easily backfire. Not only can they be costly in that the money spent on a parallel product could be lost if customers are not interested but, if the new launch goes wrong, it can even damage the credibility of the original product.

Brand stretching refers to the use of an established brand name for products in unrelated markets. When done successfully, it has several advantages. Customers will associate the quality of the original product with the new and are more likely to trust it. Launch costs usually are lower and customer awareness can build more quickly. For branding experts, the general rule of thumb is that, if the brand extension contributes more value than the original core product, ultimately it tends to fail. Pierre Cardin was criticised for over-extending its brand and lost credibility for exactly this reason. Holiday firm Club Med once launched a shower gel called Club Med and a unisex cologne of the same name. The idea had been pioneered by Disney at its theme parks, selling dolls of giant cartoon characters the children had just met in the flesh. The rationale – a good experience on holiday would be recreated at home. This is what marketing people refer to as 'memorialising' the good experience.

Further reading: International Advertising Association UK (2008) *Old Brands New Tricks, New Brands Old Tricks*, www.iaauk.com.

Market entry

Decisions about how and when to enter the market can make a substantial difference to the new product's prospects. This is illustrated with Microsoft's entry into the video-sharing market to compete with Yahoo and Google (see Illustration 17.2). Timing the entry to the market can make or break an innovation. Thoughtless positioning, with little or no distinction, can be harmful to the long-term prospects, whereas astute positioning can have a very positive effect. Entry scale and, in particular, obtaining and maintaining a strong market presence with high levels of market exposure, can ease the product introduction and stimulate the market's evolution. These three factors are explored in this section.

Entry timing has received particular attention. Commonly, it is assumed that early entry is desirable and there is evidence that 'pioneers' accrue 'first mover advantages'. They are able to influence customer expectations and shape how customers make evaluations of products in the new field. They can suggest to consumers the criteria they should employ in making their judgements, and products that are later entrants are then evaluated on that basis. Pioneers can set the standards, establish a distinctive quality position, take the lead in the continuing evolution of the technology and gain valuable experience in manufacturing and distribution. In many mature markets, the leaders are those that were the pioneering entrants. However, being too early can be as much of a disadvantage as being too late. A weak, tentative first mover, without the motivation or resources to grow the market, can spend years making losses only to be superseded by a stronger 'fast follower'. Green et al. (1995) caution that 'simple nostrums, such as early entry is best, can be dangerous oversimplifications'.

Those that come to the market early, but after the pioneer, can be successful. Procter & Gamble was not the pioneer in disposable nappies or in biological washing powders, but its Pampers and Ariel brands dominate these markets. Japanese competitors displaced Ampex, the pioneer in VCR technology (see Table 7.2 for a long list of followers who became leaders). For example: It was Creative Industries that launched the first Digital Audio Player (DAP) in 2000. It was a 6GB hard drive based player called the Creative NOMAD Jukebox. But Creative did not become the market leader. In October 2001, Apple unveiled the first generation iPod, a 5 GB hard drive based DAP with a 1.8″ Toshiba hard drive. The iPod was initially popular within the Macintosh community. In July 2002, Apple introduced the second generation update to the iPod. It was compatible with Windows computers. The iPod series has become the market leader in DAPs.

Positioning decisions can be influential and the digital camera industry illustrates this point. Eastman Kodak was the first firm to produce a digital camera for consumers in 1994. It offered 24-bit colour and the ability to connect to a desktop computer via a simple serial cable to download images directly. Today, the market is crowded by firms such as Fuji, Canon, Olympus, Hewlett-Packard, Nikon and Minolta. Sony is the market leader in terms of market share, but competition is fierce due to the mobile phone. Demand for digital cameras, which record images on memory chips instead of film, continues to grow as consumers become more comfortable with capturing, storing and printing their images. Eastman Kodak pioneered this market but has not dominated it. Indeed, competitors reacted so swiftly that there was little to distinguish the products in the marketplace.

Illustration 13.5

Generating buzz for your product launch

All product managers wish to know how to maximise the buzz and measure the impact of their new product launch. Fortunately, there are specialist firms that will help the product manager achieve his or her goal, but some knowledge of what is required is necessary. The most common and favoured way is via:

- blog posts;
- newsletters;
- videos.

Specialist internet marketing firms will analyse blog posts and media articles to prepare for the launch and monitor its impact. They should research the key influencers in both media and blogs, the competitive landscape and the key messages to the target buyer. During the launch, firms will be able to measure the impact that the positive buzz created in both media and blogs and the number of target consumers reached and how effective it was at getting the key messages across. For example, data is required from the following questions:

- Did the launch impact the market?
- How many consumers did we reach?
- Did the launch impact key media influencers?
- Did we affect both a national and local audience? How large was that impact?
- Did we reach influential Apple bloggers?

Scale of entry affects how the product performs and how the market evolves. High levels of effort and resource commitment can stimulate market evolution and a critical factor in this is market exposure. Getting prospective customers talking and thinking about the product is vital. This may mean the establishment of a strong 'market presence' through press articles, blogs, advertising, participation at exhibitions and a highly visible presence in distribution channels. Illustration 13.5 shows how to ensure successful product launch through the generation of blog buzz.

Launch and continuing improvement

From a business perspective, the innovation is not a success until it has established and fixed its place in the market. That depends upon how it is launched, its reception by customers and the continuing attention given to its improvement. The earlier discussion of market entry showed some key factors relevant to the launch strategy, but the act of putting the product on to the market is not an end: it is the beginning of a new phase. Close and constant monitoring of the reactions of customers, distributors and competitors is required to inform the proceeding strategy.

Having the product on the market allows the validation or the rejection of important estimates or assumptions about customer attitudes and behaviour that would have been made during development. It could also reveal unanticipated problems or opportunities. What do customers now understand about the product and has comprehension of its benefits spread in the predicted way? Are there still difficulties? Are they using the product in the ways envisaged? Have customers found problems in using the product that had not come to light before? Do they use it as much as expected and as frequently as expected? Are any potential customers holding back because they see risk in adopting the product, perhaps delaying their acceptance in anticipation of further developments in the technology? Are there enough of those for it to be a problem? Do customers perceive the benefits that were promised, and are these as important to them as hoped originally? Are the benefits now seen as interesting but irrelevant? And are there any problems with the product itself that customers have revealed? Unravelling these questions and dealing effectively with their implications will condition how the prospects for the product evolve.

Many assumptions will also have been built into the operations and marketing plans. Do they stand up? Was the desired positioning achieved, and was that the right positioning decision? Is it now too narrowly defined on a relatively unimportant dimension? Was it conveyed appropriately to distributors and customers? Were the pricing and distribution plans appropriate? Are customer problems being handled efficiently and is the right level of customer service in place? On all these issues the organisation should be learning and responding, tracking and improving.

Thought about how the product and the market will evolve from the launch might give attention to three areas:

1 *Product platform evolution and brand extensions.* What is the next generation of the product? Can the basic product platform be enhanced and should this lead to brand extensions?
2 *Market evolution.* How rapidly will the innovation be diffused? Will there be a lengthy introductory period before any rapid growth? Will new market segments

become apparent or can they be created? How should the geographic scope be widened?

3 *Competitive evolution.* How soon will competitors arrive? How predictable is their entry? What distinction, if any, will they bring? What kind of positioning and entry scale are they considering? What entry barriers are in place to deter rivals?

Inauguration is not enough. To be effective, the innovation must be well founded in the market and receive customer acceptance, if not their acclaim, and plans need to be made to secure, deepen and widen its market position from the initial launch.

Withdrawing products

Pruning the product range can be an important part of managing the portfolio. Chronic poor sales performance would be a first indicator that consideration should be given to **withdrawing products**. Prior to that decision, careful assessments would be needed of the reasons for the poor performance, of the possible future trends and of the costs and benefits of continuing or withdrawing. In Toyota's case, with several of its brands, it seems the firm had few options other than to organise a complete product recall, as Illustration 13.6 shows.

Illustration 13.6

How to avoid making a drama out of a crisis

Toyota was having problems. In 2010, the world's largest carmaker issued a recall – its second in three months – on 4.1 million vehicles sold in the USA and Europe to fix faulty gas pedals that have a tendency to get stuck, causing unintended acceleration. This was on top of an earlier recall of 5.3 million cars believed to have ill-fitting floor mats that have a tendency to trap pedals. In total, more than 9 million Toyota cars worldwide have been pulled back for pedal-related flaws.

Source: nitirut380/Shutterstock.com

The Japanese carmaker was strongly criticised for its response to this crisis, and the embarrassing recall of several Toyota models. Indeed, speed of response, transparency of message and visibility are the three key principles to successful crisis management.

For a brand built on the key elements of quality and reliability, the events of 2010 were disastrous. To make matters worse for the firm, US politicians leapt on to the opportunity to kick a foreign business when it was down.

So, five years later, what is the long-term damage, if any, to Toyota?

As early as 2012, things looked good; Toyota reported a ¥290 billion ($3.7 billion) net profit for

→

the first quarter, its best performance since 2008. Furthermore, Toyota was on course to regain its position at the top of the industry's volume rankings after it outsold its largest rivals, General Motors and Volkswagen. By 2015, things looked even better, as it presented impressive results: at the end of 2014, its net revenue showed a 6 per cent growth to the equivalent of $227 billion.

Operating income grew to $23 billion in 2014, a 20 per cent jump, and net income increased to $18.1 billion, a 19 per cent advancement.

Unexpected disasters can hit any company at any time. But, it seems that, if you have a fundamentally good product, the brand can withstand a crisis. So, much of the press headlines in 2010 would seem to have been trying to make a drama out of a crisis.

Investigations could first focus on how well the organisation had managed its efforts. It may have lost market share, in which case a series of questions could be posed. Is manufacturing cost out of line with others in the industry? Has there been any decline in quality relative to rivals? Has the product kept up with any evolution in the technology? Have marketing efforts tailed off? Fixing any problems that emerge from these analyses might give the product a new lease of life, and this may be associated with a repositioning exercise. However, if nothing significant is signalled, then other possibilities would need to be examined.

If market share was constant but sales were, nonetheless, in chronic decline, then this could indicate that the industry, or the particular product form, was past maturity and entering decline. Predictions about the future industry trend might confirm a pessimistic outlook and the firm would have to decide if it should withdraw quickly, more gradually or try to maintain a position in what may be a much smaller industry in the future.

Exit costs would feature strongly. There may be a complex manufacturing economy within the company with shared processes involving many products. The arbitrary removal of one may throw into jeopardy the economics of the remainder, and so it could be that the product was continued so long as it made some contribution to overheads. The firm may also become an involuntary survivor in the industry because contractual obligations tie it in. These contracts may be with suppliers, customers, distributors or other partners in the network. An inflexible manufacturing plant could also tie it. Reputation could be another issue. The company may not wish to undermine the confidence placed in it by customers or distributors. For example, customers may have high switching costs, if they had to buy alternative products and may become resentful, if they dropped the product. If the product is part of a wide portfolio, then the whole range might suffer, if the organisation's reputation were to be damaged.

Alternatively, the firm may decide to make an active commitment to stay in the declining industry in anticipation of increasing market share.

Managing mature products

As growth slows and the level of competition intensifies, profit margins will come under pressure. Product and brand managers will need to make decisions on the medium- and long-term futures of the brand. **Mature products** usually make up the majority of a firm's source of cash-generative lines (hence the term cash cow in portfolio planning). Profit margins may decline, due to increasing numbers of competitive products, cost economies used up, decline in product distinctiveness, etc. Frequently, with the loss of profit margins, industries tend to stabilise with a set of entrenched competitors. Indeed, the low margins act as a barrier to entry and those firms remaining in an industry can generate sustained profits over a long period in the maturity and decline stages of a product's life cycle. For example, the 35 mm film processing industry is declining rapidly with the introduction of digital photography. Soon, probably, there will be only a few suppliers remaining in this once enormous market. Agfa, Fuji and Kodak probably will establish positions in this declining market. Indeed, within the maturity and decline stages of a product's life cycle there are four phases to the mature phase of the traditional product life cycle:

- late growth;
- early maturity;
- mid-maturity; and
- late maturity.

They argue that firms need to be able to recognise the early signs of late growth usually characterised by aggressive price cutting. This continues into the early stages of maturity when the market becomes saturated with little or no opportunity for growth. At this stage, firms are forced into taking tactical decisions regarding additional services and promotions. It is also important for firms to be vigilant for changes that take place in the market concerning segments: some segments may decline rapidly whilst others may still be growing. As the market moves towards mid- and late maturity, customers are seen as more discerning and less loyal. Schofield and Arnold (1988) argue that several strategies are available to firms managing mature businesses and there are several positive factors:

- price is not important to everyone and probably not to the majority;
- industries that evolve gradually offer time and space for careful strategy selection;
- the market is stable;
- niches, once secured, require fewer resources to defend them; and
- sustainable real or perceived advantage in cost or performance will attract new business.

In a study of mature brands, Beverland et al. (2010) found that product innovation is vital to ongoing brand equity and has been responsible for revitalising many brands, including Apple, Dunlop Volley, Mini and Gucci.

Case study

Umbrella wars: GustBuster® and senz°

A group of friends studying at Delft University of Technology (TU Delft), developed a new type of umbrella in an attempt to build a successful business. At the time, however (2004), there was already a unique umbrella on the market called the GustBuster® and it was winning design awards and customers. It

was launched in 1995. The GustBuster® was designed and developed in the USA and its website featured a clear message:

GustBuster's award-winning design is patented and wind tunnel tested, providing the best protection

→

against the elements that an umbrella can offer. All of our umbrellas are constructed of the finest quality materials and backed by a limited lifetime guarantee.

Given this level of competition, it seems surprising that a group of MSc students would decide to enter a mature, extremely competitive market 10 years after the launch of the GustBuster®. This case study shows how the students built a successful business.

Introduction

The senz° umbrella business is one of the success stories of the YES!Delft incubator. Initiated by TU Delft and the City of Delft, YES!Delft offers university spin-outs and hi-tech start-up companies a comfortable working environment to develop their business from idea to commercial product. It is located on the university campus with easy access to the excellent TU Delft R&D facilities. It also affords to its residents: low rents, flexible contracts, active business coaching and many start-up peers nearby. In addition to Senz, there are almost 100 companies currently within the YES!Delft incubator programme, with many others that have already grown out of the incubator and are now stand-alone companies. Together with the other technological business centres in Delft, the YES!Delft incubator performs an important role for the economy in southwest Holland as a cradle for knowledge-intensive companies.

What makes this story additionally unique is the development of a new business in this industry sector that was, and still is, viewed as distinctly low-tech rather than high-tech. The umbrella business is hardly new. The word umbrella is derived from the Latin root word *umbra* meaning shade or shadow, hence it was originally designed as a method of protecting oneself from the sun. Umbrellas have been in use for over 4,000 years, originating from Ancient Egypt, Greece and China. Today, the leading global players include: Totes Isotoner (USA); GustBuster® (USA); Fulton (UK); Fox Umbrellas (UK) and Blunt (New Zealand). However, there are many other low-cost manufacturers. Most of these firms manufacture their

products in China, largely in the provinces of Guangdong, Fujian and Zhejiang. For example, Shangyu, in Zhejiang province, has more than 1,000 umbrella factories (*New Yorker*, 2008).

GustBuster®: the leading umbrella

In 1995, the GustBuster® umbrella was launched. The umbrella was based on the simple idea of a release valve. So, as with a boiler, if pressure builds too much, a valve releases pressure; the same principle is applied to the umbrella. It has a dual canopy designed to relieve wind pressure, so it will not flip inside out. The GustBuster® has two vented tiers attached with elastic secured to eliminate the potential for leakage. Fibreglass spreader rods connect a specially patented 'silver wing' to provide strength and flexibility. GustBuster® argues it developed the world's first unflippable, unflappable, unleakable umbrella. In testing, the firm revealed that the GustBuster® stood firm against 55 mile per hour winds. This generated a lot of media interest, as it also makes good television pictures. Everyone from CNN to *The New York Times* and the Fox News Channel wanted to see the umbrella in action. In addition, the firm hired the College of Aeronautics at LaGuardia Airport in New York to perform professional wind tunnel testing. Sales soared and were further helped when Arnold Palmer chose it above all other umbrellas on the golf course. The entire golfing industry, which plays rain or shine, began to take cover under the GustBuster® name. In 1998, the Gustbuster® won the 'Breakthrough Product of the Year'.

The senz° umbrella

Whilst umbrellas have been around for centuries, until very recently, the simple design has remained largely unchanged and was much the same the world over. The traditional design retained various design flaws, such as turning itself inside-out in strong winds, breaking easily, poor visibility whilst in use and having dangerous metal tips.

The senz° umbrella was designed by three students at Delft University of Technology (TU Delft) – Gerwin Hoogendoorn, Philip Hess and Gerard Kool. Their backgrounds are in product design, product development, innovation management and business administration. The three founders have skills and expertise that complement each other, providing a mix of design, engineering and commercial insight. They addressed many of the design flaws in traditional umbrellas to develop a new type of umbrella. Its aerodynamic form means that the senz° umbrella always finds the best position in the wind, making it more comfortable to use. The umbrella's design means that it can withstand winds of up to force 10 or 100 kph. The unique shape also gives the user better visibility and the specially designed 'eyesavers' make it safer.

The final finished product is the result of a two-year development project utilising facilities and expertise within the Aeronautical Faculty and the Industrial Design Faculty at TU Delft. In addition, the student start-up was one of the first to enter the TU Delft incubator in 2005. This incubator was a joint collaboration with the City of Delft and was called Young Entrepreneurs in Delft: YES!Delft.

Asymmetrical design
The basic idea came from Gerwin Hoogendoorn in 2005, who was then a student of Industrial Design Engineering. He came up with the idea of using an asymmetrical design (see earlier photo). The rear of the senz° is longer than the front. When a conventional round umbrella is caught by the wind, it will immediately tip so that the wind turns it inside-out. With the senz°, the shorter side always turns to face the wind, meaning that it will actually catch less wind. Another advantage is that the ribs are hinged at the tips, meaning that the ribs cannot break and the strength of the wind is distributed better.

At first glance, the shape looks odd, but it has logic. The cab forward aerodynamic shape does two things. First, it keeps rain off your back, an issue prevalent with traditional umbrellas. This shape also channels high winds across the surface and behind. The drag coefficient is significantly less, which helps in resisting gale force winds. This is the first umbrella to incorporate aerodynamic principles. The senz° won the American International Design Excellence Awards in 2008, a prestigious American design prize, placing it in the same league as the iPhone

from Apple. Earlier, the senz° umbrella was crowned with the Red Dot Design Award and two Dutch Design Awards.

Product development
After over a year in design and development, where numerous materials and different prototypes were built, the selected final design required manufacture. The development of prototypes used local skilled craftsmen and engineers, but scaling up production to thousands and hundreds of thousands of products required careful consideration of costs and margins. The young start-up was well aware that to the production cost they would need to add distribution costs, retailer costs, advertising and marketing costs plus their own business' overheads. They also wanted to deliver a profit and this would need to be between 10 and 20 per cent. This led to some necessary rethinking of the business plan. In particular, they needed to study gross margins. This is the percentage of profit derived from a transaction. (Both the manufacturer and the retailer will expect their own gross margin.) To get retailers and distributors interested in taking the product, the start-up had to make it financially attractive to them. This meant allowing them to have a healthy profit.

Distributor and retailer mark-ups and gross margin
Distributors are companies that typically buy products (and store inventory) from manufacturers and sell them to retailers. They are commonly used by larger retailers that handle a large volume of products, such as grocery stores. Distributor margin requirements vary by product price point, industry, segment, country and size, but 20 to 40 per cent is not uncommon.

The start-up soon realised that they needed to know a retailer's gross margin. This is because retailers often have minimum margin requirements; this helps determine what price you need to set. Although minimum requirements will vary widely, depending on the type of retailer, it is not uncommon for a retailer to expect a minimum gross margin of 50 per cent. Often, this is referred to as a 'keystone' mark-up. Thus, Senz had to double its

→

wholesale price. For example, if it sold its product wholesale to the retailer for €5, the retailer would need to charge the consumer €10 to achieve a keystone mark-up. Retailers also have large overheads and wages to pay, as well as rents and other costs. The apparent 100 per cent price increase allows the retailer to cover costs and deliver a profit, as shown below:

> Gross margin = GM
>
> €20 retail price – sold by retailer to consumer (retailer GM = 50 per cent);
>
> €10 wholesale price – sold by distributor to retailer (distributor GM = 30 per cent);
>
> €7.00 distribution price – sold by Senz to distributor (manufacturer GM = 40 per cent);
>
> €4 – cost to produce product

The start-up could begin by analysing its own costs and simply add the necessary gross margins of those in the supply chain but, in the world of fast moving consumer goods firms, they tend to start with a price point. That is, a price that they believe consumers will be willing to pay for a product. Suddenly, the business plan did not look good. The market price of a good quality umbrella was €20 but, to achieve such a price, the start-up would need to produce the product for €4. This was impossible. The unique design and carbon fibre frame meant material costs alone were almost €4. Furthermore, there was already a best-selling dominant umbrella in the market – the GustBuster®. This had a retail price of about €30. The challenge was to try and achieve a price close to this.

Manufacturing in The Netherlands was now extremely unlikely, given the pressure to achieve such a low manufacturing cost. The start-up turned to China where manufacturing costs are notoriously low. Eventually, Senz found a production partner able to deliver the product to the specifications set. This producer was experienced in manufacturing umbrellas and produced quality products for other umbrella brand owners.

Growing the business

Initially, the branded senz° umbrellas were available exclusively at www.senzumbrellas.com and large numbers were sold in and around the TU Delft campus. Unsurprisingly, the unusual shaped umbrella caused heads to turn on campus and this helped give the three students confidence that their idea would, indeed, succeed.

In May 2006, Senz Umbrellas signed an agreement with the fashion brand Mexx to introduce the senz° branded umbrellas under the Mexx brand in England, Scotland, Germany, The Netherlands, Belgium, France, Austria and Sweden. Senz° approached Mexx because their core values (optimistic, non-conformist, inspiring and fun) and its target group match the senz° brand. Additionally, it provides senz° with new and specialised distribution channels.

The senz° umbrella is now available in a range of options: foldable umbrellas include senz° smart s (€29.95) and senz° automatic (€54.95); and stick umbrellas include senz° smart (€34.95), senz° original (€54.95) and senz° XXL (€64.95). The umbrellas have been designed for both men and women.

Senz has now established a separate company called Senz Technologies to try to develop and apply their expertise in design to other products. Senz Umbrellas is a 100 per cent daughter of Senz Technologies. The plan for the future is to develop new products that can be introduced under the senz° label.

Questions

1 Explain the rationale to enter a mature market with a successful and established brand, the GustBuster®.

2 Has Senz turned its back on regional and national governments by manufacturing in China? The objective of incubators is to encourage economic growth locally.

3 This case raises important policy issues regarding how countries encourage employment and new business start-ups. Senz has decided to manufacture in China rather than The Netherlands. What, if anything, can governments do to encourage manufacturing at home?

4 Should universities be encouraging students to start their own businesses or to go and work for companies such as Shell/Unilever?

5 Was it the technology that won customers, the design or both?

6 How significant was the university association for the entrepreneurs? Could they have succeeded without the university?

7 Should Senz have sought a licensing deal with Adidas, North Face or Berghaus?

8 Senz Technologies has had limited success outside umbrellas. Why?

9 The pricing of the product seems to have limited its mass appeal. Why?

Sources: Umbrellas: A History (2010) [Accessed: September 2, 2011] http://simonesmith.hubpages.com/hub/Umbrellas-A-History; Dingjia Umbrella company website: http://www.dingjia-umbrella.com/; Senz° storm umbrella demonstration video: http://www.youtube.com/watch?v=hFzOwq5PldQ

Chapter summary

Deciding how and on what basis a company wishes to compete with its competitors is of central concern to all companies. Firms need to consider a wide range of factors in order to maximise the product's chance of success in competitive environments. This chapter has shown that a company has to identify the specific ways it can differentiate its products in order to gain competitive advantage.

First and foremost, it has to consider the market in which it is competing, the nature of the competition and how its capabilities will enable its products to be successful. The concept of platforms in new product development was introduced as a way of developing product groups for the future. The positioning of the product and the brand strategy selected were also shown to be of particular importance. Finally, marketing research offers extensive opportunities in terms of information provision. The effective use of this information often leads to the successful development of new products.

Discussion questions

1 If there was a strategic alliance between competitors for the development of a new technology, then what are the strategic issues for these firms once that technology becomes available?

2 Apply the notion of product platform to service industries. How relevant is it to financial services or to hotels? What are the issues that would need to be investigated if an idea emerged in a firm in those industries for a novel platform that had no connection with what was done before in that industry?

3 Would you agree that product portfolio analysis is too simplistic to be of much value?

4 Trace the connections between differentiation strategy, core capabilities and positioning strategy. How are they relevant to new product planning?

5 Are brand extensions as relevant in industrial markets as in consumer markets? Do they have a strategic role or are they short-term tactical exercises?

6 It seems Toyota has been successful at recalling some of its cars for modifications, without damaging the Toyota brand. How has it achieved this?

7 Apply CIM (Figure 1.9) to the case study at the end of this chapter to illustrate the innovation project.

8 Examine whether it is only the launch of technology-intensive products that can benefit from the use of 'blog buzz' or whether all product launches could benefit.

Key words and phrases

Product platform *449*

Product portfolios *455*

Product differentiation *457*

Product strategies *462*

Internal and external brand contacts *465*

Brand extensions *465*

Market entry *468*

Withdrawing products *471*

Mature products *472*

References

Beverland, M.B., Napoli, J. and Farrelly, F. (2010) Can all brands innovate in the same way? A typology of brand position and innovation effort, *Journal of Product Innovation Management*, vol. 27, 33–48.

Delbridge, R. and Mariotti, F. (2009) *Reaching for radical innovation: how motorsport companies harness network diversity for discontinuous innovation*, Advanced Institute of Management Research (AIM), London.

Gawer, A. (2014) Bridging differing perspectives on technological platforms: toward an integrative framework, *Research Policy*, vol. 43, no. 7, 1239–49.

Gawer, A. and Cusumano, M.A. (2014) Industry platforms and ecosystem innovation. *Journal of Product Innovation Management*, vol. 31, 417–33.

Green, D.H., Barclay, D.W. and Ryans, A.B. (1995) Entry strategy and long-term performance: conceptualization and empirical examination, *Journal of Marketing*, October, 1–16.

Gupta, S. (2013) For mobile devices, think apps, not ads, *Harvard Business Review*, vol. 91, no. 2, March.

Henard, D.H. and McFadyen, M.A. (2012) Resource dedication and new product performance: a resource-based view, *Journal of Product Innovation Management*, vol. 29, 193–204.

Kahn, K.B., Barczak, G., Nicholas, J., Ledwith, A. and Perks, H. (2012) An examination of new product development best practice, *Journal of Product Innovation Management*, vol. 29, 180–92.

Levitt, T. (1986) *The Marketing Imagination*, The Free Press, New York.

Mohr, J., Sengupta, S. and Slater, S. (2010) *Marketing of High-Technology Products and Innovations*, 3rd edn, Prentice Hall, Harlow.

Moore, L.M. and Pessemier, E.A. (1993) *Product Planning and Management*, McGraw-Hill, New York.

Muffatto, M. and Roveda, M. (2000) Developing product platforms: analysis of the development process, *Technovation*, vol. 20, no. 11, 617–30.

New Yorker, The (2008) Thinking in the Rain, Susan Orlean, February 11 and 18 issue. http://www.newyorker.com/magazine/2008/02/11/thinking-in-the-rain

Riezebos, R. (2003) *Brand Management: A Theoretical and Practical Approach*, Prentice Hall, Harlow.

Rubenstein, H. (1996) 'Brand first management', *Journal of Marketing Management*, vol. 12, 269–80.

Schofield, M. and Arnold, D. (1988) Strategies for mature business, *Long Range Planning*, vol. 21, no. 5, 69–76.

Schwarzkopf, S. and Gries, R. (eds) (2010) *Ernest Dichter and Motivation Research: New Perspectives on the Making of Post-War Consumer Culture*, 3–38, Palgrave Macmillan, London.

Talay, M.B., Calantone, R.J. and Voorhees, C.M. (2014) Coevolutionary dynamics of automotive competition: product innovation, change, and marketplace survival, *Journal of Product Innovation Management*, vol. 31, 61–78.

Wheelwright, S.C. and Clark, K.B. (1992) *Revolutionising Product Development*, The Free Press, New York.

Further reading

For a more detailed review of the product and brand management literature, the following develop many of the issues raised in this chapter:

Barczak, G., Griffin, A. and Kahn, K.B. (2009) perspective: Trends and drivers of success in NPD practices: results of the 2003 PDMA Best Practices Study, *Journal of Product Innovation Management*, vol. 26, no. 1, 3–23.

Biemans, W.G., Griffin, A. and Moenaert, R.K. (2007) Twenty Years of the *Journal of Product Innovation Management*: history, participants, and knowledge stocks and flows, *Journal of Product Innovation Management*, vol. 24, 193–213.

Biemans, W., Griffin, A. and Moenaert, R. (2010) In search of the classics: a study of the impact of JPIM papers from 1984 to 2003, *Journal of Product Innovation Management*, vol. 27, 461–84.

Henard, D. H. and McFadyen, M.A. (2012) Resource dedication and new product performance: a resource-based view, *Journal of Product Innovation Management*, vol. 29, 193–204.

Mohr, J., Sengupta, S. and Slater, S. (2010) *Marketing of High-Technology Products and Innovations*, 3rd edn, Prentice Hall, London.

Zirpoli, F. and Camuffo, A. (2009) Product architecture, inter-firm vertical coordination and knowledge partitioning in the auto industry, *European Management Review*, vol. 6, no. 4, 250–64.

Chapter 14
New product development

Introduction

Few business activities are heralded for their promise and approached with more justified optimism than the development of new products. Successful new products also have the added benefit of revitalising the organisation. Small wonder, then, that the concept of new product development (NPD) has received enormous attention in the management literature over the past 20 years. The result is a diverse range of literature from practitioners, management consultants and academics. This chapter explores this literature and examines the various models of NPD that have been put forward. It also explains the importance of NPD as a means of achieving growth.

The case study at the end of this chapter features one of the fastest growing brands in Europe – innocent. Its range of smoothies and other beverages has propelled it into the top flight of brands. The case explores how this start-up firm acquired funding and developed its products.

Chapter contents

Learning objectives

When you have completed this chapter you will be able to:

- examine the relationship between new products and prosperity;
- recognise the range of product development opportunities that can exist;
- recognise that a new product is a multi-dimensional concept;
- identify the different types of models of NPD;
- provide an understanding of the importance of external linkages in the new product development process.

Innovation management and NPD

When one considers a variety of different industries, a decline in product innovations is matched only by a decline in market share. For example, Table 7.2 in Chapter 7 illustrates that across a wide variety of industries product innovation has led to winning market share and leadership.

This chapter looks at the exciting process of developing new products. Part One of this book has highlighted the importance of innovation and how the effective management of that process can lead to corporate success. To many people, new products are the outputs of the innovation process, where the new product development (NPD) process is a subprocess of innovation. Managing innovation concerns the conditions that have to be in place to ensure that the organisation as a whole is given the opportunity to develop new products. The actual development of new products is the process of transforming business opportunities into tangible products.

Innovation in action

The Tangle Teezer

Shaun Pulfrey spent four years developing the Tangle Teezer. As a hairdresser, he was aware of the problems of tangled hair. Significantly, he developed a skill for untangling hair. He used a comb and a paddle brush in an unconventional manner and could detangle anything within five minutes. He made weekly visits to the British Library to expand his knowledge of brush types and flexible plastics, and then spent three years speaking to experts and researching manufacturers.

Pulfrey estimates the R&D alone cost £90,000, of which £25,000 came from remortgaging his house. His final design was for hundreds of flexible teeth on a palm-sized pad, with no handle. The cost of patenting was £15,000 and he has won a few claims.

Source: Steve Stock/Alamy Images

Interestingly, he was advised by experts to manufacture in China because it was cheaper, but he was worried something would get lost in translation. Instead, he found a British manufacturer and agreed to pay almost double the cost of a manufacturer from China. That decision brought an unexpected reward later, when he signed up Chinese retailers, who were keen because it was made in Britain.

Today, his British stockists include Selfridges, John Lewis and Topshop. The brushes, made in Oxford, are also sold to 110 countries, with exports making up more than 70 per cent of the £8.5 million revenues in 2013. Sales in 2014 reached £14 million. The business now produces 500,000 a month.

Pulfrey owns 100 per cent of the business. He told *The Sunday Times*: 'I wasn't a businessman when I started. I set out to make a product and after it launched I needed assistance to move forward. You need to build a trusted and talented team.'

His product idea was rejected by all the Dragons on the BBC's *Dragons' Den* show.

New product development concerns the management of the disciplines involved in the development of new products. These disciplines have developed their own perspectives on the subject of NPD. These are based largely on their experiences of involvement in the process. Hence, production management examines the development of new products from a manufacturing perspective, that is, how can we most effectively manufacture the product in question? Marketing, on the other hand, would take a slightly different perspective and would be concerned with trying to understand the needs of the customer and how the business could best meet these needs. However, producing what the customer wants may or may not be either possible or profitable. The lack of a common approach to the development of new products is due to this multiple perspective. This is illustrated in Figure 14.1. The variety of views presented on the subject is not a weakness. Indeed, it should be viewed as a strength, for these different perspectives illuminate the areas that are left in the dark by other perspectives.

Usually, competition between companies is assessed using financial measures such as return on capital employed (ROCE), profits and market share. Non-financial measures, such as design, innovativeness and technological supremacy, may also be used.

Theoretically, it is possible for a firm to survive without any significant developments to its products, but such firms are exceptions to the norm. Where

Figure 14.1 A variety of perspectives from which to analyse the development of new products

long-term success is dependent on the ability to compete with others, this is almost always achieved by ensuring that your company's products are superior to the competition.

Product development as a series of decisions

The existing literature on product development is vast. The Brown and Eisenhardt (1995) review provides a comprehensive overview of the literature, and an illustration of the diversity of the literature, largely adopting an organisational perspective, which is, arguably, the main focus of the existing new product literature. However, other key perspectives on new product development are evident. The reviews by Finger and Dixon (1989a; 1989b) provide an excellent insight into engineering design literature. The marketing perspective on new product development is reviewed by Barczak et al. (2009). Arguably, the paper by Krishnan and Uldrich (2001) remains one of very few papers that attempts to pull this wide and vast literature together. This review examines product development as a series of decisions. Within the product development project, the authors divide the decisions into four categories: concept development; supply chain design; product design; and production ramp-up/launch.

Focusing on the study of Krishnan and Uldrich (2001), within concept development there are five basic decisions to be made:

1 What are the target values of the product attributes?
2 What will the product concept be?
3 What variants of the product will be offered?
4 What is the product architecture?
5 What will be the overall physical form and industrial design of the product?

Within the decisions surrounding supply chain design, Krishnan and Uldrich (2001) argue that the following questions are key:

● Which components will be designed specifically for the product?
● Who will design and produce the product?
● What is the configuration of the physical supply chain?
● What type of process will be used to assemble the product?
● Who will develop and supply the process equipment?

New products and prosperity

The potential rewards of NPD are enormous. One only has to consider the rapid success of companies such as Microsoft and Facebook and Twitter in the rapidly growing social networking industry. Similar success was achieved by Apple and, prior to this, IBM, in the early development of the same industry. This example illustrates an important point, that success in one year does not ensure success in the next. Both Apple and IBM experienced severe difficulties in the 1990s.

Research by Cooper and Edgett (2008) has suggested that, on average, new products (defined here as those less than five years old) are increasingly taking a larger slice of company sales. For 3M, for example, new products contributed to

30 per cent of sales in 2015. It expects to increase this to 37% by 2017. 3M keeps careful track of new product development, using a measure called the New Product Vitality Index (NPVI), which quantifies the percentage of 3M's sales from products that were introduced during the past five years.

Considerations when developing an NPD strategy

Chapter 7 outlined many of the activities and factors that organisations need to consider in managing a business in the short and long term. In addition, Chapter 13 highlighted many of the factors that a business needs to consider if it is to manage its products successfully. It should be clear that establishing a direction for a business and the selection of strategies to achieve its goals form an ongoing, evolving process that is frequently subject to change. This is particularly evident at the product strategy level (Figure 14.2 illustrates the main inputs into the decision-making process). The process of product strategy was highlighted in Chapter 13 and is the creative process of recognising genuine business opportunities that the business might be able to exploit. It is commonly referred to as 'opportunity identification'.

Ongoing corporate planning

In large organisations this can be a very formal activity involving strategic planners and senior managers with responsibility for setting the future direction of the business. In smaller organisations this activity may be undertaken by the owner of the business in an informal, even ad hoc way. For many businesses it is somewhere in the middle of these two extremes. The effects of any corporate planning may be important and long term. For example, the decision by a sports footwear manufacturer to exit the tennis market and concentrate on the basketball market due to changing social trends will have a significant impact on the business.

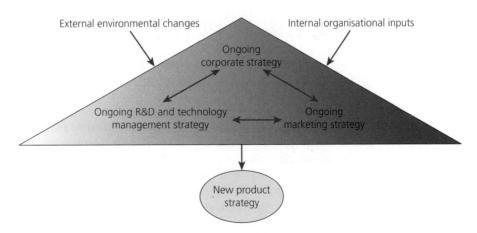

Figure 14.2 Main inputs into the decision-making process

Ongoing market planning

Decisions by market planners may have equally significant effects. For example, the realisation that a competitor is about to launch an improved tennis shoe that offers additional benefits may force the business to establish five new product development projects. Two of these projects may be established to investigate the use of new materials for the sole, one could be used to develop a series of new designs, one could look at alternative fastenings and one could be used to reduce production costs.

Ongoing technology management

In most science- and technology-intensive industries, such as the pharmaceutical and computer software industries, this activity is probably more significant than ongoing market planning. Technology awareness is very high. The continual analysis of internal R&D projects and external technology trawling will lead to numerous technical opportunities that need to be considered by the business. Say that a recent review of the patent literature has identified a patent application by one of the company's main competitors. This forces the business to establish a new project to investigate this area to ensure that it is aware of any future developments that may affect its position. This area is explored in more detail in Chapter 10.

Opportunity analysis/serendipity

In addition to the inputs that have been classified above, there are other inputs and opportunities that often are labelled miscellaneous or put down to serendipity (see Chapter 1). The vice-president of 3M remarked that 'chaos is a necessary part of an innovative culture. It's been said that 3M's competitors never know what we are going to come up with next. The fact is neither do we.'

NPD as a strategy for growth

The interest expressed by many companies in the subject of developing new products is hardly surprising, given that the majority of businesses are intent on growth. Although, as was discussed in Chapter 13, this does not apply to all companies, nonetheless, the development of new products provides an opportunity for growing the business. (It is worth reminding ourselves that new product development is only one of many options available to a business keen on growth.)

One of the clearest ways of identifying the variety of growth options available to a business is using Ansoff's (1968) directional policy matrix. This well-known matrix, shown in Figure 14.3, combines two of the key variables that enable a business to grow: an increase in market opportunities and an increase in product opportunities. Within this matrix, new product development is seen as one of four available options. Each of the four cells considers various combinations of

	Current products	New products
Current markets	1 Market penetration strategy	3 Product development strategy
New markets	2 Market development strategy	4 Diversification strategy

Figure 14.3 Ansoff matrix

Source: Adapted from Ansoff, I. (1965) *Corporate Strategy*, Penguin, Harmondsworth; (1968) *Toward a Strategy of the Theory of the Firm*, McGraw-Hill, New York.

product–market options. Growth can be achieved organically (internal development) or through external acquisition. A criticism of this matrix is that it adopts an environmental perspective that assumes that opportunities for growth exist – they may not. Indeed, often consolidation and retrenchment need to be considered, especially in times of economic downturn. Each of the cells in the matrix is discussed briefly below.

Market penetration

Opportunities are said to exist within a business's existing markets through increasing the volume of sales. Increasing the market share of a business's existing products by exploiting the full range of marketing-mix activities is the common approach adopted by many companies. This may include branding decisions. For example, the cereal manufacturer Kellogg's has increased the usage of its corn-flakes product by promoting it as a snack to be consumed at times other than at breakfast.

Market development

Growth opportunities are said to exist for a business's products through making them available to new markets. In this instance, the company maintains the security of its existing products but opts to develop and enter new markets. Market development can be achieved by opening up new segments. For example, Mercedes decided to enter the small car market (previously the company had always concentrated on the executive or luxury segment). Similarly, companies may decide to enter new geographic areas through exporting.

Product development

Ansoff proposes that growth opportunities exist through offering new or improved products to existing markets. This is the subject of this chapter and, as will become clear, trying to establish when a product is new is sometimes difficult. Nonetheless, virtually all companies try to ensure that their products are able to compete with the competition by regularly improving and updating their existing products. This is an ongoing activity for most companies.

Diversification

It hardly needs to be said that opportunities for growth exist beyond a business's existing products and markets. The selection of this option, however, would be significant in that the business would move into product areas and markets in which it currently does not operate. The development of the self-adhesive notepads (Post-it Notes) by 3M provided an opportunity for the company to enter the stationery market, a market of which it had little knowledge, with a product that was new to the company and the market.

Many companies try to utilise either their existing technical or commercial knowledge base. For example, Flymo's knowledge of the electric lawnmower market enabled it to diversify into a totally new market. Indeed, the introduction of its GardenVac product led to the creation of the 'garden-tidy' product market. Whilst this is an example of organic growth, many companies identify diversification opportunities through acquisition. For example, in the United Kingdom, some of the privatised electricity companies have purchased significant holdings in privatised water companies. The knowledge base being utilised here is the commercial know-how of the provision of a utility service (former public service).

Additional opportunities for diversified growth exist through forward, backward and horizontal diversification. A manufacturer opening retail outlets is an example of forward integration. Backward integration is involvement in activities that are inputs to the business, for example a manufacturer starting to produce components. Horizontal diversification is buying up competitors.

A range of product development opportunities

A development of Ansoff's directional policy matrix was Johnson and Jones's (1957) matrix for product development strategies (see Figure 14.4). This matrix replaces Ansoff's product variable with technology. It builds on Ansoff's matrix by offering further clarification of the range of options open to a company contemplating product decisions. In particular, the use of technology as a variable better illustrates the decisions a company needs to consider. For example, Johnson and Jones distinguish between improving existing technology and acquiring new technology, the latter being far more resource intensive with higher degrees of risk. Ansoff's directional policy matrix made no such distinction. Similarly, the market-newness scale offers a more realistic range of alternatives. Many other matrices have since been developed to try to help firms identify the range of options available.

The range of product development strategies that are open to a company introduces the notion that a new product can take many forms. This is the subject of the next section.

Increasing technology newness →

	No technological change	Improved technology	New technology To acquire scientific knowledge and production skills new to the company
Products objectives			
No market change	Sustain	Reformulation To maintain an optimum balance of cost, quality and availability in the formulae of present products	Replacement To seek new and better ingredients of formulation for present company products in technology not now employed
Strengthened market To exploit more fully the existing markets for the present company's products	Remerchandising To increase sales to consumers of types now served by the company	Improved product To improve present products for greater utility and merchandisability to consumers	Product line extension To broaden the line of products offered to present consumers through new technology
New market To increase the number of types of consumer served by the company	New use To find new classes of consumer that can utilise present company products	Market extension To reach new classes of consumer by modifying present products	Diversification To add to the classes of consumer served by developing new technology knowledge

Increasing market newness (vertical axis label)

Figure 14.4 New product development strategies

Source: Johnson, S.C. and Jones, C. (1957) How to organise for new products, *Harvard Business Review*, May–June, vol. 35, 49–62.

Illustration 14.1

New products crucial to success for Shimano

As a keen cyclist, Yoshizo Shimano knows all about the importance of keeping in touch with his company's products. Mr Shimano is president of Shimano, the world's biggest manufacturer of bicycle components.

Frequently, he borrows a bike from the company's R&D division to keep in touch with what researchers are up to. 'We won't compete with our customers by building complete bikes. But we must keep in mind how our components are going to be used and have a

→

vision of the product that is safe as well as being fun,' he says.

Mr Shimano's interest in trying out bicycles containing his company's components underlines how manufacturers must pay increasing importance to bringing out new products. These must either solve a pressing customer problem or come up with an idea that breaks completely new ground within a few years. In either case, manufacturers' strategies on new product development are crucial to their chances of long-term success in a world where competition is becoming steadily tougher.

In 1921, Shozaburo Shimano established Shimano Iron Works and began production of the bicycle freewheel. Today, some 90 years later, Shimano is a world leader in the manufacture and supply of bicycle parts, fishing tackle and rowing equipment. Sales in 2009 were ¥186 billion and profits were ¥20 billion. Shimano Inc. is the world's largest bicycle component manufacturer. Furthermore:

- Shimano has about a 70–80 per cent share of the worldwide bicycle component market;
- bicycle components make up about 78 per cent of sales, whilst fishing tackle makes up the rest of sales;
- operating margin has increased nicely for the past seven years: from 9 per cent in 2001 to 14.8 per cent in 2007;
- operating margin has averaged about 14 per cent for the past eight years;
- Shimano has a strong history of sponsoring some of the best athletes and cycling teams in the world.

Shimano is quoted on the Tokyo Stock Exchange, with the family retaining a minority stake.

Mr Shimano says Shimano keeps in touch with product development by talking continually to the 400–500 bicycle manufacturers it supplies worldwide. It

Source: Len Holsborg/Alamy Images

makes 13 main types of parts – gears, brake systems and drive chains – each of which can come in up to 100 different variants.

In the early 1990s, the company prospered through the development of products, such as specialist gears, that suited the then fashion for rugged, off-road mountain bikes. Now that the mountain bike craze has died away, Mr Shimano says the company is increasing its development of products such as automatic gears that will give cyclists, particularly on congested city roads, safer, smoother rides.

'If the cyclist does not have to bother with changing gears, he can concentrate on other aspects of controlling the bike, which is likely to lead to safer journeys,' says Mr Shimano.

What is a new product?

Attempting to define what is and what is not a new product is not a trivial task, although many students of business management have had much fun arguing over whether the Sony Walkman was, indeed, a new product or merely existing technology repackaged. Another example that illustrates this point is long-life milk, known in the United States as aspectic milk (sold without refrigeration). This product has been consumed for many years in Europe, but it is a relatively new concept for most consumers in the United States. Consumers who drink refrigerated milk may be extremely wary of milk sold from a non-refrigerated shelf. Once again, whilst clearly this product is not absolutely new, it can be seen that it is more useful, from a product manager's perspective, to adopt a relativistic view.

It is important to note, as was explained in Chapter 13, that a product is a multi-dimensional concept. It can be defined differently and can take many forms. Some dimensions will be tangible product features and others intangible. Does the provision of different packaging for a product constitute a new product? Surely the answer is no – or is it? New packaging, coupled with additional marketing effort, especially in terms of marketing communications, can help to reposition a product. This was successfully achieved by GlaxoSmithKline with its beverage product Lucozade. Today, this product is known as a sports drink, yet older readers will recall that the product was packaged originally in a distinctive bottle wrapped in yellow cellophane and commonly purchased at pharmacists for sick children. This illustrates the difficulty of attempting to offer a single definition for a new product. (Also, see the example of BMW's Mini in Illustration 14.2.)

If we accept that a product has many dimensions, then it must follow that it is theoretically possible to label a product 'new' merely by altering one of these dimensions,

Illustration 14.2

The repositioning of BMW's Mini

The Mini is one of the most established and successful product brands in the automotive industry. It has been in existence for over 45 years and had sold over 4 million units before its highly successful relaunch in 2001. The Mini was designed and manufactured in Britain; the car was launched in 1959 by the British Leyland Motor Corporation. The Mini remained under British ownership until 1994 when BMW acquired the Rover Group; though it later sold off much of the group, BMW kept the Mini. In 1999, the Mini celebrated its 40th birthday and *Autocar* named it the car of the century. The Mini itself remained relatively unchanged from its original launch until it was withdrawn completely from production in 2000. A new Mini and Mini Cooper (designed and manufactured by BMW) were launched in 2001. It has been a very successful project. For example, Mini sales were higher in March 2016 than in any previous single month in the brand's history. A total of 39,061 units were delivered to customers worldwide. In the first

Source: Mini UK

quarter of 2016, Mini sales also achieved a new record high with 78,311 units delivered, an increase of 5.4 per cent on last year.

Source: Arlidge, J. (2006) Minis maxi challenge, *The Sunday Times*, S3 Business, p. 11, 17 September; Simms, C. and Trott, P. (2006) The perceptions of the BMW Mini brand: the importance of historical associations and the development of a model, *Journal of Product & Brand Management*, vol. 15, no. 4, 228–38; https://www.press.bmwgroup.com/united-kingdom/article/detail/T0259093EN_GB/bmw-group-achieves-best-sales-month-ever

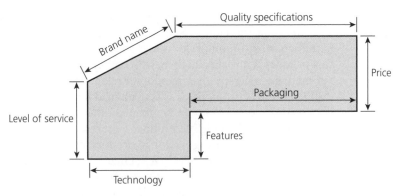

Figure 14.5 A product is multi-dimensional

for example packaging. Figure 14.5 illustrates this point. In addition, Corrocher and Zirulia (2010) found that mobile communication operators used pricing tariffs to develop innovative new services. Each dimension is capable of being altered. These alterations create a new dimension and, in theory, a new product, even if the change is very small. Indeed, Johne and Snelson (1988) suggest that the options for both new and existing product lines centre on altering the variables in the figure. Table 14.1 shows what this means in practice.

Defining a new product

Chapter 1 established a number of definitions to help with the study of this subject and provided a definition of innovation. In addition, it highlighted a quotation by Rogers and Shoemaker (1972) concerning whether or not something is new. It is useful at this juncture to revisit their argument. They stated that, whilst it may be difficult to establish whether a product is actually new as regards the passage of time, so long as it is perceived to be new it is new. This is significant because it illustrates that newness is a relative term. In the case of a new product, it is relative to what preceded the product. Moreover, the overwhelming majority of so-called new

Table 14.1 Different examples of 'newness'

1 Changing the performance capabilities of the product (for example, a new, improved washing detergent)
2 Changing the application advice for the product (for example, the use of the Persil ball in washing machines)
3 Changing the after-sales service for the product (for example, frequency of service for a motor car)
4 Changing the promoted image of the product (for example, the use of 'green'-image refill packs)
5 Changing the availability of the product (for example, the use of chocolate-vending machines)
6 Changing the price of the product (for example, the newspaper industry has experienced severe price wars)

Source: Johne, F.A. and Snelson, P.A. (1988) The role of marketing specialists in product development, Proceedings of the 21st Annual Conference of the Marketing Education Group, Huddersfield, vol. 3, 176–91.

Table 14.2 A new product has different interpretations of new

New product A
A snack manufacturer introduces a new, larger pack size for its best-selling savoury snack. Consumer research for the company revealed that a family-size pack would generate additional sales without cannibalising existing sales of the standard-size pack.

New product B
An electronics company introduces a new miniature compact disc player. The company has further developed its existing compact disc product and is now able to offer a much lighter and smaller version.

New product C
A pharmaceutical company introduces a new prescription drug for ulcer treatment. Following eight years of laboratory research and three years of clinical trials, the company recently has received approval from the government's medical authorities to launch its new ulcer drug.

products are developments or variations on existing formats. Research in this area suggests that only 10 per cent of new products introduced are new to both the market and the company (Booz, Allen & Hamilton, 1982). New to the company (in this case) means that the firm has not sold this type of product before, but other firms could have. New to the market means that the product has not appeared before in the market. However, the examples in Table 14.2 illustrate the confusion that exists in this area.

The three products in the table are all new in that they did not exist before. However, many would argue, especially technologists, that product A does not contain any new technology. Similarly, product B does not contain any new technology, although its configuration may be new. Product C contains a new patented chemical formulation, hence this is the only truly new product. Marketers would, however, contend that all three products are new, simply because they did not previously exist. Moreover, meeting the needs of the customer and offering products that are wanted is more important than whether a product represents a scientific breakthrough. Such arguments are common to many companies, especially those that have both a strong commercial and technological presence and expertise.

Pause for thought ❓

Has the BMW Mini been repositioned? Or is it a new product?

For the student of innovation and new product development, awareness of the debate and the strong feelings that are associated with it are more important than trying to resolve the polemics. Indeed, the long-term commercial success of the company should be the guiding principle on which product decisions are made. However, in some industries, the advancement of knowledge and subsequent scientific breakthroughs can lead to possible product offerings that would help certain sections of the population. Commercial pressures alone would, however, prevent these new products from being offered, as we saw in the tooth whitening case study in Chapter 12. The science and technology perspective should, therefore, not be dismissed.

Pause for thought

Is it possible to create a new product simply by changing the packaging?
Does this also apply to the dimension of price?

Classification of new products

There have been many attempts to classify new products into certain categories. Very often, the distinction between one category and another is one of degree and attempting to classify products is subject to judgement. It is worthy of note, however, that only 10 per cent of all new products are truly innovative. These products involve the greatest risk because they are new to both the company and the marketplace. Most new product activity is devoted to improving existing products. At Sony, 80 per cent of new product activity is undertaken to modify and improve the company's existing products. The following classification identifies the commonly accepted categories of new product developments.

New-to-the-world products

These represent a small proportion of all new products introduced. They are the first of their kind and create a new market. They are inventions that usually contain a significant development in technology, such as a new discovery, or manipulate existing technology in a very different way, leading to revolutionary new designs, such as Dyson's vacuum cleaner. Other examples include Apple's iPad, 3M's Post-it Notes and Guinness's 'in-can' system.

New product lines (new to the firm)

Although not new to the marketplace, these products are new to the particular company. They provide an opportunity for the company to enter an established market for the first time. For example, Google, Sony and Microsoft have all entered the smartphone market to compete with market leaders Apple and Samsung.

Additions to existing lines (line additions)

This category is a subset of new product lines above. The distinction is that, whilst the company already has a line of products in this market, the product is significantly different from the present product offering, but not so different that it is a new line. The distinction between this category and the former is one of degree. For example, Hewlett-Packard's colour ink-jet printer was an addition to its established line of ink-jet printers.

Improvements and revisions to existing products

These new products are replacements of existing products in a firm's product line. For example, Hewlett-Packard's ink-jet printer has received numerous modifications over time and, with each revision, performance and reliability have been improved.

Product

	No change	Modified	Technology change
No change	**No change** No change	**Facelift** Appearance	**Inconspicuous substitution** Technology Materials Manufacturing
Modified	**Re-merchandising** Name Promotion Price Distribution Packaging	**Relaunch** Costs Promoti… Price Distribu…	**Conspicuous substitution** Price Distribution
New market/ segment	**Intangible repositioning** Name Promotion Price Distribution Target market Competition	**Tangible repositioning** Name Appearance Costs Promotion Price Distribution Target market Competition	**Neo-innovation** Technology Materials Manufacturing Promotion Price Distribution Target market Competition

*(left axis label: **Marketing**)*

Figure 14.8 Saunders and Jobber's phasing continuity spectrum

Source: Saunders, J. and Jobber, D. (1994) Product replacement: strategies for simultaneous product deletion and launch, *Journal of Product Innovation Management*, vol. 11, no. 5, 433–50, © John Wiley & Sons Ltd.

New product development as an industry innovation cycle

Abernathy and Utterback (1978) suggested that product innovations are soon followed by process innovations in what they described as an industry innovation cycle (see Chapter 1). A similar notion can be applied to the categories of new products. The cycle can be identified in a wide variety of industries. **New-to-the-world products** (Category 1) are launched by large companies with substantial resources, especially technical or marketing resources. Other large firms react swiftly to the launch of such a product by developing their own versions (Categories 2 and 3). Many small and medium-sized companies participate by developing their own new products to compete with the originating firm's product (Category 4). Substantial success and growth can come to small companies that adopt this strategy. Hewlett-Packard grew into one of the world's leading personal computer manufacturers. This was not without difficulties along the way and included the swallowing up of Compaq computers. As competition intensifies, companies will compete in the market for profits. The result is determined efforts to reduce costs in order to improve these profits, hence there are many cost reductions (Category 5).

Overview of NPD theories

The early stages of the new product development process are most usually defined as idea generation, idea screening, concept development and concept testing. They represent the formation and development of an idea prior to its taking any physical form. In most industries, it is from this point onwards that costs will rise significantly. It is clearly far easier to change a concept than a physical product. The subsequent stages involve adding to the concept as those involved with the development (manufacturing engineers, product designers and marketers) begin to make decisions regarding how best to manufacture the product, what materials to use, possible designs and the potential market's evaluations.

The organisational activities undertaken by the company as it embarks on the actual process of new product development have been represented by numerous different models. These have attempted to capture the key activities involved in the process, from idea to commercialisation of the product. The representation of these tasks has changed significantly over the past 30 years. For example, the pharmaceutical industry is dominated by scientific and technological developments that lead to new drugs; whereas the food industry is dominated by consumer research that leads to many minor product changes. And, yet, the vast majority of textbooks that tackle this subject present the NPD process as an eight-stage linear model, regardless of these major differences (Figure 14.9 shows how the process is frequently presented.) Consequently, this simple linear model is ingrained in the minds of many people. This is largely because new product development is viewed from a financial perspective where cash outflows precede cash inflows (see Figure 14.10). This graph shows the cumulative effect on cash flow through the development phases, from the build-up of stock and work in progress in the early stages of production, when there is no balancing in-flow of cash from sales, to the phase of profitable sales that bring the cash in-flow.

Idea generation

↓

Idea screening

↓

Concept testing

↓

Business analysis

↓

Product development

↓

Test marketing

↓

Commercialisation

↓

Monitoring and evaluation

Figure 14.9 Commonly presented linear NPD model

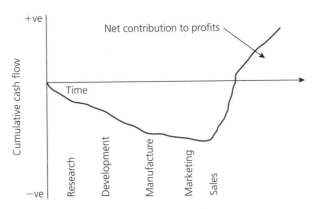

Figure 14.10 Cash flows and new product development

Virtually all those actually involved with the development of new products dismiss such simple linear models as not being a true representation of reality. More recent research suggests that the process needs to be viewed as a simultaneous and concurrent process with cross-functional interaction (Barczak et al., 2009).

For the reasons outlined above, the different perspectives on NPD have produced a wealth of literature on the subject (Barczak et al., 2009; Brown and Eisenhardt, 1995). In addition, the subject has attracted the attention of many business schools and business consultants, all interested in uncovering the secrets of successful product development. Numerous research projects have been undertaken, including in-depth case studies across many industries and single companies and broad surveys of industries (e.g. Biemans et al., 2007; Cooper and Edgett, 2008).

As a result, research on new product development is varied and fragmented, making it extremely difficult to organise for analysis. Brown and Eisenhardt (1995) produced a highly regarded review of the literature. In their analysis, they identify three main streams of literature, each having its own particular strengths and limitations (see Table 14.3). These streams have evolved around key research findings and, together, they continue to throw light on many dark areas of new product development. Slater et al. (2014) offer a more recent literature review of radical new product development.

Whilst this is an important development and a useful contribution to our understanding of the subject area, it offers little help for the practising manager on how he or she should organise and manage the new product development process. An analysis of the models that have been developed on the subject of new product development may help to identify some of the activities that need to be managed.

The fuzzy front end

Within the new product development literature, the concept of the so-called 'fuzzy front end' is the messy getting started period of new product development processes. It is at the beginning of the process, or the front end, where the organisation develops a concept of the product to be developed and decides whether or not to

Table 14.3 The three main streams of research within NPD literature

	Rational planning	Communication web	Disciplined problem solving
Aim/objective/title	Rational planning and management of the development of new products within organisations	The communication web studies the use of information and sources of information by product development teams	Disciplined problem solving focuses on how problems encountered during the NPD process were overcome
Focus of the research	The rational plan research focuses on business performance and financial performance of the product	The communication web looks at the effects of communication on project performance	The third stream tries to examine the process and the wide range of actors and activities involved
Seminal research	The work by Myers and Marquis (1969) and SAPPHO studies (Rothwell et al., 1974) was extremely influential in this field	Thomas Allen's (1969, 1977) research into communication patterns in large industrial laboratories dominates this perspective	The work by the Japanese scholars Imai et al. (1985) lies at the heart of this third stream of literature

Source: Brown, S.L. and Eisenhardt, K.M. (1995) Product development: past research, present findings and future directions, *Academy of Management Review*, vol. 20, no. 2, 343–78.

invest resources in the further development of an idea. It is the phase between first consideration of an opportunity and when it is judged ready to enter the structured development process (Kim and Wilemon, 2002; Stevens, 2014). It includes all activities from the search for new opportunities through the formation of a germ of an idea to the development of a precise concept. The fuzzy front end disappears when an organisation approves and begins formal development of the concept.

Although the fuzzy front end may not require expensive capital investment, it can consume 50 per cent of development time and it is where major commitments typically are made involving time, money and the product's nature, thus setting the course for the entire project and final end product. Consequently, this phase should be considered as an essential part of development rather than something that happens 'before development', and its cycle time should be included in the total new product development cycle time. This is even more critical for discontinuous new products, which are particularly challenging at this early stage in what is, by definition, intrinsically complex and risky, but offering high potential rewards (de Brentani and Reid, 2012).

There has been much written in NPD literature about the need to involve customers at an early stage in the process and to integrate them into the process in order to fully capture ideas (Brown and Eisenhardt, 1995; 1998; Cooper, 1999; Thomke, 2003; von Hippel, 1986). Despite this, customer involvement in NPD has been limited and largely passive in most industries (Weyland and Cole, 1997). There are many reasons for this limited utilisation of consumers in NPD and some we have touched on above, but perhaps the most limiting factor is the disconnection between customers and producers.

Nowadays, technology enables an innovative way of involving and integrating customers to the product development process. In this context, it is here that new

Table 14.4 Customer roles in NPD

Customer role	NPD phase	Key issues/managerial challenges
Customer as resource	Ideation	Appropriateness of customer as a source of innovation Selection of customer innovator Need for varied customer incentives Infrastructure for capturing customer knowledge Differential role of existing (current) and potential (future) customers
Customer as co-creator	Design and development	Involvement in a wide range of design and development tasks Nature of the NPD context: industrial/consumer products Tighter coupling with internal NPD teams Managing the attendant project uncertainty
	Product testing	Enhancing customers' product/technology knowledge Time-bound activity Ensuring customer diversity
Customer as user	Product support	Ongoing activity Infrastructure to support customer–customer interactions

Source: Adapted from Nambisan, S. (2002) Designing virtual customer environments for new product development: toward a theory, *Academy of Management Review*, vol. 27, no. 3, 395.

technologies, most notably in the form of 'toolkits', offer considerable scope for improving connection between consumers and producers. Franke and Piller's (2004) study analysed the value created by so-called 'toolkits for user innovation and design'. This was a method of integrating customers into new product development and design. The so-called toolkits allow customers to create their own product, which, in turn, is produced by the manufacturer. An example of a toolkit in its simplest form is the development of personalised products through uploading digital family photographs via the internet and having these printed on to products, such as clothing or cups, etc., thereby allowing consumers to create personalised individual products for themselves. User toolkits for innovation are specific to given product or service types and to a specified production system. Within those general constraints, they give users real freedom to innovate, allowing them to develop their custom product via iterative trial and error (Franke and Piller, 2004; von Hippel, 2001).

Nambisan (2002) offers a theoretical lens through which to view these 'virtual customer environments'. He considers the underlying knowledge creation issues and the nature of the customer interactions to identify three roles: customer as resource; customer as co-creator and customer as user. These three distinct but related roles provide a useful classification with which to examine the process of NPD. This classification recognises the considerably different management challenges for the firm if it is to utilise the customer into the NPD process (see Table 14.4).

Customer cocreation of new products

Research by Mahr (2014) sheds light on opportunities and limitations of customer cocreation. They find customer cocreation is most successful for the creation of highly relevant, but moderately novel, knowledge. Cocreation with customers who are closely related to the innovating firm results in more highly relevant knowledge at a low cost. Yet, cocreation with lead users produces novel and relevant knowledge. Recent research by Bogers and Horst (2014) shows how collaborative prototyping across functional, hierarchical and organisational boundaries can improve the overall prototyping process.

Time to market

Time to market (TTM) is the length of time it takes from a product being conceived to it reaching the market place. TTM is important in industries where products are outdated quickly. A common assumption is that TTM matters most for innovative products, but, actually, the first mover often has the luxury of time, whilst the clock clearly is running for the followers. TTM can vary widely between industries, say 15 years in aircraft and 6 months in food products. Yet, in many ways, it is a firm's TTM capability relative to its direct competitors that is far more important than the naked figure. Whilst other industries may be much faster, they do not pose a direct threat – although one may be able to learn from them and adapt their techniques.

As usual, there are some other factors that need to be considered when analysing a firm's TTM. For example, rather than reaching the market as soon as possible, delivering on schedule may be more important: to have the new product available for a trade show could be more valuable. Many managers argue that the shorter the project the less it will cost, so they attempt to use TTM as a means of cutting expenses. Unfortunately, a primary means of reducing TTM is to staff the project more heavily, so a faster project may actually be more expensive. Finally, as we have seen throughout this chapter, the need for change often appears midstream in a project. Consequently, the ability to make changes during product development without being too disruptive can be valuable. For example, one's goal could be to satisfy customers, which could be achieved by adjusting product requirements during development in response to customer feedback. Then TTM could be measured from the last change in requirements until the product is delivered. The pursuit of pure speed of TTM may also harm the business (Cooper and Edgett, 2008).

Agile NPD

Flexible product development is the ability to make changes to the product being developed or in how it is developed, even relatively late in the development process, without being too disruptive. Consequently, the later one can make changes, the more flexible the process is; and the less disruptive the change is, the greater the flexibility. Change can be expected in what the customer wants and how the customer might use the product, in how competitors might respond, and in the new technologies being applied in the product or in its manufacturing process. The more innovative a new product is, the more likely it is that the development team will have to make changes during development. In his book *Flexible Product Development* (2007), Preston Smith uses the software industry to show that having an agile NPD process enables the firm to adapt to changing markets. These days, many industrial new product development (NPD) software projects apply agile methodologies, such as Scrum, eXtreme Programming (XP) and Feature-Driven Development (FDD). Petri Kettunen from Siemens studied some of these systems and found that agility in embedded software product development can be enhanced further by following typical NPD principles (Kettunen, 2009).

Models of new product development

Amongst the burgeoning management literature on the subject, it is possible to classify the numerous models into eight distinct categories:

1 departmental-stage models;
2 activity-stage models and concurrent engineering;
3 cross-functional models (teams);
4 decision-stage models;
5 conversion-process models;
6 response models;
7 network models; and
8 outsourced (see Chapter 17).

Within this taxonomy, decision-stage models and activity-stage models are the most commonly discussed and presented in textbooks. Figure 14.13 (later) is an example of an activity-stage model and Cooper's stage-gate model is an example of a decision-stage model.

It is worthy of note that there are many companies, especially small specialist manufacturing companies, that continue to operate a craftsman-style approach to product development. This has been the traditional method of product manufacture for the past 500 years. For example, in every part of Europe, there are joinery companies manufacturing products to the specific requirements of the user. Many of these products will be single, one-off products manufactured to dimensions given on a drawing. All the activities, including the creation of drawings, collection of raw materials, manufacture and delivery, may be undertaken by one person. Today, when we are surrounded by technology that is sometimes difficult to use, never mind understand, it is possible to forget that the traditional approach to product development is still prevalent. Many activities, moreover, remain the same as they have always been.

Departmental-stage models

Departmental-stage models represent the early form of NPD models. These can be shown to be based around the linear model of innovation, where each department is responsible for certain tasks. Usually, they are represented in the following way. R&D provides the interesting technical ideas; the engineering department will then take the ideas and develop possible prototypes; the manufacturing department will explore possible ways to produce a viable product capable of mass manufacture; then the marketing department will be brought in to plan and conduct the launch. Such models are also referred to as 'over-the-wall' models, so called because departments would carry out their tasks before throwing the project over the wall to the next department (see Figure 14.11).

It is now widely accepted that this insular departmental view of the process hinders the development of new products. The process usually is characterised by a great deal

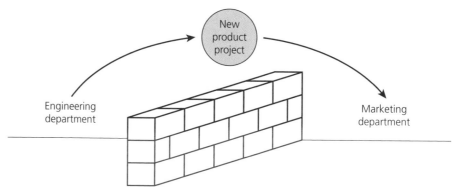

Figure 14.11 Over-the-wall model

of reworking and consultation between functions. In addition, market research provides continual inputs to the process. Furthermore, control of the project changes on a departmental basis, depending on which department currently is engaged in it. The consequence of this approach has been captured by Mike Smith's (1981) humorous tale of 'How not to design a swing, or the perils of poor coordination' (see Figure 14.12).

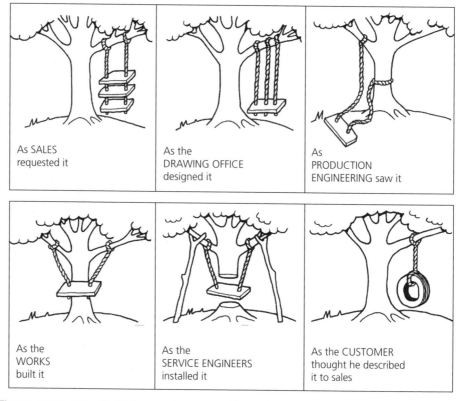

Figure 14.12 Mike Smith's secret weapon: the salutary tale of 'How not to design a swing, or the perils of poor coordination'

Source: Lorenz, C. (1990) *The Design Dimension*, Blackwell Publishing Ltd, Oxford with permission from John Wiley & Sons Ltd, permission conveyed through Copyright Clearance Center, Inc.

Activity-stage models and concurrent engineering

These are similar to departmental-stage models but, because they emphasise activities conducted, they provide a better representation of reality. They also facilitate iteration of the activities through the use of feedback loops, something that the departmental-stage models do not. Activity-stage models, however, have also received fierce criticism for perpetuating the 'over-the-wall' phenomenon. More recent activity-stage models (Crawford and Benedetto, 2014) have highlighted the simultaneous nature of the activities within the NPD process, hence emphasising the need for a cross-functional approach. Figure 14.13 shows an activity-stage model where the activities occur at the same time, but vary in their intensity.

In the late 1980s, in an attempt to address some of these problems, many manufacturing companies adopted a concurrent engineering or simultaneous engineering approach. The term was first coined by the Institute for Defense Analyses (IDA) in 1986 (IDA, 1986) to explain the systematic method of concurrently designing both the product and its downstream production and support processes. The idea is to focus attention on the project as a whole, rather than the individual stages, primarily by involving all functions from the outset of the project. This requires a major change in philosophy from functional orientation to project orientation. Furthermore, technology-intensive businesses with very specialist knowledge inputs are more difficult to manage. Such an approach introduces the need for project teams.

Cross-functional models (teams)

Common problems that occur within the product development process revolve around communications between different departments. This problem, specifically with regard to the marketing and the R&D departments, is explored more fully in Chapter 16. In addition, projects frequently would be passed back and forth between

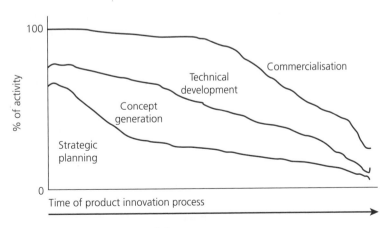

Figure 14.13 An activity-stage model

Source: Adapted from Crawford, C.M. (1997) *New Products Management*, 5th edn.

functions. Moreover, at each interface, the project would undergo increased changes, hence lengthening the product development process. The cross-functional teams (CFT) approach removes many of these limitations by having a dedicated project team representing people from a variety of functions. The use of cross-functional teams requires a fundamental modification to an organisation's structure. In particular, it places emphasis on the use of project management and interdisciplinary teams.

Decision-stage models

Decision-stage models represent the new product development process as a series of decisions that need to be taken in order to progress the project (Cooper and Edgett, 2008). Like the activity-stage models, many of these models also facilitate iteration through the use of feedback loops. However, a criticism of these models is that such feedback is implicit rather than explicit. The importance of the interaction between functions cannot be stressed enough – the use of feedback loops helps to emphasise this.

Stage-gate process

This is a widely employed product development process that divides the effort into distinct time-sequenced stages separated by management decision gates. It has been popularised by Robert Cooper's research in this area (Cooper and Edgett, 2008; www.prod-dev.com/stage-gate). Multifunctional teams must successfully complete a prescribed set of related cross-functional tasks in each stage prior to obtaining management approval to proceed to the next stage of product development. The framework of the stage-gate process includes workflow and decision-flow paths and defines the supporting systems and practices necessary to ensure the ongoing smooth operation of the process (van der Duin et al., 2014).

Over the course of an NPD process, managers learn about a new product project so as to ensure successful launch. The view is that a new product project is shaped by the path of NPD activities that it has travelled. Because learning is assumed to take place over the course of the NPD process, stage-to-stage information dependency can occur. This can, potentially, trap NPD managers rather than create effective learning from end to end of the development process. For example, because decisions at each stage rely on previous decisions, errors can be locked in. Overall, stage-to-stage information dependency seems to create inflexibility that hinders successful NPD process implementation (Jespersen, 2012).

As with any prescribed approach, the stage-gate process suffers from a number of limitations:

- The process is sequential and can be slow.
- The whole process is focused on end gates rather than on the customer.
- Product concepts can be stopped or frozen too early.
- The high level of uncertainty that accompanies discontinuous new products makes the stage-gate process unsuitable for these products.

- There is a risk of stage-to-stage information dependency.
- At each stage within the process a low level of knowledge held by the gatekeeper can lead to poor judgements being made on the project.

Conversion-process models

As the name suggests, conversion-process models view new product development as numerous inputs into a 'black box' where they are converted into an output (Schon, 1967). For example, the inputs could be customer requirements, technical ideas and manufacturing capability and the output would be the product. The concept of a variety of information inputs leading to a new product is difficult to criticise, but the lack of detail elsewhere is the biggest limitation of such models.

Response models

Response models are based on the work of Becker and Whistler (1967) who used a behaviourist approach to analyse change. In particular, these models focus on the individual's or organisation's response to a new project proposal or new idea. This approach has revealed additional factors that influence the decision to accept or reject new product proposals, especially at the screening stage.

Network models

This final classification of new product development models represents the most recent thinking on the subject. The case studies in Chapters 8 and 11 highlight the process of accumulation of knowledge from a variety of different inputs, such as marketing, R&D and manufacturing. This knowledge is built up gradually over time as the project progresses from initial idea (technical breakthrough or market opportunity) through development. It is this process that forms the basis of the network models (these models are explored more fully in Berkhout et al. (2010)).

Essentially, network models emphasise the external linkages coupled with the internal activities that have been shown to contribute to successful product development. There is substantial evidence to suggest that external linkages can facilitate additional knowledge flows into the organisation, thereby enhancing the product development process. These models suggest that NPD should be viewed as a knowledge-accumulation process that requires inputs from a wide variety of sources. The model in Figure 14.14 helps to highlight the accumulation of knowledge over time. This may be thought of as a snowball gaining in size as it rolls down a snow-covered mountain.

Pause for thought

Linear models are simple and, hence, dominate NPD, but they do not reflect reality.

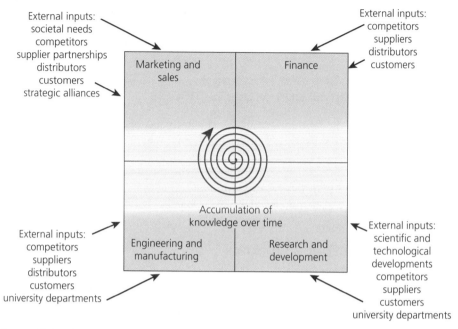

Figure 14.14 A network model of NPD

Launching innocent into the growing fruit smoothie market

Introduction

Since launching the business in 1999, innocent has not only witnessed the rise of its own business, but also the growth of the smoothie market and the rise of competitors. Whilst being the market leader with a UK market share of 80 per cent (*The Telegraph* online, 2016), it can expect fierce competition from PepsiCo as it attempts to be the dominant smoothie brand in Europe. This case study tells the story of how innocent developed a business idea into a product and launched it into the UK market with very limited funds. At that time, the smoothie market was in its infancy, although innocent was not the first into the market and could not benefit from any early entrant advantages. Nonetheless, the launch of the product coincided with the rapid growth of the market, especially in the form of own-label smoothies from Sainsbury's, Tesco and M&S.

The fruit smoothies market

Fruit smoothies are a fruit-based beverage (usually 100 per cent crushed fruit and very little else). According to the advertisements, they are nutritious and versatile, and are an excellent way of grabbing a quick meal. Smoothies have been popular in health-conscious California for many decades. They are, generally, low in fat and calories and make an excellent drink and/or snack, especially at lunchtime. Innocent is now the brand leader in the UK smoothie market, generating revenue of £80 million annually. Pete & Johnny's – the first UK smoothie company – has annual sales of £13 million whilst private-label brands make up around one-third of the market. Innocent's timing has been lucky or astute. As concern grows over rising levels of obesity in Europe, consumers are paying more attention to what they eat and drink and multinational food and beverage companies are trying to tap into changing consumer tastes by selling healthier products. Californians had been consuming fruit smoothies for a number of years before the concept was exported to the UK. It is Harry Cragoe, founder of PJ Smoothies, who is generally regarded as the first entrant into the UK in 1994. Harry had been living in California and had enjoyed fruit smoothies for lunch; when he returned to the UK he realised this drink was not available. But importing a fresh product and transporting it 8,000 miles across the world proved to be extremely difficult. Indeed, the first few years of operating were full of problems. Initially, the smoothies simply were imported in large containers. They were frozen and there were problems of them not defrosting or still being frozen when they were put on the shelves. Not surprisingly, the product was twice as expensive as other drinks at the time. Many experienced traders were doubtful such a product could succeed in such a highly competitive market. Eventually, however, Cragoe was able to establish production in Newark, Nottinghamshire, which has solved many of the initial logistical problems.

The success of the PJ Smoothie business is remarkable and unusual in that very little money has been spent on marketing and market research. This is even more remarkable for a fast-moving consumer good. Cragoe is a critic of traditional market research, arguing that 'I've never spent a penny on market research because you end up looking at it too religiously. The growth we have experienced is purely from word of mouth. People have tasted the products and told their friends. We also tried to get away from bad labelling, deciding instead to use just pictures of apples and oranges. We have always tried to be fun, relevant and interesting with our packaging.' Cragoe insists that tasting the product is the best way to experience whether it is good or bad and this has led to even more growth. He believes that 99 per cent of people like the taste and pass on the message.

Innocent and developing a new product concept

Hot on the heels of PJ Smoothies was innocent smoothies. In 2005, innocent drinks was the fastest growing food and drinks company in the UK; it was launched in 1999, and the company has grown into the No. 1 smoothie brand in the UK with 240 staff and an £80 million turnover. It has gone from making

Source: Innocent Ltd

three recipes of smoothie to seventeen different drinks. Through constant innovation and refusal to compromise, innocent continues to make an unrivalled range of totally natural fruit drinks that taste good and have health benefits. But the road to success was far from simple.

The beverage market is fiercely competitive, dominated by global players such as Coca-Cola and Pepsi. The range of beverages available is also vast, from bottled water to carbonated drinks in all flavours. The fruit smoothie product being launched was perishable, with a very short shelf life and, with a price tag at almost £2 a bottle, it was four times that of other beverages on the shelf. Achieving success was not going to be easy.

The beginnings of the business idea stretch back many years and are the result of a friendship started at university. Richard Reed, Adam Balon and Jon Wright left university and went into the obligatory milk-round professions – one into advertising, two into management consultancy. Four years later, they were still talking about their business ideas, although they still had no product. One idea they all liked and enjoyed was fruit smoothies. They all enjoyed a fruit smoothie for lunch and all had enjoyed making them at home with fresh soft fruit and an electric blender. At the time, there were very few smoothies on the shelf. In 1998, during their spare time from work and sometimes during their time at work, the three friends began planning their business idea of fruit smoothies. During this time, they continued trying out recipes on friends and developing their business plan. At the end of that time, they spent £500 on fruit, turned it into smoothies and tested their drinks on visitors to the Jazz on the Green festival in London. Their much-recounted scenario goes like this:

We put up a big sign saying, 'Do you think we should give up our jobs to make these smoothies?'

→

Figure 14.15 Innocent's own form of concept testing

and put out a bin saying 'YES' and a bin saying 'NO' and asked people to put the empty bottle in the right bin [see Figure 14.15]. At the end of the weekend the 'YES' bin was full so we went in the next day and resigned. (innocentdrinks.co.uk)

But the launch of the business took much longer than they had realised; first, there was the problem of funds. How should the entrepreneurs raise money? The options were as follows.

Raising money

When it comes to financing a business, there are two basic types of funding: debt and equity. Loans are debt financing; you borrow money and must pay it back, with interest, within a certain time frame. With equity funding, you raise money by selling a portion of your ownership in the company. This is the traditional route for people wishing to fund a start-up business, with friends and family probably the most common form of debt financiers; others are: banks, finance companies, credit unions, credit card companies and private corporations. Taking out a business loan allows the owners to remain in control of the company and not answer to investors. Getting a loan is also usually faster than searching out investors. Professional investors review thousands of investment opportunities each year, and invest in only a small fraction. Another benefit of debt financing is that as a firm repays its debts so it builds credit-worthiness. This makes the business more attractive to lenders in the future.

Overall, debt financing is typically cheaper than equity financing because the firm pays only interest and fees, and retains full ownership of the company.

Equity financing

Selling equity means taking on investors and being accountable to them. Many small business owners raise equity by bringing in relatives, friends, colleagues or customers who hope to see their businesses succeed and get a return on their investment. Other sources of equity financing include venture capitalists, which are professional investors willing to take risks on promising new businesses. These investors include individuals with substantial net worth, corporations and financial institutions (this is the group highlighted in the BBC television programme *Dragons' Den*). Most investors do not expect an immediate return on their investment, but they would expect the business to be profitable in three to seven years. Equity investors can be passive or active. Passive investors are willing to offer capital but will play little or no part in running the company, whilst active investors expect to be heavily involved in the company's operations. Personality conflicts can arise in either arrangement. Equity financing is not cheap: investors are entitled to a share of the business's profits indefinitely. Conversely, small business owners who may have difficulty securing a traditional loan or are comfortable sharing control of their business with partners may find equity financing a mutually beneficial arrangement.

Venture capital is a widely used phrase that few people properly understand. Typically, it refers to investment funds or partnerships (and, increasingly, venture capital divisions within large corporations) that focus on investing in new, promising start-up and emerging companies. Venture capitalists (VCs) have invested in some of today's most famous corporate names, including Apple, Genentech, Intel and Google. Typically, the investment is in company stock – the venture capitalist gets an ownership interest for the money invested. Beyond supplying the company with money, the VC also provides assistance and expertise with business planning – bringing industry knowledge, experience in growing businesses and expertise in taking the company public one day. Entrepreneurs should be wary; venture capitalists' primary motive is to make a lot of money on their intended investment. Furthermore, most venture capitalists are interested only in businesses that can grow very big. So, if you are a small grocery store, you should seek funds elsewhere.

Fortunately, the founders of innocent benefited from very good educations and had many business contacts from over four years working in advertising and management consultancy; hence, it was not long before they were in touch with venture capitalists. Eventually, Maurice Pinto, a wealthy US businessman, invested £250,000 and became the fourth shareholder in the group, retaining a 20 per cent stake. The money provided salaries for the three entrepreneurs, office space, cash to buy production capacity at bottling plants, promotional material and labelling for the bottles.

Product development and growing the business

Whilst, on the surface, this new business venture may seem slightly unusual, and the three founders probably would like very much to think that their business is unique, the development of their fruit smoothie product follows the well-documented process from concept to commercialisation (see Figure 14.9).

Generation of new product concepts

The three founders of innocent had been exploring and planning to start their own business ever since they met at university. They had even tried a few crazy ideas, including a gadget that would prevent baths from overflowing. It was the fruit smoothie concept, however, that seemed to appeal to the three founders the most; this is probably due largely to the fact that they were developing a new product for people like them: young urban professionals who wanted a healthy lunchtime drink to go with their sandwich. In many large cities across Europe and the USA, lunch for most is a sandwich. And, when buying your sandwich, most people usually buy a drink to wash it down. Also, the UK Government Health Department was promoting the benefits of eating more fruit and vegetables. This was a publicity campaign that innocent could use to its advantage.

Idea screening

Having a new product concept is a long way from a commercially successful new product. Moreover, this was not a completely new product; fruit smoothies had been on the market for several years, hence, innocent was entering an established market, albeit a relatively new one. Their challenge was to become more successful than the existing players. To do this,

they believed their product had to be different. They were able to achieve this through clever and very different forms of promotion. In many ways, they were developing the whole fruit smoothie market, without realising it at the time.

The main purpose of screening ideas is to select those that will be successful and drop those that will not – herein lies the difficulty. Trying to identify which ideas are going to be successful and which are not is extremely difficult. Screening product ideas is, essentially, an evaluation process. It occurs at every stage of the new product development process and involves such questions as:

1 Do we have the necessary commercial knowledge and experience?
2 Do we have the technical know-how to develop the idea further?
3 Would such a product be suitable for our business?
4 Are we sure there will be sufficient demand?

From here, more detailed evaluation checklists can be drawn up, such as the one in Table 14.5.

Concept testing

Innocent had already proved to themselves – with their unusual form of product testing using bins – that their target market liked the product. Nonetheless, starting a company from scratch is daunting. There is little room for error, so the product has to be pitched in exactly the right way. Given that this was a crowded market, innocent drinks realised early on that the product had to stand out on the shelf. Packaging is a critical issue, especially in FMCG markets. Innocent

Table 14.5 Simple evaluation checklist

	Evaluation criteria
1	Technical abilities
2	Competitive rationale
3	Patentability
4	Stability of the market
5	Integration and synergy
6	Market: growth and competition
7	Channel fit
8	Manufacturing
9	Financial
10	Longer term strategic fit

decided to develop something different. A friend of the three founders was hired to look after branding. Once again, a great deal of emphasis was placed on the fact that the three founders belonged to the target market and decisions were made based on their own thoughts and ideas, despite a lack of branding experience. Indeed, innocent confessed in interviews with the press that, 'Our user testing was done on people we knew. We'd email our friends with packaging designs.' Nonetheless, the company has always sought advice and expertise from external experts; for example, Turner Duckworth designed the original bottle shape; and innocent also used an agency for an advertising campaign in Ireland.

Design has played a big role in the product's success, from the logo and shape of the bottles to the delivery vans. Careful consideration of design and packaging has contributed to the success of the business. The brand was totally unknown, so innocent had to rely on people being intrigued enough to try the product. It is not a cheap drink, so it had to appeal to the consumer and it had to stand out and look like something you would want to pick up. Finally, like all beverage producers, innocent relied on the taste to be sufficiently good to ensure a repeat purchase.

Prototype development

Given that the three founders were the target market – young (they were all in their mid-20s), urban office workers (they all worked in Central London), affluent (they all had very well-paid jobs) – identifying what would appeal was simply a question of asking themselves: What do we like? They wanted to emphasise the purity and naturalness of the product, which is made completely from fresh fruit. This is a key point because most fruit drinks are made from concentrated juice with water – and perhaps sweeteners, colours and preservatives – added. Innocent wanted to offer pure fruit juice. This had significant manufacturing implications and problems, as they later discovered. They also wanted a bottle that would sit easily in the hand for the 'grab-a-sandwich' crowd and they wanted to introduce an element of fun. Lacking any kind of knowledge about the design process or how to go about finding and developing the right image, the company was forced to use external experts and keep things simple. According to innocent, the logo, which resembles an apple

with a halo, or a person with a halo, depending on how you look at it, was sketched on a serviette in felt-tip pen.

The creation of a brand image is crucial here and especially so for products in FMCG markets. For all new entrants into an existing market, the aim is to try to get existing users to change to your brand of fruit smoothie and to try to attract new buyers who currently purchase bottled water or Coca-Cola, for example. The brand image developed and, carefully nurtured by innocent, is one based on fun and an almost hippie approach to life. This is reflected in the packaging, promotion and logo used for the product.

Another interesting point is that, due to the high raw material costs and high production costs, initially the product offered was relatively expensive – three or four times as much as lunchtime beverage alternatives.

Market testing

Fruit is sourced from all over the world, and regular sampling is conducted at innocent's test kitchen to ensure that only the most flavoursome varieties are used in the drinks. Recipes created in the kitchen at their London offices are tested on people in surrounding office buildings. Once approved, the drinks are manufactured by one of four independent manufacturers in the UK and sold in outlets across the UK and Europe. The smoothies, which appeal to consumers whom innocent describes as 'slightly more female, slightly more affluent, slightly younger', are priced at the high end of the fruit juice market, selling for £1.79 to £1.99 in 'on the go' plastic bottles, and for £3.29 to £3.49 in larger take-home cartons. Innocent has also launched a children's range recently, retailing at £1.49.

Launch and promotion

Having developed their idea, the three founders then ran into numerous other operational difficulties that meant the launch of the product took much longer than expected. They encountered barriers, including various experts who told them their idea would not work. In particular, this was because the product's shelf life was too short. Arguments then ensued about whether or not to include preservatives or additives to lengthen its life. Ignoring most of the expert advice, innocent created a range of smoothies made from 100 per cent pure and fresh fruit. Careful quality controlled production methods and the latest packaging technology gave it the longest possible shelf life.

Innocent's first foray into the market was very modest. Out to Lunch, the local sandwich shop round the corner from their office in Ladbroke Grove, agreed to stock a few of their drinks. They supplied 20 bottles and, when they checked later, found that the drinks had sold out. Indeed, most of their early sales were through local delicatessens and sandwich shops, but it was not long before Coffee Republic, also a young and growing business, agreed to stock innocent drinks in their eight or nine shops.

Innocent has not spent large sums of money on television, press or radio promotion. Emphasis is placed on packaging design and retailers who stock and shelf the product. Advertising copy tends to be witty and straightforward, as does other communications material. The relationship with retailers has been built up through regular communication, including a newsletter, which combines product information and fun stories. Each communication is intended to reinforce the unique brand image innocent has built for itself. The copy on the labelling is intended to break down the barriers between manufacturer and customer, using humour. For example, the 'this water' labels have a section called fruit corner, which gives the fruit a personality whilst also explaining why it is good for you. See the following example about the apple:

> Apples have a long history. God put them in his garden so that Adam and Eve would have something to talk about on that awkward first date. But it all went tragically wrong; indeed, the reason why you and I feel sinful thoughts is because of that pesky apple. But apples have done a lot to improve their public image since then. William Tell did some tricks with one a few hundred years ago, and there was the one that fell out of a tree and hit Archimedes on the head, prompting him to discover fire later that day. Marvellous. (innocentdrinks.co.uk)

PepsiCo enters the smoothie market

In 2005, the maker of Pepsi dramatically entered the UK smoothie market with the purchase of the British smoothie and fruit juice brand PJ Smoothies. PepsiCo UK did not reveal the price it paid for the business, based in Newark, Nottinghamshire. PJ, launched in 1994, founded the British smoothie market and has become its leading brand. PepsiCo said PJ Smoothies is the only major brand that produces its own 100 per cent fruit smoothies and would complement its existing drinks brands Tropicana and Copella.

Future growth

Growth for many businesses can cause problems and sometimes cause a firm to fail; usually, this is because it overstretches to expand, borrows money and then runs into cash flow problems. Innocent was careful not to fall into this well-known trap, despite its dramatic growth. Innocent adopted a cautious approach with the national multiples, such as Tesco and Sainsbury's, despite the lure of multi-million-pound orders. To begin with, innocent would supply only a few of the multiples and, as sales grew and revenue came in, so the production would be increased. This is a much slower approach to growth and can sometimes allow competitors to enter the market or allow the multiples themselves to develop own-label versions. Nonetheless, innocent adopted the prudent approach, which seems to have paid off.

In 2009, innocent employed over 250 people and slowly expanded along the line of industrial units rented by the company. Innocent recorded turnover of £80 million in 2006 and was growing at an annual rate of 50 to 60 per cent. Innocent now supplies most of the major supermarkets and, this year, became Britain's leading brand of smoothie, selling, it calculates, about 72 per cent of the 50 million smoothies downed annually by British drinkers. If imitation is the sincerest form of flattery, then innocent's founders should feel very pleased. The refrigerated shelves of the nation's supermarkets are filled with own-label versions of some of the company's best sellers, such as its yogurt, vanilla bean and honey 'thickie'. But this could present a serious challenge to the firm. Innocent would not be the first manufacturer to lose out to own-label multiples like Sainsbury's, Tesco and Asda.

Also, there would seem to be many opportunities for future growth. Innocent is still aware that, whilst the business has grown extremely fast, there are still plenty of people who have not yet tasted innocent drinks. Innocent is continuing to extend its product line with new flavours of smoothies and a new product launched in 2003 called Juicy Water, whose packaging was designed by Coley Porter Bell. Innocent's main market is still the UK and Ireland, which accounts

→

for 90 per cent of its sales, but its smoothies are also sold in The Netherlands, Belgium, Luxembourg and France. It eventually plans to expand within and beyond Europe. 'We have the trademark registered in every country that we think it can become business relevant.' These include the USA, Australia, New Zealand, China, India and countries in South America.

Like any growing business, maintaining innocent's internal culture as the company expands is going to be a challenge. Much will depend on the rate of growth and whether the company will be able to control this growth. Clearly, employing the right people as the business expands, both in the UK and overseas, will be one of the significant challenges.

Many analysts argue that innocent is one of a new breed of virtual food and drink companies. Such companies develop the brand and outsource production. There is a division of labour between the owner of the brand and the manufacturer. Other such firms include: Green & Black's, the organic chocolate company; Duchy Originals, which sells organic foods; and Gu Chocolate Puds. These smaller food companies have found there is demand for products made with natural or organic ingredients and low in fats, sugars and salts. Whilst larger food companies have been altering product ingredients to try to address consumer concerns, smaller companies have been quicker at creating products that meet specific demands. The success of these companies in identifying changes in consumer tastes has made them attractive acquisition targets; for example, in May 2005 Green & Black's was bought by Cadbury Schweppes for £20 million.

The global recession blew a cold wind through the UK smoothies market. During the recession, people understandably tried to cut their costs. The high-priced fruit smoothies have, consequently, suffered. In addition, people have tended to abandon new products for ones they know and trust. For example, in 2010, Pepsi, Robinson's squash and the children's drink Fruit Shoot were amongst Britvic's best-selling brands. According to some analysts, the UK smoothies market fell by 30 per cent in value in 2010. Innocent sales fell by 28 per cent in 2008 and 29 per cent in 2009. Sales in 2009 were £94 million. More worrying is that premium high street brands such as Waitrose and M&S have introduced own label competing products. The future for innocent looks more difficult now than at any time in the past

five years. After years of growth, the going has now got tough.

Coca-Cola buys innocent

In 2010, Coca-Cola took a minority shareholding in innocent when it bought out original backer Maurice Pinto and his friend Jules Hydleman, who first invested £250,000 into the business. This cost Coca-Cola £30 million for a 20 per cent stake. Later the same year, Coca-Cola paid another £65 million to increase its ownership to 58 per cent. In 2013, Coca-Cola decided to purchase almost all of the 42 per cent stake the founders had retained for around £100 million.

The sale makes good sense. Coca-Cola has huge distribution power and should be able to ensure innocent finds its way on to more store shelves. As always with new products, the extent to which additional sales are created or new sales simply cannibalise existing sales from another brand will remain to be seen. In the long term, this brand does offer Coca-Cola a strategy to move away from a reliance on fizzy soda. The UK soft drinks market share, based on value, is shown in Table 14.6.

Conclusions

The success of innocent is remarkable, partly because this is such a competitive market in which some of the world's largest brands operate and partly

Table 14.6 UK soft drinks market share based on value

Brand	Share of market value %
Coca-Cola	26.6
Private label	18.5
Britvic	11.5
Lucozade Ribena Suntory	7.8
Danone	5.5
Tropicana UK	4.3
Red Bull	3.5
Innocent	2.8
Barrs	3.1
Nestlé Waters	2.2

Source: Britvic Soft Drinks Review 2015, with permission from The Nielsen Company.

because this success has been achieved unconventionally with minimal use of traditional advertising and promotional techniques. The development and launch of its business, and new product in particular, follows a conventional approach from concept to market, but innocent has used some very different approaches along the way. According to innocent, there are some important factors that have contributed to its success. These are:

1 Keeping your potential customer's tastes, lifestyle and personality clearly in view.
2 Keeping designs simple and practical and concentrating on the quality of the product can be the key to standing out in an overcrowded market.
3 The brand image has to consistently reflect the product and the company's values.
4 Getting the product, packaging and marketing design right before diversifying and expanding will help establish the product.
5 How should innocent respond to falling sales and market share?

The founders of innocent perhaps project an image of being hippies who have emerged from a travelling caravan to start a drinks business and who are now investing all the profits into Third World social programmes. However, these friends had a privileged upbringing (one of them attending Winchester College, one of the world's most expensive private schools), gained even more knowledge from four years at university and then gained a further four years of practical experience working for large corporate city firms in London advising others on how to run a business. Although the promotional material might suggest a 'devil may care' attitude to life, the three were involved in meticulous planning of their business idea. For example, even when they had decided on their business idea and began planning it, they adopted a cautious approach by negotiating two months' leave from their employers as opposed to simply leaving employment.

Turning to another company and a similar scenario, but this time with ice cream, two self-confessed hippies built an ice cream brand in the 1980s on their socially conscious image – Ben & Jerry's 'all natural' ice cream – and then sold to the conglomerate Unilever for $326 million. It seems innocent sold out to Coca-Cola for £200 million. This is understandable; after all, business is about making money. Let us hope few people ever believed in the 'hippie' brand and the myth that the product and brand was, in some way, different from the other drink producers.

Source: *The Telegraph* (2016) http://www.telegraph.co.uk/finance/newsbysector/retailandconsumer/11736650/The-smoothie-operator-hoping-to-gobble-market-share-from-Innocent.html

Questions

1 Innocent is very clear about the image it wishes to project to the public. This is one based on being different, fun-loving and having a care-free approach to life. This hippie-style image has helped the brand become acceptable to the young urban professionals at which it is aimed. But beneath the surface of this image there is evidence of a business that could be characterised as single-minded, profit-driven and very business orientated. Where is the evidence of the latter?
2 The success of the business is based partly on extremely good communications with retailers. How is this achieved?
3 What type of financing did innocent secure? Does it matter?
4 Would you have sold the company to Coca-Cola for £200 million? As one of the shareholders you would have pocketed tens of millions of pounds. If not, why not?
5 Innocent benefited from a key advantage: what was this and explain how it helped in the product development process.
6 How is innocent 'virtual' and how is this different from traditional food and drink manufacturers? What advantages and disadvantages does this provide?
7 Use CIM (Figure 1.9) to illustrate the innovation process.

Chapter summary

This chapter has considered the relationship between new products and prosperity and shown that new product development is one of the most common forms of organic growth strategies. The range of NPD strategies is wide indeed and can range from packaging alterations to new technological research. The chapter stressed the importance of viewing a product as a multi-dimensional concept.

The later part of the chapter focused on the various models of NPD that have emerged over the past 50 years. All of these have strengths and weaknesses. By their very nature, models attempt to capture and portray a complex notion and, in so doing, often oversimplify elements. This is the central argument of critics of the linear model of NPD, that it is too simplistic and does not provide for any feedback or concurrent activities. More recent models, such as network models, try to emphasise the importance of the external linkages in the NPD process.

Discussion questions

1 Explain why the process of new product development frequently is represented as a linear process and why this does not reflect reality.

2 Explain why screening should be viewed as a continual rather than a one-off activity.

3 Discuss how the various groups of NPD models have contributed to our understanding of the subject of NPD.

4 To what extent has BMW repositioned the Mini?

5 Examine the concept of a multi-dimensional product; how is it possible to create a new product by modifying the price dimension?

6 The software industry seems to have a very flexbile NPD process enabling changes to be made to the product at any time. Consider whether this approach could be applicable for a car production line or mobile phone handset products.

7 Explain why time to market may be less important than a flexible NPD process.

8 Discuss the strengths of network models of NPD.

Key words and phrases

New product lines *494*

Line additions *494*

Cost reductions *495*

Repositioning *495*

Line extensions *495*

New-to-the-world products *497*

Departmental-stage models *503*

Activity-stage models and concurrent engineering *503*

Cross-functional models (teams) *503*

Decision-stage models *503*

Conversion-process models *503*

Response models *503*

Network models *503*

References

Abernathy, W.L. and Utterback, J. (1978) 'Patterns of industrial innovation', in Tushman, M.L. and Moore, W.L. (eds) *Readings in Management of Innovation*, HarperCollins, New York, 97–108.

Allen, T.J. (1969) Communication networks in R&D laboratories, *R&D Management*, vol. 1, 14–21.

Allen, T.J. (1977) *Managing the Flow of Technology*, MIT Press, Cambridge, MA.

Ansoff, I. (1968) *Toward a Strategy of the Theory of the Firm*, McGraw-Hill, New York.

Arlidge, J. (2006) Versace says ciao to bling and excess, *The Sunday Times*, 28 May, 6–8.

Barczak, G., Griffin, A. and Kahn, K.B. (2009) Perspective: Trends and drivers of success in NPD practices: results of the 2003 PDMA Best Practices Study, *Journal of Product Innovation Management*, vol. 26, no. 1, 3–23.

Becker, S. and Whistler, T.I. (1967) The innovative organisation: a selective view of current theory and research, *Journal of Business*, vol. 40, no. 4, 462–9.

Berkhout, G., Hartmann, D. and Trott, P. (2010) Connecting technological capabilities with market needs using a cyclic innovation model, *R&D Management*, vol. 40, no. 5, 474–90.

Bhat, S. and Reddy, S.K. (1998) Symbolic and functional positioning of brands, *Journal of Consumer Marketing*, vol. 15, no. 1, 32–43.

Bingham, F.G. and Raffield, B.T. (1995) *Business Marketing Management*, South Western Publishing, Cincinnati, OH.

Biemans, W., Griffin, A. and Moenaert, R. (2010) In search of the classics: a study of the impact of *JPIM* papers from 1984 to 2003, *Journal of Product Innovation Management*, vol. 27, 461–84.

Bogers, M. and Horst, W. (2014) Collaborative prototyping: cross-fertilization of knowledge in prototype-driven problem solving, *Journal of Product Innovation Management*, vol. 31: 744–64.

Booz, Allen & Hamilton (1982) *New Product Management for the 1980s*, Booz, Allen & Hamilton, New York.

Brown, J.S. and Eisenhardt, K.M. (1998) *Competing on the Edge – Strategy as Structured Chaos*, Harvard Business School, Boston, MA.

Brown, S.L. and Eisenhardt, K.M. (1995) Product development: past research, present findings and future directions, *Academy of Management Review*, vol. 20, no. 2, 343–78.

Cooper, R.G. (1999) From experience: the invisible success factors in product innovation, *Journal of Product Innovation Management*, vol. 16, no. 2, 115–33.

Cooper, R.G. and Edgett, S.J. (2008) Maximizing productivity in product innovation, *Research Technology Management*, March.

Corrocher, N. and Zirulia, L. (2010) Demand and innovation in services: the case of mobile communications, *Research Policy*, vol. 39, no. 7, 945–55.

Crawford, C.M. and Di Benedetto, C.A. (2014) *New Products Management*, 11th edn, Tata McGraw-Hill Education.

de Brentani, U. and Reid, S.E. (2012) The fuzzy front-end of discontinuous innovation: insights for research and management, *Journal of Product Innovation Management*, vol. 29: 70–87.

Finger, S. and Dixon, J.R. (1989a) A review of research in mechanical engineering design, part I: Descriptive, prescriptive, and computer-based models of design processes, *Research in Engineering Design*, vol. 1, no. 1, 51–68.

Finger, S. and Dixon, J.R. (1989b) A review of research in mechanical engineering design, part II: Representations, analysis, and design for the life cycle, *Research in Engineering Design*, vol. 1, no. 2, 121–37.

Franke, N. and Piller, F. (2004) Value creation by toolkits for user innovation and design: the case of the watch market, *Journal of Product Innovation Management*, vol. 21, no. 6, 401–16.

IDA (1986) *The Role of Concurrent Engineering in Weapons Systems Acquisition*, report R–338, IDA Washington, DC.

Imai, K., Ikujiro, N. and Takeuchi, H. (1985) 'Managing the new product development process: how Japanese companies learn and unlearn', in Hayes, R.H., Clark, K. and Lorenz, C. (eds) *The Uneasy Alliance: Managing the Productivity–Technology Dilemma*, 337–75, Harvard Business School Press, Boston, MA.

Jespersen, K.R. (2012) Stage-to-stage information dependency in the NPD process: effective learning or a potential entrapment of NPD gates? *Journal of Product Innovation Management*, vol. 29, 257–74.

Johne, F.A. and Snelson, P.A. (1988) The role of marketing specialists in product development, Proceedings of the 21st Annual Conference of the Marketing Education Group, Huddersfield, vol. 3, 176–91.

Johnson, S.C. and Jones, C. (1957) How to organise for new products, *Harvard Business Review*, May–June, vol. 35, 49–62.

Kettunen, P. (2009) Adopting key lessons from agile manufacturing to agile software product development – a comparative study, *Technovation*, vol. 29, nos 6–7, 408–22.

Kim, J. and Wilemon, D. (2002) Focusing the fuzzy front end in new product development, *R&D Management*, vol. 32, no. 4, 269–79.

Krishnan, V. and Ulrich, K.T. (2001) Product development decisions: a review of the literature, *Management Science*, vol. 47, no. 1, 1–21.

Mahr, D., Lievens, A. and Blazevic, V. (2014) The value of customer cocreated knowledge during the innovation process, *Journal of Product Innovation Management*, vol. 31, 599–615.

Myers, S. and Marquis, D.G. (1969) Successful industrial innovation: a study of factors underlying innovation and selected firms, National Science Foundation, NSF 69–17, Washington.

Nambisan, S. (2002) Designing virtual customer environments for new product development: toward a theory, *Academy of Management Review*, vol. 27, no. 3, 392–413.

Nonaka, I. and Takeuchi, H. (1995) *The Knowledge Creating Company*, Oxford University Press, Oxford.

Park, J.-W., Kim, K.-H. and Kim, J. (2002) 'Acceptance of brand extensions: interactive influences of product category similarity, typicality of claimed benefits, and brand relationship quality', in Broniarczyk, S. and Nakamoto, K. (eds) *Advances in Consumer Research*, vol. 29, Association for Consumer Research, Valdosta, GA.

Rogers, E. and Shoemaker, R. (1972) *Communications of Innovations*, Free Press, New York.

Rothwell, R., Freeman, C., Horlsey, A., Jervis, V.T.P., Robertson, A.B. and Townsend, J. (1974) SAPPHO updated: Project SAPPHO phase II, *Research Policy*, vol. 3, 258–91.

Saunders, J. and Jobber, D. (1994) Product replacement: strategies for simultaneous product deletion and launch, *Journal of Product Innovation Management*, vol. 11, no. 5, 433–50.

Schon, D. (1967) Champions for radical new inventions, *Harvard Business Review*, March–April, 77–86.

Slater, S.F., Mohr, J.J. and Sengupta, S. (2014) Radical product innovation capability: literature review, synthesis, and illustrative research propositions, *Journal of Product Innovation Management*, vol. 31, no. 3, 552–66.

Smith, P.G. (2007) *Flexible Product Development: Building Agility for Changing Markets*, John Wiley and Sons, New York.

Smith, M.R.H. (1981) Paper presented to the National Conference on Quality and Competitiveness, London, November, reported in *Financial Times*, 25 November.

Stevens, E. (2014). Fuzzy front-end learning strategies: exploration of a high-tech company, *Technovation*, vol. 34, no. 8, 431–40.

Tauber, E.M. (1981) Brand franchise extension: new product benefits from existing brand names, *Business Horizons*, vol. 24, no. 2, 36–41.

Thomke, S.H. (2003) *Experimentation Matters: Unlocking the Potential of New Technologies for Innovation*, Harvard Business School Press, Boston, MA.

van der Duin, P.A., Ortt, J.R. and Aarts, W.T.M. (2014) Contextual innovation management using a stage-gate platform: the case of philips shaving and beauty, *Journal of Product Innovation Management*, vol. 31, 489–500.

von Hippel, E. (1986) Lead users: a source of novel product concepts, *Management Science*, vol. 32, no. 7, 791–805.

von Hippel, E. (2001) Perspective: user toolkits for innovation, *Journal of Product Innovation Management*, vol. 18, 247–57.

Weyland, R. and Cole, P. (1997) *Customer Connections*, Harvard Business School Press, Boston, MA.

Yakimov, R. and Beverland, M. (2004) Brand repositioning capabilities: enablers of ongoing brand management, Australia and New Zealand Marketing Academy (ANZMAC) Conference, 27 November–1 December, University of Wellington, Victoria, NZ.

Further reading

For a more detailed review of the new product development literature, the following develop many of the issues raised in this chapter:

Barczak, G., Griffin, A. and Kahn, K.B. (2009) Perspective: Trends and drivers of success in NPD practices: results of the 2003 PDMA Best Practices Study, *Journal of Product Innovation Management*, vol. 26, no. 1, 3–23.

Biemans, W., Griffin, A. and Moenaert, R. (2010) In search of the classics: A study of the impact of *JPIM* papers from 1984 to 2003, *Journal of Product Innovation Management*, vol. 27, 461–84.

Cooper R.G. and Edgett, S.J. (2008) Maximizing productivity in product innovation, *Research Technology Management*, March.

de Medeiros, J.F., Ribeiro, J.L.D. and Cortimiglia, M.N. (2014) Success factors for environmentally sustainable product innovation: a systematic literature review, *Journal of Cleaner Production*, vol. 65, 76–86.

Gmelin, H. and Seuring, S. (2014) Determinants of a sustainable new product development, *Journal of Cleaner Production*, vol. 69, 1–9.

Slater, S.F., Mohr, J.J. and Sengupta, S. (2014) Radical product innovation capability: literature review, synthesis, and illustrative research propositions, *Journal of Product Innovation Management*, vol. 31, no. 3, 552–66.

Chapter 15
New service innovation

Introduction

In Europe and the USA services now account for an increasing share of the gross domestic product of these economies, yet compared to new product development, we know relatively little about managing innovation within services. This chapter explores the growth in services and helps to explain some of the factors behind this shift in the balance of activities within economies. It identifies the pivotal role played by technology in facilitating the development of many new service opportunities, most notably internet-related technologies. This chapter also examines how new services are created and what firms need to do to enhance their new service development activities. Finally, the case study at the end of this chapter illustrates how eBay has used service innovation to grow the business and profits for the firm.

Chapter contents

Learning objectives

When you have completed this chapter you will be able to:

- recognise the reasons for the growth in services;
- recognise the wide range of different types of services;
- explain how new services have led to the creation of new business models;
- examine the pivotal role technology plays in new service innovation;
- explain the role of a classification of service innovations; and
- explain the role of the consumer in the new service development process.

The growth in services

The term knowledge-based economy has been introduced to characterise some of the main changes in the development of economies over the past 20 years. In the most advanced service economies in the world, such as the United States and the United Kingdom, services now account for up to three-quarters of the wealth and 85 per cent of employment (Barrett et al., 2015). Within the EU, services now account for 73.6 per cent of the EU-28's total gross value added in 2013 (Eurostat, 2015). But, when it comes to innovation, how should we view services?

Traditionally, the literature has viewed services as different from products; this is because 'innovation theory' has been developed around science and technological development. The **intangibility** of services clearly makes it difficult for the traditional view to embrace or understand innovation within services. But the development of internet-based firms, such as eBay (see case study at end of chapter), with its community of users driving the development of new services, is clear evidence of innovation outputs within services – even if technology is a key antecedent.

The influence of technology, in general, and information communication technologies, in particular, cannot be overstated. In virtually all industries, there has been a huge growth in specialist knowledge and skills being made available to firms. For example, in civil engineering and architecture, where previously much of the input came from the architect, now the architect employs a range of specialists from, for instance, fire engineering, acoustic engineers, lighting designers, etc. A new range of disciplines has emerged offering specialist knowledge and skills. This has been replicated in virtually all industries (Barrett et al., 2015; Papastathopoulou and Hultink, 2012).

Growth in knowledge-intensive business services (KIBS)

Occasionally, one would be forgiven for thinking that, in these advanced developed economies, services had replaced all manufacturing activities, and there had simply been a huge growth in coffee bars, smoothie bars and hair salons. The truth is that the development of these economies has led to a massive increase in the amount of specialised business services, which now provide critical inputs to firms in all sectors. It is this area of the economy (United States and Europe) that has witnessed huge expansion and development. It is not simply that people are spending more time and money in hair salons (though that may also be true). It is these **knowledge-intensive business services (KIBS)** that are the key behind the development of the service side of the economies. KIBS include traditional professional business services, such as accountancy and law, but also a new generation of KIBS. Illustration 15.1 shows how the provision of very specialist services to the oil industry has led to huge growth for Halliburton and Schlumberger, the world market leader for oil services.

The growth in information communication technologies during the 1980s and the development of the internet in the 1990s and into the twenty-first century, has led to enormous sums of money being spent by firms in order to ensure that they are equipped to compete. In addition, the introduction of some of these business systems, such as enterprise resource planning systems (ERP), has led to significant reductions in costs and improvements in efficiency. If one then adds to the KIBS the huge growth in entertainment industries, including the gaming industry (Xbox,

Illustration 15.1

Huge growth in oil services

Providing services to oil companies has been an even better business than finding and producing oil in recent years. Since the start of 2003, Exxon Mobil's shares have roughly doubled; those of Royal Dutch Shell's, now the runner-up amongst Western oil majors, have risen about 40 per cent. But shares in Halliburton and Schlumberger, the world market leader for oil services, have more than tripled. Scarcity of equipment and skilled personnel at a time of bumper investment in oil exploration and production have sent the costs of oil services soaring. Despite the slump in oil price, oil services in the global oil field services market is expected to grow from $350 billion in 2014 to $521 billion in 2018.

Source: Pearson Education Ltd/Digital Vision

Nintendo, PlayStation, PC games, etc.), the new online gambling industry (such as market leader bwin.party digital entertainment) and the more recent social networking industry (which includes Facebook, Twitter, LinkedIn, Pinterest), one begins to recognise just how much change and growth there has been to economies over the past 10 years. In painting this picture of change that continues to take place in developed economies around the world, we also need to include the biggest internet players, such as Google, Amazon, Apple and Microsoft, and we all recognise the enormous impact the online retailers and the internet search engine firms have on our lives. The transfer of knowledge is one of the key functions of knowledge intensive business services (KIBS). Research by Fernandes and Farreira (2013) shows that cooperation between KIBS and universities is increasing and has a positive impact on the company's capacity to innovate.

Pause for thought

With previously internal activities now simply being outsourced, is the growth in services simply a mirage?

Outsourcing and service growth

Outsourcing has become very widespread in the last decade and has moved on from limited applications where peripheral business functions are 'outsourced' to much more vital business functions being outsourced today, such as IT support (Edvardsson and Durst, 2014; del-Río-Ortega et al., 2015). Despite the rather mixed record of large-scale, long-term total outsourcing deals with single suppliers in particular in the IT/IS industry, such contracts are still entered into in significant numbers. The academic literature has identified a number of expected gains that companies can derive from outsourcing. These include:

- the reduction of operational costs;
- the ability to transform fixed costs into variable costs;
- the ability to focus on core competencies;
- access to the industry-leading external competencies and expertise.

There seems little doubt that the growth in services is linked to this enormous growth in outsourcing, with many firms now buying in 'services' that previously were undertaken in-house. So, whether it is catering facilities within schools now being bought from local providers by the County Education Authority or whether it is a firm buying in information technology (IT) support rather than providing the service themselves, the evidence is overwhelming that this growth in outsourcing has contributed to the growth in services (Edvardsson and Durst, 2014). Coupled to this debate, however, is the suggestion that manufacturers are now moving into highly profitable knowledge-intensive services. This is certainly the case at IBM, which has moved successfully from manufacturer to service solution provider with its profits now being dominated by IT services. For some firms, lower production costs in India and China are forcing them downstream into the provision of services. For other firms, like IBM and Ericsson, it is recognition that they can offer added value market offerings to their customers by providing additional services. Within sectors of complex products and systems (CoPS), buyers are outsourcing non-core activities and focusing on the provision of services to the final customer. In the pharmaceutical industry, for example, clinical trials that previously were undertaken by the firm are now outsourced to clinical trial specialist firms. Illustration 15.2 shows how firms, including Yahoo and Cisco, are all outsourcing activities to India. Indeed, India is now viewed as a knowledge services cluster (KSC). KSCs are defined as geographic concentrations of lower-cost skills serving global demand for increasingly commoditised knowledge services (Manning, 2013).

There is, however, also an emerging literature that highlights the weaknesses and risks associated with large-scale outsourcing arrangements, in particular, where non-peripheral business functions are concerned. This highlights the risk of becoming dependent on a supplier and draws our attention to other hidden costs of outsourcing, such as the possibility of a loss of vital know-how, in particular with respect to core competencies, as a major risk factor in outsourcing. There is also the problem of selecting the most suited supplier/service provider and their longer-term ability to offer the capabilities that are needed, in particular in business environments with rapid technology change (Edvardsson and Durst, 2014). Another risk that often is overlooked is linked to the broader area of information leakage that arises when business organisations collaborate in order to gain access to knowledge and expertise that they cannot develop on their own. Research by Hoecht and Trott (2006) has demonstrated that there is trade-off between access to cutting-edge knowledge via collaborative research and technology development in knowledge-intensive industries and the risk of losing commercially sensitive knowledge to competitors. This risk, they argue, cannot be controlled by traditional management approaches and legal contracting alone, but requires the operation of social control and, in particular, the development of trust to be contained. Table 15.1 offers a summary of the main risks.

Illustration 15.2

India and globalisation: investing in R&D for service innovation

In 2003, Yahoo set up a small office in Bangalore – its office's head count was fewer than 20 people. Today, the Bangalore office has 1,000 computer scientists and engineers in what is Yahoo's largest research and development centre outside its California headquarters. Today, Yahoo's R&D operation in Bangalore takes on advanced work, such as developing new services for Yahoo users that might be launched globally.

Large pools of highly skilled, English-speaking engineers and computer scientists hired at lower cost than in the developed world are an important factor. Yet, companies are setting up R&D centres for reasons that go beyond cost savings.

Cisco, the world's largest maker of network switches and routers, has made one of the largest R&D commitments to India. Cisco chose India as the location from which to expand its globalisation vision because India has a highly skilled workforce, supportive government, innovative customers and world-class partners.

India has benefited in a huge growth in services as it reaps the benefits of firms offshoring activities to low wage economies such as India. The extent of knowledge transfer and functional collaboration across distances and cultures is unknown, but economists would expect India to benefit in the long term. Questions remain, of course, such as: the existence and maintenance of a non-offshore corporate strategic 'core' and

Source: Chris Stowers/Getty Images

whether the movement of offshoring up the value chain, ultimately, gravely threatens that core?

Source: Norlander, P., Erickson, C., Kuruvilla, S. and Kannan-Narasimhan, R. (2015) India's outsourcing industry and the offshoring of skilled services work: a review essay, *E-Journal of International and Comparative Labour Studies*, vol. 4, no. 1

Table 15.1 Main outsourcing risks

Main negative outcomes of outsourcing
1 Dependence on the supplier
2 Hidden costs
3 Loss of competencies
4 Service provider's lack of necessary capabilities
5 Social risk
6 Inefficient management

Different types of services

The service sector is vast and it varies considerably from public services in the form of state-funded education for 97 per cent of children in the United Kingdom to specialist business services in the form of internet website design and maintenance. Each sector of the service economy (such as leisure, charities, public services, financial services) has its own set of specific challenges. Yet, at the same time, the distinctions between some of these sectors is blurring. Some charities and not-for-profit organisations are offering their services to compete with the private sector. Healthcare provision is a prime example. Similarly, some public-funded organisations, such as the BBC, offer their services in the commercial world and generate large revenue streams. The BBC iPlayer now competes with commercial players such as YouTube and others. Table 15.2 offers a classification of services and includes professional business services, such as accountancy, and public services, such as libraries. This overview helps demystify the service notion. It clarifies the different sectors within services and illustrates the different challenges facing each sector (Empson et al., 2015; Papastathopoulou and Hultink, 2012).

Table 15.2 Typology of services

	Business-to-business services (traditional)	Business-to-business services (KIBS)	Consumer services	Internal firm services	Public services	Not-for-profit services
Description	Services provided for businesses	Specialist services provided to businesses	Services provided to individuals	Services provided by internal functions	Services provided by local and national government	Services provided by charities
Examples	Accountancy Legal advice Training	Management consultancy IT consultancy	Shops Hotels Banking	Finance Personnel IT	Health Education Leisure	Hospices Counselling Aid agencies
Customers	Frequently purchased by professionals, who may not be end users	Frequently purchased by professionals, who may not be end users	Health and beauty Purchased by consumer of the service	Consumers of the service have no choice of provider	Prisons Funded Purchased by consumer of the service	Funded through charities, maybe government grants; consumers chosen or choose
Challenges	Providing high-quality tailored and personal service	Providing high-quality services to businesses that have high purchasing power	Providing a consistent service to a wide variety of customers	Delivering customised, personal service, and demonstrating value for money	Delivering acceptable public services against a backcloth of political pressures	Balancing needs of volunteers, donors and overwhelming needs of customers

Source: Adapted from Johnston, R. and Clark, G. (2012) *Service Operations Management*, 4th edn, Prentice Hall, © Pearson Education Ltd., Harlow; and Empson, L., Muzio, D., Broschak, J. and Hinings, B. (2015) *Researching Professional Service Firms: An Introduction and Overview*.

An area of service innovation that is seeing huge change and growth is that of e-healthcare services. Often, these are associated with the healthcare and wellbeing need of the elderly and/or people with chronic diseases. Yet, the current growth is in services for the 'worried well', those so-called people who are healthy, but overly concerned with their own health. This group is willing to pay a substantial premium to secure e-healthcare services, such as blood-tests and many other treatments (Chen et al., 2014).

From the perspective of innovation, however, we are less concerned with the type of organisation or even the industry sector in which it operates. We are more concerned with how the service is managed and, in particular, how it is designed and operated. In order to investigate this area, it is useful to separate out the wide range of services undertaken. For example, services in Table 15.2 range from bespoke specialist industry services to homogenised customer services found within fast-food restaurants. One way is to use the two key parameters: volume of transactions within a certain amount of time and the variety of tasks to be carried out by a given set of people and processes. At one end of the spectrum is a service we are all familiar with: that of fast-food restaurants where the volume is high and process variety is low. This type of service can be classified clearly as a commodity. Whereas, at the other end of the spectrum, we have specialist business services, such as internet website design, where the volume is low and process variety is very high (the designer can draw upon a limitless amount of imagination). Johnston and Clark (2012) have developed a simple matrix that helps to capture the different types of service processes (see Figure 15.1). On the vertical axis is process variety and on the horizontal axis is volume per unit, with fast-food restaurants sitting in the bottom right-hand quadrant as a commodity service process and internet website design sitting in the top left-hand corner. It is capability-based service processes where the

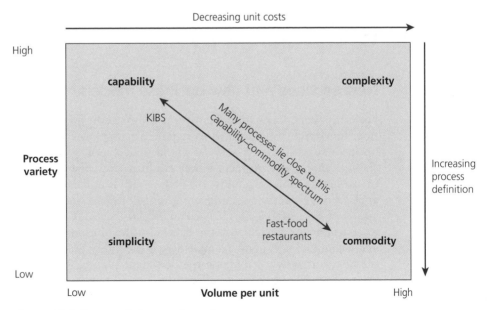

Figure 15.1 Four main types of service processes

Source: Johnston, R. and Clark, G. (2012) *Service Operations Management*, 4th edn, Prentice Hall, Harlow, © Pearson Education Ltd.

provider frequently works with the customer to clarify the problem and/or to develop a customised solution, such as management consultants and web designers.

Technology and new service development

Business opportunities based on new technology developments have been (and continue to be) identified and exploited by entrepreneurial individuals, leading to the creation of multinational businesses. Indeed, technology has become the most significant enabler of innovation in services. The application of different technologies in the context of existing service products has changed the way services are delivered and, thereby, gave rise to the development of highly innovative service products. For example, the internet technology that gave rise to the development of e-commerce has brought radical transformations in consumers' shopping practices. In contrast to the increasing significance of technology in the development of innovative services in practice, literature has largely overlooked and failed to explain the role technology plays in the development of new services (Boone, 2000; Menor et al., 2002). Technology changes the nature of service development in many ways: it can reduce the tasks of service developers by empowering customers with certain technical mechanisms, such as user toolkits. Therefore, the effect of technology is evident in transforming the roles of both employees and customers. Within this framework, technology also increases the organisational socialisation by easing the connectivity between service developers and customers (cf. Bitran and Pedrosa, 1998). Indeed, **new service development** processes that traditionally have been undertaken by marketing departments now have to involve technology teams in the development of technology-based services. Technology may also transform the structure of new service development processes. Service firms that have insufficient capabilities to develop a particular technological service may outsource service production. Illustration 15.2 shows how a variety of firms are utilising skills and resources in India to deliver and develop services.

New services and new business models

For many years, innovation literature overlooked the concept of new service innovation. Innovation was deemed to require a new physical 'thing'. But the world of business suggested new services could deliver potentially even more significant changes than new products – they could deliver new business models. The one caveat here is that, frequently, the new service is underpinned by a new technology application. Nonetheless, there are a range of firms that have introduced new services that have completely changed an industry sector. Customers usually are unable to conceptualise or visualise the benefits of revolutionary new products, concepts and technologies. A good example here is the online auction concept; eBay was not the first, but slowly it became the dominant player. Ryanair was the first in the European market to offer a budget airline service, where the price of an airfare was cut in return for a cut-down service. Ryanair identified that, within Europe, the short flying times meant that customers did not always value the extra tariff for additional services and preferred a discounted ticket price over extra services. Within the airline industry others, most notably Flybe, have continued with new service

Table 15.3 A range of new services that also create new business models

Company	Industry sector	New service/new business model
Airbnb	Accommodation	A website for people to list, find and rent lodging
eBay	Online auction	A way of buying and selling through a community of individual users
Uber	Transportation	Smartphone users can organise private trip requests from Uber drivers who use their own car
Ryanair	Airline	A way of consuming air travel with no-frills service and emphasis on economy
Zoopla	Finance	A way to lend and borrow money online
Napster; iTunes, Spotify	Music retailer	A way to buy and download music
Google	Internet search engine	A fast way to search for information on the internet
bwin.party digital entertainment	Online gambling, e.g. poker	Gambling and gaming from your own home
Facebook	Social networking	A community of users online who can chat and share music, images and news from their own home
YouTube	Online video and film archive	A community of users sharing home-made video clips plus recorded favourite film clips

innovations. In 2006, Flybe launched the first online check-in facility – Q-Buster. It was also the first to provide customers with the online ability to select seats in advance. Table 15.3 illustrates how other service innovations have revolutionised an industry sector.

Pause for thought

It seems services are so diverse that they cover almost every aspect of business. Even tangible products, such as cars, are now wrapped in services. Should we separate services from products?

Characteristics of services and how they differ from products

Within marketing literature, many differences between goods and services are discussed. Significantly, these differences are referred to as characteristics of services and are identified as intangibility, heterogeneity and simultaneity, i.e. the three key characteristics that distinguish services from products, with interaction with the consumer the key distinguishing characteristic in service development. Moreover, the literature suggests that, whilst offer development, process development and market development occur simultaneously, in those industries where services dominate it is process development that is significant. Frequently, this has involved a fundamental rethink and redesign of business processes resulting in radically new offerings, such as the purchase of airline seats using the internet, including the ability to select one's

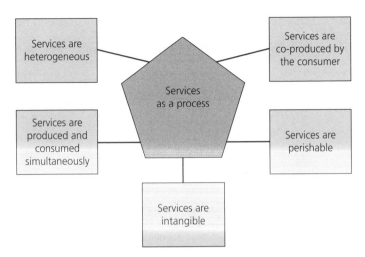

Figure 15.2 Services as a process

preferred seat on the aircraft at the time of making the reservation (see Table 15.3). Whichever service one considers, it involves a number of activities which, when linked together, can be described as a process. Figure 15.2 shows the key characteristics of services. In a study of the top 500 service firms and top 100 financial firms in Taiwan, Jaw et al. (2010) found that service characteristics of heterogeneity and perishability and market orientation positively influence a firm's resources and innovation.

Classification of service innovations

In services, often it is not feasible to distinguish product and process innovation due to the simultaneous production and consumption of services. The service product is the core of the new service offering, consisting of the essential functional benefit(s) conveyed by the service. Service process innovation, on the other hand, is a new service delivery system. Boone (2000) states that process technology innovation often is utilised to increase efficiency (reducing operational costs) and effectiveness (i.e. reducing time costs, improving quality and increasing flexibility) of firms and their offerings. Innovation in services does not always necessitate changes in the core service-offering characteristics. A service innovation can involve integration of an existing core service offering and innovative service process. For example, during the last two decades, the internet has emerged as the most innovative service process. The effects of the internet-based technologies on the way that businesses compete and manage their operations in general have also been profound (Empson et al., 2015; Lusch and Nambisan, 2015). For this reason, many service firms have been exploring ways to exploit the internet in delivering their existing service products (see Table 15.2).

In much the same way as new products are classified dependent on level of newness, services have been classified depending on the level of change. Lovelock's (1984) classification is the most widely known and usefully illustrates the different levels of change that can occur within service innovation (see Table 15.4). Yet, they are rather limited in explaining the role of technology in the identification of different innovation types.

Table 15.4 Typologies for innovations

Booz, Allen & Hamilton (1982)	Lovelock (1984)
New-to-the-world products: New products that not only represent a major new challenge to the supplier, but are also seen to be quite new in the eyes of customers	**Major innovation**: New services for markets as yet undefined; innovations usually driven by information and computer-based technologies
New product lines: New products that represent major new challenges to the supplier	**Start-up business**: New services in a market that is already served by existing services
Additions to existing product lines: New products that supplement a company's established product lines, so rounding out the product mix	**New services for the market presently served**: New service offerings to existing customers of an organisation (although the services may be available from other companies)
Improvements and revisions to existing products: New products that provide improved performance and so replace existing products	**Service line extensions**: Augmentations of the existing service line, such as adding new menu items, new routes and new courses
Repositionings: Existing products that are targeted to new markets or market segments	**Service improvements**: Changes in features of services that are currently being offered
Cost reductions: New products that provide similar performance at a lower cost of supply	**Style changes**: The most common of all 'new services'; modest forms of visible changes that have an impact on customer perceptions, emotions and attitudes, with style changes that do not change the service fundamentally, only its appearance

Source: Ozdemir, S. (2007) 'An analysis of internet banking adoption in Turkey: consumer, innovation and service developer dimensions', PhD thesis, University of Portsmouth.

Furthermore, the diffusion of innovations literature concerns the objective newness of an innovation, rather than the perceived newness of an idea, practice or physical object.

The new service development process

New service development can be defined as the overall process of developing new service offerings from idea generation to market launch (Papastathopoulou and Hultink, 2012; Ranaweera and Sigala, 2015). Offer development is a combination of the development of core product/service attributes (i.e. product or service development) and the processes by which consumers evaluate, purchase and consume the service (i.e. product or service augmentation development). Similarly, due to the nature and distinctive characteristics of services, when developing a new service, emphasis should be given not only to its core attributes but it also to the existence of other supplementary services (Papastathopoulou and Hultink, 2012). Although product augmentation or a supplementary service often brings incremental changes, it can differentiate the core service and add value to it by providing innovative support processes. This can be seen in the internet economy, where providing value added services to customers constitutes the basis of differentiation. For example, the ability to print off your boarding pass at home prior to taking a flight can remove one of the most frustrating aspects of flying: queuing.

Nonetheless, relative to new product development (NPD), the service innovation concept is little studied. This is despite the fact that the service component has become an integral part of most manufactured products. For example, the purchase of a motorcar now involves a wide range of service offerings including finance, breakdown cover, warranty, etc. In recent years, more attention has been given to innovation in services with some research expressing severe doubts about applying concepts developed in NPD to the service sector, arguing that precisely how innovation occurs in service sectors remains unclear (Ranaweera and Sigala, 2015).

Service innovation has been dominated by NPD models. The linear and more interactive models of NPD insufficiently emphasise the significance of customers and cannot capture the dynamic process of consumer involvement in the creation of innovative services. It is accepted widely that gaining an understanding of the factors that are likely to influence customer evaluations of a new product or service and how customers are likely to relate to it is necessary for ensuring a successful market outcome. Change is afoot, however, service markets are becoming global, open and competitive. Knowledge is more available, technology more complex and service life cycles are shortening. In order to satisfy this challenge, more innovation management tools are required to get better and more successful, new or improved services. Research by D'Alvano and Hidalgo (2012) suggests that leading service firms have a high use of innovation management tools.

The internet has provided the mechanism through which many more industries can now develop offerings. Indeed, the development of a service 'offer' requires far more attributes to be brought into consideration than for a tangible product. Nowhere is this more clearly visible than in the eBay case study at the end of this chapter. It is this technology dimension that now forms such a significant part of service development. This was recognised by Den Hertog (2002), who offers four dimensions of service innovations all of which are influenced by the technological options available. These are: service concept, new client interface, new service delivery system and technological options. Table 15.5 illustrates how eBay has exploited these four dimensions.

Pause for thought

It seems much of the growth in services can be attributed to the exploitation of new technology, such as the internet. Are these really services or are they products?

Table 15.5 Four dimensions of service innovation by eBay

Four service dimensions	Illustration
New service concept	Online auction community of traders
New client interface	Introduction of payment system that helps eBayers trade more easily – PayPal
New service delivery system	Huge investment in technology infrastructure to improve reliability and performance
Technological options	Introduction of voice over internet protocol service – SKYPE

Source: Adapted from Den Hertog, P. (2002) Knowledge-intensive business services as co-producers of innovation, *International Journal of Innovation Management*, vol. 4, no. 4, 491–528.

The marketing literature argues that because product development processes have not been employed in the development of new services, and because of the distinctive nature and characteristics of services, the process has been haphazard or ad hoc. However, although new product development models represent a useful framework for studying the development of new services, more research is required to integrate the influence of the unique characteristics of services into the process of new service development. **New service development models** are derived from the process models that initially were created for the development of manufactured products (Fitzsimmons and Fitzsimmons, 2000; Ranaweera and Sigala, 2015).

We have seen in Chapter 11 that the concept of open innovation captures the increasing propensity of firms to work across their traditional boundaries of operation. This phenomenon has been studied largely from the viewpoint of manufacturing businesses. Evidence is emerging that business service firms are more active open innovators than manufacturers; they are more engaged in informal relative to formal open innovation practices than manufacturers; and they attach more importance to scientific and technical knowledge than to market knowledge compared to manufacturing firms (Mina et al., 2014).

Indeed, researchers have emphasised that, with few exceptions, it is useful to integrate the models created in the study of product development into those dealing with service development. The applicability of these models depends on the nature of different services.

Sequential service development models or Stage-Gate® models

The majority of new service development models are based on the new product development framework. These stages include new product development strategy, idea generation, screening and evaluation, business analysis, development, testing and commercialisation (Figure 15.3 offers an illustration of such a sequential model). The number of these stages varies across different studies. Similarly, a widely applied approach has been the Stage-Gate model that initially was suggested by Cooper (1999) and has been used to conceptualise service activities (Stevens and Dimitriadis, 2005). Besides different stages of the product development process, the model also includes certain gates where decisions are given on the basis of the information generated in the previous groups of activities. Therefore, these gates represent the review points for the preceding stages (Phillips et al., 1999). Stage-Gate models suggest a more comprehensive and action-oriented process compared to their predecessor – sequential new product development models. However, the common point of these models is that both are characterised by a sequence of a linear progression of activities (Stevens and Dimitriadis, 2005). Indeed, limitations of these models derive from their sequential nature. One of the most important limitations is that they are very costly, time-consuming and overly bureaucratic processes. Each stage of the process is needed to be completed before proceeding to the subsequent stage. For this reason, they do not allow for parallelisation of the activities. Furthermore, because of the time-consuming nature of the process, the new market opportunity identified at

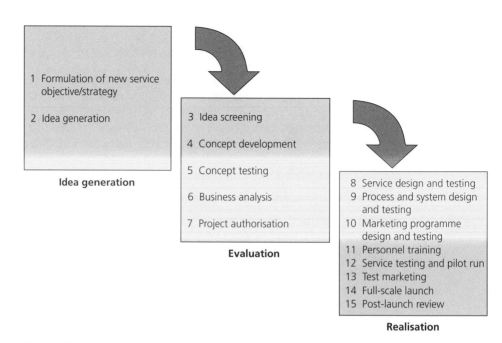

Figure 15.3 The service innovation process – a sequential model
Source: Adapted from Scheuing and Johnson, 1989.

the beginning may no longer exist when the product is commercialised. In addition, their structured and inflexible pattern gives very little chance for adaptation of the process to special service or project-specific features. Sequential models also increase the communication problems across different departments in the design and development processes. With Stage-Gate models, a failure in a particular gate may result in dropping potentially successful products.

New product or service development is an iterative process that also proceeds after the commercialisation or market launch stage. In this context, new product development models that characterise the process as being iterative in nature have also been applied in the context of services. These models are also referred to as spiral models or interactive models. They are more sophisticated models compared to linear models of product development, as each stage is repeated several times, which gives provision for feedback. The new service development model suggested by Johnson et al. (2000) conceptualises iterative stages of the service development process (see Figure 15.4). Indeed, actors, systems and technology of the process are identified as playing a significant role in the process of new service development (NSD).

However, the model still includes the limitations of sequential development processes as mentioned previously.

Concurrent service development models

Concurrent service development or simultaneous engineering overcomes the limitations of the sequential type of models and offers more flexible ways of developing innovative services. Essentially, it enables the parallelisation of the activities. The objective of this approach is to consider the whole service development processes

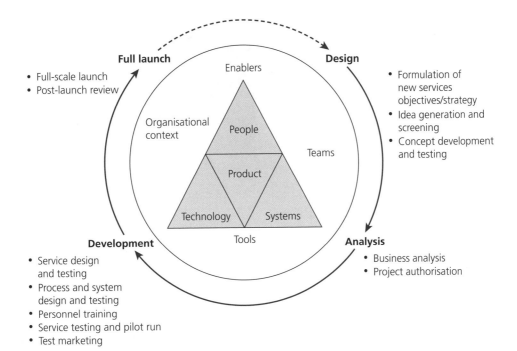

Figure 15.4 The new service development cycle

Source: Adapted from Johnson et al. (2000) 'A critical evaluation of the new service development process: integrating service innovation and service design', in Fitzsimmons, J.A. and Fitzsimmons, M.J. (eds) *New Service Development: Creating Memorable Experiences*, Sage Publications, London.

rather than individual stages. In concurrent service development, communication is improved and expertise of all departments is employed. Therefore, these types of service development processes are relatively faster and less costly compared to sequential service development models. It also avoids potential design errors that may arise in the future stages. However, specialisms of different people from different departments may also create problems during collaborative working, as these people frequently do not speak the same 'language' and they may have little understanding about each other's activities. This, in turn, may lead to an increase in time to market and costs.

Innovation in action

How a gap year led to Rat Race Adventure Sports

Jim Mee left university and took a job with Red Bull. His role included events management. He was posted to Scotland and developed a love for the outdoors. In 2003, he left Red Bull to go adventuring. He spent a year climbing in the Alps, Russia, Alaska and South America, where the idea for Rat Race Adventure Sports was formed.

He returned to Britain, envisaging playgrounds for extreme sports in towns and cities with potential for mass participation. In July 2004, he hosted his first event, a 60-mile

assault course in and around Edinburgh, and Rat Race Adventure Sports was born.

Mee sold his house to fund the £100,000 venture. The event spread to Manchester, Nottingham, Cardiff and London as part of the annual Men's Health Survival of the Fittest series, which attracts 25,000 competitors. Entry costs of up to £110 are subsidised for charity fundraisers.

Source: James Appleton/Alamy Images

Rat Race is hosting 17 events in 2014, including ultra-marathons, coast to coast trekking, biking, mountaineering and Thames river racing. The company is based in Clifton Moor, York, and has 24 staff and sales for 2014 were just over £5 million.

Rival organisers moved into the market, most notably with Tough Mudder, which started in 2010 and is now an annual 10-mile obstacle course.

Mee is also aiming to make a profit from the retail arm he added in 2013, having struggled to shift stock. The showroom and website sell branded kit, such as clothing, footwear, rucksacks and nutrition packs.

Service innovation and the consumer

One important characteristic of services that distinguishes them is that customers are **co-producers** of services. Therefore, the role customers play in services is more crucial relative to manufacturing products. Importantly, Lusch and Nambisan (2015) identified three different methods of customer involvement in the new product development process: customer as resource, customer as co-producer and customer as user. Table 15.6 illustrates further ways consumers can provide input to the new service development process at every stage. Traditionally, quality function deployment (QFD) has been the most widely known method employed during this stage. QFD has been defined as a system that is capable of linking customer requirements to design characteristics of the product or service through certain market research methods, such as direct discussion or interviews, surveys, focus groups, customer specifications, observation, etc. (cf. Zeithaml and Bitner, 2003; see also Chapter 5).

Consumer user toolkits

There has been much written in NPD literature about the need to involve customers at an early stage in the process and to integrate them into the process in order to

Table 15.6 Customers' input into the new service development process

New service development stages	Activities performed by the customer
1 Strategic planning	Thoughts and feedback on long-term plans
2 Idea generation	State needs, problems, criticise existing services; identify gaps in the market; state service requirements; state new service adoption criteria
3 Idea screening	Suggest desired features, benefits and attributes; show reactions to concepts; show level of purchase intent for concepts; indication of sales and market size
4 Business analysis	Possible feedback on financial data, including profitability of concepts; also pricing levels
5 Formation of cross-functional team	Either participate in team selection or even form part of the team
6 Service design and process system design	Review and jointly develop 'blueprints'; suggest improvements by identifying weak or fail points; observe service delivery trial by personnel
7 Personnel training	Observe and participate in simulated service delivery process and suggest improvements
8 Service testing and pilot	Participate in a simulated service delivery process and suggest final improvements and design changes
9 Test marketing	Provide feedback on the marketing plan; detailed comments about marketing mix – suggest improvements
10 Commercialisation	Adopt the service as a trial; feedback about overall performance of the service along with improvements; word-of-mouth communication to other potential customers

Source: Adapted from Allam, I. and Perry, C. (2002) A customer-oriented new service development process, *Journal of Services Marketing*, vol. 16, no. 6, 515–34.

fully capture ideas. Despite this, customer involvement in NPD has been limited and largely passive in most industries. There are many reasons for this limited utilisation of consumers in NPD, but perhaps the most limiting factor is the disconnection between customers and producers. Another reason is that research within marketing has shown, for many years, that gaining valuable insight from consumers about innovative new market offerings, especially discontinuous new products, is extremely difficult and can sometimes lead to misleading information (see Chapter 16). Indeed, frequent responses from consumers are along the lines of 'I want the same product, only cheaper and better'. Von Hippel (1986) has suggested that consumers have difficulty in understanding and articulating their needs and describes this phenomenon as 'sticky information'; that is, information that is difficult to transfer (similar to the notion of tacit knowledge). The co-creation of e-service innovations is being used by many firms to improve their performance (Chuang and Lin, 2015; Perks et al., 2012). Recent research, however, has shown that 'user toolkits' can facilitate the transfer of so-called 'sticky information' and have enabled firms to understand better the precise needs and desires of customers. Given these difficulties of utilising consumers effectively in the new service development process, how, then should firms proceed?

The earlier section on technology may provide some indications. Today, technology enables innovative ways of involving and integrating customers to the product and process development process. In this context, it is here that new technologies, most notably in the form of 'toolkits', offer considerable scope for improving connection between consumers and producers. Franke and Piller's (2004) study analysed the value created by so-called 'toolkits for user innovation and design'. This was a method of integrating customers into new product development and design.

The so-called toolkits allow customers to create their own product, which in turn is produced by the manufacturer. An example of a toolkit in its simplest form is the development of personalised products through uploading digital family photographs via the internet and having these printed onto products, such as clothing or cups, thereby allowing consumers to create personalised individual products for themselves. User toolkits for innovation are specific to a given product or service type and to a specified production system. Within these general constraints, they give users real freedom to innovate, allowing them to develop their custom product via iterative trial and error (Franke and Piller, 2004; von Hippel, 2001). Research by Thomke and von Hippel (2002) found that toolkits are particularly useful when market segments are shrinking and customers are asking increasingly for customised products. However, employment of toolkits can lead to increasing supplier costs. For example, Jeppesen (2005) found that using toolkits may be costly for suppliers due to the increased need for consumer support. This is due largely to overcoming difficulties faced by consumers. He revealed further that, under these conditions, consumer communities that enable consumer-to-consumer interaction can facilitate problem solving concerning the usage of toolkits in the consumer domain, thereby reducing operational costs.

The idea of integrating users into the design and production process is a promising strategy for companies being forced to react to the growing individualisation of demand (Franke and Piller, 2004). Over the past few years, many more firms have turned to the internet as a mechanism for communicating with their customers. Significantly, the internet enables manufacturers to communicate directly with their customers without the need for intermediaries, such as retailers and wholesalers. In some product category areas, most notably software-related ones, the internet provides the opportunity for firms to interact with customer groups and for customers to interact with customers (as eBay does with its 'community' of users). Powerful user networks can be established around product ideas, technology ideas or, most significantly, company capabilities. That is, genuine new product opportunities may be developed. This is especially so in dynamic markets where new technologies are emerging that may offer considerable advantage to firms, as in the case of online gambling, online auctions, social networking and internet banking.

Consumer testing of services

Customers also embrace the role as users in the development of new services. The role of users in this process is testing new services. As was mentioned earlier, due to the intangible nature of services, it is often easier to modify services relative to manufactured products. For this reason, consumers often test services following their market launch rather than during the initial stages of service development. For example, one of the fastest growing parts of the services sector is the software industry and it has been using lead users as active testers of their new service offerings for many years. Microsoft has been Beta testing the initial versions (prototypes) of its new software with voluntary users. Indeed, the employment of Beta testing has given rise to the emergence of online user communities that provide collaborative assistance to service firms in developing their new offerings. Internetworking giant Cisco even gives its customers open access to its information, resources and systems through an online service that enables the company's customers to engage in a dialogue. In this way, customers who access Cisco's knowledge base and user community assist other customers to solve the problems they encountered (Prahalad and Ramaswamy, 2000). Yet, involving consumers only at the end of the service development process has received criticisms from marketing literature (van Kleef et al., 2005). For example, in the field of UK commercial banking, Athanassopoulou and Johne (2004) revealed that most successful developers communicated with their lead users throughout the new service development process, whereas less successful ones concentrated their communication at the end of the process.

Case study

Developing new services at eBay

This case study explores the remarkable success of eBay and illustrates how its continual development of new services has enabled it to remain the world's leading auction site and deliver extraordinary financial results for investors. The company's decision to make PayPal independent reinforces this drive for growth.

Introduction

Founded in September 1995, eBay is The World's Online Marketplace for the sale of goods and services by a diverse community of individuals and small businesses. This eBay community includes more than 100 million registered members from around the world. According to Media Metrix, people spend more time on eBay than any other online site, making it the most popular shopping destination on the internet. On an average day, there are millions of items listed on eBay. People come to eBay to buy and sell items in thousands of categories from collectibles like trading cards, antiques, dolls and housewares to practical items like used cars, clothing, books, CDs and electronics. Buyers have the option to purchase items in an auction-style format or items can be purchased at a fixed price through a feature called Buy It Now. Currently, eBay has local sites that serve Australia,

Austria, Belgium, Canada, France, Germany, Ireland, Italy, Korea, The Netherlands, New Zealand, Singapore, Spain, Sweden, Switzerland, Taiwan and the United Kingdom. In addition, eBay has a presence in Latin America and China through its investments in MercadoLibre.com and EachNet. com respectively.

eBay, Inc. is, possibly, the most successful web-based enterprise in existence. This California-based company is known universally and is synonymous with the auction model of online selling. eBay was pivotal in helping to facilitate buying and selling between individuals and businesses. Eighty per cent of items sold are now at a fixed price and Amazon has become a fierce rival. The industry leader also created one of the first trusted online commercial communities, whereby the exchange between sellers and buyers is regulated by the evaluations and recommendations of each. eBay continues to dominate the auction industry and remains on the leading edge in innovation in services. It is now considering mobile payment services and loans.

How eBay works

Figure 15.5 illustrates how eBay works. It is, essentially, the same as that of a physical auction. Prior to

→

bidding or listing an item for sale, buyer and seller must register with eBay. All items listed by eBay can be viewed by all, including non-registered users but, to trade (i.e. buy or sell), you must register. Figure 15.5 shows the process for a typical trade:

1 Item is listed.
2 A seller's track record of selling is made available to all.
3 Potential buyers can bid.
4 Sellers view buying track record of buyers.
5 eBay notifies winning bidder and seller of winning bid.
6 Payment is made and goods shipped.
7 Buyers and sellers leave feedback on each other.

eBay receives its income from charging sellers a Final Value Fee which is a percentage of the winning bid and postage. The first 20 listings each month are free and 35p for each listing after that. The move into higher-value items, such as automobiles, has provided eBay with substantial additional income. eBay charges a vendor approximately £15, depending on vehicle value, to display a vehicle that may sell for several thousand pounds. eBay will then also take a small percentage of this winning bid.

The entire system is based upon trust and there is, clearly, an opportunity for rogue traders to operate and steal money from genuine traders. The use by eBay of the feedback system allows vendors and buyers to view the trading record of each other before agreeing to trade. This helps genuine traders to determine authentic traders from rogue ones. New traders will have to establish themselves as genuine before others will trade with them. This is possible by agreeing to pay for goods prior to receiving them or, if one is a vendor, forwarding goods prior to receiving the money.

The birth of eBay

eBay was born in September 1995. Its original name was AuctionWeb. The idea fell out of a discussion between Pierre Omidyar, a 30-something French-born computer programmer, and his fiancée, who was an avid Pez collector (sweet dispensers). With the help of his friend Jeff Skol, Omidyar launched AuctionWeb; it was incorporated in 1996 and changed its name to eBay in 1997.

After a year of trading, however, the start-up company was struggling to develop quickly. Worryingly for the founders, there were many competitors (including Yahoo's own online auction site) and the technology and internet were developing and changing rapidly. Omidyar and Skol needed significant amounts of money if they were to make eBay successful. In 1997, Omidyar drove to Silicon Valley's Sand Hill Road to seek venture capital funding for his fledgling online flea market. Though it was growing at 40 per cent a month – without any marketing – and enjoyed 30 per cent margins, eBay also needed pro-

Figure 15.5 How eBay works

fessional management. Competition was intense: there were 150 other auction sites, many of them free, unlike eBay's fee-based service. Omidyar had no PowerPoint presentation and no business plan and his company's computer server was down – meaning there was no active website for him to showcase. This was not a good start for Omidyar but, within four weeks, Benchmark, a venture capital firm, had agreed to invest $6.7 million, valuing eBay at about $20 million. According to Benchmark, it seems Odimyar recognised that he needed help. In particular, he required better qualified people to run the business. In addition to its investment, Benchmark offered its services and its industry contacts. Benchmark's investment generated a return of $4.5 billion, probably the greatest profit ever generated in the venture capital industry. But the investment paid off for eBay, too. Indeed, it was Benchmark that helped recruit Ms Whitman as CEO and Mr Swette as chief operating officer. Whilst no one doubted that the business model developed (connecting individual buyers and sellers online and taking a cut of the transaction) was excellent, it was the development of this to a public offering that has enabled eBay to become the giant it is today.

The appointment of Ms Whitman as CEO is regarded, universally, as an outstanding move by eBay. She was able to develop eBay from one of the many auction websites into the leading site. In those early days of 1997, the eBay site was in black and white and the typeface was basic courier. The company was called eBay and the website was called AuctionWeb, but both brands appeared on the site. The eBay web pages appeared amateurish compared to what Whitman was used to at P&G, Disney and Hambro; many thought she would not join, but she did. After Omidyar explained eBay's impressive growth rate, margins and profitability, Whitman realised the potential. Furthermore, when Omidyar explained that people had met their best friends on eBay, there was an emotional connection to the site and the eBay community. Whitman joined the company on 2 January 1998. The company had just 35 employees, and she began filling senior management positions. She hired auditors and set up the selection process for investment banks to lead the offer. By September 1998, she, Omidyar and Gary Bengier, eBay's then chief financial officer, began three weeks of roadshows to investors. That autumn, eBay

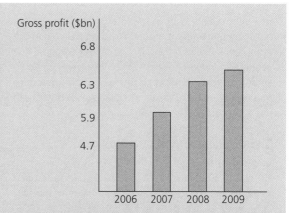

Figure 15.6 eBay profits

enjoyed a sensational IPO. The shares began trading on Nasdaq on 24 September at $18. By the close of trading, they had nearly trebled to $47. The cash raised was put to work immediately. Whilst eBay's peers burned their start-up cash, eBay became a phenomenon – a Silicon Valley company that has always made a profit and is the world's most successful internet group. Moreover, the profit potential was huge; eBay had almost no cost of goods, no inventories, few marketing costs and no large capital expenditure (see Figure 15.6).

The business model

The business model developed by eBay is unique and has evolved over time as the business has grown. The founders' intention was that eBay should be made up of a community and this vision has helped shape the business. According to the chief operating officer, Brian Swette, the business has grown by constantly responding to what the users have wanted. It is the eBay community that has designed the business model. eBay supports the desire to respond to the user community by employing approximately 5,000 people, about half of whom are involved in customer support and about 20 per cent of whom are in technology. eBay does not need to spend large sums of money trying to understand what its customers want because its customers constantly request and suggest changes. For example, over 100,000 messages from users are posted each week in which tips are shared and system glitches highlighted. The technology systems that eBay has introduced over time enables the company to trace every move of every potential customer; this yields

→

rich information that can be acted upon. In addition, category managers for eBay play a crucial role in the company's development. Unlike other positions, say product managers in large firms, these roles involve listening, adapting and enabling. It is the category managers' responsibility to develop tools to help users buy and sell more effectively.

The development of new services

International

Between 2000 and 2005, eBay expanded internationally, and had country-specific sites in the UK, Germany, Japan, Italy and Australia and, in 2005, purchased a majority stake in Korea's largest online auction site.

In 2008, the company had expanded worldwide, had hundreds of millions of registered users, more than 15,000 employees and revenues of almost $7.7 billion.

Online payment system: PayPal

In 2002, eBay purchased PayPal, the world's largest online payment system, in an all-stock deal worth about $1.5 billion. The deal was eBay's largest investment to date and it was recognition by eBay that Billpoint, its own payment system, had been unsuccessful. Furthermore, about 60 per cent of Paypal's revenues were generated on eBay; hence there was a natural association between the two firms. The acquisition of PayPal allowed eBay to expand beyond its core auction services. eBay and PayPal both prospered because their strategies capitalised on the internet's strengths. eBay has employed the 'network effect', in which new customers are added at almost zero marginal cost and to the benefit of other users. Together, eBay and PayPal enhanced the internet's potential by reducing the number of steps for buyers. This should accelerate the number of transactions, thereby improving revenues (for an interesting story on what happened to the $1.5 billion, see Illustration 1.4).

When eBay acquired PayPal in 2002, one of the main risks facing PayPal was its dependence on eBay for 60 per cent of its revenues. Since this time, PayPal has grown rapidly in line with the wider online payment market. This turned out to be a shrewd investment by eBay, as we will see later in the case.

Mobile/smart phones

Offering the ability for customers to use eBay on the move and via wireless technology is a natural development of the firm's technology. In most ways the eBay product has the necessary components to be a success in wireless markets: it delivers highly personalised content that is time-sensitive in nature.

eBay shops

In 2004, eBay began offering commercial sellers the concept of a shop on the site, where they could direct consumers to view more of their merchandise. This has proved extremely popular for the large sellers.

Dangers, threats and challenges

Competition

Whilst eBay is the internet's most successful business, the internet is, nonetheless, currently dominated by the two biggest search engine companies: Yahoo and Google. Also, there is disenchantment within certain parts of eBay's user community. This is largely because eBay is moving away from its 'user community' to keep its gross profit margins above 80 per cent. But heavier spending on marketing, including the first TV campaigns in countries like the UK and China, ate into operating profit margins, cutting them by one point to 30.4 per cent. Alibaba, the Chinese ecommerce giant, also poses a considerable threat to eBay. Alibaba provides consumer-to-consumer, business-to-consumer and business-to-business sales services via web portals. It also provides electronic payment services, a shopping search engine and data-centric cloud computing services. The group began in 1999 when Jack Ma founded the website Alibaba.com, a business-to-business portal to connect Chinese manufacturers with overseas buyers.

Fixed-price sales

The move, in 2004, to sell an increasing number of goods at fixed prices, rather than through auction, was seen as controversial amongst some suppliers. Many sellers welcome the changes because of the new buyers they attract to the site. Others, however, believe corporations will get special treatment from eBay – and destroy its culture.

Fraud

The continual coverage in the popular media of fraud on the internet in general and criminals using eBay to amass ill-gotten gains clearly does not help eBay. But, there are so many millions of users who have very positive experiences of using the site that it seems unlikely that existing users will be put off using the online auction site. Should one of its competitors develop a more foolproof trading model, however, this would be a serious threat to the business.

Maturing markets and slow growth

After a run of more than 10 years as a public company, during which it consistently turned in financial results that made every other dotcom firm green with envy, more recently, margins have declined. Worse, the company's rock-solid profit margins showed uncharacteristic signs of erosion. eBay's much-admired business model has enabled it to keep its gross profit margins above 60 per cent. eBay spent $100 million (£53 million, €77 million) in 2005 expanding its presence in China in a race to dominate what is likely to become the world's biggest Internet market.

In 2005, Visa, Microsoft and eBay announced a global service to combat identity theft on the internet, especially 'phishing' incidents. Phishing refers to the practice of emails being sent to users purporting to be from institutions such as their bank and urging them to click on a web link to update their online account information.

Shill bidding

Critics have claimed the practice of shill bidding is widespread on eBay. A shill is an associate of a person selling goods or services who pretends no association to the seller and assumes the air of an enthusiastic customer. The intention of the shill is to encourage other potential customers, unaware of the set-up, to purchase said goods or services. The word 'shill' is probably related to 'shillaber', a word of obscure early twentieth-century origin with the same meaning. eBay tried to reassure customers and stated that any such fraudulent bidding is strictly prohibited on their auction site.

Charity

eBay allows sellers to donate a portion of their auction proceeds to a charity of the seller's choice. The programme is called eBay Giving Works in the USA, and eBay for Charity in the UK. eBay provides a partial refund of seller fees for items sold through charity auctions.

eBay bans negative seller views

In 2008, eBay announced a major change to its business model. eBay said problems were occurring, and slowing down trade, when buyers left negative comments about sellers who then retaliated with their own views. The decision, which will affect users worldwide, has angered many sellers. Sellers feel it will leave them unprotected. They argue that by still allowing buyers to leave dissenting comments about sellers, eBay has skewed the whole trading process. However, eBay believes the change is necessary and is putting in additional tools to protect sellers and promote a fair marketplace:

- Sellers can add buyer requirements to their listings to prevent unwanted bidders. Sellers can block buyers with too many policy violations, unpaid items or who are not registered with PayPal. This can help dramatically reduce the number of unpaid items.
- Sellers can require buyers to pay right away. If you use Buy It Now, sellers require buyers to pay you immediately using PayPal.
- Sellers have an easy way to report problems with buyers. Sellers can use the seller reporting hub to report an unpaid item, feedback extortion, or any other problem with a buyer.

Source: Bloomua/Shutterstock.com

Growth via acquisition continues

Since its inception, eBay has used a strategy of growth via acquisition and this strategy continues, as Table 15.7 shows.

Jack Abraham, founder of Milo, helps drive innovation and profits at eBay

During the third quarter of 2007, eBay lost money for the first time as a public company. After years of astonishing growth, growth and profits were slowing. John Donahoe had been picked by Meg Whittam to be her replacement. But finding growth proved difficult.

Jack Abraham had built Milo (a specialist search engine people could use at home to find out what products were in stock at local stores) and sold it to eBay in 2010. Part of the sale involved Abraham working for eBay to integrate the Milo technology. It powered a product called 'eBay Now', which enabled shoppers to use a phone to order a product from a local store and get it delivered in under an hour. The Milo team became known as the eBay Local team, with Abraham in charge. But, he had no authority over eBay.com and the people who did had plenty of their own ideas. Abraham believed eBay should have a feed like the Facebook News Feed. It could show updates from eBay sellers and product categories. According to Abraham, eBay could turn the feed on without waiting for users to start following anybody, since it already knew search and shopping histories.

John Donahoe backed Abraham's idea and eBay launched the feed 2.0 in 2013. Since then, it has seen greater engagement amongst users who have feed, including increased visits to eBay.com, more clicks on its homepage and longer eBay sessions.

eBay to make PayPal independent

PayPal is now considerably bigger than eBay. PayPal is estimated to be valued at $45 billion, whilst eBay is valued at $30 billion. After the split, eBay has agreed to route 80 per cent of its sales through PayPal for the next five years. This is similar to present transactions.

With the growth in mobile payment, PayPal has an opportunity to capture a large chunk of this market. PayPal now provides its own electronic wallet, which lets users tap one button to check out on a website or app. PayPal's recent acquisition of mobile payments start-up Paydiant will help the company bring its wallet into physical stores. PayPal also provides the infrastructure behind the scenes, powering transactions within popular apps like Uber, Airbnb and Houzz. PayPal has the edge right now on the web as a first-person payment provider. Its challenge now is to become dominant when it comes to in-store payments. As PayPal severs its ties with eBay, it may be able to attack these challenges, step outside the shadows of apps and become a prominent payment method for consumers. Independent from eBay, it may also be able to make a genuine move into finance and offer loans, etc.

Table 15.7 eBay acquisitions

Year	Firm acquired	Business	Country
2010	Milo	Shopping engine	Unites States
2011	alaMaula	Online classifieds	Argentina
2011	Zong	Payments through mobile carrier billing	United States
2011	The Gifts Project	Group purchasing of gifts	Israel
2011	Zvents	Local events	United States
2012	Svpply	Social shopping	United States
2013	Decide.com	Price-forecasting	United States
2013	Braintree	Payments	United States
2013	Bureau of Trade	Content/Commerce	United States
2013	Shutl	Rapid fulfilment service	United Kingdom
2014	PhiSix Fashion Labs	Virtual clothing	United States

Conclusions

Meg Whitman transformed eBay from a purely domestic group that held auctions in 300 categories into a global enterprise, operating in 18 countries and offering 16,000 categories. She expanded the range of goods sold from mainly collectibles – Beanie Babies dolls accounted for 8 per cent of items sold at the time of the IPO – to include used cars, motorcycles, computers, time-share holiday homes and even golf tee-off times. A Gulfstream corporate jet has been sold on eBay for $4.9 million. The move away from auction and into mainstream sales goes against the principles on which eBay was established.

The fraud issue remains a concern. The introduction of deposit accounts would help overcome the problem of bogus bidders. The deposit account would enable a percentage of the successful bid to be automatically deducted or eBay could make an automatic deduction from users' credit cards. Whilst eBay can produce statistics showing how many auctions are successful, the numbers give no indication of how many sellers actually get paid.

During her 10 years with the company, Whitman oversaw expansion from 30 employees and $4 million in annual revenue to more than 15,000 employees and $8 billion in annual revenue when she stepped down in 2008. Since 2015, Devin Wenig has taken charge of the task of continuing to drive growth at

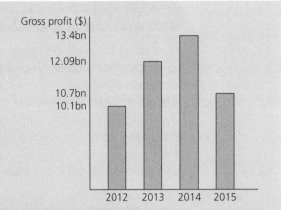

Figure 15.7 eBay profits

eBay. It seems innovation and new services will form a big part of this plan.

PayPal's rapid growth suggests a bright future for the digital-payments company. eBay, meanwhile, has considerable challenges ahead as it attempts to turn around its slow-growing online marketplace, now without PayPal helping to prop it up (see Figure 15.7).

Sources: Moules, J. and Abrahams, P. (2002) Companies and Finance, the Americas: eBay set to buy Paypal for $1.37bn, FT. com, 9 July; Nuttall, C. (2005) Visa, Microsoft, eBay combat 'phishing', FT.com, 14 February; eBay chief takes the rough with the smooth, *Financial Times*, 18 April. BBC (2008) BBC News. co.uk/eBay to ban negative seller views, 5 February; The eBay bidscam, www.thetimesonline.co.uk.

Questions

1 eBay is one of the only major internet-based firms consistently to make a profit from its inception. What is eBay's business model? Why has it been so successful?

2 Other major websites, like Amazon and Yahoo, have entered the auction marketplace with far less success than eBay. How has eBay been able to maintain its dominant position?

3 Why did eBay ban the leaving of negative feedback on sellers? What has been the impact of this change?

4 eBay makes every effort to conceptualise its users as a community (as opposed to, say, 'customers' or 'clients'). What is the purpose of this conceptual difference and does eBay gain something by doing it?

5 eBay has long been a marketplace for used goods and collectibles. Today, it is increasingly a place where major businesses come to auction their wares. Why would a brand name vendor set up shop on eBay?

6 The development of the eBay feed shows the need for eBay to continue to incorporate new services within its activities. What other mobile applications could it utilise?

7 Given the growth opportunities available to eBay, which ones and in which order should it develop?

Chapter summary

This chapter has explored the area of new service innovations. It should be clear from the chapter that there is a considerable overlap between product development and service development. There are clear differences between products and services, most notably that with services the consumer is co-producer, but so many products now incorporate services that it is sometimes unclear why we treat them separately. The chapter has reviewed the wide range of services within the economy and also shown how new technology is providing a driving force for many new services. This is illustrated very clearly in the eBay case study at the end of the chapter.

Discussion questions

1 Discuss the differences between product innovation and service innovation.

2 What are the factors that have led to the increase in services?

3 How has new technology contributed to the growth in services?

4 Discuss how some new services have created new business models.

5 Explain why manufacturing firms are increasingly involved in offering services. Discuss some examples.

6 Explain the key roles played by the consumer in new service development.

7 Explain how various groups of people in the organisation might use a service blueprint.

Key words and phrases

Intangibility *524*

Knowledge-intensive business services (KIBS) *524*

Outsourcing *525*

New service development *530*

New service development models *535*

Sequential service development *535*

Concurrent service development *536*

Co-producer *538*

Consumer user toolkits *538*

References

Athanassopoulou, P. and Johne, A. (2004) Effective communication with lead customers in developing new banking products, *International Journal of Bank Marketing*, vol. 22, no. 2, 100–125.

Barrett, M., Davidson, E., Prabhu, J. and Vargo, S.L. (2015) Service innovation in the digital age: key contributions and future directions, *MIS Quarterly*, vol. 39, no. 1, 135–54.

Bitran, G. and Pedrosa, L. (1998) A structured product development perspective for service operations, *European Management Journal*, vol. 16, no. 2, 169–89.

Boone, T. (2000) 'Exploring the link between product and process innovation in services in new service development', in Fitzsimmons, J.A. and Fitzsimmons, M.J. (eds) *New Service Development: Creating Memorable Experiences*, Sage Publications, London, 92–107.

Booz, Allen & Hamilton (1982) *New Products for Management for the 1980s*, Booz, Allen & Hamilton, New York.

Chen, S.H., Wen, P.C. and Yang, C.K. (2014) Business concepts of systemic service innovations in e-Healthcare, *Technovation*, vol. 34, no. 9, 513–24.

Chuang, S.H. and Lin, H.N. (2015) Co-creating e-service innovations: theory, practice, and impact on firm performance, *International Journal of Information Management*, vol. 35, no. 3, 277–91.

Cooper, R.G. (1999) From experience: the invisible success factors in product innovation, *Journal of Product Innovation Management*, vol. 16, no. 2, 115–33.

D'Alvano, L. and Hidalgo, A. (2012) Innovation management techniques and development degree of innovation process in service organizations, *R&D Management*, vol. 42, 60–70.

Del-Río-Ortega, A., Gutiérrez, A.M., Durán, A., Resinas, M. and Ruiz-Cortés, A. (2015) Modelling service level agreements for business process outsourcing services, *Advanced Information Systems Engineering*, June, pp. 485–500, Springer International Publishing.

Den Hertog, P. (2002) Knowledge-intensive business services as co-producers of innovation, *International Journal of Innovation Management*, vol. 4, no. 4, 491–528.

Edvardsson, R I. and Durst, S. (2014) Outsourcing of knowledge processes: a literature review, *Journal of Knowledge Management*, 18(4), 795–811.

Empson, L., Muzio, D., Broschak, J. and Hinings, B. (2015) (eds) Researching professional service firms: an introduction and overview, in *Oxford Handbook of Professional Service Firms*, Oxford University Press, Oxford.

European Union (2015) http://ec.europa.eu/eurostat/statistics-explained/index.php/Innovation_statistics#Main_statistical_findings.

Eurostat (2015) See European Union (2015).

Fernandes, C.I. and Ferreira, J.J.M. (2013) Knowledge spillovers: cooperation between universities and KIBS, *R&D Management*, vol. 43, 461–72.

Fitzsimmons, J.A. and Fitzsimmons, M.J. (2000) *New Service Development: Creating Memorable Experiences*, Sage Publications, London.

Franke, N. and Piller, F. (2004) Value creation by toolkits for user innovation and design: the case of the watch market, *Journal of Product Innovation Management*, vol. 21, no. 6, 401–16.

Hoecht, A. and Trott, P. (2006) Innovation risks of strategic outsourcing, *Technovation*, vol. 26, no. 4, 672–81.

Jaw, C., Lo, J. and Lin, Y. (2010) The determinants of new service development: service characteristics, market orientation and actualizing innovation effort, *Technovation*, vol. 30, no. 4, 265–77.

Jeppesen, L.B. (2005) User toolkits for innovation: consumers support each other, *Journal of Product Innovation Management*, vol. 22, no. 4, 347–62.

Johnson, S.P., Menor, L.J., Roth, A.V. and Chase, R.B. (2000) 'A critical evaluation of the new service development process: integrating service innovation and service design', in Fitzsimmons, J.A. and Fitzsimmons, M.J. (eds) *New Service Development: Creating Memorable Experiences*, Sage Publications, London, 1–32.

Johnston, R. and Clark, G. (2005) *Service Operations Management*, 2nd edn, Prentice Hall, Pearson Education Ltd, Harlow.

Johnston, R. and Clark, G. (2012) *Service Operations Management*, 4th edn, Prentice Hall, Pearson Education Ltd, Harlow.

Lovelock, C.H. (1984) 'Developing and implementing new services', in George, W.R. and Marshall, C.E. (eds) *Developing New Services*, American Marketing Association, Chicago, 44–64.

Lusch, R.F. and Nambisan, S. (2015) Service innovation: a service-dominant logic perspective, *MIS Quarterly*, vol. 39, no. 1, 155–75.

Manning, S. (2013) New Silicon Valleys or a new species? Commoditization of knowledge work and the rise of knowledge services clusters, *Research Policy*, vol. 42, no. 2, 379–90.

Menor, L.J., Mohan, V.T. and Sampson, S.E. (2002) New service development: areas for exploitation and exploration, *Journal of Operations Management*, vol. 20, no. 2, 135–57.

Mina, A., Bascavusoglu-Moreau, E. and Hughes, A. (2014) Open service innovation and the firm's search for external knowledge, *Research Policy*, vol. 43, no. 5, 853–66.

Papastathopoulou, P. and Hultink, E.J. (2012) New Service Development: An Analysis of 27 Years of Research, *Journal of Product Innovation Management*, 29: 705–14.

Perks, H., Gruber, T. and Edvardsson, B. (2012) Co-creation in radical service innovation: a systematic analysis of microlevel processes, *Journal of Product Innovation Management*, vol. 29, 935–51.

Phillips, R., Neailey, K. and Broughton, T. (1999) A comparative study of six stage-gate approaches to product development, *Integrated Manufacturing Systems*, vol. 10, no. 5, 289–97.

Prahalad, C.K. and Ramaswamy, V. (2000) Co-opting customer competence, *Harvard Business Review*, vol. 78, no. 1, 79–87.

Ranaweera, C. and Sigala, M. (2015) From service quality to service theory and practice, *Journal of Service Theory and Practice*, vol. 25, no. 1, 2–9.

Scheuing, E.E. and Johnson, E.M. (1989) New product development and management in financial institutions, *International Journal of Bank Marketing*, vol. 7, no. 2, 17–21.

Stevens, E. and Dimitriadis, S. (2005) Managing the new service development process: towards a systematic model, *European Journal of Marketing*, vol. 39, no. 1/2, 175–98.

Thomke, S. and von Hippel, E. (2002) Customers as innovators: a new way to create value, *Harvard Business Review*, vol. 80, no. 4, 74–81.

van Kleef, E., van Trijp, H.C.M., Luning, P., et al. (2005) Consumer research in the early stages of new product development: a critical review of methods and techniques, *Food Quality and Preference*, vol. 16, no. 3, 181–201.

von Hippel, E. (1986) Lead users: a source of novel product concepts, *Management Science*, vol. 32, no. 7, 791–805.

von Hippel, E. (2001) Perspective: user toolkits for innovation, *Journal of Product Innovation Management*, vol. 18, no. 4, 247–57.

Wang, C. and Regan, A.C. (2003) *Risks and Reduction Measures in Logistics Outsourcing*, TRB Annual Meeting.

Zeithaml, V.A. and Bitner, M.J. (2003) *Services Marketing: Integrating Customer Focus Across the Firm*, 3rd edn, McGraw-Hill, New York.

Further reading

For a more detailed review of the new service innovation literature, the following develop many of the issues raised in this chapter:

Chuang, S.H. and Lin, H. N. (2015) Co-creating e-service innovations: theory, practice, and impact on firm performance, *International Journal of Information Management*, vol. 35, no. 3, 277–91.

D'Alvano, L. and Hidalgo, A. (2012) Innovation management techniques and development degree of innovation process in service organizations, *R&D Management*, vol. 42, 60–70.

Hipp, C. and Grupp, H. (2005) Innovation in the service sector: the demand for service specific innovation measurement concepts and typologies, *Research Policy*, vol. 34, no. 4, 517–35.

Jaw, C., Lo, J. and Lin, Y. (2010) The determinants of new service development: service characteristics, market orientation and actualizing innovation effort, *Technovation*, vol. 26, no. 4, 265–77.

Papastathopoulou, P. and Hultink, E.J. (2012) New service development: an analysis of 27 years of research, *Journal of Product Innovation Management*, vol. 29, 705–14.

Chapter 16
Market research and its influence on new product development

Introduction

The role and use of market research in the development of new products is commonly accepted and well understood. There are times, however, when market research results produce negative reactions to discontinuous new products (innovative products) that later become profitable for the innovating company. Famous examples, such as the fax machine, the VCR and James Dyson's bagless vacuum cleaner are cited often to support this view. Despite this, companies continue to seek the views of consumers on their new product ideas. The debate about the use of market research and, more importantly, what type of research should be used in the development of new products is long-standing and controversial. This chapter will explore these and other related issues. It also provides a case study that shows how Dyson pursued 'unpopular' designs that later become the industry standard.

Chapter contents

Learning objectives

When you have completed this chapter you will be able to:

- understand the contribution market research can make to the new product development process;
- recognise the benefits and weaknesses of consumer new product testing;
- recognise the powerful influence of the installed base effect on new product introductions;
- understand the significance of discontinuous products; and
- recognise the role of switching costs in new product introductions.

Market research and new product development

Business students, in particular, are very familiar with the well-trodden paths of arguments about the need for **market research**. Indeed, they are warned of the dangers and pitfalls that lie ahead if firms fail to conduct sufficient market research. Compelling, and potentially alarming, stories are used to highlight the importance of market research. One of these is presented in Illustration 16.1.

Chapters 13 and 14 outlined the activities involved in the development of new products. In this chapter it is necessary to examine in more detail some of these activities and to identify areas of potential difficulty. Figure 14.9 outlined the key activities of the new product development process. Within the product concept generation stage, however, there is a significant amount of internal reviews and testing. Figure 16.1 expands this stage into a series of further activities. As can be seen from the diagram, it is extremely difficult to delineate between the activities of concept testing, prototype development and product testing. The activities are intimately related and interlinked. There is a considerable amount of iteration. Product concepts are developed into prototypes only to be quickly redeveloped following technical inputs from production or R&D. Similarly, early product prototypes may be changed almost on a daily basis as a wide variety of market inputs are received. This could include channel members who have particular requirements and early results from consumer tests may reveal a number of minor changes that can be made simply and quickly by prototype designers.

Yet, we also recognise that consumers frequently have difficulty articulating their needs. This has been confirmed by two CEOs. Steven Jobs, CEO of Apple, in an interview with *Fortune* magazine (2008) said: 'Apple does no market research, and

Illustration 16.1

The traditional view of new product testing

Even successful firms can sometimes make errors with new products, as this illustration shows from fast food giant McDonald's. Several years ago it was considering launching the McPloughman's, a cheese and pickle salad sandwich. The McPloughman's was developed to compete with the UK's supermarket chains in the cold sandwich market. Unfortunately, had the company conducted market research, it would have found that this product was not highly desirable. Indeed, their customers did not want the product and their staff were embarrassed to sell it. From now on, said the company, rather than relying on 'gut-feeling' that it knew what its customers wanted, McDonald's intended to conduct rigorous fact-based market research.

Source: Pearson Education Ltd/Burke Triolo Productions/Brand X Pictures

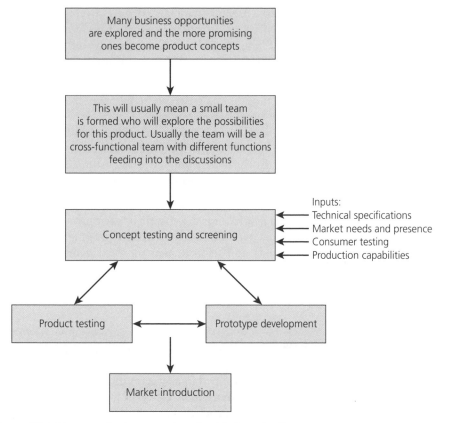

Figure 16.1 New product concept and prototype testing

in fact just wants to "make great products".' And Bart Becht, CEO of Reckitt Benckiser, said in an interview with *The Sunday Times* (2008): 'Consumers are not very good at imagining what they might want to buy if it were available . . . consumers are not very innovative.' The issue here is clear. There are some firms that wish to lead the public with new products, for they believe that the public do not know what is possible and market research frequently reinforces this lack of knowledge.

The purpose of new product testing

The main objective here is to estimate the market's reaction to the new product under consideration, prior to potentially expensive production and promotional costs. To achieve this objective, it is necessary to consider a number of other factors:

1 *The market:* current buying patterns; existing segments; and customer's view of the products available.
2 *Purchase intention:* trial and repeat purchase; barriers to changing brands; and switching costs (more about this later).
3 *Improvements to the new product:* overall product concept; and features of the product concept.

All these factors are linked and usually are covered in consumer new product testing and referred to as *customer needs and preferences*. This, however, raises an important issue: the type of needs required would, surely, depend on the type of product under consideration and the consumer. King (1985) argues needs can be classified into three types:

- *Basic needs:* those that a customer would expect. For example, a customer would expect a new car to start every time.
- *Articulated needs:* those that a customer can readily express. For example, a customer may express a desire for additional features on a motor vehicle.
- *Exciting needs:* those that will surprise customers and are not being met by any provider at present. In the example here it may be finance packages enabling easy and quick purchase of a new car.

Whilst this is helpful, it is the so-called 'exciting needs' that all new product developers want to uncover. For success surely will come to those who are able to understand these needs and use them in the next generation of new products. This, however, is extremely difficult to capture. Some of the techniques and concepts used in consumer product testing are reviewed in the following sections.

Testing new products

Have you ever been stopped in a supermarket and asked for your opinion on a new food product? This is more than a diversion from the chore of shopping – you could be tasting the next big product. For example, all food manufacturers hope it will be their company that will develop the next 'Flora' or 'Sunny Delight' (two of the most successful new food products of the past 15 years). In-store tasting is a serious business and millions of pounds are spent on this activity to create new foods that will tempt consumers. This is the accepted and well-known face of consumer research. Indeed, the food industry is one of the most prolific developers of new products and a heavy user of consumer research. Frequently, the process involves enhancing an existing winner or repackaging tried and tested products. 'Flora' was one of many 'yellow spreads' but the brand has become so successful that it has been extended to other product lines, including cheese.

Food manufacturers continually are seeking to add value to their products. This clearly enhances their profit margins, but competition in food retailing is fierce and retailers have been able to put pressure on manufacturers to keep prices down. Indeed, between 1980 and 2015 average food retail prices have fallen. Initially, manufacturers pushed down their own costs in an attempt to improve margins, but, when these could be reduced no further, manufacturers turned to new product development to enable them to add value and command a higher price. Frequently, the success of the product lies in the packaging, as Illustration 16.2 shows.

Put crudely, to command a higher price a manufacturer of, say, baked beans will have to develop different forms of packaging, add curry, meat balls, etc., all of which will have been tested by the taste buds of consumers first. But, if a product is not liked by consumers, should it always be dumped and labelled 'bad idea'? In the food industry, a disliked new flavour crisp may, indeed, be a 'bad idea' and a potential flop, if the product gets to market, but, in other industries, initial rejection by consumers may not

Illustration 16.2

Robinsons Fruit Shoot

Robinsons Fruit Shoot was launched in 2001 and is now a £100 million super brand. Britvic, owners of Fruit Shoot, delivered profits of £158 million for 2014. Its success has been attributed to the unique design and packaging of the drink. Prior to Fruit Shoot, most children's drinks were packaged in paper board cartons with a straw. Fruit Shoot revolutionised the market by using a colourful resealable plastic bottle. In the UK, Fruit Shoot was bought by 41 per cent of all households with children in 2011. Growth continued in 2012 through exports to Europe. In 2015, Britvic invested £7 million in its factory and warehousing near Leeds to help support growth. In addition, Britvic's US franchise business has pushed distribution of the brand into all 50 states.

Source: www.Britvic.com (2004 and 2007)

be a good indication of future success. The Dyson case study at the end of this chapter is a good illustration of a successful product that initially was rejected by manufacturers, retailers and some consumers, yet it turned out to be a success. There are, of course, many other well-known cases, such as the fax machine. Peter Drucker once observed that 'one can use market research only on what is already in the market'. He supported his point by saying that US companies failed to put the fax machine on the market 'because market research convinced them there was no demand for such a gadget'.

Techniques used in consumer testing of new products

The following is a brief guide to some of the research techniques used in consumer testing of new products. Some products and services go through all the stages listed, but few do or should go through all these. The techniques would have to be adapted to meet the specific requirements of the product or service under consideration.

Concept tests

Qualitative techniques, especially group discussions, are used to obtain target customer reactions to a new idea or product. Question areas would cover:

- understanding and believability in the product;
- ideas about what it would look like;

- ideas about how it would be used; and
- ideas about when and by whom it might be used.

This would help to reveal the most promising features of the new product, and groups to whom it might appeal. It might be argued that the assessment of *purchase intent* is the primary purpose of **concept testing**, so that products and services with poor potential can be removed. The most common way to assess purchase intention is to provide a description of the product or take the product to respondents and ask whether they:

- definitely would buy;
- probably would buy;
- might or might not buy;
- probably would not buy; or
- definitely would not buy.

Test centres

These are used for product testing when the product is too large, too expensive or too complicated to be taken to consumers for testing. One or more test centres will be set up and a representative sample of consumers brought to the test centre for exposure to the product and questioning about their reaction to it. See the development of the tooth whitening product in the case study at the end of Chapter 12.

Hall tests/mobile shops

These are used commonly for product testing or testing other aspects of the marketing mix, such as advertising, price, packaging, etc. A representative sample of consumers is recruited, usually in a shopping centre, and brought to a conveniently located hall or a mobile caravan, which acts as a shop. Here they are exposed to the test material and asked questions about it.

Product-use tests

These are used frequently in business-to-business markets. A small group of potential customers are selected to use the product for a limited period of time. The manufacturer's technical people watch how these customers use the product. From this test, the manufacturer learns about customer training and servicing requirements. Following the test, the customer is asked detailed questions about the product, including intent to purchase.

Trade shows

Such shows draw large numbers of buyers who view new products in a few days. The manufacturer can see how buyers react to various products on display. This technique is convenient and can deliver in-depth knowledge of the market because the buyers' views may differ considerably from those of the end-user consumers.

Monadic tests

The respondents are given only one (hence the name) product to try, and are asked their opinion of it. This is the normal situation in real life when a consumer tries a new product and draws on recent experience with the product they usually use, to judge the test product. The method is not very sensitive in comparing the test product with other products because of this.

Paired comparisons

A respondent is asked to try two or more products in pairs and asked, with each pair, to say which they prefer. This is less 'real' in terms of the way consumers normally use products, but does allow products to be deliberately tested against others.

In-home placement tests

These are used when an impression of how the product performs in normal use is required. The product(s) are placed with respondents who are asked to use the product in the normal way and complete a questionnaire about it. Products may be tested comparatively or sequentially.

Test panels

Representative panels are recruited and used for product testing. Test materials and questionnaires can be sent through the post, which cuts down the cost of conducting in-home placement tests. Business-to-business firms may also have test panels of customers or intermediaries with whom new product or service ideas or prototypes can be tested.

When market research has too much influence

It is argued by many from within the market research industry that only extensive consumer testing of new products can help to avoid large-scale losses, such as those experienced by RCA with its Videodisc, Procter & Gamble with its Pringles and General Motors with its rotary engine. Sceptics may point to the issue of vested interests in the industry, and that it is merely promoting itself. It is, however, widely accepted that most new products fail in the market because consumer needs and wants are not satisfied. Study results show that 80 per cent of newly introduced products fail to establish a market presence after two years. Indeed, cases involving international high-profile companies are cited frequently to warn of the dangers of failing to utilise market research (e.g. Unilever's Persil Power and R.J. Reynold's smokeless cigarette).

Given the inherent risk and complexity, managers have asked, for many years, whether this could be reduced by market research. Not surprisingly, the marketing literature takes a market-driven view, which has extensive market research as its key driver. That is, find out what the customer would like and then produce it (the market-pull approach to innovation). The benefits of this approach to the new product development process have been widely articulated and are commonly understood (Cooper, 1990; Kotler, 1998). Partly because of its simplicity, this view now dominates management thinking, but, unfortunately, this sometimes goes beyond the marketing department. The effect can be that major or so-called discontinuous innovations are rejected or accepted, based on consumer research.

Advocates of market research argue that such activities ensure that companies are consumer-oriented. In practice, this means that new products are more successful if they are designed to satisfy a perceived need rather than if they are designed simply to take advantage of a new technology (Ortt and Schoormans, 1993). The approach taken by many companies with regard to market research is that, if sufficient research is undertaken, the chances of failure are reduced (Barrett, 1996). Indeed, the danger that many companies wish to avoid is the development of products without any consideration of the market. Moreover, once a product has been carried through the early stages of development, it is sometimes painful to raise questions about it once money has been spent. The problem then spirals out of control, taking the company with it. Illustration 16.3 highlights many of the difficulties facing firms introducing new products.

Illustration 16.3

Neuromarketing accesses subconscious views on products and brands

Last month, I surrendered my subconscious to analysis. A red swimming cap was stretched over my head, long grey wires stuck to my skull and my innermost thoughts fed into a computer as I nervously watched an advertisement for Volkswagen.

In turn, the computer told a team of researchers which scenes I paid attention to, what I responded to emotionally and what I would go away remembering.

It was a far cry from the marketing industry's traditional method of finding out what consumers think about their brands: asking them.

The problem is, when gathered in traditional focus groups, respondents can be swayed by those sitting next to them or by the presence of researchers.

Alternatively, they may be unable to articulate their responses accurately. As a result, an increasing number of marketers now prefer to analyse the response of peoples' brainwaves to brands and advertisements by using the latest developments in neuroscience.

In recent months, these techniques have not just been applied to the marketing of finished products, but also to product development. 'It's about uncovering new undiscovered needs', says Martin Lindstrom, author of *Buyology*, who has been studying the development of neuromarketing since its inception seven years ago. 'A lot of manufacturers are struggling as it's easy to come up with ideas consumers don't feel they need.'

He cites the example of dishwasher tablets. Consumers are attracted to tablets embedded with a blue ball because, subconsciously, they believe they clean better. However, when asked in the context of traditional marketing methods, they claim no preference about colour.

'The main reason why [traditional market research often] fails is that we look at things from a conscious point of view', says Mr Lindstrom. 'We ask: "Do you like the brand?" We ask the consumer to be incredibly rational and we know today from neuroscience that 85 per cent of the decisions we make are made by the unconscious part of brain.'

Neuromarketers believe their work will be especially useful for products consumers find hard to describe – particularly when they need to know consumers' reactions to smell, taste and touch.

According to Neurofocus, the global market leader in neurological testing, consumer goods companies are even creating their own in-house testing units that mock up supermarkets. They can use them to change everything from shelf positioning to point-of-sale advertisements with the flick of a switch and monitor the shopper's brain during the few seconds it takes to select a product.

But some advertisers fear this adherence to science could stamp out 'light bulb' ideas and destroy creativity in the industry.

Neurofocus argues that mind-reading actually helps sell original thinking to companies that would otherwise stick with tried-and-tested methods.

The issue of market research in the development of new products is controversial. Marketing literature traditionally has portrayed new product development as, essentially, a market/customer-led process, but paradoxically, many major market innovations appear in practice to be technologically driven, to arise from a technology seeking a market application rather than a market opportunity seeking a technology. This, of course, is the antithesis of the marketing concept, which is to start with trying to understand customer needs. The role of market research in new product development is most clearly questionable with major product innovations, where no market exists. First, if potential customers are unable adequately to understand the product, then market research can provide only negative answers (Brown, 1991). Second, consumers frequently have difficulty articulating their needs. Hamel and Prahalad (1994: 8) argue that customers lack foresight; they refer to Akio Morita, Sony's influential leader:

> *Our plan is to lead the public with new products rather than ask them what kind of products they want. The public does not know what is possible, but we do.*

This leads many scientists and technologists to view marketing departments with scepticism. Frequently, they have seen their exciting new technology rejected, due to market research findings produced by their marketing department. Market research specialists would argue that such problems could be overcome with the use of 'benefits research'. The problem here is that the benefits may not be clearly understood, or even perceived as a benefit by respondents. King (1985: 2) sums up the research dilemma neatly:

> *Consumer research can tell you what people did and thought at one point in time: it can't tell you directly what they might do in a new set of circumstances.*

In Illustration 16.4, from GlaxoSmithKline, consumer healthcare highlights the difficulties of trying to understand consumer research.

Illustration 16.4

GlaxoSmithKline

GSK have known for many years that consumers are fickle. Many years after the launch of its very successful Aquafresh striped toothpaste GlaxoSmithKline undertook consumer research to try to explore product development opportunities. Some of the findings were surprising. Consumers questioned the need or benefit of having stripes in the paste. Yet, in store trials, when given the opportunity to purchase a single colour paste consumers continued to purchase the striped toothpaste. A similar reaction was recorded when consumers were asked about flavouring of the toothpaste. Consumers suggested that they would prefer a wider variety of flavours such as strawberry or banana rather than mint, yet when other flavours were offered few consumers purchased them. The product manager emphasised the need to check consumer rhetoric with their actions.

Source: Trott, P. and Lataste, A. (2003) The role of consumer market research in new product decision-making: some preliminary findings from European firms, Entrepreneurship, Marketing and Innovation Conference, University of Karlsrühe, 8–9 September, conference proceedings.

Discontinuous new products

Major innovations are referred to as **discontinuous new products** when they differ from existing products in that field, sometimes creating entirely new markets and when they require buyers to change their behaviour patterns. For example, the personal computer and MP3 players created entirely new markets and required consumers to change their behaviour. Such products usually require a period of learning on the part of the user. Indeed, sometimes the manufacturer has to explain and suggest to users how the product should and could be used. Rogers' (2010) study on the diffusion of innovations as a social process argues that it requires time for societies to learn and experiment with new products. This raises the problem of how to deal with consumers with limited prior knowledge and how to conduct market research on a totally new product or a major product innovation. The two major difficulties are:

1 the problem of selection of respondents; and
2 the problem of understanding the major innovation.

Due to their focus on what is currently on offer in the marketplace, customers primarily demand so-called incremental innovations. Companies, however, want to develop entry points for radical innovations. The identification of radical innovations is a difficult task whose implementation is associated often with significant risk. It is questionable if market research alone can allow innovation management to develop attractive search fields for radical innovations and whether it can also contribute to a reduction of the risk that such innovations inherently possess. Research by Lettl et al. (2006) shows that successful innovative companies tend to choose to involve specifically qualified knowledge carriers early on in the innovation process, such as lead users or external experts in their search for innovations.

Confronted with a radically new technology, consumers may not understand what needs the technology can satisfy, as was the case with the fax machine or 3M's Post-it Note. This is because consumers are not able to link physical product characteristics with the outputs of the innovation. For example, when consumers first saw a fax machine, all they saw was a bulky expensive machine that looked like a copier. They were not able to imagine using it, hence they were not receptive to the new idea. Research has shown that experts are better able to understand potential benefits than those with less product knowledge. The type of research technique selected is crucial in obtaining accurate and reliable data.

This is the key issue. Early customer input on applications that use radically new technologies is crucial for gaining an understanding of the benefits and value of these new technologies. But new technologies often are difficult to understand. Potential customers must have a clear understanding of a new technology application before they give their input on it. Otherwise, that input may be misleading. Prototypes provide a clear picture to the customer, but seldom are available in the early (predevelopment) stage. Research by van den Hende and Schoormans (2012) suggests that an easy-to-apply product narrative can explain a technology application that uses a radically new technology to a customer before prototypes have been completed.

Market research and discontinuous new products

In the case of discontinuous product innovations, the use and validity of market research methods is questionable. As far back as the early 1970s, Tauber (1974) argued that such approaches discourage the development of major innovations. It may be argued that less, rather than more, market research is required, if major product innovations are required. Such an approach is characterised by the so-called technology-push model of innovation. Products that emerge from a technology-push approach are generated with little consideration of the market. Indeed, a market may not yet exist, as with the case of the PC and many other completely new products. Frequently, consumers are unable to understand the technology in question and view new products as a threat to their existing way of operating. Martin (1995: 122) argues that:

> customers can be extremely unimaginative . . . trying to get people to change the way they do things is the biggest obstacle facing many companies.

Many writers on this subject argue that potential consumers are not able to relate the physical aspects of a major innovative product with the consequences of owning and using it (Ortt and Schoormans, 1993). Others argue that, whilst market research can help to fine-tune product concepts, it is seldom the spur for an entirely new product concept. Consequently, most conventional market research techniques deliver invalid results (Hamel and Prahalad, 1994).

New approaches are being recognised in the area of discontinuous product innovations. One technique adopts a process of probing and learning, where valuable experience is gained with every step taken and modifications are made to the product and the approach to the market based on that learning (Lynn et al., 1997). This is not trial and error but careful experimental design and exploration of the market often using the heritage of the organisation. This type of new product development is very different from traditional techniques and methods described in most marketing texts.

Circumstances when market research may hinder the development of discontinuous new products

Product developers and product testers tend to view the product offering in a classical layered view, where the product is assumed to have a core benefit and additional attributes and features are laid around it, hence layered view. Saren and Tzokas (1994) have argued that much of the problem is due to the way we view a product. They state that often we view it in isolation from:

- its context;
- the way it is used; and
- the role of the customer–supplier relationship.

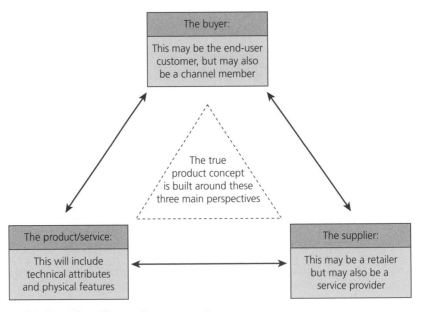

Figure 16.2 The tripartite product concept

Source: Adapted from Saren, M.A.J. and Tzokas, N. (1994) Proceedings of the Annual Conference of the European Marketing Academy, Maastricht.

This contributes to misleading views on new products. Figure 16.2 illustrates the **tripartite product concept** that captures the three views highlighted by Saren and Tzokas. The significance of this alternative view is that it highlights the reality of any product's situation. That is, product developers and product testers need to recognise that a product will be viewed differently by channel members than by end users. For example, end users will be concerned about how the product will perform, whereas channel members are more interested in how the product will *sell*, whether it will be easy to *stock and display* and, most importantly, whether it will be *profitable*. The Dyson case study at the end of this chapter illustrates the difficulties in trying to convince retailers to stock a new, slightly unusual product with which they are not familiar.

Technology-intensive products

Adopting a technology-push[1] approach to product innovations can allow a company to target and control premium market segments, establish its technology as the industry standard, build a favourable market reputation, determine the industry's future evolution, and achieve high profits. It can become the centrepiece in a company's strategy for market leadership. It is, however, costly and risky. Such an approach requires a company to develop and commercialise an emerging technology in pursuit of growth and profits. To be successful, a company needs to ensure its technology is at the heart of its competitive strategy. Merck, Microsoft and Dyson have created competitive advantage by offering unique products, lower costs or both by making technology the focal point in their strategies. These companies have understood the role of technology in differentiating their products in the marketplace. They have used their respective technologies to offer a distinct bundle of products, services and price ranges that have appealed to different market segments. Such products revolutionise product categories or define new categories, such as Hewlett-Packard's laser-jet printers and Apple's (then IBM's) personal computer. These products shift market structures, require consumer learning and induce behaviour changes, hence the difficulties for consumers when they are asked to pass judgement.

This is particularly the case if the circumstances relate to an entirely new product that is unknown to the respondent. New information is always interpreted in the light of one's prior knowledge and experience. In industrial markets, the level of information symmetry about the core technology usually is very high indeed (hence the limited use of market research), but, in consumer markets, this is not always the case. For example, industrial markets are characterised by:

- relatively few (information-rich) buyers;
- products often being customised and involving protracted negotiations regarding specifications;
- and, most importantly, the buyers usually being expert in the technology of the new product (i.e. high information symmetry about the core technology).

In situations of low information symmetry, consumers have difficulty in understanding the core product and are unable to articulate their needs and any additional

---

[1] The technology-push approach to NPD centres on trying to deliver the most effective technology available.

benefits sought. Conversely, in situations of high information symmetry, consumers are readily able to understand the core product and, hence, are able to articulate their needs and a wide range of additional benefits sought, for example in tasting new food products.

Furthermore, discontinuous product innovations or radical product innovations frequently have to overcome the currently installed technology base – usually through displacement. This is known as the **installed base effect**. The installed base effect is the massive inertial effect of an existing technology or product that tends to preclude or severely slow the adoption of a superseding technology or product. This creates an artificial adoption barrier that can become insurmountable for some socially efficient and advantageous innovations. An example of this is the DVORAK keyboard, which has been shown to provide up to 40 per cent faster typing speeds. Yet, the QWERTY keyboard remains the preference for most users because of its installed base, i.e. the widespread availability of keyboards that have the QWERTY configuration (Kay, 2013).

The idea of being shackled with an obsolete technology leads to the notion of **switching costs**. Switching is the one-time cost to the buyer who converts to the new product. Porter (1985) notes that switching costs may be a significant impediment to the adoption of a new consumer product. Buyer switching costs may arise as a result of prior commitments to a technology (a) and to a particular vendor (b). Computer software is an obvious example where problems of compatibility frequently arise. Similarly, buyers may have developed routines and procedures for dealing with a specific vendor that will need to be modified if a new relationship is established. The effect of both types of switching costs for a buyer is a disincentive to explore new vendors. There is a clear dilemma facing firms: market research may reveal genuine limitations with the new product, but also it may produce negative feedback on a truly innovative product that may create a completely new market. The uncertainty centres on two key variables:

1 information symmetry about the core technology between producer and buyer; and
2 the installed base effect and switching costs.

Breaking with convention and winning new markets

There is evidence to suggest that many successful companies were successful because they were prepared to take the risky decision to ignore their customers' views and proceed with their new product ideas because they passionately believed that it would be successful. Subsequent success for these new products suggested that the firm's existing customers were unable to peer into the future, recognise that a different product or service would be desirable and articulate this to the firm. On reflection, this seems a lot to ask of customers and, indeed, is extremely difficult.

Between 1975 and 1995, 60 per cent of the companies in the *Fortune* 500 listing were replaced. Irrespective of their industry, new entrants either created new markets or recreated existing ones. Compaq overtook IBM to become the world's largest manufacturer of personal computers; Dyson overhauled Hoover's established position of market leader to become the new market leader in vacuum

Illustration 16.5

Closures for the wine industry: the customer does not know best

Consumers made it clear time and again that they did not want a screw-cap on their bottle of wine. They preferred the theatre of the cork and pop. Yet, the international wine brands and retailers were determined to show customers that screw-cap was better: in 2011, over 90 per cent of wine bottles were sold with a screw-cap (http://www.jancisrobinson.com/articles/arent-screwcaps-mahvellous). See the case study at the end of Chapter 7.

cleaners; Xerox lost out to Canon, which quickly became the bestseller in copiers; and there are many other examples. So why is it that established highly respected firms fail to recognise the future? In the cases already mentioned, hindsight suggests that more resources should have been devoted to innovation, but that is not all. Established businesses that have been successful for many years also develop comfortable routines and become complacent. Hierarchies, systems, rulebooks and formulae work pretty well for controlling and improving the efficiency of repeated actions. They are hopeless for inventing, experimenting with and developing something that has never happened before (see 'The dilemma of innovation management', Chapter 4). Furthermore, a growing number of academics (Christensen, 1997; Hamel and Prahalad, 1994) argue that a particular problem exists because firms rely too heavily on market research and that some of the techniques reinforce the present and do not peer into the future. It is well known that market research results often produce negative reactions to discontinuous new products (innovative products) that later become profitable for the innovating company. Indeed, there are some famous examples, such as the fax machine, the VCR and James Dyson's bagless vacuum cleaner. Despite this, companies continue to seek the views of consumers on their new product ideas. The debate about the use of market research in the development of new products is long-standing and controversial.

In his award-winning 'business book of the year'[2] Clayton Christensen (1997) investigated why well-run companies that were admired by many failed to stay on top of their industry. His research showed that, in the cases of well-managed firms such as Digital, IBM, Apple and Xerox, 'good management' (sic) was the most powerful reason why they failed to remain market leaders. It was precisely because these firms listened to their customers and provided more and better products of the sort they wanted that they lost their position of leadership. He argues that there are times when it is right not to listen to customers. Indeed, many companies share the same ideas about who their customers are and what products and services they want. The more that companies share this conventional wisdom about how they compete, the more they fight for incremental improvements in cost reductions and quality, and the more they avoid the discontinuous disruptive new products. Illustration 16.5 highlights the dangers of falling into this trap.

It is not surprising that many firms try to meet the needs of their customers. After all, successful companies have established themselves and built a successful

[2] Christensen (1997) was awarded the *Financial Times* business book of the year award in 1999.

business on providing the customer with what he or she wanted. IBM and Hoover, for example, became very good at serving their customers. But, when a new, very different, technology came along, these companies struggled. These large successful companies have been fighting known competitors for many years through careful planning and reducing costs. Suddenly, they were faced with a completely different threat: new, smaller firms doing things differently and using unusual technologies. In IBM's case, it was personal computers and, in Hoover's case, it has been bagless vacuum cleaners. Table 16.1 illustrates a wide range of products that initially were rejected by consumers, but went on to be successful.

If sufficient care is not exercised by managers, market research can be used to support conservative product development decision making. The previous sections have highlighted the difficulty faced by many managers in the field of new product development. In many crucial new product development decisions, the course of action that is most desirable over the long run is not the best course of action in the short term. This is the dilemma addressed in the debate about short-termism, that is, an emphasis on cutting costs and improving efficiencies in the immediate future, rather than on creativity and the development of innovative new product ideas for the long term. What is of concern is not the desire to cut costs but the apparent disregard of the implications and damage that such policies may bring about and, in particular, the neglect of the company's ability to create new business opportunities for the future well-being of the company.

To return to a point made earlier by Akio Morita, Sony's influential leader Morita argued that the public did not know what was possible and it was the firm that should lead the customer. This point is explored more fully by Hamel and Prahalad (1994: 108) who argue that firms need to go beyond customer-led ideas if they wish

Table 16.1 Products that initially were rejected by consumers but went on to be successful

New product	Year	
Fax machines	1960s	Initially rejected by consumers who could not see any application for this product.
Microcomputers	1960s	Initially consumers could not foresee all the potential uses for microcomputers.
Benson & Hedges Gold cigarettes	1970s	Gallagher launched this product in the UK in 1978. Early consumer tests revealed indifferent support, yet the product was, eventually, a huge commercial success and brand leader in the UK.
Baileys Irish Cream Liqueur	1980s	Early consumer trials of this product suggested that it was not liked by consumers.
Dyson bagless vacuum cleaner	1990	Consumer research by retailers led them to believe consumers did not want a vacuum cleaner that displayed dirt collected in a transparent container. In fact, consumers later preferred this design.
Chryslers PT Cruiser	1990s	Actually, this product was not rejected, but Chrysler interpreted its consumer research as a niche product rather than a mass volume product. Hence, sales production could not match demand.
Screw-cap wine bottle closures	2000	Wine bottlers bowed to the demand of large retailers (buyers) to incorporate screw-caps. Consumers initially rejected screw-caps, but many now prefer it.

Source: A dirty business, *Guardian* 16/03/1999, copyright Guardian News & Media Ltd 2010.

to be successful in the future. They are brutal in their criticism of customers' ability to peer into the future:

> *Customers are notoriously lacking in foresight. Ten or fifteen years ago, how many of us were asking for cellular telephones, fax machines and copiers at home, 24 hour discount brokerage accounts, multivalve automobile engines, video dial tone, etc.?*

Successful companies of the future will be those that are part of its creation. This means developing products that will be used in the future. Companies need to continually challenge existing products and markets. This can be achieved by pushing at the boundaries of current product concepts. Some firms have recognised this and are putting the most advanced technology they have available into the hands of the world's most sophisticated and demanding customers. IBM and Xerox have learnt through bitter experience what it is like to lose out to newcomers with new ideas and new technology. They know that today's customers may not be tomorrow's.

Using a simple two-by-two matrix (Figure 16.3) showing needs and customers, Hamel and Prahalad have shown that however well a company meets the articulated needs of current customers, it runs a great risk if it does not have a view of the needs customers cannot yet articulate: in other words, the products of the future.

All this raises the problem of how to deal with consumers with limited prior knowledge and how to conduct market research on a totally new product or a major product innovation. In their research analysing successful cases of discontinuous product innovations, Lynn et al. (1997) argue that firms adopt a process of probing and learning. Valuable experience is gained with every step taken and modifications are made to the product and the approach to the market based on that learning.

This is not trial and error, but careful experimental design and exploration of the market often using the experience and heritage of the organisation. This type of new product development is very different from traditional techniques and methods described in marketing texts.

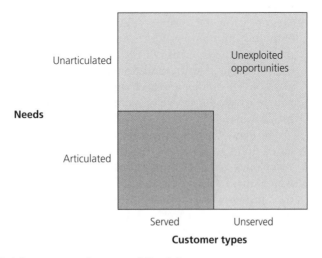

Figure 16.3 Gaining new customers of the future

Source: Hamel, S. and Prahalad, C.K. (1994) Competing for the future, *Harvard Business Review*, vol. 72, no. 4, 122–8.

Technology-intensive products present similar difficulties. Nyström (1990) described high-tech markets as marketing dependent and technologically driven. Unfortunately, there is evidence that this linkage often is not recognised by organisations (Trott et al., 2013). High-tech markets are characterised as complex. In addition, they exist under rapidly changing technological conditions, which lead to shorter life cycles and the need for rapid decisions. The importance of speed in high-tech markets is driven by increasing competition and the continually evolving expectations of customers. All of this is compounded by higher levels of risk for both the customer and the producer. Herein lies the problem: highly innovative products have an inherent high degree of uncertainty about exactly how an emerging technology may be formulated into a usable product and what the final product application will be. Market vision, or the ability to look into the future and picture products and services that will be successful, is a fundamental requirement for those firms wishing to engage in innovation, but is also very problematic (Van der Duin, 2006). It involves assessing one's own technological capability and present or future market needs and visioning a market offering that people will want to buy. Whilst this may sound simple, it lies at the heart of the innovation process and focuses attention on the need to examine not only the market but the way the new product offering is used or consumed.

When it may be correct to ignore your customers

Many industry analysts and business consultants argued that the devotion to focus groups and market research had gone too far (Christensen, 1997; Francis, 1994; Martin, 1995). Indeed, the traditional new product development process of market research, segmentation, competitive analysis and forecasting, prior to passing the resultant information to the research and development (R&D) department, leads to commonality and bland new products. This is largely because the process constrains rather than facilitates innovative thinking and creativity. Furthermore, and more alarming, these techniques are well-known and used by virtually all companies operating in consumer markets. In many of these markets, the effect is an overemphasis on minor product modifications and on competition that tends to focus on price. Indeed, critics of the market-orientated approach to new product development argue that the traditional marketing activities of branding, advertising and positioning, market research and consumer research act as an expensive obstacle course to product development rather than facilitating the development of new product ideas.

For many large multi-product companies, it seems the use of market research is based upon accepted practice in addition to being an insurance policy. Many large companies are not short of new product ideas – the problem lies in deciding in which ones to invest substantial sums of money (Cooper, 2001; Liddle, 2004), and then justifying this decision to senior managers. Against this background one can see why market research is so frequently used without hesitation, as decisions can be justified and defended. Small companies in general, and small single-product companies in particular, are in a different situation. Very often, new product ideas are scarce; hence, such companies frequently support ideas based upon their intuition and personal knowledge of the product.

The significance of discontinuous new products often is overlooked. Morone's (1993) study of successful US product innovations suggests that success was achieved through a combination of discontinuous product innovations and incremental improvements. Furthermore, in competitive, technology-intensive industries, success is achieved with discontinuous product innovations through the creation of entirely new products and businesses, whereas product line extensions and incremental improvements are necessary for maintaining leadership (Lynn et al., 1997). This, however, is only after leadership has been established through a discontinuous product innovation. This may appear to be at variance with accepted thinking that Japan secured success in the 1980s through copying and improving US and European technology. This argument is difficult to sustain on close examination of the evidence. The most successful Japanese firms have also been leaders in research and development. Furthermore, as Cohen and Levinthal (1990, 1994) have continually argued, access to technology is dependent on one's understanding of that technology.

Pause for thought

Ignoring your customers' views seems like a very high risk strategy, especially for an ambitious new manager and, if the product eventually fails, so might the career of the new manager!

Striking the balance between new technology and market research

Market research can provide a valuable contribution to the development of innovative products. The difficulties lie in the selection and implementation of research methods. It may be that market research has become a victim of its own success, that is, business and product managers now expect it to provide solutions to all difficult product management decisions. Practitioners need to view market research as a collection of techniques that can help to inform the decision process.

The development and adoption process for discontinuous or complex products is particularly difficult. The benefits to potential users may be difficult to identify and value and, usually because there are likely to be few substitute products available, it is difficult for buyers to compare and contrast. Sometimes, product developers have to lead buyers/consumers and show them the benefits, even educate them. This is where some marketing views suggest the process is no longer customer-led or driven by the market, and they would argue that what is now occurring is a technology-push approach to product development. Day (1999) suggests that, on closer examination, there are a number of false dichotomies here:

- that you must either lead or follow customers;
- that you cannot stay close to both current and potential customers; and
- that technology-push cannot be balanced with market-pull.

It is true, as we have seen in this chapter, that customers respond most positively to what is familiar and comfortable and that customers view the high costs of new technology (including switching costs) in a largely negative way. Firms need to try to understand how customers will view innovations in the marketplace; this may include adoption influences, such as consumption pattern, product capability and technological capability (Veryzer, 2003). Valid good management should be capable of selecting the appropriate market research techniques to avoid superficial consumer reactions. A thorough understanding of all aspects of the market and the needs of users should inform managers that it is possible to provide customers with what they want and lead them through education.

The argument about current markets and future markets is made powerfully by both Christensen (1997) and Hamel and Prahalad (1994). The suggestion here is that firms become myopic towards their current customers and fail to see the larger slowly changing market. The case of IBM in the 1980s is often given here. It surely is a responsibility of senior management to try to understand the wider and future environment of the firm. This may be very easy to record, but, in practice, it is extremely difficult to carry out. There are real dangers for all firms here. For example, discontinuous new technologies may require huge changes for firms and one can see that, for many, the easy option is to hope the new technology fails and the firm can carry on as normal. Failure to change and adopt may result in more cases like IBM, Xerox, Hoover and many financial service firms that failed to respond to online banking. Once again, it should be possible for a well-run company to fully exploit its current markets and develop and enter the markets of the future. For example, both Kodak and Fuji have exploited the massive changes in the photographic market with the introduction of digital photography.

Finally, the arguments about market-pull or technology-push never seem to go away. But readers of this book should now be clear that this is a stale argument. What is required is an understanding of innovation. Whilst it is clear that, in some industries, the role of science and technology is far greater than in other industries, innovation requires inputs from both. It is true there are many firms in the pharmaceutical sector that argue that their approach to product development is to start with brilliant science and to look for ways of using it in new drugs; and that the role of marketing and sales is to develop sales of these products. Whilst this approach may work for a few, even in this industry sector, there are many firms that operate differently. Some of the most successful pharmaceutical firms, including Glaxo-SmithKline, Pfizer and Merck, work very closely with buyers and users to develop new drugs and to improve many existing ones. Indeed, the success of one of the world's bestselling drugs, Viagra, is, surely, testament to the benefits of working closely with the market.

Using suppliers and lead users to improve product variety

On the suppliers' side, collaboration during the NPD process may lead to a faster and more efficient process. On the lead users' side, collaboration may provide ideas for entirely new products and/or modifications to existing ones. Research by Al-Zubi and Tsinopoulos (2012) has shown that increasing the extent of collaboration with lead users and with suppliers during the NPD process will increase the variety of products offered to customers, and that lead users have a higher impact on product variety to suppliers. (See Chapter 3 for more on lead users.)

Innovation in action

Self-service is growing in some industries. What other sectors can it be applied to?

MiNiBAR, in the heart of Amsterdam, is a self-service bar. When you arrive, a concierge gives you the key to your own fridge, which is stocked with beer, wine, spirits and snacks. You and your friends help yourselves over the course of the evening, and settle up your account before leaving. The mini-bars are stocked from the back, making for easy restocking. It's simply extending the concept of the hotel mini-bar to the high street of course – but it's new and is bound to attract interest.

From the customer perspective, it's fun, convenient and there's no more queuing at the bar. From a business perspective it also means fewer staff members, and more customers can be accommodated because less space is taken up by the bar.

Source: HSBC (2010) *100 Thoughts*, HSBC, London.

The challenge for senior management

Innovation is clearly a complex issue and, sometimes, it is a concept that sits uneasily in organisations. Indeed, some writers on the subject have argued that organisations are often the graveyard rather than the birthplace for many innovations. Applying pressure on product managers to seek high profits from quick volume sales rather than develop business opportunities for the future is a common mistake made by senior management. Similarly a heavy reliance on market research to minimise risk when developing new product ideas also contributes to an early grave for product ideas. The use of financial systems that minimise risk and avoid investment in more long-term projects is another common preference, which frequently emanates from senior management.

Correcting such ills will never be easy, but, given the strategic importance of innovation, it is a challenge senior management must take up. The adjustments that need to be made in order to encourage innovation in large companies may break some of the established rules of corporate life. They will require changes to internal systems and structures and the culture of the organisation. However, without such changes, potential innovations will continue to be squeezed out by the system, and thus rob the company of the most effective means of survival (Brown, 1991).

Case study

Dyson, Hoover and the bagless vacuum cleaner

This case study illustrates many of the obstacles and difficulties of launching a new product. The product in question used new technology that initially was rejected by existing manufacturers. It was priced at more than double that of existing products, but, eventually, captured more than 50 per cent of the UK vacuum cleaner market in less than four years.

→

Introduction

Conventional wisdom would, surely, suggest that Dyson Appliances Ltd would fail within a few months. After all, it appeared to be a small company with an eccentric manager at its helm, trying to sell an over-priced product of limited appeal in a very competitive market with less expensive, conventional, mass-market products made by respected manufacturers whose names were, quite literally, household words. The result was very different. The story of the Dyson bagless vacuum cleaner is not a classic tale of 'rags to riches'. The charismatic inventor James Dyson was afforded many privileges and opportunities not available to most. It is, nonetheless, a fascinating story and illustrates many of the difficulties and problems faced by small businesses and 'lone inventors'; and demonstrates the determination, hard work and sacrifices necessary in order to succeed. The cliché *against the odds*, which Dyson (1998) used as the title of his autobiography, is certainly appropriate and tells the story of the development and launch of the first bagless vacuum cleaner – the Dyson DC01.

This case raises several significant research questions in the field of innovation management. First, how and why did senior executives at leading appliance manufacturers across Europe, such as Electrolux, Bosch and Miele, decide not to utilise the technology offered to them by Dyson? Second, how and why did senior buyers for many retail chains across the United Kingdom fail to recognise the potential for the DC01? Third, technology transfer experts would point out that the Dyson vacuum cleaner is a classic case of technology transfer – a technology developed for one industry, i.e. dust extraction from sawmills, is applied to a different use in a new industry. Hence, it is technology transfer that needs to be championed and supported further by governments. Fourth, as a mechanism for protecting intellectual property, it seems that patents depend on the depth of your pocket. That is, they are prohibitively expensive and are, almost exclusively, for the benefit of large multinational organisations. What can be done to help small businesses without such large pockets and unlimited financial resources? And, finally, many commentators would argue that Dyson was successful partly because he had some influential contacts that he had established – he was fortunate. But there may be a hundred failed Mr Dysons littering the business

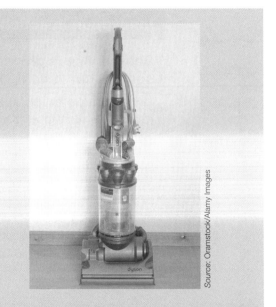

Source: Oramstock/Alamy Images

highways who did not have such contacts. How can governments try to facilitate inventors like Dyson and ensure that more innovations succeed (thereby developing the economic base of their country)?

Reaping the rewards from technological innovation

Since Dyson's entry into the domestic appliance market, two of the largest world players in the vacuum cleaner market have responded to the challenge laid down by James Dyson's bagless vacuum cleaner, launched in the United Kingdom in 1993. Dyson now accounts for a third of all vacuum cleaner sales in the United Kingdom. In 1998, Dyson Appliances sold nearly 1.4 million units worldwide. Revenues for the year were £190 million but, surprisingly, net income was £29 million – 15 per cent of sales (see Figure 16.4).

Background

Prior to the development of the bagless vacuum cleaner, James Dyson had already demonstrated his prowess as a designer and businessman. He was responsible for the 'ballbarrow', a wheelbarrow that revolutionised that market by using a ball rather than a wheel. This was to provide the financial foundation for the development of the bagless vacuum cleaner. That particular experience taught James Dyson many lessons. One in particular is worth mentioning. The patents for the ballbarrow were owned by the company that James Dyson helped to set up. He

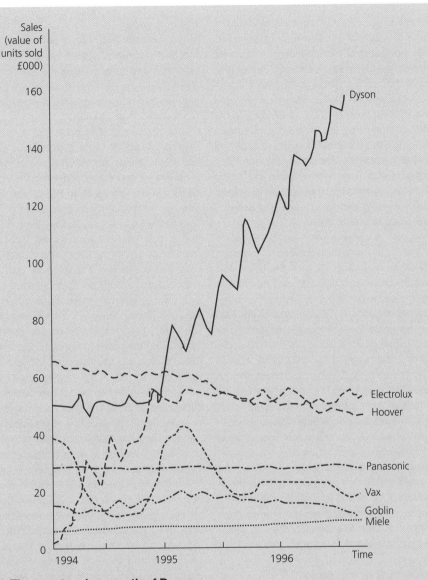

Figure 16.4 The spectacular growth of Dyson

eventually parted with this company but, unfortunately, lost all control of the patents as they belonged to the company and not to himself. Dyson was determined that any future patent would belong to him personally and not a company.

For those who may not recall their British social and economic history, Hubert Booth developed the first vacuum cleaner at the end of the nineteenth century. Vacuum technology uses the principle of a vacuum (the absence of everything, even air). Vacuum cleaners actually create a partial vacuum or, more accurately, an area of reduced air pressure as air moves outward within the fan. Airflow is created as air with normal air pressure moves towards the area with the reduced air pressure. A few years later, in 1902, the British Vacuum Cleaner Company was offering a vacuum cleaning service to the homes of the affluent and wealthy. A large horse-drawn 5-hp engine would pull up outside your home and a hose would be fed into the house where it would begin to

→

suck out all the dust. By 1904, a more mobile machine was available for use and was operated by domestic servants. As popularity of the technology increased, additional manufacturers began entering the market. Electrolux introduced a cylinder and hose vacuum cleaner in 1913 and, in 1936, Hoover an upright cleaner with rotating brushes. This was known as the Hoover Junior and was the bestselling vacuum cleaner in the United Kingdom. Indeed, virtually all vacuum cleaners since this time are variations on that Hoover Junior design. That was until the late 1970s and early 1980s when James Dyson developed a vacuum cleaner using cyclonic forces and avoided the need for a bag to collect dust.

When it comes to cleaning performance, there is a tendency to look primarily at the power of the suction motor and the amount of bristles on the brush roll. Whilst these are important considerations, the quality and size of the paper bag are very important factors as well. The paper bag in a vacuum cleaner consists of a special paper enclosure into which the dirt and air are directed as part of the filtering system. The paper used is specially processed to permit the air to pass through it whilst retaining as much of the dust and dirt as possible. The quality of the bag's filter media affects both its ability to retain the fine dust and allergens and its ability to allow air to flow easily through it. The size of the bag will also affect how easily the air flows. A good-quality paper bag is a very important vacuum cleaner component, which needs to be replaced regularly. The Dyson vacuum cleaner maintains its performance during the vacuuming process because it has no bag, hence there is no reduction in suction due to clogging of the pores of the bag, a feature that is characteristic of the bagged cleaners.

The development of a bagless vacuum cleaner

It is the bag component of a vacuum cleaner that Dyson focused on to revolutionise the vacuum cleaner appliance industry. Put simply, he tackled the key dilemma for vacuum cleaners – how to collect dirt and dust, yet, at the same time, allow clean air to pass through. This was achieved by abandoning the use of bags to collect dirt. Instead, he adapted the use of centrifugal forces. Many of us will have enjoyed cyclonic forces personally. One of the oldest fun rides at fairgrounds involves a large drum in which people stand with their backs against the outer wall. When

the drum spins, the floor is lowered and people remain pressed against the outer wall. The exhilaration and excitement clearly results from being forced against a wall, unable to move one's head or arms due to the huge forces that are created. Yet, the fascinating aspect here is that the drum's speed is no more than 33,kph (20 mph).

It is this principle that is used to separate the heavy dust particles from the air, allowing the clean air to continue through the machine. The air, which has no mass, is not forced against the side walls of the container and takes the easiest route in the centre and thus out through the hole at the bottom (see Figure 16.5). This approach had been used in a variety of industries to collect dust, for example, in sawmills, but this was on a large scale (30 m by 10 m) and involved substantial pieces of equipment. The difficulty was applying this technology to a small domestic appliance.

If anyone still thinks that innovation is about waking up in the morning with a bright idea and shouting 'Eureka!', they should consider carefully James Dyson's difficult road to success. Between 1978 and 1982, he built over 1,000 prototype vacuum cleaners, spent over £2 million and experienced many years of sweat and headaches before eventually developing a successful prototype. But this was merely the start of an even longer project to get manufacturers to buy the licence to manufacture. Indeed, over 10 years later, Dyson decided to mass produce the product for the UK market himself.

The story begins in 1978 with James Dyson at home with his young family, helping with some of the chores around the home. Like many families at the time, the Dysons owned a Hoover Junior upright vacuum cleaner. Dyson noticed that when a new bag is fitted to the vacuum cleaner it works well, but quickly loses much of its suction. He soon had the vacuum cleaner in pieces on his workbench and was amazed to realise that the standard vacuum cleaner technology relied on holes in the bag to allow clean air to pass through. As soon as these clogged up (which starts to occur immediately), suction begins to deteriorate. Moreover, he discovered quickly that all bagged vacuum cleaners operate on the same principle. How, then, can this limitation be overcome? The idea came to Dyson whilst he was investigating a problem at his ballbarrow factory. To improve toughness, the product was powder-coated and then heated. This involved spraying the powder

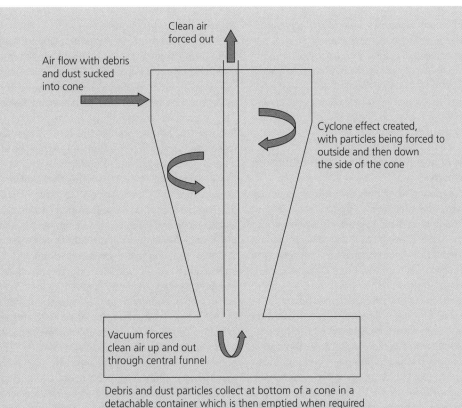

Clean air
forced out

Air flow with debris
and dust sucked
into cone

Cyclone effect created,
with particles being forced to
outside and then down
the side of the cone

Vacuum forces
clean air up and out
through central funnel

Debris and dust particles collect at bottom of a cone in a
detachable container which is then emptied when required

Figure 16.5 Basic operating principle of Dyson bagless vacuum cleaner

coating, which was messy. To overcome this problem, an industrial vacuum cleaner was required. The suppliers of the powder coating informed Dyson that most of their larger customers use cyclones to collect the powder. Such cyclones are also used in a variety of industrial settings, such as sawmills to extract dust from the air. This information was the beginning of what turned out to be a 15-year project.

Cyclonic cleaning systems separate the dust particles from the airflow by spinning the air within a separation chamber. The Dyson system operates as follows.

Any dirt and air enters the nozzle near the floor and travels through the hose towards the separation chambers. First, it enters the primary dirt-separation chamber where the larger dirt particles are deposited. From there, the air with the remaining fine dirt and dust travels to the cyclonic chamber. Once in the cyclonic chamber, the spinning action separates most of the fine dirt and dust particles from the airflow. The spinning causes centrifugal force to act upon the dust

particles, moving them outward whilst the air exits from the inner part of the chamber (see Figure 16.5).

The Dyson vacuum cleaner uses two cyclones and several filters to capture dirt and dust. Whilst the first cyclonic chamber captured large dust particles, some fine dust particles were escaping with the air. The answer was a second, smaller cyclone and Dyson spent many months developing this idea. The key problem was in the application of the theory, that is, having dust pass through one cyclone and then another, all in a small domestic appliance. After months, and eventually years, of further trials and errors, the development of a cyclone within a cyclone was born (the dual cyclone). As dirt and air is sucked into the machine, the first cyclone separates the large dust particles and these come to rest at the bottom of the canister. The remaining air and fine dust (including cigarette smoke) is then carried into a second cyclone, which separates the even finer dust particles from the air.

→

The technology also uses several replaceable filters to remove even smaller particles of dust. Since the air is quite clean, it is then allowed to flow through the motor to cool it. After leaving the motor, the air is filtered by a HEPA (High Efficiency Particulate Air) exhaust filter to remove even more fine particles and carbon from the motor brushes before it leaves the vacuum cleaner.

In search of a manufacturer – 'don't let them get you down'

Thanks to experience gained with other products, most notably the ballbarrow, Dyson was able to ensure that patent applications were in place prior to negotiations. This is essential if you wish to ensure that large multinational companies are not going to steal your intellectual property. From Dyson's experience, he would argue that they would probably try to steal it, regardless of any protection one held.

Dyson was offering a licence to manufacturing companies that included exclusive rights to his patents. In return, Dyson would receive a percentage of their profits from the sale of the manufactured product. Dyson was looking for a five- to ten-year licence with a royalty of 5 per cent of the wholesale price and £40,000 up front. In addition, he was offering his help in the development of the product from its prototype form. Unfortunately, Hoover, Electrolux, Goblin, Black and Decker, AEG, Vax and many others all declined. There were many different reasons given. Sometimes, the companies appeared to be arrogant and dismissed Dyson as a 'loony crank'. What was surprising was that, throughout, companies appeared to be obsessed with finding fault with the product. On other occasions, the company expected Dyson to hand over the patents for very little financial reward. Frequently, there were difficulties in agreeing to meet. This was due to problems of protecting the intellectual property that would flow from a meeting between the R&D experts of the company in question and Dyson.

Many of the objections, limitations and problems with the prototype may have been justified. One may even argue that the agreement sought by Dyson was ambitious. There is also one other key issue – the bags. The Dyson product was proposing to eliminate vacuum bags, but this was a very profitable business for vacuum cleaner manufacturers. They were unlikely to relish this prospect.

Breaking through in Japan

If things were not going well in the United Kingdom and Europe, fortunately Dyson had a breakthrough in Japan. Apex Inc. agreed, after several arduous weeks of negotiations, to a licence to manufacture and sell in Japan. The product was to be called 'G-Force'. The successful licensing of the technology to a Japanese manufacturer in the late 1980s helped Dyson to secure much-needed revenue at a time when he was beginning to consider throwing in the towel. This small level of income also provided the encouragement he needed to start planning the establishment of manufacturing facilities in the United Kingdom. What is interesting about the licensing arrangement in question is that Dyson was uncertain that licensing revenues received reflect the true sales figures. As with all licensing and royalty agreements, there is a significant element of trust required. For example, authors trust their publishers that sales of their book will be recorded accurately and appropriate royalties paid. There is, however, the small matter of who establishes the level of sales. This, of course, is taken by the publisher who then pays the royalties to authors. This 'high-trust' relationship also operates with other licensing agreements where royalties are paid per item sold.

Entering the UK market and manufacturing in the United Kingdom

With a small amount of revenue starting to trickle in, Dyson decided that it was time to start in Britain. The existing appliance manufacturers had expressed no interest, hence Dyson planned to manufacture the product in Britain by offering the product to existing contract manufacturers. Essentially, Dyson decided to offer a series of contracts to two existing manufacturing companies, one to mould the component parts and another to assemble. For the existing moulding and assembly companies it was additional capacity. Unfortunately, the companies selected by Dyson caused further problems. First, the quality of the completed product was not acceptable to Dyson. Second, the companies seemed to be squeezing Dyson's work in between existing long-standing contracts. In the end, Dyson decided that he would prefer to manufacture and assemble the product himself. He purchased the moulds from the plastic moulding company and attempted to establish a factory in the United Kingdom, the rationale being that this would at least ensure that he was in control of his own destiny and would not have to rely on others. Further difficulties, however, were encountered by Dyson. First, he found that it is extremely difficult to borrow money – even with a proven successful product. Dyson explored the possibility of setting up a factory in an area where government development grants are available. For example, he tried South Wales but David Hunt, the then Welsh Office Minister, refused his application for a grant.

The project had now consumed 12 years of his life and had cost £2 million. Once again, Dyson was forced to consider whether it was all worth it.

After months of negotiations, Dyson's local bank manager agreed to lend him some more money and he was able to set up his manufacturing factory in Wiltshire. Soon Dyson was producing his own product in his own factory and the first Dyson bagless vacuum cleaner rolled off the production line in 1992.

Trying to sell to the retailers

Armed with a shiny new DC01 under his arm, James Dyson began visiting the large UK white-goods retailers, such as Currys, Dixons and Comet, to arrange sales orders. Unfortunately, Dyson was disappointed at their reaction. Quite simply, the retailers were not convinced that the UK consumer would be willing to pay possibly three times as much for a vacuum cleaner. Moreover, Dyson's bagless product was twice the price of the brand leader. The response was almost universal:

> Consumers are very happy with this one – why should they pay twice as much for yours? And, anyway, if your idea was any good, Hoover or Electrolux would have thought of it years ago.

Eventually, several of the home catalogue companies agreed to feature the product. In addition, an electricity board shop in the Midlands also agreed to stock a few products. Initially, sales were slow but, gradually, they increased. Eventually, John Lewis, the national department store, agreed to take the product. From here sales began to take off.

In terms of marketing and promoting the product, what is interesting is that, to date, the company has spent virtually nothing on promotion. Dyson has always adopted a strong product orientation and has believed that, if a product is good enough, it should require very little promotion. It is this approach that Dyson adopted for the bagless vacuum cleaner. Despite the use of revolutionary technology, Dyson decided against large advertising budgets and, instead, relied upon a few press releases and features in newspapers.

The competition responds

With Dyson beginning to challenge the once-comfortable dominant position of Electrolux and Hoover, both companies mounted a strong defence of their products' technology, claiming that their traditional vacuum cleaning technology was more effective than the Dyson. Much of the debate, usually via press advertisements, centred on cleaning effectiveness. Hoover and Electrolux were able to make some headline-grabbing claims, in particular, that their products had more suction power and, hence, were better. Certainly, the traditional vacuum cleaner with a bag had an initial high level of suction power, but this was necessary because the bag soon clogged up, reducing the level of suction. There are two different ways of viewing cleaning effectiveness. The most common use has to do with the ability of a vacuum cleaner to pick up dirt from the surface being cleaned. The other is the ability of the filtering system to clean the air so that a minimum amount of dirt and allergens is recirculated back into the home. The variable that is significant in a vacuum cleaner, however, is the flow of air and is measured in cubic metres per minute (CMM). It is one of the most important aspects of vacuum cleaner performance. Airflow in a vacuum cleaner is inversely proportional to the total resistance within the system and directly proportional to the suction created by the suction motor.

Figure 16.6 depicts cleaning performance after vacuuming 1,000 grams of ASTM (American Society for Testing and Materials) test dirt. You will see that the Dyson machine maintains a steady airflow, whilst other 'bagged' machines lose airflow.

Hoover's bagless vacuum cleaner

With sales and market share continuing to decline (see Table 16.2), Miele and Hoover attempted to fight Dyson in the vacuum cleaner market by developing similar bagless vacuum technologies. Hoover embarked on a technology transfer exercise to utilise technology first developed for the oil industry. The centrifugal force technology (similar to that used by Dyson) was used to separate gas or sand from crude

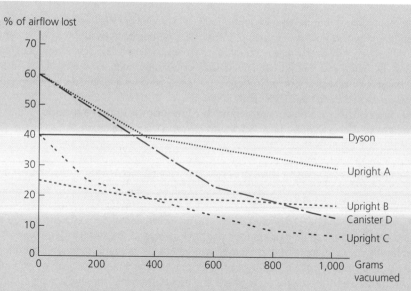

Figure 16.6 Cleaning performance of five vacuum cleaners

oil. This technology has now been applied to Hoover's range of Triple Vortex vacuum cleaners in an attempt to compete with Dyson's own patented centrifugal force technology (www.hoover.co.uk). Interestingly, Hoover's technology dispenses with the need for any filters. This may provide the advantage Hoover requires to re-establish itself as a key player in the vacuum cleaner market. Dyson, however, claimed that Hoover's technology copied its patents and sued Hoover for patent infringement in March 2000, eventually winning around £3 million in damages.

Dyson has had several legal battles with his competitors over patent infringement and advertising standards. In January 2000, the Advertising Standards Association (ASA) ruled in favour of Dyson regarding an advertisement from Electrolux that claimed its vacuum cleaner was the most powerful. The ASA ruled that power of the motor was no indication of vacuum cleaner effectiveness (*The Sunday Times*, 2000).

Table 16.2 With sales declining Miele and Hoover have attempted to take on Dyson in the vacuum cleaner market

	Volume (%)	Value (%)
Dyson		
Total market	33.5	53.5
Upright	51.6	66.9
Cylinder	13.6	29.8
Hoover		
Total market	12.3	9.2
Upright	16.5	10.2
Cylinder	8.2	7.1
Miele		
Total market	2.1	2.6
Cylinder	6.1	10.4

Hitting the big time

In 2002, Dyson entered the US market. In 2004, sales reached almost 1 million units. This contributed to a surge in profits at Dyson, which were £102.9 million in 2005, more than double 2003's figure. Sales efforts have continued and, in 2006, Dyson was the brand leader in the United States. This has been achieved with no intellectual property protection in the United States. Unusually, Dyson decided to enter the US market without any patent protection. He relied on the brand's strength that had been built and developed over the previous 10 years. Sales in 2006 were 1.5 million units. Dyson revealed that success in the United States was, partly, down to a very successful

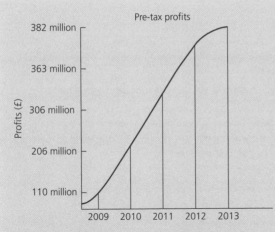

Figure 16.7 Dyson's pre-tax profits (2009–13)

$30 million ad campaign. This was a very different strategy to that used in the UK and Europe.

More recently, Dyson Appliances has been enjoying continued and improved success in one of the fiercest markets of all – Japan. Dyson became the biggest vacuum cleaner brand in Japan in 2013 by value, thanks to a 100 per cent increase in sales of its cordless cleaners, which now outsell its full-sized models in the country three to one. The company is also the market leader in Taiwan and Hong Kong. Sales in China continue to climb see Figure 16.7 and Table 16.3).

New products from Dyson

In 2013, Dyson filed patents for 'a hand-held blower with an insulating chamber' – in other words, a hairdryer, which is already being dubbed the Hairblade, playing on the name of its Airblade hand dryer. One of the key features on the diagrams within the patent is the emphasis on making it much quieter than

Table 16.3 Dyson's pre-tax profit and turnover (2009–13)

Year	Profits (£)	Turnover (£)
2013	382 million	1.3 billion
2012	363 million	1.2 billion
2011	306 million	1.05 billion
2010	206 million	0.89 billion
2009	109 million	0.77 billion

current models – rather as the Dyson bladeless fan is almost silent. Standard hairdryers are extremely loud, reaching up to 75 decibels – as loud as a vacuum cleaner, but held beside your head.

The design works by combining air pulled in through the motor element and from the sides of the machine, thus the motor could be smaller and lighter – and, perhaps crucially, less noisy. The patent claims that the product would have 'sound absorbing' and 'vibration absorbing' properties 'tuned to the resonant frequencies of the appliance'.

Conclusions

James Dyson certainly believes it was worth it in the end. But, during the 15-year period, there were probably many occasions when he felt like giving up or, more likely, would have sold out for a few hundred thousand pounds. The period 1980–92 was very difficult, not just for himself but also for his family, and enormous pressures were placed on them. Fortunately, they survived; arguably, someone without the background, resources and contacts would have failed. Many people have great ideas but only a few achieve success. Very often, it is due to the determination of the individual involved; sometimes, events seem to conspire against even the best efforts of the individual. Significantly, success has continued turning Dyson into one of the UK's most successful engineering firms.

Dyson invests heavily in R&D and believes that this is the key to success. Not all firms support this view. The level of investment in R&D varies considerably. The high value he places on creativity sets Dyson apart from other firms and helps to explain his insistence on maintaining what, in Britain, are considered insanely large annual investments in research and development. Nearly 17 per cent of revenues regularly goes to supporting the company's R&D efforts, a figure some ten times greater than the average in the United Kingdom. As a result of these ongoing research expenditures, a company that started with just one product now offers more than a dozen – all either upright or canister vacuum cleaners, each a more refined and technologically advanced model than its predecessors.

Sources: Dyson, J. (1998) *Against the Odds*, Orion Books, London; *The Sunday Times* (2000) Dyson bags ruling on Electrolux, Business Section, 24 January, 1; Wallop, H. (2006) Dyson cleans up with £31m payday, *The Daily Telegraph*, 1 November, Business Section, 4.

→

Questions

1 Explore the key problems Dyson had to overcome.

2 Characterise the type of innovation and new product development in the mature vacuum cleaner market prior to Dyson. Are there other industries in this situation?

3 Manufacturing the product has turned out to be hugely profitable, yet this was not the original plan; why not?

4 Explain the rationale behind Electrolux and Hoover's decision not to purchase the licence from Dyson. Given Hoover's development of the Triple Vortex, how do you assess this decision? What level of royalty would have been reasonable for both parties – that is, Dyson and Hoover?

5 Why is negotiating a licence for a new product so difficult?

6 What is the role of patents? To what extent is it an effective system for protecting intellectual property?

7 Not all firms invest in R&D. What should be the level of expenditure on R&D for a firm?

8 Explain the very different market entry strategy used for the United States.

9 How can Dyson succeed in the highly competitive hairdryer market?

Note: This case has been written as a basis for class discussion rather than to illustrate effective or ineffective managerial or administrative behaviour. It has been prepared from a variety of published sources, as indicated, and from observations.

Chapter summary

This chapter has shown that great care must be exercised in market research, for there are times when market research results produce negative reactions to discontinuous new products (innovative products) that later become profitable for the innovating company. Like any activity that contributes to new product development, it has strengths and weaknesses. Many of these weaknesses are highlighted when the new product is discontinuous. Finally, some new products have particularly difficult problems to overcome, if they are to be successful, like high switching costs. If these are recognised in advance, however, it is possible to overcome even these significant challenges.

Discussion questions

1 Explain why consumer market testing might not always be beneficial.

2 We are told that many new products fail, but is this because many firms are impatient? Discuss whether firms should allow more time for their product to be adopted and whether they would end up with a successful product.

3 Explain why discontinuous new products present a different challenge.

4 Show why the more radical the innovation, the greater the pertinence of qualitative market research techniques (e.g. customer visits and focus groups).

5 Examine whether there do exist innovations, typically radical, where market research of almost any kind is premature, not cost-justified or of limited value.

6 Discuss the advantages of the tripartite product concept in developing new products.

7 Discuss the dilemma faced by all firms of trying to listen to customers' needs and wants and, yet, also trying to develop new products for those customers that they do not yet serve.

8 Explain why some writers argue that organisations are the graveyard of product innovations rather than the birthplace.

Key words and phrases

Market research *554*	**Tripartite product concept** *565*
Concept testing *558*	**Installed base effect** *566*
Discontinuous new products *562*	**Switching costs** *566*

References

Al-Zu'bi, Z.M.F. and Tsinopoulos, C. (2012) Suppliers versus lead users: examining their relative impact on product variety, *Journal of Product Innovation Management*, vol. 29, 667–80.

Brown, R. (1991) Managing the S curves of innovation, *Journal of Marketing Management*, vol. 7, no. 2, 189–202.

Christensen, C.M. (1997) *The Innovator's Dilemma: When New Technologies Cause Great Firms to Fail*, HBS Press, Cambridge, MA.

Cohen, W.M. and Levinthal, D.A. (1990) A new perspective on learning and innovation, *Administrative Science Quarterly*, vol. 35, no. 1, 128–52.

Cohen, W.M. and Levinthal, D.A. (1994) Fortune favours the prepared firm, *Management Science*, vol. 40, no. 3, 227–51.

Cooper, R.G. (1990) New products: what distinguishes the winners, *Research and Technology Management*, November–December, 27–31.

Cooper, R.G. (2001) *Winning at New Products*, 3rd edn, Perseus Publishing, Cambridge, MA.

Day, G.S. (1999) *The Market Driven Organisation*, The Free Press, New York.

Fortune (2008) Steven Jobs, Apple, 3 March.

Francis, J. (1994) Rethinking NPD: giving full rein to the innovator, *Marketing*, 26 May, 6.

Gupta, A.K., Ray, S.P. and Wilemon, D.L. (1985) R & D and marketing dialogue in high-tech firms, *Industrial Marketing Management*, vol. 14, 289–300.

Hamel, G. and Prahalad, C.K. (1994) Competing for the future, *Harvard Business Review*, vol. 72, no. 4, 122–8.

Kay, N.M. (2013) Rerun the tape of history and QWERTY always wins, *Research Policy*, vol. 42, no. 6, 1175–85.

King, S. (1985) Has marketing failed or was it never really tried? *Journal of Marketing Management*, vol. 1, 1–19.

Kotler, P. (1998) *Marketing Management*, Prentice Hall, London.

Lettl, C., Herstatt, C. and Gemuenden, H.G. (2006). Users' contributions to radical innovation: evidence from four cases in the field of medical equipment technology, *R&D Management*, vol. 36, no. 3, 251–72.

Liddle, D. (2004) R&D Project Selection at Danahar, MBA Dissertation, University of Portsmouth.

Lynn, G.S., Morone, J.G. and Paulson, A.S. (1997) 'Marketing and discontinuous innovation: the probe and learn process', in Tushman, M.L. and Anderson, P. (eds) *Managing Strategic Innovation and Change, a Collection of Readings*, Oxford University Press, New York, 353–75.

Martin, J. (1995) Ignore your customer, *Fortune*, vol. 8, no. 1, 121–5.

Nyström, H. (1990) *Technological and Market Innovation: Strategies for Product and Company Development*, Wiley, Chichester.

Ortt, R.J. and Schoormans, P.L. (1993) Consumer research in the development process of a major innovation, *Journal of the Market Research Society*, vol. 35, no. 4, 375–89.

Porter, M.E. (1985) *Competitive Advantage*, Harvard Business School Press, Cambridge, MA.

Rogers, E.M. (2010). *Diffusion of Innovations*. Simon and Schuster.

Saren, M.A.J. and Tzokas, N. (1994) Proceedings of the Annual Conference of the European Marketing Academy, Maastricht.

Stewart-Knox, B., and Mitchell, P. (2003). What separates the winners from the losers in new food product development?. *Trends in Food Science & Technology*, vol. 14, no. 1, 58–64.

Sunday Times, The (2008) 17 February.

Tauber, E.M. (1974) Predictive validity in consumer research, *Journal of Advertising Research*, vol. 15, no. 5, 59–64.

Trott, P., Van Der Duin, P. and Dap Hartmann (2013) Users as innovators? Exploring the limitations of user driven innovation, *Prometheus*, vol .31, no. 2, 125–138.

Van den Hende, E. A. and Schoormans, J.P. (2012) The story is as good as the real thing: early customer input on product applications of radically new technologies, *Journal of Product Innovation Management*, vol. 29, no. 4, 655–66.

Van der Duin, P.A. (2006) *Qualitative Futures Research for Innovation*, Eburon Academic Publishers, Delft, The Netherlands.

Veryzer, R. (2003) 'Marketing and the development of innovative products', in Shavinina, L. (ed.), *The International Handbook on Innovation*, Elsevier, Oxford.

Further reading

For a more detailed review of the role of market research in new product development, the following develop many of the issues raised in this chapter:

Hutlink, E.J., Hart, S., Henery, R.S.J. and Griffin, A. (2000) Launch decisions and new product success: an empirical comparison of consumer and industrial products, *Journal of Product Innovation Management*, vol. 17, no. 1, 5–23.

Lettl, C., Herstatt, C. and Gemuenden, H.G. (2006) Users' contributions to radical innovation: evidence from four cases in the field of medical equipment technology, *R&D Management*, vol. 36, no. 3, 251–72.

Slater, S.F., Mohr, J.J. and Sengupta, S. (2014) Radical product innovation capability: literature review, synthesis, and illustrative research propositions, *Journal of Product Innovation Management*, vol. 31, no. 3, 552–66.

Swink, M. (2000) Technological innovativeness as a moderator of new product design integration and top management support, *Journal of Product Innovation Management*, vol. 17, no. 1, 208–20.

Chapter 17
Managing the new product development process

Introduction

The popular phrase 'actions speak louder than words' could be a subtitle for this chapter. Whilst the previous five chapters in Part Three of this book helped to identify some of the key factors and activities involved in the new product and service development process, it is the execution of these activities that will, inevitably, lead to the development of new market offerings. The focus of this chapter is on the management of the project as it evolves from idea into a physical form. Many companies have become very good at effective NPD, demonstrating that they are able to balance the many factors involved. The case study at the end of this chapter analyses how 3M has built a reputation for innovation and is frequently referred to as 'the innovation machine'.

Chapter contents

Learning objectives

When you have completed this chapter you will be able to:

- examine the key activities of the NPD process;
- explain that a product concept differs significantly from a product idea or business opportunity;
- recognise that screening is a continuous rather than a single activity;
- provide an understanding of the role of the knowledge base of an organisation in the new product development process; and
- recognise that the technology intensity of the industry considerably affects the NPD process.

New products as projects

Globalisation is a major market trend today, one characterised by both increased international competition as well as extensive opportunities for firms to expand their operations beyond current boundaries (see Chapter 8). Effectively dealing with this important change, however, makes the management of global new product development (NPD) a major concern. To ensure success in this complex and competitive endeavour, companies must rely on global NPD teams that make use of the talents and knowledge available in different parts of the global organisation. Thus, cohesive and well-functioning global NPD teams become a critical capability by which firms can, effectively, leverage this much more diverse set of perspectives, experiences and cultural sensitivities for the global NPD effort (Salomo et al., 2010; Bissola et al., 2014).

There is a considerable body of research examining the factors that influence a firm's ability to develop successfully and introduce new products. Recent research in this area by Sivasubramaniam et al. (2012) indicates that team leadership, team ability, external communication, goal clarity and group cohesiveness are the critical determinants of NPD team performance. Their research shows that NPD teams, with considerable experience and led by a transformational leader, are more successful at developing new products. Effective boundary spanning (Chapter 11) within and outside the organisation and a shared understanding of project objectives are paramount to success. Group cohesiveness is also an important predictor of NPD outcomes, confirming the importance of esprit de corps within the team. Unsurprisingly, the established literature on new product development (NPD) management recognises top management involvement (TMI) as one of the most critical success factors and this is confirmed in a recent comprehensive review of the literature by Felekoglu and Moultrie (2014).

The previous chapters have outlined some of the conditions that are necessary for innovation to occur and have shown various representations of the new product development process. However, whilst these conditions are necessary, they are insufficient in themselves to lead to the development of new products. This is because, as with any internal organisational process, it has to be managed by people. The concepts of strategy, marketing and technology all have to be coordinated and managed effectively. Inevitably, this raises issues in such areas as internal communications, procedures and systems. This is where the attention turns from theory and representation to operation and activities.

We have seen that a product idea may arise from a variety of sources. We have also seen that, unlike some internal operations, NPD is not the preserve of one single department. And it is because a variety of different functions and departments are involved that the process is said to be complicated and difficult to manage. Furthermore, whilst two separate new products may be similar generically, frequently there will be different product characteristics to be accommodated and different market and technology factors to be addressed. To be successful, new product development needs to occur with the participation of a variety of personnel drawn from across the organisation. This introduces the notion of a group of people working as a team to develop an idea or project proposal into a final product suitable for sale. The vast majority of large firms create new project teams to work through this process. From initial idea to launch, the project usually will flow and iterate between

Table 17.1 NPD terminology

NPD terminology	Definition
The fuzzy front end	The messy 'getting started' period of new product development processes. It is the front end where the organisation formulates a concept of the product to be developed and decides whether or not to invest resources in the further development of an idea (see Chapter 14 'The fuzzy front end section').
Business opportunity	A possible technical or commercial idea that may be transformed into a revenue-generating product.
Product concept	A physical form or a technology plus a clear statement of benefit.
Screening	A series of evaluations, including technical, commercial and business assessments of the concept.
Specifications	Precise details about the product, including features, characteristics and standards.
Prototype/pilot	A tentative physical product or system procedure, including features and benefits.
Production	The product produced by the scale-up manufacturing process.
Launch	The product actually marketed, in either market test or launch.
Co-joint analysis	A method for deriving the utility values that consumers attach to varying levels of a product's attributes.
Commercialisation	A more descriptive label would be market introduction, the phase when the product is launched and hopefully begins to generate sales revenue.
Commercial success	The end product that meets the goals set for it, usually profit.

marketing, technical and manufacturing groups and specialists. The role of the new project team is at the heart of managing new products and is the focus of the case study at the end of this chapter. Additionally, NPD has developed its own jargon and Table 17.1 offers an overview of source of the key terminology.

The Valley of Death

The Valley of Death is used as a metaphor to describe a discrete segment of development between research and product development. It is associated with a relative lack of resources and expertise in the front end of product innovation. The metaphor suggests that there are relatively more resources on each side of the valley: on one side in the form of research expertise and on the other side commercialisation expertise and resources.

The concept of the Valley of Death is shown in Figure 17.1. The y-axis maps resource availability, whilst the x-axis reflects the level of development. As Figure 17.1 suggests, if an idea makes it through the valley to NPD, there is adequate resource availability to take the idea to market. In a study of product development projects, Markham et al. (2010) found that a variety of interlocking roles are identified that move projects from one side to the other. The study revealed that significant development takes place before projects enter into a firm's formal product development process. Also, the roles of champion, sponsor and gatekeeper are seen as major actors

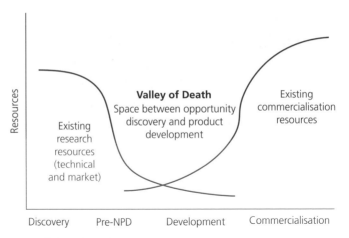

Figure 17.1 The Valley of Death

that work together to develop and promote projects for introduction into the formal NPD process. Champions make the organisation aware of opportunities by conceptualising the idea and preparing business cases. Sponsors support the development of promising ideas by providing resources to demonstrate the project's viability. Gatekeepers set criteria and make acceptance decisions. Clearly, companies need to be aware of the Valley of Death and must develop the skills and make resources available to master the front end of product innovation to ensure products do not die in the valley.

The key activities that need to be managed

The network model of NPD, shown in Figure 14.14, represents a generalised and theoretical view of the process. To the practising manager, however, this is of limited practical use. Business managers and the managers of project teams need to know what particular activities should be undertaken. From this practitioner standpoint, it is more useful to view the new product development process as a series of linked activities.

Figure 17.2 attempts to identify and link together most of the activities that have been associated with the NPD process over the years. This diagram represents a generic process model of NPD. It is not intended to be an actual representation of the process as carried out in a particular industry. Rather, it attempts to convey to the practitioner how the key activities are linked together to form a process. Some of these labels differ between industries and a good example of this is in the pharmaceutical industry. Final testing of a product is referred to as the clinical trial, where the product is used by volunteers and the effects carefully monitored. In the automotive industry, final testing may involve the use of consumers trying the product for the first time and offering their reflections on the design and ergonomics.

One of the key scholars in this area is Robert Cooper (Cooper and Edgett, 2008; Cooper and Kleinschmidt, 1993) over the past 30 years, he has undertaken extensive research in the area of new product development. His research has outlined the key

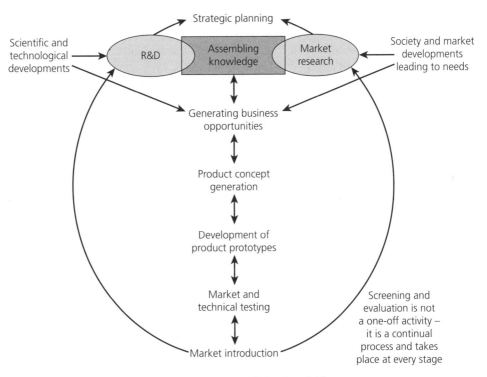

Figure 17.2 The NPD process as a series of linked activities

activities within the process: initial screening; preliminary market assessment; preliminary technical assessment; detailed market study; financial analysis; product development; product testing (in-house); product testing (with customer); test marketing; trial production; full-scale production; and product launch. Since this study, a number of different studies have highlighted the importance of some of these activities over others. Other studies have shown that firms frequently omit some of these activities. Students of new product development are left with an unclear picture of which activities are necessary and which are performed. The answer is context-dependent and, in particular, industry-dependent. Some industries no longer use test marketing, for example, whereas, for others, it is still a very important activity. This is explained below.

This section will examine the activities that need to be performed by businesses and NPD teams. The early activities are defined as the 'assembly of knowledge' and the 'generation of business opportunities'. These activities usually occur before a physical representation of the product has been developed. Up to this point, costs have been relatively low, especially when compared to subsequent activities. These activities, defined here as product concept development and development of product prototypes, transform what was previously a concept, frequently represented by text and drawings, into a physical form. The product begins to acquire physical attributes, such as size, shape, colour and mass. The final activities are market and technical testing and market introduction. It is worthy of note that these activities may occur at an earlier stage and that any of these activities can occur simultaneously.

Chapter 14 reviewed the wide range of models that have been developed to try to further our understanding of this complex area of management. Hopefully, you will recognise the new product development process as a series of activities that transform an opportunity into a tangible product that is intended to produce profits for the company. In practice, the process is difficult to identify. Visitors who ask to see a company's NPD process will not see very much because the process is intertwined with the ongoing operation of the business. Furthermore, the process is fluid and iterations are often needed. Developments by competitors may force a new product idea due for impending launch back to the laboratory for further changes. The model in Figure 17.2 highlights many of the important features and also identifies the importance played by the external environment. From an idea or a concept, the product evolves over time. This process involves extensive interaction and iteration, highlighted by the arrows in the diagram.

Assembling knowledge

The vast majority of marketing textbooks fail to identify the first activity of the NPD process, the assembling of knowledge. It is from an organisation's knowledge base that creativity and ideas for new products will flow. Part Two of this book provides extensive information on the importance of an organisation's knowledge base in underpinning its innovative ability. Without the continual accumulation of knowledge, an organisation will be hindered in its ability to create new product ideas. Part Two covered the technology side, but commercial knowledge is equally important and this is the domain of marketing and beyond the scope of this book.

Innovation in action

In business for 265 years

RS Clare was founded in Liverpool, England in 1748. It still devises and makes all its products in the city. It is a specialist grease manufacturer and lubricates the wheels of industries across the world. In its 265th year of business, its most profitable yet, the company has doubled the number of customers in its oil and gas division, focusing especially on the Middle East, North Africa and China. The firm's products are highly specialised, so it keeps a close overview of quality by keeping control of manufacturing at home in Liverpool. Survival and growth is also linked to innovation; specifically lead-user driven innovation. According to Noel Patterson, commercial director:

Source: maxuser. Shutterstock/Pearson Education Ltd

Innovation is at the heart of what we do. We have world-class chemists who work closely with our customers to formulate specific products to solve their problems.

Frequently, RS Clare's products are costlier to buy than their competitors, but the long-term cost savings outstrip the additional cost of the product. For example, curved rail tracks have to be greased to prolong life; RS Clare's product can increase re-railing periods from 7 to 23 years, saving railway companies hundreds of thousands of dollars per mile.

RS Clare does not spend large amounts of money on advertising. The type of business it is in means it has to approach customers directly. Typically, RS Clare visits the potential customer, analyses their operations and problems, and presents a technical solution. It then issues products to undertake a monitored field trial, setting performance criteria so it is clear to all how well the product has performed. This helps deliver long-term relations because engineers who have used their products move between regions – so, when they arrive in a new territory, they often turn to RS Clare to get the right solutions in their new operation.

The generation of business opportunities

The generation of business opportunities is the next activity in the process of new product development. This was discussed in Chapters 7 and 14. You should, therefore, be aware of the concept, even if the process is not fully clear. This stage in the NPD process is also referred to as opportunity identification (OI). It is the process of collecting possible business opportunities that could, realistically, be developed by the business into successful products. This definition contains several caveats, which helps to explain the difficulty that businesses face. New product ideas can emerge from many sources, such as existing products, unexploited patents, lead users, suppliers, etc., as illustrated in Figure 17.3. The case study at the end of this chapter illustrates how 3M, a company renowned for sustained innovation for over a century, develops business opportunities (Boh et al., 2014).

TRIZ (the theory of inventive problem solving) has been promoted by several enthusiasts as a systematic methodology or toolkit that provides a logical approach to developing creativity for innovation and inventive problem solving. The methodology, which emerged from Russia in the 1960s, has spread to over 35 countries across the world. It is now being taught in several universities and it has been applied by a number of global organisations who have found it particularly useful for spurring new product development (Birdi et al., 2012; Ilevbare et al., 2013).

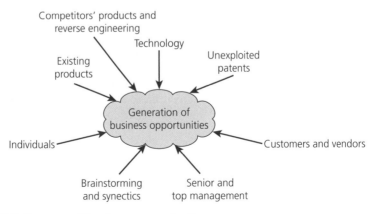

Figure 17.3 Sources of business opportunity

TRIZ research began with the hypothesis that there are universal principles of creativity that are the basis for creative innovations that advance technology. The idea was that, if these principles could be identified and codified, they could be taught to people to make the process of creativity more predictable. In other words: someone somewhere has already solved this problem (or one very similar to it.) Thus, creativity involves finding that solution and adapting it to this particular problem.

The three key principles of the TRIZ approach are:

1 Problems and solutions are repeated across industries and sciences. By classifying the 'contradictions' (or trade-offs) in each problem, you can predict good creative solutions to that problem.
2 Patterns of technical evolution tend to be repeated across industries and sciences.
3 Creative innovations often use scientific effects outside the field where they were developed, technology transfer (see Chapter 11).

Much of the practice of TRIZ consists of learning these repeating patterns of problems-solutions, patterns of technical evolution and methods of using scientific effects, and then applying the general TRIZ patterns to the specific situation that confronts the NPD team.

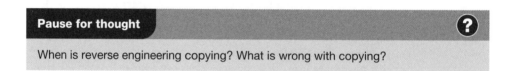

Pause for thought ?

When is reverse engineering copying? What is wrong with copying?

Developing product concepts: turning business opportunities into product concepts

This activity involves transforming a list of ideas into potential product concepts. In some cases, the identification of an opportunity is sufficient to reveal the product required. For example, a paint manufacturer may uncover a need for a new form of paint that will not drip on to carpets and clothes, is easy to apply, will wash off users' hands and clothes if spilt and is hard-wearing like conventional paints. In other cases, the concept is clear but the details need to be added. For example, a domestic appliance manufacturer may discover that some of its customers have expressed interest in a domestic water-cleaning device. In this case, the manufacturer is clear that the appliance will need to be fitted in the home but much more information is required. Sometimes, it may not be clear at all what form the product will take. For example, a chemical manufacturer may uncover an opportunity in the treatment of water for industry. The eventual product could take many different forms and use many different technologies, chemical treatment, mechanical treatment, etc. The idea is a long way from an actual product.

For a product idea to become a new product concept, Crawford and Di Benedetto (2014) argue that three inputs are required: form, technology and need.

● *Form*: this is the physical thing to be created (or, in the case of a service, the sequence of steps by which the service will be created). It may still be vague and not precisely defined.

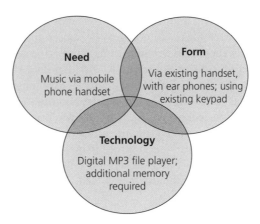

Figure 17.4 A new product concept

- *Technology*: in most cases, there is one clear technology that is at the base of the innovation (for the 3M Post-it Note, it was the adhesive; for the instamatic camera it was the chemical formulation that permitted partial development in light).
- *Need*: the benefits gained by the customer give the product value.

The following example illustrates this point. A mobile phone handset manufacturer may uncover the idea for incorporating a digital music player into its current range of handsets. All the details for the product at this stage remain unclear (some known, others not). This is simply an idea or a product concept. Once the concept starts to accumulate more information, the project team may be able to sketch out possible forms for it. Clearly, this will be influenced by the technology available from within the firm and what is available outside in the form of licensing or in the form of alliances (see Figure 17.4).

It is important to remember that an idea is just that, an idea, whereas a concept is the conjunction of all the essential characteristics of the product idea. This usually incorporates form, technology and need, but lacks detail. The underlying message here is that product ideas without details are often more like dreams and wishes. For example an aircraft manufacturer may wish for a noise-free aircraft engine, or a pharmaceutical company may wish for a cure for AIDS.

The screening of business opportunities

Screening product ideas is, essentially, an evaluation process. It is important to note that it is not a single, one-off activity as portrayed in many textbooks. It occurs at every stage of the new product development process (and is covered in Chapter 10 under 'Evaluating R&D projects') and involves such questions as:

- Do we have the necessary commercial knowledge and experience?
- Do we have the technical know-how to develop the idea further?
- Would such a product be suitable for our business?
- Are we sure there will be sufficient demand?

To help with this activity, firms often turn to product lead users and product experts (Ozer, 2009). The main purpose of screening ideas is to select those that will

be successful and drop those that will not – herein lies the difficulty. Trying to identify which ideas are going to be successful and which are not is extremely difficult.
Many successful organisations have made serious errors at this point. The Research
Corporation of America (RCA) identified the huge business opportunity of radio
and television, but failed to see the potential for videocassette recorders (VCR).
Kodak and IBM failed to see the potential in photocopying, but Xerox did not. The
list grows each year and, whilst the popular business press are quick to identify
those companies that make a mistake, they are not so quick to praise those companies that identify successful business opportunities. 3M, for example, recognised a
business opportunity in self-adhesive notes. Even here, persistence was required on
behalf of the individuals involved. This was because, initially, the company was not
sure about the idea.

Distinguishing between dreams and reality

Recognising what is a possible product and what is fantasy is an important part of
the screening process. There are many examples of businesses rejecting a new product idea (business opportunity) because they did not believe it would work. Some of
these are so famous they are known outside the world of business: Xerox and the
computer graphical interface; Dyson and the bagless vacuum cleaner; Whittle and
the jet engine. There must be a distinction between those opportunities that the business could develop into a product and those that it could not, and recognition of
those that are likely to generate revenue and those that will not.

Market research clearly will provide valuable market analysis input at this stage
to help in the decision process. This is covered in Chapter 10 along with other
activities often associated with the screening activity, such as concept testing, product testing, market testing and test marketing. Organisations use a variety of different labels for very similar activities. The following represents an overview of many
of the activities associated with the screening process.

Initial screen, entry screen or preliminary screen

This represents the first formal evaluation of the idea. Each of the ideas that came
from the pool of concepts has to be given an initial screen. This will involve a technical feasibility check and marketing feasibility test, plus a comparison with the strategic opportunity. This would include evaluating whether the particular product
would fit with the business's existing activities. The advantage of early screening is
that it can be done quickly and easily and prevents expenditure on product ideas
that clearly are not appropriate.

Customer screen, concept testing

This can vary between informal discussions with potential customers and feedback
on developed prototypes. Concept testing is extremely difficult and mistakes are
very easy to make. People have difficulty reacting to an entirely new product concept
without a learning period, as discussed below. Nonetheless, interorganisational new
product development (NPD) teams with business customers are rapidly becoming
more prevalent (Stock, 2014).

Technical screen, technical testing

This activity can vary from a few telephone calls to technical experts to extensive analysis by an in-house R&D department or an analysis by a third party, such as an independent consultant (often a university laboratory). This chapter and Chapter 10 discuss the activity of technical testing during which evaluations are continually undertaken.

Final screen

This normally involves the use of scoring models and computer assessment programs. Various new product ideas are fed into the program and a series of questions and assessments, with different weightings, are made, resulting in a scoring for each. One of the most serious criticisms of scoring models is their use of weights, because these are, necessarily, judgemental.

Business analysis

This may involve the construction of preliminary marketing plans, technical plans, financial reviews and projected budgets. All of these may raise potential problems that previously were unforeseen. It is not uncommon for new products to reach the mass-production stage only to encounter significant manufacturing difficulties, often when production is switched from one-off prototypes to high-volume manufacture.

New technology product blogs

Lead users and early adopters are often blogging or reading and commenting on blogs. Blogs, which are characterised by postings, links and readers' comments, create a virtual 'community' of blogger and readers. Members self-select, and then the community gels around a theme or idea, product, industry, hobby or any other subject. Whilst community creation is one chief function of blogs, the information-sharing, entertainment, or self- or value-expressive functions are also important. Thus, new product development (NPD) managers can glean a great deal of information about what these audiences are thinking. The significance of blogging to NPD managers also lies in the shift of focus from being separate to being immersed in these communities. Immersion enhances the potential of close relationships, sharing experiences and co-creating value with blogging communities through innovation. Droge et al. (2010) studied the roles of blogs in new product development. They found that people voluntarily join new product blogging communities and, if the manager of that product is not 'present' (at least as an observer of this 'straw poll'), an entire new product marketing agenda can be set by the community. Implicitly or explicitly, blogs can position the value proposition of the product in a prime target audience's mind. Such positioning could be advantageous or disastrous, as far as the NPD manager is concerned.

Development of product prototypes

This is the phase during which the item acquires finite form and becomes a tangible good. It is at this stage that product designers may develop several similar prototypes with different styling. Manufacturing issues will also be discussed, such as what type of process to use. For example, in the case of a tennis racket, engineers will discuss whether to manufacture using an injection-moulding or compression-moulding process. During this activity, numerous technical developments will occur. This will include all aspects of scientific research and development, engineering development and design, possible technology transfer, patent analysis and cost forecasts.

Rapid prototyping

Reducing the time to develop products is a top priority for firms, especially in consumer markets. Pamela Buxton (2000) argues that time to market is no longer measured in years but months. In the food industry 'own label' development is extremely rapid. Brand management firms like Procter & Gamble, Unilever and Biersdorf have all reduced their product development times. Ten years ago, development took eighteen months to two years. Now this has been cut to six to nine months. Industry analysts now argue that it is better to get to the market 90 per cent correct and grab the market opportunity rather than wait longer and enter the market 100 per cent correct (Buxton, 2000). It is not only the FMCG industries that are under pressure to reduce NPD times. Domestic appliance manufacturers, such as Siemens, Hoover and AEG, are also responding to the need to get new products into the marketplace more quickly.

3D printing

One area that has seen a significant development is the area of rapid prototyping. This is the process of developing a range of prototypes quickly for consideration by the firm. Stereolithography (SLA) is the most widely used rapid prototyping technology. Stereolithography or additive manufacturing (AM) builds plastic parts or objects a layer at a time by tracing a laser beam on the surface of a vat of liquid photopolymer. This class of materials, originally developed for the printing and packaging industries, quickly solidifies wherever the laser beam strikes the surface of the liquid. Once one layer is completely traced, it is lowered a small distance into the vat and a second layer is traced right on top of the first. The self-adhesive property of the material causes the layers to bond to one another and, eventually, form a complete, three-dimensional object after many such layers are formed. The term **3D printing** refers to processes that sequentially deposit material onto a powder bed with inkjet printer heads. The technology used by most 3D printers to date is fused deposition modelling, a special application of plastic extrusion. The growth of this process has led to the development of 3D printing machines for use at home.

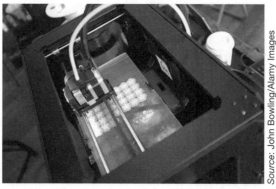

Source: John Bowling/Alamy Images

Stereolithography, or 3D printing, allows you to create almost any 3D shape you can imagine. If you can get it into a computer-aided design (CAD) program, you can probably create it. Hoover used 3D printing during the development of its Vortex vacuum cleaner. This helped it get a product from drawing board to the retailer in 12 months. It was able to develop a range of prototype vacuum cleaners and test them before deciding on the most suitable design. Once produced, the object has the strength of polystyrene plastic, which means that it can be drilled, mounted and cut. It enables the firm to try out the prototype in actual use. For example, a chair manufacturer will produce different arm-rest shapes using 3D printing and try them out on actual chairs to see how they feel.

The basic 3-D printing process goes like this:

- create a 3D model of your object in a CAD program;
- a piece of software chops the CAD model up into thin layers – typically 5–10 layers per millimetre;
- the 3D printer's laser 'paints' one of the layers, exposing the liquid plastic in the tank and hardening it;
- the platform drops down into the tank a fraction of a millimetre and the laser paints the next layer; and
- this process repeats, layer by layer, until the model is complete.

It is not a particularly quick process. Depending on the size and number of objects being created, the laser might take a minute or two for each layer. A typical run might take 6–12 hours.

3D printing is, generally, considered to provide the greatest accuracy and best surface finish of any rapid prototyping technology. Over the years, a wide range of materials with properties mimicking those of several engineering thermoplastics have been developed. In 2016, engineers found a way to create a heat-resistant ceramic material that can be 3D-printed and still retain its strength. This opens up the use of 3D printing in multiple applications in the aerospace industry, including building components for hypersonic jets and spacecraft. The technology is also notable for the large object sizes that are possible.

Technical testing

Closely linked to the development of product prototypes is the technical testing of a new product. It is sometimes difficult to distinguish between where prototype development finishes and testing begins. This is because, in many industries, it is frequently an ongoing activity. Take the motor vehicle industry as an example. Engineers may be developing a new safety system for a vehicle. This might involve a new harness for the seat belt and a new airbag system. As the engineers begin designing the system, they will be continually checking and testing that the materials for the belt are suitable, and that the sensors are not so sensitive that the airbag is inflated when the vehicle goes over a bump in the road. There will, of course, be final testing involving dummies and simulated crashes, but much of the technical testing is ongoing.

Market testing and consumer research

These activities have been covered in Chapter 16, so they will be dealt with only briefly here. The traditional approach to NPD involved a significant stage devoted to market testing. Developed products were introduced to a representative sample of the population to assess the market's reaction. Usually, this was carried out prior to a full-scale national launch of the product. The use of direct marketing and the internet has seen many new products being introduced via these developing channels. In today's fiercely competitive marketplace, products tend to go straight from consumer research and product development to national launch. Indeed, Google frequently makes beta versions of applications available for use by consumers. This enables trial and feedback. For example, Google Scholar, a search engine for academics, was a beta version for over five years.

The debate about the benefits and limitations of consumer research has raged for many years (see Chapter 16 for much more on this). Put simply, critics associated with the consumerism movement claim that most new products are actually minor variations of existing products. They further argue that consumers are not able to peer into the future and articulate what products they want. They suggest that the major innovations of the twentieth century, such as electricity, frozen food, television, microcomputers and telecommunications, have been the result of sustained technological research uninhibited by the demands of consumers. Marketers, on the other hand, argue that, without consumer research, technologists will produce products that are not what the market wants. There are many examples to support both arguments. Chapter 16 provides details on this and shows, at times, that listening to your customer actually may stifle technological innovation and be detrimental to long-term business success. For some firms in industries characterised by technological change, firms may be required to pursue innovations that are not demanded by their current customers.

How virtual worlds can help real-world innovations

By integrating users of virtual worlds into an interactive new product development process, companies can tap customers' innovative potential using the latest technology. Connecting the emerging technology of virtual worlds allows unique and inventive opportunities to capitalise on users' innovative potential and knowledge. The concept of avatar-based innovation may provide firms with new, original possibilities and enable them to take advantage of virtual worlds for innovation management. The latest advances of information and communication technologies enrich the interaction process and can improve new product development processes. Virtual worlds allow producers and consumers to swarm together with like-minded individuals to create new products and permit companies to find an audience to test, use and provide feedback on the content and products they create. A few path-finding companies have experimented with avatars as a source of innovation. In particular, the initiatives of Osram, Steelcase, Mazda and Toyota seem to have truly linked the concepts of open innovation and virtual worlds to employ the interactive technology for new product development. In a study of avatar-based innovation, Kohler et al. (2009) found that, in order to fully realise the potential of avatar-based innovation, companies need to create a compelling open innovation experience and consider the peculiarities of virtual worlds (see Illustration 17.1).

Illustration 17.1

Avatar-based innovation

Virtual worlds, such as the prominent Second Life (SL), developed by San Francisco-based Linden Lab, offer unprecedented opportunities for companies to tap the innovative potential of consumers and consumer communities. Yet, so far, initiatives have failed to attract sustained engagement amongst co-creating participants. A study by Kohler et al. (2009) showed that, only when participants experience an inspiring, intrinsically motivating, involving and fun co-creation experience, do they participate more intensely. The holy grail of the online clothes business is designing a virtual world fitting room that would allow consumers to try new clothes on avatars of themselves. Intense research is under way to develop this area of software.

Market introduction

Commercialisation is not, necessarily, the stage at which large sums of money are spent on advertising campaigns or multi-million-pound production plants, since a company can withdraw from a project following the results of test marketing.

It is important to remember that, for some products, say in the pharmaceutical business, the decision to finance a project with 10 years of research is taken fairly early on in the development of the product and this is where most of the expense is incurred. With other fast-moving consumer goods, like foods, advertising is a large part of the cost, so the decision is taken towards the launch phase.

Launch

We must not lose sight of reality. Most new products are improvements or minor line extensions and may attract almost no attention. Other new products, e.g. a major cancer breakthrough or rapid transport systems without pollution, are so important that they will receive extensive television news coverage. Illustration 17.2 shows Microsoft's new product launch of Bing, its search engine, in an attempt to compete with Google and Yahoo for a part of the search-sharing market. The promotion for this was, naturally, almost entirely web-based.

New product development (NPD) speed

New product development (NPD) speed has become increasingly important for managing innovation in fast-changing business environments, due to continuous reduction in the product life cycle time and increase in competition from technological advancements and globalisation. The existing literature suggests that the economic consequences of being late to the market are significant, including higher development and manufacturing costs, lower profit margins and lessening of the firm's market value. Therefore, traditional logic has held that new product development managers need to manage the trade-offs amongst speed to market, quality and costs. Somewhat surprisingly, however, research by Stanko et al. (2012) in a survey of 197 managers, shows that faster speed to market is related to better

Illustration 17.2

Microsoft's Bing fights Google for market share

In 2009, Microsoft rebranded its search engine (Live Search) in an attempt to compete with Google's dominance in the extremely influential search engine market. It is a profitable activity, as traffic can be routed to generate substantial revenues. One year after launch, Bing had a market share of about 10 per cent, compared to 70 per cent for Google and 15 per cent for Yahoo. In the past five years, Bing has increased its market share to 20 per cent. In 2015, the market share is divided between the following:

Google	65
Bing	20
Yahoo	13
Ask	2

Bing was launched with the aim of enabling people to find information quickly and use the information they found to accomplish tasks and make smart decisions. Bing also provides Microsoft with a starting platform for linking to its other apps, such as Outlook and Office.

Source: http://searchengineland.com/googles-search-market-share-actually-dropping-237045.

quality and lower costs; and it is not necessary to sacrifice one of these outcomes. In fast changing environments where uncertainties of market newness and market turbulence are greatest, research by Chen et al. (2012) argues that NPD teams need to pursue NPD speed as a critical strategy, but, in order to address the challenges of high uncertainty, a firm needs to probe, learn and iterate fast. In particular, NPD teams need to distinguish between the different requirements for new products in emerging and new markets and those in fast-changing markets. Moreover, NPD teams need to balance how fast they need to go with how fast they can go by considering team absorptive capacity and customer absorptive capacity. Consider the fast changing electric vehicles industry. As the technology changes so quickly, it is difficult for firms to decide which technology to support.

Aligning product development practices (PD) to radical and incremental projects

The firm's ability to vary its PD practices to develop winning products is seldom considered. In large firms, there are considerable differences in formal new PD practices with different classes of projects, such as: incremental, more innovative and radical. The management of the process varies with respect to the formal PD process, project organisation, PD strategy, organisational culture and senior management commitment. Research by Holahan et al. (2014) indicates that radical projects are managed less flexibly than incremental projects. Instead of being an offshoot of less strategic planning, radical projects are just as strategically aligned

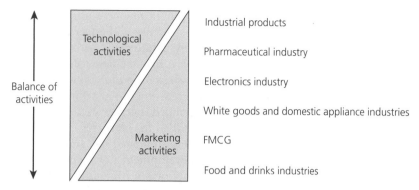

Figure 17.5 Classification of new product development activities across different industries

as incremental projects. Instead of being informally introduced as entrepreneurial adventures, radical projects are often the result of more formal ideation methods. As the level of innovativeness increased, so too did the amount of controls imposed, for example, less flexibility in the development process, more professional, full-time project leadership, centralised executive oversight for new products, and formal financial assessments of expected NP performance.

NPD across different industries

It has been stressed throughout this book that innovation and NPD, in particular, are context dependent. That is, the management of the process is dependent on the type of product being developed. A simple, but nonetheless useful, way of looking at this is to divide the wide range of activities involved in the development of a new product into technical and marketing activities. Figure 17.5 shows the NPD activities divided into the two categories. Against this are placed a variety of industries to illustrate the different balance of activities. It becomes clear that industrial products (products developed for use by other industries), such as a new gas-fired electricity generator, have many different considerations from those of a new soft drink. In the latter case, there will be much more emphasis on promotion and packaging, whereas the electricity generator will have been designed and built following extensive technical meetings with the customer concentrating on the functional aspects of the product. Clearly, in between these two extremes, the balance of activities is more equal. In a study of NPD involving 12 firms across a variety of industries, Olson et al. (1995) found that **cross-functional teams** helped shorten the development times of truly innovative products. More bureaucratic structures may provide better outcomes for less innovative products.

Organisational structures and cross-functional teams

Industrialists and academics have, for many years, been interested in the subject of how organisations are structured and the relationships that occur between individuals and functions. The nature of the industry, in general, and the product being developed, in particular, will influence significantly the choice of structure. Moreover, the organisation structure will affect considerably the way its activities are managed. It is not possible to alter one without causing an effect on the other. For example, the introduction of concurrent engineering techniques means that companies will need to be less reliant on functional operations and adopt the use of project management and cross-functional teams. Organisational structures and teams will, therefore, be examined together in this section.

The use of cross-functional teams increases creativity in new product development, leading to shorter development time and higher product innovativeness. Research in new product development has identified a number of organisational practices associated with supporting organisational creativity in cross-functional teams, including frequent and open communication, building organisational slack, attitude to risk and top management commitment (Bunduchi, 2009).

Teams and project management

The use of teams within organisations is certainly nothing new. In sport, having between five and fifteen individuals all working together has been the foundation for games all over the world. Similarly, within organisations, teams have been used for many years, especially on large projects. In industry, however, the concept of having teams of individuals from different functions with different knowledge bases is a recent development. In the field of medicine, the practice of having a group of experts from different functions working together on a project has been around for many years. In manufacturing industries, the use of cross-functional teams has occurred in parallel with the introduction of concurrent engineering.

New product project teams in small- to medium-sized organisations usually are comprised of staff from several different functions who operate on a 'part-time' basis. Membership of the project team may be just one of the many roles they perform. In larger organisations, where several projects are in progress at any one time, there may be sufficient resources to enable personnel to be wholly concerned with a project. Ideally, a project team will have a group of people with the necessary skills who are able to work together, share ideas and reach compromises. This may include external consultants or key component suppliers.

Functional structures

Unlike the production, promotion and distribution of products, NPD is a cross-disciplinary process and suffers if it is segregated by function. The traditional functional company structure allows for a strong managerial layer with information flowing up and down the organisation. Each function usually would be responsible for one or more product groups or geographical areas (see Figure 17.6).

Another common approach used by many large manufacturing companies is to organise the company by product type. Each product has its own functional activities. Some functions, however, are centralised across the whole organisation. This is to improve efficiency or provide common features (see Figure 17.7). This type of structure supports the notion of product platforms (see Chapter 13), where a generic group of technologies are used in a variety of products. Sony, Philips and

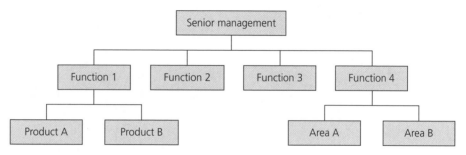

Figure 17.6 Functional company organisation

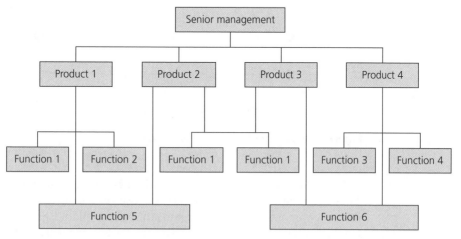

Figure 17.7 Functional company: diversification by product with centralised functions

Nokia all have centralised R&D activities where the majority of products are developed, allowing for a high degree of technology transfer between product groups. This is one of the key arguments in favour of a centralised R&D function, of which more later.

It is important to note that, whilst many organisations have clearly defined company structures, closer inspection of the actual activities within these companies will, invariably, reveal an informal structure that sits on top of the formal structure. This is made up of formal and informal communication channels and networks that help to facilitate the flow of information within the organisation (see Figure 17.8).

Matrix structures

The use of a **matrix structure** requires a project-style approach to NPD. Each team will comprise a group of between four and eight people from different functions. A matrix structure is defined as any organisation that employs a multiple-command system, including not only a multiple-command management structure but also related support mechanisms and associated organisational culture and behaviour patterns.

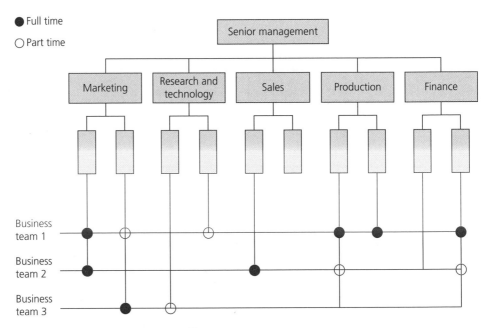

Figure 17.8 Matrix structure at Siemens

Matrix structures are associated with dual lines of communication and authority. They are seen as cross-functional because they involve bringing people together from two or more separate organisational functional areas. This can be seen in Figure 17.8, which shows the matrix structure at Siemens. The traditional hierarchy is functional, whilst the horizontal overlay consists of business areas known as business teams. Business team 1 comprises one full- and one part-time member from marketing, one part-time member from R&D, two full-time members from production and one full-time member from finance. Between them, this group would manage a number of projects. There would be a team leader for each business team. However, this person would not necessarily be, and often is not, the most senior member of the group. The choice of business team leader is based on the type of project the team is undertaking. For example, a team looking at the introduction of new products is likely to be led by someone from the marketing function, even though there will, almost certainly, be someone more 'senior' from another function within the business team (Mullins, 2013).

Matrix structure at Siemens

The following are some of the features and benefits of a matrix organisational structure that have been identified in literature. However, for a full review of matrix organisation and project management, see Mullins (2013).

● *Provision of additional channels of communication.* The combination of a matrix structure and business teams ensures that there is extensive lateral communication between functions. The diagram in Figure 17.8 shows how marketing personnel involved in business teams 1, 2 and 3 bring back to the marketing function knowledge of activities of the other functions. Communication skills are also developed as individual business team members learn the 'languages' of the other functions (Allen, 1984).

- *Increase in informal communication channels.* In addition to the increase in formal linkages, there is also an increase in informal networks between personnel from different functions. These develop from friendships and cooperation formed as a product of formal linkages.
- *Increase in information loads.* The increase in formal and informal channels of communication means that individuals collect more information. This information is brought back into the function and disseminated amongst colleagues in the group.
- *Increase in diversity for individuals.* Some individuals may be involved in two or three business teams. Their role may be part-time or full-time. This enables them to work with a variety of people from different backgrounds and disciplines across the organisation. This type of working environment enlarges an individual's experience and outlook and provides them with an improved understanding of the organisation's entire activities.

Corporate venturing

The idea behind **corporate venturing** is that fledgling businesses should be given the freedom to grow outside the constraints of an existing large, established organisation. Conventional management thinking argues that new ventures should be sheltered from the normal planning and control systems, otherwise they will be strangled. Ideally, they should be given high-level sponsorship from senior management, but must be able to manage their own relationships with other companies. Many large organisations, such as Nokia, IBM and General Electric, have a long experience of corporate venturing stretching back to the 1960s. However, following some high-profile failures, most notably by Shell in the mid-1980s, corporate venturing fell out of favour. More recent research suggests that the record of corporate venturing compared to external venture capitalists shows that the latter do no better than the corporations (Kuratko et al., 2015).

An internal corporate venture is a separate organisation or system designed to facilitate the needs of a new business. Companies usually adopt an internal corporate venture when the product involved is outside their existing activities. The case study at the end of this chapter shows how 3M uses internal corporate venturing to help transform business ideas into genuine businesses.

Project management

Whichever organisation structure is adopted, the project itself has to be well planned, managed and controlled. It is the setting of achievable targets and realistic objectives that helps to ensure a successful project. In addition, ensuring that resources are available at the appropriate time contributes to good project management.

Many organisations have tried and tested project management programmes and organisational systems to help ensure that projects are well managed. But, even in these well-run organisations, often there will be individual project managers who build a reputation for delivering on time and for being able to turn a doubtful project into a successful project. This introduces the subject of managing people within organisations. This is not the place to explore these issues that are at the heart of theories of organisational behaviour. They are comprehensively examined by others, such as Mullins (2013).

Reducing product development times through computer-aided design

When concurrent engineering is used in conjunction with other management tools, the results can be very impressive. For example, the aerospace and automobile industries have been using computer-aided design (CAD) for more than 20 years. In both these industries, product development times are relatively long, sometimes lasting 10 years. The ability to use CAD lies at the heart of broader efforts to compress product development times and share information across an organisation. This is even more important when there are several companies involved in the manufacture of a single product. The Airbus consortium of companies that manufactures aircraft has been using CAD to help with its very complicated product data management (PDM). This is particularly useful in helping speed up engineering and manufacturing processes. In addition, the Airbus Concurrent Engineering (ACE) project is helping to develop common product development processes across the consortium (Baxter, 1997).

The marketing/R&D interface

There are many difficulties in managing cross-functional teams in technology-intensive industries where the technology being used is complex and difficult to understand for those without scientific training. In such industries, scientists and engineers often are heard berating their commercial colleagues for failing to comprehend the technical aspects of the project. This introduces a common difficulty: the need to manage communication flows across the marketing and R&D boundaries. This problem was recognised as important first in the 1970s and remains a critical issue in new product development (Shin and Roh, 2015).

The main barriers to an effective **marketing/R&D interface** have been found to be related to perceptual, cultural, organisational and language factors (Shin and Roh, 2015). Marketing managers tend to focus on shorter time spans than R&D managers, who adopt much longer time frames for projects. In addition, the cultural difference results from the different training and backgrounds of the two groups. For example, scientists seek recognition from their peers in the form of published papers and, ultimately, Nobel Prizes, as well as recognition from the company that employs them. Marketing managers, on the other hand, are able to seek recognition only from their employer, usually in the form of bonuses, promotions, etc. The organisational boundaries arise out of departmental structures and the different activities of the two groups. Finally, the language barrier is soon identified in discussions with the two groups because, whilst marketers talk about product benefits and market position, R&D managers talk the quantitative language of performance and specifications.

Table 17.2 How marketing and R&D perceive each other

Marketing people about technical people	Technical people about marketing people
Have a very narrow view of the world	Want everything now
Never finish developing a product	Are focusing on customers who do not know what they want
Have no sense of time	Are quick to make promises they cannot keep
Are interested only in technology	Cannot make up their minds
Do not care about costs	Cannot possibly understand technology
Have no idea of the real world	Are superficial
Are in a different world	Are too quick in introducing new products
Are always looking for standardisation	Want to ship products before they are ready
Should be kept away from customers	Are not interested in the scientist's problems

The extent of the integration required between marketing and R&D depends on the environment within which product development occurs. In many technology-intensive industries where the customer's level of sophistication is low, the extent of integration required may be less than that needed where the customer's level of sophistication is high and the technology intensity of the industry low. For example, in the pharmaceutical industry (high level of technological intensity), customers' sophistication is low because they are unable to communicate their needs. They may want a cure for cancer, but have no idea how this can be achieved. On the other hand, in the food industry (low level of technological intensity), customers are able to articulate their needs. For example, they can explain that a particular food might taste better or look better if it contained certain ingredients. (For a more detailed discussion on the difficulties of managing the relations between R&D and marketing, see Shin and Roh, 2015.) Table 17.2 illustrates some commonly held beliefs by marketing colleagues and R&D colleagues about one another.

Pause for thought

It seems hybrid managers are necessary to bridge the communication gap between scientists and marketing! What does this mean?

High attrition rate of new products

As new product projects evolve and progress through each stage of development, many will be rightly cancelled or stopped for a wide variety of reasons. The failure of a product idea to be developed into a product is not necessarily a bad thing. Indeed, it may save the company enormous sums of money. This is explored more fully in Chapter 9. More serious problems arise when, as often happens, new products are launched in the expectation of success, but then ultimately fail, leaving high costs to be met by the company. Sometimes, a product can cause harm and suffering, but these are rare; the example of the Thalidomide drug is a chilling reminder of a product failure.

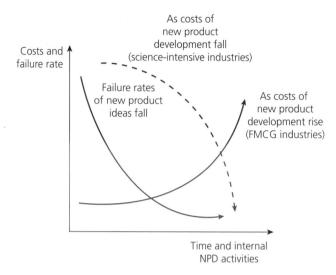

Figure 17.9 Product failures

Clearly, product ideas are rejected throughout the new product development process. Figure 17.9 shows the traditional view of the rising cost of new product development as it moves closer to launch. This is based on FMCG industries, which involve high-cost promotional campaigns. Arguably, the cost curve for science-intensive industries is inverse, with high costs being associated with R&D activities and relatively low-cost promotional activities towards the end of the development.

Studies of why new products fail are difficult to undertake. This is partly due to an unwillingness by companies to let outsiders know that they have been unsuccessful. Also, it is difficult to untangle what happened and identify the cause of failure. With hindsight, things often do not look the same. People are, in many cases, very defensive about their role in the development of a new product. There is always a reluctance to be associated with failure. Studies by Crawford and Di Benedetto (2014) have identified many of the often cited reasons for failure. These are listed in Table 17.3.

There is much debate about the failure rates of new products, which vary widely. The collection of data on this issue is problematic, with a wide range of different definitions being used across industries and countries. Some companies now claim a maximum failure rate of 10 per cent. This is a long way from the failure rate often quoted in the popular business press of 90 per cent. Products rarely fail in the marketplace: weak products usually are eliminated prior to entry to the market. Consequently, any such failures command huge publicity.

Even multinational companies with an impressive heritage of developing brands and managing products can make mistakes. For Coca-Cola, the difficulties encountered with its Dasani brand potentially highlight a poor match with its perception in Europe and the new product. Dasani has been very successful in the United States. Indeed, sales in 2015 place it second in the USA for market share of bottled water (source: http://www.statista.com/statistics/252408/market-share-of-bottled-still-water-in-the-us-by-brand/). It could simply be a combination of poor marketing communications and public relations and, maybe, some misfortune. But, it could also signify a more serious concern. That is, the reluctance on the part of the European consumer to separate Dasani from its parent brand Coca-Cola. In the bottled-water

Table 17.3 Reasons for new product failure

1 Product offers nothing new or no improved performance
2 Inadequate budget to develop ideas or market the product
3 Poor market research, positioning, misunderstanding consumer needs
4 Lack of top management support
5 Did not involve customer
6 Exceptional factors, such as government decision (e.g. new law on handgun control may seriously affect the manufacturer of a new handgun)
7 Market too small, either forecasting error with sales or insufficient demand
8 Poor match with company's capabilities, company has insufficient experience of the technology or market
9 Inadequate support from channel (a problem experienced by Dyson)
10 Competitive response was strong and competitors were able to move quickly to face the challenge of the new product (P&G highlighted weaknesses with Unilever's Persil Power)
11 Internal organisational problems, often associated with poor communication
12 Poor return on investment, forcing company to abandon project
13 Unexpected changes in consumer tastes/fashion

Source: Cooper, R.G. (1988a) The dimensions of industrial new product success and failure, *Journal of Marketing*, vol. 43, no. 3, 93–103. Crawford, M. and Di Benedetto, A. (2014) *New Products Management*, 11th (International) edn, McGraw Hill, USA. Urban, G.L., Hauser, J.R. and Dholaka, N. (1987) *Essentials of New Product Management*, Prentice-Hall, Englewood Cliffs, NJ.

market, the association with all things pure may be particularly necessary, hence Evian's association with the Alps and Buxton's association with the hills in the Peak District in Britain. In Europe, it may be that Coca-Cola may have to work particularly hard to distance itself from Dasani. This may lead some to question the financial benefits of entering the very competitive European bottled-water market. Illustration 17.3 shows another multinational that encountered a product failure.

Illustration 17.3

Microsoft's Zune

First released in November 2006, the Zune was Microsoft's answer to the iPod. Whilst it had some nifty product features that the iPod lacked (like sharing music from player to player), the Zune, despite an expensive marketing effort by Microsoft, never really caught on.

On a design level, the Zune lacked style and the simplicity of Apple's interface. The Zune seemed clunky in comparison. Perhaps, more importantly, though, the Zune could not be used with Apple's iTunes program, an even more dominant product in its market than the iPod. By integrating the music experience, Apple created strong disincentives to any competitor that just could not be overcome.

Source: Bloomberg/Getty Images

Case study

An analysis of 3M, the innovation company

Introduction

Any review of the literature on new product development and innovation management will uncover numerous references to 3M. The organisation is synonymous with innovation and has been described as 'a smooth running innovation machine' (Mitchell, 1989). Year after year, 3M is celebrated in the *Fortune* 500 rankings as the 'most respected company' and the 'most innovative company'. Management gurus from Peter Drucker to Tom Peters continually refer to the company as a shining example of an innovative company. This case study takes a look at the company behind some of the most famous brands in the marketplace, including Post-it® Notes. It examines the company's heritage and shows how it has arrived at this enviable position. Furthermore, the case study attempts to clarify what it is that makes 3M stand out from other organisations.

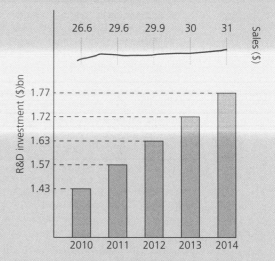

Figure 17.10 3M sales and R&D investment

Source: Compiled from data from 3M international website: www.3m.com.

Background

Originally known as the Minnesota Mining and Manufacturing Company, with its headquarters in St Paul, Minnesota, 3M was established in 1902 to mine abrasive minerals for the production of a single product, sandpaper. From these inauspicious beginnings, the company has grown organically, concentrating on the internal development of new products in a variety of different industries. The latest review of the company's position reveals that it manufactures over 60,000 products, has operations in 61 countries, employs 75,000 people and has achieved an average year-on-year growth in sales of 10 per cent (see Figure 17.10). Its products include Scotch adhesive tapes, fibre-optic connectors, abrasives, adhesives, floppy disks, aerosol inhalers, medical diagnostic products and Post-it Notes. Figure 17.10 shows the firm's continual investment in R&D, despite the economic crisis of 2009/10/11.

3M gave the world 'wet or dry' abrasives, which did so much to reduce the incidence of respiratory disease in the 1920s. It invented self-adhesive tape in 1925, light-reflective materials in the 1940s and pioneered magnetic recording and photocopying.

This heritage established the technology from which many of its products are still derived. To reinforce this impressive performance, 3M is consistently ranked amongst the top 10 of the USA's most admired companies in the US journal *Fortune*, in its annual review of the top 500 companies in the United States. 3M is a large and unusually diverse company.

The 3M approach to innovation

Many writers, academics and business leaders have argued that the key to successful innovation is good

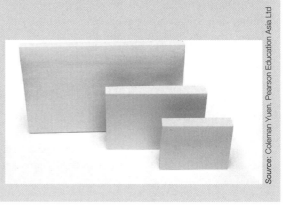

Source: Coleman Yuen. Pearson Education Asia Ltd

management (Henderson, 1994). Arguably, this is precisely what 3M has mastered. A closer inspection, however, will reveal that the company has combined a variety of management techniques, such as good communications and the setting of clear objectives with a company culture built on more than 90 years of nurturing ideas and fostering creativity. It uses a combination of structured research and individual freedom to explore ideas by allowing research scientists to spend 15 per cent of their time conducting projects of their own choosing. It is a unique combination of activities that is, by definition, difficult to replicate. They are described in this case study under the following headings:

1 Company heritage and culture
2 The demand for innovation
3 Freedom for creativity
4 Tolerating failure
5 Autonomy and small businesses
6 High profile for science and technology
7 Communication and technology transfer

Company heritage and culture

Through a combination of formal and informal processes, the company has developed a culture devoted to creating new products and building new businesses. This is based partly on the simple idea of hiring good people and trusting them. Indeed, this is the first goal that is stated in 3M's formal principles of management: 'the promotion of entrepreneurship and the insistence upon freedom in the workplace to pursue innovative ideas' (Osborn, 1988: 18).

The demand for innovation

Whilst the sales performance in Figure 17.10 is impressive, it conceals an important statistic; that is, 30 per cent of the company's sales come from products that are less than four years old. Indeed, this is a business objective that every 3M business manager has to try to achieve. What this means is that these business managers are under pressure to ensure that not only do they develop new products but that these new products will, eventually, represent 30 per cent of the business's sales. This objective has been communicated effectively throughout the organisation and is now ingrained within the management style and part of the culture of the company. Hence, the search for new ideas is part of daily activities.

Senior managers from other large manufacturing companies would, rightly, argue that a similar percentage of sales within their own companies comes from products less than four years old. However, the difference between 3M and other organisations is that 3M has developed this approach over many years and has worked hard to ensure that developing new products is much higher on the agenda in management meetings than at other companies. Moreover, the success of the approach is due to the continual reinforcement of the objective. Indeed, the performance of individual business managers is judged partly on whether they are able to achieve the objective.

The 30 per cent objective was introduced first in the 1980s when 25 per cent of sales had to come from products less than four years old. This was altered in 1992 to 30 per cent. 3M has since added another goal, which is to ensure that 10 per cent of sales come from products that have been in the market for only one year.

Freedom for creativity

Scientists and engineers are given time to work on projects and ideas that they consider to be of potential interest to the company and 15 per cent of an individual's work week time may be dedicated to such activities. This is not exclusive to 3M and is common practice in most large R&D laboratories. Nonetheless, it is an effective method of providing room for creativity and another way of showing that the organisation encourages innovative effort. Indeed, it is a method of providing resources to entrepreneurs, allowing them to work on ideas without having to seek out approval from the organisation. Another way of allocating resources is the use of grants. Known as 'genesis grants', these give researchers up to $75,000 to develop their ideas into potential product opportunities.

One of 3M's most famous new products was the result of this practice, the Post-it Note. Spencer Silver and Arthur Fry both invoked the 15 per cent rule to allow them to work on the project that eventually led to its development.

Spencer Silver was a 3M research chemist working on adhesive technology. His brief was to produce the strongest adhesive on the market. By some extraordinary mischance he developed an adhesive that had none of the properties he was looking for, but that did have two interesting properties that he had never previously encountered: it could be reused and it left no residue on the material to which it was applied. Yet, no one could find a use for it and the idea was shelved.

Art Fry, one of Spencer Silver's colleagues, sang in a choir. Every Sunday he would mark his hymn-book carefully with slips of paper and every Sunday the slips fell out. Then he remembered Spencer Silver's useless adhesive. Applied to paper strips, Art Fry found that they made fine book markers that did not fall out when he opened the book. Post-it brand technology had been developed 10 years before Art Fry discovered what to do with it!

In a lecture on the subject of innovation, the 3M vice-president for research and development (Coyne, 1996) reported that:

> *The 15 per cent rule is meaningless. Some of our technical people use more than 15 per cent of their time on projects of their own choosing. Some use less than that; some none at all. The figure is not so important as the message, which is this: the system has some slack in it. If you have a good idea, and the commitment to squirrel away time to work on it, and the raw nerve to skirt your manager's expressed desires, then fine.*

Tolerating failure

'It's easier to be critical than creative' is an adaptation of a famous quote from Benjamin Disraeli. It captures the essence of 3M's approach to tolerating failure. Most large companies with large R&D departments will have many ongoing new product research projects. Many will consume large amounts of resources and will not result in a new product. This fact is part of the new product game. Those close to the game are aware of this; at 3M it is argued that everyone is aware of the need to try new ideas. Its founder and early chief executive, W.L. Knight, stated over 60 years ago that:

> *A management that is destructively critical when mistakes are made, kills initiative, and it is essential that we have people with initiative if we are to continue to grow.*

Vasilash (1995) suggests that many of the senior managers within 3M are known to have made at least one mistake in their career whilst they tried to be innovative, thereby suggesting that W.L. Knight's philosophy continues.

3M has had its share of colossal failures. In the 1920s, one of the company's top inventors had an incredible flash of brilliance: maybe people could use sandpaper as a replacement for razor blades. Instead of shaving your face or legs, you could just sand off the whiskers. Every man and woman would need it. The company would sell the product by the ton! Not surprisingly, the idea was not realised in practice – but the inventor was not punished for following his idea. For every 1,000 ideas only 100 are written up as formal proposals. Only a fraction of these become new product ventures and over half of the company's new product ventures fail (Coyne, 1996).

Autonomy and small businesses

Like many companies, 3M realises that large organisations, with their inevitable corresponding structures and systems, can sometimes inhibit the creative dynamism often required to foster innovative effort. Hence, it has adopted an approach that enables individuals and groups within the organisation to establish small internal venture groups, with managers free to make their own decisions, develop their own product lines and take responsibility for the results, without continuous coordination across the company (Stewart, 1996). This approach attempts to offer an entrepreneurial environment under a corporate umbrella.

Provided that certain financial measures are met, such start-up venture groups follow a well-trodden path: a new business operation starts out as a project, if sales reach $1 million it becomes a fully-fledged product. At $20 million, it becomes an independent product department separate from its parent department. If it continues to grow, it will be spun off as a separate autonomous division. Currently, divisions characteristically have $200 million in sales. Experience has taught the company that, in the early days of a business's life, many decisions are taken through informal discussions amongst the individuals involved. Usually, there are insufficient resources to allow for lengthy and detailed analysis, which is more common in more established businesses.

High profile for science and technology

Although the company was formed around a single technology, sandpaper, today 3M makes use of more than 100 technologies, such as membranes, biotechnology, artificial intelligence, high-vacuum thin films and superconductivity. These technologies underpin the products that the company develops and manufactures. To support these activities, the company invests 6.5 per cent of its annual sales turnover in research and development. This is about twice that of the top 50 industrial companies in the United States. The money is used to employ over 7,500 scientists and technologists in developing new and interesting technology. It is this technological intensity that provides the company with the competitive advantage to compete with its rivals.

It is important to note that, whilst the company is technology-intensive, this does not imply a single-minded, technology-push approach to innovation. The role of the marketplace and users plays an important part in product development. For example, 3M's famous Scotch tape once was manufactured strictly as an industrial product, until a salesman got the idea of packaging it in clear plastic dispensers for home and office use.

Communication and technology transfer

The communication of ideas helps to ensure that a company can maximise the return on its substantial investments in the technology. Very often, it is the combination of apparently diverse technologies through technology transfer that has led to major product innovations. For example, microreplication technology is the creation of precise microscopic, three-dimensional patterns on a variety of surfaces, including plastic film. When the surface is changed, numerous product possibilities emerge. It was first developed for overhead projectors, its innovative feature being a lens made of a thin piece of plastic with thousands of tiny grooves on its surface. Micro-replication helped the plastic lens to perform better than the conventional lens made of heavy glass. 3M became the world's leading producer of overhead projectors. It is this technology, which can be traced back to the 1960s, that has spread throughout 3M and led to a wide range of products, including better and brighter reflective material for traffic signs; 'floptical' disks for data storage; laptop computer screens; and films.

Struggling with the innovation dilemma: efficiency vs creativity

In December 2000, James McNerney, a former General Electric executive, was selected as 3M's next CEO. McNerney was the first 3M CEO to come from outside the company and brought with him the GE playbook for achieving operational efficiency. One of his key initiatives was introducing the total quality management Six Sigma programme, a series of management techniques designed to increase efficiency. For the most part, the implementation of the Six Sigma programme was successful, as it focused on the operations (manufacturing/logistics) side of the business. However, when 3M's R&D personnel were asked to adopt Six Sigma processes, the results were less favourable. Whilst established operational processes like manufacturing require strict monitoring, measuring and a regimented set of procedures, the innovation process requires a different approach.

3M felt stifled by the new structure and pressured to produce more new products faster. The result was a greater number of incremental product-line extensions than true new product innovations. Traditionally, 3M drew at least one-third of sales from products released in the past five years but, in 2006, that fraction fell to one-quarter of sales. In 2004, 3M was ranked No. 1 on the *Business Week*/BCG list of Most Innovative Companies. In 2007, the company dropped to number seven.

After four and a half years at 3M, McNerney left to take the CEO position at Boeing. In 2005, his successor was George Buckley, who seemed to recognise the negative impact the process-focused programme had on the company's creativity. Many of the workers say they feel reinvigorated now that the corporate emphasis has shifted back to growth and innovation from McNerney's focus on process and short-term profits (see Chapter 4 for more on the innovation dilemma).

2010

'3M is everywhere,' says George Buckley, who became chairman and CEO of 3M in 2005. (He is British, with a PhD in electrical engineering.) In 2009, he said, 'even in the worst economic times in memory, we released over 1,000 new products'. Apple and many others could not do what they do without 3M. Most people do not realise that 3M products are embedded in other products and places: cars, factories, hospitals, homes and offices (Feldman and Feldman, 2010). Since 2012, Inge Thulin has been the CEO and president of 3M. He has a long history with

→

3M and has been a senior manager at the company since 1979.

3M continues to inspire and encourage innovation and creativity to accelerate growth and deliver excellent financial results. Buckley told stockholders at the company's annual meeting in St. Paul:

The people of 3M are once again driving innovation through their energy and imagination . . . At its core, 3M remains an idea company that prospers best when we commit ourselves to invest in ideas, technology development and new products.

Buckley cited increased investments in research and development – up more than 11 per cent – and the steady increase in the introduction of new products – up by about 4 per cent in 2009 and 2010 – as examples of 3M's commitment to innovation.

Why is that important? Because, as 3M's older products grow outmoded or become commodities, it must replace them. 'Our business model is literally new-product innovation', says Larry Wendling, who oversees 3M's corporate research. The company, as a result, had in place a goal to generate 30 per cent of revenue from new products introduced in the past five years. By 2005, when McNerney left to run Boeing, the percentage was down to 21 per cent, and much of the new-product revenue had come from a single category, optical films. (3M also has a history of acquisitions and has announced deals recently.)

It is safe to say that no 3M product will generate the buzz of, say, the next iPhone. But 3M has never been about inventing the Next Big Thing. It's about inventing hundreds and hundreds of Next Small Things, year after year. Things like Cubitron II. Buckley explains that Cubitron II is an industrial abrasive that cuts faster, lasts longer, sharpens itself, and requires less elbow grease than any other abrasive on the market. Introduced in 2009, it is selling like crazy, to the CEO's delight. 'How the heck do [you] innovate in abrasives?' he asks. 'A 106-year-old business for us! For goodness' sake – it's sandpaper!' Catching himself a moment later, he jokes, 'I probably need to get out more.' Maybe so, but you can understand what he is excited about: little things like grains of sand that add up to the big business that is 3M (Feldman and Feldman, 2010).

Discussion

Whilst few would argue with 3M's successful record on innovation, there may be some who would argue that, compared to companies such as Microsoft, IBM and GlaxoSmithKline, its achievements in terms of growth have not been as spectacular. However, the point here is not that 3M is the most successful company or even that it is the most innovative, although one could, surely, construct a strong case, merely that the company has a long and impressive performance when it comes to developing new products.

This case study has highlighted some of the key activities and principles that contribute to 3M's performance. Many of these are not new and are, indeed, used by other companies. In 3M's case, they may be summarised as an effective company culture that nurtures innovation and a range of management techniques and strategies that together have delivered long-term success. Many companies pay lip service to the management principles and practice set out in this case study. There is evidence that 3M supports these fine words with actions.

The struggle between efficiency and creativity is one many public companies face. The market values of company stocks are impacted more by short-term results rather than long-term prospects; and executives have an incentive to drive those results.

There are no easy answers and the best solution most likely lies somewhere between the two extremes of either process control or open-ended innovation.

Sources: Coyne, W.E. (1996) Innovation lecture given at the Royal Society, 5 March; Henderson, R. (1994) Managing innovation in the information age, *Harvard Business Review*, January–February, 100–105; Mitchell, R. (1989) Masters of innovation: how 3M keeps its new products coming, *Business Week*, April, 58–63; Osborn, T. (1988) How 3M manages innovation, *Marketing Communications*, November/December, 17–22; Stewart, T. (1996) 3M fights back, *Fortune*, vol. 133, no. 2, 5 February, 42–7; Vasilash, G.S. (1995) Heart and soul of 3M, *Production*, vol. 107, no. 6, 38–9; Feldman, A. and Feldman, B. (2010) 3M's Innovation revival, Fortune500.com, 24 February. Boh, W.F., Evaristo, R. and Ouderkirk, A. (2014) Balancing breadth and depth of expertise for innovation: A 3M story, *Research Policy*, 43(2), 349–66. For further information about 3M and its business activities, visit the 3M international website at www.3m.com.

Questions

1 There are many examples of successful companies. To what extent is 3M justifiably highlighted as the 'innovating machine'?

2 In the 3M case study, what is meant by the statement: 'the message is more important than the figures'?

3 Discuss the merits and problems with the so-called '15 per cent rule'. Consider cost implications and a busy environment with deadlines to meet. To what extent is this realistic or mere rhetoric?

4 Encouraging product and brand managers to achieve 25 per cent of sales from recently introduced products would be welcomed by shareholders, but what happens if a successful business delivers profits without 25 per cent of sales from recently introduced products?

5 Some people may argue that 3M's success is due largely to the significance given to science and technology and this is the main lesson for other firms. Discuss the merits of such a view and the extent to which this is the case.

6 Explain how the innovation dilemma affected 3M.

Note: This case has been written as a basis for class discussion rather than to illustrate effective or ineffective managerial or administrative behaviour. It has been prepared from a variety of published sources, as indicated, and from observations.

Chapter summary

The main focus of this chapter has been an examination of the activities of the NPD process. Adopting a practitioner standpoint, the new product development process is viewed as a series of linked activities. Emphasis is placed on the iterative nature of the process and many of the activities occur concurrently. A new product needs to be viewed as a project that acquires knowledge gradually over time as an idea is transformed into a physical product. The knowledge base of the organisation will provide for a diverse range of contributions to a project. Furthermore, during this process there is continual evaluation of the project.

This chapter also offered a view of NPD across a variety of industries. The key point here is that the balance of technical and commercial activities clearly will vary, depending on the nature of the industry and the product being developed.

Discussion questions

1 Explain why there is not one best organisational structure for new product development.

2 Explain how sales representatives, especially with technology-intensive products, play a crucial role in the success or not of a new product and illustrate how their image as 'second-hand car dealers' is pejorative and incorrect.

3 Examine whether the virtual world (such as Second Life) may be able to help firms trial new products.

4 Explain why the 'Valley of Death' presents a genuine challenge to product champions or project leaders.

5 'New products are a necessary evil.' From whose viewpoint are they necessary and from whose viewpoint are they evil?

6 Discuss the many reasons why so many new products fail. Are there additional reasons?

Key words and phrases

Business opportunity *589*

Product concept *589*

Screening *589*

Prototype *589*

3D printing *598*

Cross-functional teams *603*

Matrix structure *605*

Corporate venturing *607*

Marketing/R&D interface *608*

References

Allen, T. (1984) *Managing the Flow of Technology*, MIT Press, MA.

Baxter, A. (1997) Designs for survival, *Financial Times*, 20 November, 16.

Birdi, K., Leach, D. and Magadley, W. (2012) Evaluating the impact of TRIZ creativity training: an organizational field study. *R&D Management*, vol. 42, 315–26.

Bissola, R., Imperatori, B. and Colonel, R.T. (2014) Enhancing the creative performance of new product teams: an organizational configurational approach, *Journal of Product Innovation Management*, vol. 31, 375–91.

Boh, W.F., Evaristo, R. and Ouderkirk, A. (2014) Balancing breadth and depth of expertise for innovation: a 3M story, *Research Policy*, vol. 43, no. 2, 349–66.

Bunduchi, R. (2009) Implementing best practices to support creativity in NPD cross-functional teams, *International Journal of Innovation Management*, vol. 13, no. 4, 537–54.

Buxton, P. (2000) Time to market is NPD's top priority, *Marketing*, 30 March, 35–6.

Chen, J., Reilly, R.R. and Lynn, G.S. (2012) New product development speed: too much of a good thing? *Journal of Product Innovation Management*, vol. 29, 288–303.

Cooper R.G. and Edgett, S.J. (2008) Maximizing productivity in product innovation, *Research Technology Management*, March.

Cooper, R.G. and Kleinschmidt, E.J. (1993) Major new products: what distinguishes the winners in the chemical industry?, *Journal of Product Innovation Management*, vol. 10, no. 2, 90–111.

Crawford, M. and Di Benedetto, A. (2014) *New Product Management*, 11th (International) edn, McGraw-Hill, New York.

Droge, C., Stanko, M.A. and Pollitte, W.A. (2010) Lead users and early adopters on the web: the role of new technology product blogs, *Journal of Product Innovation Management*, vol. 27, 66–82.

Felekoglu, B. and Moultrie, J. (2014) Top management involvement in new product development: a review and synthesis, *Journal of Product Innovation Management*, vol. 31, 159–75.

Holahan, P.J., Sullivan, Z.Z. and Markham, S.K. (2014) Product development as core competence: how formal product development practices differ for radical, more innovative, and incremental product innovations, *Journal of Product Innovation Management*, vol. 31, 329–45.

Ilevbare, I.M., Probert, D. and Phaal, R. (2013) A review of TRIZ, and its benefits and challenges in practice, *Technovation*, vol. 33, no. 2, 30–7.

Kohler, T., Matzler, K. and Füller, J. (2009) Avatar-based innovation: using virtual worlds for real-world innovation, *Technovation*, vol. 29, nos. 6–7, 395–407.

Kuratko, D. F., Hornsby, J. S., & Hayton, J. (2015) Corporate entrepreneurship: the innovative challenge for a new global economic reality, *Small Business Economics*, 1–9.

Markham, S.K., Ward, S.J., Aiman-Smith, L. and Kingon, A.I. (2010) The Valley of Death as context for role theory in product innovation, *Journal of Product Innovation Management*, vol. 27, 402–17.

Mullins, L.J. (2013) *Management and Organisational Behaviour*, 10th edn, Financial Times Pitman Publishing, London.

Olson, E.M., Orville, C.W. and Ruekert, R.W. (1995) Organising for effective new product development: the moderating role of product innovativeness, *Journal of Marketing*, vol. 59, 48–62.

Ozer, M. (2009) The roles of product lead-users and product experts in new product evaluation, *Research Policy*, vol. 38, no. 8, 1340–9.

Salomo, S., Keinschmidt, E.J. and De Brentani, U. (2010) Managing new product development teams in a globally dispersed NPD program, *Journal of Product Innovation Management*, vol. 27, 955–71.

Shin, G.C. and Roh, J.J. (2015) Interaction of marketing, R&D and critical innovation: case study of Korean and Japanese firms, *International Journal of Business Information Systems*, vol. 18, no. 4, 437–50.

Sivasubramaniam, N., Liebowitz, S.J. and Lackman, C.L. (2012) Determinants of new product development team performance: a meta-analytic review, *Journal of Product Innovation Management*, vol. 29, 803–20.

Stanko, M.A., Molina-Castillo, F.-J. and Munuera-Aleman, J.-L. (2012) Speed to market for innovative products: blessing or curse? *Journal of Product Innovation Management*, vol. 29, 751–65.

Stock, R.M. (2014) How should customers be integrated for effective interorganizational NPD teams? An input–process–output perspective, *Journal of Product Innovation Management*, vol. 31, 535–51.

Further reading

For a more detailed review of the new product development literature, the following develop many of the issues raised in this chapter:

Barczak, G., Griffin, A. and Kahn, K.B. (2009) Perspective: Trends and drivers of success in NPD practices: results of the 2003 PDMA Best Practices Study, *Journal of Product Innovation Management*, vol. 26, no. 1, 3–23.

Biemans, W.G., Griffin, A. and Moenaert, R.K. (2007) Twenty years of the *Journal of Product Innovation Management*: history, participants, and knowledge stocks and flows, *Journal of Product Innovation Management*, vol. 24, 193–213.

Biemans, W., Griffin, A. and Moenaert, R. (2010) In search of the classics: a study of the impact of *JPIM* papers from 1984 to 2003, *Journal of Product Innovation Management*, vol. 27, 461–84.

Christensen, C.M. (2003) *The Innovator's Dilemma: When New Technologies Cause Great Firms to Fail*, 3rd edn, Harvard Business School Press, Boston, MA.

HSBC (2010) *100 Thoughts*, HSBC, London.

Salomo, S., Keinschmidt, E.J. and De Brentani, U. (2010) Managing new product development teams in a globally dispersed NPD program, *Journal of Product Innovation Management*, vol. 27, 955–71.

Index